"This comprehensive study of Bakunin's philosophy engages critically with the existing secondary literature and advances a synthetic view of Bakunin's political philosophy. Its encyclopedic scope makes it a 'go-to' text."

—**Alex Prichard**, Associate Professor of International Relations at the University of Exeter and the author of *Justice, Order and Anarchy: The International Political Theory of Pierre-Joseph Proudhon* and *Anarchism: A Very Short Introduction*.

"Mikhail Bakunin, Karl Marx's great rival, inspired labour, left, and anti-imperialist movements worldwide. For decades, his politics influenced mass movements in Africa, Asia, Europe, and the Americas. Felipe Corrêa's new book provides a vital recovery—and a critical assessment—of the ideas of this modern socialist titan. Stripped of the propaganda and myths, Bakunin remains relevant today, as the old statist projects that captured much of the left crumble, while war, inequality, and oppression endure."

—**Lucien van der Walt**, Professor of Economic and Industrial Sociology at Rhodes University, South Africa. He is editor and author of *Anarchism and Syndicalism in the Colonial and Postcolonial World, 1870–1940: The Praxis of National Liberation, Internationalism, and Social Revolution* (with Steven Hirsch) and *Politics at a Distance from the State: Radical and African Perspectives* (with Kirk Helliker).

"Among the world's foremost scholars of anarchism, Felipe Corrêa's definitive study of Bakunin's life, ideas, and works brings a renewed urgency to adapting concepts of autonomy, worker's self-management, and revolution to struggles against capitalism and the state in the twenty-first century."

—**Mark Bray**, Professor of History at Rutgers University. He is the author of *Antifa: The Anti-Fascist Manual*, *Translating Anarchy: The Anarchism of Occupy Wall Street*, and *The Anarchist Inquisition: Assassins, Activists, and Martyrs in Spain and France*.

"Felipe Corrêa is to be commended for presenting such a thorough, balanced, and perceptive analysis of the ideas and actions of Mikhail Bakunin, from Bakunin's early days as a philosophical idealist to his mature period of revolutionary anarchism. Particularly insightful is Corrêa's discussion of Bakunin's participation in the 1848 revolutions in Europe and his views on national liberation struggles."

—**Robert Graham** is a researcher, editor and author. His main works include the three volumes *Anarchism: A Documentary History of Libertarian Ideas* and *We Do Not Fear Anarchy – We Invoke It: The First International and the Origins of the Anarchist Movement*.

"Through an interdisciplinary study, Felipe Corrêa presents the result of a thorough and unprecedented investigation that covers Bakunin's political-intellectual trajectory together with a sophisticated survey of his historical context. *Freedom or Death* substantiates the relevance of Bakunin's contribution to the field of political theory, but more than that it evidences something rare nowadays: the inalienable importance of the relationship between theoretical coherence and political practice, a profound relationship that is evident in the three phases of the Russian revolutionary's life and thought."

—from the preface by Brazilian anarchist and syndicalist militant **Eloísa Benvenutti de Andrade**.

"This work by Felipe Corrêa is without a doubt a significant contribution to both political theory and the history of political thought. What prevails is the sense of complexity inherent in Bakunin's thought [...] this important work contributes a new dimension to the theoretical elaboration of this progenitor of anarchism, to understand his work in his context of production and debate. Corrêa also humanizes this figure who was above all a militant, who far from remaining on the platform of intellectual debate, constantly sought to put his analyses and proposals into practice, in a back and forth that enriches each of his elaborations."

—from the epilogue by Argentinian anarchist and syndicalist militant **Rocio Soledad Lescano**.

FREEDOM OR DEATH

FREEDOM
OR DEATH

The Theory and Practice
of Mikhail Bakunin

FELIPE CORRÊA

English translation by
Jonathan Payn

Montréal • New York • London

I dedicate this work to my family, friends, comrades, and to all those that struggle for a freer and more egalitarian world.
Arriba los que luchan!

———•———

Freedom without socialism is privilege, injustice; socialism without freedom is slavery and brutality.
Mikhail Bakunin

Black Rose Books No. WW432

Library and Archives Canada Cataloguing in Publication

Title: Freedom or death : the theory and practice of Mikhail Bakunin / Felipe Corrêa ; English translation by Jonathan Payn.
Names: Corrêa, Felipe (Felipe Corrêa Pedro), author.
Description: Original title unknown. | Includes bibliographical references.
Identifiers: Canadiana (print) 20240338952 | Canadiana (ebook) 20240339045 | ISBN 9781551648149 (hardcover) | ISBN 9781551648125 (softcover) | ISBN 9781551648163 (PDF)
Subjects: LCSH: Bakunin, Mikhail Aleksandrovich, 1814-1876—Criticism and interpretation.
Classification: LCC HX917.2.Z67 B3513 2024 | DDC 335/.83092—dc23

Cover illustration by Cristiano Suarez

Book design by Associés Libres

C.P. 42002, Succ. Roy
Montréal, QC H2W 2T3
CANADA
www.blackrosebooks.com

ORDERING INFORMATION

CANADA/US

University of Toronto Press
5201 Dufferin Street
Toronto, ON
M3H 5T8

1-800-565-9523

utpbooks@utpress.utoronto.ca

UK/INTERNATIONAL

Central Books
Freshwater Road
Dagenham
RM8 1RX

+44 20 8525 8800

contactus@centralbooks.com

TABLE OF CONTENTS

PREFACE
by Eloísa Benvenutti de Andrade 13

Note on the Translation and Quotation of Bakunin's *Complete Works* 21

INTRODUCTION 23

Chapter 1. "BAKUNIN'S LIFE AND IDEAS ARE WORTH
A THOROUGH REEXAMINATION"
1.1 Bakunin in the Twentieth Century 31
1.2 The Bakuninian *Corpus* 43
1.3 Bakunin in the Twenty-first Century 47
1.4 Bakunin in Brazil 49
1.5 Bibliographic Discussion 51
1.6 Methodological Foundations: For a History of Bakunin's Political Thought . . 54

PART I
FROM PHILOSOPHY TO PRAXIS
(1836–43)

Chapter 2. "THE PASSION FOR DESTRUCTION IS A CREATIVE
PASSION": FROM PHILOSOPHY TO PRAXIS (1814–43)
2.1 Russia, The Bakunins, First Years in Premukhino
· and Saint Petersburg (1814–35) 71
2.2 Philosophy and Stankevitch's Circle in Moscow (1836–40) 77
2.3 The Hegelian Left in Germany (1840–42) 81
2.4 Communism in Switzerland (1843) 84
2.5 Bakuninian Political Theory between 1836 and 1843 85

Chapter 3. LOVE-FREEDOM AND EMANCIPATION (1836–37)
3.1 Interior World and Exterior World 97
3.2 God and Religion of Humanity: Anthropocentric Immanentism 98
3.3 Rational Ethical Action 100

Chapter 4. ALIENATION VS. RECONCILIATION WITH
REALITY AND THEORY-PRACTICE UNITY (1837–40)

4.1 Knowledge, Subjectivism, and Alienation 103

4.2 Reality and Theory-Practice 109

4.3 Critical-Dialectic Method 117

4.4 Philosophy of Action and Education 119

Chapter 5. THEORY OF REVOLUTION AND NEGATIVE
DIALECTICS (1841–42)

5.1 Negative Dialectics: Revolutionary Theory of History 127

5.2 Europe, Early 1840s: Contradictions, Revolutionary Crisis
and Decomposition of the Old World 130

5.3 Reactionary Party and Democratic Party 133

5.4 Negative Dialectics: Revolutionary Logic 143

Chapter 6. PRIMACY OF PRACTICE AND SELF-GOVERNMENT
OF THE PEOPLE (1843)

6.1 Insufficiency of Philosophy, New Theory, and Concrete Practice 149

6.2 Radicalism and Communism 152

PART II
REVOLUTIONARY PAN-SLAVISM
(1844–63)

Chapter 7. "FREEDOM, EQUALITY, AND FRATERNITY OF
NATIONS": REVOLUTIONARY PAN-SLAVISM (1843–63)

7.1 Socialism and the Revolutionary Movement
in the Switzerland-Belgium-France Triangle (1843–45) 159

7.2 The Russian-Polish Cause in Paris and Brussels (1845–48) 163

7.3 The February Revolution and Internationalization (1848) 168

7.4 Slavism and National Liberation in the Austria-Poland-Prussia
Triangle (1848–49) 171

7.5 Prisons, Exile, and Escape (1849–61) 176

7.6 Resumption of the Slavic Cause in London and Frustration
with the Polish Insurrection (1862–63) 184

7.7 Bakuninian Political Theory between 1844 and 1863 189

Chapter 8. STATE, NATION-RACE, AND IMPERIALISM (1844–63)

8.1 Europe in the Years 1848–49, Context of the Peoples' Spring 199

8.2 Social Classes, State, Nation-race, and Imperialism 204

8.3 Political Power and Social Stratification in Imperial Russia 210

8.4 National Oppression of Russian and Non-Russian Slavs 220

Chapter 9. NATIONAL LIBERATION AND
SELF-DETERMINATION OF PEOPLES (1844–63)

9.1 Pan-Slavism, Nationalism, and Patriotism 229

9.2 Slav Federation and Revolution: From the Old to the New World 231

9.3 Centralism, Dictatorship, Role of the Tsar and the Bourgeoisie
in the Emancipation of the Slavs and Anti-Germanism 237

PART III
FROM SOCIALISM TO ANARCHISM
(1864–76)

Chapter 10. "FREEDOM WITHOUT SOCIALISM IS PRIVILEGE,
INJUSTICE: SOCIALISM WITHOUT FREEDOM IS SLAVERY AND
BRUTALITY": FROM SOCIALISM TO ANARCHISM (1864–76)

10.1 International Fraternity: Socialism, Federalism, and
Anti-theologism in Italy (1864–67) 253

10.2 Anarchism, the Alliance, and International in Switzerland (1867–76) 258

10.3 Bakuninian Political Theory between 1864 and 1876 296

Chapter 11. SCIENTIFIC-NATURALIST MATERIALISM,
SCIENCE, AND FREEDOM (1864–76)

11.1 Nature-matter and Science 313

11.2 Animality and Humanity 320

11.3 Genesis of Religion: Divine Authority and Human Authority 326

11.4 Different Forms of Idealism 330

11.5 Freedom, Society, and the Individual 337

Chapter 12. HISTORY, SOCIAL FORCE,
AND DOMINATION (1867–76)

12.1 History and Society 345

12.2 Social Forces and Conflict 349

12.3 Domination, Social Classes, and Class Struggle 354

12.4 The Statist-capitalist System: Domination at All Levels 360

Chapter 13. SOCIAL REVOLUTION, MASS ORGANIZATION,
AND CADRE ORGANIZATION (1868–76)

13.1 Destruction-Construction Dialectics: Collectivist-federalist
Socialism and Social Revolution 385

13.2 Social Force, Organization, and Federalism 390

13.3 Mass Organization: The International 396

13.4 Cadre Organization: The Alliance 410

13.5 Dictatorship of Allies and Anti-Semitism 423

Final Considerations.
"IN POLITICS THERE IS NO POSSIBILITY OF HONEST AND
USEFUL PRACTICE WITHOUT A THEORY": AN ASSESSMENT
OF BAKUNIN'S POLITICAL THEORY AND TRAJECTORY 431

Epilogue.
FROM ANARCHISM: BAKUNIN FOR THE TWENTY-FIRST CENTURY
by Rocio Soledad Lescano 435

Bibliographic References 439

Appendix I. BAKUNIN'S WRITINGS (1837–76) 467

Appendix II. BAKUNIN'S PERIODIZATION, THEORETICAL
AND POLITICAL POSITIONS (1836–76) 475

by Eloísa Benvenutti de Andrade

In *Freedom or Death: The Theory and Practice of Mikhail Bakunin*, the work and life of Russian revolutionary Mikhail Aleksandrovitch Bakunin (1814–76) is discussed by Felipe Corrêa in light of a rigorous analysis of Bakunin's political theory, produced between 1836 and 1876. Through an interdisciplinary study, the author presents the result of a thorough and unprecedented investigation that covers Bakunin's political-intellectual trajectory together with a sophisticated survey of his historical context.

The task undertaken by Corrêa, refined in this book, substantiates the relevance of Bakunin's contribution to the field of political theory, but more than that it evidences something rare nowadays: the inalienable importance of the relationship between theoretical coherence and political practice, a profound relationship that is evident in the three phases of the Russian revolutionary's life and thought.

In thirteen chapters, divided into three parts, followed by a rich collection of bibliographical references and appendices, Corrêa develops a careful reflection based on a treatment of Bakunin's books, letters, articles, and speeches. These texts, taken together, present Bakunin's interest in Hegelian philosophy; his involvement in the Slavic national liberation struggle; his ties to the International Working Men's Association and the development of revolutionary syndicalism; and, finally, a concluding comment on Bakunin's defense of anarchism. In the book at hand, Corrêa's successful attempt to delve into Bakunin's theoretical contributions as a militant and intellectual becomes evident, as well as his concern to situate them historically so that a better understanding of their development and changes may be possible. In this way, the author also reveals the extreme importance of Bakunin and of anarchism to—as well as the lack thereof in—the constitution of contemporary political theory and practice.

Corrêa is an anarchist professor and militant, coordinator and researcher of the Institute for Anarchist Theory and History (IATH), and a scholar of Social Change and Political Participation as well as Social Sciences in Education. Through this experience, it seems to have been possible for Corrêa to elaborate this fruitful work, which fulfilled the double task announced above: to discuss both the internal coherence of Bakunin's political theory, and the coherence, both fundamental and necessary, between theory and practice in politics.

This book refutes several arguments usually sustained by traditional studies on Bakunin. It helps us understand the origin of his revolutionary conceptions and discard unjustifiable speculations about his work. In his text, Corrêa is adamant about at least three of the most frequent chimeras concerning Bakunin's life and thought: 1) "Bakunin was not a conservative, reactionary, precursor of fascism, apostle of destruction and chaos, individualist, and disciple of Stirner or Rousseau"; 2) "In his anarchist period, he was not idealistic, opposed to organization, or a pan-Slavist (in the sense of defending a Slavism under the hegemony of the tsar), and neither can his ideas and actions be considered petty bourgeois"; 3) "Bakunin and the Alliance never intended to disorganize or destroy the International"; and it "was not a Jacobin organization nor (anachronistically speaking) a precursor to Bolshevism, but a federalist cadre organization..." (p. 434).

In the first Bakuninian period analyzed by the author, specifically the years 1836–43, one can notice "Bakunin's rapid and constant evolution," observable in the changes that occurred in his philosophical frame of reference between 1837 and 1841, and, above all in 1841, in his political frame of reference. In this way, it is possible to conclude that there is coherence both in the philosophical interests chosen as priorities by the Russian revolutionary, and in his reflections "that take as their theme the human interpretation of reality, the problems of man and the modern world, and the paths to change" (p. 433).

In the second period analyzed in the book, from 1844 until 1863, the conclusion is that there is coherence in the priority that practice acquires over theory and philosophy, that is, in the philosophical referential that supports both Bakuninian voluntarist realism, as well as the thematic centrality of the national question, in the period under review. Corrêa's argument is that in the passage from the Russian-Polish cause to the Slav cause, the emerging modification of the political referential "which complements French republican radicalism with Slavism resulting in revolutionary pan-Slavism" is evidenced. At this time, it is mainly the development of Bakunin's thought and work that is observed, rather than its contradictions, although these appear in some significant moments of his work. In this period, Bakunin's defense, between 1851 and 1862, of the Jacobin model of political organization stands out, as well, in 1851 and 1860, as "dictatorship as a model of post-revolutionary government (in 1851 and 1860); in the flirtation with the tsar and with exclusivist and narrow nationalism in 1851 and 1860–62; in the anti-Germanic and even Germanophobic aspects of 1850–51 and 1862" (ibid.).

Concerning the third period (1864–76), Corrêa finds coherence in Bakunin's "philosophical defense of scientific-naturalist materialism, in the materialist conciliation between theory and practice, in the treatment of the national question as part of the social question, and in the thematic focus on the emancipation of workers" (ibid.). The author also argues that, especially in this period, the Bakuninian passage from socialism to anarchism occurs, between the years 1864 and 1867, not as an element of contradiction, but as an expression of the enrichment of the thought and revolutionary practice of the Russian intellectual and militant. However, Corrêa points out that there is an important contradiction in Bakunin's positive claim to the term "dictatorship" in 1870, and "in the anti-Semitic and, in some cases, anti-German positions" he enunciates, which "were exacerbated from 1869 onwards" (ibid.).

It is therefore through this path investigated by Corrêa that some important points about Bakunin's theory and practice are clarified in his text, among them: Hegelianism, Pan-Slavism, the idea of anarchism, and the embryonic participation in the formation of syndicalism of revolutionary intent.

*   *   *

In the course of his research, Corrêa shows that Bakunin was deeply devoted to the study of Hegel's work, and that Hegel was the greatest theoretical-philosophical influence of the Russian revolutionary; an influence that guided his thought and intellectual production, especially between the years 1837 and 1842. This period can be defined as Bakunin's properly "Hegelian period, in which he is more concerned with the issues of society and community, and moves from the influence of Fichte's subjective and ethical idealism to Hegel's objective idealism" (p. 79). In the meantime, Bakunin establishes himself as the greatest Hegelian in Russia. This influence appears mainly with the idea of *reconciliation with reality*, accompanied by Bakunin's harsh criticism of abstraction and philosophical subjectivism, which would favour the interrelation between theory and practice, allowing the reintegration of the individual into the social totality and offering conditions for rational action. The idea is that this would be possible through education, through becoming aware of objective reality and its concrete manifestations.

Corrêa shows in his research that between 1841 and 1843, Bakunin adopted French radicalism as an expression of German idealism in the form of praxis, and "concomitantly, uses Hegelianism as a dialectic method, as he understands '*dialectics as a driving force for development and historical change*'" (p. 118 *apud* Del Giudice, 1981, p. 339, emphasis added). Through the ideas of conflict and progress, Bakunin would have emphasized the role that contradiction and negation play in placing historical forms in a state of opposition to each other, conflicts that lead to higher stages of "reconciliation." In this way, Bakunin would also have understood history as dialectical, which requires a dialectical method to embrace it, as proposed by Hegel.

In his book Corrêa explains that, since 1844, Bakunin occupied himself with the cause of revolutionary Pan-Slavism, on which occasion he came to know the cause of Poland through the historian Joachim Lelewel. From this, the Russian revolutionary moves on to the defense of the Russian-Polish cause and then to the cause of the national liberation of the Slavs. It was the ideas of a democratic Slavism of revolutionary inclination that led Bakunin to the question of the Polish national struggle and the Slavic cause, consistent with his democratic convictions. And this, "the cause of the Poles, which would soon become the Russian-Polish cause and finally the cause of the Slavs," was the occasion of Bakunin's first practical engagement and the conception of his revolutionary pan-Slavism (p. 164). However, the author stresses that between these years, 1844 and 1863, "it should be noted that Bakunin's pan-Slavism is not just revolutionary; he is also anti-centralist, anti-imperialist, classist, democratic, and federalist" (p. 194), as well as accompanying Bakunin's assertion that freedom must be the way to freedom, and from this, one must understand the defense of the need to build up the autonomy of the Slavic people.

Corrêa shows, therefore, that this initial period from 1843 to 1844 ended for Bakunin the interest exclusively in philosophical questions and theoretical reflections about the world and man, and "a new period of rupture with philosophy opened up, in which the national (Russian-Polish and then Slavic) question replaced the previous theme and supported a concrete political practice" (p. 432). Between 1863 and 1864, the period of rupture with philosophy and theory in general, as well as the focus on the national question, came to an end, and a period of priority on workers' emancipation and conciliation between theory and practice, and between national and the social questions is given priority (p. 433).

For Corrêa, it is finally on the basis of these ruptures "that one can speak of the three great periods of Bakunin: that in which he proceeds from philosophy to praxis (1836–43), that in which he sustains revolutionary pan-Slavism (1844–63), and that in which he proceeds from socialism to anarchism (1864–76)" (p. 432). Corrêa argues that it is possible to identify

the less drastic changes in Bakunin's philosophical-political thinking. In philosophical terms, his change from subjective idealism to objective idealism in 1837; from this to voluntarist realism in 1841; and from this to scientific-naturalist materialism in 1864. In political terms, his change from progressive romantic idealism to French republican radicalism in 1841; the complementing of this with revolutionary pan-Slavism in 1844; and the change from this to revolutionary socialism in 1864 and finally to anarchism in 1868. (Ibid.)

On the question of anarchism, Corrêa defends, together with Berthier, that Bakunin became an anarchist in 1868, and that *Federalism, Socialism and Anti-theologism* (1867–68) is his passage to anarchism. The author explains that it is a methodological mistake to affirm that anarchism is a Bakuninian creation and that everything produced by Bakunin is considered anarchist. For Corrêa, to speak of anarchism requires "a group of people with relatively homogeneous thoughts and actions, people who relate to each other, who have common references and who participate in some way in the social struggles of their time" (p. 302) and this, still, cannot be identified before 1868. Therefore, the author argues that, from a historical perspective, it is reasonable to establish 1868 "as a milestone from which it is possible to situate both the emergence of anarchism and Bakunin's passage to anarchism" (ibid.). However, it is important to consider that this does not mean the development of an absolute and atomized anarchist notion on Bakunin's part since, historically, it is observed that the fundamental characteristic of the anarchist tradition is that it always emerges "through the inseparable relationship between thinkers and popular movements, between anarchists and social struggles, in which both are influenced" (ibid.).

As to Bakunin's political theory in the years 1864–76, Corrêa points out that both the practical experiences of the Russian revolutionary and the work of Proudhon and the theoretical-philosophical contributions of Feuerbach, Comte, Darwin, Marx, and De Paepe were fundamental. However, Bakunin's anarchist conception is considered, by the Russian revolutionary himself, as an extension and radicalization of Proudhon's anarchist system, stripping it of its metaphysical and idealist garb, and occupying itself with privileging "matter [nature] in science and social economy in history as the basis for all further developments" (ibid., p. 297 *apud* Bakunin, 2014, p. 93). From this, the author stresses that both Bakunin's revolutionary socialism and his anarchism must be understood in their entirety, considering their theoretical-philosophical and political-strategic positions. However, Corrêa points out that one must not lose sight of the fact that Bakunin's appropriation of different authors and various practical experiences "is done in a critical way and does not mean, therefore, unrestricted adhesion" (p. 298).

Thus, in political terms, "Bakunin is a proponent of revolutionary socialism, collectivist socialism, or anarchism." This can be defended as, "starting from the concepts of history, society, social force, and social conflict," Bakunin "elaborates a harsh critique of domination in all its forms and of the statist-capitalist system, the modern expression of this historical domination" (ibid.), although some incongruities often appear in his project. Corrêa argues:

> It should be remembered that between 1868 and 1876, Bakunin, supported by scientific-naturalist materialism, harshly criticized both domination in general, national domination, and imperialism in particular, and narrow nationalism and patriotism. In contrast, he defends popular emancipation, national liberation, anti-imperialism, internationalism, classism, and the self-determination of peoples. From such bases, both the call for a collective dictatorship of the allies and the demonstration of frankly anti-Semitic positions seem incongruous with his political theory. (p. 423)

Finally, Côrrea also places Bakunin in the elaboration of revolutionary syndicalism and its diffusion around the world. The author recalls that Leval (2007, p.19) had already stated that "the true founder of revolutionary syndicalism was Bakunin." For the author, even if this statement is exaggerated in relation to the real role of the Russian revolutionary in the embryonic formation of revolutionary syndicalism, due to the fact that this movement was built by the very workers who were part of it, the discussion undertaken by Bakunin about the International in fact contains, in political-strategic terms, what will be called, years later, revolutionary syndicalism.

According to the author, taking into consideration Bakuninian organizational theory, it is possible to adequately understand the enigma of the complex relationship between anarchism and revolutionary syndicalism usually discussed. In this regard, Corrêa already stated in his writings that, "like anarcho-syndicalism, revolutionary syndicalism constitutes an anarchist strategy and cannot be, by means of a rigorous historical study, detached from anarchism" (Corrêa, 2015, p. 109). For the author, the crucial point for an adequate understanding of anarchism, mainly during the twentieth century, would be to understand how and why anarchists proposed revolutionary syndicalism as a model of mass organization that does not require a necessarily anarchist nor antireligious composition. And such an understanding is found precisely in the considerations elaborated by Bakunin.

Another fundamental characteristic of Bakunin's presence in the formation and spread of revolutionary syndicalism is carried out in his historical context of action. The author recalls that in the early 1870s, Bakunin took part in two insurrectionary uprisings: the Lyon Commune in France in 1870, which preceded the Paris Commune, and the Bologna Insurrection in Italy in 1874. On these occasions it was through the influence of Bakunin, and his Alliance followers, that anarchism and syndicalism of revolutionary intent, namely revolutionary syndicalism and anarcho-syndicalism, became established in Switzerland, Spain, Italy, France, and Portugal and spread to other continents.

*   *   *

Finally, it is worth emphasizing the importance of the research carried out by Corrêa, published in this book, as material capable of properly grounding the process of consolidation of radical political thought and especially the revision of the concept of freedom, now no longer restricted to the State. The analysis presented by the researcher, starting from the passage from the metaphysical understanding of man to the radical understanding of class and its historical nature, to scientific materialism, allows us to understand some of the steps taken to think about the emergence of a critical ontology of philosophical idealism, which was the basis of most liberal political theories, and which was concerned, from the context analyzed by Corrêa, with orienting itself to struggle and revolution. Here, then, is available to the academic community, militants, and appreciators—not only of the history and work of Bakunin and anarchism, but also of the history of the construction of political-social theory in the nineteenth century—a very rich resource, capable of shedding light on many historical ruptures, as well as encouraging new research and new problems. But more than that, one finds in the reader's hands a fundamental contribution to the memory of the conception of revolutionary life for the global permanence of radicalism in the left camp that further fuels the living flame of anarchism as one of the main forces in the history of struggle of the working class and subaltern individuals in capitalist and ultraliberal conservative society. Certainly, Corrêa's work, beyond the historical record, is an invitation to critical thinking and to organizing the popular struggle against domination and exploitation.

Arriba l@s que luchan!

Eloísa Benvenutti de Andrade is a Brazilian anarchist and syndicalist militant who holds a PhD in Philosophy and is a professor at Cásper Libero University.

NOTES

BAKUNIN, Mikhail. "Aos Irmãos da Aliança na Espanha (12–13 de junho de 1872)". In: *Escritos Contra Marx*. São Paulo: Imaginário, 2014.

CORRÊA, Felipe. *Bandeira Negra: Rediscutindo o Anarquismo*. Curitiba: Prismas, 2015.

_____. *Freedom or Death: The Theory and Practice of Mikhail Bakunin*. Montreal: Black Rose Books, 2024.

DEL GIUDICE, Martine. *The Young Bakunin and Left Hegelianism: Origins of Russian Radicalism and Theory of Praxis (1814–42)*. Montreal: McGill University (Philosophy PhD), 1981.

LEVAL, Gaston. *Bakunin, Fundador do Sindicalismo Revolucionário*. São Paulo: Imaginário/Faísca, 2007.

Note on the Translation and Quotation of Bakunin's *Complete Works*

Bearing in mind that the greater part of the works and studies of Bakunin are in other languages, numerous translations were necessary in this book. As a result, it was impossible to quote the passages in the original language in an endnote, as is usually done in academic studies. I also considered it inadequate and to some extent disrespectful to readers, to do all the quotations in the original languages. So, despite the tiresome task, I translated all the excerpts into Portuguese to fulfil the requirements of this type of work. Therefore, the translations for this book were done by me and I take responsibility for any problems.

For citations, I prioritized the bibliography in Portuguese—when available—which, in general, is well-translated. In cases where it was necessary to resort to bibliographies in other languages, I gave priority, with a few exceptions, to the authors' original languages, in the case of commentators, and the French texts of the *Complete Works* (International Institute of Social History, Amsterdam, 2000), in the case of Bakunin.[1]

This fundamental source divides Bakunin's work into writings, letters, and other works, and numbers all of these texts. For practical reasons, I decided to follow this division and numbering, both in the bibliography and in the quotations. According to this division it is specified in the quotations whether the texts are: writings [e], letters [c], or other works [o]. According to this numbering, the referencing of the texts is always made by a sequence of five numbers; the first two representing the year of production, and the other three, the number of that text in the year. For example, the text 48020[e] is the twentieth writing of 1848. In all cases of the *Complete Works*, the pages that appear in the references are from the original manuscripts. When, under the same numbering, there are different extracts or versions of the same text I do not mention the page number.

Finally, regarding the spelling of Russian and non-Russian names, I have given preference, in several cases, to the way in which they were consecrated or are used more frequently. I did not necessarily follow the recommendation of transliteration or updated contemporary translation.

NOTE

1 Since more than 60% of Bakunin's writings and nearly 40% of his letters were originally written in French (Péchoux, 1979, pp. 58–59), this was the language chosen for the publication of the *Complete Works* (Bakunin, 2000a). In these, in addition to the French originals, other texts, written mainly in Russian, German, and Italian are found, in the originals and in translations.

INTRODUCTION

This book is a version of the doctoral dissertation "'Real Unity of Thought and Action': Mikhail Bakunin's political theory and trajectory" ("'Unidade Real de Pensamento e Ação': teoria política e trajetória de Mikhail Bakunin"), defended in 2019 in the Postgraduate Program in Education ("Social Sciences in Education" focus area) of the State University of Campinas (UNICAMP), Brazil. It constitutes an *interdisciplinary study of the life and work of the Russian revolutionary Mikhail Aleksandrovitch Bakunin (1814–76). More specifically, it formalizes and discusses, in a relatively in-depth way, Bakunin's political theory produced between 1836 and 1876, anchoring it in the author's political-intellectual trajectory and in the context that surrounded his existence. It is a history of Bakunin's political thought, which encompasses all of his writings, his most important letters, and dialogue with his principal commentators.*

It locates itself in the camp of works by authors sympathetic to anarchism that, without losing their critical capacity, have become increasingly frequent and that, after the publication of Bakunin's *Complete Works*—in 2000, by the International Institute of Social History (Amsterdam)—have been taking a renewed breath. Contrary to several Marxist and liberal studies, and even some of these sympathetic authors, *I maintain in this work that Bakunin has relevant contributions in the field of political theory, systematically exposing them and dividing them into three major periods, in order to locate them historically and such that it is possible to understand his development and changes over time.* Furthermore, I argue that, *if properly periodized, this political theory bears considerable coherence, both internally and in relation to Bakunin's political practice.*

* * *

But, why study Bakunin in the twenty-first century? For two reasons: for his historical importance in the past and for the contributions that he can bring to the present.

When we analyze his historical importance, different aspects can be highlighted. The greatest of which, without a doubt, has to do with the reason that he became a globally known classic thinker: his contributions to the shaping of anarchism (as well as of revolutionary syndicalism and anarcho-syndicalism) and his influence within a considerable group of militants and within a sector of the European workers' movement; an influence that spread, during his life and afterwards, to all continents.

According to renowned academics Benedict Anderson and Lucien van der Walt and Steven Hirsch, after the end of the International Workers' Association (IWA)—

and, most importantly, after the death of Karl Marx, in 1883—anarchism became the predominant element in the internationalist left. A position that, primarily due to the strength of revolutionary syndicalism and anarcho-syndicalism, both mass expressions of anarchism, lasted until after the 1917 Russian Revolution and continued, in many cases, into the 1930s (Anderson, 2014; Van der Walt and Hirsch, 2010a). As I have argued elsewhere,[1] until the 1930s anarchists played a leading role in four revolutions—Mexico (1910–13), Ukraine (1919–21), Manchuria (1929–32), and Spain (1936–39)—and intervened decisively in popular struggles in the Americas, Europe, Africa, Asia, and Oceania (Corrêa, 2015).

Such expression, although it has decreased significantly since then, has continued to stand out in countries like Bulgaria (1940s), Cuba (in the context of the 1959 revolution), Uruguay (1960s–70s)—in these three cases, anarchists were present in union and armed struggles—Algeria (in the context of the liberation struggle, from 1954 to 1962), and France (during "May 1968") (Van der Walt and Hirsch, 2010b; Corrêa, 2015).

Accompanying this movement, anarchism was among the main forces of the workers' movement in Brazil, during the first decades of the twentieth century. It was determinant in the development of revolutionary syndicalism and in episodes such as the 1917 General Strike in São Paulo and the 1918 Anarchist Insurrection in Rio de Janeiro. Even after that, until the 1964 civil-military coup, anarchism continued—particularly through specific groups and organizations—to have a notable presence and influence among workers and students, which were greater or lesser depending on the context (Santos and Silva, 2018; Samis, 2004; Silva [Rafael], 2017).

Although there are valuable exceptions—and they exist, both in the militant and the academic world—in general, anarchism has not been properly studied, inside or outside the university (Van der Walt and Hirsch, 2010a, p. xxxviii). It can be said that the opposition between the political-ideological alternatives that were presented to the world during the twentieth century—capitalist liberalism and Marxist socialism, culminating in the Cold War—contributed directly to this problem. Anarchism, as a type of socialism, did not arouse interest (unless it was critical) on the part of the liberals. As a libertarian doctrine and an alternative in the anti-capitalist camp, it did not arouse interest (again, unless it was critical) on the part of the Marxists. Anarchism often ended up being ignored or simply erased from history.

Through an adequate analysis of the anarchist canon, it is proved, without much effort, that "anarchism and syndicalism [revolutionary syndicalism and anarcho-syndicalism] were formulated principally by two of their imposing figures: [Mikhail] Bakunin and [Piotr] Kropotkin." Thus, Bakunin must be considered one of the two greatest anarchists in history, especially for his role as a precursor and because of the influence he exercised, both during his time and afterwards, directly and indirectly (Van der Walt, 2016a, pp. 85–88).

A charismatic man of immense oratorical and persuasive capacity, Bakunin was the creator of the Alliance, the first anarchist political organization in history, and through it he intervened pointedly in the International Workers' Association after 1868. He had relations with central figures of the European workers' movement and contributed in a determinant way to the direction of that movement in Switzerland, where he lived from 1867 until the end of his life, and in other countries. From 1869 onwards, he headed the hegemonic current of the (federalist-collectivist) International and was Marx's greatest adversary until the so-called "split" of 1872. The so-called Anti-authoritarian International, created that year, and which gave continuity to the work of the International until 1877, found in Bakunin its greatest inspiration. Many of its militants were called "Bakuninists" and, not rarely, this whole anti-authoritarian internationalist camp was referred to as "Bakuninism." In the early 1870s, Bakunin participated in two insurrectionary uprisings: the Lyon Commune in 1870 in France, which preceded the Paris Commune, and the Bologna Uprising in Italy in 1874. It was, finally, through his influence and his Alliance followers that anarchism and syndicalism of revolutionary intent (revolutionary syndicalism and anarcho-syndicalism) established themselves in Switzerland, Spain, Italy, France, and Portugal and extended to other continents.

With Bakunin, more or less the same happens as with studies of anarchism. During the twentieth century, also with valuable exceptions, there were a significant number of studies about him, including by renowned intellectuals, that oscillate between common sense, reproduction of the positions of the opponents and enemies of Bakunin and anarchism, and inadequate theoretical and methodological approaches. There is an impressive collection of nonsense sustained with a veneer of seriousness that was—and, in some cases, continues to be—promoted by scholars from the Marxist, liberal, and even libertarian camp, that lacks any basis in history. As an example, the following characterizations of Bakunin can be mentioned: revolutionary due to sexual impotence and love for his sister (Carr, 1961, pp. 24–25, 35–36); thinker without any intellectual seriousness or originality in the field of thought (Berlin, 1978, p. 108); advocate of the dictatorship of the intelligentsia and moved by the will to take control of or destroy the International (Draper, 1978, pp. 93–96); reactionary and precursor of fascism (Arvon, 1971, pp. 9, 15).

The fact alone that anarchism and Bakunin have such an historical scope, and have not been studied accordingly, would already justify contemporary works on them. But, when it comes to Bakunin, there are still other reasons of an historical order. In 1887, the Italian sociologist and socialist Filippo Turati wrote that, "to tell the life of Bakunin is to tell the life of socialism and of revolution in Europe for more than 30 years (1840–76), as he contributed to or participated in all the progress of revolutionary idea and facts" (Lehning, 1999, p. 7). In the anarchist period mentioned, which goes from 1868 onwards, such contributions and participation are better known. But, in addition to them, there are others, earlier, which correspond to the pre-anarchist period, and which can be mentioned here to reinforce Bakunin's historical importance in those years. A brief passing over the initiatives he undertook, the people he related to, the causes in which he was involved, the struggles in which he participated, and the influence he exercised, gives an idea of his political scope.

Bakunin was the greatest figure of Hegelianism in Russia between 1838 and 1840, standing out as a member of the circle stimulated by Nikolai Stankevitch, who, together with the circle of Aleksandr Herzen and Nikolai Ogarev, was responsible for the formation of a substantial part of the Russian intelligentsia of those times. There, he had relations with the important Russian literary critics Vissarion Belinski and Pavel Annenkov. The latter pointed out at the end of his life that "Bakunin showed proof of the greatest aptitude for dialectics, of qualities indispensable for giving a living form to the formulas of abstract logic, of drawing from it deductions that could be applied to life." He further stated: "We all turned to him to clarify one or other obscure or difficult aspect of Hegel's system," such that, "ten years later (in 1846), Belinski still told me that he did not know anyone who knew better than Bakunin how to dispel [. ..] any doubt regarding the meaning [...] of Hegel's philosophical system" (Lehning, 1999, pp. 31–32).

In Germany between 1840 and 1842 he rose to a prominent, albeit heterodox, position on the Hegelian left. He took classes with Karl Werder, Friedrich Schelling, and Leopold von Ranke, and was an influential colleague of musician Adolf Reichel, artist Bettina von Arnim, columnist Arnold Ruge, communist Wilhelm Weitling, and novelist Ivan Turgueniev, who claimed to have used Bakunin as inspiration for his novel *Rudin*. His abilities in Hegel, praised by Annenkov and Belinski, would also be recognized over time by allies like Pierre-Joseph Proudhon, Ruge and Herzen, and by opponents like Karl Marx and Friedrich Engels.

In 1844 France, Bakunin met several personalities who, in addition to Marx and Proudhon—over whom he would exercise some influence in the following years— included the novelist George Sand, the historian Jules Michelet, and even HFR de Lamennais, Pierre Leroux, Étienne Cabet, Ferdinand Flocon, Louis Blanc, and Victor Considerant. In 1848, he participated actively, weapons in hand, in the barricades and demonstrations of the February Revolution in France. In the context of the Peoples' Spring, he also involved himself in two other uprisings: the Prague Uprising (June 1848)—carried out shortly after the Slavic Congress, in which Bakunin participated and which would later be known as the first pan-Slavist Congress in history—and the Dresden Insurrection (May 1849), in which he distinguished himself as a military commander and had the collaboration of his musician friend Richard Wagner. Arrested, he remains in prison and exile for a long period, from 1849 to 1861, when he makes a spectacular escape, leaving Siberia, passing through Japan, the United States and arriving back in Europe.

He then again takes up the cause of revolutionary pan-Slavism, which had occupied the greater part of his political efforts since 1844, when he learned of the cause of Poland through the historian Joachim Lelewel. He then moves on to the defense of the Russian-Polish cause and, after, to the cause of the national liberation of the Slavs. In 1862, in England, he joined the newspaper *Kolokol,* with Herzen and Ogarev, in an initiative the impact of which was directly felt by populism in Russia— in 1860, it came to be defended by Nikolai Tchernichevski himself, in a controversy about the aforementioned novel by Turgueniev (Lehning, 1999, p. 183). At that time, he was close to the Italian nationalists Giuseppe Mazzini and Giuseppe Garibaldi, he met the Polish general Ludwik Mierosławski and the King of Sweden Carlos XV, through the poet Emil von Qvanten.

He participated, alongside Garibaldi, in the Peace Congress held in Switzerland in 1867, which had been endorsed, among other personalities, by John Stuart Mill and Victor Hugo. He intervened there as a member of the International Fraternity, a secret society he had founded during his time in Italy (1864–67), when he was linked to Princess Zoe S. Obolensky. He was elected to the central committee of the International League of Peace and Freedom, created at the Congress. In 1868, when a considerable progress in political-strategic terms culminated, he joined the International Workers' Association and converted definitively to anarchism.

However, as I stated before, Bakunin is not only important in these historical terms, but also for the contributions he can bring to the contemporary world. First, with regard to contributions to the political-ideological camp of anarchism itself, which has experienced a resurgence at the global level since the 1980s, gaining strength with the end of the bipolarization after the fall of the Berlin Wall and the end of the former Soviet Union.

In this context, anarchism has been growing in presence and strength. Different sectors of popular societies and movements have been influenced, such as Peoples' Global Action (PGA, an international network that stimulated the Global Resistance Movement or "anti-globalization" in different parts of the world) and the Oaxaca Commune, in Mexico, in 2006 (Van der Walt and Hirsch, 2010b; Corrêa, 2015). In Brazil, this resurgence, which started in the late 1970s, has depended on numerous initiatives, such as: journals, athenaeum and cultural centres, political organizations, publishers, study groups, libraries, events of different types, more and less organized participation in the union and popular movements, and in the feminist, black, LGBT, and youth subculture movements. In recent years, Brazilian anarchism has played an important role, directly and indirectly, in the struggles against neoliberalism led by the PGA, in the formation and concepts of the Movimento Passe-Livre (Free Pass Movement, MPL), in the resumption and practice of Black Bloc tactics, as well as in the so-called "June Days" of 2013[2] (Rocha et al, 2018; Ortellado et al, 2013; Solano et al, 2014; Ferreira, 2016; Moraes, 2016).

But Bakunin's contributions need not be restricted to the anarchists. His practical achievements and theoretical works seem to be able to provide analytical and strategic elements for a renewal of broader sectors of the left, whether they are linked to the building of critical thinking or to organization and popular struggle. Especially in the case of those who believe, even today, that it is necessary to confront the consequences of capitalism, neoliberalism, and the modern State by means of a conciliation between equality and freedom. In the end, several themes discussed by Bakunin throughout his life continue to have relevance in the present: the problems of alienation and domination/exploitation, as well as alternatives for combating and overcoming these problems; the desirable relations and mediations between theory and practice; the most appropriate analytical and conceptual tools for a critical interpretation of society; the possibilities of anti-imperialist struggles, including those that do not point toward statist solutions; the perspectives of syndicalism and political organizations. Many others could be cited.

∗   ∗   ∗

This book is divided according to the following axes.

In the opening Chapter 1: "Bakunin's Life and Ideas Are Worth a Thorough Reexamination," I carry out a critical bibliographic review of the studies on the author that were produced during the twentieth and twenty-first centuries, as well as a history of the reestablishment and publication of the Bakuninian *corpus*, which took more than a century to complete. In addition, particularly when I approach Brazil, I invest in drawing up an almost exhaustive inventory of studies of Bakunin, which had previously not existed. Finally, I present the methodological foundations of this work.[3]

Following this, the book has three parts, which correspond to the proposed periodization of Bakunin's life and work: From Philosophy to Praxis (1836–43); Revolutionary Pan-Slavism (1844–63); From Socialism to Anarchism (1864–76). In each of these parts there is an opening chapter with the author's political-intellectual trajectory at that time and the historical context that surrounded his existence. These are the chapters: 2. "The Passion for Destruction Is a Creative Passion"[4]: From Philosophy to Praxis (1814–43); 7. "Freedom, Equality, and Fraternity of Nations"[5]: Revolutionary Pan-Slavism (1843–63); 10. "Freedom Without Socialism Is Privilege, Injustice; Socialism Without Freedom Is Slavery and Brutality"[6]: From Socialism to Anarchism (1864–76)."[7] At the end of each of these, I present certain comments important for the understanding of the Bakuninian political theory of the period in question. I proceeded with writing these chapters while taking into account the relevance of the period in the author's life, such that they deliberately differ from each other in size and depth.

The other chapters of the book correspond to Bakunin's contributions to political theory; the concepts discussed are in the titles, giving a general idea of the content covered. In Part I, these chapters are divided chronologically and thematically; in Parts II and III they are divided by theme only. In Part I, the chapters are: 3. Love-Freedom and Emancipation (1836–37); 4. Alienation Vs. Reconciliation with Reality and Theory-Practice Unity (1837–40); 5. Theory of Revolution and Negative Dialectics

(1841–42); 6. Primacy of Practice and Self-Government of the People (1843). In Part II, 8. State, Nation-Race, and Imperialism (1844–63); 9. National Liberation and Self-Determination of Peoples (1844–63). In Part III, 11. Scientific-Naturalist Materialism, Science, and Freedom (1864–76); 12. History, Social Force, and Domination (1867–76); 13. Social Revolution, Mass Organization, and Cadre Organization (1868–76).

The book has two appendices. The first is a list of all of Bakunin's writings (not including letters and other material), with their titles translated into English and with a coding that classifies them into books and more and less important articles. The second is a summary table, which outlines the periodization (periods and sub-periods) of Bakunin's life and work and, in each of them, the main countries of residence, theoretical-philosophical positions, political-strategic positions, and the main concepts.

*　*　*

Finally, I would like to mention some challenges that I faced in carrying out the research behind this book. First, the fact that I did research without a scholarship for almost the entire year of 2014 and from mid-2016 until the beginning of 2019, a period in which I continued working as a university lecturer. Second, because most of the work and almost all the commentators are in other languages, mainly in French and English, and in some cases in Spanish. It would have been impossible to do this work without knowledge of these languages. Not only for consulting the works, but, above all, for the countless quotations, which, as I mentioned, I preferred to translate in order to facilitate the readers' understanding.

Third, the fact that Bakunin's *Complete Works* were published on CD-ROM, while on the one hand facilitating the digital consultation of texts and searches for terms, on the other hand also caused difficulties. By choice of the editors responsible, the texts on the CD-ROM are very "dirty": in addition to including all the excerpts removed or modified by Bakunin (properly marked), the pagination, which follows the original manuscripts, is much more difficult to locate than a book or article. Fourth, the thematic obstacles that such an interdisciplinary study implies. During his life, Bakunin dealt with very varied topics that, taking into account my training, ended up presenting me with great challenges. If at certain times I found it easier—especially with the political theory of the third period, the one I knew best, as well as with Bakunin's trajectory, which I had been studying since 2010—I also had difficulties with such varied historical contexts and, above all, with the toughest parts of philosophy and those that addressed the Slavic question.

I hope, in the end, that I have managed to carry out a serious study that, despite its limitations, provides the public with a good starting point for understanding Bakunin's life and work, his political theory and his trajectory.

NOTES

1   I refer, in particular, to my master's thesis *Rediscutindo o Anarquismo: uma abordagem teórica* ("Rediscussing Anarchism: a theoretical approach," Corrêa, 2012), later modified and published in book form under the title *Bandeira Negra: rediscutindo o anarquismo* ("Black Flag: rediscussing anarchism," Corrêa, 2015). In these, it and other studies of anarchism are utilized for a work in which: 1) I do a critical review of the most influential literature of studies on anarchism in Portuguese, English, Spanish, and French; 2) I identify the problems and gaps in these studies; 3) I propose a new theoretical-methodological approach capable of solving these problems and filling these gaps; 4) Through this approach, I perform a rereading of anarchism, based on 80 authors and organizations that have existed around the world for the past 150 years, and propose a redefinition by answering what anarchism is and what its main debates and currents are.

2   It is still curious that, in 2014, in a Civil Police investigation that incriminated 23 militants for violent protests in Rio de Janeiro, Bakunin was among the suspects (cf. https://www1.folha.uol.com.br/poder/2014/07/1492074-acusada-de-articular-atos-violentos-professora-diz-que-inquerito-e-ficcao.shtml)

3   Leier, 2006, p. xiv.

4   Bakunin, 2007a[e], p. 136.

5   Bakunin, 48020[e], p. 10.

6   Bakunin, 1988a[e], p. 38.

7   The quotes used to name these chapters were written by Bakunin during the period being studied; cf. references noted to sources.

CHAPTER 1

"BAKUNIN'S LIFE AND IDEAS ARE WORTH A THOROUGH REEXAMINATION"

1.1 BAKUNIN IN THE TWENTIETH CENTURY

It is possible to organize the bibliographic inventory of studies on Bakunin in the twentieth century according to different criteria: type of study (biographies, philosophical or theoretical studies, themes, etc.), region of production (Romanesque, Slavic, Germanic traditions, etc.),[1] language,[2] chronological order (date and/or period in which they were written),[3] or ideological current (Marxist, liberal, anarchist, etc.). This last criterion—which supports the brief bibliographic critique made by Brian Morris in *Bakunin: The Philosophy of Freedom* (Morris, 1998, pp. vii–4, 71–77)—seems to offer good possibilities for briefly surveying the studies of the life and the work of Bakunin during the twentieth century.

1.1.1 Approaches by Marxist Authors

Among the Marxists, an unavoidable starting point is a document entitled "L'Alliance de la Démocratie Socialiste et l'Association Internationale des Travailleurs" ["The Alliance of Socialist Democracy and the International Workers' Association"] written by Paul Lafargue, Friedrich Engels, and Karl Marx,[4] and published in England in 1873.[5] This text formalizes a series of accusations related to Bakunin and makes public secret documents (statute, program, regulations, etc.) of the Alliance, a political organization of which he was a member, with the intention of proving the existence of this organization in different countries—which contradicted the resolutions of the London Conference of 1871—and to show its incompatibilities with the International, and Bakunin's role as its authoritarian and Machiavellian chief.[6]

This writing, which can only be properly understood in the context of the conflicts within the IWA, was intended to support the expulsion of Bakunin and his comrade James Guillaume from the International Workers' Association (IWA)—later called the "First International" (1864–77)[7]—which took place at The Hague Congress in 1872, as well as the consequent "split" of the association.

The text by Lafargue, Engels, and Marx (1978, pp. 297–301) says that, "the Alliance of Socialist Democracy is of a completely bourgeois origin," and that its "efforts, instead of being directed against the bourgeoisie and existing governments, have turned against the International itself" and "against revolutionaries who do not accept its orthodoxy and its direction." The Alliance "tries, initially, to govern it [the International], and works to disorganize it the moment it realizes the failure of its plan." "It shamelessly substitutes the broad program, the great aspirations of our organization, with its sectarian program and narrow ideas." And "to achieve its ends, it refuses no means, no disloyalty; lying, slander, intimidation, ambush serve them equally." Thus, they conclude that the Alliance is the "mortal enemy" of the International.

According to the authors, in articulating secret and public instances, the Alliance was nothing more than a structure to propagate Bakunin's dictatorial concepts: "But this public Alliance hid behind it another which, in turn, was led by the even more secretive Alliance of international brothers, the Hundred Guardians of the dictator Bakunin." The direct attacks on Bakunin run throughout the text, including other accusations. In the anarchist period, responsibility for everything the young Russian Sergei Netchaiev did and produced, the dissociation between discourse and practice and defense of destruction. Before that, the denunciation of revolutionaries, defense of a racist pan-Slavism subordinate to the tsar, enjoyment of government favours, lies in the context of his escape from Siberia in 1861 and flirtation with the tsar in 1862.

As much as Marxist scholars themselves recognize the empirical fragility of this document,[8] not to mention the anarchists,[9] it did not fail to synthesize and propagate much of what, to this day, is attributed to Bakunin in the political and intellectual circles of Marxism.

With the Russian Revolution of 1917, the relationship of Russians with Bakunin took on other shapes, and interest in the life and work of the Russian revolutionary, which had been reviving since 1905–1907, grew considerably. Yuri M. Steklov (born O. Nakhamkis)—a Bolshevik who, after the revolution, became editor of *Izvestia* between 1917 and 1925, collaborated with *Pravda* and was elected a member of the Party's Central Committee—published a biography of Bakunin in four volumes, between 1926 and 1927. In *Михаил Александрович Бакунин: Его жизнь и деятельность* [*Mikhail Aleksandrovitch Bakunin: His Life and His Work*], Steklov, in addition to exposing a wide range of biographical elements of Bakunin's life, promotes the thesis that his trajectory is relevant to Russian revolutionaries, especially because of his influence among the populists, and that he should be considered a precursor to Bolshevism. Leaning on an excerpt from the 1851 "Confession,"[10] written many years before Bakunin became an anarchist, the Bolshevik argues that he had created the concept of Soviet power in this writing, foreseeing the political form that the dictatorship of the proletariat would take. Although with reservations, he believed that Bakunin's legacy should be assumed as part of the prehistory of Bolshevism (Steklov, 1926–27).

In "Michel Bakounine et les Historiens: Un Aperçu Historiographique" ["Mikhail Bakunin and the Historians: An Historiographic Summary"], Arthur Lehning (1979a, pp. 25–29) maintains that this relationship between Bakunin and Bolshevism, although nuanced in Russia by Steklov himself, or even refuted by other Bolsheviks like Vyacheslav Polonsky, was also reinforced by theoreticians and historians of German social democracy. By associating Leninist Bolshevism with Bakunin's tradition, the Social Democrats accused Lenin's supporters of a veritable deviation from the Marxist tradition. In the Soviet Union, although until the early 1920s there had been an immense repression by the Bolsheviks against all dissident currents in the revolutionary camp, including anarchists,[11] there was still some possibility of debate and disagreement.

In 1923, the State Publishers decided—following Lenin's acceptance, in 1920–21, of the request of Michel Sajine (Armand Ross), a former comrade of Bakunin—to publish the complete works of Bakunin, under the direction of Steklov. In a complicated process that involved the refusal of the anarchists (especially Max Nettlau) to provide the originals thanks to the deviations of the revolution, the first volume was only released in 1934, followed by three others, published until the following year. However, the process that had begun in 1931, with Stalin's letter on "some issues on the history of Bolshevism" to the editorial staff of the *Proletarian Revolution* magazine, ended between 1935 and 1936; already in the context of the Great Stalinist Purge, with the deepening of censorship, repression and persecution of dissidence. With this the Soviet regime's interest in Bakunin's life and work ended, and Steklov himself, an enthusiast of this project, was arrested in 1938 and died in one of Stalin's concentration camps.

After that, the respectable studies of Bakunin carried out by Steklov, Polonsky, and other Russians like Evgueni Tarle and Aleksandr Kornilov[12]—which, even though they were produced in a time of immense adversity, particularly due to the complicated access to the sources, and even though they suffered certain "adjustments" to suit the interests of the Communist Party, had a certain historiographical seriousness—gave way to completely ideological works, without any correspondence with reality, and which responded only to political interests.

> In 1950, the second edition of the *Great Soviet Encyclopedia*, rejecting all aspects of the rich Soviet historiography about Bakunin, describes him as a "petty-bourgeois rebel, unable to prove his consistency, his discipline, and his revolutionary stoicism. His petit bourgeois versatility caused him to betray the fundamental interests of the revolutionary movement. Despite his 'revolutionary' phraseology, his role was that of a traitor, averse to the Russian revolutionary Democrats. His struggle against Marx was aimed at destroying the international political party of the working class." (Lehning, 1979a, p. 31)

With rare exceptions, the later writings of the Marxist camp followed this same path in addressing Bakunin and anarchism. This happened both in the political field and in the academic field; both in the case of Stalinist authors and currents and that of non-Stalinists.

In the epilogue of the compilation of texts by Marx, Engels, and Lenin on anarchism and anarcho-syndicalism, published by the Soviet Union with a view to promoting Marxism-Leninism, NY Kolpinsky (1976, p. 333) states that anarchism is a petit bourgeois doctrine, "alien to the proletariat because of its class content," that has no theoretical or practical basis, and which is characterized by "adventurism, born of voluntarist conceptions." It is, moreover, an idealistic and individualistic doctrine, which substitutes "the scientific analysis of the laws of social development with utopian dreams about the absolute freedom of the individual."

In *Revolutionaries: Contemporary Essays*, Eric Hobsbawm (2003, pp. 96, 84) links Bakunin to individualistic liberalism and to a pre-political form, which, according to him, could only have found space in "backward countries" like Spain. In *The Age of Capital (1848-1875)*, the same Hobsbawm (2004a, pp. 227–28), referring to Bakunin as "a peripatetic Russian aristocrat who launched himself into agitation at every opportunity that arose" maintains that he was an apostle of destruction who "nurtured reckless enthusiasm for the potential of criminals and outcasts in society," even though his analyses of the peasantry and some institutions had some basis. For the Marxist historian, Bakunin "was not a great thinker, but a prophet and [... a] formidable conspiratorial organizer," a quality that contributed to the spread of anarchism in countries with specific socio-economic characteristics, such as Italy, Switzerland, and Spain.

In *Karl Marx's Theory of Revolution, Vol. 4: Critique of Other Socialisms*, Hal Draper (1990, pp. 130, 270–304) argues that Bakuninian anarchism was characterized by a "combination of three vaguely mixed ingredients": the first, "a social theory suggested by Proudhon, with at least a little Stirner"; the second, "a socio-economic program that was a (modified) vision of the anti-capitalist collectivism that prevailed in socialist circles, including eclectic appropriations of Marxian theory to fill in the gaps"; the third, in strategic terms, "the conspirator *putschism* of the left Jacobinism of the time," linked to "Babeuf, Buonarroti, Blanqui, Barbès" and called "Blanquism" by historians, and this doctrine was still "distorted by nihilist terrorism with a Russian accent." Bakunin is characterized by Draper as an authoritarian, lying and racist (anti-Semitic) conspirator who wanted to split the International Workers' Association.

In *Beyond Capital: Toward a Theory of Transition*, István Mészáros (2006, pp. 577, 573, 812) also emphasizes the liberal and bourgeois ascendancy of Bakuninian concepts, as well as their contradictions. According to this intellectual, Bakunin did not have a theoretical understanding of society, based his positions on voluntarism without mediation with the socio-historical reality, and did not offer strategic alternatives to reconcile the struggles for immediate improvements (reforms) with the struggle for revolution.

When analyzing the sources of these works, it appears that *none of them take Bakunin's writings into account* and/or the historiography produced by authors sympathetic to anarchism. Kolpinsky takes the writings and letters of Marx and his companions as a basis, interpreted in the key of the Soviet Leninist-Stalinist tradition. Hobsbawm does not explain his sources, but, judging from his arguments, they are not much different from Kolpinsky's. Draper, in turn, uses everything from extensive Marxist documentation to work by liberal historians such as Edward Hallet Carr, Arthur P. Mendel, and Eugene Pyziur (who are deployed to support his thesis). Mészáros takes as a basis only Marx's critical notes on Bakunin's book *Statism and Anarchy* (Marx, 2012).

As can be seen, after almost a century, except for the Russian interregnum in the context of the October Revolution, the camp of Marxism has remained tied to the arguments maintained in the 1873 document written by Lafargue, Engels, and Marx. As I intend to demonstrate later, almost all of these statements are false and are not supported when confronted by history.

1.1.2 Approaches by Liberal Authors

Among liberals, the first relevant effort to systematically address Bakunin occurred in Edward Hallet Carr's biography *Michael Bakunin*, published in 1937 in London. Carr was an English diplomat and intellectual (historian and theorist of international relations) who became interested in Russia and, from the 1930s, wrote copiously. He stood out for his biographies (which, in addition to Bakunin, include Fiódor Dostoiévski and Marx), for his books on international politics and the theory of history, and for the work *A History of Soviet Russia*, published in 14 volumes between 1950 and 1978. For decades *Michael Bakunin* remained the most influential biography of the Russian revolutionary, primarily in English- and Spanish- speaking countries (due to the translation into Spanish in the 1970s by Ediciones Grijalbo).[13]

In addition to the primary sources, Carr bases his study mainly on the Russian authors; in most cases Steklov, but also Kornilov, Polonsky, and Mikhail Dragomanov. For the period of his later life, there are important references to the four volumes of James Guillaume's *L'Internationale: Documents et Souvenirs* [*The International: Documents and Memoirs*]. Carr ended up producing a work rich in detail that contributes a lot to understanding different elements of Bakunin's life trajectory; however, his central concern for the peculiarities of Bakunin's *sui generis* personality had complicated consequences. Bakunin is explained by means of countless politically irrelevant details of his life and in a psychologizing key, poorly founded and unconvincing, which often ignores the historical context, his political thinking and even his rationality.

Carr (1961) dedicates himself to the minute exposition of this intriguing character, highlighting his "enormous dimensions" and "his appearance and his way of walking," which resembled those of "an elephant" (p. 475); his enormous pleasure in cigarettes, drinking, and food (p. 215), with "the vulgar way of eating and drinking" shocking the most unsuspecting company (p. 255); his complete detachment from material goods (p. 133), being, "as always, carelessly dressed" (p. 343), and being irresponsible with his finances, which "were always irreparably complicated and a tangle of confusion" (p. 123); his strange habits, which included sleeping "fully dressed, on a board or on a foldout bed" and with his "famous gray hat, with which he always appeared in public" (p. 497), or, as at the end of his life that, due to diseases, he was always found "sleeping folded in half on a table" (p. 502); as well as his marital relationship, which included a comrade from his militancy, his wife's lover, living in his house, sharing a bed with her, and being the true father of his children (p. 368).

In this book, Bakunin's revolutionary positions in the field of theory and practice are explained by sexual impotence, a forbidden love for his sister and a rebellious temperament made explicit since his early years. Such positions are reproduced based on the judgments of others without proof and an apparent causal relationship with Bakunin's political behavior.

Carr maintains (1961, pp. 24, 73, 37) that, as early as his youth, "[Bakunin's] sexual development is strangely repressed." For him, "at the end of his life, Mikhail was certainly impotent. When he was in his twenties, some of his contemporaries already suspected his inability; and he is not known to have had sex with any woman." The author bases his arguments on statements by the Russian writer Belinski, an old friend of Bakunin: "Belinski appears to have been the only one of his contemporaries attentive enough to relate the scholastic and particularly abstract nature of Mikhail's attitudes in relation to his comrades with his lack of sexual experience." And still, "there must be no doubt, however, that Mikhail found in the jealous furor of his passion [according to him, corresponded] for Tatiana [his sister] a compensation for his exclusion from normal sexual love."

Carr (1961, pp. 111–12) characterizes Bakunin as someone who, since his youth, was a "rebel in terms of temperament" and that this rebellion manifested in the impulsiveness and turbulence of his relationships. For the biographer, "in a character as obstinate as that of Mikhail Bakunin, long-term temperament generally has more importance than tradition and reason," and therefore "his conversion to the revolutionary cause can reasonably be considered a previous conclusion." It was, as he points out, in 1842 that Bakunin went through this "process of converting from family rebellion to political rebellion," which occurred because of his temperament.

With regard to Bakunin's political thought, especially in his anarchist period, the impression is that Carr did not read his biography—although he quotes from the Œuvres edited by Max Nettlau and James Guillaume—or, if he did, that he understood almost nothing. He does not even mention Statism and Anarchy, one of Bakunin's four books, written in 1873, and carries out a very reduced theoretical discussion in comparison to the extent of his study. But the most serious thing is that many of his statements have no basis in Bakuninian work.

For Carr (1961), Bakunin "remained a Hegelian idealist" (p. 451), being the "most complete individualist that has ever existed"; "individualism remains the essence [of his] political and social system [...] and of his opposition to Marx" (p. 452), being derived, in large part, from the influence of the "extreme idealist and individualist Max Stirner." His "conception of freedom was, in the final analysis, extreme individualism" (p. 451), and "he accepts Rousseau's hypothesis that man, not being perverted by social or political authority, is inherently virtuous" since "the more primitive is man, the closer he comes to that ideal" (p. 452).

Bakunin's political thought "is not perfectly consistent, even after 1867, when it no longer underwent substantial changes" (p. 452); "his writings," continues Carr, "although vigorous, were inconsistent; and both in his writings and in his actions, he rarely finished what he had started" (p. 150). This inconsistency is characterized, among other things, by Bakunin contradicting himself in terms of theory and practice, and by trying to reconcile the irreconcilable: freedom and dictatorship. "It is less frequently remembered that he [Bakunin] was the first creator of the concept of a select and intimately organized revolutionary party, maintained not only by common ideals, but by the implicit bonds of obedience to an absolute and revolutionary dictator" (p. 455). Added to the defense of individualism, such a claim of dictatorship contributes to explaining not only that "Bakunin's influence on subsequent history [has] been incomparably weaker than that of Marx" but also that "if Bakunin has a place in history [...], it is as one of the dark ancestors of an aspect of fascism" (p. 456).

The Doctrine of Anarchism of Michael A. Bakunin by Eugene Pyziur came to light in 1955, and was republished countless times until the end of the following decade. In this book, which uses Bakunin's writings and the biographies of Carr and the Russians as sources, Pyziur addresses the Russian revolutionary's theory and political thought in his anarchist period. Although it is a reasonable book, it also reinforces the arguments about the ancestry of Bolshevism and the personal and political contradictions. For Pyziur (1968), Bakunin did not contribute to the ideas of anarchism and proposed a purely destructive program in which "the task of building a new order [should], therefore, be left to posterity." (pp. 15–17). He considers that "despite the vitriolic anti-statist phraseology, Bakunin's doctrine, in reality, reintroduces political power." His anarchism "represents a strange amalgamation of utopian and of non-utopian theorems about freedom, appropriate to the conquest of political power and the establishment of the most severe social discipline." And, in the search for the realization of anarchism, this contradiction is resolved in an authoritarian way: "utopian elements [...] would not be feasible" and "disciplinary [... elements] would undoubtedly predominate," culminating in "complete despotism" (p. 146).

Another reference in the liberal camp is the book *Russian Thinkers* by the Russian-British intellectual Isaiah Berlin, published in 1978, which gathers a collection of texts by the author on the subject. In the essay "Herzen and Bakunin on Individual Liberty"—whose sources are testimonials from people who knew Bakunin, particularly Aleksandr Herzen and Arnold Ruge, Polonsky's biography (that of Carr is not in the references) and some of the revolutionary's books and writings—Berlin analyzes Bakunin in a very critical way, even though he recognizes some of his qualities. For him, Bakunin makes no contributions to the fields of social theory or political doctrine. In terms of political thought, he makes no notable contribution.

In terms of action, he aims only to satisfy his personal, sometimes pathological impulses—his praxis in general is profoundly contradictory.

Bakunin, Berlin posits (1978), is a "talented journalist" (p. 82) who, despite "all his wonderful eloquence, his lucid, skillful, vigorous and, at times, devastating critical power, rarely says anything precise, profound or authentic" (p. 83); his thought "is never original, serious or specific" (p. 108). In truth, what should be sought in Bakunin, according to him, "is not social theory or political doctrine, but a mentality [outlook] and a temperament" (p. 110). For the liberal intellectual, "there are no coherent ideas to be extracted from his [Bakunin's] writings from any period" but "only fire and imagination, violence and poetry, and an uncontrollable desire for strong sensations, for life in high voltage"; for the Russian revolutionary, "any kind of chaos, violence, revolt" was stimulating (p. 111).

Berlin even considers Bakunin to oscillate between captivating "childishness" and the "pathological and inhuman" (p. 113), and that his revolutionary rhetoric, in reality, masks his own contradictions, which involve: the concurrent and uncritical defense of freedom (very poorly defined) and dictatorship (constantly defended); and reprehensible practices in the social camp—when he shows his "infantile enthusiasm to play with human lives in function of social experiments, an appetite for revolution by revolution" (p. 103)—and when he shows himself to be a defender, in the theoretical field, of an "absolute historical and sociological determinism" (p. 109), irreconcilable with the freedom he claims to profess.

During the 1980s, the last major interests in Bakunin in the liberal camp took place. *Mikhail Bakunin: A Study in the Psychology and Politics of Utopianism* by Aileen Kelly—one of the organizers of the reedition of *Russian Thinkers*, in Berlin in 2008, and author of the introduction to the collection—published in 1982, and Arthur P. Mendel's *Michael Bakunin: Roots of the Apocalypse*, published the previous year, are psychobiographies that propose to explain the Russian revolutionary according to psychological theories. Both books—as pointed out in the excellent critique "Bakunin and the Psychobiographers: The Anarchist As Mythical and Historical Object" by Robert M. Cutler (1990)—on the one hand have qualities and on the other have severe limitations, due to the approach used (psychobiography) and methodological problems of different orders, and which end up not able to contextualize Bakunin's positions historically and, therefore, to really understand his ideas and actions[14] (Kelly, 1982; Mendel, 1981).

Kelly (1982) portrays Bakunin as a solipsistic dilettante whose existence, influenced by Stirner, intends to reinforce his own ego in an idealized process of self-deception and fantasy that places itself outside reality. The Russian revolutionary is, for her, an example of those people who, having an introverted, divided, and incomplete personality, choose consciously or not to make mass movements the vehicles for the satisfaction of their aspirations, which derive from their own frustrations. In this way Bakunin, in fact, "applies a combination of moral passion and dialectical ingenuity to the task of presenting cruelty, cynicism, and the desire for power as altruistic satisfaction," and appeals to "his audience to take part in his self-deception, in his fantasies of self-realization and to accept a simulation of paradise" (pp. 292–93); he is, therefore, someone whose behavior has despotic implications.

Mendel (1981)—less contextualized, although more rigorous than Kelly in psycho-historical terms—attempts a psychoanalytical interpretation of Bakunin who, according to him, projected models developed in childhood and adolescence, within family relationships, onto the political relations of adult life. Bakunin's life is understood to be the result of the combination of a pathological narcissism and a poorly resolved Oedipus complex, this combination being "the ultimate source of Bakunin's millenarian aims and destructive means, the roots of his apocalypse" (p. 31).

As can be seen, the liberal authors based their studies on broader and more pertinent sources than the Marxists (such as, for example, the Russian biographers and Bakunin's own writings). Among other issues, the foci adopted ended up contributing to conclusions that emphasized Bakunin's contradictions and the irrelevance of his political thinking.

1.1.3 Approaches by Authors Sympathetic to Anarchism

Among authors sympathetic to anarchism—both openly anarchist militants and scholars, and scholars sympathetic to libertarians in general and Bakunin in particular—there have been studies that, while not problem-free, can in general be considered more honest and rigorous than Marxist and liberal studies.

It was from the anarchist camp that the first biography of the revolutionary emerged: *Michael Bakunin, eine Biographie* [*Mikhail Bakunin, a Biography*] by Max Nettlau was published in three volumes between 1896 and 1900. Nettlau was one of the most important historians and archivists of anarchism. An Austrian, he lived between 1865 and 1943 and, at the end of his life, his collection was acquired by the International Institute of Social History (IISH), Amsterdam. The German-language biography he produced saw the light of day in only 50 copies, collecting biographical information (much of it obtained in testimonies by people who knew Bakunin), documents, writings (several of them in full), notes, and comments by the author. Inaccessible and extremely complicated to understand,[15] this work was fundamental for the establishment of the Bakuninian *corpus* and to substantiate, in addition to Nettlau's own writings (cf., among others: Nettlau, 1964), those of Steklov and Guillaume (cf., among others: Guillaume, 1907a[16]).

Another fundamental work in this camp is the aforementioned *The International: Documents and Memoirs* by James Guillaume, published in Paris in four volumes between 1905 and 1910. Guillaume was a Swiss anarchist militant who lived between 1844 and 1916 and was active with Bakunin in the Alliance and the International. His work focuses on the history of the International Workers' Association between 1864 and 1878 from a collectivist and federalist perspective, and draws on his experience as a militant, which is supported by unpublished reports, documents, statutes, newspaper articles, and letters. This study highlights the contributions related to Bakunin's thought and action, particularly in his anarchist period, which are considered by Guillaume to be fundamental to the development of anarchism in the workers' movement during and after his life (Guillaume, 1985).

In 1913, Fritz Brupbacher, a Swiss social democrat sympathetic to anarchism, published the comparative study *Marx und Bakunin* [*Marx and Bakunin*], which provided the basis for his 1929 biography *Michael Bakunin: der Satan der Revolte* [*Mikhail Bakunin: the Satan of Revolt*]. Without mention of sources, this is, in general, a mediocre biography. Although it offers good information for understanding Bakunin's historical trajectory and the socioeconomic context in which he was inserted, it emphasizes arguments generally associated with the Marxist camp—for example, it relates anarchism to the backward world; considers there to be despotism in the model of political organization defended by Bakunin, and a contradiction between this and the model of mass organization advocated for by the International; takes Bakunin as a precursor to Bolshevism—which were stimulated, to some extent, by the inaccessibility of documents that would come to light years later. Published in France in 1971, this biography received a supplement of notes and texts from Jean Barrué, which contributed to complementing and updating it considerably (Brupbacher, 1955, 2015).

The camp of anarchist syndicalism has also produced other important authors and works throughout the twentieth century. As a founding member of the IISH, Arthur Lehning (1899–2000) was responsible for reestablishing a considerable part of Bakunin's work and for publishing in the Netherlands between 1961 and 1981 seven volumes of the *Archives Bakounine* [*Bakunin Archives*] series, which gave continuity to Nettlau and Guillaume's *Œuvres* (published in Paris between 1895 and 1913), and which were soon republished in France. In addition to the very rich supplements written for these books[17] and other articles, Lehning published: in 1970, *From Buonarroti to Bakunin: Studies in International Socialism*, which contains a chapter on the conflict between Bakunin and Marx in the International; in 1976, *Bakounine et les Autres* [*Bakunin and the Others*], containing letters and fragments of letters written or addressed to the Russian revolutionary, in addition to articles, notes, memoirs, documents, and police reports relating to him; in 1979, the aforementioned "Mikhail Bakunin and the Historians: a historiographical summary," which lists and analyses the studies produced until the late 1970s (Lehning, 1970, 1976/1999, 1979a).

In this camp of anarchist syndicalists there are three other authors who deserve to be mentioned. Gastón Leval published *La Pensée Constructive de Bakounine* [*Bakunin's Constructive Thought*] in 1976, focusing theoretically and very strictly on Bakunin's work from the anarchist period (Leval, 1976). Part of that same tradition, René Berthier published in 1991 *Bakounine Politique: Révolution et Contre-révolution* en Europe Centrale [*Political Bakunin: Revolution and Counterrevolution in Central Europe*], politically discussing the history of Germany and German-Slavic relations from Bakunin's perspective (Berthier, 1991). Ramón Liarte published in 1995 *Bakunin: La Emancipación del Pueblo* [*Bakunin: The Emancipation of the People*], in which he makes a biographical sketch of the Russian revolutionary (Liarte, 1995).

Among academics sympathetic to anarchism and/or Bakunin, there were also a series of studies of greater or lesser quality. In France, two biographies were published during the 1930s: *La Vie de Bakounine* [*The Life of Bakunin*] by Hélène Iswolsky (1930) and *Michel Bakounine: La Vie d'un Révolutionnaire* [*Mikhail Bakunin: The Life of a Revolutionary*] by Hanns-Erich Kaminski (1938). In 1950, the study *Bakounine et le Panslavisme Révolutionnaire* [*Bakunin and Revolutionary Pan-Slavism*] by Benoît-P. Hepner (1950) came to light—an important reference that, despite insisting on the thesis of Bakunin's inconsistency, portrays his period of struggle for the national liberation of the Slavs very well. And, in 1972, *Bakounine: Absolu et Révolution* [*Bakunin: Absolute and Revolution*] by Henri Arvon (1972), who links Bakunin's thinking with religion and argues that the engagement of the Russian revolutionary was motivated by an existential search for the absolute.

A work that constitutes a certain landmark is *Bakounine: Combats & Débats* [*Bakunin: Battles and Debates*] organized by Jacques Catteau and published in 1979 as a result of the International Bakunin Colloquium held in Paris in January 1977. It has 15 articles that discuss issues related to historiography, trajectory, political and personal relations, and Bakunin's international struggles,[18] and has two of his own texts (Catteau, 1979).

In Russia, between the 1960s and the 1990s, despite the immense difficulties of the Soviet regime, Natalia Pirumova was the greatest scholar and promoter of Bakunin's work. In addition to a series of articles, she published the biography Бакунин [*Bakunin*] in 1970 and Социальная доктрина М. А. Бакунина [*The Social Doctrine of M. A. Bakunin*] in 1990, in which she elaborates a very rigorous debate of Bakunin's political-social thought (Pirumova, 1970, 1990).

In the 1980s, three works in the field of philosophy and political theory stand out and one in the field of history. *The Young Bakunin and Left Hegelianism: Origins of Russian Radicalism and Theory of Praxis (1814–42)* by Martine Del Giudice is an excellent doctoral dissertation in philosophy defended in 1981 at McGill University in Canada. In this thesis, the author contests that Bakunin was conservative in the pre-1840 period and argues that "the concern with the practical application of philosophy as a political tool for revolutionary action constitutes the principal theme of [his] first works," located in the camp of left Hegelianism (Del Giudice, 1981, p. ii).

The Social and Political Thought of Michael Bakunin by Richard B. Saltman, published in 1983 in the United States, aims to introduce Bakunin academically into the field of political theory, opposing Marxist and liberal critics. To this end the author, emphasizing Bakunin's coherence, analyses his texts from the anarchist period and systematically and rigorously discusses his political and social thinking. The most questionable aspect of his work is the link he holds there to be between Bakunin and the work of naturalist J.B. de Lamarck (Saltman, 1983). In *Bakunin y el Socialismo Libertario* [*Bakunin and Libertarian Socialism*] published in 1986 in the Hispanic world, Angel Cappelletti produces a work similar to that of Saltman, expounding, after a brief biographical sketch, theoretical aspects of Bakunin's mature work (Cappelletti, 1986). *Bakunin and the Italians* by T.R. Ravindranathan (1988) discusses Bakunin's history in Italy and his influence among Italians starting from 1864 (Ravindranathan, 1988).

Robert Cutler, a North American academic, produced some interesting articles about Bakunin from the 1980s on that are worth mentioning (Cutler, 1990, 1992, 2014). In 1990, in France, Madeleine Grawitz published the biography *Michel Bakounine* [*Mikhail Bakunin*] which, although recent, extensive, and favourable to Bakunin, drinks deeply from Carr's fountain and, as pointed out by Eckhardt (2000), has numerous problems, among which are the limitations of sources and inaccuracies in the data presented (Grawitz, 1990). Although synthetic, the book *Bakunin: The Philosophy of Freedom* by Brian Morris, published in 1993, constitutes an important reference when approaching Bakunin's biography and summarizing the theoretical aspects of his anarchism. Morris defends Bakunin from liberal and Marxist criticism, and argues in favour of his theoretical coherence, his link with anarchism, and his contemporary relevance (Morris, 1993). In that same year, Demétrio Criado published *Ética y Poder Político en Mijail Bakunin* [*Ethics and Political Power in Mikhail Bakunin*], focusing on Bakunin's anarchist period and discussing his thinking starting from his concepts of materialism, ethics/morals, and power/politics (Criado; 1993).

Authors sympathetic to anarchism have tended to portray a Bakunin more in line with historical reality and, while recognizing his complexities, ambiguities and complications, have highlighted the aspects of his life and work that influenced the circles of workers and revolutionaries in nineteenth-century Europe. Bakuninian praxis had a significant impact in countries such as Switzerland, Spain, Italy, France, Portugal, and Russia, and this historical repercussion cannot be explained by Bakunin's personal characteristics and not even due to several aspects highlighted by his critics, such as his authoritarianism or his contradictions.[19] Being more interested in Bakunin due to such influence, these authors, whose intellectual productions are not without problems, had, however, much more depth and honesty in the treatment of his trajectory, his writings, and his correspondence. They produced much more rigorous studies than the Marxists and liberals and, from the 1970s–80s, they were at the forefront of the first, more careful, efforts to profoundly systematize his political-philosophical thought.

1.2 THE BAKUNINIAN *CORPUS*

The Bakuninian work, if compared to that of other thinkers of the same size, stands out for some peculiarities. It is known that Bakunin wrote copiously; his work consists of writings (books, pamphlets, articles, drafts, excerpts), letters and other productions (autobiographical excerpts, studies, personal notes, etc.). However, this *corpus* is rather complicated, mainly for two reasons: those related to Bakunin's life—and which encompass his personal and political interests, his type of militancy, his relationship with intellectual production, and his conditions for this production—and those related to the process of compiling and disseminating Bakuninian work.[20]

Despite having received a solid family education and having graduated from the great philosophical circles of Russia and Germany, Bakunin never considered himself an intellectual. In a 7 May, 1872 letter sent to his comrade Anselmo Lorenzo, he states: "I am not a philosopher, nor a system inventor like Marx" (Bakunin, 72013[c], p. 3). This explains, to some extent, his relationship with intellectual production itself, which, especially after 1842–43, in the context of his break with philosophy, gains more uncompromised outlines from the point of view of systematization and even the care of the original manuscripts. Besides this, because Bakunin was undoubtedly and in accordance with his reading of himself, a man of action—with participation in insurrections and armed uprisings, long years in prison, activity in social struggles, popular movements, and secret societies—it was necessary, during his life, to destroy an important part of his own texts to escape repressive persecution or to keep unrevealable secrets.[21]

Bakunin never completed a book that could have exposed his thinking in a systematic way. In his later life, he tried to do this on four occasions, but the manuscripts remained incomplete and unstructured: 1) *Fédéralisme, Socialisme et Antithéologisme* [*Federalism, Socialism and Anti-theologism*], of 1867–68[22]; 2) *L'Empire Knouto-germanique et la Révolution Sociale* [*The Knouto-Germanic Empire and the Social Revolution*], of 1870–71[23]; 3) *La Théologie Politique de Mazzini et l'Internationale* [*The Political Theology of Mazzini and the International*] of 1871[24]; 4) *Государственность и анархия: Борьба двух партий в Интернациональном обществе рабочих* [*Statism and Anarchy: The Struggle Between the Two Parties in the International Workers' Association*] of 1873.[25]

In these cases, as in all his intellectual production after 1843, Bakunin's writings have a profound relationship with the context in which they were inserted. They were never disinterested or turned to posterity—they intended, permanently, to propagate ideas, persuade people, intervene in debates. In the four books in question, Bakunin's interests were profoundly political: persuading members of the International League of Peace and Freedom, in the first; analyzing the Franco-Prussian War and its consequences for the workers' movement, in the second; responding to Giuseppe Mazzini's attacks on the Paris Commune to the International and criticizing his thinking, in the third; formulating and disseminating the federalist-collectivist critique of the State in the context of the conflict with Marx and the centralists in the International, in the fourth (Angaut, 2005, p. 13).

Because of this intentionality contained in the writings, and taking into account the dynamism of the political conjuncture of the time and of his own life, besides certain personal characteristics, Bakunin ended up producing a body of work that, although very rich, is fragmented and little- (in some cases ill-) structured or systematized (Avrich, 1970, p. 130). During his lifetime, he moved houses numerous times, often from one country to another. The multiple projects, struggles, and conflicts in which he was involved often required changes in intellectual priorities. His peculiar way of being, which so attracted liberal historians, adds to these other factors in explaining the constant changes in intellectual plans—when writings were interrupted to make way for others or simply abandoned[26]; when articles were expanded to become pamphlets, and these were expanded to constitute books; when themes came into and went out of the field of interest—and Bakunin's detachment with material goods in general, including books.[27] He never had a significant library, nor did he produce in places that offered adequate conditions, with due access to the literature.

To these aspects of Bakunin's life are added others, related to the reconstitution of the Bakuninian *corpus*. According to Lehning (1979a), lots of his writing and letters were lost.[28] In addition to the material destroyed by Bakunin himself, there were other documents lost during his life, such as those that were burned by his comrade Carlo Cafiero in 1874 when he left Baronata, the property where he lived on the Swiss border with Italy. With Bakunin's death, in addition to the normal circumstances that involved the loss of an unprecedented part of his production, writings and letters were compromised in other episodes: the death of comrade Alfred Andrié, who found himself with all the documents left by Michel Sajine (Armand Ross), and whose son later informed Guillaume that his mother had used them to light the house fire; the fire in 1893 at the house of comrade Errico Malatesta, which compromised the material that was there; the destruction of documents by James Guillaume in 1898 due to the depression caused by the death of his daughter; the loss of material that was at the University of Naples when in 1943 the archive building was destroyed by the German army.

In "Écrits et Correspondance de Bakounine: Bilan des Publications" ["Bakunin's Writings and Correspondence: Audit of Publications"], Pierre Péchoux (1979) states that at the time of his death Bakunin's work was practically nonexistent due to the near impossibility of being found. As he argues, just over half of his writings were published during his lifetime (65%); the rest came to light posthumously. Of the published material, with the exception of the French publications made in Geneva or Zurich, everything was found in other countries: Italy, Spain, France, England, Sweden, Russia, Germany, Bohemia, Switzerland, and Belgium. Only 38 texts had been published in pamphlets or books and, of these, only 16 with the author's name.

After Bakunin's death there was therefore a need to reconstruct his work and bring together both published (and rarely found) and unpublished material.

According to Jaap Kloosterman in the article "Les Papiers de Michel Bakounine à Amsterdam" ["The Papers of Mikhail Bakunin in Amsterdam"] (Kloosterman, 1985/2004), after 1876 there were huge efforts, at the demand of anarchist militants, to compile and disseminate Bakunin's work. With his death that year, his documents remained with his wife Antonia K. Bakunin, divided into two packages: one of intimate, non-political letters, and another with unpublished political and philosophical writings.[29] After negotiation with Antonia the militants, headed by Guillaume, managed to obtain in 1876 the package of the political and philosophical texts. They committed themselves to working towards the publication of Bakunin's complete works. Guillaume commented on the occasion: they are "papers that form a real chaos and that are difficult to classify" (*apud* Kloosterman, 1985/2004, p. 6). Antonia remained with the personal documents, which were partially copied by Nettlau in 1899 and 1902, and later destroyed at the University of Naples in 1943.

That is, if the difficulty in accessing the published material was not enough, there was still an enormous challenge relating to the unpublished writings: it was necessary to understand all the disorder of the manuscripts and, literally, to gradually reconstruct the complex Bakuninian *corpus*. In 1878, Guillaume sent the political documents to the anarchist geographer and comrade Élisée Reclus, who selected two excerpts from the second unpublished part of *The Knouto-Germanic Empire* and published them independently: "La Commune de Paris et la Notion de l'État" ["The Paris Commune and the Notion of the State"] in 1878 (Reclus's selection with considerable changes in the text and title) and "Dieu et l'État" ["God and the State"] in 1881 (Reclus and Carlo Cafiero's selection and title).[30] This procedure—of comrades who selected, modified, and corrected the writings—already underway during Bakunin's life constituted yet another complicating factor after his death.[31]

It was in this interim that Max Nettlau became interested in Bakunin and continued the work of retrieving and publishing the manuscripts; he coordinated the first volume of the *Œuvres*, which was published in 1895 in Paris, the same year that Mikhail Dragomanov published a set of 105 unpublished letters from Bakunin in Germany, almost all addressed to the Russians Aleksandr Herzen and Nikolai Ogarev[32] (Dragomanov, 1895). As stated, in addition to addressing Bakunin's trajectory, the biography that Nettlau published between 1896 and 1900 made 127 unpublished letters available (Nettlau, 1896–1900). Guillaume coordinated the next five volumes of the *Œuvres*, continuing Nettlau's work and presenting them to the public in 1907, 1908, 1910, 1911, and 1913 respectively. The six volumes of the *Œuvres*[33] provided a collection of 34 writings from his later life (Bakunin, 1895–1913).

Michel Sajine—who had undertaken initiatives with Kropotkin to publish Bakunin's complete works in Russian, and who published their first volume in 1915 in London—wrote to Lenin in 1920 asking for funding to finish the project. Although he seemed to have been favourable, the funds were not released and the project was not taken forward. In 1923—after the discovery in 1920 of the "Confession"—the State Publishers decided to edit Bakunin's works, which had four volumes published between 1934 and 1935, under the responsibility of Steklov. With the foundation of the IISH and the incorporation of the Nettlau archives, not without immense difficulties due to the rise of Nazism,[34] the IISH continued the recovery, maintenance, and translation of Bakunin's work. The aforementioned volumes of the *Bakunin Archive* organized by Lehning between the 1960s and 1980s are an important part of the result of this work (Lehning, 1979a).

Between 1919 and 1935—with the exception of the publication of the three volumes in German of the *Gesammelte Werke* [*Selected Works*] organized by Erwin Rholfs and Nettlau, which made 31 new letters available—all new publications were done in Russia. Between 1919 and 1921, the Union of Russian Anarchists published five volumes of the *Избранные сочинения* [*Selected Works*], with 24 new writings; Polonsky, between 1923 and 1933, three volumes of the *Материалы для биографии М. Бакунина* [*Materials for M. Bakunin's Biography*], with 25 new writings; Kornilov, in 1925, *Годы странствии Михаила Бакунина* [*Mikhail Bakunin's Pilgrimage Years*], with 193 new letters; Steklov, in 1934–35, the four volumes of the *Собрание сочинений и писем* [*Complete Works and Correspondence*], with 30 new writings and 341 new letters. In 1938–39, Nettlau published four volumes of the *Works*, with 24 new writings, in Spain.

From the 1960s to the 1980s, the publication in the Netherlands, and then in France, of the *Bakunin Archives*, organized and commented on by Lehning, with 60 new writings, stands out. However, it was the last great wave of the discovery of letters, which took place between 1944 and 1976—in which Bakunin's correspondence with the Swedes, the Finns, and Serguei Netchaiev was recovered—which contributed towards a new milestone in the discussions.

In 1962, when Natalie Herzen's archives could be accessed, historian Michael Confino found a letter that Bakunin sent to Netchaiev in June 1870. Until then, the famous and controversial 1869 document "Катехизиса Революционера" ["The Catechism of a Revolutionary"] was considered to have been written by Bakunin. In general terms, this text—the letter of which found by Confino proved to have been produced by Netchaiev (although it is likely that he relied on contributions from Bakunin in the redaction)—defended, in addition to an exclusively destructive conception of revolution, a notion of an amoral revolutionary, who should be willing to do anything to advance the revolution, including killing, exploiting, deceiving, and blackmailing allies and potential allies.[35] The attribution of this document to Bakunin was what contributed to a large part of the arguments about his authoritarianism and his inconsistency, when, for example, the proposals of the 1869 "Catechism" were compared to his public writings of the anarchist period.

From the 1960s, due to this new wave of letters in general and the correspondence with Netchaiev in particular—which, among other themes, addresses Bakunin's conception of revolutionary political organization in some depth—it became necessary to revise the investigations and put into question a good part of the judgments that had been made about Bakunin.[36]

However, although the reconstitution of the Bakuninian *corpus* was then in the process of being concluded, there was another problem: access. During the 1980s, to consult his complete work it was still necessary to resort to countless books in different languages. In the two decades that followed, the IISH endeavoured to finish compiling everything that had been found and to digitize and translate the writings. Bakunin wrote mainly in four languages: French, Russian, German, and Italian. The writings were, for the most part, originally written in French; the letters were written, generally, in Russian and French. This was the reason that contributed to the IISH's decision to publish the complete works in French.

This effort to compile, digitize, and translate the work culminated in 2000, with the publication of the *Bakounine: Œuvres Complètes* [*Bakunin: Complete Works*] CD-ROM by the International Institute of Social History itself.[37] More than 120 years after his death, Bakunin's complete work (at least, what was left of it) was finally made available to the public, with images and transcriptions of 1,200 letters and 350 writings penned between 1823 and 1876.[38] With this, all that remained of the Bakuninian *corpus* was reconstituted and available to scholars on the subject.

1.3 BAKUNIN IN THE TWENTY-FIRST CENTURY

The publication of the *Complete Works* in 2000 gave new wind to research on Bakunin, especially in the camp of authors sympathetic to anarchism. Since then, great studies, many of them innovative, which have established themselves as the best in the area in which they were produced have come to light.

In 2002, Paul McLaughlin published *Mikhail Bakunin: The Philosophical Basis of His Anarchism*, which constitutes the best study in the *stricto sensu* philosophical field so far, and which is dedicated to systematically exposing Bakunin's conceptions of naturalist materialism and negative dialectics, comparing them to the thought of other philosophers. The foundations of the discussion are Bakunin's more specifically philosophical writings: the famous 1842 article "Die Reaktion in Deutschland, Ein Fragment von einem Franzosen" ["The Reaction in Germany, a Fragment from a Frenchman"][39] and the late 1870 text titled "Considérations Philosophiques sur le Fantôme Divin, sur le Monde Réel et sur l'Homme" ["Philosophical Considerations on the Divine Phantom, the Real World and on Man"], which should be an appendix to the second part of *The Knouto-Germanic Empire*.[40] The only complicating factor in this study is that it is based on two writings from very different periods; it is not necessarily possible to understand, exactly, the extent to which the negative dialectic of the Hegelian period of 1842 has continuity in the naturalist materialism of the anarchist period of 1870. Such that not everything that is discussed in the book can, without due precautions, be considered as the "philosophical foundations of his [Bakunin's] anarchism" (McLaughlin, 2002).

In 2005, Jean-Christophe Angaut completed his doctorate in philosophy at the Nancy 2 University in France, titled *Liberté et Histoire chez Michel Bakounine* [*Freedom and History in Mikhail Bakunin*]. Said study—the most rigorous and complete in the field of political philosophy today—based on Bakunin's complete work, articulated an excellent theoretical-philosophical assessment, and discussed Bakuninian political thought in the different periods of his life over more than 600 pages. Among its few problems are: the argument that Bakunin was conservative until 1840, and the discussion of the Alliance and its relationship with the International. Among its (also few) limitations are: the lack of a more complete and linear exposition of Bakunin's history (which the author did not intend to do) and the author's choice, especially in the Hegelian and pan-Slavic period, to discuss Bakunin's texts almost individually— which, if on the one hand allowed us to understand them in more depth, on the other deprived the reader of a more unified understanding of the period (Angaut, 2005).[41]

In 2006, Mark Leier published the biography *Bakunin: The Creative Passion*, enjoying use of the *Complete Works* as well as of recent studies, which sought to update the discussions after the discoveries of the 1960s. Contrasting, to a large extent, Carr's biography and the premises of Marxist critics, Leier (2006, pp. xii-xiii) proposes studying Bakunin by focusing "both on the evolution of his ideas and on the details of his life" and offering an "interpretation [...] useful for those interested in understanding anarchism and social change." In recent years, this study has been elevated to the top of historiographical productions on the life of Bakunin. Even so, it is worth mentioning that it is a study that, at times, is not very critical, refraining from mentioning some facts and issues that are uncomfortable to libertarians (Leier, 2006).

René Berthier published a wide and also very rigorous collection of writings and articles focusing on Bakunin, amongst which are: a considerable part of his 2008 *Essai sur les Fondements Théoriques de l'Anarchisme* [*Essay on the Theoretical Foundations of Anarchism*], which discusses Bakunin in the light of comparisons with Proudhon and Marx; the three volumes of *L'Autre Bakounine* [*The Other Bakunin* (2010), which cover Bakunin's history and theory from the pre-anarchist period, between 1836 and 1868; the interview "Political Theory and Method of Analysis in Bakunin's Thought," which focuses on Bakuninian theoretical-methodological contributions; various articles, some of which have been translated into Portuguese (Berthier, 2008, 2010, 2014b).[42] Some of these writings have that characteristic of Leier's biography—of, at certain times, omitting or attenuating elements that are uncomfortable to libertarians—and are supported by a permanent parallel with Marx and Engels, which, at certain moments, is excessive.

In 2016, Wolfgang Eckhardt—in addition to the 2005 compilation *Von der Dresdner Mairevolution zur Ersten Internationale. Untersuchungen zu Leben und Werk*

Michail Bakunins. [*From the Dresden Revolution to the First International: Studies on the Life and work of Mikhail Bakunin*] and numerous articles[43]—published the book *The First Socialist Schism: Bakunin vs. Marx in the International Working Men's Association*, which over 600 pages discusses, very carefully, the conflicts between federalists and centralists in the IWA in the light of the relations between Bakunin and Marx (Eckhardt, 2016).

Finally, mention should be made of the publication of *Actualité de Bakounine, 1814-2014* [*News of Bakunin, 1814–2014*], a compilation of texts coordinated by Philippe Pelletier on the occasion of the bicentenary of Bakunin's birth (Pelletier, 2014)[44]; and also of *Reconciliación y Revolución: la Juventud Hegeliana de Mijaíl Bakunin* [*Reconciliation and Revolution: Mikhail Bakunin's Hegelian Youth*], an academic study by Pablo Abufom Silva, performed in 2010 in the area of philosophy at Universidad ARCIS, Chile (Silva [Pablo], 2010).

1.4 BAKUNIN IN BRAZIL

As I pointed out in my article "A Bibliografia de Mikhail Bakunin" ["The Bibliography of Mikhail Bakunin"] (Corrêa, 2010b), in Brazil the publication of Bakunin's writings and letters began in 1979, focusing on his anarchist period and, in a certain sense, giving continuity to the Portuguese publications that had appeared in 1975.

There are still very few writings and letters from Bakunin's pre-anarchist period in Portuguese. From the period of transition to anarchism and anarchist (1867 onwards), the following audit can be made: of the four books, practically three were published (Bakunin, 1988a [e]; Bakunin 2014d [e], 2014e [e], 2014f [e]; Bakunin, 2003a [e]); of the most important writings, about 60% are published; of all letters, less than 10%. The vast majority of publications were made by the publisher Novos Tempos/Imaginário/Intermezzo, although others (Hedra, Faísca, Cortez, Alternativa, and L&PM) have had some relevance.

One can inventory the following about Bakunin. In addition to the translation of some excerpts from statements contained in *Bakunin and the Others* (Lehning, 1976)—published in Brazil in 1994 under the title *Bakunin* (Coêlho, 1994)[45]—there are some studies produced by Brazilian authors and others that were translated. Today, there are two biographies in Portuguese: the first, brief and introductory, *Bakunin: Sangue, Suor e Barricadas* [*Bakunin: Blood, Sweat and Barricades*] was published in 1988 by the Brazilian Sérgio Norte (Norte, 1988); the second is a translation of the aforementioned *Bakunin: The Satan of Revolt* by Fritz Brupbacher, published in 2015 containing Jean Barrué's appendix of notes and texts from the French edition (Brupbacher, 2015). Smaller studies that are also dedicated to the discussion of his trajectory are my "Introduction" to the compilation of letters *Revolução e Liberdade: Cartas de 1845 a 1875* [*Revolution and Freedom: Letters from 1845 to 1875*] (Corrêa, 2010b), which is accompanied by a chronology of his life at the end of the volume (Corrêa, 2010a); and the first part of the book *Introdução ao Pensamento Político de*

Bakunin [*Introduction to Bakunin's Political Thought*] written by the Brazilian Alex Buzeli Bonomo (Bonomo, 2017).

There is also a collection of studies that are not very in-depth, which aim, in some way, to discuss some specific aspect of Bakunin's political thought from his later life,[46] among which are the following: of my own authorship, I point out the book *Teoria Bakuniniana do Estado* [*Bakuninian Theory of the State*] (Corrêa, 2014c) and some chapters and articles that I produced in the field of history and political theory[47]; of other authors, I highlight the second part of the previously mentioned book by Bonomo (2017) and *Bakunin, Fundador do Sindicalismo Revolucionário* [*Bakunin, Founder of Revolutionary Syndicalism*] by Gastón Leval, which is the translation of an excerpt from the aforementioned book *Bakunin's Constructive Thought* (Leval, 2007). I also highlight the work by Selmo N. Silva, which includes the chapter "O Bakuninismo: Ideologia, Teoria, Estratégia e Programa Revolucionário Anarquista" ["Bakuninism: Ideology, Theory, Strategy and Anarchist Revolutionary Program"] and the article "A Anarquia Social: Resistência, Insurgência e Revolução Social na Teoria de Bakunin" ["Social Anarchy: Resistance, Insurgency and Social Revolution in Bakunin's Theory"] (Silva [Selmo], 2016, 2014); Rafael Abrunhosa's master's thesis, *Fundamentos Político-Pedagógicos a Partir do Pensamento de Mikhail Bakunin* [*Political-Pedagogical Foundations Starting from Michael Bakunin's Thought*] (Abrunhosa, 2015); the translated chapters of Francesco Codello, "Mikhail Bakunin: a Educação como Paixão e Revolta" ["Mikhail Bakunin: Education as Passion and Revolt"] (Codello, 2007) and of René Berthier, "Elementos de uma Análise Bakuniniana da Burocracia" ["Elements of a Bakuninian Analysis of Bureaucracy"], "Bakunin Fazia Política?" ["Did Bakunin Do Politics?"], as well as his texts "O Emprego do Termo 'Anarquia' em Bakunin" ["Use of the Term 'Anarchy' in Bakunin"] and "Atualidade de Bakunin" ["News of Bakunin"] (Berthier, 2011d, 2011e, 2014a, 2015a).

Among the material that was published as an appendix of Bakunin's publications, I highlight: Berthier, "Introduction to *Writing Against Marx*" (Berthier, 2015b); Jean Barrué, "Bakunin and Education," the notebook of Brupbacher's book, "Bakunin and the 'Franco-German Annals' (1843)," "Pan-Slavist Bakunin?" and "Bakunin and Netchaiev" (Barrué, 2003, 2015a, 2015b, 2015c, 2015d); Maurício Tragtenberg, "Introduction to *Federalism, Socialism, and Anti-theologism*" and "Introduction to *God and the State*" (Tragtenberg, 1988a, 1988b); Maurice Joyeux, "Bakunin in France" (Joyeux, 2015); Thyde Rossell, "The International in Italy" (Rossell, 2015); Anatol Gorelik, "Bakunin and the Dictatorship of the Proletariat" (Gorelik, 2015); Alexandre Samis, "Bakunin, Science and Revolution" (Samis, 2015a); Amédée Dunois, "Mikhail Bakunin" (Dunois, 2016); Alexis Vencia, "Bakunin and Revolutionary Action in Russia" (Vencia, 2016); Jean-Marc Raynaud, "Mikhail Bakunin and Libertarian Education" (Raynaud, 2003); Alex B. Bonomo, "Introduction to *God and the State*" (Bonomo, 2011); Paulo-Edgar Resende, "Introduction to *Statism and Anarchy*: 'The Struggle Between the Two Tendencies in the International Workers' Association'"

(Resende, 2003); Sérgio Norte, "Bakunin Versus Marx: Conflict of Titans in the International Workers' Association" (Norte, 2001); Eduardo Colombo, "Introduction to *The State Principle*" (Colombo, 2008).

It is also important to emphasize a collection of articles: two by Andrey C. Ferreira, "Work and Action: The Debate Between Bakunin and Marx and its Contribution to a Contemporary Critical Sociology" and "Materialism, Anarchism and Social Revolution: Bakuninism as Philosophy and Politics of the Workers' and Socialist Movement," as well as its introduction "Anarchism, Insurgent Thought and Practices: Phenomenon of the 'First International'?" (Ferreira, 2010, 2013, 2014); two by Nildo Viana, "The Paris Commune According to Marx and Bakunin" and "Genesis and Meaning of Religion According to Bakunin" (Viana, 2004, 2015).

And more: "Bakunin's Political Philosophy and Libertarian Pedagogy: Reflections on Integral Education and Barcelona's Modern School" by Ivan Oliveira (Oliveira, 2014); "From Reconciliation with Reality to Integral Instruction: Mikhail Bakunin's Philosophical Contributions to Educational Questions" by Luciana Brito (Brito, 2014); "Mikhail Bakunin and Education in the IWA: Notes on Integral Education" by José D. de Moraes (Moraes, s/d); "Revolt and Anti-politics in Bakunin" by Acácio Augusto (Augusto, 2014); "The Construction of Social 'Theory' as Construction of Social Relations: The Historical Materialism of Mikhail Bakunin" by Fabrício Monteiro (Monteiro, 2013); "The Concept of 'Freedom' in Mikhail Bakunin" by João G. Mateus (Mateus, 2011); "Libertarian Pedagogy and Integral Education" by Angela Martins (Martins 2009); "Libertarian Education: Integral Instruction in Mikhail Bakunin" by João G. Mateus, Wanderson Sousa, and Rafael Saddi (Mateus, Sousa, and Saddi, 2009); "Mikhail Alexandrovitch Bakunin" by Ramon Pino (Pino, 2002); the 13 writings found in the Memories of the International Mikhail Bakunin and the IWA Colloquium, organized in November 2014 by Biblioteca Terra Livre.[48]

Finally, the monographs of course completion: *Bakunin e a Educação* [*Bakunin and Education*] by Fabiana Nascimento (Nascimento, 2005); *O Bakuninismo: um Estudo Sobre o Coletivismo* [*Bakuninism: A Study on Collectivism*] by Gabriel Cornélius (Cornélius, 2008); *Bakunin e a Gênese Histórica da Ideia de Divindade na Consciência dos Homens* [*Bakunin and the Historic Genesis of the Idea of Divinity in the Consciousness of Men*] by Jonathan Nascimento (Nascimento, 2014) and, finally, some productions from the militant camp.[49]

1.5 BIBLIOGRAPHIC DISCUSSION

In a review of the bibliography about Bakunin it can be said that, among Marxists and liberals, the Russian revolutionary has received quite problematic treatment. In both cases, the approaches are deeply ideological and have a political intentionality. In most cases they serve, consciously or not, to disqualify Bakunin—and, with this, anarchism—and almost always shy away from scientific seriousness or the most appropriate approaches to an understanding of his life and work.

As pointed out well by Saltman (1983, p. 16), "these authors [Marxists and liberals] were more interested in discarding Bakunin's arguments for political reasons than in evaluating his thought in order to seek contributions to the field of the theory or history of socialism." It never ceases to amaze, in this sense, that on dealing with anarchism and Bakunin notable scholars such as Hobsbawm and Berlin demonstrate a complete lack of scientific rigour.

In the case of Marxists, with the exception of the Russians of the time of the 1917 Revolution, there is only repetition of the claims by Marx and his supporters, reproduction of documents written by them or even of the ideologically defined party lines; certainly, they did not read Bakunin and did not look for counterpoints and alternative sources, contextual information, and did not question party orthodoxies. In other words, among Marxists, despite the claim of "scientific socialism," science was normally not done about Bakunin and anarchism, but politics—ideology was produced. This also occurred, albeit less crudely, in the case of Steklov who, exalting Bakunin, sought through an interpretive distortion to include him in the canon of Marxism-Leninism.

In the case of liberals, with the exception of Pyziur, Bakunin's political thought was largely left out; and, even with regard to his life, studies prioritized his personality and personal aspects in all cases. Despite having certain qualities,[50] liberal studies generally run into methodological problems that support their mistaken or deeply limited conclusions. The focus on Bakunin's *sui generis* personality and his psychological traits—which, according to these authors, would have been marked by issues such as impotence, Oedipus complex/love for his sister, which do not even have historical evidence and seem quite unlikely[51]—is insufficient for contextualizing and explaining Bakunin's thought and trajectory, primarily in its political aspects, which gave him his historical scope.

Brian Morris summarizes his conclusions about Marxist and liberal approaches to Bakunin like this:

> Marxists repudiate him, accusing him of being a deluded romantic, prone to destruction and secret societies, and despise his alleged "elitist despotism." Liberal academics, on the other hand, continue to find Bakunin fascinating—but only as an object for studies in Utopian or Freudian psychology. (Morris, 1993, p. vii)

It seems pertinent to point out that, although deeply opposed in terms of reading and projecting the world, when they focused on Bakunin, Marxists and liberals showed aspects of congruence.

As Saltman (1983, pp. 3, 7, 11) pointed out, both treatments offered to Bakunin, in portraying him as "a paradoxical figure," highlighted the "extremely contradictory and inconsistent course" of his actions, his thinking and of the relationship between the two. For this reason, the author groups Marxist and liberal approaches into a single camp, which he calls "School of Paradox," which agrees that "in the final analysis, Bakunin's political thought was theoretically inconsistent and contradictory, without intellectual merits or serious politics." In addition, recognizing the problems and difficulties in the treatment of the Bakuninian *corpus*, as well as some of Bakunin's conceptual inaccuracies, Saltman points out three reasons that explain a considerable part of the problems with these studies: 1) "The false imposition of a theoretical coherence for life," since Bakunin modified his conceptions a few times and only became anarchist at the end of his life; 2) "The incorrect attribution of Bakunin's intellectual lineage," attributing to him nonexistent influences, such as that of Stirner, and minimizing or ignoring others that were relevant, such as that of Ludwig Feuerbach; 3) "The psycho-historical solution," the limits of which have been pointed out and which are added to the "additional problem of the evident lack of familiarity with Bakunin's manuscripts." To this one could also add: 4) The foundation in works or data that are now considered outdated.

It was among the authors sympathetic to anarchism that, with the reconstitution of the Bakuninian *corpus*, the most serious and scientifically based studies on Bakunin's documents and on his history were produced. However, this camp is also not without its problems. As evidence of this one can mention, for example, the conclusions of Brupbacher's biography (which emphasize the despotism and contradictions of the Russian revolutionary, in line with the School of Paradox); and also others, which appear in some studies by these authors: the arbitrary omissions of Bakunin's uncomfortable or condemnable aspects (such as his defense of dictatorship in the pan-Slavic period and his anti-Semitism in the anarchist period) or of precious information aimed at political ends (such as in the case of the existence of the secret Alliance after 1868). Even so, this camp is certainly the one that best serves a serious discussion of Bakunin's life and work, creating conditions for a fruitful critical dialogue.

When analyzing Brazilian production, it is possible to say that, contrary to other countries, the approach to Bakunin here was, almost exclusively, carried out by sympathetic authors from the academic and militant camp.

With regard to the biographical studies available in Portuguese, Norte (1988) is an introductory study and Brupbacher (2015) has several problems, and even with Barrué's contribution it cannot be considered a satisfactory study of Bakunin's trajectory. The biographical summaries—like my own "Introduction" to the volume of letters published by Hedra (Corrêa 2010a) and also the first part of *Introdução ao Pensamento Político de Bakunin* [*Introduction to Bakunin's Political Thought*] by Alex B. Bonomo (Bonomo, 2017)—are quite succinct and lack depth. It is therefore possible to say that, today in Brazil, there are no historiographical references of greater impetus and depth about Bakunin's political and intellectual trajectory. Furthermore, studies that have looked at his intellectual production in the 1830s, 1840s, 1850s, and early 1860s are very rare, with only two more substantial exceptions (Barrué, 2015b, 2015c).

When looking at the writings in Portuguese that discuss aspects of Bakunin's anarchist thought, it appears that the production of the 1980s and 1990s is almost non-existent—here there are also two more substantial exceptions (Tragtenberg, 1988a, 1988b). It was in the 2000s that these studies began to come to light and in the 2010s that the vast majority of them were produced. Such writings have accompanied the growth in translations of Bakunin's work into Portuguese, and interest in anarchism in general and in Bakunin in particular. Moreover, they have a characteristic feature: although, as a rule, they are good studies, they are not in-depth. All of them have introductory traits, although it must be said that some are much better than others. Themes such as education and science, the concept of freedom, conflicts with Marx and Marxism, politics, and the State have received the most attention. In terms of sources, we see a limitation of translations of Bakunin and some commentators into Portuguese; few writings and letters in other languages, as well as commentators in foreign languages have been used concretely.

1.6 METHODOLOGICAL FOUNDATIONS: FOR A HISTORY OF BAKUNIN'S POLITICAL THOUGHT

Taking into account the previous bibliographic summary I can say that, on the one hand, this book contrasts the School of Paradox's studies, showing the insufficiency of its approaches and contesting most of its theses. On the other hand, it is located in the camp of publications by authors sympathetic to anarchism, establishing a dialogue with some of them. Agreeing that, undoubtedly, Bakunin was a man of action, I maintain that he also makes contributions in the field of political theory. Contrary to the Marxist authors, who did not study Bakunin's writings or letters, I looked at all of his writings and his main letters. Unlike the liberal authors, who focused on Bakunin's personal life and personality, I prioritized his political theory and his political-intellectual trajectory. I did this, of course, taking advantage of the context of the beginning of the twenty-first century—in which, after a long time, the Bakuninian *corpus* is reconstituted and accessible—and supported by the findings and contributions of previous research.

In challenging the claims of Marxist and liberal critics, and even of authors sympathetic to anarchism, I argue that Bakunin is not a completely contradictory figure, nor irrelevant in terms of his action and thought; he was not merely an apologist for destruction, an individualist, or a primitivist; he cannot be properly considered a precursor to Bolshevism or fascism; he was not influenced by Stirner nor can he be held responsible for everything Netchaiev did and wrote; he did not live, in his anarchist period, with a contradiction between the defense of freedom and dictatorship; he was not, also in the anarchist period, a conspirator, a supporter of dictatorship, who intended to destroy the International and was unable to reconcile the struggles for reforms and revolution; he cannot be explained solely in terms of his psychological aspects.

With regard to the bibliography in Portuguese (including translations), this book, with all its limitations—which I assume are not a few—offers the Portuguese-speaking public the most complete study carried out up until now in the field of political-intellectual trajectory, and even of Bakunin's biography. In the field of political theory, this is the first work in Portuguese that methodically focuses on the complete works of Bakunin and his principal foreign commentators. I believe I have made some original contributions in this field, as I discuss themes from the Bakuninian work that had not received much attention. In particular, those which, chronologically, are prior to Bakunin's definitive conversion to socialism in 1864. There is very little literature debating Bakunin's intellectual production in the period in which he moves from philosophy to praxis—and which is divided, internally, into a Fichtean period (1836–37), the first Hegelian period (1837–40), the second Hegelian period (1841–42), and his break with philosophy in favour of the primacy of practice (1843)—and in his revolutionary pan-Slavic period (1844–63).

Still based on the bibliography in Portuguese, when taking into account the period in which Bakunin goes from socialism to anarchism (1864–76) this book contributes both to systematizing (and, in some cases, to deepening) themes and concepts that have been receiving more attention—among which are freedom, religion, the State, education, social revolution, and syndicalism (mass organization) —as well as to developing less discussed themes and concepts—among which are materialism-naturalism, social force, domination, social classes, imperialism, capitalism, and cadre organization (party).

As you can see, this research took advantage of several previous Lusophone studies. It is my intention that, alongside them, it can become a complementary reference with some innovations. Evidently, both in the field of political theory and in the field of political-intellectual trajectory, it must be taken into account that this is an introductory study, albeit long, which can and must be deepened in the future. Such is, precisely, my purpose: to forge the bases for further research capable of examining more specific questions, complementing the theme studied and correcting possible problems.

* * *

In order not to fall into the mistakes mentioned above, I relied on certain methodological foundations, set out below.

First, I believe it is necessary to point out that I am aware of the risks that exist when I research an author for whom I have a deep admiration and to which I am linked politically and ideologically. When I challenged the authors of the School of Paradox, I never wanted, by the same means they used, to substitute scientific production with ideological production, exchanging what *was* for that which *I would have wished to have been.*

In other words, I was constantly concerned with not producing a hagiography, an uncritical work that ignored or arbitrarily modified facts and positions. I tried not to carry out an idolizing study that would put Bakunin in the position of a perfect classic to be worshiped. I sincerely tried not to omit or change what I did not agree with—I disagree with various practical actions and theoretical contributions that were exposed throughout the book—or that, to some extent, could harm Bakunin's image or even the lines of argument developed by me. I sought to expose Bakunin's political theory and political-intellectual trajectory in the most objective way possible, and always exercising ideological control, honesty, and self-criticism.[52] Still, it should be mentioned that my closeness with Bakunin offered possibilities that I enjoyed during these years of research.[53]

Taking Bakunin's complete work into account I consider that, during his life, he produced relevant contributions to the field of political theory. Like other theoretical contributions that were based on politics, Bakuninian political theory has philosophical foundations and empirical elements—generalizations that are made based on historical and/or normative facts, and/or events—that encompass the ends and the means, the political strategies that are guided by certain values and ethical foundations. Therefore, I understand that a book like this, which is dedicated to the study of Bakuninian political theory, is naturally inserted in the academic field of political theory itself.

Political theory can be defined as an "interdisciplinary effort [...] united by a commitment to theorize, criticize, and diagnose the norms, practices and organization of political action in the past and in the present, in our locations and in others" (Dryzek, Honig, and Phillips, 2006, p. 4). It theoretically addresses "conceptual, normative and evaluative issues related to politics and society" and seeks in its exposition, "logical rigor, terminological precision, and clear exposition" (List and Valentini, 2016, p. 525). In general, political theory is divided into two subareas: contemporary political philosophy, or normative political theory, and the history of political thought (Frazer, 2010, p. 2; Tozo, 2016, p. 137).

Now, however much it is possible to highlight Bakunin's contributions to the field of political theory it is also necessary to point out that the fact that he was not and did not want to be an academic, and because his texts have a mainly political intent they differ in many aspects from productions of political theory with an academic profile, produced inside or outside universities. But what matters, at this point, is to underline that this book falls exactly into this second subarea of political theory: *it is a work of the history of Bakunin's political thought*, or, in the terms of Terence Ball (2004, p. 12) of a "second-order theorization," which takes his intellectual production as raw material.

The main elements of this methodological foundation are therefore related to the history of political thought. I start with the contributions of John G. A. Pocock, one of the greatest international names in this field who with Quentin Skinner and others composes the so-called Cambridge School, a reference in contemporary methodological debate of the history of political thought (Silva [Ricardo], 2010). In "Theory in History: Problems of Context and Narrative," Pocock highlights the historical nature of political theory and states that political thought must be considered an action that takes place in history. There is no doubt that Bakunin's political thought must be considered accordingly. It is impossible to separate his theoretical production from his political practice, as it is his concrete political interests that normally explain his intellectual contributions. His writings and letters are part of a set of practical actions, which take place to intervene in reality in order to modify it.

Moreover, for Pockock, a history of political thought must be able to "characterize, evaluate, expose [...] and, consequently, in the last analysis, narrate actions carried out in the registered past." It must be able to "examine the actions and activities of political theory", assuming that it "is and has been an ongoing activity, about which generalizations can be made, and that [...] has undergone changes in its general character over time"; changes that can be narrated historically (Pocock, 2006, pp. 166–67, 198–99).

The concern of a historian of political thought has to be

with *what the author was doing*, with *what was happening and what had happened when the text was written*, published, read, and responded to. The concern [of the historian] is with *contexts*. [...] The historian is interested in the *multiplicity of things that happened and in the contexts in which they happened*. (Pocock, 2006, p. 171, emphasis added)

According to Pocock's recommendations, there is, therefore, a clear need for contextualization when addressing a thinker's political theory. In this book, in addition to exposing and systematizing Bakunin's intellectual production throughout his life, in a generalized way whenever possible, I devote considerable effort precisely to this task of contextualization, passing mainly through the author's political-intellectual trajectory, but also through the social context in which he was inserted.

However, I did not prioritize discussion of the linguistic context, of those "articulations made by the authors in the language or in the diversity of languages available to them," as recommended by the Cambridge School.[54] This is because, from my point of view, this discussion is much less essential to understanding Bakuninian political theory than that about what Bakunin "was doing" in political and intellectual terms, and what "was happening and had happened when the text was written" in terms of the "political, religious, [...] social and historical contexts" (Pocock, 2006, p. 168, 171).

When I say that I take Pocock as my starting point, it is because I believe that his contributions, however central, have limitations. One of them, which is also found in Skinner, is the claim of a division, in my view exaggerated, between history and theory. Such positions, which were consolidated in the second half of the twentieth century, profess that history must necessarily be linked to the past and to particular questions, and theory must discuss the present and general/universal questions (Pocock, 2006, 2012).

Thus, for the historian, political thought should be approached as something from the past and, precisely contextualized, it could not be generalized nor used as a supplement for the reflection of certain *perennial problems*, to use one of Skinner's expressions. I understand that this contextualism, for me extreme, has its *raison d'être*, when one takes into account that textualism—taking the text as something autonomous, treating it in a totally ahistorical way—against which the members of the Cambridge School arose. But even so, I think that it is too restricted and implies different problems, both for historians and theorists.[55]

As different authors, historians, and social scientists such as William Sewell Jr. and Peter Burke have argued, the relationship between theory and history need not be conceived in these terms. I believe there is no need, today, for this *disciplinary militantism*, typical of the second half of the twentieth century. It seems to me necessary, therefore, to rely on interdisciplinarity to rethink this and other questions.

In this book, I seek to promote that which Sewell Jr. (2005, p. 5) called a "genuine dialogue" between history and theory, which concretizes Peter Burke's (2011, p. 278) proposal, "to persuade the historians to take theory [...] more seriously than many of them do today, and the theorists [...] to be more interested in history." I tried to take advantage of the best contributions of historians—the focus on the temporalities of social life and its complexities, which encompass continuities and changes, as well as on the prioritization of causal heterogeneity, on historical context, and the importance of chronology—and of theorists (social scientists, philosophers among others)— greater proximity to theoretical discussions and their systematization, structural thinking, and the focus on grand objects (Sewell Jr., 2005, pp. 6–18).

In the field of the history of political thought, the propositions of Rafael S. Vega (2016, p. 157) concerning the "focus on the double meaning of classical texts," which aim to substantiate the interpretation of "writings of political thinkers of the past," seem to me to be correct. In order to minimize the distance between history and theory, Vega maintains that

> every classic text has a double level of meaning, one concrete and the other universal. And that taking this approach [...] allows us to reconcile two types of inquiry about the writings of authors from the past that, in fact, are not antagonistic. Understood in this way, the classics can be approached, simultaneously, as thinkers whose writings pose serious questions and specific and original answers to the problems of the political life of their own time and, moreover, as writers who enable us, through the reading of their works, to illuminate our present in order to understand it. (Vega, 2016, pp. 176–77)

Even so, and despite these recommendations, advancing this approach concretely is not simple, and there are several possibilities for it to be undertaken. Some recent studies of Bakunin have confronted this challenge, all achieving very satisfactory results in their own way. Leier (2006) opted for a mostly historical focus on Bakunin's contextualized trajectory, devoting only a few pages to the discussion of his political thought. Angaut (2005) and Berthier (2010), following another path, prioritized a theoretical focus and presented elements of Bakunin's trajectory and context in the middle of the systematization of his political thought. Angaut and Berthier opted for a more particular contextualization and, although they rely on a broader periodization of Bakuninian work, in terms of theoretical exposition they prioritize the short intervals of time in relation to the long ones. Anyway, I believe that there is no exact answer as to how to make this approach between history and theory operational.

In this work, with the intention of promoting this approach, I started from the contributions of Pocock and the Cambridge School and complemented them with the propositions of Sewell Jr., Burke, and Vega. It was definitely not my goal to produce a study of history without theory, or of theory without history. And I did this in order to distinguish my contribution from the studies of Leier, Angaut, and Berthier, such that my book could function as a complementary production to theirs. Moreover, I believe that Bakunin's political thought certainly has a connection with the past and addresses particular questions, relative to that context in which he was inserted during the nineteenth century. But, at the same time, I believe that his theoretical production still has something to say at the beginning of the twenty-first century, in as much as it offers answers to a series of questions that we continue to ask ourselves.

In more concrete terms, seeking to respond to the demands of contextualization, I establish a periodization of Bakunin's life and work that, as I understand it, can be done in this way for a historicized and adequate understanding of his political theory. As I pointed out in the Introduction, there are three parts: "From Philosophy to Praxis (1836–43)," "Revolutionary pan-Slavism (1844–63)," and "From Socialism to Anarchism (1864–76)." As I also mentioned in the Introduction, I produced a chapter of historical contextualization, with Bakunin's trajectory and the environment in which he was inserted, for each of these parts. They are Chapter 2 for Part I, Chapter 7 for Part II, and Chapter 10 for Part III. These chapters were written based on works of social history, Bakunin's letters, and biographical writings about Bakunin. Four authors accompanied me permanently: Leier (2006), Carr (1961), Nettlau (1964, 1977a), and Grawitz (1990); for Chapter 7, I sought reinforcement from Hepner (1950); for Chapter 10, I sought help mainly from Guillaume (1985), but also from Lehning (1973, 1977, 1999) and Berthier (2015c).

The solution I found for the exposition of the chapters of political theory responds to the dilemma of the relationship between history and theory and seeks to avoid two extremes. One, completely problematic and mistaken, of putting together all of Bakunin's written contributions between 1836 and 1876 as a supposedly coherent whole, systematizing them without taking into account the period in which they were elaborated. Such was the error of authors who, like Pyziur (1968), attributed to Bakunin the position of anarchist, which he assumes only at the end of his life, and discussed the totality of his political thinking as if it were part of this "anarchism." An important part of the claims of Bakunin's inconsistency comes from this misunderstanding. Another extreme that I avoided and that, it should be noted, does not have more serious implications in methodological terms, was to make an even more historicized and contextualized study discussing, almost text by text, Bakunin's most important productions—a path chosen by Berthier (2010).

In these political theory chapters, I ended up opting for the following. Firstly, I defined a periodization of Bakunin's life and work, taking into account his historical trajectory, the theoretical-epistemological foundations of his thought, and the themes addressed by him. This was done considering that the development of Bakuninian political thought has two major ruptures, in 1843–44 and in 1863–64, which support the definition of the three periods, corresponding to the parts previously stated in the book. This periodization was the way I found by which to establish, historically, what in Bakuninian political theory could be systematized together and what would need to be systematized separately.

Within each of the parts, based on the criteria of trajectory and/or theoretical-epistemological foundations and/or themes, I established the division of the chapters, specifying in each of them to which period the contributions of political theory correspond. It was, above all, when there was a theoretical-epistemological break, as in the case of Part I, that I chose, within the part itself, to divide the chapters chronologically and by themes. When there was no such rupture, as in the case of Parts II and III, I preferred to divide the chapters in each of them only by themes, seeking the best way to systematize Bakunin's contributions according to a certain logic. This allowed for a further deepening of the themes within each of the parts. For, in the countless cases in which Bakunin approaches the same themes in different texts, or in which, from a logical point of view, he discusses themes that should/could be exposed later and vice versa, this could be solved. Whenever there was unity from the theoretical-epistemological point of view, I looked for the best way to gather and organize the thematic contributions present in Bakunin's writings and letters.

I based my systematization of Bakunin's work on two procedures; one, more common, of synthesizing the contributions that were originally theoretical; another, less common, of seeking in the productions that did not have this theoretical character, as in concrete analyses of reality, the aspects of political theory embedded therein.[56] For this formalization I took advantage of the contributions of Christian List and Laura Valentini (2016), seeking to expose and articulate concepts, principles, and theories. I tried to locate the most important concepts of each period, and to describe the principles and theories that were formulated from them. In adjunct, I chose those that, for me, are the most rigorous studies on the theory of the periods in question. In Part I (1836–43), for the Fichtean period and the first Hegelian period, I sought support in Del Giudice (1981, 1982); for the second Hegelian period, in addition to Del Giudice, I relied on Angaut (2007a) and McLaughlin (2002). In Part II (1844–63), I sought support in Angaut (2009, 2005) and in Berthier (2010, vol. 2). In Part III (1864–76), I relied on McLaughlin (2002), Berthier (2011b, 2012, 2014c, 2015c,), Angaut (2005), Saltman (1983), and Leval (1976, 2007). Finally, I was guided, in more general terms, by some intellectual biographies: *Max Weber: Um Perfil Intelectual* [*Max Weber: An Intellectual Profile*] by R. Bendix (UNB, 1986), *A Teoria da Revolução no Jovem Marx* [*The Theory of Revolution in the Young Marx*] by Michael Löwy (Vozes, 2002), and *Edward Palmer Thompson* by Bryan Palmer (Paz e Terra, 1996).

In terms of narrative, usually, in the chapters of political-intellectual trajectory (2, 7 and 10), I favoured the third person, referring to Bakunin by his name, a pronoun or variables (the Russian, the revolutionary, etc.). In the chapters of political theory (3–6, 8–9, 11–13), I prioritized another style, to avoid the incalculable repetitions, referring to Bakunin in the third person only in the notes and in the excerpts in which it seemed indispensable. I hope the text has become less tiring for the reader with this. In these chapters, two precautions are necessary: the positions exposed are Bakunin's, not mine; the time in which the narrative is inserted is, obviously, the nineteenth century.

I enjoy both the indicated interdisciplinary character of political theory and the interdisciplinarity that underlies the "Social Sciences in Education" concentration area, to which I am connected in the Post-Graduate Program in Education. This book is, equally, an interdisciplinary effort which dialogues not only with political science and philosophy, but with history, sociology, and education. I think, in accordance with the position that Gildo M. Brandão expressed at the end of the 1990s, that interdisciplinarity is an important challenge today, and that the strengthening of political theory, as an interdisciplinary area, is necessary because, among other reasons, it can strengthen the development of the Social Sciences in Brazil (Brandão, 1998).

Finally, it is necessary to point out what I did not do and did not intend to do in this book. Because my subject is already very large, and due to limited space and time, I did not perform evaluative judgments of Bakuninian political theory. For this reason, and regardless of the aforementioned narrative that I adopted in the chapters of political theory (3–6, 8–9, 11–13), as I have already pointed out, I do not necessarily agree with everything that is expounded in the text. Even though I believe that there are theoretical elements in this book that can support an understanding of our past and our present, and which can support strategies for social change for the future, I did not make an assessment of which elements would be more or less pertinent to this. Nor did I resort to works of social, political, or economic history to assess if whether, in the chapters of theory, when Bakunin approaches history (of Europe, Russia, the Slavs,[57] the Franco-Prussian War, the modern State and bureaucracy, capitalism and the bourgeoisie, German imperialism) his characterizations are accurate or not, whether they correspond to what specialized literature says or not. Finally, I did not make comparative discussions with the political theory of other thinkers, who agree or disagree with what is supported by Bakunin. I dedicated myself only to the task of pointing out, in a note, some quotes from authors that influenced (or probably influenced) him, showing the similarity of his ideas with those of such thinkers.

NOTES

1   Such is the case with Robert Cutler who, in "Bakunin and the Psychobiographers: The Anarchist as Mythical and Historical Object," maintains that there are three traditions in the historiography about the revolutionary: Romanesque, mostly French, which "is the most sympathetic to Bakunin"; the Germanic, mainly American-English, which "is the most hostile"; and Slavic, mostly Russian, which is "the most controversial" (Cutler, 1990, p. 17).

2   This is the case with Jon Bekken in "Bakunin and the Historians," 1992 (updated and republished in 2015), for publications in English (Bekken, 1992, 2015), and with my article "A Bibliografia de Bakunin" ["The Bibliography of Bakunin"], 2010, for publications in Portuguese (Corrêa, 2010b).

3   Such is the case with Arthur Lehning, in "Michel Bakounine et les Historiens: Un Aperçu Historiographique" ["Mikhail Bakunin and the Historians: A Historiographic Summary"] which, even today—although it was produced and published in the late 1970s and needs to be updated—is the best bibliographic assessment of studies on it (Lehning, 1979a).

4   On the authorship of this text—originally signed by E. Dupont, F. Engels, Léo Frankel, C. Le Moussu, K. Marx, and A. Serralier, but later attributed to Lafargue, Engels, and Marx—cf. Guillaume, 1985, vol. 3, p. 148. As Guillaume puts it in a letter to the General Council of 1873, Engels affirms "the report on the Alliance is being written at the moment; Lafargue and I are working every day." On July 26, Engels writes to Sorge: "The brochure will drop like a bomb on the autonomists, and Bakunin will be a dead man. [...] Lafargue and I wrote it and only the conclusion was written by Marx and myself."

5   This document can be found in facsimile edition of the original in French at the Gallica Library, of the National Library of France [http://gallica.bnf.fr/ark:/12148/bpt6k65650545], or in Castilian, in the work *Marx/Bakunin: Authoritarian Socialism, Libertarian Socialism*, which was organized and commented on by Georges Ribeill (1978, pp. 296-402). The original French version of Ribeill's book, published in 1975 by the Union Générale d'Éditions in Paris, does not include the document.

6   Marx and Engels' judgments about Bakunin and anarchism prior to this document are compiled in the book *Acerca del Anarquismo y el Anarcosindicalismo* [*About Anarchism and Anarcho-Syndicalism*] (Marx, Engels, Lenin, 1976).

7   I take the date of 1877 as the end of the International because I understand, as I will argue later, that the sector that continued the work of this association was the one known as "anti-authoritarian," and not the one linked to the General Council that, from 1872 onwards, practically ceased to exist, declaring its end formally in 1876.

8   Franz Mehring (2014, p. 530), for example, a Marxist and Marx's principal biographer, considers this document to be "at a level below anything else ever published by Marx and Engels" and that it "is not an historical document, but an accusation, whose tendentious character is apparent on every page."

9   Max Nettlau (2008, pp. 148, 174-75), for example, a historian partisan to the anarchists, is more emphatic in the criticism. For him, this document is "a plot without evidence, a web of lies" and part of the "astonishing lack of honesty that is characteristic of *all* their polemics [of Marx and Engels], based on insufficient documentation that, according to their [the authors] habit, they completed by arbitrary statements that their disciples considered true, when, in fact, they were only deplorable deformations, errors or unscrupulous disguises."

10 It is a long letter that Bakunin—imprisoned in the Peter and Paul Fortress in Russia and without any prospect of leaving—wrote to Nicholas I, as demanded by the tsar himself, taking stock of his life until prison in 1849. With the Russian Revolution of 1917 this writing was discovered and, shortly afterwards, it became public.

11 On the Bolsheviks' repression of anarchists in the Russian Revolution until 1921, cf., among many others Tragtenberg, 2007. The *Dossiê 100 Anos da Revolução Russa: Anarquismo, Revoluções Russa e Ucraniana*, [*100 Years of the Russian Revolution Dossier: Anarchism, Russian and Ukrainian revolutions*] organized by Pablo Mizraji at the Institute for Anarchist Theory and History (IATH), has other materials on the subject. [https://ithanarquista.wordpress.com/revolucao-russa/]

12 According to Lehning (1979a, pp. 22–26), on Bakunin were published: a short biography by Eugene Tarle, in 1907; a study on his youth, in 1915, and a work on his years of pilgrimage, in 1925, both by Alexandr Kornilov; and another short biography, this time by Vyacheslav Polonsky, in 1920 (reedited in 1924 and 1926), which provided the basis for the publication, in 1922–25, of another broader biographical study.

13 I include Carr among the liberals because that was his position when he wrote Bakunin's biography (as well as that of Marx), although he recognizes the complexity of his thinking and that his positions had been moving increasingly to the left throughout his life.

14 In light of Kelly and Mendel's studies, Cutler (1990) discusses the problem of psychobiographies or the psychological tradition in modern historiography. He points out the challenges in the field, showing not only the limits of this approach, but how both authors commit compromising errors in terms of the actual methodology recommended for this type of study. Cutler's harsh criticisms of Kelly's work are joined by others, also very harsh, by Brian Morris (1993) and Paul McLaughlin (2002).

15 There are only 15 copies available for consultation in the world. As pointed out by Steklov, Nettlau's work poses immense difficulties for the researcher: the tiny and often illegible letters, the passages in other languages with incomprehensible transcriptions/transliterations, the disorder of the documents, the numerous notes—which include notes of notes, notes of notes of notes etc. (cf. Lehning, 1979a, pp. 36, 20). Today, there are very few researchers in the world able to use and understand this biography by Nettlau, among whom is Jaap Kloosterman.

16 There is a Portuguese translation of this writing: Guillaume, 2015.

17 The whole of these rigorous supplements is the length of one work: more than 500 pages. The content of the eight volumes, which follows the theme of editing Bakunin's texts, is as follows: 1) Italy (1871–72): the polemic with Mazzini (Lehning, 1973); 2) Italy (1871–72): the First International in Italy and the conflict with Marx (Lehning, 1974a); 3) Conflicts in the International (1872): the German-Slav question and state communism (Lehning, 1975); 4) *Statism and Anarchy* book (1873) (Lehning, 1976); 5) Relations with S. Netchaiev (1870–72) (Lehning, 1977); 6) Slavic relations (1870–75) (Lehning, 1978); 7) Franco-Prussian war and social revolution in France (1870–71) (Lehning, 1979b); 8) *Knouto-Germanic Empire and the Social Revolution* book (1870–71) (Lehning, 1982).

18 The authors and topics covered, in order of presentation and always relating to Bakunin, are as follows: Arthur Lehning and the aforementioned historiographical assessment, Pierre Péchoux and publications, Alexandre Bourmeyster and the young Bakunin, Henri Arvon and the Hegelian left, Marcel Body and the period of imprisonment and deportation, Daniel Guérin and the relationship with Proudhon, Daria Olivier and the relationship with Herzen, Jacques Catteau and the relationship with Dostoiévski, Michel Mervaud and secret societies, Marc Vuilleumier and the workers' movement, Georges Haupt and the conflict with Marx, Wiktoria Śliwowska and René Śliwowski and the relationship with the Poles, Robert Paris and the relationship with the Italians, Jean Barrué and education, Miklós Molnár and Marianne Enckel and international politics.

19 What is the point of trying to explain the positions of the majority of the European workers' movement between 1869 and 1877, federalist and profoundly influenced by Bakunin, as a result of an Oedipus complex and sexual impotence? If he was an aspirant dictator, how did he so determinedly influence a whole political-ideological tradition—anarchism, revolutionary unionism (revolutionary syndicalism and anarcho-syndicalism)—which does not have dictatorial and authoritarian experiences in history? If Bakunin was contradictory, how did such an influence, on spreading, produce a significantly coherent global movement (cf. Corrêa, 2015)?

20 Lehning (1979a), Péchoux (1979), and Kloosterman (1985/2004) are the best sources to discover the saga of the efforts of compiling and disseminating Bakunin's work. Lehning and Kloosterman were involved, at the IISH, with the *Bakunin Archives* and with the publication of the complete works. Péchoux specialised academically in the trajectory of the Bakuninian *corpus*, such is its complexity.

21   Even so, as I shall expand on below, I do not agree with the widespread idea in libertarian circles that
      Bakunin was only a man of action, nor that his political practice explains all the problems and
      limitations of his writings. As I intend to demonstrate, I consider, in addition to being a man of action,
      him to have been a theorist of breadth and substance. However, I agree that his work has numerous
      problems and limitations, several of which (although not all) can be explained by the two aspects being
      discussed.

22   According to Nettlau (1895, pp. xxvi–xxvii; 1979a, pp. 26–27) said text, originally written in French, was
      initially entitled "Proposition Motivée des Russes, Membres du Permanent Committee de la Ligue de
      la Paix et de la Liberté" ["Justified Proposal of the Russians, Members of the Standing Committee of
      the League of Peace and Freedom"] and then changed to "Proposition Motivée au Comité Central de la
      Ligue de la Paix et de la Liberté par M. Bakounine" ["Justified Proposal to the Central Committee of
      the League of Peace and Freedom, by M. Bakunin"]; then, the title La Question Révolutionnaire,
      Fédéralisme, Socialisme et Antithéologisme [The Revolutionary Question, Federalism, Socialism and
      Anti-theologism] was adopted, keeping the previous title, "Justified Proposal... by M. Bakunin" as a
      subtitle. Finally, "The Revolutionary Question" was removed. The text was published in 3,000 copies in
      Switzerland in late 1867. In Portuguese, cf. Bakunin, 1988a[e].

23   According to Guillaume (1907b, p. 277–82), the first part (or "delivery") [livraison] of this book—
      originally penned in French, at first titled La Révolution Sociale ou la Dictature Militaire [Social
      Revolution or Military Dictatorship] and which had its title modified during the editing process—was
      published in 1,000 copies in Switzerland in 1871, presenting a series of problems in the publishing. The
      second part of the book remained unpublished during Bakunin's life. In Portuguese (almost complete),
      cf. Bakunin, 2014d[e], 2014e[e], 2014f[e].

24   According to Guillaume (1985, vol. 2, p. 253) and Lehning (1973, p. xlvi), this text, written in French,
      was partially published in Switzerland in late 1871 as part of a larger book, which had a circulation of
      1,000 copies. The excerpt published contained the subtitle "Première Partie: L'Internationale et
      Mazzini" ["First Part: The International and Mazzini"]; the second part, composed of a series of
      fragments, remained unpublished during Bakunin's life. Unpublished in Portuguese; in French, cf.
      Bakunin, 1973b[e].

25   According to Nettlau (1986) this text, written in Russian and accompanied by two appendices, had
      1,200 copies made in Switzerland between the end of 1873 and the beginning of 1874. Commissioned by
      young Russians, the book was smuggled into Tsarist Russia (several copies were seized in the process),
      where it exercised considerable influence. It remained unpublished in other languages until the death
      of Bakunin, who, everything indicates, never wrote the other volume(s) he foresaw for the completion
      of the work. In Portuguese, cf. Bakunin, 2003a[e].

26   Incomplete writings are a constant in Bakunin's work, as in the case of the four books previously
      mentioned.

27   Carr (1961, p. 133) highlights, for example, that when moving to Paris in 1844 Bakunin stayed with a
      brother of Bernstein (editor of Vorwärts) who "was surprised to discover that all the possessions of
      that unusual aristocrat were limited to a suitcase, a folding bed and a zinc sink."

28   To substantiate his finding, he provides three examples: "Bakunin's manuscripts from the 1940s—one
      of which is written on Feuerbach—have never been found and must be considered lost. His carnet
      [notebook], an excellent source, from the years 1871–72, gives us an idea of his vast epistolary relations,
      of which we have discovered only a few traces until today. On 11 August, 1870, for example, he wrote to
      Nikolai Ogarev saying that he had written 23 long letters in the previous three days: only two were
      found. His correspondence with Spain and Italy was almost entirely lost" (Lehning, 1979a, p. 18).

29   When Bakunin prepared both packages before leaving for the Bologna Uprising in 1874, in which he
      believed he was going to die, he most likely disposed of part of the documents that were secret,
      organizational, and/or that could be said to be compromising.

30   In Portuguese, cf. Bakunin, 2008[e], 2011a[e].

31   Such is the case with the aforementioned God and the State, which became Bakunin's most translated
      and widespread writing. The most well-known version, which was established as the definitive one, is
      that of 1882, selected by Reclus and Cafiero. However, this same title was used on three other occasions:
      in 1895, by Nettlau, for a selection different to the unpublished part of The Knouto-Germanic Empire;

after that, when editors combined excerpts from the two versions (Reclus/Cafiero and Nettlau); and in 1938–39, also by Nettlau, as the title of volume IV of the *Works*, which contains the whole unpublished part of *The Knouto-Germanic Empire* and other writings of 1870 and 1871 (Péchoux, 1979, p. 53).

32   The numbers of letters and writings, as well as the waves of publication, can be found in Péchoux, 1979.

33   The six volumes of Bakunin's *Œuvres* can be found in full online at
https://fr.wikisource.org/wiki/Bakounine/%C5%92uvres

34   Which includes the flight from Austria, led by the institute's first librarian, Annie Adama van Scheltema-Kleefstra, carrying Bakunin's manuscripts obtained by Nettlau, when the Nazis occupied Vienna. Cf. https://socialhistory.org/en/about/history-iish.

35   In Portuguese, cf. Netchaiev, 1976.

36   Bakunin and Netchaiev's June 1870 letter was first published as part of Michael Confino's "Bakunin and Netchaiev Dossier" in the *Cahiers du Monde Russe et Soviétique* [*Notebooks of the Russian and Soviet World*] between 1966 and 1967. In Portuguese, cf. Bakunin, 2017a[c]. Confino's dossier, which discusses the relationship between the two Russian revolutionaries, was later expanded and published as a book (Confino, 1973). Volume 4 of the *Bakunin Archives*, titled "Michel Bakounine e ses Relations avec Serguej Necaev" ["Mikhail Bakunin and His Relations with Serguei Netchaiev"] was published by Arthur Lehning in 1971. The relationship between the two, in light of the correspondences that surfaced in the 1960s, was also discussed by Paul Avrich (1974/1987) and Philip Pomper (1976).

37   All previous efforts that called themselves Bakunin's "complete works" or "works" do not contain the entirety of his writings and letters. *The IISH CD-ROM is the only publication with Bakunin's complete works.* Many of its documents are digitized and can be accessed at: https://search.socialhistory.org/Record/ARCH00018.

38   Péchoux (1979) counts 166 of Bakunin's writings and there are 350 on the CD-ROM. This difference is due to the form of presentation of the texts, which was modified by the IISH in the *Complete Works*.

39   In Portuguese, cf. Bakunin, 1976[e]. However, attention should be paid to Angaut's comments (2007a) regarding Jean Barrué's translation (done from German into French, and conforming to the text from which the Portuguese translation was made). According to Angaut, primarily because Barrué has no intimacy with philosophical concepts, several parts of "The Reaction in Germany" were poorly translated, which is why he presents a new translation of this text into French (Bakunin, 2007a [and]) at the end of his book.

40   In Portuguese, cf. Bakunin, 2014c[e].

41   Two excerpts from this thesis were published as a book in France: *Bakounine Jeune Hégélien: la Philosophie et son Dehors* [*Young Hegelian Bakunin: Philosophy and its Exterior*] (Angaut, 2007a) and *La Liberté des Peuples: Bakounine et les Révolutions de 1848* [*The Freedom of Peoples: Bakunin and the Revolutions of 1848*] (Angaut, 2009).

42   A large part of René Berthier's writings can be found on the site *Monde Nouveau*: http://monde-nouveau.net. For a more detailed list of his articles on Bakunin (including those translated into Portuguese), cf. the bibliography of this book.

43   A complete biography of this author's writings about Bakunin can be found at
http://www.bakunin.de/forschung/eckhardt/index.html.

44   The authors and topics covered, in order of appearance and always relating to Bakunin, are as follows: Frank Mintz and militancy, René Berthier and political theory and method of analysis, Maurizio Antonioli and syndicalism, Gaetano Manfredonia and the Italian period (1864–67), Jean-Christophe Angaut and anti-theologism, Philippe Pelletier and geopolitics, Philippe Corcuff and political philosophy.

45   The book features testimonies about Bakunin by Ivan Turgueniev, Leopold Sacher-Masoch, Arnold Ruge, August Röckel, Richard Wagner, Aleksandr Herzen, Piotr Kropotkin, Errico Malatesta, James Guillaume, and Alexandrina Bauler.

46   Several of these studies also appear in other publications and part of them can be found in the Bakunin Archive online, http://arquivobakunin.blogspot.com.br.

47   The interview "Bakunin Yesterday and Today: interview with Hedra publisher" published online on the occasion of the launch of the compilation of letters *Revolução e Liberdade: Cartas de 1845 a 1875*

[*Revolution and Freedom: Letters from 1845 to 1875*] (Corrêa, 2010c); the chapter "Mikhail Bakunin e o Anarquismo" ["Mikhail Bakunin and Anarchism"] from the book *Filosofia: Um Panorama Histórico-temático* [*Philosophy: a Historical-thematic Panorama*] (Corrêa, 2013); the chapter "A Lógica do Estado em Bakunin" ["The Logic of the State in Bakunin"] from the book *A Destruição do Leviatã: Críticas Anarquistas ao Estado* [*Destruction of the Leviathan: Anarchist Critiques of the State*] (Corrêa, 2014e); the article "Federalismo, Socialismo e Antiteologismo de Bakunin" ["Bakunin's Federalism, Socialism, and Anti-theologism"] (Corrêa, 2014b); the article "Social Classes and Bureaucracy in Bakunin" (Corrêa, 2016b); the introduction "Contexto e Implicações da Relação Bakunin-Netchaiev" ["Context and Implications of the Bakunin-Netchaiev Relationship"] to the translation of Paul Avrich's book *Bakunin & Netchaiev* (Corrêa, 2017); a series of interviews with PraxisTV in 2017, as well as lectures and events on the topic.

48 The authors and topics covered, always relating to Bakunin, are as follows: Jan de Freitas and Victor Soliz, two works on the concept of freedom; Felipe Corrêa and theory of the State; Ricardo Rugai and political organization; Selmo da Silva and strikes; Ivan Oliveira, Luciana Brito, and Paulo Marques, three works on the conception of education; Márcio Leme, Bruno Gandin, and Gustavo Pose, two works on conception of science; Jonathan Nascimento and religion/anti-theologism; Marcelo Mazzoni and Marcus Faria and the workers' movement in Switzerland; José da Silva, Marcos Ataídes, and Renato Coelho and inheritance in contemporary militancy. Memories of the International Mikhail Bakunin and the IWA Colloquium, https://coloquiobakuninait.wordpress.com/memorias.

49 Among which stand out: Luta Libertária, 2002; UNIPA 2003, 2009; COPOAG, 2005/2013.

50 Among which I highlight: in Carr, the rigorous research of Bakunin's trajectory (dates, locations, contacts, etc.) and the consultation of Russian material; in Pyziur, the approach to political thought and the discussion of some of his political writings; in Kelly and Mendel, the in-depth study of correspondence.

51 Cf., for example, the article "Mikhail Bakunin and his Biographers: The Question of Bakunin's Sexual Impotence" by Marshall Shatz, which discusses the impotence argument in depth and concludes that it is a fallacy (Shatz, 1988). Regarding the romance between Bakunin and his sister Tatiana, I can affirm that, through a detailed analysis of the correspondence between them from 1836—the year that Carr (1961, pp. 35–36) and other authors maintain the romance having occurred—there is no evidence whatsoever that this "forbidden passion" existed.

52 For that, I relied on Pedro Demo's concept of "objectification" (2011, pp. 80, 28), understood as the "effort to know reality in what it is," even recognizing that in the human and social sciences "objectivity does not exist." It is, therefore, a permanent search for objectivity that we know will never be fully achieved, and a conscious departure from productions that "make of scientific activity an *invented* production of reality." This seems important in order to "control ideology, but without disguising the fact that [it] is intrinsically part of the scene." I based myself, at the same time, on Ralf Dahrendorf's three recommendations (1981, p. 28): the permanent effort of ideological control, honesty with my own values, self-criticism and mutual criticism, facilitated when there are no hidden premises.

53 Due to this proximity—and my interest in a more systematic study of Bakunin, which I've had for about ten years—I was able to take advantage of accumulated years of reading and a lot of bibliography obtained in that period. All the translations of Bakunin into Portuguese, the CD-ROM of the *Complete Works* (very rare today) and a considerable part of the commentators' texts and books were obtained before the doctorate. In addition, due to this proximity, I have maintained and maintain an ethical commitment regarding intellectual work that—according to Douglas Bevington and Chris Dixon's (2005) notion of "theory relevant to movements"—demands that a book like this be useful not just to my professional career or even to scholars of Bakunin, but to anarchists and their political project.

54 In terms of the linguistic context, I make brief comments regarding the use of certain concepts—like, for example, in the case of the concept of *people*, during the revolutions of 1848 and 1849 in Europe. But my biggest concern, in linguistic terms, was to work primarily with the terminology used by Bakunin. Even when I named concepts that had not been nominally used by him, I was careful to only give shape to something the content of which he had already formulated. I was also concerned with not using conceptual nomenclatures that would be enshrined after the author's life—such as, for example, in the case of concepts of *race* (which, in a contemporary approach, it would be more appropriate to treat as *ethnics* or *ethnicity*) and of *social tradition* and *eduction in the broad sense* (which, in a contemporary approach, would be more appropriately treated as socialization).

55   It is enough to observe how, especially during the twentieth century, the distancing between historians and theorists ended up prejudicing the intellectual production of both. It was common for many historians to end up disconnecting themselves from theory, avoiding it and/or demonstrating a lack of intimacy in their discussion; and many theorists ended up detaching themselves from history and producing studies completely out of context. On another occasion, I demonstrated how, in the case of studies of anarchism, this distancing was responsible for numerous problems (Corrêa, 2015, pp. 57–100).

56   A procedure that was presented to me by Ricardo Musse, in the case of Marx and Marxist studies, and which I used at various times in Part II and in some of Part III of the book.

57   The literature specializing in the history of the Slavic peoples (Cf., for example: Portal, 1968) demonstrates that—the same way as in many other types of nationalism, as Anderson's (2013) studies show—Slavic nationalism, particularly during the nineteenth century, often maintained that there was a history and common ties between Slavs that were only imagined, without any foot in the real world. When Bakunin discusses the national oppression of the Slavs, I do not assess to what extent he operates in the field of real or imagined history.

PART I

FROM PHILOSOPHY TO PRAXIS
(1836–43)

CHAPTER 2

"THE PASSION FOR DESTRUCTION
IS A CREATIVE PASSION":
FROM PHILOSOPHY TO PRAXIS (1814-43)

This chapter discusses Bakunin's trajectory from 1814 to 1843, divided into four parts: 1) Russia, the Bakunins, First Years in Premukhino and Saint Petersburg (1814-35); 2) Philosophy and Stankevitch's Circle in Moscow (1836-40); 3) The Hegelian Left in Germany (1840-42); 4) Communism in Switzerland (1843). Finally, in a fifth part, it presents important elements for the understanding of Bakuninian political theory during the period in question.

2.1 RUSSIA, THE BAKUNINS, FIRST YEARS IN PREMUKHINO AND SAINT PETERSBURG (1814-35)

Mikhail Aleksandrovitch Bakunin was born in Russia, on 30 May, 1814[1] to a family of nobles in Premukhino, a property located in the province of Tver, between Moscow and Saint Petersburg. His parents Alexander (Aleksandr) and Varvara Bakunin (born Varvara Muravieva) had eleven children, with Mikhail being the third oldest and the first male.

At the beginning of the nineteenth century, the Russian Empire had as its main foundation the relation of serfdom between noble landowners and peasant serfs, who constituted 85% of the population. The Russian economy, with a predominantly agrarian base, was characterized by low productivity, finding in international trade (especially in cereals, minerals, wood, and hemp) the indispensable resources for its survival. The Empire was governed in an absolute and centralized manner by the tsar—in those years, Alexander I (1801-25) and Nicholas I (1825-55) respectively—in a regime of almost unlimited state power, in which violence and arbitrariness constituted a rule, without providing any freedoms even to the nobility; the land was considered the property of the tsar and there was an obligation for services on the part of the subjects in general (Tragtenberg, 2007, pp. 43, 86-87).

The Bakunin family had been part of the Russian nobility since the sixteenth century, when they had ascended the social hierarchy and had members occupying prominent posts in the State. In 1779, Mikhail Bakunin and Liubov P. Myshetskaya (Mikhail's grandparents) acquired the Premukhino estate, where they moved with their children—but Alexander Bakunin (father) followed a different path from his brothers. Born in 1768, he was sent to Italy at the age of nine due to a physical weakness; the family thought that the young man could benefit from the milder climate in that country. While there, he enrolled at the University of Padua, completed his doctorate in natural history and then worked in Russian diplomacy in Florence and Turin. He witnessed not only at the university, but also on his travels, a liberal political and intellectual environment profoundly different from that which prevailed in Russia and was positively influenced by the French Revolution, which was then taking place.

Due to a health problem of his father's, Alexander had to return to Russia to dedicate himself to managing the family property. Premukhino was part of a larger property, made up of three villas, which together had 16 km² of forest, 3 km² of agricultural land, and 1.5 km² of pasture. In addition, the Bakunins had 500 adult male serfs. There were 35 just to serve the Premukhino house; another 30 were dedicated to serving the other houses and the rest worked on the land, cutting wood, breeding animals, fishing, producing clothes, and other goods. When Alexander returned, the property had enormous management problems and huge debts. Significant efforts on his part were needed to remedy them.

Around 1801, thanks to an inheritance received by his mother, family domains could be improved and the number of serfs reached a thousand. Two years later, with the death of his father, Alexander became lord of Premukhino, and part of his endeavour as the head of the property was an attempt at liberal modernization. He proposed an "agreement between lord and peasants" to his serfs which, characterized by moderation against tyranny but obviously not calling into question his status as lord, intended to implement mutual rights and duties in addition to guaranteeing lands and hereditary rights for serfs. Thus, it aimed not only at increasing productivity, peasant loyalty, and class conciliation, but also at promoting progress and tranquility, guaranteeing a harmonious, prosperous, and happy coexistence among all (Leier, 2006, pp. 3–10; Carr, 1961, pp. 3–6).

In 1810, at 42 years of age, Alexander fell in love with the young Varvara Muravieva, aged 18. Born in 1791, she also came from a noble family. Her father Alexander F. Muraviev died shortly after the birth of his daughter and after a few years her mother, a widow, married Paul Poltoratsky—who owned a property, Bakhovkino, near Premukhino—and took Varvara with her (Randolph, 2007, p. 94). Alexander and Varvara were married in that same year, 1810, and soon had their first children. There were, as previously mentioned, 11 in total: the oldest, Liubov, was born in 1811, followed by Varvara in 1812; Mikhail Bakunin, the first boy, in 1814; Tatiana and Alexandra in 1815 and 1816; Nikolai, Ilya, Pavel, Alexander, and Alexei between 1818 and 1823, and Sofia in 1824, who died of dysentery at the age of two (Nettlau, 1964, pp. 29–30).

Regarding the children's education process, Alexander established guidelines similar to those adopted in relation to serfs, resolving

to include the children in Premukhino's liberal experiment. Inspired by Jean-Jacques Rousseau's *Emile*, Alexander sincerely tried not to make the mistakes that had transformed his childhood into "boredom and captivity." Instead of his mother's coldness and his father's authoritarianism, he would encourage his children to disagree with him; when it was necessary to instruct or correct them, he would use reason, guidance, suggestion. Most impressive in Orthodox Russia, he would not insist that his children be religious, but "would only try to show them that religion is the sole basis of all virtue and of our complete prosperity." (Leier, 2006, p. 13)

Such a model of education, which was the same adopted for sons and daughters, was very different from that which prevailed in the Russian nobility, especially in stimulating rationality and critical thinking.

Reflecting on this in an autobiographical sketch started in 1871 and never finished,[2] Bakunin, describing his father as "a very shrewd man, very learned and even erudite, very liberal, very philanthropist, deist not atheist, but free thinker" understood that, for this very reason, he was a man "in complete contradiction with everything that existed and that he breathed in his time in Russia." Raised and educated abroad, Alexander reproduced Western modes and values in Premukhino, which had little to do with the reality of most Russians: his children, educated mainly in French, enjoyed conditions almost nonexistent in Russia and practically did not know their own country (Bakunin, 71030[0], pp. 1–2).

Bakunin's education, carried out by his father and tutors of different nationalities, included classes in natural sciences, history, geography, philosophy, mathematics, Western literature, arts, religion, and music (Carr, 1961, pp. 8–9). In moral terms, Bakunin recalls in the aforementioned autobiographical sketch not to have cultivated in those years any more robust basis of values, norms, and standards, capable of substantiating a more consistent judgment of the world around him. However, he considers, in an analysis much more critical than that of the time, that there was in that context a distortion of his moral education, since all his "material, intellectual, and moral existence was based on a blatant injustice, on an absolute immorality, on the slavery of our peasants who supported our leisure" (Bakunin, 71030[0], p. 3). That is, the premises that made their education possible were guaranteed by the exploitation of the serfs' work and there was, undeniably, a contradiction between the values advocated by Alexander and the situation to which the serfs were subjected.

In general, the progressive and liberalizing education received by Bakunin provided him with a certain solidity in different areas of knowledge. It even enabled conditions to maintain the family's social position, to broaden horizons and even to question certain aspects of the status quo. However, this educational paradigm was only in effect until 1825, when Bakunin was only eleven years old. After that, due to the unfolding of the Decembrist Revolt, Alexander, with apprehension and fear of what could happen in the future, radically changed his positions.

Said uprising took place on 26 December, 1825 when with the sudden death of Alexander I and the scenario of uncertainties that followed, two secret societies of progressive officers linked to the lower and middle nobility led an attempted *coup d'état*, aiming to solve the economic and political crisis that was plaguing Russia.[3] There was an imminent need for modernization of the country, which was taken over by these clandestine political groups that had emerged in 1816 as a result of the hardening of Alexander I after the victory in the war against France.

Two groupings formed in 1821 out of a split—the Northern Society, politically more moderate, which advocated an English-inspired constitutional monarchy[4] and the Southern Society, politically more radical, which advocated a republic of French and American inspiration—led the Decembrist movement (so called according to the month of its occurrence). This should, according to its protagonists, mark this modernizing change in Russia—through the seizure of state power—and start with the troops' refusal to make an oath to the new Tsar Nicholas I. On the day of the oath, the seditious officers managed to gather 3,000 military personnel in the Senate Square in Saint Petersburg and, without consistent planning, occupied it, remaining there. The tsar's troops positioned themselves in front of the rebels awaiting orders and remained so for a few hours. After a time of hesitation, Nicholas I ordered the massacre: the insurgents were severely repressed with cannon fire and pursued, until, by the end of the day, the uprising was completely contained. The insurgents were harshly punished with loss of rights, forced labour, deportations to Siberia and the Caucasus, and even death. Furthermore, a generalized regime of profound political and intellectual repression was put in place by Nicholas I (Brupbacher, 2015, pp. 21–26; Tragtenberg, 2007, p. 54; Hepner, 1950, pp. 37–48).

The Bakunins' proximity to the rebels—among them Sergei Muraviev-Apostol, Varvara's (mother) second cousin, who ended up being hanged—and the family environment known for liberal ideas contributed to Alexander's aforementioned conservative turn. As for the serfs, he came to see the relationship with the masters as something natural; as for the education of his children, he began to reinforce his fidelity to the new tsar. However, a different seed had already been planted and, at least in Mikhail, it would have more lasting effects than these new positions.

In November 1828, Bakunin, aged 14, left for Saint Petersburg with the intention of pursuing a military career. He joined in late 1829 as a cadet at the Saint Petersburg artillery school, a position he held until the end of 1832. In his three years as a cadet he remained confined in the school; nostalgic, demotivated, and little applied, he, like the other cadets, adopted heterodox behaviors that, without having a public or articulate character, served to minimize the impacts of the authoritarian environment in which he lived.

Bakunin was experiencing a cultural shock in what was, after all, his first deep contact with Russian reality: on the one hand, he admired the patriotism of his colleagues, who "love their country, adore their sovereign, and his will is a law for them; none of them would hesitate to sacrifice their dearest interests, and even their lives, for the sake of the tsar and the country" (Bakunin, 31005 [c], p. 6); on the other hand, he was surprised by their moral positions, saying a few years later to his father: "At the artillery school I learned at once everything gloomy, dirty, and hateful that life can present" (Bakunin, 37055[c], p. 19). In those years, he began to face a great dilemma, central in the subsequent period of his life: Was it inevitable to follow the necessities of duty? Or was there a possibility of enjoying some freedom?

In January 1833, at the age of 18, Bakunin was promoted to officer, which brought him greater autonomy. On a visit to Premukhino in August he became involved in the controversy over the marriage of his sister Liubov, who was deeply unhappy about having accepted marriage to Baron Renne out of a sense of sacrifice and submission to the family. Sometime later Bakunin would achieve what he understood as his sister's liberation: his parents were persuaded by him and the marriage was canceled. The Bakunin sisters—who had received the same education as him, and who participated actively and equally in family discussions and early philosophical conversations with Mikhail and the sisters Alexandra and Nathalie Beer—also experienced this dilemma regarding their class obligations (Shatz, 1999). They questioned whether familial marriage designs should really be followed, or if there was a possibility of romantic love. And, to some extent, the outcome of the Liubov case showed everyone that it was possible to find happiness and personal achievements outside social and familial duties. In addition, Mikhail stimulated markedly progressive reflections about the relations between men and women, marriage, sexuality, and love in general.

There seems to be no doubt that Liubov's episode helped Bakunin to start thinking more seriously about his own destiny. He wrote to the sisters in January 1834 saying that the beginning of the year had been a period of "intellectual revolution" for him. He felt out of place in relation to his own class, analyzed himself and decided to dedicate himself completely to his own intellectual improvement: "Now I study passionately because it is only in the science of nature that one can seek pleasure on Earth," he wrote. This process was strengthened by Nikolai N. Muraviev, his mother's cousin, who welcomed him into his home and encouraged the study of politics and philosophy (Bakunin, 34002[c], pp. 1–5).

But in February 1834, Bakunin was severely punished. He was walking around the city in civilian clothes and, when questioned by his commander, gave him an angry answer. For this, he was expelled from the artillery school and, although he remained in the army, was condemned to remain three years without promotions and to be transferred to a distant border region with Poland. In his new routine, marked again by boredom and difficulties relating, he met the doctor Danylo Vellansky, who maintained contact with romantic and idealistic thinkers from Russia and who had studied with Schelling in Germany. Under his influence, he approached romanticism and devoted himself to reading Dmitry Venevitinov, Friedrich Schiller, and Alexander Pushkin, and to the appreciation of Beethoven.

Romanticism played a peculiar role for Bakunin. Differently to the interpretation of Carr (1961, p. 21) and Grawitz (1990, p. 54), who observed in Bakunin's relationship with romanticism an attempt to escape from reality, one should consider, like Leier (2006, p. 47), that at least in Russia the process was different. This was not a "withdrawal to a languid dream world" but an "engagement in the real world," which resulted from the "regime's inability to change": "Nicholas I's refuge in orthodoxy, autocracy and nationality made thinkers and artists from the Russian youth look to the West for inspiration." Russians like Pushkin, Venevitinov, and the Decembrist Alexander Bestuzhev, all read by Bakunin, had, in addition to their romanticism, concerns about political issues—and were repressed for it. During the 1830s, when Bakunin's main traits of thought were patriotism and Christianity, this contact with romanticism allowed him to get closer to reality, questioning his own life and devising to some extent critical solutions.

On the Polish border, Bakunin took advantage of long periods of time with nothing to do. He had access to a library, which allowed him to continue his studies in philosophy, history, mathematics, statistics, physics, and military strategy.[5] Sad and unmotivated by the doldrums, and affirming that "everything in me requires activity, movement," Bakunin would say he was willing to break with his duties in order to dedicate himself to science and civil service (Bakunin, 34012[c], pp. 3-5). Such inclination, in fact, at that time was already a decision made. Bakunin just waited for the right circumstance to leave the army.

They appeared in early 1835 when he was assigned to go to Tver to buy some horses and, on his way, went to Premukhino under the pretext of illness. He would never return to the army again. Not even his father—who secured him a civil service post in Tver afterwards (not accepted by Mikhail) and, then, his dismissal from the army without punishment—was able to dissuade him from the decision to dedicate himself to studies.

At Premukhino, where he spent the entire year of 1835, Bakunin tried to continue his project but had difficulties, mainly because of family conflicts. During that year he established relations with Nikolai Stankevitch, a young member of the Russian *intelligentsia* who coordinated an important philosophical-literary circle that brought young people together weekly to consume and discuss Western music, romantic poetry, and philosophy. This circle was historically known as "Stankevitch's Circle" and, together with the "Herzen-Ogarev Circle"—which, also founded in 1831, brought together other young people from the Russian intelligentsia—was responsible for the promotion of Western thought (especially French and German) in Russia.[6] Stankevitch, who became Bakunin's intellectual mentor, introduced him to German philosophy, especially the work of Immanuel Kant—they studied the *Critique of Pure Reason* together, not without immense difficulties on Bakunin's part (Angaut, 2010a; Del Giudice, 1981, pp. 99-100).

2.2 PHILOSOPHY AND STANKEVITCH'S CIRCLE IN MOSCOW (1836–40)

In January 1836, without pleasing his parents, without luggage, without a job, and without money, Bakunin left Premukhino and went to Moscow, settling in Stankevitch's house and immediately joining his circle. He was thinking of working as a math teacher. For the next four years, from 1836 to 1840, he remained between Moscow and Premukhino, going deeper into the study of the German philosophers Goethe, Schiller, Jean-Paul Richter, E. T. A. Hoffman; and, then, from Kant to Johann G. Fichte, and from there to Hegel (Bakunin, 36030[c]; Del Giudice, 1981, p. xv; Barrué, 2015a, p. 149).

Although Bakunin never attended the Moscow University, he attended some classes and enjoyed the atmosphere of that city, which, far from the capital, was to some extent able to avoid the repression and stimulate democratic discussions of literary, philosophical, and even political issues among members of different social classes (Nettlau, 1964, p. 33; Grawitz, 1990, pp. 51–53). The fundamental features of Bakunin's correspondence from that period are efforts to use philosophy to think about himself, others, and personal relationships.

In this Moscow-Premukhino period, two personal conflicts also stand out: that with Belinski—a member of Stankevitch's Circle who, despite huge differences, was greatly influenced by Bakunin and later became the most celebrated Russian literary critic of his generation—whose relations were marked by instability and conflict, and subsequently supplemented a considerable part of the liberal criticisms of Bakunin. And that with Alexander, who considered the path chosen by his son "full of obstacles and pitfalls" (*apud* Brupbacher, 2015, p. 42) and scolded him for his choices; while his son, in contrast, pointed out: "my freedom is not for sale, nor my dignity as a man" (Bakunin, 36014 [c], p. 2). The intensification of these disagreements culminated in 1836, with the father "expelling" Bakunin from the family.

When considering the most consistent philosophical development, taking place between 1836 and 1840 based on Fichte and, mainly, Hegel, Bakunin's trajectory fits directly into the framework of German idealism and the interpretation consumed by the Russians in the 1830s.

> In Russia, it was clear that the autocracy should be rejected for being repressive, inefficient, and gross. But it was not so obvious what could or should be put in its place; so, it was quite natural for Russian intellectuals to plunge into the new wave of European philosophers—the German idealists, ranging from Schiller and Fichte to Hegel—looking for answers. [...] From romantic literature and music, it was rational and obvious to turn to the philosophy that supported it. In it, Bakunin and his colleagues discovered authors who spoke of the real issues of duty and freedom. (Leier, 2006, pp. 67–68)

It was not, therefore, an abstract and metaphysical philosophy, but a search, at least on the part of the members of Stankevitch's Circle, for answers to real and concrete questions of modern life, especially about the meager realizations of the promises of the bourgeois revolutions. With that, these young people intended to self-educate themselves ideologically, in the sense of social and political liberation in Russia, even though a more concrete practice in this direction was extremely difficult, in view of the repressive context that prevailed in the country. It was for this reason that, choosing critical journalism as a field of action, the members of the circle had to "camouflage themselves in complex philosophical jargon" that, in addition to the complexities of the field, demonstrated an attempt to escape censorship (Del Giudice, 1981, pp. 69–76).

Bakunin's closeness to Fichte was intense and brief, although it can be said that it had lasting effects. It would be appropriate to speak of a properly Fichtean period in Bakunin during 1836, with some reminiscences during the first months of 1837 (McLaughlin, 2002, pp. 23–24). From the German philosopher Bakunin translated the 1794 *Einige Vorlesungen über die Bestimmung des Gelehrten* [*Conferences on the Vocation of the Scholar*] into Russian,[7] publishing them in the literary journal Телескоп [*Telescope*], which had been founded five years earlier by Nikolai Nadezhdin, and on which Belinski worked. In these lectures, Fichte discusses the vocation of man as an individual and in society and, based on the dilemma between freedom and necessity, proposes a reconciliation starting from freedom and harmonizing it with equality. He also makes a call for rational action with a view to improving society, towards deepening enlightenment ideals. For him, it is the ethical ideal that allows us to judge reality and guide this change, which must occur as a result of action in the real world. Thus, he considers theory to be inseparable from rational action, from practice. In this process, he maintains that education is a fundamental element for qualifying choices, and the ("wise") educators or intellectuals—intermediaries between the ideally and ethically established future, and their practical implementation—are people who are so committed to educating society as to contributing to human liberation (Fichte, s/d; Leier, 2006, pp. 68–72).

Bakunin was also influenced by the reading of *Die Anweisung zum seligen Leben* [*The Way towards the Blessed Life*] from 1806, a text in which Fichte explains his philosophical-religious concepts (Bakunin, 36034[c], p. 2; Nettlau, 1964, p. 33). Bakunin's references, frequent in the 1836 letters, underscore the conception of love advanced by Fichte:

> Life is love, and the whole form and force of life is none other than love, it comes only from love. Tell me what you truly love, what you seek, what you aspire to with all your might, in the hope of reaching the true fullness of your being, and you will have explained your life to me. Live what you love. [...] To love, to act under the influence of some thoughts enlivened by feeling—such is

the purpose of life. [...] The purpose of life, the object of true love is God... Not that which is prayed to in churches, not that which is believed to contemplate with their own humiliation, not that which, apart from the world, judges the living and the dead. No! But the one who lives among men, the one who is elevated by the elevation of men, the one who spoke through the mouth of Jesus Christ the sacred words of the Gospel, the one who speaks through the voice of the poet. (Bakunin, 36017[c], pp. 2–3)

From Fichte, members of Stankevitch's Circle—many of whom had been converted by Bakunin to Fichtism—passed on to Hegel; its members were the greatest spreaders of Hegelianism in Russia. Bakunin, already dissatisfied with the excess of subjectivism in Fichtean thought, was introduced to the study of Hegelian work by Stankevitch in November 1836, when he brought thirteen volumes of the German philosopher to the group, in the original in German. Hegel would then become Bakunin's greatest theoretical-philosophical influence and would determine his thought and his intellectual production between 1837 and 1842. This is Bakunin's Hegelian period, in which he is more concerned with the issues of society and community, and moves from the influence of Fichte's subjective and ethical idealism to Hegel's objective idealism.

From 1837 Bakunin devoted himself dedicatedly and methodically to Hegel, studying his main works, until 1839: *Encyclopedia of the Philosophical Sciences, Science of Logic, The Philosophy of Nature, Philosophy of the Spirit* (*Phenomenology of Spirit, Elements of the Philosophy of Right, The Philosophy of History, Lectures on the Philosophy of Religion,* and *Lectures on the History of Philosophy*). Between 1838 and 1839, these studies were systematized in a few hundred pages that are part of Bakunin's complete work (Hepner, 1950, p. 89; Del Giudice, 1981, pp. 177–180, 232, 281, 283; Bakunin, 2000a). With Stankevitch's departure for abroad in September 1837, Bakunin became the circle's main reference and, between 1838 and 1840, established himself as the largest Hegelian in Russia. He stood out for his immense philosophical and dialectical ability, which was demonstrated orally and in writing, and which would be recognized by Herzen, Marx, Engels, Proudhon, and Ruge (Hepner, 1950, pp. 82–89; Del Giudice, 1981, pp. xi, xvii, 234–35). However, even though the intellectual production of those years had Hegel as its greatest reference, Bakunin, in his first Hegelian period, also incorporated other influences; among them Fichte and possibly August Cieszkowski (Del Giudice, 1981, pp. 317–18, 360).

This outstanding position of Bakunin's was achieved through his influence on other Russian thinkers and consolidated in two publications. The "Preface" to Hegel's 1838 *Gymnasialreden* [*Gymnasium Lectures*], and "О философии" [*Of Philosophy*] of 1839–40.[8] The "Preface"—which preceded Hegel's lectures (held at the Nuremberg Gymnasium, between 1809 and 1815, when he was then rector), which were translated by Bakunin himself—was published, along with the lectures, in the *Московский наблюдатель* [*Moscow Observer*] in March 1838. It is probably Bakunin's most misunderstood writing, due to his proposal for a *reconciliation with reality*, a Hegelian concept that he himself introduced in Russia (Del Giudice, 1982, pp. 161–62). In this text, Bakunin proposes such a reconciliation, not in a conservative key, in defense of Russian absolutism, as frequently interpreted, but as a harsh critique of philosophical abstraction and subjectivism.[9] Through a defense of the interrelationship between theory and practice, Bakunin investigates the phenomenon of *alienation* in modernity and offers *education* as an answer—this would allow the individual to be reintegrated into the social totality and offer the conditions for rational action.

"Of Philosophy" gives continuity to the "Preface"[10] and originally has two parts, which were written in 1839; the first was published in 1840 in the magazine *Отечественные записки* [*Notes from the Fatherland*], edited by Andrei Kraevsky in Saint Petersburg (where Bakunin lived from July to November 1839), and the second remained unfinished and unpublished. This writing is one of Russia's greatest philosophical contributions of the 1840s, having collaborated in that country for the development of philosophy, especially of objective Hegelian idealism (Del Giudice, 1981, p. 311). Marking a transition from philosophy to praxis, the first part of the article discusses philosophical knowledge and, starting from a critical-dialectical method, elaborates in depth the concept of *unity between theory and practice* as a path to social change. The second part formalizes a *theory of action*, maintaining that change must aim at freedom and be conceived in terms of a transformation of the practical world, the result of the realization of the rational idea through rational will.

Even so, it must be pointed out that, in his Hegelian period, Bakunin was not orthodox. He took the German philosopher as a point of departure, but quickly went beyond him, understanding that there were revolutionary elements in his thinking, but which lacked development; and for that, Fichte's contributions were fundamental. As you can see, this is a movement similar to that of the young German Hegelians, of whose existence Bakunin knew in 1838. Even if unfolding independently, the ideas of Bakunin and of that Hegelian left find parallels and similarities (Del Giudice, 1981, p. xx).

In 1840, Bakunin's situation in Moscow was complicated: Stankevitch's Circle had practically dissolved and, since his arrival, he had lived on favours and on other people's money. At the same time, the reality in Germany was promising, not only in professional terms but mainly in philosophical terms. Bakunin decided, then, to move to Berlin. He intended to obtain a doctorate and return to be a professor at Moscow University. He convinced his father, already reconciled with him, and Aleksandr Herzen—whom he had met with Nikolai Ogarev a year earlier—to commit to a future financial contribution and planned the move (Nettlau, 1964, p. 34; Carr, 1961, pp. 82–93).

2.3 THE HEGELIAN LEFT IN GERMANY (1840–42)

At the age of 26, Bakunin left Premukhino in June, passed through Saint Petersburg and arrived in Berlin in late July 1840.[11] He remained in Germany until the beginning of 1843, sharing for some time the company of the brothers Varvara and Pavel, living initially in Berlin and, from April 1842, in Dresden.

Germany in the early 1840s was experiencing reflections of the conservative ebb after Napoleon's defeat. Compared to France, it remained a politically archaic country, the structures of which prevented economic progress and modernization. On the one hand, the economic backwardness was beginning to be overcome—without this implying a reduction in social inequality—with modernizing measures such as the Zollverein, a customs alliance between 39 states that stimulated trade liberalization and conditions for industrialization, as well as construction of the first railway lines and scientific development. On the other hand, the political backwardness complicated this overcoming, fostering the formation of progressive national and democratic movements, composed mostly of a radicalized fraction of the bourgeoisie, which faced a conservative sector of the landed nobility, often supported by the governments of the order.

However, in that context, in a sense, all classes turned their interests back to state policy: the bourgeoisie sought protection of property, landowners claimed guarantees for bad harvests, and both wanted conditions and protection for international competition; educated professionals wanted conditions for intellectual development and aspired to influence the direction of the State; the bureaucracy defended parliamentarism and supplanted the old ruling elites; the proletariat sought protection, regulation of trade, and work; the rural workers—former peasant serfs who, with their change of condition, were forced to compensate the landowners without any means to do so—in addition to protection, yearned for reparation and land.

Germany did not yet form a unified power bloc—the difference between Prussia and the other German states was striking. The latter, fragmented in the fictitious unity of the German Confederation, created at the Vienna Congress in 1815, faced a Prussia that, although politically backward, had growing power and stood out as a European power. With Frederick Guilherme IV's ascension to the Prussian throne in 1840, and the consequent frustration that followed in light of his economically anti-liberal and politically conservative direction (especially regarding freedom of the press and teaching), a traditionalist sector was strengthened which, in addition to defending political centralization, considered Prussia to have the historic mission of governing the other German states (Guillaume, 1907a, p. vii; Angaut, 2007a, pp. 21–25; Leier, 2006, pp. 97–98).

Bakunin had the excitement of his arrival in Berlin interrupted by news of Stankevitch's untimely death. A few days before, still in the month of his arrival, he met Ivan Turgueniev—who, after a few years, would rise to the pantheon of Russian novelists—to whom he was closely linked and with whom he began his insertion in German intellectual and philosophical circles[12] (Coêlho, 1994, pp. 33–34). His first point of contact with German and immigrant intellectuals was at the University of Berlin, where he enrolled shortly after his arrival in the city. There, he attended lectures by the philosopher Karl Werder, Schelling, and the historian Leopold von Ranke, which were soon criticized due to their lack of depth and their conservatism aligned with Germany in that context. Such impressions announced, in a way, a feeling relative to the academic world, which ended up becoming more accentuated in the months after the beginning of classes. University was unable to meet Bakunin's expectations, which were more properly achieved with the literature and personal ties of the period, especially in Dresden.[13]

The studies of Hegel seemed to him to be most useful, undoubtedly his greatest theoretical-philosophical influence of the period. But the reading of other authors complemented his development: that of the French philosopher Lamennais—in particular, the *Politique à l'Usage du Peuple* [*Politics for the Use of the People*] of 1839, whose progressive synthesis of religion and politics was praised by Bakunin—and the German economist Lorenz von Stein—whose 1842 book *Der Sozialismus und Kommunismus des Heutigen Frankreich* [*Socialism and Communism in Contemporary France*] popularized ideas by Fourier, Saint-Simon, and Proudhon and brought Bakunin closer to French socialism (Bakunin, 41009[c], p. 1; Bakunin, 42019[c], p. 1). In addition to the musician Adolf Reichel—whose friendship was preserved by Bakunin until the end of his life—relevant links of that time were: the romantic writer Bettina von Arnim—a friend of Goethe and Beethoven, with whose work Bakunin had contact in Russia and who, during the 1840s, was involved with progressive politics—and the German revolutionary poet Georg Herwegh—whose *Gedichte eines Lebendigen* [*Poems of One Living*] published in 1841, embodied, to a large extent, the path taken by the Hegelian left and Bakunin himself (Carr, 1961, pp. 99–101, 116–117).

Since Hegel's death in 1831, a tradition heir to his thought had formed in Germany that, a few years later, split into two parts. One side was conservative and had older members who held university chairs and government positions. The other was progressive and composed of young students and professors, especially from the University of Berlin. The first group was called "old Hegelians" or "Hegelian right" and the second "young Hegelians" or "Hegelian left," for whom the work *Das Leben Jesu* [*The Life of Jesus*] by David Strauss, published in 1835, was a founding landmark. Still in Russia, in March 1839, Bakunin (39008 [c], pp. 1–2) said to his sister Varvara: "do not be afraid of the Strauss book"—which proposed a historical and not divinized understanding of Jesus, explaining Christianity in the key of the myth of Christ. It was, in Bakunin's interpretation, "the last and most powerful manifestation of skepticism, and that is a good thing." He also explained to his sister that the German Hegelians "had divided into two groups, one taking Strauss' side and the other opposing him strongly and solemnly."

After Strauss, this philosophical field was strengthened by the philosophical production of Ludwig Feuerbach and Bruno Bauer. In 1841, the first sustains in *Das Wesen des Christentums* [*The Essence of Christianity*] that the essence of the Christian religion is human and proposes an anthropological understanding of theological foundations. The second argues in *Die Posaune des Jüngsten Gerichts über Hegel, den Atheisten und Antichristen* [*The Doomsday Trumpet against Hegel, the Atheist, and Antichrist*] that Hegelian philosophy is praxis, revolution itself, and that its core is the destruction of religion. In fact, this criticism of religion forged the basis for political criticism insofar as it challenged divine law, one of the main foundations on which the power of the German aristocracy rested. It established an inseparable relationship between religion and politics, similarly to that maintained by Bakunin (1981a [e], p. 432) in the "Preface" of 1838, in which he emphasized that "where there is no religion, there cannot be a State" and that "religion is the substance, the essence of the life of any State."

During his period in Germany, Bakunin, under the profound influence of Hegel—according to his own recollection in the "Confession" of 1851 he would say that, at the time, he "studied the sciences, especially German metaphysics, in which I immersed myself exclusively, almost until madness; day and night I saw nothing but Hegel's categories" (Bakunin, 1976b[e], p. 43)[14]—and instigated by the Hegelian left, deepened the path started in Russia, in the sense of giving abstract philosophy a political content. For that, the reading of Edgar and Bruno Bauer, as well as of Feuerbach—to whom Bakunin (2017f [e], p. 439) will refer, in the 1870s, as "the most notable thinker and most original of the entire Hegelian School"—were determinant to him; the contact established with Arnold Ruge was also striking.[15]

Ruge had been responsible, between 1838 and 1840, for the publication of the *Hallische Jahrbücher* [*Halle Annals*], the main organ of the Hegelian left, which Bakunin had known in Moscow. Under the repression of Frederick William IV, Ruge had moved to Dresden, Saxony, continuing the publication under the title *Deutsche Jahrbücher* [*German Annals*]. Bakunin (41010 [c], p. 1) met him in 1841, referring to him as an "interesting, remarkable man" and highlighting his materialistic approach to life, which made him "hostile to everything, without exception, that has the slightest appearance of mysticism." Between late 1841 and early 1842, Bakunin, still in Berlin, visited Dresden a few times, getting close to Ruge, and then decided to take a new direction in his life. He decided to abandon university, the project of becoming a teacher and even returning to Russia—he moved to Dresden, hoping to share the presence of his new comrade (Grawitz, 1990, pp. 96–103).

In October of that year, Bakunin published "Die Reaktion in Deutschland: Fragment von einem Franzose" ["The Reaction in Germany: Fragment of a Frenchman"] in Ruge's *German Annals*, signing it with the pseudonym Jules Elysard. "The Reaction in Germany" marks Bakunin's transition from theoretical-philosophical reflection on praxis to properly political thought with a view to practice.

For the first time he discusses a historical and concrete theme: Europe in the early 1840s. In this writing Bakunin elaborates a *theory of revolution*, which is anchored in a *negative dialectic*. Explaining this theory, he expounds the historical and logical foundations of this dialectic and characterizes the historical moment in question: it is, as he argues, a moment of revolutionary crisis and decomposition of the old world. On reflecting on the forces at play, it signals the existence of a conflict between two contradictory poles—one positive (order/reaction) and the other negative (revolution/democracy) or "reactionary party" and "democratic party"—which are characterized and analyzed in their fundamental features and in the relationship they establish with each other. Bakunin advances, also, from a normative perspective to the political tasks of the democratic party, aiming to consolidate its victory in this conflict. The famous and controversial passage that closes this writing—"the passion for destruction is, at the same time, a creative passion" (Bakunin, 2007a [e], p. 136)—highlights the need to destroy the old world so that the new can be built up. In other words, a preponderance of the negative—or the victory of the democratic party—that supports this whole concept of dialectics.

The impact of this writing was enormous. It circulated widely in the progressive European media and raised Bakunin to the position of one of the most prominent left Hegelians at that time (Carr, 1961, p. 116; Grawitz, 1990, p. 104; Leier, 2006, p. 104).[16] But the political possibilities in Germany were quite limited and the repression intense at the end of 1842. The *German Annals* were closed down by the government, Ruge went to Paris seeking to continue his editorial work with Marx, and Herwegh was expelled from Prussia due to a disagreement with the king.

2.4 COMMUNISM IN SWITZERLAND (1843)

Apprehensive that the repression of Herwegh might have some consequence for him, Bakunin decided to follow the poet to Zurich, where he remained from January to June 1843.

But on Swiss soil intellectual and political life proved to be limited. Bakunin was in a time of transition and, as much as he advocated practice and had established certain lines of action in "The Reaction in Germany," he still did not have concrete political work, and his contacts were quite restricted—until then he had not had any contact with the European popular sectors.

The most important relationship of the period in Zurich was established with the Christian communist Wilhelm Weitling, who met Bakunin personally in May 1843. Since then, there had been mutual empathy. His newly published book *Garantien der Harmonie und Freiheit [Guarantees of Harmony and Freedom]* had been read by Bakunin and made a great impression. In a letter to Ruge from the beginning of 1843 he commented that this book was "really, a remarkable work" and that its first part, with the "critique of the present situation" was "alive and often true and profound," highlighting an excerpt which he found interesting: "a finished [perfect] society has no government, but administration; it has no laws, but obligations; there are no penalties, but remedies" (Bakunin, 2007[c], pp. 139–40).

For Bakunin, the relationship with Weitling was remarkable for two reasons. First, unlike all previous connections, Weitling was a poor craftsman who worked many hours a day and experienced the problems and possibilities of the popular universe on a daily basis. Second, Weitling reconciled work with political militancy and studies—he became known in Paris, where he spent some years, getting involved politically with German immigrants, participating in the League of the Just and the May 1839 insurrection.

This relationship gave Bakunin, for the first time, the strengthening of ties with a worker who reconciled revolutionary ideas and actions, and whose positions provided a certain understanding of the reality of the oppressed in general and of programmatic notions of communism such as violent revolution, the end of property, and equal privilege, recompense, and education. Still, there were also political disagreements between them: for Bakunin, Weitling's project was authoritarian, and its corollary would be not a free society but a new regime of oppression, particularly because of its exclusively material and strictly hierarchical foundations (Barrué, 2015a, pp. 158–61; Bakunin, 1976b[e], pp. 48–49; Bakunin, 2007b[e], pp. 150–51).

Bakunin's reflections on this relationship with Weitling were formalized in the article "Der Kommunismus" ["Communism"], published anonymously in three parts in the journal Der Schweizerischer Republikaner [The Swiss Republican] in June 1843. In this text Bakunin reflects on the possibilities and limits of philosophy, considering Hegel the culmination of modern theory, but unable to offer answers to the present need for concrete political practice. Professing the primacy of practice, he proposes, through Hegelian philosophy, a way out of philosophy itself and the adoption of a new theory, now conceived as a practical awareness of the present. Bakunin still ponders two expressions of modernity: political radicalism, of which he is a supporter and the foundation of which is the notion of self-government of the people, and communism, which is critically discussed in the light of Weitling. Bakunin does not claim to be a communist and sees in this doctrine—although he considers it practical, emanating from the people and a legitimate descendant of Christianity—a risk of particularism and authoritarianism. However, he understands it to have important aspects and legitimate demands (Bakunin, 2007b[e]).

2.5 BAKUNINIAN POLITICAL THEORY BETWEEN 1836 AND 1843

At this point, some elements relevant to the understanding of Bakuninian political theory will be presented in the period in question. They introduce the theoretical discussion, which will be explained in more detail in the following chapters.

2.5.1 Fichtean period (1836–37)

The first theoretical discussions of relevance in Bakunin's political-philosophical thought were produced between the beginning of 1836 and the first months of 1837 when he was between Moscow and Premukhino and beginning his adult life. At that time, he broke with the conservative romanticism that had influenced him in the previous two years and moved from a fruitless prior contact with Kant to Fichte's ethical and subjective idealism. This *Fichtean period*, although brief, allowed him to develop a set of ideas that, at least in part, were continuous in his political theory.

In appropriating Fichte, Bakunin did so by prioritizing his writings on political, social, and religious philosophy, rather than those epistemological ones, more focused on the theory of knowledge. His primary influences were first the *Conferences on the Vocation of the Scholar*, which he translated and published, and second *The Way Towards the Blessed Life* a text that discusses theory and praxis and presents an immanent and anthropocentric concept of religion. Starting from these writings, Bakunin outlines the foundations of a *philosophy of love-freedom and emancipation*.

According to Fichte's subjective and ethical idealism, the ideal (morally active individual) is not separate from the real (social community) but constitutes a more important or original element than it. When considering the metaphysics of Kantian subjectivity adopted by Fichte, the ideal assumes the role that classical philosophy relegated to the essence, while the real would be mere appearance. Thus, there is a priority of the subject in relation to the object or, in Fichte's terms, of the self in relation to the non-self, of the internal world and the internal life in relation to the external world and the external life. The subject (self) assures itself in particular through its activity, its action, and the object (non-self) is only a field for the subject's activity or a foreign resistance to that activity, to that action.

Such a dichotomy between subject and object (self and non-self) can only be overcome through the action of the subject, which is based on will and moral conscience and is guided by imperatives of practical reason. For this action, the individual must turn to himself and, becoming conscious through formalization in his inner experience, find the ethical reasons and the moral attitude for the duty of his task. It is only then that external action can be performed and, with it, proceed to the realization of *love-freedom* (Del Giudice, 1981, pp. 104, 107, 147).

2.5.2 First Hegelian Period (1837-40)

Between 1837 and 1840, Bakunin, still in Russia, is in his *first Hegelian period* in which, mainly in two writings—the "Preface" from 1838 and "Of Philosophy" from 1839-40—he developed the foundation of his political and philosophical thinking, which will culminate in 1842. In these years, the greatest reference for Bakunin is Hegel—in particular his concepts of *reason* and *reality*—which are complemented by him with contributions from Fichte and, possibly, from Cieszkowski, generating a thought that if at first it is faithful to Hegel, it   overtakes him and finds parallels in the German Hegelian left.[17]

Between 1837 and 1840, Bakunin, widely studied in his most relevant works, already has a solid command of Hegelian philosophy. The central question of these years is the solution, through a *critical-dialectical method*, to the problem that places *alienation* (or alienated life) on one side and *reconciliation with reality* and the *unity between theory and practice* (or real, effective life) on the other. Based on Hegel, he reflects on the process of *knowledge* construction, in which he criticizes modern subjectivism harshly and asserts the need to overcome sensible certainty through a *dialectic of knowledge* and to proceed to reason—or, that is, to overcome appearance and seek an understanding of the essence of social totality. Extrapolating Hegel, Bakunin, through a *philosophy of action*, derives from the knowledge of truth the need for rational ethical action that, as an effectuation of thought, has possibilities for the realization of freedom—for this, *education* is a primary tool.

Bakuninian *objective idealism* derives from the critique of Fichte's subjective and ethical idealism and has in Hegel its greatest foundation. Bakunin quickly realizes that the Fichtean priority given to the ideal, to the subject, and to the subjective self, reinforces modern alienation and, as he understands it, ends up distancing man from nature and from forms of social existence, from objective and external phenomena to the cognizant subject: society, state, politics, economy, history, institutions. In this way, subjectivism is considered an abstraction responsible for splitting ideal and real, subject and object, thought and being, theory and life, philosophy and practice, individual and community, life/internal world and life/external world. Such an abstraction is at the root of the withdrawal of the self (subject) from objective existence (world), causing a rupture in life, a social dichotomy, and expressing a conflict with no prospect of a solution.

Reconciliation with reality and unity between theory and practice (in this case, between ideas and facts, thought and empirical data) are Bakuninian objective idealism's responses to subjective and abstract idealism. It is a matter of reconciling these divided elements—ideal and real, subject and object, being and thought, theory and life, philosophy and practice, individual and community, life/internal world, and life/external world—overcoming the particular and the subjective finite and reaching totality and infinite objectives. With this, the dichotomy between subjective consciousness and objective reality is overcome, and the self is reintegrated into reality, the subject into the world. The abstract self changes to the concrete community of us and love (feeling) changes to reason (thought). The foundation of ethics is now considered universal and not particular, individual. In this way, the external reality is raised to a prominent position not only as something that must be taken into consideration, but as an essential philosophical component.

However, while this objective idealism is more realistic than other idealisms, it remains linked to the premise of German idealism as a whole, generally more concerned with the idea of things than with things themselves. For Bakunin (1981d

[e], p. 419) in this period, reality is more the knowledge of reality than reality itself, and freedom is the sense of freedom of human consciousness: "Consciousness is liberation [...]. The level of consciousness in man is the level of his freedom." Freedom, humanity's ultimate goal, is achieved through thought, through speculative (philosophical) understanding. Even if it opposes the premises of other idealisms—by denying that the external reality (of nature and society) is non-existent and that only the ideal (of human perception) has reality; by refusing that the subject is the principle of everything and that it produces the object, the external reality—Bakuninian objective idealism remains linked to the notion that the external reality (object) has no autonomy in relation to the subject's perception of knowledge.

In fact, like Hegel, he understands that ideal and real, subject and object, being and thought, thought and reality are identical. They constitute only different facets of the same thing, of the same totality, insofar as there is unity between ideal-real, subject-object, being-thought, thought-reality. Thought is the ultimate reality that man must discover within himself, bearing in mind that his conscience is equivalent to the reason that governs the world. Thought must be the refuge of reason and freedom. This is the key to understanding why, for Bakunin (1981b [e], p. 468), "the real world is, in fact, nothing more than an effective, accomplished, implemented thought." Reality is the realization of thought and to understand it is to find thought existing within it. Reality (the real and even matter) is not independent of the (ideal) mind; on the contrary, because it is indeterminate, universal, and only accessible by thought, it is a thought. More than dependent on the mind, the world (nature and society) resembles it. In seeking to understand the truth, philosophy needs to access reason, because with this it becomes able to understand the world inside and outside consciousness. After all, the content of consciousness is reality itself and the truth must be found within the subject itself. Thus, access to reason allows an understanding of reality. But, as will be seen, this is not a simple process (Del Giudice, 1981, pp. 151–53, 162–72, 188–97; Arantes, 1999).

Bakunin extrapolates Hegel when he argues that, when the process of understanding is complete and reason is reached, it must be dialectically put into effect—from which emerges the Bakuninian philosophy of action. *The unity between theory and practice acquires, then, a sense of reconciliation between knowledge and praxis, rational understanding and human action.* It is evident here that the transition from Fichte to Hegel does not mean, for Bakunin, an absolute break with Fichte in favour of Hegel. As stated, Fichtean elements remain that will allow, among other things, the development of this notion. It should also be noted that, in the end, there remains in Bakuninian objective idealism a certain possibility of understanding the object as the basis of the subject, or even that subjective functions are only objective ones, a path that will be followed from 1842 onwards (McLaughlin, 2002, pp. 66–67).

As in Hegel, some effort is required to understand Bakunin's political-philosophical ideas, which are expounded through idealistic and religious jargon.

According to Bakunin himself (1981d [e])—and also with Del Giudice (1981, pp. 154, 173–74, 195–200, 229, 261–63) and McLaughlin (2002, p. 27)—the notion of an immanent God, incompatible with transcendence and superiority, remains and is deepened in the writings of those years, with the religious substance changing progressively towards an anthropocentric humanism.

For Bakunin, *religion*—determinant in the character of a people together with aesthetics—is the conscience of the absolute and *God* is the absolute itself. God/Absolute is the effective reality, the living whole, the social totality, ethical life as a whole, the expression of the real-ideal unity. At the same time, religion is the understanding of this whole, of this totality—the understanding of the unity between theory and practice and the reconciliation with reality itself—thus equating with reason and concomitantly the criterion for the moral and normative evaluation of this totality. This becomes evident when Bakunin proposes to reconcile the religious (as a form of reason of itself) and the political (in its effectiveness, as the State, because it is). *Divine will* is this elevation to the totality and to non-alienated action, it is the rational process of history itself, the human reason taking effect in the world. The *religious ideal* is freedom, the political and social reconciliation of the free man in the rational state (Christianity, absolute religion), which is based on truth and the freedom of all.

Bakunin (1981d[e], pp. 419, 421) wrote that the *spirit* is "absolute knowledge, absolute freedom, absolute love and, consequently, absolute blessing." It is "absolute power, the source of all power. Reality is its life and, consequently, reality is all-powerful, such like the will and the action of the spirit." Finally, "all existence is the life of the spirit; everything is permeated by the spirit; there is nothing outside the spirit." There is the *objective spirit*, of a social group, which is embodied in customs, laws, and institutions, and there is the *absolute spirit*, which encompasses art, religion, and philosophy, and conforms to a rational social community, self-consciousness of God.

2.5.3 Second Hegelian Period (1841–42)

Between 1841 and 1842, Bakunin, in Germany and in his *second Hegelian period*, elaborates a radicalized continuity of his political and philosophical thinking—especially in "The Reaction in Germany" of 1842. In these years, his main intellectual reference remains, undoubtedly, Hegel—whose concepts of *reason* and *reality* remain central and to which is added a third, *revolution*—who is critically read by him and complemented by the influence of the young members of the Hegelian left, especially Ruge, Bauer, and Feuerbach.

During this period, Bakunin must be considered a young Hegelian. However, both in comparison with Hegel and with the Hegelian left itself, he cannot be regarded as orthodox. In relation to Hegel, he continues the radicalization movement based on the master's ideas and, although without major ruptures, the first open critiques of him are made. In relation to the young Hegelians, Bakunin shares a set of ideas with them but he also ends up going further, particularly with regard to the deployments of his realism, which are more evident in the discussion about the relationship between theory and practice.

For him, the central question of this period and his greatest contribution in the field of political theory is the elaboration of a *theory of revolution*, which allows, at the same time, for analyzing social and political history, past and present, and devising a revolutionary strategy from it. As an essential element of this theory, he formalizes a *negative dialectic*, which improves his critical-dialectical method, supports his first political analysis—about the conflicts that took place in Europe in the 1840s between the enemies and defenders of freedom—and indicates the means to action for those who, like him, understood themselves supporters of freedom and the democratic principle.

In the field of dialectics, the biggest change refers to the role of the negative element of contradiction. In the previous period, Bakunin advocated reconciliation, in which the past was retained as a necessary and integral moment. Distinctly, in this period, the external mediation is refuted in favour of a preponderance of the negative, in which the past is absolutely denied in service of a new future. Negation—for him the engine of history and the vital impulse of life—stands out even more as an essential criterion and necessary prerequisite for the rational human action that will emancipate man (Del Giudice, 1981, pp. 391–92, 413). In the analysis of European politics the fundamental contradiction between the reactionary party and the democratic party is dissected, allowing a broader understanding of the forces at play and the establishment of programmatic lines of action on the part of those who intended to radicalize this contradiction and guarantee the establishment of the democratic principle or principle of freedom.

From 1838 onwards, there is a growing emphasis on realism, which has considerable effects. In the "Preface" Bakunin proposes a reconciliation with reality in philosophical terms. In "Of Philosophy" he reflects, also in these terms, on the process of knowing and of changing reality. In "The Reaction in Germany," entering the field of politics, he analyzes concrete issues of European reality theoretically and recommends ways to intervene in that dispute of forces—preparing the terrain for practice and effective action. The subtitle of this writing ("Fragment from a Frenchman") and the French pseudonym that undersigns the text (Jules Elysard) clearly reflect Bakunin's interest in French political philosophy and its conception of revolutionary and democratic practice. Even the style of this writing explains this intentionality, as it is much clearer and more concrete than that of the preceding texts. Subsequent developments of this emphasis seem logical: it will be a matter of increasingly assuming the primacy of practice and progressively approaching a real and concrete political practice.

In philosophical terms this movement means, between 1841 and 1843, a departure from the more orthodox objective idealism in favour of a *voluntarist realism*, which

Bakunin himself recognizes as part of the idealist camp and whose consequences are decisive. In addition to the aforementioned negative conception of dialectics this realism implies that the previous attempt to reconcile opposites—ideal and real, subject and object, thought and being, theory and life, philosophy and practice, individual and community, life/internal world, and life/external world—gives way, increasingly, to prioritizing the second elements over the first. Progressively, concrete reality starts to differentiate itself from knowledge about it and to acquire autonomy in relation to the subject's perception of knowledge. Reality acquires more importance than theoretical and abstract constructions, even those that have it as their object. Object, being, life, practice, community, and external life/world come to have more relevance than subject, thought, theory, philosophy, individual, and internal life/world. In the wake of the philosophy of action, for example, the concept of unity between theory and practice starts to give way to a preponderance of practice to the detriment of theory, which will mark the end of this period, when Bakunin moves from the theoretical discussion about practice to concrete practice.

However, it is not yet a break with idealism in the sense of materialism. If Bakunin intensifies his criticism of subjectivism and accentuates the realistic aspects of his thinking, this is not done through an emphasis on the material foundations of nature and society. It is done, distinctly, in the direction of a reality that is conceived, as explained by Del Giudice (1981, p. 389), "in terms of the human personality that expresses itself concretely and practically through free action in the historical process." For him, this "affirmation of the concept of personality gave concrete expression to the roles that *action* and *will* would play in the emancipation of the human person."

> The idea of the individual and *concrete* human personality, which had overcome the limitations of its "immediacy" and, asserting itself through free and creative action, would constitute the bridge by which Bakunin would reach the field of revolutionary politics and activity. The free personality, removed from the confines of Hegelian historical determinism and linked by Bakunin to the concepts of *reality*, *will*, and *action*, constituted the key factor in this gradual transition. (Del Giudice, 1981, p. 388)

Reality is thus understood as a historical result of the voluntary and practical action of people within certain limits of necessity. If this reality is certainly not conceived in deterministic terms, it is also not understood as a pure result of human will. Bakunin (1976a [e], p. 106) emphasizes, in this sense: "In general, I do not recognize [contingency as] a real influence on history; history is a free, but also necessary, development of the free [spirit]." Thus, the Bakuninian voluntarism of those years asserts itself on the notion that the historical process imposes certain limits on the human will in shaping reality, even though the will has enormous possibilities. Personality is conceptualized as the unity between individuality and effective reality, social totality. It is not a question of pure individuality, much less of selfishness, but of a concrete and rational human being who expresses their will through practical action to affect the knowledge of reality and the realization of freedom. Action is understood as life itself, as the practical attempt, carried out by means of will, to bring about the knowledge of reality and the realization of freedom. Finally, will is conceptualized as freedom, the ability to produce historical effects through active negation and action, following rational purposes; it is the engine, the fuel of action.

In discussing these concepts Bakunin asserts the need to become "completely free from theoretical drunkenness" with an exclusively abstract basis and to see "reality in all its pitiful nakedness." For him, it is crucial "to move from the indeterminate sphere of fantasy to reality, [...] in which he [the negative party] must live, suffer in order to finally triumph." The existing reality must be understood as it actually is, since it constitutes the historical terrain for the realization of freedom. "Only reality can satisfy us" because "only reality is the strong and energetic truth, that is, true. Everything else is [...] idiotic idealism." In asserting a more realistic idealism he understands that "idealism is holy and true only because it is the idealism of a real, living world." And that the true idealist is one who "throws himself passionately and boldly into the waves of real life" realizes "his inner world in living love and in real work" and submits "his wise ideal world to the evangelical simplicity of reality" (Bakunin, 42026[c], pp. 1–2; Bakunin, 42016[c], pp. 2–3).

He defines personality in religious jargon, emphasizing that "the true self is the *personality* of man, a personality that cannot be sinful or deceptive, because it is the individual's immediate unity with God," "the original diversity of each man in God." The personality differs from "individuality precisely because it [the personality] is the original incarnation of God in the individuality of each one." Every man must "purify himself definitively of all individual selfishness ... to achieve a radiant and immortal personality." Seeing as this immortality "should not be a demand for egoism, of unhealthy individuality" but of "fortunate self-consciousness," "individuality must pass, disappear, in order to become a personality; not a personality in general, but *that* undivided personality." In order to be able to express its will through action, in a concrete sense, "the personalities of human beings must be absolutely autonomous and free" (Bakunin, 40024[c], pp. 3–5; Bakunin, 41002[c], p. 3; Bakunin, 42001[c], p. 7).

When Bakunin discusses "the practical and free actions of man" he does so considering that "to live is to be, to live is to act truly and actively," such that "only action is life." And to act implies "not being stuck in words" but "proving practically that you understand and that you love life." Life "is not accessible to abstract theory, to impassive calculation, because it is more than a theory," it "is the supreme action, the free unleashing of holy passion." And "action is only known through action, freedom through freedom and love through love. Knowing freedom does not only mean thinking, but also living; and life is more than thought: life is the miraculous realization of thought" (Bakunin, 43012[c], p. 3; Bakunin, 42010[c], p. 1; Bakunin, 43015[c], pp. 1–2).

He also maintains that "fierce and religious will" makes it possible to "overcome all difficulties" insofar as a determined existence can be modified "according to my ideas and my beliefs." Thus, will continues to be defined the same way as in the previous period, as active and rational negation: "Will is the infinite force of self-negation of the truth, the negation of all narrow instincts that disgust the nature of man and of finite thinking contrary to the truth" (Bakunin, 43010[c], p. 3; Bakunin, 42002[c], p. 2; Bakunin, 40057[c], p. 3).

In political terms, between 1841 and 1843 Bakunin adopted French *radicalism* as a political-doctrinal foundation. Adhesion to this type of republicanism, according to his understanding, does not necessarily mean a break with the German way (theoretical, idealistic) in favour of the French way (practical, materialistic), as argued by Angaut (2007a, pp. 13–14) but more precisely the understanding that France's revolutionary and socialist tradition did nothing more than put into practice the ideas of Germany's philosophical idealism, as Del Giudice proves (1981, pp. 384–86, 405–408). It is therefore a fusion or continuity between the French and German routes according to an understanding that French radicalism is the expression of German idealism in the form of praxis. As a result, Bakuninian Hegelianism becomes not only a tool for analyzing reality, but also a political-doctrinal instrument and philosophy adjusted to praxis.

This republican radicalism aims to promote the fulfillment of the promises of the French Revolution—Freedom, Equality, and Fraternity—which, according to his understanding, had not been extended to the whole of humanity, especially to workers and the poor. In Bakunin (1976a [e], p. 108), this objective is summed up in the concretization of a principle: "the equality of men being realized [in] freedom." It is in these years in general, and in "The Reaction in Germany" in particular, that Bakunin (1976a [e], p. 127) manifests, for the first time, the conception that the "people"—in the sense of an exploited-dominated class, of the workers and the poor in general—whose radicalized demands would culminate in the revolutions of 1848, will be a prominent subject in this revolutionary process.

The holy spirit of freedom and equality, the spirit of pure humanity [...] was revealed to humanity by the French Revolution amid thunder and lightning, and [...] was sown everywhere in the storm of revolutionary wars as the germ of new life. The French Revolution is the beginning of a new life; many are so blind that they think they have overcome and domesticated its powerful spirit. How terrible the awakening of these unfortunates will be! No, the revolutionary drama is not yet over. We were born under the star of the revolution; we live and move under its influence and we will also die, all those who live today, without exception, under its influence. We are on the eve of a great historical world transmutation, on the eve of a new and even more dangerous struggle, because it will no longer have a purely political, but principled, religious character. We must not deceive ourselves: it will be nothing less than a new religion, the religion of democracy, one that, under its old banner with the slogan "*Freedom, equality, fraternity*" will fight its new struggle, a struggle to the death. (Bakunin, 2007b[e], pp. 158–59)

As can be seen, the idealistic and religious jargon persists in these years, although much less emphasized. References to God and the divine are much scarcer, unlike references to the spirit, which are still constant. When they appear, they have a similar meaning to that of the past period, provided the aforementioned modifications corresponding to the transition from objective idealism to voluntarist realism are understood.

Between 1841 and 1842, Bakunin accompanies the movement of other young Hegelians, such as Ruge, who move more clearly from religious to political critique. In this way, Bakunin (41009 [c], p. 3) equates religion and politics, writing that "politics is religion, and religion is politics," freedom being the objective of both. Politics is interpreted as a new, practical religion, capable of supporting the praxis towards the future (thus relating to the previous concept of religion as an actualized socio-religious life); and religion is the source of a universal principle and the way it can penetrate life, supporting the creation of a new totality, a "Church [...] of the free humanity." The transition from theory to practice is interpreted as conversion.

He declares himself an enemy of the existing churches and Christianity, claiming a religion of freedom, equality, democracy, and rediscussing the relationship between politics and religion. He advocates a "true Christianity" as an effective realization of freedom synonymous with reason, which is synonymous with a policy of freedom and democracy (Angaut, 2007b, pp. 43–47; Del Giudice, 1981, p. 411).

Bakunin recognizes that man

only becomes conscious of God in free action, in unlimited freedom. God is freedom, and we only become conscious of the recognized freedom through freedom. Freedom is the supreme activity that produces itself, that creates itself. The person of God, as with immortality, the dignity of man—and, in my opinion, all this is inseparable—can only be known practically, by free action, produced and fruited by the original depths of an individual spirit, seeing as God himself is nothing but the miraculous action of himself. [...] constantly putting God in motion in itself: such is the nature of action. This action —and only it, this action of consuming itself—represents the supreme pride and the greatest humility of man before God, the simple and innocent heart, the translucent fulfillment of the eternal person of man. (Bakunin, 42014[c], pp. 3–4)

In such terms, it is the free action of the person, which has placed within him the movement of God, which allows the consciousness of God, of freedom. That is, it is only through the action of the personality that freedom can be known and to effect it in reality through will.

2.5.4 Moment of Departure from Philosophy (1843)

In terms of political theory, the corollary of this Bakuninian theory of revolution and its implications can be drawn from the texts Bakunin produced in 1843.

First, these texts formalize the *primacy of practice* over theory—previously indicated, when the limits of philosophy and the tasks of the democratic party were pointed out—and the abandonment of philosophy by Bakunin, which will extend for many years. It is thus the end of his Hegelian period. But it should be noted that this passage he makes from theory to practice does not mean a complete abandonment of theory, but a new conception of it, understood in a different key and deeply interwoven with practice.

Second, they present the centrality of the concept of *self-government of the people* as the objective of political radicalism, and allow a critical analysis of communism, which emerged at the time as a political-doctrinal alternative.

NOTES

1   Date relative to the Gregorian calendar, adopted in Russia only in 1918; according to the Julian calendar, which was in force in Bakunin's time, his date of birth is 18 May.

2   "Histoire de ma vie: Première Partie – 1815–1840" ["My Life Story: first part – 1815–1840"] (Bakunin, 71030[o]) is a short text written in 1871, in which Bakunin begins an exposition of his life story. Like several other productions, this one also remained unfinished. Only twelve pages were written, in which Bakunin discusses his early years in Premukhino. In this text, still, a slightly more detailed discussion of the 1825 Decembrist Revolt stands out.

3   Economically, conditions for international trade worsened and exports of agricultural products were complicated. Even with the growth of industrialization, the almost entirely agrarian model of production was still marked by low productivity and relations of servitude. Politically, the war with France had shown weaknesses in the Empire and the needs of a larger army with greater operative capacity, greater amounts of money, and a more modern model of government (Brupbacher, 2015, p. 19; Leier, 2006, p. 25).

4   As pointed out by Leier (2006, p. 24), Bakunin's claim (71030 [o], p. 1) that his father was a member of the Northern Society is unlikely.

5   From the period 1833–34 in the field of literature, in addition to the aforementioned romantics, the following stand out: *The Wealth of Nations* by Adam Smith; *Tableau des Révolutions de l'Europe dans le Moyen Âge* [*Table of European Revolutions in the Middle Ages*] by Christophe-Guillaume Koch; fictions by Faddey Bulgarin, Nicholas Grech, and Mikhail Zagoskin (Bakunin, 33016[c], p. 2; Leier, 2006, pp. 43, 54).

6   To these two circles, Marshall Shatz—in his article "Mikhail Bakunin and the Primukhino Circle: love and liberation in the Russian Intelligentsia of the 1830s"—believes it to be possible to add a third, constituted later, but also in that first half of the 1830s: the "Premukhino Circle": "Bakunin, his sisters, his closest friends, Nathalie and Alexandra Beer, and, to a lesser extent, his five younger brothers, formed an intimate group. Even if its members would not call it that, it can reasonably be called the Premukhino Circle" (Shatz, 1999, p. 1). It should also be noted that Herzen's account, constantly reproduced by historians—that Stankevitch's Circle was more focused on German philosophy, more abstract and reactionary, and that the Herzen-Ogarev Circle was more focused on French thinking, more concrete and progressive—does not correspond to reality (Del Giudice, 1981, pp. 78–84). This indicates an important aspect, since Herzen's reports on Bakunin, often used as a source, are not always accurate or even correct.

7   With the exception of the Fifth Lecture, entitled "Examination of Rousseau's Theses on the Influence of Arts and Sciences on the Goodness of Humanity" (Del Giudice, 1981, p. 119).

8   These were Bakunin's first published texts. But his first written production is from 1837: an article on Shakespeare's *Hamlet*, in which he analyses the tragedy in the key of justice, reflected in its implications in the fields of law and morals (Bakunin, 37003[e]).

9   This position is supported by the pioneering work of Del Giudice (1981), which, to this day, remains the best study of Bakunin's first Hegelian period (1837–40). In this study, she devoted herself to exquisitely opposing what seemed to be a consensus among a whole generation of scholars of Bakunin and of the Russian Hegelian left (Carr, Steklov, Polonsky, Pirumova, Annenkov, Martin Malia, and Hepner, among others): the notion that the 1838 "Preface" shows a conservative, reactionary Bakunin; a Hegelian right-wing defender of Russian absolutism. Even contemporary authors—as or more rigorous than those others mentioned here, such as J.C. Angaut (2005, pp. 46–47) and René Berthier (2010, vol. I, p. 6)—support this view. As Del Giudice demonstrates, this text, if properly interpreted, shows a break with the period of aesthetic metaphysics and "interiority" inspired by Schelling, and the coming to consciousness of objective reality and its concrete manifestations. In the "Preface" Bakunin is critical of reality and in favour of social change (Del Giudice, 1981, pp. 242–43).

10   Still, according to Del Giudice (1981), Bakunin's thought between 1838 and 1842 has continuity. This thesis also breaks with the argument that it was only after going to Germany in 1840 that Bakunin broke with conservatism and, due to the influence of the Hegelian left, took a revolutionary position. For Del Giudice (1981, p. vii), there is "logical continuity in the evolution of Mikhail Bakunin's thought before and after the 'crucial' date of 1840," that is, from the "Preface" of 1838 to "The Reaction in Germany" from 1842, going through "Of Philosophy" from 1839–40.

11   The arrival date in Berlin is 13 July (Julian calendar, used in Russia) or 25 July (Gregorian calendar, used in Germany) (Carr, 1961, p. 93).

12   The relationship between the two contributed directly to Turgueniev's construction of the main character of his 1856 romance novel *Rudin*. It seems certain that this was to some extent inspired by Bakunin, but it is worth highlighting, based on Shatz (1992), that this novel should not be considered a document capable of contributing to the historical or psychological clarification of Bakunin.

13   Bakunin stayed in Berlin for a year and a half: from July 1840 to February 1842. In a 10 February, 1842 letter, he finds himself in Berlin and mentions that in a week he will go to Dresden (Bakunin, 42005 [c], p. 2); in the following letter, of 7 April, 1842 and in the subsequent ones, he is definitively in Dresden. According to another letter from Bakunin (40061 [c], p. 3) his classes began in late October 1840. Initially, he studied logic and history of philosophy with Werder, and aesthetics, theology, physics, fencing, and horse riding with other teachers. Thus, those 15–16 months between November 1840 and February 1842 were probably the period in which he attended the University of Berlin, after which he abandoned it. Even so, according to Grawitz (1990, p. 92), Bakunin received a diploma recognizing him as *vir juvenis ornatissimus* [a talented young man] for the duration of his university stay.

14   For the "Confession" quotes, I used the Spanish translation as a basis of reference (Bakunin, 1976b [e]). However, I have often compared it with the French translation and, in some cases, with the original Russian version, adjusting what I deemed necessary (Bakunin, 2000a).

15   ʿAs Berthier (2008, pp. 203–209) demonstrates, Max Stirner (pseudonym of Johann Kaspar Schmidt), also a member of the Hegelian left, had no influence on Bakunin in the 1840s and beyond. In all of Bakunin's writings and letters, Stirner—who in 1845 published the book *Der Einzige und sein Eigenthum* [*The Ego and Its Own*], which was reintroduced at the end of the nineteenth century by the individualist John Henry Mackay, with the mistaken intention of incorporating it into the anarchist canon—gets only one mention (in the book *Statism and Anarchy*) without any relevance. The argument about the nonexistent link between Stirner and Bakunin is due to Engels, who promoted it in his writings and letters in order to disqualify his political opponent.

16   Herzen, before knowing that Bakunin was the author of this text, stated, "It is a masterpiece; the author is the first Frenchman I have encountered who understood Hegel" (*apud* Grawitz, 1990, p. 104). Engels, another member of the Hegelian left at the time, confessed to Charles Rappoport in 1893 that Bakunin "understood Hegel" (Lehning, 1999, p. 394).

17   With regards to the discussion on education, two translations by Bakunin, which deal precisely with this theme, were important: Fichte's *Conferences on the Vocation of the Scholar* and Hegel's *Gymnasium Lectures*.

CHAPTER 3

LOVE-FREEDOM AND EMANCIPATION
(1836–37)

This chapter, divided into three parts, expounds Bakunin's political theory in his *Fichtean period*, which runs from 1836 to 1837: 1) Interior World and Exterior World; 2) God and Religion of Humanity: Anthropocentric Immanentism; 3) Rational Ethical Action.[1]

3.1 INTERIOR WORLD AND EXTERIOR WORLD

Life consists of two elements: the "spiritual element" interior to the individual, and the "exterior element" of other individuals, society, and nature in general. In the first stage, of becoming aware of and shaping the ethical assumptions for action, the "interior life" based on the first element must take precedence over the "exterior life," based on the second. "The less man depends on the exterior world, the more the interior world is accessible to him," and such access is indispensable, since "outside of spiritual life there is no true life." Thus, the good existence, in that first moment, implies a dedication to the interior life, into which the individual absorbs himself with a view to his own improvement in the search for love and freedom, which are the true foundations of religion and life (Bakunin, 36017[c], pp. 1–2).

This search for life and inner religion may imply a certain egoism, but not in the sense of "material egoism that separates men" from the "common egoism." It can only be understood in this way, since it requires a return of the individual to himself, in a procedure that makes it possible to find this ethical principle, love-freedom. But when the individual is penetrated by religious feeling, when he becomes aware of his divine nature and destiny, he obtains the conditions to transform his individual self into an ideal, collective self of all men. The return of the individual to himself thus allows him to establish the possibilities for finding and recognizing others (Bakunin, 36049[c], p. 3; Bakunin, 36074[c], p. 9).

In a second moment, through action, activity, the subject is able to effectively realize love-freedom not only individually but collectively. Freedom is achieved through absolute love and the emancipation from external constraints, allowing individuals to develop fully and cause their moral will to coincide with the divine will (Bakunin, 36074[c], p. 4). However, for collective realization any form of egoism must be abandoned.[2] This is because, to the extent that freedom is the ultimate end of all society and to which all men tend, it involves aspects not only related to interior life (individual) but also to exterior life (collective), and carries with it a certain notion of equality. Love exists only in freedom, so that "only the free man can love the free man"; to love the other is to want your freedom. Those who find the path of love begin to free themselves and, then, are destined for the liberation of others—their destiny is "to liberate humanity and the entire universe." In absolute freedom, men, by growing closer to God, converted their passion into love; they are equal to both God and each other. Therefore, seeking freedom means to a certain extent seeking equality; individual progress is linked to the advancement of the emancipation of humanity (Bakunin, 36033[c], p. 4; Bakunin, 37055[c], p. 7).[3]

Such freedom must also find ways to reconcile with necessity. It is not carried out by a purely abstract mental exercise, nor is it supposed to be pure, as a freedom capable of imposing itself on all kinds of necessity. In accordance with what Fichte advocated, "human beings exist in a real, physical, material, and limited world, not in that of the mind or spirit, in which everything is possible" (Leier, 2006, p. 69). In other words, there are limits to freedom, even though individuals can, through their rational action, expand them.

> The inner mission is to morally transform the outside world, [...] requiring a severe moral commitment on the part of all self-conscious individuals. Freedom cannot be imposed from outside; it can only emerge from the most intimate depths of the will, acting in accordance with the precepts of practical reason. Only after an inner change has been made can ethical life be practically applied to all aspects of existing society. [...] Instead of seeking a complete annihilation of the concrete "external" reality in favor of his "speculative" and "pure" self, Bakunin, under the influence of Fichte, is concerned with the "establishment of harmony between internal and external life—the external is absorbed in the internal, not to dissolve in it, but to *regenerate itself* and recover a new external expression." (Del Giudice, 1981, p. 125)

The greatest human duty is, in this sense, to "understand [this] his mission and follow the path that it indicates" (Bakunin, 36033 [c], p. 4). As can be seen, this mission and this path are based on an ethical principle of action (love-freedom) and imply a religious practice, even though the belief in God is found in the recognition of the subject's moral dynamics.

3.2 GOD AND RELIGION OF HUMANITY: ANTHROPOCENTRIC IMMANENTISM

"The object of true love is God" but not that God "cut off from the world," rather the one "who lives among men," "who is elevated by the elevation of men" (Bakunin, 36017 [c], p. 3). "True religion" is interior—which can only be found in the interior life, "that religion of the soul that feels its God in itself" (Bakunin, 36052 [c], p. 5)— that of love for humanity—"my love for humanity constitutes my religion" (Bakunin, 36019 [c], p. 1). From this conception of God and religion, the basis for a critique of institutional religion is forged, understood as "inversion or destruction of this free inner life and its development." Institutional religion is, in fact, a false religion that "distorted the real meaning of Christianity," replacing Christian morality and its ethical values with dogmatism and rhetoric (Del Giudice, 1981, p. 127).

Thus, one can distinguish the true from the false religion:

> May religion be the foundation and essence of your life and actions. But let it be the *pure and only true religion of divine reason and love*, and not that religion that you professed before, not that religion that strives to separate you from everything that constitutes the content and life of true moral existence. Not that narrow idea of a capricious God; not that limited and cold feeling, which denies all that is beautiful in the moral and intellectual world, and which threatens to be absorbed in a miserable sphere of actions without ideas and feelings without love. Not that religion that, in the end, can only kill such a burning soul, sublime and eager for love as yours, that no moral force can quicken, and that is irreconcilable with true love. (Bakunin, 36074[c], p. 6, emphasis added)

This religion—"of divine reason and love," of Jesus Christ, Christianity—is the only one capable of reconciling being, life, and morals, constituting morally active individuals who progressively approach "a new world—a world of absolute freedom and love." Such a religion, by guiding the individual in the direction intended by divine Providence, can provide his improvement in the sense of a life of freedom, love, and happiness. And the feeling that marks this improvement is inevitable suffering because "whoever has not suffered cannot truly love" and only those who really love can be free and happy. The human purpose, the vocation of man, is to find inner and divine life and, with that, to rise to love, freedom, and happiness—man was born to love, to be free and happy (Bakunin, 36074[c], pp. 3–8).

The essence of God and religion is love-freedom (absolute, spirit), which leads man to reason and which becomes effective through the encounter of divine life in man, of true religion, with the accomplishment of the task, of ethical action, moral will. The essence of the ideal is freedom, and the essence of freedom is this task, the realization of which is motivated by freedom itself. There is no God in slavery and divinity is emancipation; divine life manifests itself in all man's moral acts, through which God reveals himself to humanity and man attains freedom, not without first experiencing suffering, that negative moment of the realization of the will, of dialectical progress (Del Giudice, 1981, pp. 114, 122, 147–48).

In this way, the objective of the task, that love-freedom, is equivalent to the fusion between man and God[4]—"man will become God" (Bakunin, 36043 [c], p. 3)—to the human realization of divinity, the reconciliation between heaven and earth:

Man's destiny is not to suffer on this earth with folded arms in order to deserve a mythological paradise. His destiny is, instead, to transport that heaven, that God that he has within him, to the earth; and to elevate practical [life], the earth, towards the sky. This is his high mission. (Bakunin, 36029[c], p. 5, emphasis added)

In the key of this anthropocentric immanentism nothing is considered superior to man, and his salvation is found within himself, in the autonomous individual in commitment with his moral autonomy. The path taken by Christ is the inspiration in this sense, since he incorporated the conversion of passion (man) into love (God) and thus indicated, through his life and suffering, the destiny of the good life. For a life of love, freedom, and happiness to be achieved, human passion must, as in Jesus' indicative, be directed towards divine love, purifying man and his ulterior path.

3.3 RATIONAL ETHICAL ACTION

Once the ethical basis for action is found, it is then a matter of acting morally: "to love, to act under the influence of some thoughts enlivened by feeling" (Bakunin, 36017 [c], p. 2), thus giving reason a concrete dimension, uniting theory and praxis, applying philosophical knowledge to life. It is a question of knowing the world, evaluating it critically and acting to transform it,[5] since it is only through the task, through action, that man expresses and realizes his essence (Del Giudice, 1981, pp. 103–21). In this way, "action is not only the necessary consequence of our conscience, but it is the necessary condition of our conscience: without action, without external expression from the inner world, there is no consciousness, there is no life" (Bakunin, 36088[c], pp. 1–2).

Ethical action must be propagated through words and above all deeds, as the force of example is indispensable to it. You must find means corresponding to the ends you want to achieve because "only noble means can lead to noble ends; only the truth can lead to the truth." That is why reciprocal and free "persuasion, and not [...] force [or] violence that leads to nothing" is recommended and, understanding that "love and slavery are diametrically opposed," "submission to [exterior] will" is rejected because "submission is not love."[6] When a person's action involves a request or an order that puts another person's individual beliefs at stake, or even when he or she deviates from those assumptions, there is "not only the right, but even the duty not to obey." "Education founded on Christian love" stands out as a form of action (Bakunin, 37055[c], pp. 5, 8, 12–13).[7]

Education is an activity capable of morally reforming society, and the educator (wise, *philosopher*) has an important role in establishing a link between the moral idea and its implementation in society. The philosopher is therefore capable of driving this process, establishing himself as a pedagogue of humanity, an educator of society, and a guide of individuals towards love-freedom (Del Giudice, 1981, pp. 103–12).[8]

NOTES

1 From this period, the Bakunin documents used (letters) can be found on the IISH CD-ROM (Bakunin, 2000a); the quotes were translated from the French texts.

2 It was in this sense that Bakunin (37007 [c], p. 4) emphasized, "I feel that I am capable of great things, but for that I must forget myself, because otherwise my egoism will destroy my mission."

3 Cf. Fichte (s/d, pp. 18, 23): "Free is only the one who wants to make everything free around him" and "all who considers himself master of others is himself a slave"; "the ultimate goal of the whole society [... is] the full equality of all its members."

4 Cf. Fichte (s/d, p. 10): The equalization of man with God is perfection, which must ethically guide the conduct of individuals: "*Perfection* is the supreme and inaccessible goal of man; but *betterment* to infinity is his vocation."

5 Cf. Fichte (s/d, pp. 2, 9): "We affirm only that the effective reality must be evaluated by them [ethical ideals], and be modified by those who feel the strength for that" since "without morality no happiness is possible."

6 Cf. Fichte (s/d, pp. 17–20, 38), who advocates "reciprocal influence, mutual giving and receiving, mutual action and passion," the "universal influence of all human kind on itself," and the "acting on others as free beings." Regarding the ethical foundations of this action, he recommends: man "should not act on them [rational beings] as on inert matter or the animal, in order to accomplish with them only their end, without taking into account their freedom"; in the case of the wise man, for example, he "cannot deal with it [society] except by moral means" and "must not fall into the temptation to lead men to admit their convictions through embarrassment, through the use of physical force."

7 Cf. Fichte (s/d, pp. 50, 13, 39), who emphatically supports the need for action: "Act! Act! That's what we're here for." He also reinforces—like Bakunin (37055 [c], p. 6), who considered that "love moves and expresses itself necessarily in its actions"—the importance of going beyond theory and discourse: "The theoretical scope of philosophy has arguably been exhausted by the critical inquiries of critics; all questions so far unanswered must be answered based on practical principles"; "we don't teach only through words; we also teach, and much more profoundly, through our example."

8 Cf. Fichte (s/d, pp. 36–38): "The wise man [...] is the educator of humanity" who "exists only thanks to society and for society." The knowledge acquired in society must return to it in the form of education: the educator "must lead men to the feeling of their true needs and make known to them the means to satisfy them", with the goal of "the moral ennoblement of the whole of man."

CHAPTER 4

ALIENATION VS. RECONCILIATION WITH REALITY AND THEORY-PRACTICE UNITY (1837-40)

This chapter examines Bakunin's political theory in his *first Hegelian period*, which lasted from 1837 to 1840, divided into four parts: 1) Knowledge, Subjectivism, and Alienation; 2) Reality and Theory-practice; 3) Critical-dialectic Method; 4) Philosophy of Action and Education.[1]

4.1 KNOWLEDGE, SUBJECTIVISM, AND ALIENATION

Alienation is a fundamental aspect of modernity. It is characterized by the dissociation between man and reality, by the estrangement arising from the schism between theory and practice, between subject and object. It is a type of illusion or abstraction through which man places himself outside of reality or abandons it and thus separates himself from the totality, from the essence, from life. Alienated, man mistakenly believes that the truth can be found outside the living whole. Alienation manifests itself in both philosophical and social terms and has disastrous consequences in the contemporary world (Del Giudice, 1981, pp. 164, 270).

> Bakunin uses "abstraction" as a pejorative term, as a synonym for "illusion"— since, in abstraction, he places himself outside concrete reality or leaves it behind. Abstraction and alienation are types of "illusion" or ignorance because they embody the *belief of the particular subject, that his truth can be found in isolation from the real totality. Consequently, abstraction is the separation from life, the social whole or essence*; and Bakunin insists on the fact that reality, the totality, the absolute, is concrete and universal life. (Del Giudice, 1981, p. 270, emphasis added)

Alienation, abstraction, illusion; such is "the main disease of our new generation" [young Russian intelligentsia of the 1830s]. Historically, the origins of this disease of modern alienation are found in the Protestant Reformation: "the beginning of this evil [alienation] is camouflaged in the Reformation." This is because "the Reformation shook his [the Pope's] authority, but it also shook all the other authorities" and, with that, it established the basis for the emergence of the principles of individual conscience, morality and freedom, as well as the notion of autonomous subjectivity, which culminated in the French Revolution. The concrete results of the Protestant Reformation were "unlimited investigations in all walks of life" and "the revival of the empirical sciences and of philosophy" (Bakunin, 1981a[e], pp. 424, 426).

The empirical sciences, limited to the observation of the finite world, a world accessible to sensible finitude, from inside and outside, and to contemplation, progressed rapidly and in a short time achieved brilliant successes. But outside this finite world there is another sphere, inaccessible to sensible observation, the sphere of the spirit, absolute and unconditional, and that sphere has become the object of philosophy. The awakened intellect, released from the restrictions of authority, expected nothing more from faith and, separating itself from the real world, immersing itself in itself, wished to derive everything from itself, to find the origin and the basis of knowledge itself.

"I think therefore I am."

This is how the new philosophy began in the person of Descartes. Doubt in the face of all existing things, refutation of everything that was not known and established by philosophical cognition. And this, together with the essential principle of experimental knowledge, empiricism, which maintained that all knowledge is necessarily conditioned by the immediate presence of the cognizant subject, constituted the main attribute of the mind, liberated from papal authority by the Reformation, a characteristic that was expressed preeminently in the XVIII century. (Bakunin, 1981a[e], pp. 426–27)

A movement of paradoxical results followed the Protestant Reformation. Before the Reformation, there was a certain tendency towards universality—albeit abstract— that "was limited only to abstract understanding, to the abstract universal, abstracting itself from all reality." It was a *moment of truth without reality*, in which there was a concern with the human *genus* (gender, human species) in general (universality), but this was done in a way completely dissociated from the concreteness of life. With the Reformation, the obscurity of theology and of the doctrine of the Catholic Church is increasingly broken, and interests in the secular world are renewed. At the same time, as a derivation of this secularization, the fragmentation of knowledge (analytical division of reality, of proceedings and of those responsible for analysis) is promoted. This movement, on the one hand, allowed certain aspects of reality to become more deeply known; but, on the other hand, it implied a rupture with universality, with totality, establishing the primacy of particularity, of the subject's singularity. Thus forming a *moment of truth without reality*, in which there was greater concern with the concreteness of life, but this was done through a limited subjectivism (particularity). Such is the picture that explains the historical origins of modern alienation (Bakunin, 1981b[e], p. 448).

Therefore, if the Protestant Reformation allowed knowledge to come closer to reality, it also broke with universality, with totality and with that "completely destroyed the living connection that united knowledge and life, giving rise to enormous suffering, limitations" (Bakunin, 1981b [e], p. 447). The Reformation marks the passage from a premodern form of abstraction, abstract universality, to the modern form of alienation, illusory subjectivism. Thus, man and reality, theory and practice, subject and object are dissociated. Hence, "rationalism and empiricism—which are called 'philosophy of understanding'—are considered responsible for the general illness of the eighteenth and early nineteenth centuries." This disease, modern alienation, has as symptoms "emptiness," "separation from reality," "moral alienation," and "loss of 'substance,' of 'totality' or of 'life'" (Del Giudice, 1981, p. 270).

Although rationalism and empiricism differ in terms of the source of knowledge (reason in rationalism and experience in empiricism) and method of knowledge (deduction in rationalism and induction in empiricism), both have in common an excess of subjectivism that results in alienation. For rationalists, the object can be known to us, insofar as it is produced by us. For empiricists, all the concepts and laws of reason cannot aspire to universality (Arantes, 1999). For the understanding of an object, focusing both on reason and on the subject's experience means subjectivism, a subject's priority in relation to the object, a split, a knowledge that depends exclusively on the cognizant subject, its sensitivity, and its individual understanding. Even the traditions of German idealism (particularly of Kant and Fichte) and French materialism were not enough to break this framework of subjectivism and alienation.

Premodern knowledge, under the tutelage of the Catholic Church, and modern knowledge, under the aegis of rationalism, were considerably reduced to abstract theoretical studies without any empirical foundation. But modern knowledge also relied largely on empirical studies without any theoretical basis (empiricism). In a sense, before modernity and rationalism it was theory without practice, and in empiricist modernity, practice without theory. Even the studies that, in a third way, sought to reconcile empirical thinking and data in a certain manner—and with that, manifested advances in relation to the two other forms of knowledge —have their limitations. It seems necessary, therefore, to proceed to a more profound critique of the latter two forms of modern knowledge: empiricism and theory.

Empiricism had an undeniable merit compared to previous forms of knowledge, which was that it "turned the thinking spirit's attention to the reality of the universal, to the finite moment of the infinite, to the diversity of natural and spiritual life." It managed to get closer to reality but only to understand it in its finite aspects. It gave up universality through a notion of autonomous subject and a focus on individual particularity. With that, it lost sight of the infinite, falling into another extreme: "knowledge of facts without thought and without unity is not true knowledge, but a dead pile of inanimate matter." Empiricism is unable to "destroy all limitations, all unilateralities" and "to embrace the past, present and future appearances of the real world." Therefore, it is "unable to know the absolute truth." And such limitations cannot be overcome because empiricism, "experimental knowledge," is prisoner "to the finite conditions of space and time." As a matter of fact, empiricism means an advance in relation to ordinary consciousness since it invests in the process of knowledge of science. But it does so by restricting itself to the finite, manifesting itself as a collector of particular data and reaching, at most, particular laws (Bakunin, 1981b[e], pp. 448–49, 455, 460–61).

However, in seeking universal truth some thinkers were able to extrapolate this tougher empiricism and arrive at theoretical formulations. Then, as a historical product of modernity, a controversy between empiricists and theorists was formed:

> *Theorists* claim that empiricism, by limiting itself to facts alone, does not find spirit in them and does not satisfy the main criterion of knowledge, which requires thought and not arid facts; *empiricists*, on the other hand, claim that theories are useless, no more than fantastic flashes that are based on nothing and prove nothing. *Both are right.* (Bakunin, 1981b[e], p. 457, emphasis added)

Facts cannot be understood without unifying and universal ideas, and those who proceed without such thinking should be considered, more appropriately, mere "fact collectors." However, this does not make the theorists right either because, although they managed to break with the superficiality of the object—as were the cases of Goethe, Georges Cuvier, Johann Gottfried von Herder, Montesquieu and Pierre-Simon Ballanche — their theories have as their starting point "experimental observation, diversity of the facts, particular laws, as observed by empiricism". (Bakunin, 1981b[e], pp. 457, 461).

What theorists do is to try, based on this observation, to find these facts or laws, possible generalizations—they seek confirmation of their theories in them. Theorists do not break with subjectivism; they remain tied to the particular (me, rational individuality), they do not relate the particularities among themselves, to each other, nor those particularities with the universal (we, *genus*, social community). This impossibility of encompassing the universal and infinite totality is explained by the fact that

> all theories, without exception, not only emerge from the realm of empiricism, but in essence are their necessary continuation; every theorist is at the same time an empiricist. Empiricism, the experimental world, is the beginning and the end of any theory; the theorist begins with the diversity of the real world, discovers thought, which in his mind must explain and encompass that world, and returns to that same diversity in order to find in it the justification and proof of his thoughts. Theory is the necessary result and—if one can express it that way—the flower of empiricism, in that there is no theorist who is not an empiricist, just as there is no empiricist who is not a theorist; and the struggle between empiricists and theorists is nothing more than an internal struggle, an internal contradiction of empiricism itself. (Bakunin, 1981b[e], p. 459)

In other words, theory, however much an advance, a superior form of knowledge when compared to empiricism, continues to be unable to encompass the totality of the real world and to penetrate the universal principle, which constitutes all the infinity of the real.

This insufficiency of empiricism in both its forms is sustained because in a thought it can only be proven in two ways: *a posteriori*, in the field of the experimental world of facts, without being able to break with partiality; or *a priori*, in the field of thought, which requires philosophy (and not the empiric and/or theory), the only tool of knowledge capable of solving this dilemma. Understanding a particular phenomenon or law requires "understanding its development and its necessary origin, from a single and universal principle." And, for that, "knowledge of the universal as pure thought and which develops itself is necessary." This is only possible with philosophy (Bakunin, 1981a[e], p. 458).

Modern alienation was highlighted during the eighteenth century, "the century of the second fall of man in the field of thought." There, in the middle of the Enlightenment, it was already more than evident that man had lost "his contemplation of the infinite" and was swallowed up by "finite contemplation of the finite world" (Bakunin, 1981a [e], p. 428). At that time, the rupture with universality-totality was manifested "in two different spheres, opposite, but inextricably linked, both in theory and in practice"; the first, the "philosophy of Kant, Fichte and [Friedrich] Jacobi, in Germany"; the second, the "philosophical reflections and reasoning of Voltaire, Rousseau, Diderot, D'Alembert, and other French writers, who invested in themselves the thunderous and undeserved title of philosophers" (Bakunin, 1981a[e], p. 427).

In the case of Kant's subjectivism in *Critique of Pure Reason*, the German philosopher considers "the beginning of all knowledge as the original identity between *the self and the thought*" and that "the differences between objects also do not belong to objects, but in essence are nothing more than pure forms of knowledge." Thus, there is nothing left of the "knowable object" but an "abstraction, the thing itself!" Knowledge has its origin in experience, the source of matter, and is concerned with impressions, making it impossible to know the thing itself that gave rise to such impressions. In this way, reason is subjective and has no power over the objective structure of reality—the world is split between subjectivity and objectivity. Fichte, following the Kantian tradition, "destroyed this final illusion of external existence," demonstrating "that the thing itself is also a production, an appearance, of the pure self." In this way, he began to consider "the whole external world and all nature" an illusion, so that "only the self was real" and "all determination, all content had to be destroyed in the face of this abstract and empty identity" (Bakunin, 1981a[e], pp. 428–29; Arantes, 1999).

"The result of Kant and Fichte's subjective systems was the destruction of all objectivity, all reality, and the immersion of the empty and abstract *self* in egoist and vain self-contemplation, the destruction of all love." This because love does not exist "where one abstracts from the other and immerses themself in self-contemplation"; it only lives in a relationship between subjects who are external to each other (Bakunin, 1981a [e], pp. 429–31). Kantian and Fichtean subjectivisms resulted in social terms in individualism and atomism, and with that started to articulate social alienation and the disintegration of social relations.

> Bakunin criticizes the notions of subjectivity and individuality, particularly those that are expressed in the Kantian-Fichtean tradition of the legislative and autonomous self. The individual, believing himself to be the only source of truth, separates himself from objective reality and perceives the real world only as a series of facts or objects that can be changed through the exercise of his independent will. The relationship between individualism and the faculty of understanding that cannot encompass the whole in its entirety makes the individual abstract from objective life, believing that it alone has real and positive value. This point of view, Bakunin alleges, following the Hegelian tradition, is mistaken since it unduly emphasizes the side of the subjective self and thus widens the gap between the thinking subject and the objective reality. By placing itself outside the ontological unity between being and thought, the self, affirming its autonomy, alienates itself and separates itself from the world. From its perspective of finite understanding, it fails to see that reality is infinitely more "concrete" than its subjective individuality and that the empirical world conjectured by this autonomous subject. For reason, says Bakunin, is not a possession that is held individually, but a historically and communally elaborated process, from which individual will cannot be abstracted. (Del Giudice, 1981, pp. 248–49)

This theoretical dilemma of Kant and Fichte posed two possibilities to be solved. A first, inadequate, was to renounce thought and embrace an even greater abstraction, the immediacy of subjective feeling, which was adopted by Jacobi. A second, more adequate, was to resolve the contradiction in the camp of thought itself, which was adopted by Schiller. The road opened by Schiller towards reconciliation with reality, insofar as he proposed to rediscover the unity between subject and object, was continued in Schelling and was crowned by Hegel, summarizing it in the maxim, "What is real is rational, and what is rational is real."[2] On this road lie the foundations and the source of inspiration for the rupture with alienation and the formation of a *moment of truth in reality*, with a universal concern (with the human *genus* in general) with the concreteness of life.

In the case of the French thinkers, they acquired a distinct and even less developed path than that of the Germans. In the eighteenth century, their reflections were "an immediate result of empirical investigations" and never managed to go beyond "arbitrary reasoning." This, at least, had been overcome by the Germans when they managed to put themselves "above empiricism" and in the direction of the "abstract element of pure understanding." This focus of the French, exclusive in finitude, coupled with their rejection of Christianity and their aesthetic formalism, resulted in limited materialism. An "uninspired celebration of the flesh," its correlations in society were liberalism, atheism, individualism, and egoism, which culminated in the French Revolution and were responsible for the excesses of Terror. In this way, philosophical empiricism led to religious, social, and political alienation. In France, the revolution and its exaggerations resulted from this "spiritual depravity" since "where there is no religion, there can be no State" because "religion is the substance, the essence of the State." By having a more consistent link with religion and a less limited concept of aesthetics, Germany distinctly managed to be spared the revolutionary consequences (Bakunin, 1981a[e], pp. 431–32).

However, it should be noted that this "French disease is not limited to France" and, "unfortunately, it has also spread to our country [Russia]." Links between France and Russia, especially regarding the education of the young intelligentsia, were enormous in the early nineteenth century. This youth was "raised in a French way, in the French language and ideas" and, as a result, it uncritically imported its limited philosophical perspectives and experienced their social and political consequences. The "emptiness of our [Russian] national education is the main reason for the illusory nature of our new generation." In other words, due to the adoption of the French model of education, Russia's intelligentsia was experiencing philosophical, social, and political alienation. This dissociation from reality is "the main disease of our new generation—a generation that is abstract, illusory, and foreign to all reality" (Bakunin, 1981a[e], pp. 424, 434–36).

4.2 REALITY AND THEORY-PRACTICE

The dialectical solution to the problem of alienation is "reconciliation with reality, in all its aspects and in all spheres of life"—this "is the great question of our time." The nineteenth century, "as opposed to the last [eighteenth] century," featured, notably on the basis of Hegel's contributions, an effort towards the abandonment of "isolated particularities" and the resumption of "living, universal knowledge," thereby offering the conditions for such reconciliation (Bakunin, 1981a[e], p. 439; Bakunin, 1981b[e], p. 448).

Reconciliation with reality is the integration between man and reality and the *unity between theory and practice*. It is therefore a rupture with alienation—and thus with abstraction, illusion, finitude, and particularity—and an encounter with reality, infinity, universality-totality. Reconciliation and unity that imply, in this sense, a dialectical unity between ideal and real, subject and object, being and thought, theory and life, philosophy and practice, individual and community, life/internal world, and life/external world. In other words, by means of the "almighty dialectic of the historical development of the spirit" one can adequately proceed to reconciliation with reality, that is, this "rational and indissoluble unity of the universal and the particular, of the infinite and the finite, the single and the multiple" (Bakunin, 1981b

[e], p. 449). In the key of the passage from subjective idealism to objective idealism, what is claimed is the transition from abstract to concrete, from illusion to absolute truth—it is the grasp of the concrete universal. It is also the reintegration of the individual in his true substance (social totality) and the coming to consciousness of the *genus* or of this totality as a whole. This is because reality is supra-individual, the individual is part of a whole and is involved in social relations. It is, finally, to overcome the finite understanding and to advance in the understanding of infinite truth, it is to overcome voluntarism and to adopt a concept of will with a rational and real base.

Therefore, we work with "two great contradictory poles of attraction." One of them, "abstraction, under which Bakunin includes the principle of subjectivism and alienation, the ontological division between subject and object, which is the source and origin of the culture of individualism and selfishness"; another, "effectiveness or reality, that is, reason or unity between subject and object; both Bakunin and Hegel refer to this unity as reconciliation." This reconciliation must be understood as rational understanding or consciousness (Del Giudice, 1981, pp. 194, 265–66). And thus reconciliation with reality means overcoming abstraction, subjectivism, alienation, the subject-object divide, individualism, and selfishness.

However, understanding this proposition of reconciliation more properly requires understanding how the concept of reality is conceived. It involves, as in Hegel, a distinction between reality (or existing reality) and effective reality (or effectiveness).

> What is real [effective] is rational, and what is rational is real [effective]. This proposition, enunciated for the first time in the preface to *Philosophy of Right* [by Hegel], was and continues to be attacked from all sides. However, [to understand it properly] we must first define what reality is and distinguish it from chance and contingency, which may or may not exist. In religion, this proposition is clearly articulated in the notion that God rules the world. This proposition is opposed to the thought that ideas are nothing but chimeras, that all philosophy is a system of these chimeras, and that ideals are too perfect to exist in reality. But this separation between reality and ideas occurs mainly in understanding, which takes your abstract dreams to something true and prescribes duty. If the world were as it should be, according to that opinion, then what would have happened to your notorious duty? And if not, wouldn't that truth be weak, so as not to have the strength to subdue reality itself? This judgment may in some cases be right when, together with your duty, it is directed to objects, dispositions, propositions, etc.—external, contingent, and vulgar—which, in certain particular spheres, at certain times, may have a great relative reality. But in the sphere of philosophy this is absurd, because philosophy has as its object the idea, which is too powerful to be able to manifest itself in reality. (Bakunin, 37001[o], pp. 8–9)

Thus, a substantial distinction is made between *reality* (*Realität*)—as an existing, casual, contingent, empirical reality—and *effective reality* or *effectiveness* (*Wirklichkeit*)—as a rational and necessary order, coincidence of the rational idea with its historical manifestations.[3] *When the rationality of the real is recognized here and the reconciliation with reality is claimed, one has in mind not the existing reality, but the actual reality.* The latter concerns the self-realization of reason—understood as a dialectical development inherent to the world and the subject's understanding of this process, as the greatest principle of being—which "in the Hegelian framework, considered as historical progress, implies the movement of factors that must be seen in dialectical interrelationship." It concerns therefore a convergence between "external modes of existence—religious, social, political institutions—and internal substance or principle" or a confluence between rational idea and its historical manifestations. Because to the extent that "reason is both concrete and effective, it must necessarily manifest itself or be incorporated into the external reality," reaching the unity called "life," which is inseparable from knowledge (Del Giudice, 1981, pp. 181, 199; Del Giudice, 1982, pp. 179, 448).

The existing reality cannot be considered effective or rational as it is a contingent, limited historical form. It must certainly be known through reason, when it comes to understanding things as they really are, in essence, and not as they appear in theories or in more or less illustrated artificial constructions. But the existing reality can only find its effective reality, its rationality, when conformed to the rational idea. In this sense, an existing reality cannot and should not be considered necessarily effective and rational. And, if not, this existing reality must be modified in the sense of the effective reality, with the rational idea guiding this movement of change. For this reason, the recognition of the rationality of the real and the call for reconciliation with reality do not in any way mean the defense of the existing society, of Russian tsarism, and do not even express a conservative or reactionary position, a tributary of a right-wing Hegelianism.[4] It does not mean the elaboration of a justification for accepting the present society uncritically but, quite the contrary, the formation of a theoretical-philosophical tool so that the existing reality can be known, evaluated, and modified.[5]

Therefore, reconciliation with reality is the foundation of the unity between theory and practice, through which it is possible to break with an alienated understanding of life and alienated social life. And if the alienation and dissociation between theory and practice have their philosophical and social correlates— abstraction, individualism, selfishness—then reconciliation with reality and the unity between theory and practice have them too. In philosophical terms, it is a question of achieving knowledge of the absolute truth; in social terms, it is a question of conforming social life, society, to the rational idea. An adequate theory leads to an adequate practice; a mistaken theory leads to a mistaken practice. The proposed reconciliation and unity allow, at the same time, to provide support for the knowledge of the truth, the assessment of reality, and social change. This reconciliation and this unity, in knowledge, imply the reconciliation between ideas and facts; in society, they imply the conciliation of knowledge and praxis, the primary form of which is education.

The process referred to was initiated with the Protestant Reformation, which peaked in the eighteenth century, and despite advancing towards knowledge of the truth, it did not achieve its objectives. In the sphere of knowledge, reconciliation with reality and unity between theory and practice is only possible through philosophy. Not that abstract, alienated philosophy that continued to be produced in Russia and other countries, but another philosophy. This philosophy must be conceived as a "methodical, self-contained, and positive science," the object of which "is not the finite abstract, nor is it the infinite non-abstract, but the indissoluble and concrete unity of both: *the real truth and the true reality*." Thus understood, this "philosophy is knowledge of the truth," "knowledge of the absolute truth."[6] This is because the truth is defined as "the absolute, that is, the infinite, universal, necessary and unique truth, which occurs in the diversity and finitude of the real world." This truth is the idea that exists in reality, the synthesis between thought and action, theory and practice, the realization of potentiality. One of the foundations of this truth is necessity and, therefore, in the truth of history there is necessity. In this, a counterpoint to empiricism and its variants is posed by denying that history is only a contingent and accidental succession of facts. In reality, history has a meaning, a coherence, the search of which for its necessary truth it must be able to grasp (Bakunin, 1981b[e], pp. 443, 445, 449).

If hard empiricists "prepare materials for theorists" and these "elaborate and work them in all directions, elevating them to relatively universal thoughts," it is philosophy that, drawing on the knowledge elaborated by theorists, produces "from these fragments, a united, organic and absolutely transparent whole." In this way, philosophical knowledge is that which has managed to overcome ordinary consciousness, empiricism, theory, and has succeeded in embracing the totality of absolute truth and proving the need for its content—it is that which, finally, has ascended to reason (Bakunin, 1981b[e], p. 462).

However, would this knowledge of the absolute truth be possible? Yes, and the *dialectic of knowledge* (dialectic of consciousness) can explain how the conditions are created so that one can ascend from ordinary consciousness to reason. Knowledge involves four stages—1) Sensible certainty (ordinary conscience), 2) Experimental observation (empiricism), 3) Judgment, and 4) Reason—the first being the most elementary and the fourth the most complex. Progress in these stages is motivated by a dialectical movement inherent to the knowledge process itself, the foundations of which are those that substantiate *Hegelian dialectics*, devoid of its formula of vulgarization (thesis–antithesis–synthesis): *in the attempt to be realized, a principle produces its negation and, with it, a contradiction, which ends up destroying it; in return to itself, this principle resumes its movement, integrating what seemed to negate it and rising to another stage of reconciliation.*

This dialectic of knowledge takes as a starting point the notion that everything that potentially exists in man must develop, and that this development is motivated by the contradiction that is established between what is realized in a limited fashion (existing reality) and of potentiality (of that which may become an effective reality). In other words, the motor of the dialectic of knowledge is the dialectic *between existing reality and the potential for effectiveness* (or between real and potential) in man, which can be explained as follows:

> The human spirit cannot stay for long at this low, limited level of its development [that of the animal's sensible and instinctive needs]. In itself, *in potentiality, man is the infinite truth and, therefore, there is a contradiction between his potentiality and his limited effectiveness.* This contradiction does not allow him to exist in limitation for a long time; it continually pushes him forward, towards the realization of internal, potential truth, and continually lifts him above that temporary, external limitation. (Bakunin, 1981c[e], p. 480, emphasis added)

Truth, freedom, reason are human potentialities; they are the essence of man. And it is the contradiction between these potentialities and their existent realization that moves humanity towards developing them, in a march that always involves some suffering. In the field of knowledge, man, by means of an increasingly greater abstraction, proceeds from sensible certainty to experimental observation, from this to judgment, and from that to reason. With that, consciousness knows itself, it knows the world and seeks unity in the diversity that surrounds it, absolute and universal unity. This is "an objective—that is, necessary—result of the development of consciousness, which passes through all these levels as necessary stages of its development" (Bakunin, 1981c[e], p. 488).

Then, this development, initiated in sensible certainty, passes to experimental observation and "finally, it denies them at the highest level, at the level of the universal, of abstract judgment, at which it, however, does not stop" (Bakunin, 1981c [e], p. 488). In a rigorous dialectical argument, it is possible to explain this transition from sensible certainty to judgment:

> The object of experimental observation, on the one hand, is already abstraction, thought, since it is an object without universal existence and which exists only in the plurality of transient and insignificant singularities that correspond to it and of which it is an abstraction; on the other hand, this abstraction is not a pure abstraction, because it has in itself a moment of sensible diversity, its essence is contained in the plurality of sensible attributes. [...] Observant consciousness appears, on the one hand, as sensible certainty, because the

previous levels of development are preserved in the latter as moments, but, on the other hand, it rises above this and seeks its truth not in the singular object, but in its species [universal in relation to particular]. [...] Consequently, experimental observation constitutes a transition from sensible certainty, the truth of what *this* singular and sensitive is, to the kingdom of reflected and abstract judgment, which has its truth in the inner, invisible world of power and laws, and that manifests itself in exteriority. [...] But the object of observation is not preserved, just as the object of sensible certainty is not preserved, and like the latter, it is destroyed by its own dialectical movement, because it is precisely an internal contradiction. (Bakunin, 1981c[e], p. 484; cf., also: Del Giudice, 1981, p. 351)

As pointed out, this dialectic of knowledge continues after that: "judgment, through its own dialectical movement, is elevated to reason and is negated in it and in the sphere of true, absolute knowledge" (Bakunin, 1981c[e], p. 488).

But for this complete movement, and even this quoted excerpt, to be properly grasped, it is mandatory to identify, in greater depth, how each of these four stages of knowledge is understood—1) Sensible certainty (ordinary conscience), 2) Experimental observation (empiricism), 3) Judgment, and 4) Reason—as well as the movement of passage from one to another.

Sensible certainty (ordinary consciousness) is the "first level of consciousness." It is the "immediate awareness of the sensible singularity of objects: this table, this tree, etc." and therefore is restricted to the infinite diversity of the sensible world, which has spatial and temporal limits. At this level, "truth is contained in the diversity of sensible objects that exist in externality." Sensible certainty is knowledge "based on immediate perception" and which "is the representation of objects separate and different from the sensible and spiritual world." Its object is *this* singular and its subject the *singular self* (Bakunin, 1981b[e], p. 451; Bakunin, 1981c[e], pp. 471, 482–85).

Thus sensible certainty presents huge limits for knowledge since it only relates to appearance and never to the essence of things. Knowledge is not neutral but mediated, and is deeply influenced by society and culture.

All men are formed under the immediate influence of the society in which they were born. But each nation, each State, has its own particular moral sphere, its popular beliefs, its prejudices, its particular limitations, which depend, in part, on its individual character, its historical development, and its relationship with the history of all humanity. Every State and time has its own particular concepts and its own worldview; moreover, every State is fragmented into different social strata, and each of these strata, in turn, into its individual character, its own particularity, so that ordinary consciousness develops under the most diverse influences. With the education of the mind, vulgar concepts and a vulgar moral and spiritual sphere are absorbed, and its activity, which in its nature is essentially always the same, alters the physical and spiritual circumstances that surround it. Consequently, its development is always limited, partial, and unable to encompass the absolute truth. (Bakunin, 1981b[e], p. 454)

Realizing its singular, immediate, and partial limitations, sensible certainty ascends to experimental observation, in the sense of finding dialectically greater universality and totality.

Experimental observation (empiricism) is the second level of consciousness. It is a stage of knowledge that, taking advantage of a greater abstraction than in sensible certainty, and also of scientific elements, manages to break with the singularity of the object and move towards greater universality. It is no longer "of this tree" but "of the tree," a "universal object of observation [...] inaccessible to my sensible perception (for example, a tree in general)." With this, "consciousness is elevated [from the external world] to the internal, invisible, universal, and infinite world"; it seeks the relationship between objects, the universal, the necessary in its diversity; seeking to penetrate the object with thought, seeking laws that can be formulated from experience. Its object is thought ("tree"), which has a moment of sensible diversity ("this tree")—its subject is still the singular self. As pointed out, theory is a superior form of empiricism, but it remains stuck in experimental observation, in the diversity of facts, in particular laws. Realizing its limitations, in view of not being able to encompass the relationship between particular laws and their relationship with the universal, experimental observation, also in the sense of finding dialectically greater universality and totality, ascends to judgment (Bakunin, 1981c[e], pp. 483–84, 487; Bakunin, 1981b[e], pp. 460–61).

Judgment (abstract and reflected) is the third level of consciousness and also the moment in which consciousness ascends to the first form of self-consciousness. It is a stage of knowledge that continues to benefit from greater abstraction than in experimental observation and is moving towards greater universality. Its object is "the internal world of immutable and universal laws," that is, the "essence of the physical world, as well as the spiritual world," which can be accessed with the abstraction "of the insignificant diversity of exteriority"; its subject passes from the singular self to the universal self (with the transition from consciousness to self-consciousness). These laws are internal thoughts ("pure, super-sensible universalities") —thoughts both objective and subjective at the same time. Thoughts that exist in the real world, that were not invented by man, but can be found and apprehended by him in real existing facts (Bakunin, 1981c[e], pp. 487, 490).

However, this internal world "only exists in relation to the world of external appearances." There is no difference between both worlds, inner and outer, because a law is the constant and universal expression of changing appearance. "The external world has no existence independent of the interior, since it is nothing more than a manifestation of the internal world." In other words, "the content of the sensible exteriority and the super-sensible interiority is completely identical"; the relation with the inner world of laws is, at the same time, the relation with "the outer world of appearances." Insofar as the content of the internal and external worlds is the same, on knowing the external world, the inner world is also known. "The awareness of another external object is transformed into consciousness of your *own* thoughts, of your *own* essence, of *yourself* as truth, and it becomes self-consciousness" (Bakunin, 1981c[e], pp. 488–91).

Synthesizing this dialectic of knowledge so far, it is possible to say that:

> In its phenomenological process, consciousness, beginning with sensible certainty, taking as truth the diversity of the sensible, singular being, has been preserved as a subordinate moment in *self-consciousness*. The sensible diversity of the singular being disappeared in the universal and was discarded as a transient and insignificant *appearance* of the essential and universal laws of the physical and spiritual world. [...] These universal laws, which contain in themselves the whole infinite world of truth and reality, are in essence nothing more than *determined thoughts*, particular universalities. [...] These determined thoughts are essentially nothing more than productions of the abstract universality of cognitive judgment, such that, in knowing them, the judgment knows itself and consciousness becomes *self-consciousness*. (Bakunin, 1981c[e], pp. 505–506)

Self-consciousness has two forms: the abstract and the universal, the first preceding the second and the second being equivalent to reason.

In abstract self-consciousness, the subject, even though he knows his own thoughts and his own essence, does so in his singularity, in his finite individuality, in abstraction. And for this very reason, he constitutes a contentless and abstract identity with himself: "The expression of individual abstract self-consciousness is I = I." In this way, universality, truth and freedom appear only as potential, and not as reality. "These singular individualities are different from each other and relate to each other in exteriority and strangeness, all of their concrete content is contained in their singular individuality" and this poses the risk of a "criminal egoism." "The individual spirit is, at the same time, a singular organism, a finite individual that, like everything that is finite, is subjected to inescapable slavery, destruction, and death." In this external relationship between individualities, the subjects "enter into a struggle with each other" due to their tendency towards universality, which leads to the negation of the subjects' own immediate individuality and their "reciprocal recognition"; thus arriving at universal self-consciousness, at reason (Bakunin, 1981c[e], pp. 506–11).

In universal self-consciousness this mutual recognition is consolidated. There is the "universal recognition of the subjects" and the singular differences between them disappear—the subjects "merge into an indivisible unit." The *"identity between subject and object,"* which had been found and lost since the transition from consciousness to self-consciousness, is also consolidated. With the subject–object unity, the subject recognizes himself in others and recognizes others in himself; the self and the other are understood in terms of self-consciousness. "All virtues are based on this *unity* of self-consciousness with oneself and with others. 'I' is 'we', or I = us. This "reason occurred as a simple *identity between subject and object,* as a unity between being and thought, as infinite truth and freedom." For this reason, the mastery of philosophy was achieved: "the whole infinite totality of reason is accessible to its knowledge; in this totality, the whole truth and reality of both the physical and spiritual world are contained" (Bakunin, 1981c[e], pp. 514–16).

True (necessary, absolute, and real) knowledge is the understanding of the real figure that the totality must assume, the true manifestations of the real. To access such knowledge philosophy needs to recognize these manifestations of the real and, among them, identify what is necessary in the midst of the contingent—finding the internal connection in the facts in exteriority, negating the contingency and finding, in the midst of it, the necessary and rational—grasping the concept in a state of historical change to arrive at a rational understanding of the real in motion (Del Giudice, 1981, pp. 315–17).

At the beginning of "From Philosophy," Bakunin (1981b [e], p. 442) had proposed to answer three questions: What is philosophy? Is philosophy useful? Is philosophy possible? It can be understood that they were answered and that they can be summarized here. Philosophy is the science that seeks knowledge of reality, of truth. It is useful since, in order to develop and progress, society needs knowledge of reality, and this can only be adequately obtained with philosophy; it can and must function as a social and political tool by making man a conscious part of the social totality and a useful member of society. It is possible because, through the dialectic of knowledge (of consciousness), it is possible to ascend from ordinary consciousness to reason and to reconcile theory and practice (Leier, 2006, p. 86).

4.3 CRITICAL-DIALECTIC METHOD

In his reflections from this period, Bakunin makes use of a *critical-dialectic method.* He uses Hegelianism as a critical method to on the one hand provide a harsh critique of alienation in modernity, which encompasses the process of knowledge and its social and political correlates. Regarding the process of knowledge, Bakunin establishes a break with common sense by questioning what appears to be true, and also with the notion of neutrality of knowledge, arguing that access to the object is always mediated. Furthermore, as stated by Del Giudice (1981, p. 258), Bakunin also performs "a very comprehensive analysis of the interrelationship between theory and practice, and the way that philosophical and theoretical ideas have an immediate and direct impact on political, social, and practical existence." Starting from "a philosophical concept," he continues, "Bakunin arrived at the deduction of cultural and socio-political implications; the philosophy of idealism and subjectivism had as a logical and necessary conclusion a condition of *social alienation*."

On the other hand, this critical method allowed Bakunin to elaborate his proposition of reconciliation with reality and of unity between theory and practice, which, in the same way, involve the process of knowledge and its social and political correlates. His analysis of the phenomenological development of consciousness sought to demonstrate the possibility of accessing the totality of truth through a dialectic of knowledge, which would make it possible to overcome the appearance of phenomena and access their essence. As will be seen below, this method also provided the basis for drawing up a reference for the critical assessment of reality and for social change to proceed.

Bakunin, concomitantly, uses Hegelianism as a dialectical method, as he understands

> *dialectics as a driving force for development and historical change.* In his analysis, Bakunin examines the ideas of *conflict and progress*, continually emphasizing the role that *contradiction and negation* play in putting historical forms in a state of opposition to each other, which ultimately leads to higher stages of "reconciliation." (Del Giudice, 1981, p. 339, emphasis added)

In other words, for Bakunin history is dialectical and therefore to comprehend it, a method that is dialectical and capable of articulating concepts for understanding the world is essential. In terms of method, he understands dialectics in the same way as Hegel—who conceptualized it, when asked by Goethe—as a "spirit of organized contradiction" (Safatle, 2015), as a history of movement, of the experience of contradiction.[7] Dialectics is thus the description of the movement of thought that, set in motion by contradiction, seeks to grasp the process of historical reality that takes effect in the form of contradiction. It is based on a set of related categories that guide the thinking and analysis of reality. This dialectical method, which is concomitantly historical, permeates all Bakuninian writings from that period (cf. alienation-effectiveness dialectic, theory–practice dialectic, dialectic of knowledge, real effective existent–potential dialectic, etc.). For Bakunin (1981c [e], p. 499), "contradiction [...] is the source of movement, of development, striving to obtain its resolution"; contradiction moves the world and thought. Thought is the negation of negativity (subjectivism, particularity, finitude), the spiritualization of negativity, the negation of negation. The concept of negation thus acquires centrality, as Leier explains:

> The positive, for Hegel and Bakunin, was that which already existed. Negation was a critique of what existed. [...] For Hegel, "thinking is, in fact, essentially the negation of that which is immediately before us." From this criticism comes

new thinking, new ideas, and the determination of what is real and rational. Consequently, negation was the first step in resolving contradictions. [...] Bakunin [...] emphasized negation and contradiction—in other words, struggle—as the way in which humanity advanced to discover the truth and the reality of its progress towards freedom. (Leier, 2006, pp. 87–88)

This dialectic—by which Bakunin intends to understand the contradictions of a totality, of a historical reality—as mentioned, does not end with understanding. In a process that surpasses Hegel, it advances as a tool that allows a critical assessment of the existing reality and the conception of historical social change, both of which, supported by a determined concept of subject, constitute the foundations of Bakunin's *philosophy of action*, amid which *education* continues to stand out.

4.4 PHILOSOPHY OF ACTION AND EDUCATION

The tool for critical and normative assessment of existing reality was previously outlined when the difference between effective and rational reality and existing reality was expounded. The proposed reconciliation with reality and the unity between theory and practice, "far from being a reactionary and conservative doctrine, [...] with its identity of the real and the rational, provided Bakunin with a philosophical tool" that, among other things, offered the support for such an evaluation. His doctrine of the interrelationship between theory and practice established a concept that "functions as a criterion by which to measure events." With it, for example, it is possible to "critically examine the external, political and social manifestations" of the "Modern State", "in terms of its correspondence—or lack of correspondence—with the rational idea." In comparison with the rational idea, this state may not be considered effective and rational, in which case it must be modified.

Thus "by juxtaposing dialectical historicism and the conservative 'preservation' of the past, Bakunin deftly highlighted the potential dialectical transformation of all existing and historical forms." Counterposing the passive and uncritical acceptance of existing reality as something rational, he "presents a radical departure from this conservative attitude, insofar as he establishes the criteria for evaluating change, in accordance with its internal principle of progress." This position, although not being able to be explained more clearly due to the censorship that prevailed in Russia, has clear implications: "those facts that are not rational must be modified in order to conform to the rational idea." Reality must be rationally understood and then the subject must apply this knowledge dialectically to life, through practical activity, historical rational action. After all, "the vocation of man is to infuse reality with thought and endow thought with reality." However, to do so, the truth had to previously be achieved through philosophy and reason could then establish the lines of this social change (Del Giudice, 1981, pp. 179, 336, 339–40).

Finally, reconciliation with reality and the unity between theory and practice find their corollary. In the existing reality it is not enough to know, it is not enough to evaluate critically: it is necessary to act. At first, man must identify his will and his reason with the rationality of the universe; in a second moment, he must act, giving concrete substance to the universal principle. "In order to act, one must already be in truth, so that the action is the expression and the realization of the truth, and not the lie." "One must act on the path of truth, one must act in love and for love, and it is in this union of the grace of God with the action of man that the complete truth rests" (Bakunin, 37039[c], p. 7).

> He [man] must *know the infinite truth* that constitutes his substance, his essence, and *realize it in his actions*, so that, in the *identity of the true knowledge and actions of man*, in the truth of his theoretical world and in the *correspondence of the practical world with the theoretical*, all its reality is contained. (Bakunin, 1981c[e], pp. 498–99, emphasis added)

To effect reality, reason is also to reconcile theory and practice, thought and action; it means knowing, critically evaluating, and making that which should be correspond with that which is. Even if in the knowledge process there is already a certain content of action, to the extent that the very act of thinking reconfigures propositions and provides the basis for conceiving change, this is not enough.

It is necessary to proceed to a solution that can, in fact, guarantee this effectiveness. Such a solution is rational ethical action, that expression and realization of the truth that proposes "transforming [...] everything according to our will (Bakunin, 37038 [c], p. 2)."[8] Will is therefore the factor that drives action. Its possibilities are enormous; in the face of feelings, for example, "will can do anything; for it, nothing is impossible, because it has an infinite nature, because it is, in essence, infinite freedom." Will can be defined as "infinite force of self-negation of the truth, the negation of all the narrow instincts that disgust the nature of man and of finite thought contrary to the truth" (Bakunin, 40057 [c], p. 3). In the context of rational ethical action, will is given centrality. As part of human freedom, it supports rational self-negation based on truth to drive action.

> Within the framework of Hegelian philosophy, Bakunin established the foundations of his *philosophy of action*, which presented a solution to one of the most urgent questions of his time—the problem of the dynamic interrelationship between theory and praxis, and the active and conscious realization of the known truth through reason and speculative philosophy. The notion of *change*, based on a rational understanding of the world, and which allows reality to correspond to the theoretical cognition of truth, becomes the dominant theme in Bakunin's work. Theory is henceforth approached in terms of a rational prelude to action in the real world; thus, once man has *understood*

reality, he must exercise his conscious will, act, transform the world into a "rational reality." (Del Giudice, 1981, p. 357)

This notion of historical social change means that external social forms must correspond to the internal, rational idea. And if there is a human potential in freedom (since freedom is the essence of the human spirit), and if it is a human necessity that must take effect, historical social change must take place in the direction of freedom. But wouldn't defending this position also mean subjectivism, voluntarism, by breaking with the notion of necessity?

The entire existence of the physical world, as well as the spiritual world, happens, develops, lives, and passes according to determined and necessary laws. [...] We are not yet talking about the organic development of man, completely submitted to the laws of organic life, but about spiritual development, which, as development and self-realization that contain reason in itself, is subject to necessity, and precisely to the necessity of the development of reason, of the universal. [...] From this, it could be concluded that man is not a free creature, and that this would contradict the essential determination of the human spirit, the essence of which is freedom. But does necessity really exclude freedom? No, not at all. In submitting to *external* necessity, I am not free, but conditioned and limited externally, because the laws that condition and determine my existence are not within, but outside of me. [...] The universal develops, lives and isolates itself according to immutable and necessary laws; but this need does not restrict its freedom, because it is not fixed, and does not limit it externally, but constitutes its own and unique essence, which encompasses everything in itself, and which is not externally conditioned. [...] The dual nature of the human spirit, which is infinite totality and freedom from universal truth, on the one hand, and transient, finite, and singular individuality, on the other. [...] Only those who are in themselves, in potential, who have already elevated themselves beyond their limitations, can feel their limitations and suffer. [...] As a singular and natural organism, man is subjected to the same fate. Like the animal, he also feels needs, but because he contains within himself the *real* possibility of the totality of the universal, and because he is capable of self-consciousness and unlimited freedom, man is capable of suffering more strongly than the animal. (Bakunin, 1981c[e], pp. 500–505)

Necessity, even though it may be conditioned (relative, hypothetical) or unconditioned, is defined here as a synonym for something essential, not contingent and of inevitable existence or development. Necessity is present in the world of things and of people (in nature, in society, in history, in man) and can be identified in the laws that operate in both worlds. Man, as a natural being who thinks and lives in society, in space and time, is subject to such necessary laws. This necessity and these laws subject the world of things and people unconditionally—they are part of universal reason and, therefore, are also inside the subject. Therefore, they are concomitantly external and internal necessities, among which are found that of the development of reason and of freedom.

Freedom, like reason, exists in man as potential, and its realization, marked by suffering, is a necessity. Therefore, in this case, necessity constitutes a vehicle for freedom. Freedom is possible in necessity since man (individual) identifies his will with the social totality (ethical whole); when he identifies his subjective self and the other individuals of the totality, of the social community. Freedom, as effective reason, is therefore not completely subjective but at the same time subjective and objective. Freedom is called into question only when the exclusively external, artificial necessities are imposed on man, in order to condition and limit him.

Now, how to promote this social change in the direction of freedom? The most propitious way to do so seems to be education.[9] In religious terms, it is possible to say that "Christian education aims to endow man with a second spiritual birth," for him to develop "an autonomous and free life that will prepare him for the hard career of life, to endure all pain and all the sufferings he will not cease to encounter." This education should not "make him a slave without any independence, a complacent and blind executioner of arbitrary and blind wills" (Bakunin, 37055 [c], p. 13). Education is then considered as a means that unites theory and practice for spiritual and moral regeneration, with the ultimate goal being freedom, here understood as secular redemption. However, as mentioned, this path to freedom is not without suffering, which is not necessarily a bad thing: "Yes, suffering is good: it is that purifying flame, which transforms and gives strength to the spirit"; in this way, suffering itself is educational—it is "education, the rational experience of the spirit" inherent in the process of liberation (Bakunin, 1981a[e], p. 428).

Education is a key component both for the learning of philosophy and with it for the improvement of knowledge, as well as for the assessment of existing reality and social change. With it, the identification of contradictions and their negation are substantially facilitated. It is also education, a central tool to promote reconciliation with reality and the unity between theory and practice, which contributes in a decisive way so that this knowledge is transmitted and shared with other people. Education proves to be indispensable for overcoming philosophical and social alienation, and for the individual to be reintegrated into the social totality, forging the conditions for his rational action and a truly effective life in freedom. Education is the remedy capable of curing the modern disease of alienation.

Alienation, as a loss of reality, accentuates the need for a spiritual and moral regeneration of humanity; *Bakunin's theory of education* constitutes his *response to this crisis in society.* The tragic condition of alienation, brought into sharp focus by Bakunin's analysis, is one in which rational and meaningful action becomes completely problematic. His formulation of the ideal of *education* is intended to be the vital link between theory and practice; this is because education, as the *reintegration of the individual into the social totality,* constitutes the *presupposition and the essential condition of rational action.* [...] The idea of education (*obrazovanie-Bildung*) was always primordial for Bakunin, who saw in it an *ideological instrument for social and political change.* Consequently, it is no small matter that, in presenting Fichte and Hegel to the Russian public, he chose to translate works that were dedicated to this central question of education. (Del Giudice, 1982, pp. 164–65, emphasis added)

In this way, education is understood as an outstanding type of non-alienated rational human action with liberating potential. Specifically, in Russia, it seemed paramount to overcoming the alienation of the young intelligentsia, which had been educated according to abstract and subjective French presuppositions, and to establish this reinvigorated Hegelianism as their doctrine, thereby allowing Russian society to be properly understood and evaluated, and that the foundations for its change can be laid. Again, philosophers stand out as agents of this educational process. Due to their ability to access reason, they have a role to play in this process, and they must place themselves as guides, educators, to stimulate and facilitate this development of knowledge and social and political praxis. Philosophers were then understood to be the potential educators of the Russian intelligentsia (Del Giudice, 1981, p. 340).

In terms of the specific objectives that this education should assume in Russia, it is maintained that it must "light the divine flame in the young heart, placed there by Providence itself," "awaken deep religious feelings in it," and "form a deep aesthetic feeling in it." This is because, as stated, a religion, aesthetics, and philosophy—the latter of which, in the texts of that period, acquires an ever-greater centrality, establishing itself as the greatest manifestation of the absolute spirit—are the most significant aspects in the definition of the character of a people. Furthermore, this education must "train the young mind to do real work," "stimulate the love of knowledge in it," and "inspire in it the idea that knowledge is its own end, that it is the source of great, inexhaustible satisfaction, and that using it as a means of standing out in society is sacrilege." Finally, this education must also be an ethical education, which can develop certain values in individuals, among which are morality, anti-individualism/anti-egoism, and the love of freedom. With all this, there is the possibility of creating a "real Russian man" in identity with the reality in which he lives and with the possibility of intervening freely and rationally in this totality. Such is the key to freedom, the regeneration of Russian society (Bakunin, 1981a[e], p. 436).

NOTES

1   From this period, the documents of Bakunin used (writings, letters, and other productions) are found as appendices to Martine del Giudice's thesis (Bakunin, 1981a [e], 1981b [e], 1981c [e], 1981d [e]) and on the IISH CD-ROM (Bakunin, 2000a); the quotations were translated from the documents in English (in the case of the appendices by Del Giudice) and in French (in the case of the CD-ROM).

2   Or, in the translation used by Angaut (2005, p. 41), who is concerned with distinguishing between the Hegelian concepts of reality (*Realität*) and effective reality or effectiveness (*Wirklichkeit*): "What is rational is effective, and what is effective is rational."

3   A distinction that Bakunin also makes explicit in an 1838 letter sent to his sisters and in the 1839 "From Philosophy." In the letter, Bakunin (38014 [c], p. 3) emphasizes, "Understanding and loving reality, such is man's vocation. I do not speak here of what we have the habit of understanding by the term reality: the chair, the table, the dog, Varvara Dmitrieva, Alexandra Ivanovna; all of this is a dead, illusory reality, with nothing of life or truth." For this reality is that existing, casual, contingent, empirical reality. Bakunin (1981c [e], p. 517) understands that "the meaning given [by Hegel] to the term 'reality' has been misunderstood." To call "everything" that exists, any finite being, 'real' [...] is an error." "Only that being in which exists the totality of reason, idea, truth, is real; everything else is an illusion and a lie." In this sense, Del Giudice (1982, pp. 180–81) states that Bakunin works with the "distinction between contingent existence [reality] and reality or effectiveness [effective reality]." So that "[effective] reality cannot be considered in terms of merely immediate, contingent existence—which, according to Hegel, is chance, illusion, partiality." Cf., also: Hegel, *Encyclopedia*, paragraphs 142 to 159.

4   Bakunin's texts from this period certainly have certain passages that give the impression of this conservatism. In criticizing the education system in Russia, for example, Bakunin (1981a [e], p. 436) wrote that "this education does not form a real and strong Russian man, devoted to the tsar and his country." As Leier (2006, p. 80) explained, the "Preface" of 1838 "was written in double coding, familiar to Bakunin's colleagues and comrades. First, Bakunin codified the article in Hegelian language and definitions, and then recoded his controversial ideas in Aesop's language [hiding its real meaning for uninitiated people], using the rhetoric of patriotism, indirect metaphors, irony, and sarcasm to hide the real message from the tsar's censors. The real meaning, however, was evident to the informed." Finally, as Del Giudice (1981, pp. 288–303) rigorously demonstrated, although Bakunin was instrumental in influencing Belinski with the ideas of Fichte and Hegel, there is no way—as Herzen, for example, incorrectly did, being repeated by countless historians—of attributing Belinski's conservative interpretation of the formula "reconciliation with reality" to Bakunin (whose progressive position was shared by Stankevitch). This difference of interpretation was even a central aspect of the rupture between the two.

5   However, one must proceed with some care in this denial of Bakunin's conservatism and reactionaryism in this period so as not to incur anachronism. If it seems evident that this conservatism/reactionaryism has no consistency in Bakuninian work from the years 1837 to 1840, it also seems evident that the positions that will be adopted in his later life (1860s) are still very distant. For Bakunin (1981b [e], p. 444), "philosophy will never be atheistic and anarchic, because the essence of his life and movement is contained in the search for God and the rational and eternal order." At that time, Bakunin (1981a [e], p. 431; 1981b [e], p. 452; 1981c [e], pp. 472, 491, 497) criticizes both atheism and "anarchy" (as opposed to order). Whenever it appears, the adjective "anarchic" is used disparagingly; similarly, whenever it is mentioned, materialism receives disapproval, also being considered subjective and implying the end of living religion.

6   When disagreeing that philosophy could be defined as love through knowledge, Bakunin (1981b [e], p. 442), in 1839, made his first criticism of the monopoly of knowledge, saying that "it would be a great pity if by it knowledge and love became the exclusive property of only a small number of people who study philosophy."

7   Cf. Hegel (1992, p. 80, emphasis added): "It is clear that the *dialectic* of sensible certainty is nothing more than the simple *history of its movement or experience*; and the same sensible certainty is nothing other than this history alone." This passage is cited by Bakunin himself (1981c [e], p. 475).

8 Cf. Cieszkowski, in *Prolegomena zur Historiosophie* [*Prolegomena to Historiosophy*]: "Consciousness, it is true, occupies a specific place in the true system of philosophy; but the universe does not *end* with it. What lies behind it is unconsciousness, that is, the fact; but what lies ahead must develop consciously, and that is action. [...] Practical philosophy or, more precisely, the *philosophy of practice*— its most concrete influence on life and social relations, the development of truth in concrete activity—such is the future destiny of philosophy as a whole" (*apud* Del Giudice, 1981, pp. 326, 331).

9 Cf. Hegel (s/d, p. 35): "Scientific teaching [scientific education] [...] exercises the meaning of relationships and constitutes a permanent passage for the elevation of the particular point of view to the universal and conversely for the application of the universal to the particular. Scientific formation [education] has, in general, this effect on the spirit, to separate it from itself, to remove it from its immediate natural existence, from the sphere not free of feeling and impulse, and to situate it in thought. With this, it [the spirit] acquires an awareness of the reaction to external expressions that otherwise is merely necessary and instinctive. And through this liberation, it is converted into power over immediate representations and sensations; this liberation constitutes the formal foundation of moral conduct [of action in general]."

CHAPTER 5

THEORY OF REVOLUTION AND NEGATIVE DIALECTICS (1841–42)

This chapter exposes Bakunin's political theory in his *second Hegelian period*, which runs from 1841 to 1842, dividing it into four parts: 1) Negative Dialectics: Revolutionary Theory of History; 2) Europe, Early 1840s: Contradictions, Revolutionary Crisis, and Decomposition of the Old World; 3) Reactionary Party and Democratic Party; 4) Negative Dialectics: Revolutionary Logic.[1]

5.1 NEGATIVE DIALECTICS: REVOLUTIONARY THEORY OF HISTORY

At this point, it seems necessary to take as a basis the comprehension of the theoretical-logical aspects of history, such that they permit describing the process of historical reality that takes effect in the form of contradiction. History is considered a dialectical process of realizing freedom,[2] and development and change are understood as a result of contradiction and negation. The historical reality, always contradictory, is in permanent dialectical movement and can be explained by the negative dialectic. The elements referring to the theory of history (historical logic), which proceed according to this negative dialectic, are decisive in a theory of revolution.

History in general and socio-political history in particular normally move in terms of a dynamic development animated by contradictions. Among these stands out that "eternal contradiction, which has always existed [...], between freedom and non-freedom" and which, "throughout history, has done nothing more than grow and develop" (Bakunin, 1976a [e], p. 124). In its normality, history almost always works in a conservative way, seeking to reinforce the aspects that constitute its own foundations; there is an apparent consensus around them, commonly conceived by the defenders of the status quo. Such a consensus is apparent because, as a rule, the historical process coexists within itself with different, opposing, and even contradictory elements—elements of resistance, which express anomalies and problems in relation to the dominant historical or socio-political paradigm and which contribute decisively to its quantitative changes in the direction of freedom—which, however, in these normal times, remain more or less covered up by the forces of order, of reaction. However, in this process of containing change and forging consensus, the conservative and reactionary forces, in seeking to assert themselves positively, end up stimulating the forces of negative resistance, of revolutionary potential, which act gradually and underground in opposition to the order. In this sense, it is possible to say that, even in its normality, history carries with it the germs of revolutionary change (McLaughlin, 2002, pp. 41–45; Angaut, 2007a, pp. 50, 88).

The dialectic of history occurs, then, due to the contradiction between two principles, two terms, two elements: on the one hand, the positive (order/reaction); on the other, the negative (revolution/freedom). It is explained by the perspective that there is a

> cosmic opposition between the old and the new world, with each of these two worlds being supported by its own principle. This cosmic opposition supports a *historical opposition between reaction and revolution*, and the latter opposition itself constitutes an articulation with the political domain within which the parties are in contradiction. (Angaut, 2009, p. 47, emphasis added)

This dialectic between the old world (order/reaction) and the new world (revolution/ freedom) translates into a contradiction of *principles, that is, propositions on which the dynamic organic totality of the political and social world rests.* Historically, these principles are incorporated by *parties, which are partial organs of society that confront each other in order to conserve or modify the world* (Bakunin, 1976a [e], pp. 107, 111). Therefore, a party is the historical and partial organ that represents the existence of a principle, and principle is the essence of the party: "This distinction between principle and party, essence and existence, universal and particular, now asserts itself as a difference between logic and history" (Angaut, 2007a, p. 52).

As the current socio-political historical structure becomes unable to provide adequate answers to the questions posed by society—which this same structure, at least in part, contributed to create—and its anomalies and problems can no longer be hidden, a moment of crisis opens. If this crisis is not avoided by the forces of order (repressing, disintegrating dissent, etc.) and if the elements of resistance do not remain subordinate to be resumed only in the future, then a new historical socio-political paradigm, generally claimed by younger people and that tends to win adherents, will emerge. In this way, there is a split in society, with a polarization of rival camps, in which one defends the permanence of the old structure (positive) and the other the emergence of the new (negative).

At a certain point in this conflict, the contradiction between positive and negative reaches such a limit that mediation becomes impossible; the contradiction becomes a revolutionary contradiction, an incompatibility between positive and negative, and announces the decomposition and overthrow of the positive. There, the contradiction can only be apprehended in relational terms and necessarily points to the destruction of the positive by the negative, to the preponderance of the negative which, in a return to itself, becomes a new positive, with nothing of the old—it is that which is understood by revolution, the formation of a new social and historical totality. As can be seen, in this contradiction there are only two elements: the positive and the negative, and the revolution is not conceived in terms of a third element of external mediation, supersumption, or synthesis. This revolutionary and negative dialectic is therefore dyadic and not triadic. And its emphasis on negation allows it to be considered a negative dialectic.

Thus conceived, revolution is the result of the overcoming of reactionary forces (supporters of the old) by revolutionary forces (supporters of the new). It does not constitute a quantitative, gradual change, which brings to the new elements of the old; but it is, distinctly, a qualitative transformation, which forges a paradigm of nature that is incompatible with new foundations. Therefore, the revolution is not just a negative revolution since the negative forces, in negating the old, concomitantly affirm the new. Their negation requires a parameter of comparison, whereby they reject one paradigm in favour of another. With this, the revolutionary future is not conceived speculatively, but from this negation of the past and present socio-political historical structure (McLaughlin, 2002, pp. 41–45; Angaut, 2007a, pp. 50, 53, 88).

In the history of religion there is a case in which this negative dialectical process has manifested itself.

For example, the principle of theoretical freedom has awakened in the Catholic world of the past since the first years of its existence. This principle was the source of all the heresies so numerous in Catholicism. Without this principle, Catholicism would have been [deprived of movement]; it was, therefore, at the same time, the principle of its vitality, but only as long as it was kept in its entirety as a simple [moment]. And so, Protestantism made its appearance, little by little; its origin even goes back to the origin of Catholicism, but [at a given moment], its progression suddenly stopped being gradual and the principle of theoretical freedom was elevated until it became an autonomous and independent principle. It is only then that the contradiction appears in its purity, and you know it well, gentlemen, you who call yourselves Protestants, what Luther replied to the [mediators] of his time when they came to offer their services.

As we can see, the idea I have about the nature of contradiction lends itself to a confirmation that is not only logical, but also historical. (Bakunin, 1976a[e], p. 123)

One can understand, from what has been discussed, the historical foundations of negative dialectics. From time to time, "the gradual movement of history, bringing the revolutionary germ within itself, is interrupted by moments of revolution," which transform the socio-political historical bases of society in qualitative terms, as a rule in the direction "of the extension of the scope of freedom," being responsible for progress and historical change (McLaughlin, 2002, p. 41).

5.2 EUROPE, EARLY 1840s: CONTRADICTIONS, REVOLUTIONARY CRISIS, AND DECOMPOSITION OF THE OLD WORLD

As a result of its fierce social conflicts, the French Revolution, a decisive landmark of modernity, gave birth to the germs of a new world. It pointed to the burial of the old aristocratic world and its representatives and announced a future of freedom, equality, and fraternity for all. However, after the revolution, what was seen was the growing dissociation between the discourse of the bourgeoisie and its concrete posture in the course of these conflicts. It had risen to power allied with the people and promising the universalization of these revolutionary ideals, but it was increasingly evident that it intended to interrupt the results of this process, subjecting workers, artisans, peasants, the marginalized, and poor to its own interests.

One of the crucial means for this was the dissociation between discourse and concrete posture. In theory, the bourgeois recognize the ideals of the French Revolution and advocate its universalization. In practice, they prevent the people from enjoying them. Freedom, the greatest revolutionary ideal, is now promoted theoretically by many in Europe in the early nineteenth century. But at the same time it was practiced very little, such that "no one dares to declare themselves openly and boldly [an enemy] of freedom." However, "talking about something and recognizing it does not give it a real existence; in reality, there is unfortunately still a crowd that truly does not believe in the depths of their hearts, in freedom." These many do not truly believe in freedom; they do not contribute to its effective realization. That is why the words "freedom, *realization of freedom* [...] are now at the top of the agenda of history" (Bakunin, 1976a [e], p. 105). For it is only a question of proceeding to an effective realization of that abstractly promoted freedom, of practically realizing the revolutionary promises made in theories and discourses.[3]

Such realization of freedom found, in the Europe of the early 1840s, a considerable opportunity to consolidate itself, in light of a favourable context, with the culmination of contradictions and the indication of a new crisis and a new revolutionary cycle. "Contradictions have never been more accentuated than at present"—in the case of the aforementioned "contradiction [...] between freedom and non-freedom," it "took its impulse in our time, so analogous to the periods of the decomposition of the pagan world and reached its peak!" It was certainly not yet a definitive moment of revolutionary war, and that was what made it possible for some less attentive observers to argue that "there are contradictions in our time, but they are not so dangerous" because "calm reigns everywhere, and the hustle and bustle is quiet; no one thinks about war and most nations and living men today use all their might to maintain peace." For such observers, since the July 1830 Revolution in France, "excellent occasions [...] for waging war and destroying the existing regime" had arisen, many of which "it was never believed possible for them to find a peaceful solution." But in spite of that "the difficulties, little by little, disappeared, everything became calm and peace seems to have been established forever on earth!" Nothing could be more incorrect than this interpretation.

As a matter of fact, it would not be appropriate to even consider the beginning of the 1840s a period of peace: "as if that could be called peace!" Even with the conflicts less evident, this did not mean the absence of huge contradictions and even an underground war, about to emerge again. This supposed peace stemmed from an attempt, made by tiny sectors of society that benefited from the effects of the French Revolution, to guarantee their privileges before the people. Such sectors "know that, without peace, their material interests cannot be favoured, which seems to have become the main business of politics and [universal culture]". In other words, peacekeeping meant containing social conflicts and ensuring, in political and cultural terms, the conditions for the predominance of the material interests of privileged minorities (Bakunin, 1976a [e], p. 124). Even though, in principle, "peace was preferable to conflict and struggle, the peace sought by the conciliators was that imposed by the conqueror on the conquered, the master's peace imposed on the slave. That peace could not end the conflict" (Leier, 2006, p. 103). Although temporarily contained, these contradictions showed the latency of a war about to be unleashed; it was just a matter of time. One could ask, then:

Did they not read on the pediment of the temple of liberty erected by the revolution these mysterious and terrible words: Liberty, Equality, Fraternity? Do you not know and feel that these words mean the total destruction of the present political and social order? Have they never heard that Napoleon, that alleged victor of democratic principles, has, as a son worthy of the revolution, propagated throughout Europe, by his victorious hand, the [leveling] principles? Perhaps you ignore everything about Kant, Fichte, Schelling, and Hegel, and you don't really know anything about a philosophy that, in the intellectual world, established the principle of the autonomy of the spirit, identical to the [leveling] principle of revolution? Do you not understand that this principle is in complete contradiction with all the current positive religions, with all the existing Churches?

"Yes," you answer, "but these contradictions are precisely from ancient history; in France, the revolution was won by the wise government of Louis-Philippe, and it was Schelling himself who recently overthrew modern philosophy, when he had been one of its greatest founders. Everywhere, and now in all walks of life, the contradiction will be overcome!" Do you truly believe in this resolution, in this victory over the revolutionary spirit? Are you, therefore, blind or deaf? Do you have no eyes or ears to understand what is going on around you? No, gentlemen, the revolutionary spirit was not defeated; its first appearance shook the whole world to its foundations, then only [it returned to itself, doing no more than absorbing itself] to announce itself once again as the affirmative and creative principle, and now digs under the earth like a mole, according to Hegel's expression! Not to work uselessly, is what all these ruins show that join the soil of the religious, political, and social building. And you speak of overcoming contradiction and of reconciliation! Look around you and tell me what is still alive of the old Catholic and Protestant world? You speak of victory over the negative principle! Have you not read anything from Strauss, Feuerbach, and Bruno Bauer, don't you know that their works are in everyone's hands? Do you not see that all the German literature, all the books, newspapers, and brochures are penetrated by this negative spirit and that even the works of the positivists [members of the reactionary party], unconsciously and involuntarily, are too? And this is what you call peace and reconciliation! (Bakunin, 1976a[e], pp. 124–25)

Effectively realized, the ideals of the French Revolution would imply a revolution, a complete destruction of the existing socio-political historical order. Even if in an apparently peaceful context, the penetration into European society of both French politics and German philosophy—notably that produced by young Hegelians—would be a demonstration of the vivacity of revolutionary ideals, invisibly deteriorating the old structures of society by germinating a new one, without political and/or religious precedents. The revolutionary process of 1789 had exacerbated the contradictions between the negative and the positive principle, and the early nineteenth century was nothing more than a moment of hidden, underground warfare, a moment when the negative principle was preparing itself for inner progress to emerge and overcome the positive, itself becoming, finally, a new positive.[4]

However, even more decisive than French Napoleonic politics and German Hegelian philosophy for triggering this revolutionary war were two other factors: on the one hand, the emergence of secret socialist and religious political associations; on the other, the growing public unrest of workers and the development of their class consciousness.

Precursor phenomena are manifesting around us: they are the sign that the spirit, this old mole, has finished its underground work and will soon reappear to do its justice. Everywhere, and especially in France and England, *associations of a type that are both socialist and religious*, are being formed which, entirely [foreign to] the current political world, will seek their vitality in new and unknown sources, developing and propagating themselves secretly. *The people, the class of poor people who undoubtedly constitute the immense majority of humanity, this class the rights of which have already been recognized in theory, but which [until now, by their birth and their relations, are condemned to misery (lack of property) and ignorance] and, in the same way, to a de facto slavery,* this class that constitutes the people proper, is taking an offensive attitude everywhere; it is beginning to enumerate its enemies, whose forces are inferior to its, and to claim the realization of its rights that everyone has already recognized for it. All the peoples and individuals are filled with a vague foreboding, and every normally constituted being eagerly awaits this near future, where the liberating words will be spoken. Even in Russia, this immense empire of snow-covered steppes that we know so little and to which perhaps a great future is opening, even in this Russia, dark clouds pile up, precursors of the storm. Oh! The atmosphere suffocates and is full of storms! (Bakunin, 1976a[e], pp. 126–27, emphasis added)

These two factors provided the necessary resources for the destruction of the old world. Organizational resources, on the one hand, allowing revolutionaries to articulate, train, and act safely and effectively. Human resources, on the other, making an interaction between revolutionaries and people possible, this new collective source of power, without which revolutionary vitality was impossible.

Here, it is worth highlighting what is meant by the concept of people. It is not, as can be seen, a bourgeois conception of a group of people or community living in the same territory, nor of citizens living under the same state. It is also not a question of people in the ethnic-racial or cultural sense. The people are conceptualized here in terms of social class and understood as the whole of the dispossessed of society (workers, artisans, peasants, the marginalized and poor in general); the majority of members of society that are deprived of wealth and education, and that are condemned to exploitation and domination by other minority classes. In other words, people are "the greatest number, the greatest mass, the poor and the oppressed" (Bakunin, 2007b [e], p. 156). A people who, after the French Revolution, showed themselves to be increasingly autonomous as a class and acting according to their own interests. A people who articulated, claimed, understood themselves and their class enemies—who, at the same time, acted and became aware.

5.3 REACTIONARY PARTY AND DEMOCRATIC PARTY

In order to lay the foundations for the continuity and strengthening of this revolutionary movement, it seemed necessary to produce an analysis that would make it possible to understand, concretely, the main social and political contradictions, the conflict between the old and the new world, this historical dispute involving freedom. After all, it seemed urgent to make negative dialectics a practical tool.[5] It was also necessary to unfold, from this analysis, the strategic paths for political action. And, for this analysis and this line to be properly elaborated, a set of procedures should be taken into account—employed quite concisely by Bakunin in "The Reaction in Germany" in his discussion of Europe from the early 1840s, which will be discussed below.

This *political analysis*, at the same time dialectical and realistic, has to take into account the forces at play, the parties and principles in dispute in a given historical context, encompassing the totality of fundamental contradictions, especially that between freedom and non-freedom. It must map and typify these camps, pointing out which is the opposing party (of the enemies of freedom) and the party itself (of the supporters of freedom), as well as the functioning of relations between them. In relation to each of the camps, and taking care to distinguish discourse and reality, theory and practice, it must apprehend: the political positions and interests at stake; the capacity for advocacy and expression in reality; relations with society in general; strengths, weaknesses, risks, and potential; morality and ethical parameters; the social positions and the demographic and behavioral profile of the members. Such an analysis must be able to map a determined socio-political conjuncture and relate it, more broadly, to the necessary directions of history, pointing out the political possibilities of action and will. It must be able to characterize the period in question—whether it is normality or crisis, quantitative or qualitative changes, underground or open—and the moment of contradiction—whether it is a moment when positive and negative can be conceived separately or not, whether mediations are possible or not, whether there is an ongoing revolutionary period or not. With this analysis elaborated, one should start from this knowledge produced to build avenues for action, which involve policies of treatment of opponents and enemies, for the party's own performance, with a view to its victory in the final outcome.[6]

In mapping out and typifying the forces at play and the contradictory camps, there are three forces in the opposing camp, of the enemies of freedom, whose members rely on the principle of maintaining order and of reaction, and opposing freedom, equality, democracy, and revolution. The first two are less relevant. "Firstly, well-placed people, loaded with years and experience who, in their youth, were even dilettantes of political freedom," rich and distinguished men who find "a certain exquisite pleasure in talking about freedom and equality," something that makes them "doubly important in society." But now, distant from youth, "they try to hide their physical and intellectual weakening under the veil of 'experience.'" Second, several "young people who share the same convictions with the people in the first group, or rather, the absence of all conviction." People who "belong, for the most part, [to] this aristocracy, which by its nature has been marked for a long time in Germany by political death, be it the bourgeois and merchant class, or that of the officials."

Due to its irrelevance, with regard to the former, "it is a waste of time to talk to these people" because "they never took freedom seriously, freedom was never for them the religion that only leads to the greatest pleasures and the supreme happiness by the way of the most terrible contradictions, at the price of the most cruel sufferings and of total and unreserved selflessness"; moreover, because "they are old and [...] will die soon." In relation to the second, also irrelevant, "there is nothing to undertake" with them, as they are "born of non-existent beings, dead men"; they are "all embarrassed by their sordid interests of vanity or money and solely concerned with their daily lives, they ignore everything in life and what is happening around them" (Bakunin, 1976a[e], pp. 105–06).

The third and most relevant force is that of the "reactionary party, which emerged shortly after the Restoration throughout Europe, and which is called conservatism in politics, historical school in the science of law, and positive philosophy in the speculative sciences" (Bakunin, 1976a [e], p. 106). That is, politically, Frederick William IV's Prussia and all the reaction that followed in Europe after the defeat of Napoleon; philosophically, old Schelling's counterpoint to Hegelianism as demanded by the king; legally, the traditional reaction of lawyers such as Gustav Hugo, Frierich Karl von Savigny, and Friedrich Julius Stahl to the attempt to found a rationally based law (Angaut, 2007a, pp. 21–35). Unlike the other two, this party "is now, everywhere, the ruling party, and, much more, we are about to grant it that its present strength is not a game [of contingency], but that it has deep roots [in the development] of the modern spirit." The crucial feature of the present is the "current [domination] of the reactionary party" as a whole and, therefore, it is necessary to seek to "discuss with this party" and understand its functioning because "it would be absurd on our part to ignore its existence and consider it insignificant" (Bakunin, 1976a[e], p. 106).

On the other hand there is, in the other camp, the supporters of freedom, only one force: the "democratic party." It is, for the moment, the negative element, which contradicts the positive element headed by the reactionary party, in front of which it is still insufficient, and that is found in the defenders of the principle of "equality of men being realized [in] freedom," of the revolution, and in the people its greatest justification and source of revolutionary power (Bakunin, 1976a[e], pp. 107–08).

The central confrontation that is announced, as a socio-political historical contradiction, is therefore that between the reactionary party and the democratic party, of which the features and relations between them will be discussed below.

The reactionary party is the historical organ of the principle of non-freedom; it is composed of two internal forces, that of the pure reactionaries (consequential), a minority, and that of the mediator reactionaries (inconsequential), the majority.

The pure reactionaries, who make up a sizeable force, claim to be "sincere, honest and want to be whole men" and often in fact are. In general, these reactionaries clearly and openly defend their side of the conflict. They are "fanatics" and "intransigent," they have "purity full of energy" and nurture "like us, hatred of every half-measure, because they know that only a whole man can be good." They are consequential, since they usually exhibit a certain coherence between what they think, say, and do. They know and apply the "strict consequences of their own principles." This coherence guides the notion that "they simply reject the negative as an absolute evil." In the present moment of contradiction, however, "it is very difficult, if not impossible, to remain in the pure positive" such that they abstract themselves "from their own reason" and not infrequently "substitute the word for injury" (Bakunin, 1976a[e], pp. 110, 113).

These reactionaries

conceive of opposition in all its purity; they know well that you can no longer
[mediate] the positive and the negative, like water and fire; not seeing in the
negative the affirmative side of its [essence], they cannot believe it and
correctly deduce that the positive cannot be sustained except by the total
[oppression] of the negative. [...] These fanatical reactionaries accuse us of
heresy, and, if it were possible, they would make the Inquisition's hidden force
emerge from the arsenal of history to use it against us; they deny us any good
or human feeling and see in us hardened anti-christs whom it is allowed to
combat by all means. [...] They see in the principle of freedom nothing more
than a cold and vulgar abstraction—[for which] the vulgarity and dryness of
several defenders of this principle actively collaborated—an empty abstraction
of all life, of all beauty and of all holiness. [...] Finding no more than the
humiliation of this life in the negative, they return to the past, to the past as it
existed before the opposition between the negative and the positive arose.
(Bakunin, 1976a[e], pp. 110, 112)

In sum, pure reactionaries, despite being avowed enemies of freedom, and being
willing to use all possible means for victory, still have certain qualities: their
intransigence, contrary to mediation, and their coherence. Furthermore, their
aspiration to return to the past has its *raison d'être* since, long ago, "that past was a
whole animated of its own life, presenting itself, as such, much more alive and richer
than the present torn by its contradictions."

However, these reactionaries did not understand the moment of historical
contradiction and the dialectic corresponding to it. They think that this return to the
past is possible, when in fact it is not. "They make a big mistake when they think they
can resurrect that past," constituting such an aspiration that is nothing more than a
distorted view of reality: "they forget that the [totality] of the past can only appear to
them in the form of [a distorted and fragmented reflection] of current contradictions
that they fatally engendered." This "past, belonging to the positive, is nothing more
than a corpse without a soul" (Bakunin, 1976a[e], p. 112).

The reactionary mediators, "principal representatives of the current age," despite
being "intelligent and prudent" "theoreticians par excellence" and having "more
intelligence and penetration than the consequentials," are "malicious individuals" and
more "corrupted" than pure reactionaries, without having "the same purity full of
energy" as these. They do not clearly and openly state their positions in the conflict;
they do not deny the negative absolutely, even granting it "a relative and momentary
justification." They are cunning, and with them "it is difficult to get anything straight,
because, like the German constitutions, they take with the right hand what they give
with the left; they never answer with a yes or a no." They like to say, "'To a certain

extent you are right, but nevertheless... ', and when they have no arguments then say: 'Yes, it's a sensitive issue.'"

The attitude of these reactionaries is inconsequential as they do not exhibit coherence between what they think, say, and do, between what they advocate in theory and do in practice, and the position they end up finally assuming in the dispute of forces. This conciliatory position, which is often sought through the State, far from ending contradictions, often leads to misunderstanding, reproducing a crude logic and favouring one side of the contradiction. "The left side says: two times two makes four; the right side: two times two makes six... And the [*juste milieu*, the "fair middle ground"] says: two times two makes five" (Bakunin, 1976a[e], pp. 113–14).

> We can define the point of view of the [mediators] as that of dishonesty in the domain of theory; I say well: of theory. [...] However, it is necessary to recognize that theoretical dishonesty, due to its own [essence], necessarily leads almost always to practical dishonesty. [... The Mediators] never allow [the practical impulse towards truth, to destroy] the artificial building of their theories; they are too experienced, too intelligent to listen to the imperative voice of simple practical consciousness. Assured of their points of view, they throw on it looks full of distinction, and when we say that only what is simple is true and [effective], because only it can play a creative role, they pretend, on the contrary, that only the complex is true. They had, in fact, the greatest difficulties in patching it up, and it is the only sign that allows us to distinguish them—the intelligent individuals—from the imbecile and uneducated plebs. And it's very difficult to overcome these individuals because, precisely, they know everything! Other reasons for their attitude: being skillful politicians, they resist an unforgivable weakness to be taken in by any event. Finally, helped by reflection, they slipped into every nook and cranny of the world of nature and spirit and, after this long and painful intellectual journey, they acquired the conviction that it is not worth keeping [relations effectively alive] with the real world. (Bakunin, 1976a[e], pp. 113–14)

After all, the reactionary mediators embody the authority of theoretical knowledge, which is accompanied by a lack of realism and practical and ethical spirit. They want to box reality into their preformulated ideas and distance themselves from practice in the name of a pure theory without support in the real world. Their concealed moderation is a factor that complicates relations because, unlike pure reactionaries, who are openly exposed as declared enemies, they can pass as adversaries or even as allies, when in fact they are also enemies.

Pure reactionaries are obvious enemies, willing to do anything to suppress the democratic party and therefore the situation with them is one of open conflict, although there are limits to this struggle. Even if they have no ethical criteria for the conflict, the democratic party must have: "Do we pay them in kind? No, it would be undignified for us and the great cause we defend." The great principle defended by the democratic party gives us "the good privilege of being just and impartial without doing any harm to our cause." Even in the face of the toughest enemies, we have to "effectively practice love, even in the most obstinate battles, this love that is the highest power of Christ and [the unique essence] of true Christianity."[7] As far as they are concerned, the politics must be of combat and ethical confrontation (Bakunin, 1976a [e], pp. 110–11). The reactionary mediators, even because of the difficulties related to their profile, and "despite [their lack of position and their inability to produce anything that that be]" cannot be despised. As they form "today, a strong party, even the strongest" in numerical terms, you cannot "ignore this party or pass it in silence." It is, therefore, necessary to "try to enter into relationships" with these reactionaries in order to persuade and convert them, but offer those who remain in the enemy camp the due combat and ethical confrontation (Bakunin, 1976a[e], p. 114).

The democratic party is the historical organ of the democratic principle, of the principle of freedom, previously enunciated as "the equality of men occurring [in] freedom," and which can also be considered "the universal principle of [uncon-ditional] freedom." It represents such a principle that in short it is nothing more than the movement of history itself, and has considerable political possibilities, insofar as this principle corresponds to the most fundamental desires of society. It provides the conditions for this principle, an essential theoretical foundation, to function as a motor for a practical and conscious existence and to be realized in history. It establishes the possibilities for politics to rise to the condition of religion, going from partisan particularity to human universality, and for morality to be converted into ethics. Therefore, the democratic party carries within itself dialectical oppositions between essence and existence, principle and party, morality and ethics, universality and particularity (Bakunin, 1976a[e], pp. 108, 111, 122; Angaut, 2007a, pp. 45, 49).

Coming into consciousness relative to its essence, its principle, is a sine qua non condition for its victory, in the first place; in the second place, the effective realization of this essence, this principle.

For such coming into consciousness, it is necessary to break with abstraction, take reality as it really is, and take part in it. The party must "know its momentary weakness and the relative strength of its adversaries" and enemies. "This knowledge will make it leave, firstly, the [indetermination of fantasy] and enter this [effective reality] where it must live, suffer and finally win." In this "painful contact with reality" the party acquires "consciousness of its sacred and priestly mission" and finds that "its enemy is not only outside it, but also, and above all, in itself." This is because its insufficiency is explained less by the imperfection of its principle and more by the fact that it has not yet reached the consciousness of its principle. Thus, the democratic party must know that victory depends on a triumph in the face of external and internal enemies.

Becoming conscious of the democratic principle means, among other things, understanding that "democracy does not consist only of an opposition to the governors, it is not a particular, constitutional, political, or economic [transformation], but that it announces a total transformation of the current [state] of the world and an [originally] new life, previously unknown in history." In other words, awareness of the democratic principle implies the adoption of a revolutionary perspective, which extrapolates the most limited changes and finds their corollary in generalized transformation and in the new society.

It implies, at the same time, the understanding that "democracy is a religion," it being therefore essential that the party itself becomes religious, "not only [penetrated by] its principle in thought and reasoning, but also true to this principle in real life, even in the smallest manifestations." To understand politics as a religion means to convert the democratic party into a religious organ, not in the sense of strengthening any existing religion, but of promoting the religion of freedom politically. With that, it will be penetrated by its essential principle and will be able to realize it effectively in history (Bakunin, 1976a[e], p. 107).[8]

In the first place, giving this religious meaning to politics requires that the democratic party convert it into a practical politics, one that permeates its principle in all spheres of life. Turning to practice, the party goes beyond the limits of morality and reaches ethics, since those who "are not penetrated by the practical spirit of the time" are "men without [ethics]" because "outside this Church of free humanity there would be no possibility [of ethics], without which there is no salvation" (Bakunin, 1976a[e], p. 122).

"From the Hegelian distinction between *Moralität* [morality] and *Sittlichkeit* [ethics]" there is a difference, on the one hand, "a subjective morality, which must be apprehended at the strict level of individuality" and on the other "an objective or social morality, which refers to the way in which a historical process is incorporated into individuals." Ethics exists only with the penetration of certain moral elements into customs, strengthening the notion of a religion of freedom. Moving into practice thus breaks from this abstract and individual morality and gives access to a perspective of concrete and collective ethics, of ethical life constituted by a practical attitude in the face of historical contradictions. It expresses with conviction an entry into the universe of politics; the ethical being. Ethics comes into being as the democratic principle penetrates life, giving it a religious dimension (Angaut, 2007a, pp. 41–42).

In the second place, making politics religious implies breaking with the partiality of partisan proposals and accessing universality.

As a party we only do politics, but we find our [legitimacy] only in our principle, otherwise our cause would be no better than that of the positive, and it is necessary, for our own conservation, to remain true to our principle, [as the only foundation of our strength and of our life, that is, to continually supersede ourselves] from this [unilateral] and only political existence until the religion of our universal and [multilateral] principle on life. We must act not only politically, but also religiously in our politics, [religiously, in the sense of freedom as the only true expression of justice and love]. Yes, it is with us, that we are treated as enemies of the Christian religion, it is only with us that this task of which we do supreme duty is reserved: to effectively practice love even in the most obstinate struggles, this love which is the highest power of Christ and [the only essence] of true Christianity. (Bakunin, 1976a[e], p. 111)

The democratic party does politics since it is one of the forces at play in the existing society. However, in this society, its politics is nothing if not particular, insofar as the democratic party (negative element) is only the partial opposition to the reactionary party (positive element), which is also partial. Thus, it is possible to say that "according to its existence as a party, [the democratic party] is only something particular—the negative—opposing anything else particular—the positive"; but "according to its [essence] and its principle, the democratic party aspires to the general and the universal" (Bakunin, 1976a[e], p. 108).

Politics are given a religious sense here when it proceeds from party existence and moves towards its essence, the democratic principle—when it goes from faith to love.

The question of religion and the relationship between love and faith approaches the central question of the relationship between party and principle, and the religion of freedom desired by Bakunin has the following characteristics: it takes Christianity back to its essence (love), which is secularized to give it its true extent; it corresponds to it a faith that certainly has the character of partiality, but which is inhabited by a tension towards universality; this religion demands only to incarnate itself in a church, that of "free humanity"; moreover, the object of this religion is a principle, that of "the equality of men realizing themselves in freedom." (Angaut, 2007a, p. 46)

This religious content of the democratic party's politics calls into question not only its partial existence as a party, but opens up two possibilities for criticism of the State. Considering that "the State without religion and without [a strong universal conviction is impossible]," it is possible to affirm that the existing state, by its partiality, is incompatible with the universality of the true religion of freedom (Bakunin, 1976a [e], p. 126). It follows from this that, on the one hand, this new religion requires a new state, a new political form (Angaut, 2007a, p. 47). On the other hand, it is possible to question the State itself as a privileged space for politics. Like the parties, the State as such is a partial organism; and if the democratic party is to seek universality in its essence, state politics can only find its universality in the religion of freedom. Thus, this religious element of the democratic party can be considered anti-political, or at least form the basis of a new politics, pointing out that the realization of the democratic principle is only possible outside the State apparatus (McLaughlin, 2002, p. 27).[9]

In this way, the relationships between religion, politics, the democratic party, and the democratic principle can be more precisely understood. Love—found as the essence of Christianity and then secularized—is freedom, and freedom is the only true expression of love and the basis of the democratic principle, which constitutes the essence of the democratic party. Having found this essence (love–freedom), it must be actualized, practically realized, and this is done through a faith, initially partial/particular, but which tends to universality. The democratic party, partial and particular insofar as it is negative, contains this possibility in itself, since it has the potential to become a new positive and support the creation of a new totality, a new socio-religious life for all humanity.

Starting from the elements of theory of history and the European political context previously presented, it is possible to foresee a new revolutionary wave, the outcome of which would occur as a result of this contradiction between the reactionary party (positive) and democratic party (negative). In this confrontation, according to the foundations of his negative dialectic, Bakunin (2007a [e], p. 136, p. 136) understands that the democratic party will win, and for this reason he reclaims, in religious jargon: "Do penance! Do penance! The Kingdom of the Lord is at hand."

This is because, among other things, the moment of contradiction placed the contradictory elements in such a relationship that they could no longer be conceived independently. "The negative, by isolating itself from its opposition to the positive and considering itself, seems to be [without content] and without life"; at this stage, "the negative cannot be taken in isolation" because "as such, it would be absolutely nothing!" The negative can be taken "only in opposition to the positive." In other words, the terms of the contradictory relationship—positive and negative, reactionary party and democratic party—are inseparable here.[10] For this reason, there is no sense in censoring the seconds for any "[apparent lack of content]" in view of its momentary and exclusively negative perspective, in which "all its being, its content, [consist of] the destruction of the positive." At that moment, "all the importance and all the irresistible force of the negative" consists of "the annihilation of the positive"—the democratic party, in this exclusive negation, has "a particular nature" but is "imperfect and unsuited to its essence" (Bakunin 1976a[e], pp. 108–109).

> The democratic party does not exist as such, in the fullness of its affirmation, but only as the negation of the positive: it is because it must, in this imperfect form, disappear at the same time as the positive, in order to be spontaneously reborn in a regenerated form and in the living fullness of its being. Thus, the democratic party [becomes itself], and this transformation is not only quantitative, it is not a simple extension of its current, [particular and] imperfect

existence: God save us! Because such an enlargement would lead to universal humiliation and the final term of history would be nothing at all. This transformation is, on the contrary, qualitative, it is a revelation that lives and that announces life, it is a new heaven and a new earth, a young and magnificent world in which all current dissonances will become a harmonious unity. (Bakunin 1976a[e], pp. 108–109)

Being so, the democratic party exists only as a negation in contradiction with the reactionary party. "The negative is dedicated to the destruction of the positive in this contradiction. Its whole existence is either negation or revolution." But by destroying the reactionary party, the democratic party also destroys itself, since, in this moment of contradiction, both are inseparable. "The negative is also dedicated to the destruction of itself as merely negative, revolutionary and (anti-)political." The democratic party "is dedicated, then, to destroying not only its antithesis, but also [itself], insofar as [it] depends on its antithesis, and is only an antithetical political or anti-political existence" (McLaughlin, 2002, p. 29).

In this way, the negative is reborn as a new positive, the democratic party returns to itself and resurfaces, no longer in a particular, partisan way, but as a new socio-political historical totality, fullness of life, affirmative awareness of its principle and effective realization of freedom (Angaut, 2007a, p. 87). This dialectical process in which the negative destroys the positive and itself, "[assuming the one-sidedness of] its existence as a party" and emerging as a new positive, is a revolutionary process of qualitative transformation, which points to the end of the present historical contradictions (Bakunin, 1976a[e], p. 109).

If you want to quote Hegel, it is necessary to do so in full. You will then see that the negative is not a vital condition of a given organism until the time that it appears in that organism as [a moment preserved in] its totality. You will see that a moment comes when the gradual action of the negative is abruptly broken, [returning to itself as an autonomous principle], that this moment means the death of this organism, and that Hegelian philosophy characterizes this moment as the passage of nature to a qualitatively new world, to the free world of the spirit. (Bakunin 1976a[e], p. 123)

As mentioned, the democratic party's exclusively destructive position is momentary and, as this party develops its negative politics against the reactionary party, it prepares, with this return to itself, the ground for a creative, constructive, positive position. It is in this perspective that "the passion for destruction is, at the same time, a creative passion" (Bakunin, 2007a [e], p. 136). Negating the old, the new is affirmed and created. In the refusal of the old, a paradigm of new emerges, which does not appear speculatively, but through contrasting the old in the negation. That is why the criticism of the old has to be made from a negative perspective, arriving at certain rejections that contain in themselves the affirmation of the future. In other words, in this negative dialectic, to negate is also to affirm, to destroy is also to create, to construct (McLaughlin, 2002, p. 34). By destroying the reactionary party and the old world, the democratic party also destroys itself as a party and creates a new world, a free, egalitarian and democratic totality. As can be seen, such a position does not imply any nihilism or defense of total and absolute destruction.[11]

In this process, the "[external mediation]" between the democratic party and the reactionary party, advocated by the reactionary mediators, is not viable "because the positive and the negative are, once and for all, incompatible."[12] The negative exists only in contradiction to the positive and, in truth, when these reactionaries insist on the conciliatory proposition they do nothing more than preserve themselves as a privileged force of the social totality. The mediators "say to the positives: 'Keep what is old, but at the same time allow the negatives to break it down little by little.'" And, at the same time, they say "to the negatives: 'Destroy what is old, but not in one stroke nor totally, so that you can always have some work to do.'" In other words, "stay each one in your [unilateralism], while we, the elect, will save for ourselves the enjoyment of the totality!" That is, this supposed middle ground of the mediators is not neutral or objective but a restricted political conception that does not carry within it the general interests of humanity (Bakunin, 1976a[e], pp. 109, 121–22).

The "only [mediation] possible" between both parties is the "self-decomposition of the positive," the "[tireless self-combustion of the positive] in the pure flame of the negative" "because [it is the movement and the immanent, total energy of the contradiction itself]." Any other mediation is arbitrary and "all those who tend to [another mediation] demonstrate [thereby] only that they are not penetrated by the spirit of the time and that they are stupid, or without character" (Bakunin, 1976a [e], pp. 118–19). The external mediation between the reactionary party and the democratic party, between "a partial political existence and the universal religion of freedom"— mediation that is "promoted by the reactionary mediators, the paladins of the statist principle" and which contradicts the very notion of a dialectical movement—not only does not exist historically: it is a logical impossibility (McLaughlin, 2002, p. 47).

There is therefore no absolute and complete refusal of any and all mediation, but only that mediation outside contradiction, which aims to "progress indefinitely by degrees to unite the two opposites" (Angaut, 2007a, p. 77). The recommended and accepted mediation, in this case, is that of the destruction of the positive by the negative and the transformation of the negative into a new positive. Thus, the primacy of negative logic, of destruction, in relation to positive logic, of mediation, is assumed.

5.4 NEGATIVE DIALECTICS: REVOLUTIONARY LOGIC

With what has been discussed it is possible to say that for Bakunin the foundations of negative dialectics, unlike what he advocated in the previous period, become in the period from 1841 to 1843 the following: *in the attempt to be realized a principle produces its negation and with it a contradiction, which ends up destroying it; in a return to itself, this principle resumes its movement,* but not (as in the previous conception) integrating what seemed to negate it and rising to another stage of reconciliation, *but* (in this new conception) *asserting itself as a new principle, evidencing the preponderance of negation without relation to the old.* Thus *the positive principle produces the negative and therefore constitutes a contradiction that, in a given historical moment, aims at the destruction of the positive by the negative and the formation of a new positive.* It is not the synthesis mediated between negative and positive nor does it conserve any aspect of the old positive, but it incorporates the revolutionary transformation of the old negation into a renewed affirmation.

This dialectic, understood as a negative movement, can then be formalized in terms of its logical and revolutionary foundations.

The contradiction between positive and negative—when it is elevated from mere difference, annoyance, to opposition, shaping the contradiction and reaching its climax—can only be considered in its entirety, in an inseparable relationship between the contradictory parts—it is no longer possible to understand the parts separately. In other words, it is necessary, at that moment, to "understand the contradiction in its entirety in order to know the truth." In agreement with "Hegel's Logic, where he makes such a remarkable study on the category of contradiction," it is from the "nature of contradiction" itself that "the existence of a term of contradiction [presupposes] the existence of the other," and this "[is not a positive assumption, but a negative, dissolving assumption]." As a relational totality "the contradiction itself, which as such includes the two [unilateral] terms, is total, absolute, true"; its terms, positive and negative, cannot be understood separately, unilaterally. The contradiction "is not only the negative, but it is also the positive and, encompassing them entirely, it is the total, absolute plenitude, leaving nothing outside of it."[13]

However, embracing the contradiction in its entirety is not a simple matter. This is because contradiction does not exist as a totality; "it is only a totality in itself and hidden, and its existence [is] precisely [the contradictory division] of its two terms: the positive and the negative." In a way that "contradiction, while a total truth, is the indissoluble union of its simplicity and its own division." The totality of the contradiction as such cannot be immediately perceived, since it appears in a partial existence, in the exclusivity of its positive and negative terms. It "exists only in the form of the division of its terms and is nothing more than the addition of the positive and the negative." However, "these terms exclude one another so categorically, that this reciprocal exclusion constitutes their whole nature" (Bakunin, 1976a[e], pp. 115–16).

If one proceeds incorrectly, taking into account only the positive principle, in an autonomous way, one can believe that it is the static term of the relationship. However, when approaching the contradiction in its entirety, it appears that it can only be conceived as a dynamic relationship between both terms, and that the mere existence of the contradiction implies dialectical movement.

The positive appears, firstly, to be the calm and immobile element; and even it is positive only because there is no cause for disturbance in it and there is nothing in it that could be a negation, because, finally, within the positive there is no movement, since the whole movement is a negation. But precisely because the positive is such that in it the absence of movement is established as such, and thus, taken in itself, the total absence of movement is imagined; now, the image that evokes immobility in us is inextricably linked to that of movement, or rather, they are nothing more than one and the same image, and so the positive, absolute repose, is only positive in opposition to the negative, absolute agitation; [within itself, the positive is related to the negative as its own living determination]. The situation of the positive in relation to the negative is presented in two ways: on the one hand, it brings repose, and this apathetic calm that characterizes it has no trace of the negative itself; on the other hand, in order to preserve this rest, the negative is energetically removed from it, as if it had something opposed to the negative. But the activity it develops to exclude the negative is a movement, and so the positive, taken in itself and precisely because of its positivity, is no longer the positive, but the negative; eliminating the negative from it, it eliminates itself and runs towards its own [ruin]. (Bakunin, 1976a[e], p. 117)

In contradiction the positive, apparently absolute repose, is only positive insofar as it is opposed to the negative, agitation or absolute movement. But in opposing the negative the positive puts itself and the whole contradiction in motion. Trying to remove the negative, the positive sets itself in motion and denies its positivity; it becomes the negative itself, so that when it eliminates the negative it does nothing but destroy itself. "The positive and the negative are, therefore, not equal in rights" and "*the contradiction is not a balance, but a preponderance of the negative*, which is the moment of superposition." It is not therefore a contradiction that reaches a certain point of equilibrium of the contradictory parts, but a contradiction that resolves itself with the preponderance of the negative, which, "[as the determinant life of the positive itself,] contains only within itself the totality of the contradiction" and is "the only one that [is absolutely legitimate]" (Bakunin, 1976a[e], p. 117, emphasis added).

It is only with the abstraction of the negative, when it is excluded from the positive, that the negative becomes as partial as the positive. When the positive, as a negative force, negates the negative it fulfills a logical and sacred function without knowing that it does. The movement of the positive awakens the negative from its sleep and puts it back in the direction of its vocation: the negation and destruction of everything that has a positive existence. The positive, then, makes it possible for the negative to effectuate this vocation.

The negative must not be egoist, [but must surrender] with love to the positive in order to absorb it and, in this act of religious [negation], full of faith and life, reveal its intimate nature, inexhaustible and full of future. The positive is negated by the negative and [conversely] the negative [is negated] by the positive. So, what is common to both and who dominates them? [Negation, ruin, passionate absorption of the positive], even when it seeks [finely] to hide itself under traces of the negative. The negative [is legitimized] in this [merciless] negation—and as such it is absolutely [legitimized]: [because, as such, it is the act of] the practical spirit [invisibly present] in contradiction, the spirit that, by this storm of destruction, fervently exhorts the penance of the [mediators'] sinful souls and announces its next coming [and its] next [manifestation] in a Church of Freedom [effectively democratic and universally human]. (Bakunin, 1976a[e], p. 118)

It is, therefore, in negation, in destruction, that the practical possibilities of a new future are found—denial and destruction are prerequisites for the new affirmation and revolutionary reconstruction. In its negation, the negative term of contradiction has as its essence the democratic principle, which works as an antithesis to the reactionary principle of the positive element. As a revolutionary force, democracy, equality occurring in freedom, can only be understood through the negative reference to non-freedom, and can only be effectuated by the negation of that non-freedom. When, finally, the negative destroys the positive in this contradiction, absorbing it, it shapes a new future and the democratic principle is effectively realized as a new positive principle. It is not, as you can see, of a supersumption or synthesis, but of destruction of the positive by the negative. It is the effective realization of freedom, equality, democracy. Therefore, this conflict is resolved with the self-expression of the negative, with the destruction, on the part of the negative, of its dialectical counterpart, the positive. With this, the negative ceases to be another, a negative term, to disappear along with the positive and re-emerge as a new positive (McLaughlin, 2002, pp. 48–49).

NOTES

1   From this period, Bakunin's main writing is "The Reaction in Germany," which has been translated into several languages, including Portuguese (Bakunin, 1976a [e]). This, however, is a regular translation, based on the French version of the text, produced by Jean Barrué from the German. The biggest problem with the Portuguese edition is, without a doubt, that it does not have the last three paragraphs of Bakunin's text. But another problem is the fact that some Hegelian concepts and certain passages are not adequately translated—probably, according to Angaut's hypothesis (2007a), due to Barrué's lack of intimacy with Hegel's philosophy. In quoting this writing I gave preference to the Portuguese translation, but made corrections as necessary based on the version by Angaut (Bakunin, 2007a [e]) or sometimes on the original in German, indicating the changes in brackets. The only concept that I chose not to make this adjustment to was "contradiction," which Angaut proposes to translate as "opposition," taking sides in a Hegelian controversy—whether contrariety or opposition is or is not contradiction, and to what extent this changes when it comes to logical or historical contradiction/opposition—in which I preferred not to take a position. I chose to follow McLaughlin (2002), whom I consider to be very rigorous and who treats this concept as "contradiction." The

quotations from Bakunin's documents on the IISH CD-ROM (Bakunin, 2000a) have been translated from the French texts.

2 Cf. Hegel (2001, pp. 65–66): "The history of the world is the advance of the consciousness of freedom. [...] Freedom itself is its own goal and the spirit's unique purpose. It is the ultimate end to which all the history of the world has always been turned. [...] The question of the means by which freedom develops in a world takes us directly to the phenomenon of history. Although freedom itself is essentially an undeveloped internal idea, the means that it uses are the external phenomena that in history present themselves directly to our eyes."

3 Cf. Ruge: "Our times are political, and our politics seeks the freedom of this world" (*apud* McLaughlin, 2002, p. 70).

4 Cf. Hegel (1805/6), about the mole metaphor, later also taken up by Marx: "Often, the spirit seems to have forgotten and lost itself; but inwardly, it is constantly in opposition to itself. It is always inner progress—like when Hamlet says, about his father's ghost: 'Bravo, old mole! And how you drill the earth, good miner!'—until it finds the strength in itself to break the earth's crust that separates it from the sun. [...] With that, the earth collapses."

5 Cf. Bruno Bauer, in *The Trumpet of the Last Judgment...*: "A theoretical principle must [...] arrive at the act, the practical opposition, transform directly into praxis and action. [...] The opposition must be serious, sharp, effective, unrestricted, and its main objective must be to overthrow the established order" (*apud* McLaughlin, 2002, p. 69).

6 I believe that embedded in "The Reaction in Germany" is a model of analysis of socio-political conjuncture and a programmatic-strategic line. Although, in terms of analysis and program, Bakunin's answers are brief and even in some cases limited or problematic—especially in the cases of the most evident manifestation of his idealism—it seems possible to extract from the answers he offers in this writing the questions that guided its elaboration. What are the forces at play? How are they articulated in the formation of the major camps/parties in conflict/dispute? Internally to these camps/parties, how do the correlations of forces occur? What are the principles of these camps/parties? Are they consciously defended? To what extent are they put into practice? Who makes up our camp/party and who the enemy? Who are our adversaries and enemies and how do they think and act? What are our conjunctural and historical possibilities? And our limits? How should we characterize the present period and the moment we find ourselves in? What can and should we do, in strategic and tactical terms, to defeat our enemies?

7 Cf. Feuerbach (2007, p. 260): "God is love. This is the highest principle in Christianity."

8 Cf. Feuerbach (2008, p. 5, emphasis added): "We must therefore become religious again—*politics must become our religion*—but it can only become such if we have in our intuition a supreme principle that can transform politics into religion. You can, by instinct, make of politics a religion, but here it is a last declared foundation, an official principle."

9 Cf. Bruno Bauer, in *The Trumpet of the Last Judgement…*: "Hegel is not only against the State, the Church and religion, but he opposes everything that is firm and that is established" (*apud* McLaughlin, 2002, p. 69). And Hegel has some contributions that can be interpreted in this direction: "I will demonstrate that, just as there is no idea of a machine, there is no idea of the State, because the State is something mechanical. Only that which is the object of freedom can be called an idea. We must, therefore, transcend the State, since each State is limited to treating man as if he were a cog in a gear; and this would be exactly what the State should not be doing; it must therefore perish" (*apud* Marcuse, 1969, p. 23).

10 Cf. Hegel (1982, vol. I, book II, pp. 55–56): "The positive and the negative are not just some post, nor purely an indifferent, but a being-post, that is, their reference to the other in a single unit, which is not constituted by themselves, is recovered in each one. Each is, in itself, positive and negative; the positive and the negative are the reflexive determination in and of itself; only in this reflection of the opposites themselves do they become positive and negative. The positive has in itself the relationship with the other, which consists in determining the positive; likewise, the negative is not negative vis-à-vis another, but it also has determination within itself, through which it becomes negative."

11 Cf. Feuerbach (2008, p. 2, emphasis added): "In periods of the decadence of a historical world view, there are certainly contrary necessities—for some it is, or seems, necessary to preserve the old and banish what is new; for others, it is imperative to achieve the new. On which side does real necessity

lie? In those who demand the future—the anticipated future: in those who are moving forward. The necessity of conservation is just an artificial, created necessity—it is just a reaction. Hegelian philosophy was the arbitrary synthesis of several existing systems, of insufficiencies—without positive force, because without absolute negativity. *Only those who have the courage to be absolutely negative have the strength to create newness.*"

12   Cf. Bruno Bauer, in *The Trumpet of the Last Judgement...*: "Away with these modern notions, these verbose exchanges and this unsettling give and take back; it all rests on a principle—that truth and error can be reconciled. Away with this desire for reconciliation, with this sentimental nonsense, with this disgusting and lying secularism." To the "Hegelian mediators" with their dialectic of "reconciliation" or "of half measures" is counterposed the notion that "negative dialectic [is] the central principle of Hegelianism" (*apud* McLaughlin, 2002, pp. 21, 69). Cf. Edgar Bauer, in an article in the *Gazeta Renana* of June 1842: "Every principle is particular. The *juste milieu* has no principle, but it evokes as a threat two principles that are on its left and its right: on the right, absolute royalty, on the left, the republic. The *juste milieu* is precisely the opposite of history. History strives to push principles to the extreme, and the *juste milieu* fears principles and its barricade against it. History loves opposites because it evolves thanks to them. The *juste milieu* hates opponents because it would always love to remain in an indeterminate and insignificant environment" (*apud* Arvon, 1979, p. 76).

13   Cf. Hegel, *Science of Logic*, first volume, second book: "The doctrine of essence."

CHAPTER 6

PRIMACY OF PRACTICE AND SELF-GOVERNMENT
OF THE PEOPLE (1843)

This chapter discusses Bakunin's political theory *at the moment of his departure from philosophy* in 1843, dividing it into two parts: 1) Insufficiency of Philosophy, New Theory, and Concrete Practice; 2) Radicalism and Communism.[1]

6.1 INSUFFICIENCY OF PHILOSOPHY, NEW THEORY, AND CONCRETE PRACTICE

Analyzing the purposes and achievements of philosophy during the eighteenth century, it can be said that, without a doubt, it has virtues and possibilities. Philosophy aims at "knowledge of the truth, and the truth is not so abstract and ethereal that it cannot or should not have a significant influence on social relations, on the organization of society." In other words, philosophy, by promoting knowledge of the truth, is able to influence the directions of the world, in the direction recommended in the gospel: "you will know the truth, and the truth will set you free" (Bakunin, 2007b[e], pp. 152–53).

Such potential can be seen, in its concrete results, when looking at the history of the French Revolution, notably the history of the French people.

> Shortly before the revolution, the best part of the people, its laboring part, was still, in France, in the saddest situation. It barely possessed a third of the soil, its own labour, this only means of existence; it was weakened by disturbing obstacles, it had to bear the full burden of taxes and, moreover, pay particular taxes to the clergy and aristocrats. We will not mention the other obligations, often humiliating, to which the poor people were subjected. The courts were organized in such a way that the great lords always ended up being right against the people. In a word, the people were trampled underfoot by the great lords in all possible circumstances. And why? Not because the people were weak, God forbid! The people are never weak. This happened because the people were ignorant and allowed themselves to be deceived by Catholic priests, who told them that the king and these lords of the nobility and clergy were their teachers by the grace of God, and that they should serve them, bow down to and humble themselves before them, in order to reach the kingdom of heaven. "You are stupid, you are unable to understand what is just; rely on us and we will guide you". Thus, spoke the priests to the people, to the poor people, within which this faculty of belief and intelligence is always to be

found. The people effectively believed that they were stupid and fought every
suspicion, every liberating thought within themselves, as if they were the work
of the devil. (Bakunin, 2007b[e], p. 153)

The lack of access to land, poverty, abusive taxes, legal injustices, and other forms of
domination were accepted by the people due to their lack of knowledge. They had the
quantitative advantage in relation to the lords, but at the same time, their submission
was legitimized by a set of ideas that were produced and promoted by Catholic
Christianity.

"Who liberated the people from this holy slavery? Philosophy." Despite their
mistakes, the eighteenth-century philosophers fulfilled their "providential destiny,
which was to raise the people to self-esteem, to consciousness of their dignity and
their sacred and immutable right." Thus it was the philosophers who through their
initiatives managed to elevate the condition of people's consciousness—a fact that
demands guaranteeing, in history, the name of these philosophers "among the
liberators and the best servants of humanity." And even during the nineteenth century,
philosophy still had a role to play: "its persevering struggle, its struggle to the death,
against all prejudices, against everything that prevents men from reaching their high
and holy goal, *realization of the free and fraternal community*, the realization of heaven
on earth." And more: the fight against the interested lies that were promoted against
the people. After all, philosophy strives "for the liberation of man" and "knowledge
of the truth is his only weapon."

However, despite this realized potential and what could still be achieved in the field
of knowledge, philosophy also has considerable limits. "According to its essence,
philosophy is only theoretical; it moves and develops only inside consciousness." It is
true that "thought and action, truth and ethics, theory and *praxis* are, ultimately, one
and the same inseparable essence." And it is true, in the same way, that "the greatest
merit of philosophy is to have conceived and known this unity," but to know is not
enough. "With this knowledge, it [philosophy] reaches a frontier, a frontier that it cannot
cross as philosophy," a frontier that marks the passage from knowledge of the world
(theory) to the changing of the world (practice), and it is exactly in the latter sense that
philosophy finds its shortcomings. "After that frontier an essence more elevated than
itself begins—the *effective community of free men*, stimulated by love and born of the
divine essence of original equality." For the realization of this essence, theory is not
enough; practice is demanded (Bakunin, 2007b[e], pp. 153–54, emphasis added).

But what did this practice mean, after all? Even if other young Hegelians spoke of
practice and recognized its importance, it seemed necessary to make certain critical
notes. Asserting this need for practice did not mean conceiving theory as practice nor
theorizing about practice. It was not a question—as in the cases of Bruno Bauer,
Feuerbach and others[2]—of remaining in the "theoretical-abstract" or "practical-
abstract" camp without being able to break with theoretical abstraction. More precisely,

it was a question of finding in the *concrete practice of action* an answer to this dilemma. And for that, philosophy proved to be insufficient (Bakunin, 41016[c], p. 3).

"Our poor present," as can be seen, "requires practice" and therefore we must "break with our own past," leaving the "isolated life in the sky of learned theory" and entering the promising camp of practice. We must assume the primacy of practice over theory. That is why "the French," due to their practical conception of politics, "are still our teachers" and should remain so in the next period (Bakunin, 2007[c], p. 139; Bakunin, 2007c[e], pp. 144–45).

This practice involved, among other things, proceeding to the "action of liberating truth," "working day and night to live as men among men, to be free," "to take possession of our time with our thoughts," "to communicate [to our] contemporaries this movement of heart and mind," to win "the people to our side," to become "the voice of freedom and to captivate the world" (Bakunin, 2007c [e], pp. 144–45). It should move in the direction not only of raising awareness among the people, but of guaranteeing the conditions for freedom, equality, and democracy to materialize— in order to actualize that free and fraternal community, that heaven on Earth.

Even Hegelian philosophy, which was the culmination of modern theory, did not have the conditions in itself to provide adequate responses to such demands. This philosophy certainly had virtues and possibilities but, at the same time, when it came to the concrete practice of action it showed weaknesses and limitations.

> Contradiction and its immanent development form one of the main nodes of the entire Hegelian system, and since this category is the main category, the [dominant essence of] our time, Hegel is [unconditionally] the greatest philosopher of our time, the highest summit of our modern culture, considered only from a theoretical point of view. And it is precisely because he [constituted] this summit; [it is precisely because he understood and, at the same time, indicated the dissolution of this category; it is precisely for these reasons that] he is at the origin of a necessary self-decomposition of modern culture. [In constituting this summit, he has already surpassed theory—in fact, firstly, within theory itself—and postulated] a new practical world; a world that will not be realized, by any means, through formal application and the [diffusion of readymade theories], but only through an [original] action of the autonomous practical spirit. Contradiction is the most intimate essence, not only of all determined or particular theory, but also of theory in general. Thus, the moment [of understanding the theory is also, at the same time, the end of its role as a theory. And that is theory's self-decomposition in a practical, original and new world, in the effective present of freedom]. (Bakunin, 1976a[e], pp. 115–16)

That is, with Hegel, theory reached its peak. With Hegelian philosophy it was possible, in theoretical terms: to understand the past and the present, especially in what concerns the historical and logical understanding of contradictions; to point the way to a harmonious future of freedom; to comprehend the importance and necessity of practice. In short, theory provided the conditions for the knowledge of reality and ended up pointing out the relevance of and indicating the path of practice. Such are its virtues and possibilities.

However, Hegelian philosophy also showed its limits, and even the limits of philosophy itself and of theory in general. This is because the "world of practice" was increasingly announcing itself as something that was beyond the philosophical and theoretical domains. Philosophy and theory were proving to be increasingly insufficient to change the direction of this world. Curiously, Hegel provided the conditions for this problem to be posed, and for a solution to this aforementioned dilemma to be found. The need for a concrete practice of action in order that the practical world could be transformed implied the recognition of the limits of philosophy and with that the inevitability of the "exit from philosophy" by those who intended not only to know the world but primarily to modify it, to transform it.[3] And the solution found in Hegelian philosophy was paradoxically the abandonment of philosophy: "Philosophy itself indicates to us the exit door of philosophy," the abandonment of exclusively theoretical perspectives. Such that, through theory, one discovers the indispensability of giving space to practice, of moving to practice, of admitting the primacy of practice. The effective realization of freedom then becomes perceived as a more practical than theoretical task; and, for that reason, philosophy becomes a dispensable tool (Angaut, 2007a, p. 95).

However, affirming this primacy of practice does not mean a complete abandonment of theory. This should not be discarded but readapted in this perspective—it has to find a new status, a new conception that takes account of these new challenges that have been posed. For that, Weitling's intellectual production, in particular his *Guarantees of Harmony and Freedom*, provides a reference: "when you read the book, you feel that Weitling expresses what he feels, thinks and must think about his condition as a proletarian." His reflections and intellectual productions are interesting because "they are not productions of an erudite and useless theory, but the expression *of a new practice that seeks to rise to consciousness*"; they are "a *practical consciousness* of the present" (Bakunin, 2007 [c], pp. 139–40, emphasis added). Here the sought-after status and conception are obtained. With the primacy of practice, theory is then conceived as a "direct expression of practice that is elevated to self-consciousness" or even as a practical consciousness of the present (Angaut, 2007a, p. 104). Theory has to end in practice; one must "defend practice against any interference from theory," refusing to "mobilize theory for something other than to strengthen a practical engagement" (Angaut, 2009, p. 27).

6.2 RADICALISM AND COMMUNISM

With philosophy showing its insufficiencies and indicating the need and path for its own overcoming, through a practice that found its expression in theory, political doctrines such as political radicalism and communism started receiving greater attention. Both necessary products of modernity finding their justification in society itself, they intend to respond practically to this challenge imposed by the contemporary world and to liberate humanity.

In the case of radicalism, it offers the most appropriate frameworks for conceiving this practice:

> The self-government of the people is the principle that underlies all of the other positions of the radicals, who are concerned with improving schools and promoting the education of the people, because they are convinced that the people cannot govern themselves until they are more mature and autonomous, and that they cannot be elevated to maturity and autonomy except through education. [...] The principal objective of the radicals is the liberation of the people from the tutelage of the great and the rich. (Bakunin, 2007b[e], p. 152, emphasis added)

Here, in general terms, the principle, objective, and strategy of political radicalism, of which Bakunin is a supporter at the time, stand out. The most important concept, which constitutes the radicals' fundamental principle, this historical phenomenon, is the notion of *self-government of the people*, that is, the administration or direction of the people exercised by the people themselves—or as it would be said from the 1960s on, their self-management as a people. The radicals' goal is to find this, their essence, and realize it: popular emancipation, which is the realization of freedom in relation to the holders of political and economic power. Their strategy is mainly in the field of propaganda and education. Their positions must be publicized, schools must be improved, and the people must be widely educated. Promoting maturity and popular autonomy implies freeing the people from the tutelage of those above, ensuring that they can think and act for themselves and promote their own interests.

In the case of communism, it is an essentially practical doctrine that, like others, is the legitimate daughter of true Christianity. Having emanated from the people, containing "highly [...] significant elements" based on the "most sacred rights" and "most human demands," it has been acquiring more and more importance. It is increasingly able to "exercise this great potency, remarkable and even surprisingly active on souls." As a descendant of true Christianity communism has "an unconditional right, because, according to the principles of Christianity itself, everything that opposes the spirit of love must be destroyed." Since communism proposes to break with existing society, seeing in it nothing more than injustice and privilege, its criticism is legitimate insofar as it contains the proposition of erecting another society based on love. Those who call themselves Christians, but are opposed to communism and advocate hatred, are not true Christians (Bakunin, 2007b[e], pp. 151, 159).

Furthermore, it is not only through this affiliation with the spirit of love that communism demonstrates its Christian roots. It is also evident in its defense of the "idea of humanity," that "all men—all, without exception—are brothers" as "the Gospel teaches, and if they love one another, the invisible God and the redemptive and liberating truth are present in them." In other words, the emphasis of original Christianity on the notion of humanity, as well as its opposition to the "isolated and hermetically closed nations of paganism" is assimilated into the communists' denial of individualism and the notion of nationality, understood as the "narrow egoism of nations" (Bakunin, 2007b[e], p. 157).

In both cases, it seems true that

> the isolated man, even if he has beautiful and ethical intentions, cannot take part in the truth if he does not live in community. God is not present in the isolated individual, but only in the community, and thus the virtue of an individual, the living and fruitful virtue, is only possible through the sacred and miraculous bond of love, but in the community. Outside the community, man is nothing; in the community, he is everything. And when the bible speaks of community, it is not at all a matter of communes or narrow, isolated nations, separate from the others; original Christianity knows nothing of national differences, and the community exalted by it is the community of all men, humanity. (Bakunin, 2007b[e], p. 157)

This defense of a single and indivisible humanity, contrary to individualism and narrow nationalism, differs well from the critique of eighteenth-century cosmopolitanism, which distinguished itself for being theoretical and abstract. Contrary to this, "communism does not speak from theory, but from practical instinct, the popular instinct." And for that very reason its positions must be valued (Bakunin, 2007b [e], p. 157). Even so, both in the case of Christianity and communism, this critique of nationality was a necessary step in their trajectory. When Christianity emerged, it had this negative character, which gave it a condition of relative, partial, unilateral truth. Likewise, communism, as a recent phenomenon at that time, also had this character; it rejected nationality as it existed, especially since it did not satisfy its concept, but not as a principle in and of itself. Something similar to what happened with Christianity, when it initially rejected art for seeing in it something inextricably linked to paganism.

Another outstanding factor that provides legitimacy to communism is the fact that it emerged as a practical expression of the people themselves, since "the people [...] have always been the only creative basis on which [...] all dignity, all historical actions, all revolutions that liberated the world were born." In other words, all "that which is foreign to the people, their deeds and their actions" is nothing more than something marked by "impotence." The only way to "effectively create" is "through effective, electric contact with the people." And this is demonstrated by the history of religions and in modern history: "Christ and Luther were born of the people, of the lower people" and "the heroes of the French Revolution" powerfully established "the first foundation of the future temple of freedom and equality" only because "they regenerated themselves in the stormy ocean of popular life."

For these reasons, and because it has spread to various parts of the world, communism can no longer be ignored. Even though it is still "little theoretically and scientifically developed" such that "it is still a long way from having conceived its own principle in its truth and to the full extent of its consequence," communism will have to receive attention from the dominant classes and the states. It could even become a dangerous risk to existing society, if the "privileged and educated classes" do not facilitate its journey with love and sacrifice, recognizing that it has a "historic world mission." And also, if states, due to this legitimacy, do not satisfy its demands (Bakunin, 2007b[e], pp. 156–57).

It is known that "all the power and vitality of a state consists, precisely, in that it maintains itself and can maintain itself in the face of the thousand contingencies of daily life." And that "the State can and must impose itself on all the evils that arise from the evil of some individuals." After all, "the police exist for this, the laws and the courts exist for this, its entire organization exists for this." "A thief, and even a large band of thieves," even though they are "dangerous for more than one individual in the State" is not dangerous "for the State itself, as long as it is a healthy and well-organized body." That is, contingencies in general and crimes in particular are normally contained by a functioning state. They can put some people's lives at stake, but not the State itself.

But it is very different when considering modern doctrines such as radicalism and communism, phenomena that have "their source, not in the caprice, in the ill will of some individuals, but in the deficiencies of the State organism, of the State institutions of a political body." These doctrines can in fact become dangerous for the State. And insofar as their "legitimate claims are not recognized and satisfied by the State" they must not be "repressed by force." In general, when such phenomena and demands arise, the State faces two possibilities: using the "recourse to force" and running the risk of completely dismantling itself, or acceding to demands and "reforming itself peacefully." But the State can also seek ways to undermine the possibilities of these doctrines.

In the case of communism, which supports this position of a single and indivisible humanity, states, even if proclaiming themselves as Christian, stimulate "national sentiment among the people, to the detriment of humanity and love," preaching "hatred and murder in the name of nationality!" They use national sentiment as a way of dividing and opposing members of that same humanity. For this reason, it seems central, as communists have done, to oppose "supposedly Christian governments and all princes and power holders, republicans and monarchists" who claim to profess Christianity. This because "their Christianity is nothing more than an appearance; only its non-Christian elements are really effective" (Bakunin, 2007b[e], pp. 150, 159).

However, even if we must recognize all these merits of communism—the fact that it is a practical doctrine, emanating from the people and descendant of Christianity, and that its demands, in particular of humanity/community, are legitimate—it cannot be uncritically endorsed. Bakunin makes this very explicit when he states: "We are not communists; we could not live [...] in a society organized according to the plans of a Weitling." This is because the future advocated by the communists "would not be a free society, [...] an effective, living society of free men, but an insufferable constraint." Freedom would definitely not be its foundation. This society would be, more correctly, "a flock gathered by the force of beasts that would have in view only material things and would know nothing of what is spiritual and of the great pleasures of the spirit." Such a society "can never be realized," as human needs are material and spiritual. And in view of the "sacred power of truth, inherent in all men, in a more or less conscious way," it is possible to emphasize that the self-government of the people, responding to these material and spiritual demands of humanity, is still the best answer to modern dilemmas (Bakunin, 2007b[e], pp. 150–51).

NOTES

1   From this period, Bakunin's main writing is "Communism," of which Angaut's new translation into French (Bakunin, 2007b [e]) was taken as the basis for the quotations. The quotations from Bakunin's documents found on the IISH CD-ROM (Bakunin, 2000a) have been translated from the French texts.

2   Cf. Bruno Bauer in *The Trumpet of the Last Judgement...*: "The clique of young Hegelians would love to tell us that Hegel was absorbed only in considerations of theory, and that he never thought of extending the theory to praxis. As if Hegel had not attacked religion with hellish fury, as if he had not gone to war against the existing order. His theory is, in itself, praxis, and that is why it is the most dangerous, the most vast and the most destructive. It is the revolution itself" (*apud* Angaut, 2007a, p. 91). When discussing an article by Feuerbach in the beginning of 1843, Bakunin considers that his expectation to safeguard theory against practice doesn't make sense. For him, Feuerbach's text is an "attempt to save theory, that which must, in its totality, abdicate itself; that is its only salvation." And there was no point in recommending practice in theory: "practice *within* theory; that is the biggest contradiction" (Bakunin, 2007[c], p. 139).

3   It seems inevitable to compare this passage with Marx, in particular in his "Theses on Feuerbach," written in 1845, two years after these contributions by Bakunin. Marx's theses 8 and 11 dialogue with what Bakunin maintained between 1842 and 1843. Thesis 8: "Social life is essentially practical. All the mysteries that seduce theory into mysticism find their rational solution in human praxis and in the understanding of this praxis." Thesis 11: "Philosophers have only interpreted the world in different ways; the question, however, is to transform it" (Marx, 1845). Marx, like Bakunin, highlights in these theses the role of practice in human life and also points out the need to cross the frontiers of knowledge of reality, moving on to the question of how to transform it. However, even with such similarities, both have different positions about philosophy. In 1843 and 1844, Marx intends to effectively perform philosophy, as pointed out in *Critique of Hegel's Philosophy of Right*: "Philosophy cannot be realized without the supersumption of the proletariat, the proletariat cannot be fulfilled without the effectiveness of philosophy" (Marx, 2010, p. 157). Bakunin, distinctly, indicates the limits of philosophy and proposes that it be abandoned in favour of a new type of theory (cf., also: Angaut, 2007a, pp. 92–93).

PART II

REVOLUTIONARY PAN-SLAVISM
(1844–63)

CHAPTER 7

"FREEDOM, EQUALITY, AND FRATERNITY OF NATIONS": REVOLUTIONARY PAN-SLAVISM (1843-63)

This chapter discusses Bakunin's political-intellectual trajectory from 1843 to 1863, divided into six parts: 1) Socialism and the Revolutionary Movement in the Switzerland-Belgium-France triangle (1843-45); 2) The Russian-Polish Cause in Paris and Brussels (1845-48); 3) The February Revolution and Internationalization (1848); 4) Slavism and National Liberation in the Austria-Poland-Prussia Triangle (1848-49); 5) Prisons, Exile, and Escape (1849-61); 6) Resumption of the Slavic Cause in London and Frustration with the Polish Insurrection (1862-63). Finally, in a seventh part, it presents important elements for the understanding of Bakuninian political theory during the period in question.

7.1 SOCIALISM AND THE REVOLUTIONARY MOVEMENT IN THE SWITZERLAND-BELGIUM-FRANCE TRIANGLE (1843-45)

It was still 1843 and Bakunin was still in Switzerland. Before the last part of his article "Communism" was published, Weitling ended up in prison due to a new book that maintained that Jesus, besides being Mary's illegitimate son, was the first communist in history. Weitling, accused by the Swiss government of violating political and religious orthodoxy, had all his papers seized and Bakunin was identified as a member of his circle of relations.[1] Fearing repression, Bakunin, although unaware of the machinations running against him and that was being articulated by the Swiss and Russian authorities, left Zurich. He remained however in Switzerland: he lived in Nyon and then in Bern, where he stayed until the beginning of 1844 and met the Vogt family, with whom he maintained ties until the end of his life.

In February, Bakunin received a summons to return to Russia immediately but decided not to. He was aware that this was most likely an irreversible decision for life, differing from the one that had been made in Berlin. After passing through Baden, he headed for Brussels with his friend Reichel, where he stayed for the next few months.

The period in Brussels, though brief, was marked by decisive contact with Poles, among them the Polish democrat and historian Joachim Lelewel, who had participated in the 1830 revolution—in which the Poles demanded Poland's national liberation from Russia and were brutally repressed for it. His ideas of a "democratic Slavism with a frankly revolutionary inclination" had been set out in an 1832 manifesto (Hepner, 1950, pp. 225-26). This contact—which Nettlau (1976, p. 198) characterized as "a dismal event in Bakunin's life" that would cause him to fall "from the heights of internationalism [...] to the depths of nationalism"—was decisive, as it introduced

Bakunin to the question of the Polish national struggle, which corresponded to his democratic convictions and was the prelude to his engagement in the Slavic cause.

Bakunin had visited Paris in March 1844, impressed by the French revolutionary atmosphere and his reunion with Ruge, Herwegh, Vasili Botkin (former companion of the Stankevitch Circle), and Grigori Tolstoy (a liberal Russian aristocrat he met in Dresden). In search of a more politically stimulating environment he moved with Reichel to the French capital, where he lived from July 1844 to December 1847 (Carr, 1961, pp. 129, 131-32; Leier, 2006, p. 107; Bakunin, 1976b[e], pp. 53-54).

Still under the July Monarchy, France in the 1840s was, from a political point of view, a bomb about to explode. That interlude between the revolutions of 1830 and 1848, in which the bourgeoisie sought to establish itself definitively as a ruling class, strengthened social conflicts and provided immense politicization in which the defenses of the republic, democracy and socialism had a prominent place. In this movement, the masses of workers continued to be prominent actors, often relating with philosophers and thinkers from other social classes and articulating with them publicly and/or in secret societies. All layers of French society realized that a social revolution was imminent.

Luís Filipe's accession to the throne in 1830 marked the end of a stage of social conflict in France. With it the bourgeoisie gained strength and the workers were properly contained. According to Samis (2011, pp. 47-48) "there is no doubt that the July Monarchy is the representation of the bourgeoisie in power." However, it was not the bourgeoisie as a whole but particularly the financial bourgeoisie: "bankers, speculators of the stock exchange, owners of the [coal] mines, iron, forest exploiters and even large landowners." The majority of the industrial bourgeoisie—as well as small producers, workers, and peasants—remained without power and political representation in the government.

Until the mid-1840s, France had invested heavily in its economic development, which was accompanied by an intense process of industrialization and urbanization. The productive and commercial infrastructure, as well as transport (with the creation of channels and railways) were widely developed; new mines and industries were created in the cities; the steam engine contributed an important part of it all. Countryside residents migrated to the cities and there was an intense demographic growth; the population was becoming younger. In the cities, working and housing conditions were very precarious: low wages, strenuous hours, lack of basic sanitation, diseases... The social camp reconstituted itself, with workers gaining more and more protagonism and class consciousness, according to the mobilizations—which include insurrections, organization of mutual aid, and *Carbonari* societies—and repressions. The picture of the conflicts got worse with the economic crisis that started in 1846; insufficiency in the wheat harvest and increases in the price of bread, a plague impacting potatoes, recession in industry and transport and state indebtedness. Thus, a picture was formed that would point to the revolutions of 1848 (Samis, 2011, pp. 35–49; Beer, 2006, pp. 457–63; Hobsbawm, 2004b, pp. 409–23).

Bakunin knew this context, and when he arrived in Paris, he was determined to join the revolutionary movement. After all, it was time to start taking advantage of that admired practice, characteristic of the French. During that period he made contact with members of the local political circles representing a wide range of concepts ranging from the constitutionalists to the socialists, including Republicans and Democrats. Among them the following stand out: Lamennais, George Sand, Pierre Leroux, Étienne Cabet, Ferdinand Flocon, Louis Blanc, Victor Considerant, Pascal Duprat, Félix Pyat, Victor Schoelcher, Jules Michelet, and Edgar Quinet.[2]

Still in 1844, Bakunin met Marx, who had recently moved to Paris with a view to publishing the *Deutsch-Französische Jahrbücher* [*Franco-German Annals*] with Ruge.[3] With only one issue published at the beginning of the year the magazine ceased to exist, and Marx then joined the *Vorwärts!* [*Onward!*] newspaper, around which a group that approached Bakunin and introduced him to the Parisian socialist media was connected (Carr, 1961, pp. 132–37).

Almost 30 years later, in 1871, Bakunin recalled that moment, writing about Marx:

I met him for the first time in Paris in 1844. I had already emigrated. We were quite friendly. He was, at that time, much more advanced, as he remains today, not more advanced, but incomparably more learned than me. I knew nothing, then, of political economy; I still hadn't gotten rid of metaphysical abstractions, and my socialism was only instinctual. He, although younger than me, was already an atheist, a learned materialist, and a circumspect socialist. It was precisely at this time that he developed the first fundamentals of his current system. We saw each other quite often because I respected him a lot for his knowledge and for his passionate and serious devotion, although always mixed with personal vanity, to the cause of the proletariat, and I eagerly sought conversation with him, always instructive and spiritual, when he was not inspired by petty hatred, which, unfortunately, happened all too often. Therefore, there was never any intimacy between us. Our temperaments didn't match. He called me a sentimental idealist, and he was right; I called him a perfidious and hypocritical narcissist, and I was also right. (Bakunin, 2014h[e], pp. 240–41)

Bakunin maintained this admiration for Marx's thought and intellectual production throughout his life, as well as this personal antipathy, which would be accentuated according to the intensification of political conflicts and the spread of calumnies about Bakunin. Even so, there seems to be no doubt that already in 1844 Marx had some influence on Bakunin's positions.[4] However, as Nettlau (1964, p. 37) and several other researchers point out, the main link of the period in Paris was certainly that with Pierre-Joseph Proudhon, a self-taught French socialist who by then already had some notoriety.

Like Weitling, Proudhon was a legitimate child of the people. Of poor origin, he had worked as a printer and in 1838 obtained a scholarship to resume his studies at the Academy of Besançon. His 1840 book *Qu'est-ce que la Propriété?* [*What Is Property?*]—a critique of capitalist private property and the exploitation of labour, which, elaborated through a theory of the social force of collective labour, concluded that "property is theft" due to misappropriation of the surplus of collective labour— exerted a significant influence on progressive European circles, having been considered by Marx as the "first decisive analysis of truth, relentless and at the same time scientific" about property (Marx and Engels, 2003, p. 43) and preceded the rupture between the two that would occur in 1846.

This book was followed by two other memoirs on property—published in 1841 and 1842, responding to the criticisms of Blanqui and a Fourierist opponent, respectively—and the book *De la Création de l'Ordre dans l'Humanité* [*From the Creation of Order in Humanity*], from 1843—in which Proudhon sought to establish the foundations of a social science capable of contributing to the understanding of society, in terms of genesis and structure, mobilizing Fourier's serial method and Comte's philosophy of history.

Bakunin's relationship with Proudhon began in 1844 in Paris and continued until the Frenchman's death in 1865. It played a central role in Bakunin's political development, both for the heated and long-lasting face-to-face debates and for reading his works.[5] Until the 1870s, Proudhon would remain an unavoidable reference for Bakunin, who, despite objecting to him with harsh criticisms in his later life—such as, for example, that he "remained an incorrigible idealist all his life" and that he remained in "perpetual contradiction"—never failed to recognize that he "was a great revolution- ary thinker, who rendered immense services to the development of socialist ideas," in addition to "understanding freedom" much better than his authoritarian adversaries and, therefore, demonstrating himself a prominent anti-statist, markedly after his experience as a deputy in 1848 (Bakunin, 2014b[e], pp. 91–93; Berthier, 2008, pp. 113–23).

However, this was not yet Bakunin's position in his Parisian period. At that time both met, became affectionate and influenced each other. Proudhon knew of Hegel through Bakunin, even though he never was nor pretended to be Hegelian. Bakunin was exposed to Proudhon's criticisms of political economy, private property, and the idea of God. They discussed theoretical-philosophical foundations for understanding reality, conjunctural and structural analyses of society, and political perspectives for revolutionary transformation. In this respect, the admiration that Proudhon had come to have in those years for the mutualists of Lyon who had led insurrections in 1831 and 1834 was certainly felt in his arguments.

In December 1844, Bakunin was sentenced in Russia for noncompliance with the return order. The tsar condemned him to the loss of the title of nobility, confiscation of property and deportation to Siberia, where he was to dedicate himself to forced labour. Even if it was not Bakunin's desire, the possibility of returning to his homeland was ended.

7.2 THE RUSSIAN-POLISH CAUSE IN PARIS AND BRUSSELS (1845–48)

In France, Bakunin hoped to find the possibilities for revolutionary practice. But if there was much willingness on his part to do so, there were also difficulties in consolidating ties and giving political concreteness to this project. Even the attempt to link in 1845 with Freemasonry—to which Bakunin associated himself through the Scottish lodge of the Grand Orient of Paris, hoping to enjoy the relations with progressive members—did not bring the desired fruits (Grawitz, 1990, pp. 121–22).

In the "Confession," Bakunin recalls that period in France:

> My life in Paris was hard, very hard, sir! Not so much because of the misery, which I endured with indifference, but because I had finally awakened from the delirium of youth and fantastic hopes. Suddenly, I found myself in a foreign country, in an atmosphere without moral warmth, without family, relatives, without a field of action, without a job and without the slightest hope for a better future. Having detached myself from my homeland and ended any possibility of return, I was unable to become German or French; on the contrary, *the longer I stayed abroad, the more deeply I felt that I was a Russian and that I would never cease to be one.* (Bakunin, 1976b[e], pp. 59–60, emphasis added)

In addition to failing to connect with Parisian revolutionaries, Bakunin had other issues that concerned him. Not only the lack of financial resources and the condemnation in Russia, but also the restriction of contacts with other Russians, the distance and lack of communication with his family that in 1845 would turn into a new rupture with his father, into hatred for his mother and into estrangement from his brothers (Bakunin, 45001 [c]). In some way, this picture resulted in a progressive reinforcement of his Russian identity, which seems to have been strengthened with the arrival in Paris of Herzen, Ogarev, and Turgenev, and with the presence of another Russian, ex-member of the Moscow veterans' circle Nikolai Sazonov (Carr, 1961, pp. 142–45).

Added to this background were the events linked to Poland and the relationships forged with Polish immigrants. These, in particular Lelewel, had introduced Bakunin to the Polish question during his time in Brussels. Poland, which had been invaded and divided by the empires of Russia, Austria, and Prussia, completely ending its independence in 1795, had been a subjugated nation for years. Since then, there had been several struggles in favour of independence and self-determination, which culminated in an insurrection in 1830:

Like the rest of Europe, Poland was also hit by waves of nationalism and romanticism, and in November 1830 it promoted an insurrection to free itself from Russia [which had taken over most of its territory]. Initially an ill-planned attempt at a *coup d'état* by the Warsaw cadets, similar to the Decembrist Revolt of 1825, it turned into a full-blown revolt when rank-and-file workers and soldiers, arising from the peasantry, took up arms and gave them to the people. These few conspirators quickly found themselves at the forefront of a spontaneous militia of 30,000 members. Soon after, Poland declared its independence. The tsar's reaction was fierce and resolute. Nicholas I sent in the Russian army with orders to crush the revolt decisively. But [...] it took the army nine months to suppress the insurrection. The brutal consequence shocked much of Europe and confirmed Nicholas I as the leader of the reaction and the exterminator of nationalities. (Leier, 2006, p. 114, square brackets added)

In the mid-1840s, Europe still felt the effects of this process very emphatically, and in progressive circles Poland was considered a symbol of resistance (Hepner, 1950, pp. 218–20). Complemented by the previously acquired political conceptions, such a framework—involving the search for revolutionary practice, lack of integration with the Paris radicals, reinforcement of Russian identity, knowledge of the Polish issue and Polish immigrants, among which the idea of Poland's "national independence" prevailed (Hepner, 1950, p. 219)—offered Bakunin the conditions for his first practical engagement: the cause of the Poles, which would soon become the Russian-Polish cause and finally the cause of the Slavs. Thus, the main features of his "revolutionary pan-Slavism" would be forged.[6]

Opposing a position manifested in his youth,[7] Bakunin was in favour of Poland's cause in 1845, although only briefly. In a letter written to the Republican newspaper *La Réforme*, published in January of that year, Bakunin demonstrates publicly, protesting for the first time against his condemnation in Russia, advocating Poland's independence and denouncing the Russian government, which he considers an obstacle to Polish democracy (Bakunin, 45001[e]).

Regarding the different currents that advocated for the liberation of Poland, Bakunin remained closer to the "radical current" led by Lelewel. Even so, the position defended in that letter to *La Réforme* had a positive impact, even among members of other currents; among them Prince Adam Czartoryski, leader of the "conservative current," and poet Adam Mickiewicz, leader of the "messianic current," who tried unsuccessfully to attract Bakunin to his mystical federalist circle (Angaut, 2009, pp. 26–27; Nettlau, 1964, p. 38).

Bakunin's position was strengthened in early 1846 by the intensification of the struggles of the Polish resistance: in Krakow, the rebels demanded the liberation of Prussian and Austrian Poland; in Galicia, serfs rebelled against their masters. Recalling these facts and the consequences they had in Paris's radical circles, Bakunin puts in the "Confession":

> The Poznan projects, the attempts made in the kingdom of Poland, the Krakow uprising and the events in Galicia surprised me, at least, as much as everyone; the impression that these events produced in Paris was unimaginable: for two or three days the entire population lived on the street; people talked to each other without knowing each other, all demanding, all waiting, with feverish impatience, for news from Poland. This sudden awakening, this general movement of spirits and passions, also took possession of me; I, in turn, had the impression of awakening, and decided, whatever the cost, to get out of my inaction and play an active part in the events that were being prepared. (Bakunin, 1976b[e], pp. 62–63)

That was, in addition to the *La Réforme* article, Bakunin's first experience with a concrete action, and there were two measures taken to strengthen it. The first was to send a letter to the newspaper *Le Constitutionnel*, which was published in March 1846, in which he devoted himself entirely to denouncing Russia's role in the oppression of Poland (Bakunin, 46001 [e]). Its text is a protest against the political violence carried out by the Russian government with a view to extinguishing the Polish language, submitting Poland to the laws of Russia and imposing a state religion on the Poles, an issue that is discussed more specifically. The second was to go to Versailles to meet the members of the Polish democratic party and seek an agreement to act together. As he points out, he proposed an action among Russians living in the region of Poland with a view to a "Russian revolution and the federative republic of all Slavic States; federative, in any case, only from an administrative point of view, but centralized from a political point of view" (Bakunin, 1976b[e], p. 64).

For him, it was then the time to try to deepen political relations and to be able to articulate from France the Russian-Polish resistance, which became a priority between 1845 and 1847. Corroborating this position in an August 1847 correspondence, Bakunin (47001[c], p. 4) emphasized: "I live almost exclusively among Poles, I put body and soul into the Russian-Polish movement." However, this articulation was not easy to achieve. As much as the *Le Constitutionnel* article had some repercussions, there were no allies and not even an action plan. In addition, Bakunin (1976b[e], p. 64) had problems of understanding with the Poles of Versailles, due to an exclusive and narrow nationalism advocated by them, and a probable distrust expressed by them (Carr, 1961, pp. 148–49).[8]

In spite of this, in November 1847, Bakunin was invited by two young Poles to speak at the banquet commemorating the seventeenth anniversary of the 1830 uprising, which would take place that same month in Paris and would be chaired by radical deputy Hippolyte Vavin. Bakunin accepted the invitation, prepared his speech in three days and delivered it on that occasion, his first public speech. Published the following month in *La Réforme*, the "Discourse: 17th Anniversary of the Polish Revolution" takes up and deepens the themes of the writings of 1845 and 1846. Recovering aspects of Slavic history, Bakunin draws a parallel between the domination of the Russian people and Poland, showing how both were victims of the same executioner of the peoples' freedom: Nicholas I's "official Russia." He considers Russians and Poles part of the same people, of the same nation, of the same race, and points out the need for a Russian-Polish alliance to combat European despotism in favour of democracy.

The speech, ended with the words *Jeszcze Polska nie zginela!* [Poland is not dead yet!], was acclaimed by the 1,500 present, and placed Bakunin's name not only among the great Russian Slavists but among the greatest revolutionary speakers in nineteenth-century Europe, a position that would be consolidated in the following years (Bakunin, 47003[e]).[9] It cost him the expulsion from France, requested by the Russian ambassador, who took the opportunity to spread the rumour that Bakunin was a provocateur of his government. It remained for Bakunin to return to Brussels, where he stayed from December 1847 to February 1848 (Bakunin, 47003[c]).

During this second stay in Brussels, Bakunin (1976b[e], p. 66) found Lelewel again and resumed contacts with the Polish immigration. As he wrote in the "Confession", he "frequented aristocratic circles more" and "found himself at the center of Jesuit propaganda"—he had met General Jan Skrzynecki (who had also participated in the 1830 Insurrection), Count Xavier de Merode, and Count Charles de Montalembert. This was certainly a conservative circle, and as much as Bakunin's ties were ephemeral and without further continuity, they have something to say. If on the one hand it seems an exaggeration to state, as Carr (1961, p. 154) and Grawitz (1990, p. 133) do, that in Brussels Bakunin abandoned the communists to articulate with the extreme right, on the other, it seems it was correct to understand that to some extent and as will be discussed below, the banner of national liberation raised by Bakunin flirted on some occasions with nationalism. In these circumstances, it was marked by multi-class, anti-democratic, exclusivist, or even conservative traits.

Bakunin received another invitation from the Poles, this time to speak at a banquet organized by them in commemoration of the anniversary of the Decembrist Uprising. In what was his second public speech Bakunin resumed in February 1848 the theme of the previous speech, pointing to the liberation of the Slavs (with a focus on the Russians and Poles) as the key to the ending of oppression in the Western world. But Bakunin's difficulties in establishing more organic ties with the Poles continued and were now compounded by rumours from France that he was an agent of the Russian government (Bakunin, 1976b[e], pp. 65–67; Carr, 1961, pp. 151–52).

Another reunion in Brussels occurred with Marx, who lived there since 1845 after an expulsion from France. Since then, Marx had established with Engels the foundations of his historical materialism in *The German Ideology*—which, however, would only come to light in the 1930s—criticized Proudhon's economic theory in *The*

Poverty of Philosophy, and worked on the writing and publication of the *Communist Manifesto*. Marx was a member of the League of Communists and with Lelewel made up the vice-presidency of the Democratic Association. Bakunin attended two meetings of this association, which were important as they allowed him to get to know the German communists and Marx himself a little more closely.

The experiment did not have good results. Commenting on it with Herwegh, Bakunin wrote:

> The Democratic [Association] Alliance could really lead to something good, but these Germans—the worker Bornstädt, Marx and Engels, especially Marx—are still here, as usual, creating disasters. Vanity, hatred, gossip, *arrogance in theory and cowardice in practice*; reflections on life, action and simplicity, and a total lack of life, action, and simplicity. [...] Feuerbach is a *bourgeois* and this term "bourgeois" has become a slogan that is repeated until exhaustion—all of them being, from head to toe, viscerally provincial petty bourgeois. In two words, nothing but lies and stupidity, stupidity and lies. [...] I remain aloof and have explained to you very firmly that I will not join your association of communist workers and that I do not want to have anything in common with it. (Bakunin, 47011[c], pp. 1–2, emphasis added)

In order to point out the similarities and differences that existed between Bakunin and Marx in the passage of 1847 to 1848, it is necessary to not anticipate the polemics of the 1860s and 1870s, as Leier to some extent does (2006, pp. 118–30). At that time, Bakunin was far from being anarchist, and his positions would change much more than those of Marx. It is therefore inadequate to interpret this relationship in the key of a conflict between "anarchism" and "Marxism."

During the Brussels period, there were differences of opinion between them in the personal and theoretical-political fields. Bakunin considered Marx vain, arrogant, and hypocritical, and accused him of raising himself by the destructive criticism of others and attacking those who refused to associate with or submit to him. He believed that Marx was running away from revolutionary practice, hiding behind his intellectual production. Marx's judgments on Bakunin were not positive either. Moreover, even if they pursued the same goal—the ending of oppression by revolutionary means—both had different readings of reality and their political projects were very different. Bakunin was approximating a revolutionary pan-Slavic, whose focus was on the practice of the Slavic people's national liberation struggle to establish political federalism in Slavic countries (Central and Eastern Europe). Marx advocated a statist communism, whose focus was on the production of a critical theoretical tool that offered conditions of liberation to the (mainly urban-industrial) proletariat, aiming at change through the conquest of the State initiated in the most advanced countries of Western Europe.[10]

According to Leier (2006, p. 130), the differences between Bakunin and Marx in the context of the Peoples' Spring can be noticed in the direction they give to the course of their lives: "In 1848, their differences of theory, personality, and philosophy led them to different paths. As Europe boiled over, Bakunin threw himself at the barricades of Paris and Dresden, while Marx began his long journey at the British Museum."

7.3 THE FEBRUARY REVOLUTION AND INTERNATIONALIZATION (1848)

In February, the revolution broke out in Paris, giving way to the aspirations of the population for greater freedom and social change. Within the framework of the economic crisis and the escalation of social conflicts described above, the February Revolution began with the government banning a banquet on 22 February, 1848 and the respective resistance of the dissatisfied population. For two days, there was hard fighting in the streets and, following a massacre of hundreds of demonstrators, the National Guard sympathized with the insurgents.

As Leier (2006, pp. 131–33) points out, "on February 24, workers, artisans, radicals, democrats and middle-class republicans declared the end of the monarchy and proclaimed the Second Republic." It was the end of the July Monarchy and the reign of Louis Philip. Revolutionary workers and bourgeois "held elections with universal male suffrage," "abolished the death penalty and declared work for all as an essential right that the government had to maintain"; moreover "they organized a popular militia, headed by Marc Caussidière, to replace the police and defend the revolution."

Thirsty for action, Bakunin decided to leave Brussels and join the uprising in Paris—it was finally time for revolutionary action. His excitement was such that, the train having left him at the border with France as the railway had been destroyed, Bakunin walked 200 kilometers over three days to reach Paris, which occurred on 26 February, when the barricades were still standing. Profoundly impressed by what he was witnessing, he placed himself "alongside the extreme left," more specifically in the Caussidière militia (Hepner, 1950, p. 213).[11] He participated frenetically in barricades, demonstrations, meetings, and he met the French workers, who made a deep impression on him, as he reported in his "Confession":

In every street, practically everywhere, the barricades rose up like mountains and reached the rooftops, and on them, among stones and broken furniture [...], were the workers with their picturesque blouses, dirty with gunpowder and armed to the teeth. [...] For more than a week I was living with the workers in the barracks on Tournon Street. [...] So I had the opportunity to see the workers and study them from morning till night. I assure you, sir, never and nowhere in any other social class have I found such noble abnegation, such truly touching integrity, and such delicate manners and kindly joy united to such heroism, as among those simple and uncultured people, who were and always will be worth a thousand times more than their bosses! What most draws attention to them is their deep instinct for discipline; in their barracks there could be no established order, no laws, no coercion, but it pleased God that any regular soldier could obey so accurately, could guess so well the desires of his chiefs and keep order as strictly as these free men; they asked for orders, they demanded chiefs, they obeyed meticulously, with passion; in their painful service for whole days they endured hunger and were no less kind for it, they were always cheerful. If these people, if these French workers had found a chief who was worthy of them, capable of understanding and loving them, this chief, together with them, could have performed miracles. Sir, I cannot give you an exact account of that month I spent in Paris, for it was a month of drunkenness of the soul. It was not only me who was drunk, but everyone: some with terror, others with ecstasy, with foolish hopes. I would get up at four or five in the morning and go to sleep at two; I would stand all day long, going to all assemblies, meetings, clubs, parades, walks or demonstrations; in a word, I absorbed in all my senses and in all my pores the drunkenness of the revolutionary atmosphere. It was a festival with no beginning and no end; I saw everyone and saw no one, for each individual was lost in the same innumerable and wandering crowd; I spoke to everyone, without remembering my words or those of others, for attention was absorbed at every step by the new events, the new things, the unexpected news. (Bakunin, 1976b[e], pp. 67–69)

This was Bakunin's first armed insurrectionary-revolutionary experiment, whose prolonged relationship with workers would directly affect his political perspectives. The "people" returned again to the scene and became understood as an indispensable actor in confrontations for the freedom of peoples. As he wrote in a new letter to the *La Réforme* journal published in March: yesterday's utopia—the complete democratization of France and Europe—was, then, the only possible alternative (Bakunin, 48002[e], p. 1).

Bakunin began to support the demands of the French insurgents, who proclaimed the need to internationalize the revolution. After all, he advocated a *permanent revolution*.[12] This should, according to them, come from France and lay the foundations for a complete democratization of Europe, involving Italy, Germany, Poland, and even Russia. And indeed, as Berthier (2010, vol. 2, p. 12) explains, the French Peoples' Spring was spreading rapidly and, beyond the social traits it carried in France, was acquiring national characteristics in other countries. "The Italians expel the Austrians from Milan and Venice. Mazzini proclaims the republic in Rome. The majority of Italian sovereigns grant constitutions (the constitution of Ferdinand II on

February 10, 1848, and that of Pius IX on March 14)." Austria, which had become the centre of conservative Europe at the Vienna Congress was in 1848 bound by a "legacy of the Old Regime: the national minorities—Czech in Bohemia, Polish in Galicia, Serbs in the Danube region, Romanians in Transylvania, Italians in Trieste and Trentino—questioning the domination to which they were subjected." Metternich, the protagonist of Europe's absolutist reaction, is forced to resign thanks to a radicalized mobilization in Vienna. In Germany, "the revolutionary movements in the South lead to the abdication of King Louis I of Bavaria; political freedoms are established in Saxony, in Württemberg, in Hesse-Nassau." To the north, the movements reach "Frankfurt, Hamburg, Bremen, and Prussia. A parliament is convened in Frankfurt to discuss the future of Germany."

Still in France, Bakunin was informed in March 1848 of some of these developments. He then planned to go to Poznan, where a Polish National Committee had been established. From there, he intended to seek a means to contribute to this internationalization of the revolution by mobilizing Poland and, through it, Russia. Supported by Flocon in the provisional government and by Caussidière, he obtained money and two passports (one of them false) and left at the end of March 1848. He would stay, in the end, for one month in Paris.

He passed through Frankfurt and other surrounding cities and went on to Berlin. But soon after his arrival he was arrested, as the Russian authorities in Germany somehow became aware of his plans. They proposed an agreement: Bakunin would be released if he accepted, instead of going to Poznan, where the Polish resistance would be against the Prussian government, to go to Breslau, where it would be directed at the Russian and Austrian governments. Bakunin accepted and, left in Leipzig by the police, moved on to Breslávia, arriving in May and establishing himself there. There, he was disappointed not only by the Germans who, he thought, talked a lot and acted little, but also by the news coming from France, reporting the conservative positions adopted by the provisional government against the workers. He tried to connect with the Poles but their mistrust, still because of the rumour that he might be a Russian agent, complicated his plans (Carr, 1961, pp. 158–63). Bakunin (1976b[e], p. 81) eventually preferred to accompany the German democrats, among whom he enjoyed a certain prestige, for, in his own words, "it was only through my influence that my old friend Arnold Ruge was elected to the National Assembly in Frankfurt as a member of parliament for Breslávia."

But the South still seemed to offer certain hopes. As Carr recalls (1961, p. 163), "it was only in Austria that the revolution was still progressing" as the popular uprisings of March and May in Vienna demonstrated. Moreover, "Hungary was practically independent," the "Slavs of the empire were restless," "Jelačić insurged the Croats against their Hungarian masters," and "in Prague, a Czech National Committee was taking over the functions of a provisional government"; in other words, it seemed the "time for the Slavs to unite."

7.4 SLAVISM AND NATIONAL LIBERATION IN THE
AUSTRIA-POLAND-RUSSIA TRIANGLE (1848–49)

With this intention of strengthening the union of the Slavic peoples, a Czech committee had initiated the articulation of a Slavic congress, which was to take place in
Prague in the first days of June 1848. With no prospects in Breslávia, Bakunin decided
to participate in this event, arriving in Prague at the beginning of the sessions. The
Slavic Congress, chaired by František Palacký, brought together 340 Slavic delegates—
including Czechs, Slovaks, Moravians, Silesians, Ruthenes, Poles, Croats, Serbs, and
Dalmatians; Bakunin was one of the two Russians present—from 2–12 June, 1848. It
was a pioneering event, which brought Slavs together to discuss the various oppressions they had been subjected to and to find possible ways out for the future; it would
later become known as the First Pan-Slavic Congress.

In the first moment, the congress allowed Bakunin (1976b[e], p. 82) to meet other
Slavs: "until then—with the exception of the Poles and certainly the Russians—I had
not met any Slavs." It was also useful for him to attend the emotional meeting of his
Slavic compatriots. "It seemed that the members of the same family [...] were gathered
for the first time after a great and painful separation. They cried, they laughed, they
hugged." But then, the enormous cultural and political differences forged over
centuries made themselves felt. They were evident in the historical and conjunctural
characterizations, as well as in the propositions and paths conceived for the solution
of the problems that the congress intended to solve. The Slavs, despite the hopeful
impression caused by the meeting, were deeply marked by discord, and this
complicated any communion in terms of analysis, projects, or interests.

Grawitz offers some elements for understanding this complex and conflicting
chess:

> The Poles, who were the most nationalistic and ambitious, wanted to take over
> the leadership of a Slavic federation, eliminating its enemies and rivals:
> Germany, Austria, and Russia. [...] Many Ukrainians also wanted to separate
> from Russia. The southern Slavs understood the Slovenes, who had never had
> autonomy, and, Catholics, were more or less integrated with Austria and Italy.
> Croatia was annexed to Hungary in 1102, while Bulgaria, Serbia and Bosnia,
> which had been subjected to the Greek Orthodox religion, became part of the
> Ottoman Empire after the 14th and 15th centuries. The Russians' advance
> towards the Black Sea raised hopes of being freed from the yoke of the Turks.
> But the dream of a great Serbia clashed with that of a great Croatia; Serbs and
> Croats competed in Bosnia and Herzegovina, composed of Muslims, Orthodox
> Greeks and Roman Catholics. The Slovaks agreed to speak Latin, the official
> language of the Kingdom of Hungary, but not the language of their enemies,
> the Magyars, who were allies of the Poles and together distrusted the other

Slavs. Finally, the Czechs of Bohemia and Moravia were part of the German Confederation, but as a true German nationalist State emerged, they also sought to regain their independence. In this imbroglio of languages, religions, traditions, past, influences, interests and hopes, how can a common will be recovered? (Grawitz, 1990, p. 145)

In political terms, such differences in projects and interests help to explain, to some extent, the positions that were adopted at the Slavic Congress. According to Berthier (2010, vol. 2, pp. 76–79) and Cipko (1990, p. 4), the meeting was mostly marked by nationalist and conservative positions. On the one hand, it was intended to promote the interest of one nation over another—the Czechs, for example, who made up the largest delegation, wanted to promote their hegemony and impose their language and nationality on the other Slavs. On the other hand, it was to find a solution to the Slav question in the major empires, with two tendencies being accepted: to transform the Austrian monarchy into a Slavic monarchy with Czech hegemony, and the other, to bring together the Slavic lands of Austria and Russia, and even to place the fate of all Slavs in the hands of the latter (cf., also: Hepner, 1950, pp. 250–56).

For Bakunin the congress and these positions had ambiguous impacts and directions. Even immersed in so many conflicts, the Slavs showed themselves to be part of the same nationality, the same family; and, at the same time, they seemed to embody an enormous potential in revolutionary and democratic terms. This, to some extent, relativized the Parisian experience of February for Bakunin (1976b[e], p. 82): "In Paris, I had allowed myself to be dragged along by democratic exaltation, by the heroism of the popular masses, but here I found myself seduced by the warmth and sincerity of this I but profound Slavic feeling. I felt a Slavic heart beat in me." This provided support for an expansion of the horizons of the Russian-Polish cause, making it something more comprehensive and ambitious: the Slav cause.

For Bakunin, a project for the liberation of the Slavs required working hard to resolve the differences and minimize the conflicts mentioned above, and also to find appropriate ways of doing so. In the meantime, the discussions at the congress had been taking place, on the contrary, in order to exalt national particularisms and to find in the greatest enemies, the empires, the solution to the Slavic dilemma. Bakunin disagreed because he understood that the Slavs were one people, and that their liberation was one of solidarity. For him, one nation, one "race" would only be free with the liberation of all the others. It was not a question of discussing who should dominate, but of putting domination itself in check. And there was another problem: the discussions seemed to him to be very impractical, not pointing to directions capable of realizing any project.

Bakunin (1976b[e], pp. 111, 115)—who on that occasion stressed his "need for movement and action" under the banner "love of freedom and invincible hatred of all oppression"—maintained that the freedom of the Slavic peoples could only be achieved through a revolutionary practice in which all Slavs had to be allies, and empires, especially those of Austria and Russia, had to be regarded as irreconcilable enemies. This additional freedom would only be found in the post-revolutionary construction of a Slavic federation, which, according to Hepner (1950, pp. 210, 218) was a "half political, half revolutionary" initiative, and whose inspirations were as much in the Polish Decembrists and liberals as in Proudhon. Such positions would be formalized in an article entitled "Principes Fondamentaux de la Nouvelle Politique Slave" ["Fundamental Principles of the New Slav Politics"], published throughout 1848 in different languages.[13]

Understanding that the Slavic Congress did not offer conditions for this project, either because of the direction of the discussions or because of its public character, Bakunin, under the inspiration of *Carbonari*, articulated for the first time a secret society called The Slavic Friends, composed of Slovaks, Moravians, Croats, and Serbs, which ended up lasting a few days, depending on the course of events.

On 12 June, 1848 the congress was interrupted by an uprising in the city of Prague itself. It was precisely one of the developments of the Peoples' Spring, which now involved the Czech struggle against Austria. Articulated by Czech students and democrats, with the participation of artisans and workers, the Prague Uprising erupted in outrage at the action of Austrian troops, who had fired on a peaceful demonstration. It was not, however, a totally spontaneous insurrection since it had been prepared for some time, including with the pretense of involving the peasants. Bakunin, contrary to what was later claimed, was not the greatest articulator of the insurrection—he became aware of the plans only one day before the eruption. And, judging them deeply unsatisfactory, he even tried to dissuade the insurgents. For him, despite the favourable revolutionary context, Commander Windisch-Graetz had, on that occasion, full conditions for a rapid victory and this would guarantee his troops a rise in morale and reinforcement of discipline. But, without being able to convince the insurgents, he decided, with other Slavic congressmen, to join the uprising, participating in what would be his second armed insurrectionary-revolutionary experience.

Still in the "Confession," Bakunin (1976b[e], pp. 116–17) reported: "Armed with a rifle, I went from one barricade to another, I fired several times, but without ceasing to be, in all this, a kind of guest." He suggested to the revolutionaries to oust the local government by preventing negotiations with Windisch-Graetz and that this government be replaced "by a military committee with dictatorial powers." But there was no time for that, and after a mediation in which Palacký took part the insurgents capitulated on 17 June, and Bakunin had to flee (cf., also: Bakunin, 48019[e]).

Between June and September 1848, Bakunin went to Wroclaw and then to Berlin, from where he sent a letter to Herwegh harshly criticizing parliamentary strategies (Bakunin, 2010b[c]). He felt, through the Germans, a huge impact of the rumour that he could be an agent of the Russian government, which was reinforced by a publication in July in Marx's *Neue Rheinische Zeitung* [*New Rhineland Gazette*].[14] Accused of having plans to assassinate the tsar, Bakunin was arrested and expelled from Prussia. He went to Wroclaw, making contact with the local Freemasonry and, under threat of deportation, passed through Dresden and found refuge in October in the principality of Anhalt-Köthen, whose autonomy from Prussian and Saxon legislation offered possibilities to many exiles. He would remain there until December (Hepner, 1950, p. 241).

In those months, he dedicated himself to writing his "Appeal to the Slavs by a Russian Patriot," initially in French ["Appel aux Peuples Slaves par un Patriote Russe"] and then in German ["Aufruf an die Slaven von einem russischen Patrioten"], a version which was published, and whose broad impact was felt among Germans, Czechs, Poles, and French, becoming his second major writing (Leier, 2006, p. 139). Still based on the theoretical-philosophical framework of "The Reaction in Germany," Bakunin analyzes the revolution–reaction dialectic in Europe with a focus on the Slav question, and further formalizes the positions defended in Prague, with a view to contributing to the minimization of fights among Slavs and their rapprochement with German democrats.[15] It also combats the possibility of an alliance with the Austrian Empire and preaches its destruction, as well as that of the empires of Russia, Prussia, and Turkey. It advocates the *freedom and self-determination of peoples*, in the key of a *national liberation* opposed to nationalism, which could only be achieved collectively and as a result of a revolutionary and democratic policy with implications for external relations (national question) and internal relations (social question) (Bakunin, 48020[e]).[16]

Still in Anhalt-Köthen, Bakunin joined German democrats William Hexamer and Karl D'Ester, working to minimize disagreements between Germans and Slavs. He went with them to Leipzig at the end of December 1848, where he met the Czech students Gustav and Adolf Straka, and tried to establish links with democrats in Prague, including Emmanuel Arnold. In Leipzig, where he stayed until March 1849, he learned of plans in democratic circles for a general uprising, which was to be carried out during the first half of the year and to involve various territories in Germany. The episodes that would agitate the country from February onwards were announced, including the *Märzerrungenschaften* [conquests of March] and the insurrectionary uprisings of May and June.

At that time, the neighbouring region of Bohemia came to attract Bakunin's attention and political efforts. As part of the German insurrectionary plans for 1849, it had already impressed him when, in solidarity with the Prague Uprising a few months earlier, they had stood up in arms. In addition, Bakunin understood that the region had not been strongly affected by the European reaction, it had the will, the motivation, and the means necessary for a revolution. This position was confirmed during his brief visit to Prague in March, where he was impressed by the lively spirit of the *Märzerrungenschaften*, popular freedom, the people in arms, and solidarity between students and soldiers. For Bakunin, Poland, previously considered a focus for the insurrectionary outburst, was possibly exhausted, demoralized, trapped in its restricted nationalism and more prone to relations with the West than with the Slav world. It was thus, at least temporarily, replaced as the *locus* of the revolutionary spark, which was to set fire to the Slav world and to Europe.

From March 1849 onwards, Bakunin was in Dresden, where he established ties with August Röckel, editor of the radical journal *Volksblatt* and through him with the musician Richard Wagner. During the period in Leipzig and Dresden, Bakunin dedicated himself to the preparation of the Bohemian Uprising, efforts of which are described in detail in a long passage of the "Confession" (Bakunin, 1976b[e], pp. 128–63). His project, which he would try to implement by the end of April, was to bring together Germans, Slavs, and Hungarians in a broad movement capable of breaking with the restricted involvement of the cities and moving towards a massive mobilization of peasants. It was intended to forge the basis for a mass revolution, the aim of which was to form a revolutionary government with dictatorial powers.

To this end, Bakunin became involved in an attempt at understanding between Germans and Czechs by writing an "Aufruf an die Czechen" ["Appeal to the Czechs"], which was published in April 1849 in *Dresdner Zeitung* (Bakunin, 49001[e]). In addition, he produced a series of articles that same month entitled "Russische Zustände" ["The Situation in Russia"], the first two of which were also published in *Dresdner Zeitung*. The series was devoted to explaining the Russian political situation through analyses of the army, the people, the nobility, the Church, the bureaucracy, and the finances of their homeland (Bakunin, 49005[e], 49006[e], 49007[e], 49008[e], 49009[e], 49010[e]).

He tried, for the second time, to articulate highly hierarchical and disciplined secret societies in Prague and throughout Bohemia, as well as to mobilize workers and involve the Tilo Slavic Czech nationalist society in his plans. However, things did not turn out as planned. The only concrete achievement of Bakunin and his associates was an improvement in the relationship of the Slavs with Germans, French, Polish, and Italians. But as far as the insurrectionary project in Bohemia is concerned, it did not materialize, among other reasons, for lack of members, involvement, responsibility, and financial resources.[17]

As part of the episodes of May 1849 in Germany, the Dresden Uprising burst open at the beginning of that month. According to Grawitz's contextualization, the origin of this uprising lies in the will expressed by the Chamber of Deputies to have the King of Saxony also accept a constitution like that of Frankfurt. On 22 April, 1849 the *Vaterlandsverein*, comprising approximately 75,000 citizens, voted to refuse to pay taxes until the constitutional demands were met. The King of Prussia having promised military aid to all royal authorities in difficulty, the King of Saxony decided to dissolve the chamber and appeal to the Prussian army. The angry mob gathered in front of the arsenal, demanding weapons against the invading enemies. The National Guard fired, leaving five dead (Grawitz, 1990, pp. 169–70).

On 3 May, the population spontaneously took to the streets and built more than a hundred barricades. The next day they proclaimed a provisional government of three members: the democrat Samuel Tzschirner and the constitutionalists Otto L. Heubner and Carl Todt. In its early days, that movement of a few thousand insurgents fought the forces of law and order and set fire to buildings, advancing their demands. It was quickly radicalized, and the constitutional banner was replaced by the democratic one, thus driving away the moderate bourgeoisie.

In what would be his third insurrectionary-revolutionary experience, Bakunin acted in this German uprising as a political and military leader. Outside the interim government, he devised strategies and advised Tzschirner, with whom he even made plans concerning the Slavs, should the revolution prosper. He commanded—in constant confrontation with the official leader of the revolutionary militia, Alexander Heinze—the unprepared insurgents at the barricades, stimulating them and contributing, as far as possible, to their organization. His performance was even praised by adversaries Marx and Engels.[18] In prison, Bakunin (2010c[c], p. 60) would confide in his lawyer Franz Otto: "If I had not been Russian, if I had found myself in a different situation, and if I had had a better knowledge of the places, I would probably have done a lot more."

With a lack of resources (mainly ammunition) on the part of the insurgents and increased repression, many deserted—including Tzschirner and the Poles Heltman and Krzyzanowski. Bakunin remained in the confrontation thanks to the persistence of Heubner, whom he had grown fond of, and the accusations of a Russian agent, which he wanted to dispell—he hoped that, with that attitude, he could prove in practice that he was an honest revolutionary. However, the Saxon and Prussian armies repressed the insurgents severely and cruelly.[19] On the brink of defeat, which became increasingly evident between the 6th and 9th, Bakunin even proposed blowing up the prefecture building, but without support, he articulated the withdrawal of the insurgents. The insurrection ended with more than 200 people dead and a thousand arrested. On the way to the withdrawal, Bakunin, in the passage through Freiberg, even proposed resuming the war, but everyone was exhausted and demoralized and there was no agreement on this.

Exhausted, while sleeping in a boarding house in Chemnitz on the night of 9–10 May, 1849 he was arrested with Röckel and Heubner by conservative bourgeoisie and handed over to the Prussian authorities in Altembourg—Wagner managed to escape. The worst phase of his life began there (Bakunin, 1976b[e], pp. 170–79; Guillaume, 1907a, p. xxiii; Berthier, 2010, vol. 2, pp. 132–33).

7.5 PRISONS, EXILE, AND ESCAPE (1849–61)
Captured, Bakunin and his comrades were taken back to Dresden, staying one night in the local prison and then in the custody of the Saxon army on the outskirts of the city. Interrogations began and the Russian government was notified of the arrest.

However, the risk of communication with potential sympathizers in the city resulted in Bakunin being transferred at the end of August 1849 to the Fortress of Königstein, southeast of Dresden on the border of Saxony, where he would spend his last ten months on German soil. During both interrogation and transfer, Bakunin was chained and escorted by armed soldiers.

In Königstein he remained in solitary confinement awaiting trial. The conditions were calm, as Bakunin himself (2010d[c]) reported in an early 1850 letter to Mathilde Reichel (Adolf's sister). He said he was calm, devoted to literature, mathematics, and English studies, and that he could walk, although in chains. He was also able to focus on the history of France through the works of Adolphe Thiers (*History of the Consulate and the Empire*), François Guizot, and A. de Lamartine (Carr, 1961, pp. 207–209).

After the interrogations in October, the defense preparation followed, which was done by Franz Otto, a lawyer appointed by the government. It was presented in November but was not successful. In January 1850, Bakunin, Heubner, and Röckel were sentenced to death by the Saxony court. In order to provide the lawyer with more information, Bakunin drew up a balance sheet of his activities between January and March: "Meine Vertheidigung" ["My Defense"] is an 88-page memoir that to some extent anticipates aspects of the "Confession" of 1851. In it, Bakunin takes up elements of the history of Europe and the Slavic world, discusses and propagandizes political strategies, and reports on his political activities of the recent period (Bakunin, 50001[e]). Without access to this document, which remained inconclusive, Otto appealed on his own, but in April the death sentence was confirmed.

Bakunin (2010e[c]) had confessed in another letter to Mathilde that he preferred death to life imprisonment. However, the governments of Austria and Russia had a keen interest in him. When consulted, the tsar eventually agreed that Bakunin should be extradited to Austria, and that he should be held responsible for his crimes there, provided that he was then sent to Russia for the same purposes. Thus, contrary to Bakunin's preference, in June 1850 his death sentence was commuted to life imprisonment. He was led to Prague by a detachment of armoured men and was incarcerated in St. George's Basilica, located in Prague Castle, where G. Straka and E. Arnold were also imprisoned. Conditions in Prague worsened considerably. Bakunin was considered a highly dangerous prisoner and, under court martial, was in a solitary, permanently and highly guarded facility. The cell was observed every 15 minutes and could only be opened with the presence of six armed guards; he was not allowed to write or receive letters. Moreover, he had to find another lawyer willing to defend him.

In mid-March 1851, because of rumours that the Czechs were preparing an operation to rescue him, the authorities decided to transfer him, again under a strong security detail, to the Fortress of Olmütz (Olomouc) further east in Moravia. In that prison he remained chained to the walls and deteriorated physically and mentally; he had severe toothache, insomnia, and the suffering was so great that he even attempted suicide. In April, he was subjected to a long interrogation and in mid-May, when he had already lost hope, he received his second death sentence, this time by hanging, from the Austrian government. However, on the same day, in accordance with the agreement with Russia, the sentence was commuted to life imprisonment (Grawitz, 1990, pp. 179–86).

Bakunin was then finally taken to Russia. For more than ten years he had been away from his homeland and when he crossed the border he became emotional. He entered under condemnation in December 1844 and was therefore directly imprisoned in the fortification of Aleksei in the Fortress of Peter and Paul in Saint Petersburg. There he was imprisoned in solitary confinement from May 1851 to March 1854. For a while he couldn't even go out, read, or receive visitors. As reported to Herzen in 1860, Bakunin (60006[c], pp. 7–8) was imprisoned for two months without any referral until, in July, he received a visit from Count Orlov, chief of political police and chief assistant to the tsar. He brought him Nicolas's proposal of writing to him a kind of confession of his sins, "as a spiritual son" he writes "to his spiritual father." Bakunin reflected for some time and decided to write. He would seek to "sweeten the forms" of the text, taking advantage of "polite terms" and account, in a kind of political autobiography, for only what was self-related or public knowledge. After all, for him "no one is obliged to confess the sins of others" and therefore he would not betray any companion. He indicated in that direction: "After my wreckage I have only one treasure left: the honour and the feeling that I have not betrayed any of those who have trusted me."[20]

As a result, between July and August 1851, Bakunin's "Исповедь" ["Confession"] was produced, which only became public in 1921 during the Bolshevik government, and would become the object of controversy thereafter.[21] It is a 96-page manuscript, written in a formal tone and even praising the tsar, in which Bakunin makes something like a biography of his philosophical and political life, covering the period from 1828 to 1849, in which he describes his trajectory, his thoughts and his actions. As much as most of the information is true, the document should be regarded with caution in view of the context in which it was produced and the strategy adopted by Bakunin to defend himself.

In the "Confession" Bakunin is characterized as an adventurous and foolish revolutionary who, repentant, wants to achieve a commutation of his life sentence. Seeking the tsar's sympathy with criticisms of the Germans—who received assurances from him, written in the margins of the original document—and claims of that Russian pan-Slavism promoted under his tutelage, Bakunin also makes analyses of the European situation, promotes harsh criticism of Russia, the tsar, and proposes solutions to internal and external dilemmas, with a frankness that probably had no precedent until then (Bakunin, 1976b[e]).

The tone of "Confession", Bakunin's feelings and claims can be picked up in the final section of the document:

I am a great criminal and I do not deserve forgiveness! I know this, and if I had been given the death penalty, I would have accepted it as a deserved punishment and almost with joy, for it would have freed me from an unbearable, intolerable existence. But Count Orlov let me know from Your Imperial Majesty that capital punishment does not exist in Russia. However, I beg you, sir, if the law does not oppose it, and if the supplication of a criminal can touch Your Imperial Majesty's heart, do not let me be consumed in prison for life! Do not punish my German sins with a German punishment. If the hardest jobs could be my fate, I would accept them with recognition and as a grace; the more painful the work, the easier I will forget myself. But in prison one remembers everything, and one remembers uselessly. Intelligence and memory become there an unspeakable torment; one lives a long time, one lives in spite of everything and, without dying, one dies day after day of inactivity and anguish. Nowhere, neither in the fortress of Königstein nor in Austria, have I been as well as here, in the Peter and Paul fortress; may God permit every free man to find a leader as good and human as the one I have found here, for my invaluable happiness. However, if I could choose, instead of life imprisonment in the fortress, I believe I would prefer not only death, but even corporal punishment.

Another plea, sir! Allow me, for once and for all, to see my family and say goodbye to them, if not all of them, at least my old father, my mother and my favorite sister (Tatiana A.), who I do not know, however, is still alive.

Grant me, O most gracious of sovereigns, these two great graces and I will bless the Providence that freed me from the hands of the Germans to give myself into the paternal hands of Your Imperial Majesty.

Having lost the right to call me Your Imperial Majesty's faithful subject, I subscribe with a sincere heart,

The repentant sinner,

Mikhail Bakunin. (Bakunin, 1976b[e], pp. 179–80)

This manuscript was forwarded to Nicolas with Orlov's recommendation that Bakunin's principal request—that his imprisonment be replaced by perpetual forced labour—not be met. The count understood that the prisoner was "a very dangerous man" who had not "completely healed himself of his false opinions" and who, in contact with others, could be "dangerous and harmful because of his ardent and resolute spirit." At the same time, Orlov approved of the possibility of improving Bakunin's conditions in prison and of allowing him to see his relatives at a later date. These recommendations were broadly followed by Nicolas. According to his resolution of August 1851, Bakunin was to "remain where he is" but he could see his father and sister, accompanied by the authorities (Guillaume, 1907a, p. xxv).[22]

Contact with his family, which had not occurred since 1845, was stimulating and from October 1851 Bakunin received visits from Tatiana and his brothers and sisters, who were standing in for their father, too old to travel. In those years, Bakunin tried to reconcile with his family and gained access to Russian books (novels and scientific papers), periodicals, and newspapers, and to *Revue des Deux Mondes* [*Two Worlds Magazine*]. But at the same time, the passing of the years had had a considerable impact on the deterioration of his health conditions.

In a brief letter, delivered secretly to his brothers in February 1854, Bakunin (2010f[c], pp. 73–75) provided a portrait of his physical and psychological condition on that occasion. Even though he was "always in a good mood" and "always laughing," he reported "twenty times a day I would like to die, so much so that my life has become painful. I feel that my strength is exhausted; my soul is still strong, but my body weakens." This was, according to his assessment, due to the inhumane conditions to which he was subjected: "immobility, forced inaction, lack of air." He had hemorrhoids, fevers, headaches, ringing in his ears, and difficulty breathing. In addition, malnutrition in prison had caused scurvy, which was the reason for the appearance of wounds on his body and the loss of all his teeth. Meanwhile, the sanity of the mind was still preserved—"my head is lucid, in spite of all the evils which, as a rule, make it their residence"—as well as the will to act—"my will, I hope, will never bend; my heart seems like a stone, it is true, but give me the possibility to act and it will resist." After all, he stressed that he still had many ideas and a "burning desire for movement and action," concluding: "I am not yet completely dead."

In March 1854, Bakunin was transferred to the Shlisselburg Fortress (Oreshek), almost 50 km east of Saint Petersburg on the shores of Lake Ladoga, where he would remain for the next three years. It was a preventative measure by the Russian authorities who, thanks to the development of the Crimean War, feared that the British might attack the Gulf of Finland and somehow facilitate Bakunin's release. With the death of Alexandre Bakunin in December of that year, Varvara mustered the strength and conditions to help her son, a task to which she would commit herself over the next two years of her life. Concerned by Bakunin's deteriorating conditions—he would even, because of the intense suffering, settle the procedures for suicide with his brother at the end of 1856—Varvara used her position and influence with the nobility to intervene with the authorities on several occasions. To this end, the death of Nicolas in 1855 and the coronation of his first-born, Alexander II, seemed to offer hope given the more liberal positions of the heir.

Even so, the broad amnesty that marked the beginning of Alexander's government did not include Bakunin, personally removed by the new tsar from the list of amnesties. Varvara, intervening again, received the following response: "Know, madam, that as long as your child lives, he can never be free" (Guillaume, 1907a, p. xxvii). But her collaborative, direct efforts continued so that in early 1857 Bakunin received permission to write again to the tsar.

Dated February 1857, the letter to Alexander II is much shorter than the "Confession." In it, Bakunin (2015b[c], pp. 90–92), referring to the previous document, assumed what he pointed out as his past mistakes and apologized. In addition, he highlighted his desperate condition in prison and his lack of future prospects: "Imprisonment is the most terrible penalty, without hope it would be worse than death; it makes dead of a living being and destroys in him consciously, slowly, and day after day, all physical, moral and intellectual forces." Moreover, he thought that the last years of imprisonment had exhausted his strength and destroyed his youth and health: "I consider myself an old man and I feel that I no longer have much time left to live." He was certain that living with others, of which he was deprived, was indispensable for any happiness or well-being. Because of all this, he asked for only one thing: "freedom or death."

A week later, in February 1857, the government granted Bakunin the possibility of commuting his sentence to a perpetual exile in Siberia, and also of making a final visit to Premukhino. During the month of March, he made what would be his last visit to the family estate and was taken in the following weeks to Siberia, arriving in Omsk at the end of the month and then going on to Tomsk, the capital of Western Siberia. His Siberian period would extend until mid-1861 (Bakunin, 60006[c]; Carr, 1961, pp. 231–36).

Life in exile in Tomsk, even with its difficulties, was much better than life in prison and no doubt contributed to the re-establishment of Bakunin's physical and psychological condition, which in a few months completely recovered. Living with other exiles, merchants, and officials, he sought ways to support himself financially. To this end, he considered the possibility of employment in the gold mining industry, which was developing in the Lena River region. But faced with a ban on traveling long distances, he had to devote himself to private French lessons. On that occasion he fell in love with one of his students, Antonia Ksaverievna Kwiatkowska—a 17-year-old Polish woman (and therefore, 27 years younger than him), the daughter of an auriferous merchant—to whom he was married in October 1858.

They lived a few months in Tomsk and moved in March 1859 to Irkutsk on the border with Mongolia. There, Bakunin got a job at the Amur River Company, which promoted trade in the newly conquered region. Change and employment were made possible with the help of a powerful and well-connected relative: Varvara's (mother) cousin, General Nikolai N. Muraviev-Amurski, whom Bakunin approached personally and politically. Governor of Eastern Siberia since 1847, Muraviev, as Leier characterized him (2006, p. 155), was a "Russian imperialist and patriot" who was "largely responsible for the annexation of large parts of northern China above the Amur River." Between 1854 and 1858 he had undertaken expeditions along the Amur River, with which he secured the expansion of the Russian Empire—and with it, in addition to a huge territory, river access to the Pacific—"extend[ing] the trade networks of Russia along and beyond the river and coloniz[ing] new territories for the tsar," especially with the transfer of Cossacks from the Dauriya region (Transbaikalia). The general "considered himself a liberal, and in the context of nineteenth century Russia he really was." But if he "appreciated American democratic institutions and lamented servitude," "the political beliefs he professed were often contradicted by his actions."

From the end of 1858, still in Tomsk, Bakunin had begun to re-establish his political contacts, which were strengthened during the period in Irkutsk. An important relationship was established with Muraviev, with whom he met frequently and in whom he saw possibilities of strong leadership, capable of pushing the banner of revolution or even of reforms in Russia from above (Leier, 2006, pp. 154–56). He also re-established a relationship with former comrades Herzen and Ogarev, who since 1857 had published the radical newspaper Колокол/Kolokol [The Bell] in London, read by Russian immigrants in Europe, smuggled into Russia, and consumed even on Siberian soil (Bakunin, 58004[c]; Grawitz, 1990, p. 235). In addition to these relationships, which were the most striking of his period of exile, Bakunin lived with other exiles, including several Decembrists.

In 1860, Kolokol dedicated some of its columns to the analysis of Siberia and, among the criticisms, were some against Muraviev. Initially, he was accused of violation of correspondence and then, in an article entitled "Muraviev's Tyranny in Siberia," he was condemned for his expansionist initiatives in Amur. During that year, Bakunin came out in defense of Muraviev, sending two letters to Kolokol and two more to Herzen, in which he interceded over more than 50 pages in the defense of the general and the disqualification of his opponents. In a letter to Herzen in November 1860, Bakunin (60005[c], p. 2) claims that Muraviev is "one of the best men, one of the most useful in Russia" who "wants the greatness and glory of Russia in freedom"; he was, he argued, "a determined democrat," "a man whom we can consider absolutely our own and by whom Russia today can hope to be effectively served and perhaps even saved." The positions on Muraviev echo what Bakunin would later call "Petersburger pan-Slavism" or "Russian imperial pan-Slavism," which he himself had defended in some passages of "Confession"—thus marking a new flirtation with narrow nationalism.

Still on Siberian soil, Bakunin published in April 1861—soon after the emancipation of the serfs granted by Alexander II—two articles in Амур [Amur], the first political-literary newspaper in Eastern Siberia, created the year before by Mikhail Petratchevski. In the first, he discusses aspects of Irkutsk's social life; in the second, longer, he analyzes the dynamics of social classes in Mongolia, highlighting the contribution of the Chinese governor (ambam) and especially of merchants and young people to what he called the "popular resurrection" in the region, which was based on instruction and practical initiative. The case of Mongolia, after all, showed possible ways forward for a Russia that seemed susceptible to reforms from above (Bakunin 61001[e]; Bakunin, 61002[e]).

However, from the beginning of 1861, Bakunin no longer planned to remain in Siberia. With Muraviev's retirement in January, it became more feasible to articulate an escape. Moreover, the arrival of the acting governor, General Mikhail S. Korsakov, who also had a tie with him not far from kinship, did not seem to be a hindrance. From a businessman in Kyakhta, Bakunin got a job and an advance on his salary to contribute to the commercial expansion along the Amur River; from the governor, on the word that he would return to Irkutsk, he got a permit to board ships in the region and an indemnity offered to political exiles (Grawitz, 1990, pp. 224–25).

Bakunin began his escape in June 1861 when he left Irkutsk and conquered, over almost a month, more than 3,000 kilometers, traveling down the Amur in a steamboat to the port of Nikolaevsk, near the access to the Okhotsk sea. Until that moment, he did nothing that was forbidden to him; the next step, however, would be more complicated and would in fact constitute a crime in light of his escape from Siberia. Bakunin stayed in Nikolaevsk for a week when, in early July, he managed to board the government ship *Strelok*, which was heading for De-Kastri, claiming that he would change his initial route and then return to Siberia via China. When, in the La Pérouse Strait, which separates the island of Sacalina from the mainland, the Russian vessel started towing an American clipper, *Vickery*, dedicated to trade on Japanese soil, Bakunin was able to continue his escape. He was able to switch to the US vessel and continue his journey to Japan. Through the port of Olga, the last stop on Russian territory, it entered the Sea of Japan, landing at Hakodate and then Yokohama, where it arrived in early September.

From Yokohama he sent a letter to Korsakov informing him of his escape, justifying himself and asking him not to stop his wife from meeting him in London later (Bakunin, 61006[c]). In September, he boarded the US ship the *SS Carrigton* and traveled over 8,000 kilometers via the Pacific to the west coast of the United States. During the trip, he met the cleric Koe, with whom he discussed religion and other topics and got some money to go on the trip—they kept in touch. He arrived in San Francisco in October, staying there for a week, from where he wrote to Herzen and Ogarev. In this letter, Bakunin (2010g[c], p. 88) informed his companions that he had managed to escape from Siberia and asked Herzen for money to get to London. He showed interest in the episodes of the War of Secession, affirming his sympathy for the northern states, and emphasizing his political project for the next period: "Friends, I aspire to join you in all my being, and from my arrival I will set to work, I will take charge among you of the Polish-Slav question, which has been my fixed idea since 1846 and practically my specialty in 1848 and 1849." He thought he could do this through *Kolokol*, and gave notice that he had made connections with a view to facilitating sending the periodical to Siberia.

Bakunin left San Francisco by boat at the end of October for Panama. He crossed the Isthmus and boarded for New York, where he arrived in mid-November. He stayed there for almost a month; he reestablished contact with German exiles, visited Boston, and received the funds sent by Herzen. He then managed to embark for Europe in mid-December, appearing in London on the evening of 27 December, 1861. In six months of escape, he covered more than 30,000 kilometers. But at last he was free.

7.6 RESUMPTION OF THE SLAVIC CAUSE IN LONDON AND FRUSTRATION WITH THE POLISH INSURRECTION (1862–63)

In London, where he remained from late 1861 to early 1863, Bakunin joined Herzen and Ogarev, his main interlocutors from that period, and became involved with them in the *Kolokol* project. He resumed contacts with his family, the Reichels, the Vogts, and also with Sand, Turgueniev, Ruge, A. Straka, and Koe; he also made contact with Giuseppe Garibaldi.

At first, Bakunin, still poorly informed and politically displaced, sought to reintegrate into this new scenario. He did this in a frenetic way, as Herzen reported: Bakunin "discussed, preached, gave orders, shouted, decided, articulated, organized, incited, all day, all night, finally all 24 hours" (*apud* Carr, 1961, p. 254). However, this reintegration was not so simple since the situation had changed immensely and the twelve years of imprisonment and exile had deprived Bakunin of a more refined knowledge of reality. On his arrival in London, he maintained "not only the spirit, but the opinions of the furious 1840s. He returned to the world like a ghost from the past." In other words, he was a man "who was trying to resume life from the point where it had been abandoned and hoped to find everything around him in the same position" (Carr, 1961, p. 252). While Bakunin's assessment of the economic situation and the political program were largely the same as in 1848 and 1849, both the European and Slavic worlds had since undergone considerable changes.

In Europe, with the end of the Peoples' Spring, radicalized movements and hopes for more significant social change were increasingly giving way to the growth of reaction and to more moderate forces. Politically, transformation projects weakened while under the bourgeoisie an unprecedented industrial capitalism expanded economically. At least in the countries further west, as Hobsbawm (2004a, p. 21) points out, these were times when "the (English) industrial revolution had swallowed the (French) political revolution." For many progressives, revolutionary times—at least in the "advanced countries"—seemed over.

In Russia, the emancipation of serfs granted by Alexander II in 1861 had not only profoundly changed the country's social relations but also stimulated in many people the expectation that he could lead the way in other reforms. It was a time when the political forces were reconfiguring themselves, and if the differences between conservatives and progressives became more marked, among the progressives themselves a moderate and a revolutionary sector began to distinguish themselves. As recently as 1861, this revolutionary sector was embodied in populism, which was emerging in large cities; its main organization was Земля и воля [Land and Freedom] and its inspirations came, besides the members of *Kolokol*, from Blanc, Proudhon, and Nikolai Tchernichevski. Its members, the *narodniks*, were young people from the middle classes of society (*raznochintsy*) who, alleging the insufficiency of spoken and written propaganda, decided to devote themselves to the practice of the peasant revolution by raising the flags of land and freedom. In 1862, the government attributed a series of fires in Saint Petersburg to the populists.

Because of his continued attachment to the Slavic cause, Bakunin, even though he was in London—the capital of the country which, during its industrial development, witnessed the rise of a workers' movement some decades before that, despite its moderation, was gaining ground in trade unionist initiatives—knew little and established few links with English social struggles. With the exception of a meeting organized by Herzen on the occasion of his arrival, to which a delegation of workers went to welcome him and congratulate him, later publishing his greeting in the pages of *The Cosmopolitan*, Bakunin devoted himself almost entirely to the Slavic cause and contacts. The only exception to this rule was the link established with Italian nationalists, particularly Garibaldi and Giuseppe Mazzini, who motivated Bakunin's interest in Italy and its national liberation struggle against Austria (Nettlau, 1964, p. 43; Leier, 2006, pp. 156–57, 163–64).

In February 1862, Bakunin published, in the pages of *Kolokol*, "Русским, польским и всем славянским друзьям" ["To the Russians, Poles and All Slavic Friends"]. In this text he tries to answer the question of the time, which would be eternalized in the title of the novel by Tchernichevski of the same year: What to do? The response, as well as taking up the ideas of the 1840s, is a brief outline of the land and freedom program for the peasant revolution in Russia. For this mobilization of the Russian people, Bakunin understood that the tradition of the Old Believers would have a role to play (Bakunin, 62002[e]). In a way, this article marked a more radical approach from *Kolokol* which, with Bakunin's presence and in spite of Herzen's moderate and skeptical liberalism, was acquiring a more left-wing position and intended to foster dialogue with the new young Russian revolutionaries (Brupbacher, 2015, p. 98). According to Herzen himself (1982, p. 572), after his arrival in London Bakunin proposed to "revolutionize *Kolokol*," arguing that "propaganda was not enough," that "there should be immediate action" and that "centers and committees should be organized."

Having to deal with the resurgence of rumours returning to England[23] that he was an agent of the Russian government, Bakunin began to look for a link with the Slavs, especially the Russians who visited London and had Herzen as a reference. This occurred with some of those who, between May and November of 1862, visited the city to participate in the Universal Exhibition. But the official Russian repression of the revolutionary movement, taking advantage of London's connections, prevented this link from continuing and resulted in the arrest of several Russians, including Nikolai Serno-Solovievich, the leader of Land and Freedom who had been with Herzen in London shortly before Bakunin's arrival. It was also at the time of the Universal

Exhibition that Bakunin first expressed clearly anti-Germanic positions, giving in to that feeling of hatred for the Germans which, for him, was the basis of Slavic unity.[24]

At that moment, Bakunin made contact with Martyanov, a Russian peasant who had been a servant and who had sought Herzen out for a meeting. This was an unusual situation, as the circle of Russians in London had not yet established links with the Russian people. Bakunin saw in this opportunity not only the chance to educate the peasant politically, but to link himself with him and improve his own knowledge about the realities and demands of the Russian people.[25] Like most of his companions, Martyanov loved the tsar and did not conceive of a Russia outside the authority of the Romanovs. Nevertheless, he defended the need (and believed in the possibility) for Alexander to head the changes in Russia, breaking with his aristocratic role as emperor and calling a National Assembly (Carr, 1961, pp. 272–73, 276–77; Leier, 2006, pp. 165–69).

Bakunin established some dialogue with Martyanov's positions in a June–July 1862 article: "Народное дело: Романов, Пугачев или Пестель?" ["The People's Cause: Romanov, Pugachev or Pestel?"]. This text was intended for *Kolokol* but was eventually rejected by Herzen and published independently in London—a process that strained relations between them. In it, Bakunin carries out an analysis of the new Russia, under intense transformation, and points out a program of revolutionary and democratic transformation, based on Land and Freedom and demanding the socialization of property, the national liberation of the Slavs, and self-determination of peoples, which would conform to a new society marked by the autonomy of communes. In discussing the possible paths to such transformation, Bakunin assesses three ways: the first, led by Tsar Alexander, who, by radically changing his political perspective and breaking with his tradition, could become a tsar of the people, convening an Assembly of the *zemstvo* [local government institution] and thus securing peace; the second, headed by the people themselves, in the perspective of the peasant uprisings led by Iemelian Pugachev between 1773 and 1775, in which the social revolution would take place in an extremely violent way; the third, headed by the illustrious youth, in the perspective of the Decembrist Uprising of 1825, in which the State would be taken over by a Jacobin-type coup, also involving a bloodbath (Bakunin, 62006[e]).

Another relevant article from 1862 was "Bakunin on the Slavs," published in Czech under the title "Bakunin the Slovanstvu" (Bakunin, 62008[e]). The translation and publication went to Josef Václav Frič, a Slavic revolutionary of Czech origin, who took part in the Prague Uprising and who was, especially in 1862, a privileged interlocutor in Bakunin's pan-Slavic discussions.

Even with the repression, Russian populism grew in 1862, and Bakunin conceived ways of contributing more directly to the movement. After all, as Barrué (2015a, p. 186) points out, his "appeal to the youth to go to the people," not with the aim of commanding or indoctrinating them but of contributing to their revolutionary project, had found echoes among the young Russians, many of whom decided "to follow Bakunin with enthusiasm." In view of this contribution, Bakunin approached a young Russian newcomer, Nikolai Jukovski, with whom he planned trips to strategic border regions and the use of *Kolokol* as an organ of support for the struggle.

In early 1863, Sleptsov, a member of the Executive Committee on Land and Freedom, came to London and proposed that *Kolokol* become the representative of his organization abroad. Persuaded by Bakunin, Herzen and Ogarev agreed and in the March issue, *Kolokol* welcomed the initiative of the young Russian revolutionaries (Grawitz, 1990, pp. 246–47). However, this episode, together with Herzen's refusal to publish "The People's Cause" and the fact that Bakunin never really succeeded in integrating himself into the *Kolokol* leadership, contributed to further worsening the relations between the two, gradually shaken by the wear and tear of coexistence and political differences.

But in early 1863 Bakunin's attention turned again to Poland. In the middle of the previous year he had spent a few days in Paris, where he had met General Ludwik Mierosławski, a former combatant of the 1830 Insurrection, with whom he discussed the Polish question. He had also received a delegation from the National Central Committee in Warsaw shortly after that, which proposed to the publishers of *Kolokol* an alliance for the liberation struggle in Poland. According to Leier (2006, pp. 169–70) this committee, which had been founded in the same year of 1862, expressed a polarization in the national movement in Poland, which was divided. On the one hand, there was a sector led by the nobility (*szlachta*), which was looking for a state that could offer conditions for the aggrandizement of its properties and for guaranteeing the exploitation of those who worked on them; among the Russians, they found in the tsarist government their potential allies. On the other hand was this National Central Committee, which understood that the national liberation of Poland demanded not only to struggle against Russian tsarism, but also against Polish landowners; among the Russians, they found potential allies in the Democrats—and it was in order to strengthen this alliance that they had sought out *Kolokol* in London.

Anticipating the expectations of the national movement itself, the Polish uprising of 1863 broke out in January, once again pitting the might of the Poles against the oppression of tsarist Russia. Initiated with a protest against the compulsory enlistment of young urban workers in the Russian army, this revolt became an insurrection of vast proportions, receiving support from different sectors of society and finding in the guerrillas its main form of combat. The outbreak of this uprising immediately gave many progressives, especially Europeans, the impression that the era of revolutions had finally returned.

Such was Bakunin's assessment that he rushed to get money and a fake passport to join the insurgency. He wrote to the central committee offering his help, but was discouraged—even so, he decided to go to Poland. He left London at the end of February, passed through Copenhagen (Denmark) and arrived in Gothenburg

(Sweden) at the beginning of March.[26] On Swedish soil, Bakunin was invited to board the Ward Jackson ship, which had left Paris for Poland with guns and 200 insurgents who wanted to join the uprising. He agreed, and headed for Helsingborg, where he boarded the vessel. However, the continuity of the voyage was prevented by, among other things, the discovery of the rebels' plans by the Russian government and by the conduct of the ship's captain who, fearfully, refused to leave Sweden. The rebels still managed to reach Malmö at the end of March 1863, where Bakunin gave his third public speech, this time to Swedes sympathetic to the uprising, highlighting the importance of their support for the Polish cause (Bakunin, 63002[e]). But from there they were prevented from continuing their journey. It was already the beginning of April, and the Polish Uprising, which had not received the expected solidarity from the Russian peasantry, was suffering from the intense repression. Although it extended in the form of open warfare until the following year, the uprising had, at that moment, already shown its limits in revolutionary terms. Its defeat would have a decisive impact on Bakunin's political positions (cf., also: Brupbacher, 2015, p. 99).

Bakunin would remain in Sweden for a few more months, until October 1863. In Stockholm, he finally met Antonia, who had arrived from Russia in April after agreeing with the government never to return. According to Carr (1961, p. 302–307), while in London Bakunin had received little attention. In Sweden the scenario was different; he was received as a hero and a relevant political personality, especially by members of the Swedish Radical Party. He had links with the *Aftonbladet* newspaper, in which he published a number of articles. At the end of May 1863, he was honoured in Stockholm at a banquet at the Phoenix Hotel with 140 radicals present, where he gave his fourth public speech, now dealing with Russia and based on the Land and Freedom program. He was interested in the cause of the liberation of Finland, which had been taken from Sweden by Russia in 1809. In defense of this cause, he found support from the Finnish poet Emil von Qvanten, through whom he was presented to the King of Sweden, Charles XV.

Despite the warm welcome, Sweden had no prospects for revolutionary practice in Bakunin's view. In addition to the constant financial problems, the conditions for militancy with the Slavic cause were becoming increasingly complicated. It was not only a matter of frustration with the Polish Uprising, but also of the significant loss of force in Russia of Land and Freedom and *Kolokol*, whose positions were now considered outdated by most radicals, inside and outside that country. With this, the prioritizing of pan-Slavism was beginning to be put in check (Bakunin, 63037[c]). The idea of a move to Italy, which had previously arisen for exclusively political reasons, was then taken up again. In addition to political possibilities, Italy offered prospects of a better life with Antonia due to the climate and people. Leaving Sweden in October, Bakunin passed through England (London), Belgium (Brussels), France (Paris), Switzerland (Geneva, Vevey and Bern), and arrived in Italy in January 1864 (cf., also: Nettlau, 1964, pp. 43–44; Grawitz, 1990, pp. 253–59).

7.7 BAKUNINIAN POLITICAL THEORY BETWEEN 1844 AND 1863

At this time, some elements relevant to the understanding of Bakunin's political theory in the period in question will be presented. They introduce the theoretical discussion, which will be set out in more detail in the following chapters.

7.7.1 Revolutionary Pan-Slavic Period (1844–63)

Between 1844 and 1863—during which he spent twelve years in prison and exile (1849–61)—Bakunin finds himself in his *revolutionary pan-Slavic* period,[27] which has considerable continuity as well as ruptures compared with previous periods.

From 1841–42, Bakunin maintained theoretical-philosophical concepts and notable aspects of more general analyses of Europe. From 1843, he maintained the notions of the primacy of practice and self-government of the people. In this period, he breaks with philosophy and redirects his theoretical production—his greatest intention is that it may express and support revolutionary praxis. In thematic terms, the national issue becomes central, expressing itself in reflections and actions that initially involve the Russian-Polish cause and then move on to the Slavic cause.

In these 20 years, Bakunin, either in liberty or in prison, passed through numerous countries: Austria, Belgium, Denmark, France, England, Prussia, Russia, Sweden, and Switzerland. He actively participated in insurrectionary and revolutionary uprisings—the February Revolution of 1848, the Prague Uprising (June 1848), prepared for the Bohemian Uprising (the passage from 1848–49), and the Dresden Uprising (May 1849)—tried to articulate himself politically, and intervened in European political debates through speeches and writings.

Although he did not produce new philosophical reflections or more in-depth analyses of Europe as a whole, he took up in his writings and letters elements of his theory of revolution and his negative dialectics of 1841–42. Most of these elements, especially those of "The Reaction in Germany," are still considered correct and are therefore taken as background and starting point for concrete discussions (Angaut, 2009, p. 48). It can thus be said that, in philosophical terms, Bakunin continues to operate within the framework of the *voluntarist realism* of previous years. As Berthier points out (2010, vol. 2, pp. 14, 83, 105), the readings of the reality of this period continue the method developed in "The Reaction in Germany" and are carried out by means of "extremely elaborated and realistic strategic thinking, taking into consideration the forces present." Such realism needs to be understood as an analytical foundation that "starts from an objective analysis" of reality, in particular of "the situation of the Slavs."

However, this realism does not mean that Bakunin's project of the emancipation of the Slavs "was achievable" at that time. In this regard, Angaut (2009, pp. 24, 30) points out that between 1844 and 1863, Bakunin had "a practical relationship with history: to the theoretical pessimism of understanding [...], he opposed the practical optimism of the will." In other words, the realization of his political project, in line with the very context of the Peoples' Spring, seems to point to a "confusion between what is possible and what is necessary" so that his desire for transformation goes— all too often—beyond the structural and conjunctural conditions for its realization. Moreover, the ideas and political positions of the actors remain the greatest analytical determinants, even if considered within certain limits imposed by the historical needs and social and national realities in question.

According to Angaut (2009, p. 47), during this period Bakunin undertook a "practical attempt to prolong the cosmic and historical opposition between revolution and reaction in political opposition." But this was done with a view to giving priority to the national question in these two decades—the very notion of self-government of the people of 1843 is adapted in this direction. It should also be pointed out that, if Hegel's influences can still be noticed in Bakuninian political theory, it would hardly be possible to consider the Bakunin of those years as a Hegelian, especially because of the ruptures from 1843 onwards.

In 1848, already after the failure of the revolutionary experiences of February and June, Bakunin considered that "today, more than ever, Europe is divided into two camps." For him, although defeated, "the revolution has dealt a terrible blow to old politics; a blow from which it will never recover." It seemed obvious to him that "the old order is breaking down everywhere with a frightening noise, everywhere people are waking up, everywhere they cry out for their long-forgotten rights and for their freedom" (Bakunin, 48019[e]). Thus it was clear that Europe was deepening its division between an "old world in ruins" and a "new world," between two contradictory camps, "counterrevolution" and "revolution." It was then necessary to choose between one or the other, deciding whether he would contribute to the approach or to the delay of this inevitable change, bearing in mind that on this choice "the realization of the destinies of the world will depend."

The same position regarding mediators is reproduced: playing an important role for diplomacy, they are "mistaken if they believe this lie" that it is possible to escape this contradiction "by granting something small to each of the two parties in struggle in order to slow them down and thus prevent the explosion of the inevitable, necessary battle" between them (Bakunin, 48020[e], pp. 3–4). Similarly, reforms are seen as insufficient remedies so that only revolution, a complete transformation, can solve the dilemma of the European conflict. The "party of reform" should therefore be rejected and the "party of a radical revolution" embraced (Bakunin, 62002[e], p. 1).

The concept of "the people," widely deployed in this period, especially when the *freedom of peoples* is demanded, relates both to this historical context and to Hegelian philosophical production. It

> is not only the axis of the revolutions of 1848; it is also one of the central terms in the philosophy of Hegel's history, and it can be said that by wielding the banner of the freedom of peoples [...], Bakunin does nothing more than

prolong Hegelian questioning, which claims that the peoples are the main actors in history and that it is at the level of the peoples that history develops. Here the question is that of the mediations through which freedom is realized in history: for Hegel, history is the place where the spirit realizes its freedom, in the sense that it becomes aware of itself and of its autonomy. And "in history, the spirit is an individual of both universal and determined nature: a people; and the spirit with which we deal is the spirit of a people (Volksgeist)." (Angaut, 2009, pp. 11–12)

Although claiming Hegel's notion that freedom takes place in history, it is possible to question to what extent Bakunin's pan-Slavic reflections are anchored in Hegelian philosophy.

> When he thinks of the emancipation of Slavic nations, Bakunin seeks to recover this scheme, which sees the spirits of the peoples commit themselves to a process "by which the spirit reaches the free conscience of itself"? [Hegel, "Reason in History"] That would mean several things. First, it would imply that he goes further than his texts of the Hegelian period, in which Hegel is claimed to think of the historical contradictions that manifest themselves in a political conflict (the thesis defended in "The Reaction in Germany" that nothing or nobody can reconcile these contradictions from outside, which must inescapably lead to a revolution). Subsequently, this means that he goes beyond Hegel himself, who did not assign a particular destiny to the Slavic nations in the chapters of his philosophy of history consecrated to the nations of Europe: they had at most the vocation to build an intermediate zone between Asia and Europe (he thought mainly of Russia). Finally, it would involve returning to the Slavs a particular historical mission, for example, that of embodying social transformation after the religious revolution in Germany and the political revolution in France— according to a scheme very common at the time. (Angaut, 2009, p. 12)

That is to say, as has been mentioned, if it is true that some influence of Hegel remains in the Bakuninian political theory of those years, this is very unorthodox. It involves not only going beyond what Hegel[28] advocated, but extrapolating Bakunin's own earlier ideas.

In those years, despite considerable written production, Bakunin did not develop intellectual formulations exclusively aimed at the field of philosophy or theory in general. In the wake of the positions previously held on the relationship between theory and practice, he continues to regard philosophy as an insufficient means for change and, to a certain extent, believes that what has been elaborated in this field is sufficient to support an understanding of reality and to conceive the means for concrete action. His writings and letters of these years should be understood, more precisely, as part of the consolidation of that project of the primacy of revolutionary praxis, which had been proclaimed in 1843 (Bakunin, 45002[c], pp. 4–5; Bakunin, 50001[e], p. 28).

On this Bakunin emphasized (62006[e], p. 32): "In theory, everything is arranged. In practice, especially at a time like ours, what is not useful is harmful." However, such a position does not mean that there is an absolute rejection of theoretical and philosophical questions. They will be adapted—in a more utilitarian sense, it is true—to support a transformative praxis or even express themselves as such. Philosophy will continue to underpin intellectual production and theory will be adjusted to become, as practical awareness of the present, a tool for the intervention in reality.

In some way, this allows us to understand some questions related to the study of the Bakuninian work of those years. First, this intentionality of the writings and letters explains the fact that there are no authors who receive much attention. From an intellectual point of view, only a few influences can be noted: Hegel, mentioned a few times and whose ideas appear residually in the texts; Weitling, regarding the notion of the primacy of practice; Proudhon, especially regarding his conception of federalism, which will be adapted to the discussions of the national question; Herzen, in his conception of Slavic socialism and of the role of the Slavic peasantry in the struggle for transformation. Also relevant were the works of the history of Europe and the Slavic world, as well as magazines and newspapers of conjunctural polemic. Second, it explains why the texts are even less complex and far more realistic than their predecessors. Third, it makes explicit the deep attachment of these texts to the political and geopolitical situation in Europe at that time, making it possible to note that evaluations, predictions, and positions change depending on contexts of short duration. All the theoretical and methodological aspects of these texts are embedded in these assessments, predictions, and positions. Fourth, and finally, it makes it possible to identify that in certain cases, as Angaut (2009, p. 30) mentions, past and present historical analysis, as well as future historical necessity, is confused with political possibilities and intentions.

With regard to the themes under discussion, Bakunin also made a considerable change from 1844 onwards. The social issue now receives less attention than the *national question*, which is the central concern of the period, not without some difficulty in adapting the previous analytical model. With this, the central concepts of *State, nation-race, imperialism, national liberation*, and peoples' self-determination emerge. The already mentioned concept of *people*—related to the conjuncture of the Peoples' Spring, and which evidenced some Hegelian inspiration—is in most cases replaced by *peoples* and used in a triple sense. Sometimes the most common conception of the previous period remains, in the sense of oppressed classes; several other times, this concept is used in the ethnic-racial sense; finally, at other times, there is a hybrid sense or even its use to refer to the population in general (Bakunin, 48019[e]; Bakunin, 1976b[e], pp. 68, 70; Bakunin, 50001[e], p. 41).

In political terms, French radicalism—which remains, at least as regards the struggle of the democratic and social republic against despotism, and the universalization of the ideals of the French Revolution (Bakunin, 48019[e]; Bakunin, 48004[e], p. 3)—is adapted to this centrality of the national question, leading to Slavism or revolutionary pan-Slavism. At the end of the period, in the year 1862, Bakunin referred to his doctrine as "Slavic socialism," expressing that somehow it corresponds to the very nature of the Slavic people.[29] As political principles, freedom and democracy remain, but they go beyond the situation of one state or another and extend mainly to the relationship between states and peoples.

He also dedicates himself to analyzing Russia and the Slavic world in a concrete way, seeking to understand the national forces at play and, on the basis of these analyses, to devise the most appropriate means of promoting a revolution that would guarantee, in national terms, the national liberation of the Slavs and peoples' self-determination, and, in social terms, the popular emancipation of Europeans. To achieve these objectives, Bakunin thinks that the Slavs must form a movement capable of promoting this revolution and thus destroying the old world, opening up the possibilities for building a Slav federation, the foundation of the new world. He sets out the strategic foundations for this, reflecting on the subjects capable of leading this transformation, the base that could forge the union of the Slavs and be their main allies. But although the years in question (1844–63) present a certain homogeneity in these lines, there are some ideas that highlight certain uncertainties and dilemmas of his project.

Moreover, this is the last period in which religious jargon, which is used less and less, will be deployed more frequently. The Bakuninian notion of faith, for example, already completely secularized, is part of the framework of his voluntarism:

> I had only one companion, faith, and I told myself that it can move mountains, remove obstacles, overcome the invincible and do the impossible, that it alone is half the victory; united to a strong will, it engenders circumstances, awakens men, gathers and merges the masses into a single soul and a single force alone. (Bakunin, 1976b[e], pp. 96–97)

Bakunin still claims a "religion of humanity" and the "holy cause of revolution." But at the same time he emphasizes that religion can become the "opium" to "stupidify and deceive the people" (Bakunin, 60005[c], p. 22; Bakunin, 48019[e]; Bakunin, 50001[e] p. 21).

NOTES

1   Since his arrival, Bakunin had been under investigation by the Swiss authorities and the Russian embassy in Switzerland, which ended up involving the Third Section in the process. The evidence of the Weitling connection only complicated matters. For this reason, Alexander Bakunin was ordered, in Russia, in November 1843, to no longer provide his son with any financial resources and to ensure that

he returned to Russia. But Alexander had not sent Bakunin any more money for some time and he also had no ability to compel him to return (Carr, 1961, p. 129).

2   In the 1851 "Confession," Bakunin (1976b [e], p. 57) provides a more complete list of his relations in Paris: F.-A. de Chambolle (*Le Siècle*), Merruceau (*Le Constitutionnel*), Émile de Girardin (*La Presse*), Durieux [X. Durrieu?] (*Le Courrier Français*), the economists Frédéric Bastiat and L. Wolowski, P.-J. Béranger, the Arago family, A. Marrast and J. Bastide (*Le National*), Godefroi Cavaignac, F. Flocon and L. Blanc (*La Réforme*), Victor Considerant (*La Démocratie Pacifique*), Pascal Duprat (*La Revue Indépendante*), Félix Pyat, Victor Schoelcher, J. Michelet, and E. Quinet.

3   In the only issue of the *Franco-German Annals*, of February 1844—which featured two famous essays by Marx, "On the Jewish Question" and the introduction of his "Critique of Hegel's Philosophy of Right"—a letter from Bakunin to Ruge from May 1843 is found, in which, continuing the arguments of "The Reaction in Germany," he asserts the need for a liberating political practice inspired by the French (Bakunin, 2007c[e]).

4   Just before arriving in Paris (and therefore before meeting Marx), while still in Brussels, Bakunin sent a letter to August Becker in June 1844, in which he states: "I am progressing in communism to the point of beginning to admit certain communist ideas." Already in Paris, he wrote in a letter of 14 October, 1844 to Reinhold Solger: "I became French and work, with application, on an *Exhibition and Development of Feuerbach's Ideas*. I study political economy a lot and I am a communist with all my heart" (Bakunin, 44002 [c], p. 1; Bakunin, 44004 [c], p. 3). Apparently, Bakunin had a brief moment of flirtation with communism between 1843 and 1844, to which the work of Stein and relations with Weitling and Marx probably counted. The only claim of communism that Bakunin makes without reservations is this, from October 1844. Even so, it serves to relativize, at least to some extent, the statement of the 1851 "Confession" in which Bakunin (1976b [e], p. 48) wrote: "I was never a communist." This book on Feuerbach was never found, but it reinforces the thesis of Bakunin's closeness with his writings.

5   In Bakunin's work there are references to the following works by Proudhon, followed by the year of their original publication: *What is Property?* (1840), *Idées Révolutionnaires [Revolutionary Ideas]* (1849), *Les Confessions d'un Révolutionnaire [Confessions of a Revolutionary]* (1849), *Idée Générale de la Révolution au XIXe Siècle [General Idea of Revolution in the Nineteenth Century]* (1851), and *De la Justice dans la Révolution et dans l'Église [Justice in the Revolution and the Church]* (1858).

6   In this period, I give preference to the term "revolutionary pan-Slavism," following Hepner (1950, p. 233). However, it should be noted that, between 1844 and 1863, as much as Bakunin's ideas have remained relatively homogeneous, he takes different positions regarding the use of the term "pan-Slavism." After all, not only was the movement in dispute, but also the terms that would be used to refer to it. Initially, Bakunin refuses to identify his views with pan-Slavism; it is only in 1862 that he does so, claiming the term positively. In that period, he considers that his concept of Slavism is, in fact, a type of pan-Slavism, which differs from others. Finally, it should be noted that Bakunin's pan-Slavism is not just revolutionary; he is also anti-centralist, anti-imperialist, classist, democratic, and federalist, such that the adjectives of Bakuninian pan-Slavism could be others. After that period, as the term became more and more linked to a purely Russian Slavism, imperialist and headed by the tsar, Bakunin started to refuse it definitively.

7   In January 1835, when he was living on the border with Poland due to the punishment received in the army, Bakunin was against the Polish cause, albeit in a very superficial way. In a letter to Nikolai N. Muraviev wrote: "not only do I apologize, but I think the measures he took were truly necessary"; he was referring here to the actions of Mikhail, Nikolai's brother and Varvara's cousin (mother), who directly contributed, four years earlier, to the Russian repression of insurgent Poles (Bakunin, 35001[c], p. 7).

8   Of his meeting with members of the Polish democratic party, Bakunin (1976b[e], p. 64) stated: "My attempt was unsuccessful. I have seen Polish Democrats on several occasions, but I have not been able to get along with them. First, because of the disagreement between our conceptions and our national feelings; they seemed to me limited, petty, exclusive, they saw nothing in the world except Poland and were unable to understand the changes that took place in Poland, even after their complete subjection; on the other hand, they were suspicious of me and probably didn't expect much from my cooperation." Leier (2006, p. 116), explaining these differences, considers that "although he offered himself to the Polish community in Versailles and supported the local unrest, the defeat of the uprising threw the movement into a wave of chaos and recriminations. It was difficult for Poles to trust each other, not to

mention a Russian nobleman. Bakunin's revolutionary democracy was of less interest to noble Polish immigrants, many of whom saw the revolution as only an opportunity to replace the Russian nobility. Furthermore, for Bakunin, national liberation was about liberation and not nationalism."

9   According to Carr (1961, pp. 150–51), Bakunin was probably "one of the greatest speakers of all time." Even speaking in several languages, "his solidity and his ardent seriousness," added to his enormous charisma, "left the audience mesmerized." The speech at the banquet on the seventeenth anniversary of the Polish Uprising "was the first and most surprising display of his power as a speaker."

10 However, it is important to point out, so as not to focus on anachronism, that Bakunin's social impact at that time was far greater than Marx's. Corroborating this fact, Leier (2006, p. 119) states: "Marx's work as a writer and editor had attracted some attention to him, but nothing he had done up until then had had the impact of Bakunin's 'The Reaction in Germany.' Even Marx's best-known work, the *Communist Manifesto*, first published in 1848, was practically ignored outside the small circles of German artisans and intellectuals until the 1870s. It was Bakunin, not Marx, who had the crowd at his feet. Marx, with his high, nasal, and academic speech could impress by his logic, but rarely by his presence. Bakunin had an effective discourse style aimed at convincing people by vigorous expression of his ideas and not by meticulous exposure. However, he benevolently perceived and recognized Marx's talent and ability."

11 According to Herzen's account, the position taken by Bakunin, of taking the revolution to its final consequences, would have motivated Caussidière to say about him: "What a man! On the first day of the revolution it is luck to meet him, but the next day it would be necessary to shoot him" (Coêlho, 1994, p. 88). On that same occasion, Flocon said that "if there were 300 Bakunin it would be impossible to govern France" (*apud* Carr, 1961, p. 157).

12 According to Herzen, on that occasion Bakunin defended the "revolution 'in permanence'" (*apud* Dragomanov, 1896, p. 41). In 1868 and 1872, Bakunin takes up this notion when he argues in favour of the "federation of permanent barricades" (Bakunin, 68016[e]), of the "permanence of the barricades and the whole centre of resistance" (Bakunin, 68022[e], p. 3), and of the "permanence of the barricades and the revolutionary uprising" (Bakunin, 72016[e], p. 5).

13 This text was published: in July in *Dziennik Domowy* (Poznan), in Polish; in September in *Wcela* (Prague), in Czech; in December in *Jahrbücher für Slawische Literatur, Kunst und Wissenschaft* (Leipzig), in German; and later, in November 1861, in *Cech* (Geneva), in Czech (Nettlau, 1976, p. 212).

14 The publication, dated 6 July, 1848—which was widely circulated, not only among Germans—reported that George Sand had documents proving that Bakunin was an agent of the Russian government. However much the *New Rhineland Gazette* printed Bakunin's protest and Sand's public denial (made at Bakunin's own request) in its pages, this fact greatly harmed Bakunin's political activities. For Barrué, the rumour probably came from Engels (Barrué, 2015a, pp. 173–74).

15 Speaking of the Slavic Congress, Bakunin (1976b[e], p. 83) pointed out that "among the Slavs, the predominant feeling is hatred of the Germans"; a feeling which met with reciprocity, in that there was also an aversion to the Slavs on the part of the Germans.

16 In the German version, which was circulated in publications, the entire section discussing the "social question" was deleted (for all the deleted passages, cf. Bakunin, 48019[e]). This was at the suggestion of Berlin's democratic friends, depending on the purposes of the text. Thus, Bakunin's view on the subject was only partially known to the public (Berthier, 2010, vol. 2, p. 103). Among other factors, this contributed to the insistence by authors that, in this period, Bakunin replaced the social question with the national question. The "Appeal to the Slavs" was harshly criticized by Engels in the article "Der demokratische Panslawismus" ["Democratic Pan-Slavism"], published in the *New Rhineland Gazette* in February 1849. The article, to which Bakunin probably did not have access, was based on two criticisms: 1) That Bakunin's project was chimerical, based on abstractions and therefore unrealizable. 2) That the Slavs were a people without history and intrinsically counterrevolutionary, without national perspectives. For this reason, Engels advocated, as a historical necessity, the Germanization and Magyarization of the Slavs. This national oppression and even imperialism—Engels openly defends, as a civilizing project, the takeover of Mexican territory from California by the United States in 1848— were necessary for the development of the productive forces and with it the realization of socialism (Engels, 2010). For good commentary on the controversy, cf. Angaut, 2009, pp. 52–61; Berthier, 2010, vol. 2, pp. 101–17; Leier, 2006, pp. 139–42.

17   For a more in-depth commentary on Bakunin's project of the Insurrection in Bohemia, cf. Berthier, 2010, vol. 2, pp. 117–28. Note the similarity, highlighted by Berthier in these pages, between the insurrectionary model advocated by Bakunin for this region and the project concretized in the Russian Revolution of 1917.

18   See Marx's letter to the *New York Daily Tribune* of 2 October, 1852 and Engels' 1851–52 book *Revolution and Counterrevolution in Germany*.

19   In the "Confession", Bakunin (1976b[e], p. 176) ponders the question of violence: "I could never conceive of lamenting more for houses and inanimate objects than for men. The Saxon and Prussian soldiers had fun shooting innocent women looking out of windows, and that did not surprise anyone; but when the democrats set fire to houses in their own defense, everyone shouted to the heavens, describing it as barbarism."

20   This letter to Herzen contains an interesting account of the period when Bakunin was in prison and in exile (Bakunin, 60006[c]).

21   As Grawitz explains (1990, p. 197): "The publication of the text [the 'Confession'] in 1921 was a scandal (some excerpts had been published in 1919). The image of the revolutionary hero was replaced by that of the 'repentant sinner,' the admirer of the Tsar, the courtier. [...] Then several Marxists, mainly Stalinists, began to consider Bakunin a traitor." These controversies ended over the course of the twentieth century, and my evaluation is the object of agreement by practically all scholars in Bakunin.

22   The letter from Count Orlov to Nicholas, as well as the comments and resolutions of the tsar are attached: Bakunin, 1976b[e].

23   The return of the rumour to England was due to the publication in March 1862 of an anonymous article in the pages of David Urquhart's *Free Press*. On that occasion, Ruge, Herzen, and Bakunin himself publicly protested against the unjust charges. These took up the arguments of another article of similar content published in 1853 in the *Morning Advertiser*, also from London, by Urquhart himself. Bakunin tried to put the pieces of the puzzle together and, influenced by Herzen, began to identify Marx's strange proximity to the false accusations. The *New Rheinland Gazette*, which had published them in July 1848, was directed by Marx; Urquhart, who had published them twice, was close to Marx. Bakunin thus began to consider, at least privately, that Marx was most likely involved in the spread of these rumours (Grawitz, 1990, p. 238). But, it should be noted, there has never been any proof that this was true.

24   In a letter of June 1862 to his sister-in-law Natalia, Bakunin (62043[c], p. 3) states: "I preach systematically and by ardent conviction hatred of the Germans, and I say, as Voltaire with regard to God: 'If the Germans did not exist, it would be necessary to invent them,' for nothing is more appropriate to the union of the Slavs than this their fundamental hatred."

25   It is interesting to note the surprise—quite elitist even—of Carr (1961, p. 277) who, in dealing with the influence that Martyanov had on Bakunin, wrote: "This [the greatest importance often given by Bakunin to the people in relation to renowned intellectuals] was part of that inherent simplicity which distinguished Bakunin from all the other radicals and revolutionaries of that time. Herzen idealized the Russian people and Marx the proletariat. But it is impossible to imagine Herzen appropriating the ideas of a field worker, or Marx of a factory worker. Only Bakunin, the aristocrat, was free enough of his class consciousness to be perfectly at ease in his relations with a former serf, and to find that this was so natural that he could be influenced by Martyanov in the same way that Martyanov could be influenced by him."

26   According to Carr (1961, p. 294), it was on that voyage, onboard the ship heading from Copenhagen to Gothenburg, that Bakunin met one such "Mr. Britto," a Brazilian diplomat in charge of business in the Scandinavian capitals; it seems that this was the only Brazilian that Bakunin met in his life.

27   It should be recalled, as already commented in a note, that Bakunin only claims the term "pan-Slavism" from 1862 onwards, when he distinguishes his propositions from other types of pan-Slavism. It should also be remembered that the adjective "revolutionary" could be replaced or supplemented by others, such as "anti-centralist," "anti-imperialist," "classist," "democratic," or "federalist." More important than the term here is the content behind it, which will be further elaborated below.

28   Another reference to Hegel from that period can be found in "Appeal to the Slavs." In this text, when Bakunin (48020[e], p. 27) reflects on the revolutionary possibilities in Europe, he alludes again to the Hegelian metaphor of the mole, when he speaks in the presence of a revolutionary spirit that has become a power capable of dissolving the old world and creating the new (cf., also: Angaut, 2009, p. 49).

29 In that year, Bakunin (62008[e], pp. 7, 9, emphasis added) emphasizes the need to build "the free community of brothers, a totally Slavic community." He emphasizes that "this confirms once again the idea that *socialism, this faith in the future*, is part of the character of the Slavs, is their nature and their mission; this is why they are radically opposed to the Germanic world, which finds its natural expression in the petit bourgeois spirit. By the term *socialism*, we understand a simple and fertile truth: *every intellectual and moral achievement necessitates the development of the material means and advantages on which it is based*. There can be no freedom if everyone does not have enough to eat; the noble goal of generalized *political freedom* will not be achieved until society is organized on the basis of *justice* and *equality*. Every man who comes into the world must find his place on earth, our common mother, and have the means to realize himself according to his capacities." Slavs are a "nation of the future" and must "appropriate this heritage" because "they are socialists by nature." In sum, "the future belongs to *Slavic socialism*; it alone will serve as a vehicle for the patriotic aspirations of all branches of our great family."

CHAPTER 8

STATE, NATION-RACE, AND IMPERIALISM
(1844–63)

This chapter begins the presentation of Bakunin's political theory in his *revolutionary pan-Slavic period*, which runs from 1844 to 1863, and is divided into four parts: 1) Europe in the Years 1848–49, Context of the Peoples' Spring; 2) Social Classes, State, Nation-race, and Imperialism; 3) Political Power and Social Stratification in Imperial Russia; 4) National Oppression of Russian and Non-Russian Slavs.[1]

8.1 EUROPE IN THE YEARS 1848–49, CONTEXT OF THE PEOPLES' SPRING

For a reflection on the European reality, one can start from the foundations of the *method of political analysis* of "The Reaction in Germany," which were explained at the beginning of the theme "Reactionary Party and Democratic Party" (Chapter 5.3) and which are at least partially maintained. In short, it is a question of mapping the forces at play, the parties and principles in dispute, and of understanding the historical context and all the contradictions, especially that between freedom and non-freedom. These foundations are complemented and, to a certain extent, adapted to take into account the national question, which is emerging as a central concern, but not without some considerable difficulties, especially with regard to the relationship between party and principle.[2]

Reality continues to be conceived as the result of a dispute of forces, a confrontation between forces. When there is conflict in society, certain agents—notably "individuals, classes and nations" (Bakunin, 48019[e])—organize themselves and use resources to make themselves preponderant according to certain objectives. As one or some forces manage to impose themselves on another, a new reality is formed. And that reality will be preserved as a status quo as long as the dominant force succeeds in maintaining itself as such. Power relations, oppression, and domination are thus explained as a result of this process and are therefore nothing more than relations of force (Bakunin, 48020[e], pp. 5–7, 21). Even the "influence" that certain agents have over others is explained by these forces (Bakunin, 62002[e], p. 3).

However, force cannot be understood purely and simply as violence. It is not always that a conflict between forces or even an imposition of force involves violence; conflict and imposition can take place in a context of apparent peace or even preserve an apparent situation of peace. But this does not mean that there is no conflict, so that peace is, in general, a "beneficial peace" that works for the benefit of the hegemonic force (Bakunin, 62008[e], p. 2).

Therefore, to understand a reality, violent or peaceful, politically requires analyzing a certain "balance of forces" from a "strategic point of view." Notions such as force, influence, power, oppression, domination, and strategy thus becoming essential (Bakunin, 50001[e], p. 48). In historical terms, it can be said, for example, that the monarchic power established over the peoples was the result of a confrontation in which one force (of the monarchs) imposed itself on the other (of the peoples)—to this end, the resources mobilized by the former and some conditions imposed on the latter (misery, disagreements, political, and moral isolation) were important (Bakunin, 48019[e]).

The forces in conflict in society are both material and moral forces, and ideas are important factors in this dispute (Bakunin, 48007[c], p. 2). Usually, the forces are at play in a social scenario, which is society itself, structured according to a certain "historical development" (Bakunin, 62002[e], p. 4). It is this development that lays the foundations of society by forging, according to the confrontation between forces, social positions that have specific roles and are necessary for the functioning of society. Such a structure, such positions, place certain limits on human will, and impose a certain morality on political actions (Bakunin, 63008[e]).

To occupy a hierarchical position in class society—as in the case of a master of serfs in Russia, for example—means to reproduce oppression and to do evil, regardless of the will of those who do it. "There are men and parties who never correct themselves and who, because of the *very necessity of their position*, based on the slavery of the masses, cannot but do evil unless they cease to exist; for them, to live means to oppress" (Bakunin, 48019[e], emphasis added). Another example is the case of the bureaucracy which, in Russia's case, because of its position in society, is condemned to corruption: "From the top of this pyramid to its base, all officials are the most cynical thieves"; that is "the rule," that which is "inscribed as a principle inherent to their function" (Bakunin, 49009[e], p. 4).

Nevertheless, even within these limits, *will* has enormous possibilities. Understanding the play of forces and adopting a position in the face of it remains the most relevant criterion for the formation of these forces. Human resources are those which have the most centrality in the analysis (Bakunin, 50001[e], p. 49). The increase or decrease of force is in most cases linked to the union or disunion of people according to certain objectives (Bakunin, 48004[e], p. 1). "Public opinion" is an important factor in this game, as is "consciousness of its strength" on the part of the agents. Both increase the possibilities for certain agents to impose themselves on others, taking what they consider to be theirs by right (Bakunin, 62006[e], pp. 4, 39).

At the same time as there have been historical impositions of force between individuals, classes, and nations, which explain the formation of different relations of oppression and domination, there have also been confrontations between forces in order to combat and transform these relations. Faced with this, the prospect of breaking with oppression and domination necessarily involves intervening in this dispute of forces—the oppressed and dominated must accumulate force to break with their submission. This implies, therefore, stimulating the "popular consciousness" (Bakunin, 50001[e], p. 7), mobilizing the "power [Macht] of the people"[3] (Bakunin, 49001[e], p. 1) and the "force of the revolutionary movement" (Bakunin, 48019[e]). This was the case, for example, when popular pressure in Europe imposed a series of defeats on European absolutism: "With a knife to the throat [of Europe's absolute monarchs], they were forced to *generously* make the broadest concessions" (Bakunin, 48019[e]).

*   *   *

Utilizing this analytical tool to understand Europe in the context of the Peoples' Spring and immediately thereafter, some notes can be made. In the early 1840s, it seemed right to predict that the culmination of the contradictions—which, in a way, were still unfolding in that new context—heralded a new revolutionary cycle, which in fact opened up in 1848. It was no longer an underground war but an open conflict in which the new world imposed itself on the old.

"The revolution that took place in France [February 1848] radically changed all the issues. Without any exaggeration, it can be said today that the ancient world is dead; what remains of it will soon disappear. We are at the birth of a new world." This opening up of the transforming cycle of 1848 drastically changed the perspectives of the agents in conflict when it came to revolutionary possibilities: "the practical men of the Old Regime have today become the utopians, and the utopia of yesterday is, from now on, the only thing possible, reasonable, practicable. This utopia is pure, absolute democracy for France and for the whole of Europe." The idea that this would be impossible was therefore outdated: "that word [impossible] is no longer from today, it is from yesterday. Impossible today is royalty, aristocracy, inequality, slavery" (Bakunin, 48002[e], p. 1).

There also seems to be no doubt that the June Revolution continued to contribute to this idea and to show that the negative principle was emerging, testing its overcoming of the positive. But would this old negative become a new positive? The question was posed. In any case, right after June, there was evidence that "the revolution is there [...], it is everywhere, acting and fermenting" (Bakunin, 48009[c], pp. 3–4). Between 1848 and 1849, the contradiction between freedom and non-freedom culminated in a revolutionary process which, directed towards the realization of freedom and the overcoming of the old world by the new, put social and national questions on the agenda, as well as the problem of the concomitant realization of "social democracy" and "national democracy" (Bakunin, 62008[e], p. 12; Bakunin, 63008[e]; Berthier, 2010, vol. 2, p. 16).

Two major questions arose [...] in the first days of spring: the social question
and that of the independence of all nations—the emancipation of peoples
internally [from the States] and externally [from other States] at the same time.
It was not a few individuals, nor a party, but the admirable instinct of the masses
that put these two questions above all others and demanded an immediate solution. Everyone had understood that freedom is a lie when the majority of the
population is condemned to a miserable existence, when, deprived of education,
leisure and bread, it is, so to speak, destined to serve as a step for the rich and
powerful. The social revolution is therefore a natural consequence of the political revolution. In the same way, it was felt that as long as there is even one
persecuted nation in Europe, the decisive and complete triumph of democracy
will not be possible anywhere: the oppression of one people or even of a single
individual is the oppression of all, and one cannot violate the freedom of one
without violating the freedom of each and every one. (Bakunin, 48019[e],
emphasis added)

First of all, the Peoples' Spring and the insurgent initiatives that unfolded during that
time were therefore not only social. The problem of inequality, directly linked to social
classes, was undoubtedly a central axis of this process; the political change begun in
February and deepened in June should lead to a transformation that, by means of a
social revolution, would resolve it.

But the Peoples' Spring also counted on national initiatives: "The revolutions of
1848 were also often correctly called the 'Spring of Nations,' since the events of 1848
gave expression to the aspirations of submerged nations." Here, the problem of national
oppression between states and peoples, imperialism, was the central axis. With regard
to this problem, changes should lead to national liberation or independence, which
could point toward the freedom and self-determination of peoples.

In other words, "the experience of 1848 forged the basis for the crystallization of
two forces in Europe: socialism and nationalism." It was, therefore, a problem that
was both social and national, and its solution required efforts on both fronts (Cipko,
1990, p. 3).

Secondly, when it is emphasized that the domination of a people or an individual
means the domination of all and that, at the same time, the freedom of all demands
the freedom of each one, it is indispensable to understand the collective and solidarity
aspects in the freedom-oppression/domination dialectic. In accordance with what
Fichte and Hegel advocated—the latter, particularly in his well-known Master–Slave
Dialectic—freedom (as well as oppression/domination) has a collective, solidary
foundation, demanding that for a person to be free, all others around him must also
be free. The realization of freedom, thus understood, implies a project that is not and
cannot be individual, involving only one or a few individuals.

This concept of freedom was exposed when Bakunin spoke of his beliefs up to
the time of his arrest:

This need [for movement and action], later united to democratic exaltation, was, so to speak, my only cause. This exaltation can be defined in a few words: love of freedom and invincible hatred of all oppression, hatred which is even more intense when it is exercised over another and not over me. *To seek my happiness in the happiness of others, my personal dignity in the dignity of all those around me, to be free in the freedom of others*; this is my whole belief, the aspiration of all my life. (Bakunin, 1976b[e], pp. 111–12, emphasis added)

Democracy, or the democratic principle, is then seen as a project for the collective struggle against oppression in favour of freedom, happiness, and dignity. Freedom is understood as solidarity and something that does not exist partially; either it is collective or it is not freedom. In this way, the possibilities of individual and even sectoral social ascension or mobility in social structures of domination are discarded.

The conquest of democracy and freedom in social and national terms therefore implies guaranteeing "the greatness, freedom and happiness of all, based on a sacred and fraternal solidarity of individuals and nations." Not even those who are protagonists of social and/or national oppression can be effectively free. In the case of the domination of one nation by another, for example, there is "oppression not only of the oppressed" but also "for he who oppresses" so that liberation can only occur if there is an end to oppression. "Respect and love for the freedom of others is [...] the first condition of one's own freedom" (Bakunin, 48004[e], p. 1). That is: "the freedom of all peoples is in solidarity" (Bakunin, 48019[e]); "the freedom of each people in particular is guaranteed only by the freedom of all peoples" (Bakunin, 48020[e], p. 30).[4]

The revolutionary wave of 1848 and 1849 made it possible to understand this principle even more concretely. It became evident that domination and oppression, as well as freedom, are collective and in solidarity. So Europe, in analytical and political terms, had to be considered not in part, but in its entirety.

After all, these were very different times from those which, following the fall of the Middle Ages, had marked the "golden age of absolutism" in which "the peoples of Europe fell into mortal apathy." At that time, when "the monarchies of Europe were consolidated" and "princes reigned with unlimited authority," peoples were "completely engrossed in the vain speculations of the Jesuits or the pietists" and even seemed to have "lost all force, all vital impetus and even a leftover conscience of free men." These peoples were treated as "inert and servile masses" and the despots disposed of them "according to their pleasures and whims, dividing them among themselves, robbing them, selling them." They enjoyed of them "as if the peoples existed only to serve, to be a vulgar instrument designed to satisfy the power and appetites of a few families"; they enjoyed of them "as if the honor and life of princes depended on the shame and death of peoples" (Bakunin, 50001[e], p. 62).

However, the history of the seventeenth century, and especially of the eighteenth, has profoundly changed this picture.

The philosophy of the Enlightenment of the 18th century, the great French
Revolution that emerged, and later Napoleon's victories, shook people from
their mortal sleep. They awoke to a new life, to independence, to freedom, to
morality. New demands and new needs made themselves felt everywhere. A
new world was born, a world in which men were aware of themselves and of
their dignity; in a word, it was humanity, in its noblest and broadest sense, the
only and highest objective to which every form of society and every history
tends. Until then, peoples were divided, often enemies of each other, victims o
f stupid and artificially preserved prejudices. They then felt the need to come
closer; guided by a certain instinct, they understood that this great goal to
which everyone aspired—and which could set them free, make them men—
could only be attained by the union of their forces. Thus, bit by bit, a general
movement was born in Europe: sometimes hidden in the deepest layers of
society, sometimes manifesting itself again by some thunderous action,
stimulated by the progress of general culture, but above all by the increasing
extension of industry and commerce, invisible but powerful. It united all the
peoples of Europe in a great indivisible organism and, little by little, created
among them that solidarity which is the characteristic sign, the capital feature
of contemporary history. (Bakunin, 50001[e], pp. 62–63)

Deeply marked by the French Revolution, crowned by the Peoples' Spring and
deriving from a general development in economic, political, and cultural terms,
European modernity was then characterized by a "general movement" which, in a
latent or manifest way, demonstrated the importance of solidarity between peoples.
    This solidarity was growing in the nineteenth century and caused "the destinies
of all the European peoples [to be] entangled" with "no human power [able] to
disunite them." Thus, it would be possible to say that "there are no longer, in our time,
several different histories, but only one great history" (Bakunin, 50001[e], p. 40). In such
a transnational history, the various oppressed peoples of Europe had an important
role to play, both for their national liberation and for their social emancipation.

8.2 SOCIAL CLASSES, STATE, NATION-RACE, AND IMPERIALISM

For the political analyses carried out in the period in question, the most important
concepts are *State*, *nation-race*, and *imperialism*, which will be discussed next.
However, it should be noted that these concepts are related to another, *social classes*,
which will initially be elucidated in order to support the consecutive exposition.
    *Social classes are human groupings formed on the basis of the relative social position
of large collectivities, defined according to whether or not they possess certain privileges:
ownership (including, and in some cases mainly, land), money, knowledge, power, and
status.* These privileges—which, as can be seen, are not only economic—are
responsible for the division of society into classes and for the conflict between classes

which, in permanent existence, must also be interpreted as a relationship between forces. This conflict involves not only the social question but also the national question in more and less developed societies (Bakunin, 48019[e]; Bakunin, 50001[e], Bakunin, 1976b[e], Bakunin, 62002[e], p. 4).

Class conflict usually involves two contradictory sets of classes—it is not just the struggle of one class against another, but of some classes against others. And in this conflict, not only the origin or position of the class is decisive, but also and in some cases mainly, the stance taken in the face of the conflict analyzed. However, while classes and class conflicts in general can be found in diverse contexts, their particular concreteness is specific to each historical context. In every society, at every moment, different social classes are formed, allied, and confronted. And it is in these precise contexts that the particular expressions of the classes and their conflicts can be identified.[5]

The State—building on its modern dimension, incorporated into the European powers of the mid-nineteenth century[6]—is a centralized political instrument that imposes its might and authority on a geographical territory and on the people as a whole, in order to administer and govern people, classes, nations, and races oppressively and through its power. It is an artificial and mechanical power, managed by a bureaucracy and other ruling classes, which has imposed itself on the people to the detriment of their individual and national freedoms, and which is constantly seeking to preserve itself (Bakunin, 48004[e], p. 1; Bakunin, 50001[e], pp. 15, 44, 61). There is therefore a clear distinction between the State and the social community that is subordinated to it (Bakunin, 49001[e], p. 1). Now, while on the one hand it can be said that all states dominate an important part of their own populations, on the other, some of these states—the great states, the powers—also oppress other peoples, nationally, by means of conquest and imperialist policies (Bakunin, 50001[e], p. 6).

In terms of the "nature" and "purpose of its organism," the State "was created not to liberate, but to oppress peoples"—its force "is based solely on the subjugation of the people." And this political domination is generally carried out by means of a range of procedures, which include "lying, hypocrisy, corruption, ruthless murder, demoralization" as well as "the buying of consciences by money, fear, misery, superstition, and religious obscurantism." In short, the State is founded and established with "all that which could be invented for the harm and unhappiness of the people." In the case of a great state, a "state-machine," which succeeds in imposing itself on its population and still "extends its territory by conquest," it "can only demand three things from its people: money, soldiers, and internal peace and, for the latter, the means to guarantee it matter little. Such a State treats its own people as a conquered people and is a dictatorial State both internally and externally." Thus, it can be said that the state-machine subjugates its own population, as well as those of other states which are dominated by it (Bakunin, 50001[e], pp. 6, 15, 61; Bakunin, 48002[e], p. 1; Bakunin, 49001[e], p. 1).

When the State is understood as an artificial and mechanical power, this opposes certain ideas involving not only states but also national unity and borders. *Artificial and mechanical is all that which is produced from outside in, from top to bottom.* Such that the State, by subjugating a territory and a social collectivity, must be considered an artificial and mechanical political instrument. This is because its force and authority are historically established from the outside in—it is not a political body created according to the national and cultural criteria of the peoples themselves— and from the top down—which have been imposed on the peoples by rulers, who have subjugated their ruled (Bakunin, 48019[e]; Bakunin, 50001[e], p. 45; Angaut, 2009, pp. 39, 72, 81).

For the same reasons, the national unity and borders forged by the State are artificial and mechanical. The State establishes "artificial, monstrous borders, violently determined by the congresses of the despots [as in the case of the Vienna Congress in 1815], according to so-called historical, geographical, commercial, strategic needs" (Bakunin, 48019[e]). In the historical case of German unity, the State and its representatives "are at most capable of promoting a purely mechanical and still very problematic union" (Bakunin, 50001[e], p. 45).

However, the State is not an automaton, but an organism formed and maintained under the management of people, groups, and social classes. The State is run by *the "bureaucracy, that power of administrations," a managing power which, depending on the context, can be more or less centralized, more or less absolute.* And the bureaucracy does this in association with other upper classes of society, such as "the aristocracy" and "the privileged bourgeoisie." The State is always under the management of this "minority of privileged bureaucrats," of its "powerful bureaucratic hierarchy," as well as of the dominant strata of society and their corresponding hierarchy. Bureaucracy and the upper classes are responsible for the oppression of the people (Bakunin, 62008[e], pp. 1, 7–8, emphasis added).

The bureaucracy has "a dual nature, a dual system following its French and German origins." It accompanies the different types of state, French or German, and is also divided into two types: French bureaucracy and German bureaucracy. But, as will be explained below, the French and German nations do not necessarily correspond to the states of France and Germany. Although the typical French state is France, the typical German state is the Austrian Empire, later being increasingly replaced by Prussia; although the typical French bureaucracy is France, the typical German bureaucracy is Austrian. The oppression exercised by France and Austria on their peoples have distinct foundations and legitimizing bases.

What marks the French state is the "centralizing tendency" which shaped—from its emergence "in 1793, starting with the great revolution" to the beginning of the 1860s—"modern French society," which became largely "docile and passionately devoted" to state power so that such fidelity is "the engine of current power." The French state has "a simple, understandable and practical system which leads all the components of the governed society to a single center." It "subdues every personal initiative, abolishes every form of communal or regional autonomy, causing them to be absorbed by an autocratic state, the only admitted power." A typical member of the French bureaucracy is "esteemed, reputed and capricious, but does not demand a religious reverence before his own person," he is like a "conductor who drives his train to a funeral." "This kind of bureaucracy can suit a people who no longer want to take control of themselves, who do not feel comfortable expressing their own will, acting according to their ideas, or simply living, especially if they want nothing more than to be guided." But it does not suit a "young and new nation" that wants its own self-government.

What marks the Austrian state, a typical German state before the rise of Prussia, is not modern centralization, but its "quasi-religious system," which is explained by the "abstract Germanic spirit," "a kind of temple, where the whole great German nation bows before the divine power of the 'State.'" It is more properly a "nation-killing State," which "does not recognize in itself any notion of homeland" that is not "incarnated by the State." The term *Gesammtvaterlanden* itself, which appeared between 1848 and 1849, supports this thesis in that it reflects the notion of an Austrian patriotism disconnected from the State. The Austrian bureaucracy, a typical German bureaucracy, whose member "reminds us of a priest who sacrifices the sweat and blood of the people, the independence, the law and the very being of nations, on the altar of the supreme idol, his majesty, the State." This bureaucrat is "a fanatic, a cruel man by conviction, as true priests often are"; "forced to labor for a low wage, he is ready to renounce humanism, friendship, family, homeland, in the name of his supreme ideal—the State" (Bakunin, 62008[e], pp. 8–9).

Again insisting on the distinction between state and people, some notes need to be made. Internally, it is the bureaucracy and other ruling classes that oppress the population under state management. It is not therefore a question of the domination of the people over the people. Externally, it is not the whole people of the oppressing state who dominate another state or nation, but the bureaucracy and other upper classes of this state. So, in discussing national domination, imperialism, it cannot be conceivable that such oppression is equally led by all strata and classes of the oppressing state.

This is the case when considering Russia, a great conquering state externally and oppressing one internally, distinguishing between two Russias within it. On the one hand, there is an "official Russia, the only one known in Europe" made up of the tsar, the nobility, the bureaucracy, and the clergy, who are the real Russian tyrants. On the other, there is a "popular Russia," a national one, much less known internationally because it is composed of the Russian people, and which has nothing in common with the official Russia. Between the two, "there has never been anything in common." The second is not the explanation of oppression, but the liberating power of the Russians (Bakunin, 63003[e], p. 6; Bakunin, 63008[e]).

Finally, the quest for state preservation by the State itself, driven in particular by bureaucracy and the sectors that benefit from it, obeys one rule: every state, "every power, even if it is small or limited, or if it is the most iniquitous and the most malignant in the world, seeks to maintain itself as much as it can." A state, small or large, always wants to remain a state. "There has never been an example in history of voluntary political suicide" by the State "for the benefit of a community"—"this is completely contrary to its nature." The State is maintained internally and externally, to the detriment of individual and national freedoms (Bakunin, 50001[e], p. 44).

As mentioned, it must be kept in mind that a state is not synonymous with a nation, and a nation cannot and should not be considered only an idea promoted by the State in favour of its own constitution. The intention is now to conceptualize nation-race and then to compare this concept with that of the State so as to make such differences evident.

Nation-race is a social collectivity whose members share a specific national identity, which differs from others and which expresses itself in terms of their way of living, acting and thinking (Bakunin, 50001[e], pp. 48, 60; Bakunin, 62008[e], p. 7; Bakunin, 62025[c], p. 5). It is thus a concept that expresses a natural and organic potential: the culture and cultural identity of a people, as well as the way in which it is concretely manifested through the community of: language, customs, and lifestyle (traditions, clothing, food, music, literature, art, etc.), national feelings, religion, institutions, values, blood and historical ties (real or imagined), and/or shared hopes for the future (Bakunin, 48020[e], p. 16; Bakunin, 50001[e], pp. 70, 76).

A nation-race is that collectivity which possesses "unity in its conscience," "unity in its political life," "the feeling of its force, the sufficient potential to make its talents prevail and to protect its isolated members, divided among themselves, against foreign influence, against conquests and divisions." It is that collectivity which possesses identity, national feeling, "effective feeling of its living unity" (Bakunin, 50001[e], pp. 41, 60). Therefore, nation-race resembles the idea of people in the ethnic-racial or cultural sense (not in the sense of class), and even what in the twentieth century will be called ethnics and ethnicity, or what has been called spontaneous nationality, stateless nationality, ethnic, and linguistic community. Slavs are an example of a nation-race, of a people, which includes within itself other nation-races, other peoples (Bakunin, 48019[e]).[7]

When talking about natural and organic potency, one must be careful not to take the concept in question in biological terms when in fact it is a cultural concept. The nation-race is natural because it opposes the artificial, and it is organic because it opposes the mechanical. *Natural and organic is everything here that is produced from the inside out, from the bottom up.* National unity and the borders forged by the nation-races are therefore considered natural and organic. Their force and potential are established on the basis of national identities and feelings, from the inside out, from the bottom up, from the national and cultural criteria of the peoples themselves, representing their self-determination. This unity implies that "people [...] can create organic unity [...], for only the people themselves contain blood, sap, and life" (Bakunin, 50001[e], p. 45). Such borders are a "natural, just, democratic delimitation, based on the sovereign will of the peoples themselves and on their different nationalities" (Bakunin, 48019[e]). Thus, when one speaks, for example, of "the nature of a people" or of a homeland as a natural notion, it is not a question of biological determinism but of a cultural nature, forged and maintained historically by social relations (Bakunin, 50001[e], pp. 70, 76; Bakunin, 62002[e], p. 1).[8]

In distinguishing between the concepts of State and nation-race, it is understood first of all that a nation-race can have a presence in several states—as in the case of the Slavs, who live in the countries of Eastern and Southeastern Europe—and that a state can have several nation-races within its territory—as in the case of Austria, which has Slavs, Magyars/Hungarians, and Germans among its population (Bakunin, 48004[e]; Bakunin, 49001[e], p. 1). Secondly, it is understood that historically it was not states that created the notion of nationality as a means of legitimizing themselves. On the contrary, it is modern states that have imposed their forces on nation-races, often stimulating conflict and fragmentation between these peoples, which predate states (Bakunin, 49001[e], p. 1). It is in this perspective that the previous statement that the nation-state is nothing more than a murderous state of nations must be understood. As has been argued, if the State forges its unity and its borders artificially and mechanically, the nation-race establishes them in a natural and organic way. In the case of Russia, for example, this distinction between State and nation-race is clear. "The Russian state is not the Russian nation"; it is, rather, only "an abstract principle that weighs on this nation" (Bakunin, 50001[e], p. 25). An abstract principle because it is artificial and mechanical, yet has very concrete consequences.

Imperialism or national oppression/domination is the imposition of force by the bureaucracy and other upper classes of one state on the entire population of another state or of a nation-race, for the benefit of those who impose themselves and to the detriment of those who are subjected.[9] It is achieved by different means derived from conquest and/or political influence and, among other cases, when a people, according to its nationality, is the victim of persecution, discrimination, imprisonment, murder; when it experiences the subordination of its culture, its religion, its institutions; when it is the victim of dependence, and/or when economic exploitation may be noted (Bakunin, 49001[e], p. 1; Bakunin, 50001[e], pp. 58, 74–75, 84).

In such a relationship, which can be considered a "foreign oppression," a "foreign yoke," an imposition of the State on a "foreign race," the protagonist of national domination is not the people of the imperialist state (Bakunin, 48004[e], p. 1). In the case of Russian imperialism, for example, it is not the Russian people (popular Russia) but the Russian state allied to the dominant strata (official Russia) that is the protagonist of the conquests—the Russian state, more precisely, is also hostile to its own people (Bakunin, 63003[e], p. 6; Bakunin, 63008[e]).

When one investigates the reason for national domination, one finds that it exists according to a dynamic characteristic of modern states. To preserve itself, the State is obliged to constantly increase its force in order not to be conquered and to guarantee internal order. And the "conquests" are carried out by the great states, by the powers, for this reason. It is not, therefore, only the will of the imperialists. The great state conquers "because it is obliged to do so. It does so for its own preservation." In Russia, because internal oppression is insufficient for the necessary gain of force, the State "turns to the exterior, and only this perpetual expansion, only these tireless efforts to extend its borders give it its force" (Bakunin, 50001[e], p. 25).

8.3 POLITICAL POWER AND SOCIAL STRATIFICATION IN IMPERIAL RUSSIA

On the basis of the above concepts, it is possible to invest in an "objective analysis of the situation in Russia," which explains the role of classes, the State, the nation, and imperialism in that country's history (Bakunin, 49006[e], p. 1).

In imperial Russia, during the 1840s–60s, the State can be characterized as a centralized, autocratic, absolutist political instrument, imposing itself on a territory of millions of square kilometers—forming, in physical dimensions, the largest state in the world—and on a population of tens of millions of inhabitants belonging to different nation-races—the largest being the Russians themselves, but including, among others, Poles, Ukrainians, Belarussians, Tartars, Jews, and Germans. The Russian state is "the principle of a power founded on absolutism and seeking only selfish ends, a principle that submerges peoples in darkness and crushes them in the name of divine law. It is the devil of despotism" (Bakunin, 50001[e], p. 25).

This absolutist state is a "monstrous machine of oppression and conquest," that is, an instrument that dominates the Russians themselves and also other peoples, inside and outside its territory (Bakunin, 47003[e], p. 2). Even with the numerous problems of its army—among which are: its means of recruiting, the lack of adequate preparation, and the frequent demoralization of troops, which often cause soldiers to desert or join their enemies during battles—this state, through the social classes that control it, is able to maintain the order of the Russian people and advance over other states and peoples (Bakunin, 49006[e], p. 2).

The Russian state is "synonymous with brutal oppression and shameful slavery" as well as "a vile instrument of conquest" constituting "an increasing danger to the freedom of peoples" throughout Europe. The Russians, under the empire, are "still a slave people" for whom "there is no freedom, no respect for human dignity. It is hideous despotism, without a brake on its whims, without limits on its action. Without rights, without justice, without resources against arbitrariness." "Abroad," the position of the Russian state "is no less deplorable" since official Russia, these "masters" of the Russian people, uses its force "to subject peoples, and each of their successes is a new shame." In its history of domination of foreign peoples, the case of "Poland, where since 1772, and especially after 1831, we have been dishonoured daily by atrocious violence, by nameless infamy" stands out (Bakunin, 47003[e], p. 1). To understand the "why of these conquests" of Russia, it is necessary to understand that, as pointed out, "it is obliged" to do so since these conquests are "necessary for its own preservation" as a state. With limited resources to be exploited within its own territory, Russia—because it does not have enough "interior life," "activity," "progress," and "objective"—"turns to the outside world, and only its perpetual expansion, its tireless efforts to extend its borders give it its everlasting force and monstrous vitality" (Bakunin, 50001[e], p. 25).

Noting this double oppression of the Russian state makes it possible not only to understand its own nature, but also, on the basis of the concept of solidaristic and collective freedom explained above, to point out certain challenges for the realization of the freedom of peoples.

> On the one hand, the theme of the executioner slave, omnipresent in the texts about Poland, finds a wider application here [in "My Defense"]: it is better understood how the freedom of Poland, for example—but also that of Finland, the Baltic provinces and even the recent conquests in the Caucasus and Central Asia—is a necessary condition for the freedom of Russia and how its subjection is founded on the subjection of the Russian people. On the other hand, the analysis of the Russian State as a machine of exploitation, developed in "The Situation in Russia," finds its realization here. What unites these two themes is essentially the nature of the Russian State as an expansionist force which is mobilizing on the interior to expand abroad. (Angaut, 2009, p. 75)

The domination of its own people allows the Russian state to invest in an imperialist expansionism that oppresses other states and other peoples, other nation-races. In other words, the oppression of the Russian people is directly linked to the domination of Poles, Finns, Lithuanians, Latvians, Estonians, and Greeks. So, the liberation of one people demands the liberation of the others; ending the submission of one people demands the ending of the submission of the others.

In historical terms, it was under Peter the Great, particularly between 1721 and 1725, that the imperial state imposed itself on the Russian nation or people. It was a model of political power that had been imported from Europe and which was foreign to the local political culture. "The regime and society which Peter I founded had nothing pleasant for the people" and everything about them "was foreign to them: laws, classes, institutions, customs, language, religion, the tsar himself, who called himself Emperor, and whom the people, on the other hand, named the servant of the Antichrist" (Bakunin, 62002[e], p. 2). After that, "the Russian nation" remained "increasingly alien to the imperial State" (Bakunin, 50001[e], p. 5). From 1762 onwards, this process became even worse when the Romanovs were replaced by the Holstein-

Gottorp-Romanovs, of German origin. As a result, Germanic elements were imposed on the Russians, as was the case with Tsar Nicholas I's own rise to power. In Russia, his government must be considered the power of "a foreign hand" and a "unique mixture of Mongolian brutality and Prussian pedantism, [which] completely excludes the national element," and the tsar "a sovereign of German origin, who will never understand the needs and character of the Russian people" (Bakunin, 47003[e], p. 2).

The fact is that, through this formula of internal and external oppression, and under the imperial rule of Germanic origin, the Russian state, especially after the Congress of Vienna, became the greatest European power, leading the international reaction. In this "geopolitics of reaction," "it is not Germany [...] which constitutes the center, the reservoir of power and archetype of European reaction, but Russia" (Angaut, 2009, p. 62). Its role in defending the old world in the conflict with the new had been decisive—a "miserable role," which could be observed, for example, in the stance adopted by Russia "in Germany, Italy, Spain, and France itself" (Bakunin, 47003[e], pp. 1–2).

To understand the Russian state better, it is necessary at this time to relate it to the social classes of imperial Russia. However much land ownership and money were central privileges of that society, putting masters and serfs in contradictory positions, other privileges—such as access to political power, knowledge, and social prestige—also existed. On the basis of this range of privileges one can map the structure of social classes and class conflicts in Russia.

In general terms, taking into account the size of the classes and the social relations of that society, it can be said that the central class conflict is expressed in the contradiction that involves "on the one hand, a very numerous nobility, and on the other, the great mass of peasants" (Bakunin, 48019[e]). However, the picture of the dominant and oppressed classes in Russia was broader than that. The dominant strata in imperial Russia were: the nobility (civil and military), the bureaucracy (civil and military), and the clergy. The oppressed social strata were mainly the peasants, who constitute the vast majority of society, but also workers, craftsmen, soldiers, and sailors. Intermediate strata were made up of merchants and skilled workers, also in small numbers (Bakunin, 62002[e], p. 3, Bakunin, 62006[e], p. 17).

The classes that control the Russian state are these upper classes—the nobility, the bureaucracy, and the clergy—i.e. official Russia.

With a much greater power than the others is the emperor, Tsars Nicholas I and then Alexander II, belonging to the Romanov dynasty that ruled Russia from 1613 onwards. In tsarist imperial Russia there is to a large extent only the "unlimited will of the emperor," who concentrates practically "all political powers in his person, being free from all control." In general, and in everything that is done publicly, the tsar "has to respect no privileges or rights" and therefore "he is, in fact and in law, the absolute master of life and honour of all his subjects without exception" (Bakunin, 45001[e], p. 1). Even the Senate is not in any position to limit the absolute power of the tsar and must be considered "the most humble and obedient servant of the tsar," having never had "the audacity to manifest any inclination to autonomy. The emperor is the sole source of all legislative and executive power. He is the one who appoints and revokes senators" (Bakunin, 49008[e], p. 6).

However, internal oppression in Russia was obviously not instrumentalized by the tsar himself alone; the upper classes, who were subjected to him, played a fundamental role. These classes even had some representation in the Council of State, which despite its rather limited influence contributed to the consolidation of imperial power.

> For two centuries, the Russian people suffered under the rule of Moscow and Saint Petersburg; they endured torments and difficulties unimaginable to a foreigner. The first cause of all the calamities were the tsars. They created this monstrous autocratic centralization and baptized it with the blood of the people. They formed castes hostile to the people, the clergy, the officials [bureaucracy], and the nobility, who served as a weapon to the tsars for their disastrous despotism, and handed over to them the people under the religious servitude of some and physical (servitude) of others. It is only by their force, by their will, by their direct protection that the furious will of the half-wild nobleman and the oppressive barbarism of the official are perpetuated. The tsars, until the last moment, have considered the Russian people with the same contempt that the potter holds for his clay, considering it an inanimate raw material, forced to take any form, according to his good will. (Bakunin, 62006[e], p. 17)

Nobility, bureaucracy, and clergy are therefore the enemy classes of the Russian people and contribute directly to their political-religious submission. Despite the conflicts of more or less significant sectors of these classes with the tsar himself, they generally serve as intermediaries between the tsar and the people and are concretely responsible for implementing domination at all levels. In the history of imperial Russia, it was this intermediation that, on various occasions, caused popular hatred to be channeled against the members of these classes and not against the tsar—in these cases it was common for the tsar to receive admiration and fidelity from the Russian people (Bakunin, 49008[e], p. 3).

The Russian nobility and bureaucracy were deeply impacted by the creation of the Table of Ranks by Peter the Great in 1722. This table provided 14 levels for careers in military service, public service, and court service; the nobility held the highest positions on such a scale, and the bureaucracy the lowest (Bakunin, 49008[e], pp. 3–4). From then on, during the period analyzed here, the nobility encompassed the highest military (e.g.: general-marshal, general, lieutenant, major, brigadier, etc.) and civilian (chancellor, marshal, procurator, adviser, master, director, etc.) levels. And the bureaucracy is now composed of the intermediate military (e.g.: captain, second lieutenant, commissioner, merchant, etc.) and civilians (master, executor, prosecutor, advisor, judge, senator, court employee, etc.) levels.[10]

Two episodes have been remarkable in the history of Russian nobility: the war between Russia and France (1812–14) and the Decembrist Uprising (1825). During that war, some educated nobles visited Europe and had access to progressive (reforming and modernizing) political concepts. This had a significant "influence on the nobility" and made certain nobles "aware of their value"; they developed "an aspiration for freedom" and embodied the promotion of such political concepts in Russia (Bakunin, 49008[e], p. 5).

From 1816 onwards, the first Russian secret societies, which would lead the Decembrist movement, were derived from this.

> This conspiracy was remarkable because it represented the first awakening of the Russian nobility and not a simple conspiracy of courtiers. It was above all in the corps of officers, in which the elite of the nobility were represented, that this conspiracy was born, erupted in 1825 and was repressed with blood. [...] Everything in this conspiracy was full of youth and romanticism, but its initial objective, a constitution for the empire, was quickly surpassed by its most prominent leaders, like Pestle, Ryleyev and Muraviev, who established principles which are still essential for a revolution in Russia. In particular: the declaration of national ownership of land and soil, the liberation of peasants, the expulsion of the Romanov house and, with the dismantling of the Russian empire, the foundation of a Slavic federal republic. (Bakunin, 49008[e], p. 5)

Nicholas I's repression of this conspiracy was based on "terrorism," which put an end to the "noble spirit of youth through the restoration of censorship, secret police and the inquisition." The "young progressive nobility," which was harshly repressed, began to devote itself to German literature and philosophy after the repression, condemning itself to paralysis. Sometime later, part of this nobility realized "that it has no value, that it has no future" if it relies only on itself, if it acts on its own. In other words, some progressive nobles finally grasped that "it is only in the people that Russia's energy and future life reside." It is precisely this part of Moscow's "radical youth," of noble origin, "which refuses to serve the State" and, betraying its class origin, "allies itself with the people, seeking, in the fields, to dissolve itself into the people" (Bakunin, 49008[e], p. 6).[11]

Obviously, this position taken by the radicalized nobles did not change class relations in Russia. Even after that, the nobility continued to form an oppressive class. Yet the trajectory of these radicals seemed to show that there was among them a certain potential for change.

In the case of the Russian bureaucracy, this "world of officials," it embraces a "incorrigible" universe marked by "corruption," which continues to "oppress the people." Such "corruption is the inevitable consequence of the low salaries received by the poor mass of civil servants and the sad state of affairs" to which they are subjected. These bureaucrats simply "cannot have the moral sense of honour, because of the unconditional obedience and complete lack of independence that are required as the first and only duty of every good Russian official." The socialization to which bureaucrats are subjected in the exercise of their profession serves them as a practical education, which teaches this very corruption through everyday activities (Bakunin, 49009[e], pp. 4–5; Bakunin, 1976b[e], p. 102).

Moreover, it should be remembered that it is "through his powerful hierarchy that the orders of the emperor go down to the people, and that the complaints and claims of the people go up to the emperor, obviously subject to the consent of the officials." This function is used by bureaucrats for their own benefit. In addition to being the ones who guarantee the execution of the tsar's orders and thus instrumentalize popular oppression, the bureaucrats also make Russia "a great field of application of his system, based on theft and pillage." That is, they exploit the population subjected to them. This is why "the people feel an infinite animosity against them that far outweighs the hatred they feel for the nobles."

This function is also used by officials to have not only power over the people, but also a determining influence on how superior decisions will be fulfilled—as they are many, articulate, and nurture a common feeling, they see this potential being fostered. Of course, this is not about any open confrontation or even any interest in sharing decisions with the tsar or the nobility. After all, the bureaucracy is responsible only for the instrumentalization of oppression, whose main source is the emperor. More precisely, it is a question of passive resistance on the part of civil servants, for their own benefit, enabled by their position as the closest intermediary of the people. In the field of compliance with decisions, the monitoring of procedures, and the transmission of information, everything is done in accordance with the interests of the bureaucracy. This corruption of officials and even the direct robbery of peasants are common practices. Therefore, in a way, this functionalism ends up as an "unconscious corruptor of the whole system" and contributes to the "ruin of the State" that it is supposed to safeguard. Its dubiousness is exactly this; the bureaucracy is a dominant class but one which, by virtue of its class-driven behavior, insofar as it places its class interests above the interests of the State, "becomes a powerful instrument at the service of the revolution" because it helps to weaken the State itself. In other words, "everywhere, the bureaucracy kills, and does not give life to, the government" (Bakunin, 49009[e], pp. 7–8; Bakunin, 1976b[e], p. 102; Bakunin, 62002[e], p. 3).

During the years 1840–60, the Orthodox Church was the official religion of the state and the tsar was also the head of the church. At that time "the emperor was both a secular prince and a dignitary of the Church." The church was subordinated to the state and depended on it, forming a crucial tool for the legitimization of autocratic power, above all through the conformist and resigned Christianity that it preached.

The clergy, represented by the parish priests (*popes*), were the social class that directly promoted this legitimization by spreading religious knowledge. Moreover, the church is an important source of financing for the tsar since "the emperor appropriates the high income of the Church," often depriving the clergy themselves of funds (Bakunin, 49009[e], pp. 1–3, 7).

The most numerous social class that is oppressed by the Russian state is the peasantry. However, less numerous classes are also oppressed, such as the low-level military and the few urban workers in existence at the time, classes which make up popular Russia, the Russian people.[12]

In the period in question, the main characteristic of the Russian people was servitude, which marked the lives not only of the peasants, who were the vast majority, but also of a large number of traders and workers. Serfs were subjected to the harshest exploitation by masters and the cruelest oppression by the State; freedom was completely lacking and this, in a way, was the concrete situation that united the Russian people. "All the people [...] are in agreement and intimately united by something that concerns them to the same extent: *the total lack of freedom, subjugation* in which they find themselves and from which they try to free themselves" (Bakunin, 49007[e], p. 1).

These workers became definitive serfs during the seventeenth century. As far as the peasants were concerned, this action was aimed at "charging the landowner with a double responsibility: to keep the peasants quiet and to guarantee the exact delivery of the rents and the conscripts" (Bakunin, 50001[e], p. 6). With this, the peasants were bound to the land without owning it—they could be bought and sold from the lands on which they worked, as well as deported or physically punished. Serfdom existed in Russia until 1861, when it was abolished by one of the liberalizing measures adopted by Alexander II.

Contrary to what was often imagined in Europe, the Russian people are not "an uncultured mass, without conscience or will, a heap of nullities that is linked to the person of the Tsar and gives him an imposing position. This idea is completely false." For this very reason, despite the various moments of popular support for the tsar, it cannot be considered that the peasants and other workers are in their entirety subordinate to the emperor, so that there is no possibility of harder and more radicalized confrontations. "The Russian people do not identify at all with the emperor." There is no great unanimity in such a direction among the peasants and other workers.

The contradiction between the people, on the one hand, and the dominant classes and the State on the other, can be observed historically both in the dissident religious sects and in the indigenous community traditions of the peasants and their understanding of their rights, which have been inspiring impressive and radicalized mobilizations.

In the religious camp, the Russian people is "divided into more than 200 sects, all with a political component and unanimously thinking that the present order of things must be rejected and that the sovereignty of the emperor must be considered the kingdom of the antichrist." Such sects, which "are scattered all over the empire," are "very oppressed" and "the most fanatical"; many of them are "communist in nature." Because they were contrary to the Orthodox Church and questioned the power of the emperor, they were brutally persecuted by Catherine II, had a certain truce under Alexander I, and were once again persecuted by Nicholas I, tending to rebel (Bakunin, 49007[e], p. 1; Bakunin, 50001[e], p. 9).

These sects make up the Raskol, a schism of 1667 that placed the Orthodox Church on one side and its dissenters on the other. "It is in the Raskol that the history of popular Russia continues and is preserved for the people." In it "are its martyrs, its sacred heroes, its intimate beliefs and its hopes; in it are its prophetic consolations." With this schism, "the people have received their social education, a political organization—secret, but even more powerful; it is it that has consolidated their force. The Raskol will make the flag of freedom to save Russia wave" (Bakunin, 62002[e], p. 2). Part of the Raskol sects were, for example, the Dukhobors (духоборцы), whose members "recognize absolutely no authority" (Bakunin, 49007[e], p. 1).

In the field of indigenous culture, "the peasant," subjected to relations of servitude and deprived of land ownership, knows that "he has the right to a better destiny, more worthy of his condition as a human being"—he also realizes that "the land he cultivates in the name of the emperor, the State or his lord, in reality belongs to him." To this end, the tradition of the *mir*, a communal and autonomous organization of land ownership prior to servitude, which remained a communal practice and cultural trait for a considerable part of the Russian people, who "have completely democratic instincts and ways" contributed. This not only contradicted the model of society in Russia, but also gave revolutionary perspectives a social character, inasmuch as, beyond the questioning of servitude and the demand for freedom, it raised the question of land ownership. The *mir* could even inspire a prefiguration of the post-revolutionary society in Russia (Bakunin, 49007[e], pp. 1–2; Bakunin, 45001[e], p. 3; Angaut, 2009, p. 68).[13]

> The Russian people, in the midst of the horrible slavery they endured for over two centuries, have preserved three primitive dogmas that form the deeply historical basis of their entire future. 1) First, the universally propagated belief among the popular masses that *the land, all the land, belongs to the people.* [...] 2) The second dogma [...] is *the commune.* Not the western commune, which forms an agglomeration of individual owners, but the commune with economic solidarity, the sole owner of the land it occupies and shares equally with each new generation. [...] 3) The third dogma, finally [...] is the *self-government* of the commune. Even in times of servitude, the vast majority of communes govern themselves. After a public debate in the streets, the [*mir*]

always unanimously elects all the communal administration officials as well as the political head of the commune for one, two or three years. It also discusses its budget and distributes among its members, according to each one's strength and means, amicably, all the income, be it in cash or *in kind*; such as taxes, annual rents to be paid to the lords, oats and recruits. It also distributes communal land, conducts trials and imposes punishments for all offences that do not go beyond its jurisdiction. (Bakunin, 63003[e], pp. 8–10)

The contradiction between what the peasants believed to be dignified and just and what was practiced in imperial Russia had led to a series of more or less violent pushback. "Rebellions" and "uprisings" were the Russian people's answers to this fundamental contradiction; answers that not only constituted important historical precedents, but were at the same time "the most explicit proof of the social effervescence, which has progressed in Russia much more than is believed abroad" (Bakunin, 49007[e], p. 1).

A striking case was the insurrection led by Iemelian Pugachev between 1773 and 1775.

Pugachev's uprising has not been appreciated in Europe for a long time. It was in Russia that the first peasant revolution took place, but not the last. While Catherine II was busy partitioning Poland, Pugachev, a simple Don's Cossack, gathered large masses of peasants on the border of Siberia and proclaimed himself emperor under the name of Peter III: with his flocks—whose numbers grew ceaselessly, sweeping everything in their path, devastating everything in their fulminating march—he went on to the wall of Kazan, which he took and set on fire. With his undisciplined bands, he defeated disciplined armies; his name made the whole empire tremble and spread among the people with the speed of lightning. In Moscow, the rising masses awaited him impatiently, and if he had reached there, who knows if Poland and Russia would not have had another fate. In the beginning, his troops were composed mostly of sect supporters; his watchword was the liberation of the peasants and his name still lives on in the memory of the Russian people. (Bakunin, 50001[e], p. 11)

The popular mobilizations during the war against France in 1812 were also significant and continued in subsequent years. "Russia freed itself from Napoleon's yoke, less by the resistance of its armies—which, in fact, were almost always defeated—than by the uprising of its people." The "rigor of the climate would not have triumphed over Napoleon if he had found a people in Russia willing to assist him, and ready to provide him with winter supplies and lodgings free of surprises." But the Russian people, who "had risen en masse, destroying and burning their own villages," took refuge "in the forests, leaving Napoleon destroyed fields and waging a terrible *partisan* war against him." Consequently, it was the Russian people "who had the greatest part to play in liberating the country and their consciousness of their role is strongly rooted within them" (Bakunin, 50001[e], pp. 11–12).

These mobilizations of 1812 had consequences in the following years. "During the years 1813 and 1814, there were important popular uprisings in all parts of Europe": those "peasants who had risen up" against the Napoleonic troops "declared that they had contributed to expelling the enemy, deserving their freedom and no longer wanting to return to forced labor." The year 1812 ushered in a period of intensification of the struggles of the Russian people, especially the peasants: "from 1812 onwards, peasant revolts took place in Russia without interruption—they spread, threateningly extending and gaining force and depth every year" (Bakunin, 50001[e], p. 12). This cycle of revolts goes on until the 1840s, being that "after 1842 the peasant uprisings were permanent" in various localities (Bakunin, 49001[e], p. 2). So that, by the end of the 1840s, it could be said that in Russia "the people now have a conscience, a clearly expressed common will, and demand first and foremost their freedom from the yoke of servitude and their own freedom" (Bakunin, 50001[e], p. 12).

The low-ranking military, although few in relation to the peasantry, are also a considerable part of the Russian people. Their living conditions, especially with regard to the work routine, are very hard. Apart from low wages, "the soldier on duty is constantly harassed" and has "not a moment's rest." "His whole life is nothing but marches, guards, inspections, cleaning uniforms and weapons" and "the only word he can say, rightly or wrongly, is *sluschy*, that is, I obey." Moreover, during the fighting, the mortality rate of these soldiers is quite high, especially with hunger and frequent exposure to the cold. That is why, when they were summoned to combat popular uprisings, they often joined them, and in some cases even headed the mobilization of the peasantry (Bakunin, 49006[e], pp. 1–2).

In short, one must not confuse official Russia with popular Russia, both when it comes to social classes and the relationship between state and peoples. Both Russias are not an "indivisible whole" (Bakunin, 47003[e], p. 2). Because of its social formation, Russia is split between a set of oppressive classes (nobility, including the tsar, bureaucracy, and clergy) and another of inferior classes (people, especially peasants). They are the first to hold political power through the control they exercise over the state apparatus. Thus, when it comes to the oppression of the Russian state over the Russian nation, over the Russian people, it is important to emphasize that this constitutes class domination. They are not "Russians" dominating "Russians," but a minority and dominant sector of Russians (and even oppressors of other nationalities such as the Holstein-Gottorp-Romanov, of German descent) oppressing a majority and subjugated sector of Russians and other nation-races present in Russia.

Moreover, when it comes to the oppression of the Russian state upon other states or nation-races, peoples, it is fundamental to point out that it is also class domination. It is not the "Russians" dominating other peoples, but this same minority and

dominant sector oppressing other whole states, whole nation-races, that is, all their
social classes.

> The Russian people do not participate as a people in Russia's conquests; they
> are pushed against foreign peoples with the same knute[14] that, even today, serves
> to force them into servile labor in their own country. [... Russia is] a State eager
> for conquests, a State which, strange and hostile to its own people, uses it to
> subjugate other peoples. [...] Is there a single conquest of Russia that was the
> work of an entire people? Never, and nowhere. All the conquests were the work
> of the State alone, with the help of well-disciplined armies and, above all, of a
> diplomacy well-known for its particular tricks and its uninterrupted spirit.
> [... In religious terms, for example,] the Russian people are, on the contrary,
> the most tolerant in the world; they have friendly and peaceful relations with
> the Tartars, the Jews, the Catholics and the Protestants, and even with the
> pagans. [...] The Russian people have never undertaken or will undertake
> a conquest, whether by religious fanaticism or for any other reason; on the
> contrary, the Russian State does so because its only *raison d'être* is to conquer
> and subject. (Bakunin, 50001[e], pp. 20–23)

In this way, it must be stressed that a people does not play a leading role in
imperialism; it is its upper classes who do so through the State. In other words, Russia's
imperialism is not the result of national oppression led by popular Russia, but by the
Russian ruling classes and their state, including the tsar himself, i.e. official Russia.
The state of Russia, hostile to the Russian nation-race itself, subjects the latter, while
dominating other nation-races abroad (Bakunin, 48020[e], pp. 20, 25; Bakunin,
63003[e], p. 6; Bakunin, 63008[e]).

8.4 NATIONAL OPPRESSION OF RUSSIAN AND NON-RUSSIAN SLAVS

The Slavs are a large nation-race that mainly occupies territories in Central, Eastern,
and Southeastern Europe, bringing together other smaller nation-races as part of
themselves. There are three subgroups of Slavic nation-races, among them: in the east,
Russians, Ukrainians, and Belarussians (Eastern Slavs); in the centre, Poles, Czechs,
Slovaks, and Moravians (Western Slavs); in the southeast (the Balkan region),
Slovenes, Croats, Serbs, Bosnians, and Bulgarians (Southern Slavs) (Bakunin,
62008[e], pp. 1, 11). Such peoples share a certain Slavic national identity expressed,
among other ways, in language, condition, and national sentiment.

Slavic languages come from the same Indo-European origin and are spoken,
accompanying to some extent the division of these subgroups, "from the banks of the
Adriatic and the Black Sea to the ends of the White Sea and Siberia" (Bakunin,
48004[e], p. 1). Nevertheless, in the nineteenth century there was a considerable
variety of these languages and a class issue surrounding them. With a few exceptions,

The Slavic languages of Europe differed greatly; they were neglected by the upper classes and perceived as dialects spoken by the people. It was no longer known how to write them and they were not printed. The state of dissolution of Slavic culture was such that a Czech patriot, Jungmann, wrote in 1828: "We have had the sad fate of being witnesses to the definitive annihilation of our language." (Berthier, 2010, vol. 2, p. 62)

Moreover, the Slav peoples share a historical and concrete condition of national oppression: "our great Slav family, oppressed for centuries [...], seeks its rightful place on earth" and "there is not a branch of our family that has not been subjected to hard trials" because of this national oppression (Bakunin, 62008[e], pp. 1, 3). Therefore, the Slavs must be considered together as a *"great oppressed race"* (Bakunin, 48019[e]). They also cultivate a common national sentiment, understanding themselves as peoples with bonds of origin, blood, and history. They are oppressed peoples who form part of the same larger nation-race. There are therefore common interests among all Slavic peoples, especially those relating to their national liberation (Bakunin, 48004[e], p. 1).

"The Slavic peoples of Eastern Europe as a whole are subject to political systems imposed on them from outside" (Berthier, 2010, vol. 2, p. 62). The greatest oppressors of Slavic peoples are the states and upper classes of Russia, Prussia, and Austria as far as the Eastern and Western Slavs are concerned, and the dominant Turkish classes and the Ottoman Empire as far as the Southern Slavs are concerned. They are the protagonists of the imperialism that perpetuates the national domination of the Slavic peoples (Bakunin, 62025[c], p. 10).

This imperialism means, in concrete terms, Slavic submission to an artificial nationality, with consequences in various aspects of life: language, habits, customs, religion, labour, political conduct, justice, territory, political organization, etc. Generally speaking, it can be said that a culture that is not their own is more or less violently imposed, by different means, on the Slavs. Russia oppresses the following Slavs: Russians, Ukrainians/Ruthenes, Belarussians, and Poles; the Russian empire controls territories of Ukraine, Belarus, Poland, Lithuania, Latvia, and Finland. "The Slavic peoples [...] who are dominated [...] by Russia are in a state of total domination" (Berthier, 2010, vol. 2, p. 62).

When discussing Russia's role in the oppression of the Slavs, it should be pointed out, as argued above, that the first great oppression it engages in is in relation to its own people. Although it is not "oppressed by any foreign people," Russia, or specifically official Russia, "plays the role of oppressor" both internally—for popular Russia is "succumbed to the lowest level of slavery"—and externally (Bakunin, 50001[e], p. 55).

Externally, the second great oppression that Russia exerted is over Poland. Russian imperialism in Poland, allied with Austrian and Prussian imperialism, aims not only to put an end to the State, but to the Polish nation-race itself. This is evidenced by the ending of independence in 1795 and by "the constant thought of Emperor Nicholas" who "from 1811 onwards" intends to "*break* Poland." Something that could be characterized as "a perfectly logical thought, since, him not wanting an independent and free Poland, must necessarily proceed to the destruction of its nationality." And Russia does this, above all, by investing in three imperialist procedures: "1st. The extinction of the Polish language; 2nd. The submission of Poland to Russian legislation; 3rd. The establishment of the State religion on the ruins of the Catholic and Greek churches" (Bakunin, 46001[e], p. 1).

It is clear that this is an attack on the "Polish nation," in particular "its customs, its religion, even its language." Worse still, in the event of resistance from the Poles, they are susceptible to "quite arbitrary forms of accusation and condemnation" since "the smallest official in the Russian administration enjoys almost absolute power over all Poles" (Bakunin, 46001[e], p. 2). This when the Poles are not directly repressed or even murdered by force of arms, as happened in the insurrection of 1830–31, which demanded Polish independence and was harshly repressed by the Russian army. For a member of popular Russia, such repression should be considered a "national disgrace" because, besides being "an unjust attack on a neighboring country," it is at the same time "a monstrous attack on a brother's freedom." This "war of 1831 was [...] an absurd, criminal, fratricidal war," which only served the upper classes and the Russian state (Bakunin, 47003[e], p. 1).

By imposing itself on the Poles, Russian imperialism imposes itself on Ukrainians and Belarusians, as well as a considerable part of the people of Lithuania, Latvia, and Finland (Bakunin, 62006[e], pp. 34–35; Bakunin, 46001[e], pp. 1–2).

Prussia oppresses mainly the Polish Slavs. But the Prussian kingdom also dominates other non-Slavonic peoples, such as Silesians and Saxons; it controls territories not only in Poland, but also in Pomerania, Silesia, Rhineland, Westphalia, part of Saxony, and the Ruhr. "The Slav peoples [...] who are dominated by Prussia" are also "in a state of total domination" (Berthier, 2010, vol. 2, p. 62).

Even during the eighteenth century, when it becomes a kingdom, Prussia is gaining more and more force both within Europe and in relation to Austria, which, despite seeing its power decline progressively since the Peace of Westphalia in the seventeenth century, was then the hegemonic German power. In the second half of the nineteenth century, Prussia will take over the former position of Austria, establishing itself as the hegemonic German power (Bakunin, 50001[e], p. 57). This strengthening of Prussia and its oppression of the Slavs in Poland shows an enormous Germanizing potential, which may even be able to extend to other German states during the unification process.

Austria oppresses the following Slavs: Poles, Czechs, Moravians, Slovaks, Croats, and part of the Serbs; but the Austrian empire also oppresses other non-Slavic peoples such as Italians, Magyars, Walloons, and Germans. It controls territories not only in

Poland but also in Bohemia, Moravia, Slovakia, Slovenia, Croatia, part of Serbia, Italy (in the process of unification), Hungary, Wallachia, Silesia, Galicia, Dalmatia, and Transylvania (Hepner, 1950, pp. 243–44).

As a result, and even with the growth of Prussia, during the 1840s Austria still had to be characterized as a "monstrous and violent conglomeration of foreign peoples" whose oppression extends to different nation-races (Bakunin, 48019[e]; Bakunin, 49001[e], p. 1). In the midst of effective strategies for this national domination to be perpetuated are repression and censorship, promoted in a very severe way. There is also, on the part of the dominant strata and the Austrian state, the stimulation of national hatred, so that the peoples subjected to it are not in a position to put their power in check (Bakunin, 48019[e]).

Unlike those "who are dominated by Prussia and Russia," the Slavs subject to "the Austrian empire" experience a "kind of original relationship" in a peculiar sense. "The Austrian empire had this particularity of dominating peoples who dominated others," as in "the case of Hungary" (Berthier, 2010, vol. 2, p. 62). The Hungarians (Magyars) are subject to Austria, but at the same time they oppress the Slavs.

As a result of the revolutionary process of 1848–49, Hungary briefly gained its independence from Austria. The Magyars, protagonists of this revolution even though they received support from members of other nation-races, strengthened sub-imperialist relations with them. Among the peoples subjected were Slavs, mainly Slovaks (whose ruling class had disappeared, merging into the Hungarian nobility), Serbs, and Croats, many of whom, still during the Hungarian revolution, rebelled against the process of *Magyarization* to which they were being subjected (Bakunin, 49001[e], p. 1; Berthier, 2010, vol. 2, pp. 63, 108). But the frustration of the revolutionary intent, the fruit of a coordinated attack by Austria with the help of Russia, removed the protagonism of the Magyars in mid-1849, and prepared the ground for the process of Germanization of Hungary, which took shape in the 1850s.

This was what motivated, within the revolution, a "war of the Slavs in Hungary [...] against a handful of Magyars" who denied the "existence of Slav nationality." In fact, that confrontation of the Slavs against the Magyars must be considered "a legitimate and just war, a popular war, a war eminently democratic" since the "Slavic peasant"—"from whom it was intended to take everything: freedom, property and even the native language"—sought to overcome Hungarian oppression (Bakunin, 48019[e]). "Despite the pressure of several centuries, no one managed to Germanize or Magyarize" these "Slavs living on Hungarian soil." Their "resistance to multiple aggressions" has been admirable, for they cannot—like "the Italians, the Poles or the Czechs"—"seek strength in the memory of a glorious past." Their opposition to "permanent persecution" is based only on "their authenticity, their language, their habits and their customs"—and their survival can perhaps be explained by "the presentiment of a great near future" (Bakunin, 62008[e], p. 3).

Also prominent as victims of Austrian imperialism are the Czechs and the

Moravians; Bohemia and Moravia, the territories of these peoples, have a sad history of submission. "Among the Slavic homelands, Bohemia and Moravia were those that endured the cruelest fate." In the seventeenth century, Bohemia-Moravia was launched "into a desperate war," losing two thirds of its numerous inhabitants and witnessing the disappearance of the best part of its *intelligentsia*." In the period that followed, "that country, once famous, fell into oblivion" and "the Czechs who survived the disaster became slaves." Ceded to "the nefarious domination of the Jesuits", "their land, once Slavic—the cradle of Jan Huss, of Jan Žižka, of the king of Poděbrady, of the brothers Chelčický and Comenius"—was later "subjected to the arrogant brutality of new masters who had denied all belonging to the Czech nation"—it also became "governed and constantly watched over by the imperial administration." A few decades later it "began to become a Germanic province," which was consolidated "already in the first quarter of our century" (Bakunin, 62008[e], p. 3).

"The Czech and Moravian peoples were subjected by German officials"; "they were tyrannized and persecuted in their language, in their faith and even in the sacred character of their national sentiment." And the Austrian government did this allied to the upper classes, to the "great lords," to the "aristocrats," to the "clergy," that is, to the "privileged of all classes," composing "an alliance which still persists, to squeeze out from the poor people all their sap, to the last drop of their blood" (Bakunin, 49001[e], p. 1). Among Slovenians, the linguistic Germanization that had been taking place since the fifteenth century had a decisive impact as it struck at the heart of their language.

When it comes to the national conflict between the Germans and the Slavs, it is necessary to emphasize the process of *Germanization*, led above all by Prussia and Austria, whose results directly affect the Slav peoples, but not only them. *Germanization is the imposition, by various means, of an artificial Germanic nationality on peoples who are not naturally Germanic* (Bakunin, 50001[e], pp. 58, 75, 84; Bakunin, 62008[e], pp. 5–6, 12; Bakunin, 63003[e], p. 5).

It is a form of German imperialism, which began in the Middle Ages with the Ostsiedlung (German Expansion to the East) and experienced its second great wave in the nineteenth century. The Prussian and Austrian peoples themselves were Germanized, the states of Prussia and Austria being, in a way, living expressions of this process as they continue it. An important landmark for this was the Congress of Vienna in 1815, which "made Germany, within the framework of the Holy Alliance, a German Confederation of 39 sovereign States, under the leadership of a Federal Diet made up of the representatives of these States, of which the two main ones were of course Prussia and Austria" (Berthier, 2010, vol. 2, p. 11).

With regard to the Germanization of the Slavs, it should be noted that "after the Middle Ages, the Slav territories were the object of systematic invasions by the Germans." And "the Germans carried out a policy of systematic Germanization of the Slavic populations," which was successful in that the Slavs, "a rural population," proved incapable of "resisting the expansionist designs of the Germanic States, Prussia and Austria." The Christianization movement, headed by "advanced strongholds of Christianity" such as "Ratisbon, Passau, Salzburg, Halberstadt, Magdeburg," was relevant to this Germanization. They "sent missionaries to convert Czech and Polish Slavic pagans" and were successful, mainly because they managed to convince Slavic leaders who then converted their own populations. The "German clergy" in both Bohemia and Poland "played a decisive role" in "unifying the populations around the indigenous ruling classes" who joined the Germanic Church. "By becoming Christian, the Slavic nobility [...] gained a great deal of power" (Berthier, 2010, vol. 2, pp. 64–65).[15]

The Ottoman Empire oppresses the following Slavs: Serbs, Bosnians, and Bulgarians; but this Turkish state also oppresses other non-Slavic peoples, such as the Greeks; it controls territories of Serbia, Bosnia, Bulgaria, Greece, Albania, Moldova, Romania (Wallachia), and Montenegro. "From the fourteenth century onwards, the Balkans gradually succumbed to Turkish domination. This domination is exercised in different ways, depending on the circumstances." Some peoples "retain relative autonomy, like the Albanians, and others, like the Serbs, endure a very strict regime of submission. In the cities, the garrisons isolate strategic points, especially the crossroads of circulation." And the submission of controlled territories "manifests itself in the payment of a tax, which also varies according to circumstances" (Berthier, 2010, vol. 2, pp. 55–56).

During the nineteenth century, the positions taken by England and its proximity to the Turks, as was the case in the Crimean War, also made it an enemy state of the Slavs (Bakunin, 62008[e], p. 4).

As a result of this national oppression of Russian and non-Russian Slavs, forms of Slavic nationalism have developed since the eighteenth century. The principles of the French Revolution and German romanticism were influential factors in this. From then on, "the Slavs knew that they had a history and literature that left nothing to be desired by those of their oppressors." Such nationalisms took more definite form during the nineteenth century, this being the century of the Slavs' national awakening (Berthier, 2010, vol. 2, pp. 58, 62). Several insurrectionary movements—in particular Polish, in places such as Warsaw, Krakow and Galicia—contributed to this awakening.

In the mid-1840s, the position of the Slavs was delicate, "particularly for those who, among them, [were] democrats or simply liberals." This was because these Slavs did not identify with the "two national movements, German and Hungarian," since neither recognized "the national rights of the Slavs." There was a risk that "Slavic national sentiment [would be] instrumentalized by the reaction," concentrated in Innsbruck, Austria, and be set against the "revolutionary governments of Vienna and the Pest." In March 1848, the Czechs petitioned Emperor Ferdinand of Austria with the "signatures of bourgeois, intellectuals, students and workers, calling for the abolition of the corvée, the reconstitution of the Bohemian Kingdom and equality between Germans and Czechs" (Angaut, 2009, p. 35).

Seeking a place for the Slavic cause in this context, marked by German and Hungarian nationalism, the Slavic Congress in Prague in 1848 ended up as a definitive landmark for the strengthening of Slavic nationalism and as one of the first initiatives of what would, a few years later, be called pan-Slavic. "The Prague Congress marks the beginning of a new life, a new history for the Slavs" (Bakunin, 62025[c], p. 1). There, Slavs of various nationalities meet for the first time and forge the foundations of a movement of considerable proportions, based on mutual recognition, common interests and feelings, and a shared expectation for the future:

> When they arrived in Prague, [... the Slavs] met, recognized each other and felt like brothers and sisters, a feeling understood not only in their hearts but also in their languages. [...] They were united around their common interests and, even more so, around the feeling of the great destiny that the future holds for them. They bowed down before God, thanking him for putting an end to their hard trials, for having been able to preserve in all its purity that fraternal sentiment; they forgave themselves with regard to the past, and, seeing before them only the present and the future, they swore never again to separate their destinies. (Bakunin, 48004[e], p. 1)

In other words, "the importance of the Slavic Congress was that it constituted the first meeting, the first contact, the first attempt by the Slavs to unite and understand each other" (Bakunin, 1976b[e], p. 84). But this congress also showed that, despite a certain common national identity, there were several contradictory interests.

This became clear when "the Slav delegates there, representing the various nationalities, could not overcome their differences and act as a homogeneous whole towards a single goal: the liberation from foreign control through a pan-Slav effort." The Czechs "were more concerned with establishing a hegemony over the Slavs in a reformed Austrian monarchy, the Poles wanted dominance over the Ukrainians in Galicia, while the Slavs in Hungary were only concerned with what directly affected them—the Magyar occupation." Moreover, "certain Slavic groups in the Balkans [...] had succumbed to the Tsar's pan-Slavic propaganda, which proposed liberating these groups under the imperial cloak of Russia" (Cipko, 1990, p. 4).

NOTES

1   Bakunin's main writings from this period, discussed in this and the next chapter, are: "Appeal to the Slavic Peoples," "The Situation in Russia," "Confession," "To the Russians, the Poles and All My Slavic Friends," and "The People's Cause." With the exception of "Confession," which was cited from the Spanish edition (Bakunin, 1976b[e]), these other writings, as well as the other Bakunin documents on the IISH CD-ROM (Bakunin, 2000a), have been translated from the French texts.

2   Considering that Bakunin prioritized the national question in his activities between 1844 and 1863, it is not possible, without certain difficulties, to completely transpose his analytical methodology and even the analyses of "The Reaction in Germany," established with a focus on the social issue, for the aforementioned period. It is possible that the biggest problem in this movement concerns Bakunin's

reflections on party and principle. Something that was pointed out by Angaut (2009, p. 47), when he argued that "the latter [the opposing parties] were parties only because they were penetrated by the principle of the world that they demanded." In the social sense of "The Reaction in Germany," the democratic party became a party insofar as it was penetrated by the principle of democracy or freedom. But when the national question is introduced and prioritized, would it still be possible to speak in these terms of party and principle? Did the democratic party finally embrace the social and national questions raised by the emergence of the Peoples' Spring? Or were they both, although they were concomitantly posed by this movement, claimed by different sectors of the European population? To what extent did those who advocated extending democracy and freedom to national relations exist as a party? For Angaut, in the "Appeal to the Slavs," such a difficulty—which I consider pertinent to the whole period 1844–63—is evident, for there is "a lack of an objective correlate to that party of the negative which Bakunin described" in 1842; "even if a certain number of people, and perhaps even the spirit of the time, conspired to destroy the old world, this does not mean that these people were constituted into a party." That is to say, however much part of the foundations of the political analysis method of "The Reaction in Germany" is maintained in this period, it would not be correct to say that all the methodological and analytical aspects of 1842 should still be considered valid.

3   The notion of "power" will be deployed by Bakunin until the end of his life. In this case, where Bakunin writes in German, the term in question is "Macht"; when he writes in French, the term used is "puissance." Taking into account Francophone writings, which make up the greater part, despite the other possibilities of translation, "power" really seems to be the best option because Bakunin differentiates this notion from others. In his work, the notions of "puissance" [capacity] and "force" are generally used in a more neutral tone, and often serve to refer to the relations of the oppressed in the perspective of their liberation. On the other hand, the notions of "pouvoir" [power], "oppression," and "domination" are usually associated with the relations imposed by the oppressors.

4   Taking this notion of collective freedom and solidarity as a basis, Bakunin (45002[c], p. 6) wrote on the question of women: "Women are almost everywhere slaves, and we ourselves are slaves to their slavery. Without their liberation, without their total and unlimited freedom, our freedom is impossible; without freedom there is no beauty, no dignity, and no true love. Man loves only to the extent that he desires and demands the freedom and independence of the other—total independence from everything and even (and above all) from himself. Love is the union of free beings and it is only this love which educates and ennobles man. Every other love demeans the oppressed, the oppressor, and is a source of depravity." Years later, Bakunin (62008[e], p. 11) returned to the question of women, criticizing prostitution: "It is impressive to see how prostitution, the most repugnant servitude in modern society, proliferates today! The trade in blacks has been abolished in America, but a slavery of a new kind—even more degrading, that in which body and soul are sold to low lust for a piece of bread—blatantly proliferates among us."

5   In the writings from 1844 to 1863, looking at Russia and Western Europe, the actually existing classes identified by Bakunin are, above all: nobility, bourgeoisie, peasants, proletariat, bureaucracy, and clergy (cf., for example: Bakunin, 48019[e]; Bakunin, 62008[e]). Referring to the Slavic world, he points out: "Among us [...] we do not exactly have proletarians or bourgeois; but, on the one hand, a very numerous nobility, and, on the other, the great mass of peasants" (Bakunin, 48019[e]). Referring to the more developed countries, he considers that there is an undeniable contradiction of the "bourgeois against the proletarian" (Bakunin, 48019[e]). When analyzing class conflicts, Bakunin refers with some frequency to the range of "privileged classes" (51001[e], p. 8) and "oppressed classes" (48014[e], p. 1). He also refers to the former as "upper classes" (49009[e], p. 5), "elevated/high classes" (1976b[e], p. 50), "ruling classes" (50001[e], p. 69), or, on the basis of their privilege in the field of knowledge, "savant [intellectual] classes" (50001[e], p. 74), "educated classes" (1976b[e], p. 61), "enlightened classes" (63008[e]). From that moment on, there is a concern with the relations of oppression established on the basis of knowledge, as factors of class domination and which are pointed out as "the domination of scholars" (62008[e], p. 3) or of "doctrinal wise men" (62002[e], p. 5). The bourgeoisie is in some cases still called the "middle class" (48019[e]) and distinguishes, according to the postures and ideas of its members, between a backward and a progressive bourgeoisie (48019[e]). Bakunin also refers to the latter as a "people," as discussed, as a "dispossessed/poor class" (1976b[e], pp. 132; 51001[e], p. 61). The proletariat is in some cases called the "working class" (48019[e]; 51001[e], p. 8), and the peasantry is called the "peasant class" (51001[e], pp. 60–61).

6   Bakunin's reflections of the State are in most cases based on Russia, but also on other major European powers: Austria, Prussia, England, France, and the Ottoman Empire. Between 1844 and 1863, his criticism of the State was still directed at the "great States"; sometime later, an important part of this criticism will be generalized to all states.

7   Bakunin does not speak exactly of a nation-race concept, but uses the notions of nation, race and people with the same meaning, referring to the different ethnicities (cf., for example: Bakunin, 48019[e], 48020[e], 62002[e]).

8   Nevertheless, it should be noted that at different times in this period and afterwards, Bakunin seems to essentialize and generalize this notion of nature.

9   Although Bakunin discussed the issue of national oppression/domination since 1844, especially that of Russia, he will only call it "imperialism" from 1862. And in almost all cases he does so to refer to Russian imperialism, always in a critical and denouncing tone. Bakunin speaks of "Saint Petersburg imperialism," "Petersburger imperialism," "Russian imperialism," etc. (Bakunin, 63003[e], p. 8; Bakunin, 62011[e], p. 19; Bakunin, 62025[c], p. 9). Even if it emerged late in his pan-Slavic period, this use of the concept of imperialism is early, considering its more widespread use, which dates back to the 1870s.

10 For details, see the first full Portuguese version of this Table of Patents, published in 2016: http://www.usp.br/lea/arquivos/russiaoh_lea.pdf.

11 In this passage, Bakunin takes his own trajectory as a typical example of this sector of Russian nobility.

12 It seems relevant to mention here Angaut's considerations (2009, p. 67) about the notion of "people" which is used by Bakunin in that period, and which applies here to his analysis of Russia. According to him: "It is clear, however, that [Bakunin's] gaze on Russia takes up the constituent elements of the myth of the people as it was elaborated in the revolutionary Europe of the nineteenth century: a mixture of primitive barbarism and potential for general emancipation. Adapted to Russia, this myth translates in practice into a constant concern to direct popular 'bad passions,' in particular fanaticism and superstition, against the Tsar's power. Here we find the figure, recurrent in Bakunin and never discussed as such, of religion as a practical power par excellence, as an example of an adherence that produces maximum practical effects. This is evidenced by the adaptation to Russia of the European myth of the people."

13 This defense of the traditional community organization of the Russian people motivated Bakunin (63006[e], pp. 3–5) to say in 1863: "Who are [...] we who fight the government of Saint Petersburg? We are the true conservatives." And that, for this reason, the program for Land and Freedom had a "conservative" objective.

14 The term knute means "whip" in Russian (кнут); with this instrument, the servants were punished by their masters during Imperial Russia. Bakunin used this term from 1845–46 and gradually it gained relevance in his work, even becoming an adjective concept for states and powers of an absolute/destructive type. According to Bakunin "knute is the symbol of absolute power" and it is with this meaning that he will speak of "Knuto-Austrian unitary State" or, in his anarchist period, of "Knuto-Germanic empire" (Bakunin, 50001[e], p. 5; Bakunin, 49003[e], p. 2; Bakunin, 2014d[e]).

15 According to Berthier (2010, vol. 2, pp. 4–6, 68, 110), an important key to understanding the political differences between Bakunin and Engels (and to some extent Marx)—in the context of the Peoples' Spring and as far as the national issue in general and the Slavs in particular are concerned—is the way they understood and valued this process of Germanization. Bakunin saw Germanization as an imperialist process responsible for the national oppression of the Slavs and therefore to be destroyed in favour of Slav national liberation; Engels understood this Germanization of the Slavs as an inevitable and even positive process, as it strengthened the development of the productive forces and thus improved the conditions for the advent of socialism.

CHAPTER 9

NATIONAL LIBERATION AND SELF-DETERMINATION
OF PEOPLES (1844–63)

This chapter concludes the presentation of Bakunin's political theory in his *revolutionary pan-Slavic period*, which spanned from 1844 to 1863, divided into three parts: 1) Pan-Slavism, Nationalism, and Patriotism; 2) Slav Federation and Revolution: From the Old to the New World; 3) Centralism, Dictatorship, Role of the Tsar and the Bourgeoisie in the Emancipation of the Slavs, and Anti-Germanism.

9.1 PAN-SLAVISM, NATIONALISM, AND PATRIOTISM

In order to realize this emancipatory project, it is essential to invest in a *"reestablishment of Slavism,"* for which it is essential "that all Slavic branches understand, *again*, that they can only have power through a powerful union. And this union is called *pan-Slavism*" (Bakunin, 62025[c], pp. 7, 9).

Pan-Slavism can be defined in a double key: one negative, of common opposition to German oppression, and the other positive, of the expectation of a future of freedom. "In its negative sense, pan-Slavism means first of all *hatred of Germans*. Since the Germans are the original oppressors, the sworn enemies of all Slavs." This is because it was through Germanization that the Germans "founded their entire existence, all their power on the Slavic vestiges," both of which were forged "by violence"; it was through Germanization that the Germans imposed "their civilization on the Slavs." "From a positive point of view, pan-Slavism is the faith and certainty of a great Slavic common future." In other words, "together we, the Slavs, form a world for ourselves," a culture of our own, a people which "for a thousand years has been oppressed by different enemies and yet has not been annihilated." This nation-race "has preserved its unity in the form of an instinctive brotherhood (*Bratrstvo*, a sacred word for the Slavs)" (Bakunin, 62025[c], pp. 14–15).

However, it is necessary to point out that there is not much consensus when talking generically about "Slavism" or "pan-Slavism." Different conceptions compete and contribute, more or less adequately depending on the case, to the emancipation of the Slavs in particular and the freedom of peoples in general. It is necessary, therefore, to explain the essential aspects of the Bakuninian pan-Slavism of 1844–63. First of all, it should be mentioned that *this pan-Slavism is revolutionary, anti-centralist, anti-imperialist, classist, democratic, and federalist*.[1]

This pan-Slavism breaks with the prospects for the hegemony of large states, particularly Austria and Russia, or of a particular nation-race, as in the case of certain Czech and Polish claims (Hepner, 1950, p. 211). "The empire of Austria [...] must be dissolved"— since "a Slavic Austria, an Austrian Slavism" would be nothing more than "a freedom breathing slavery"—and Slavism cannot move in the direction of "the ancient Russian hegemony and domination" nor of any other state or nation-race, even if it is Slavic (Bakunin, 48019[e]; Bakunin, 62025[c], pp. 3, 6). This obviously includes the prospect of replacing Russian domination with German domination (Bakunin, 50001[e], p. 35). A Slavic movement which claims to be emancipatory, distinctly, must develop "in the direction of the most complete freedom," preserving the independence of each people, its own determination, and ensuring that none of them will be subject to a state or any other people (Bakunin, 62025[c], pp. 6–7).

This is the only way to guarantee *national liberation* and *peoples' self-determination* for the Slavs, avoiding centralist and imperialist solutions which favour specific nations or states and which strengthen new ties of oppression. This means asserting the principle of "*freedom and self-determination* absolutely free for all, both for the *nations* and the *provinces*" (Bakunin, 63025[c], p. 2, emphasis added). This notion is reinforced by taking into account the collective and solidarity-based assumptions of freedom, which were previously presented (Bakunin, 1976b[e], pp. 111–12). Such a process of emancipation cannot be individual, group-based, or sectoral; it cannot involve only one Slavic nation-race and not even only Slavic ones. It must expand and embrace all peoples. To achieve *peoples' freedom* means precisely to achieve "both the liberation of nations as well as democracy and social revolution." It is precisely that which encompassed the "three dimensions of the revolutions of 1848" (Angaut, 2009, p. 9).

For this reason, when one considers that this pan-Slavism is a form of nationalism supported by a certain patriotism, as in the case of Nettlau (1976, p. 198), a certain care is needed. Such a pan-Slavism can be understood as a form of nationalism only if it is considered not to be a state nationalism, but a *nation-race nationalism*, a *Slavic nationalism* that prescinds and transcends states: "The new politics of the Slavic race will, therefore, *not be a politics of States, but a politics of nations, a politics of free and independent peoples*" (Bakunin, 48004[e], p. 1, emphasis added; cf., also: Bakunin, 48020[e], pp. 22–23). What is more, it can only be considered as such if it is understood as a *federalist and democratic nationalism*, insofar as it does not advocate, with regard to its ends, any preponderance of specific nation-races and states, centralist and imperialist solutions nor even new relations of domination. State nationalisms or nationalisms based on the notion of the superiority of a nation-race or a state— what can be called "national exclusivism" or narrow nationalism (Bakunin, 60005[c], p. 39)— are limited and inadequate forms of nationalism, and should therefore be discarded.

Similarly, this pan-Slavism can only be understood as a doctrine that advocates patriotism if it is also considered to be a *nation-race patriotism*, a *Slavic patriotism*, a feeling of love and devotion to Slavic peoples that supports a federalist and democratic nationalism that is contrary to national domination and imperialism (Bakunin,

49001[e], p. 2; Bakunin, 62008[e], p. 2). Also state, centralist, imperialist, and/or oppressive patriotisms—that which can be called "narrow patriotism" or patriotic exclusivism (Bakunin, 50001[e], p. 55)—should be overlooked. Homeland is thus synonymous with a nation-race or people (Bakunin, 63003[e], pp. 3, 5).

Therefore, pan-Slavic nationalism and patriotism must be regarded as natural and organic (Bakunin, 62002[e], p. 1). They do not mean doctrines or feelings that are based on upholding one state over another, one people over another. And they are only justified when they are linked to nationally oppressed peoples (Bakunin, 50001[e], p. 55).

9.2 SLAV FEDERATION AND REVOLUTION: FROM THE OLD TO THE NEW WORLD

In this process of transformation and on the basis of this pan-Slavism, the destructive task was up to the Slavic generations of the 1840s–60s: "Let us at least be the destroyers of the old iniquity," since there is no certainty at all that we will "be allowed to be the builders of the new world" (Bakunin, 47012[c], p. 4). One could even say to these generations: "Our mission is to destroy, not to build"; very likely "others will be the men who build, better than us, more intelligently" (Bakunin, 1976b[e], p. 112). Thus, the most urgent task was to invest in a rupture with the old world, destroying its foundations and paving the way for future construction. But according to any relevant notion of strategy, to establish the appropriate means of change, one must keep in mind the aims to be attained, at least in general terms.

These aims are, firstly, the formation of a "federation of all Slavic peoples" and, secondly, the formation of a "universal federation of European republics" (Bakunin, 48020[e], pp. 9, 19). These solutions would make it possible to realize a project of national democracy, whose unity and borders would be natural and organic, reflecting the sovereign will of the peoples and forging the foundations of an "autonomous national culture." It is precisely the realization of what could be called "*people's self-administration*" or "*self-government of the commune*" (Bakunin, 62008[e], p. 7; Bakunin, 62006[e], p. 13; Bakunin, 63003[e], p. 9, emphasis added). The support for this project would be found in the notion of a "liberated commune," an articulation of the different communes in a social and political federation, capable of ensuring both a national coexistence without oppression, and the freedom, equality, and fraternity of nations (Bakunin, 48019[e]).

On the Slav federation, it can be affirmed that

> unlike Western city life, the new Slavic world will be that of a peasant
> democracy. It will be based on our self-administered rural community, without
> social differentiation and living according to the "one for all and all for one"
> principle: government, justice and administration will be ensured by
> democratically elected officials. These communes, federated, will together form

the provinces. The provinces will be freely united into countries, having an executive power, a judiciary and the entire administrative hierarchy, with all their members also democratically elected. These countries, always self-administered, will be able to unite in a common statist unity. This is our future organization, which will encompass all Slavic countries in a single federation, autonomous but united. (Bakunin, 62008[e], p. 10)

Such a federation is conceived on a rural basis, as these correspond to the cultural tradition of the Slavic peoples and the social formation of the territories that were occupied by them in the nineteenth century.[2] Furthermore, it is hoped that such a socio-political initiative could guarantee solidarity and reciprocity between Slavic nations without depriving them of their autonomy, their capacity for self-determination and, at the same time, without leaving them isolated and powerless, vulnerable to foreign domination.

"Another centralization if not that of the Slavic federation" is not sought (Bakunin, 48004[e], p. 1). "From a political point of view" it is a "centralized" initiative; "from an administrative point of view" it is a "federalist" initiative (Bakunin, 1976b[e], p. 64; Angaut, 2005, p. 216). Such a federation by locality or territory has internal democracy, in that its rulers, magistrates and officials are elected, and seeing as each people is prevented from oppressing another. It is articulated from the communes, through the provinces and countries, into the federation, which is conceived as a Slavic state (Bakunin, 62025[c], pp. 13–14, 16; Hepner, 1950, p. 298; Angaut, 2009, p. 48).[3]

This federation differs from the great powers, the "machine states," for two reasons: internally, besides having democratic elections, this state does not oppress its own people; externally, it does not seek or achieve conquest and is therefore not and cannot be imperialist. Thus, this Slavic state cannot be considered an empire or an imperialist state. The proposition of certain Slavs to transform the Austrian empire into a "Slavic empire," for example, would mean the preservation of a political instrument that could only be "maintained by violence." And for this very reason it is necessary to warn the Slavs who are promoting this initiative: If this Slavism wins, "you will be the oppressors of your brothers of foreign nationality, the despots of the Italians, the Magyars, the Germans of Austria" (Bakunin, 48019[e]; Bakunin, 48020[e], p. 17).

Nor was it fair for certain Poles to propose, by liberating Poland, to annex "Ukraine in anticipation, without consulting the Ukrainians and on the basis of their historical rights alone." For "Polish Ukraine, as well as the Russians of Galicia and our Little Russia—with 15 million inhabitants who speak the same language, who have the same religion, will not belong to Poland, nor to Russia, but to themselves" (Bakunin, 62002[e], p. 9).

In the Slav federation, the different peoples are independent: "each can freely give itself constitutions adapted to its customs, its interests, its position." However, "there are principles inherent in the Slavic nature which must therefore form the fundamental basis of the new existence of Slavic peoples." These "principles are: equality of all, freedom of all and fraternal love." In this federation "there are no slaves (in law or in fact). Subjugation in all its forms is outlawed forever. There are no inequalities other than those which nature has created. There are no castes." In the cases of peoples who still have "an aristocracy" or "a privileged nobility," they must "merge with and lose themselves entirely in the popular masses." Every Slav "must have a share in national property and in the well-being of all"; property must be "the property of the whole people" and "every right to the soil must be abolished," allowing widespread access to land. And finally, property must be replaced by "communal ownership"[4] (Bakunin, 48004[e], p. 2; Bakunin, 62002[e], p. 5).

Every Slav must have his "right as a citizen," ensuring that he is "treated by all as a brother." Among Slavs, in the federation, "internal war [...] is outlawed forever" and is considered a crime. All these organizational aspects, as well as internal problems and conflicts, including those between two or more peoples, are to be arbitrated by a "Slav Council" which is "above all Slav peoples as an authority and supreme tribunal." This Council is the only institution which has the "right to declare war on foreign powers" (Bakunin, 48004[e], p. 2).

Indeed, this model of federation could serve as a paradigm for a political restructuring of Europe. This is because it offers the conditions to support the post-revolutionary construction of a federation of European republics, solving national and social conflicts throughout Europe.

The most appropriate means for the destruction of the old world is a revolutionary conflict, a revolutionary war. "No longer wars of conquest, but the last supreme war, the war of revolution for the liberation of all peoples." For the Slavs, "revolution is everything"—"it is their awakening, their resurrection, their hope, their salvation, their future." This means staking on a mobilization for "revolution, and nothing less than revolution." Through it, the Slavs, and even the peoples of Europe, will be able to liberate themselves and emancipate themselves nationally and socially (Bakunin, 48020[e], pp. 7, 26). It would undoubtedly be a "horrible and unprecedented revolution, even if it were directed more against things than against people" (Bakunin, 1976b[e], p. 134). This transformation would mark the implementation of a new politics, destroying all the great state powers responsible for the imperialist oppression of the Slavic peoples and guaranteeing the conditions for popular emancipation on the continent.

The old policy of kings disappeared and a new one, that of the peoples, emerged. The revolution, in all its omnipotence, declared the States of the despots dissolved. The Prussian empire was dissolved, abandoning one part of Poland. The empire of Austria was dissolved, that monster composed of diverse nations which were chained together by cunning, force and crime. The Turkish empire was dissolved, in which 700,000 Ottomans trampled on a population of 12 million Slavs,

Walachians and Greeks. Finally, the last consolation of despotism was
dissolved, the last refuge of Machiavellianism and diplomacy, struck at its
heart: the Russian empire, so that the three great nations long held in its
bosom—Great Russia, Little Russia and Poland—freed themselves and
surrendered themselves, being able to extend their free hand to all their
brothers of the Slavic race. In this way, dissolution, change and regeneration
throughout Northern and Eastern Europe, free Italy and, as a last result: the
universal federation of European republics. (Bakunin, 48020[e], pp. 8–9)

But who should undertake this revolution and how? It would result from the struggle
of the Slavic people and their allies against their enemies. "It is in the most oppressed
fraction of the population that both the conditions of destruction of the old world
and the conditions of emergence of the future world reside." And so it is among "the
'populace' of Western nations and the Slavs" that the conditions for the "regeneration
of societies" are found. In social terms, this revolution must be led by the European
people; in national terms, the Slavs, as historically oppressed people, are privileged
agents. "The Slavs are charged with this historic mission [of promoting emancipation]
because they are this European people who 'have gone through centuries of slavery,
painful struggles and suffering.'" Because they are "those who have endured foreign
oppression for the longest time, the Slavs are charged by history with being the first
nation to emancipate themselves without oppressing another." This is because the
Slavs "abhorred the foreign yoke very deeply, so as never to impose their [yoke] on a
foreign race'"[5] (Angaut, 2009, pp. 37–39).

Among the Slavs, who are the potentially revolutionary subjects and how can
they undertake this revolutionary war? Taking the Slavic world into account, this
Slavic disposition of undeniably classist traits realizes that the main popular force is
that of the peasants—this "formidable mass of peasants" is a "restless, turbulent class,
which will launch itself passionately into the first revolutionary movement" (Bakunin,
47003[e], p. 2). The Slavic peasantry is the most oppressed class and has historically
demonstrated its revolutionary capacity. In the specific case of Russia, there is no
doubt that there the revolution will be a peasant revolution. In the case of urban
workers, they have also shown their transformative potential, despite their very
limited number, especially among the Slavs (Bakunin, 50001[e], pp. 17, 32). The low-
level military, particularly the "soldiers," are also relevant subjects in this conflict; in
Russia, these soldiers "are the people themselves"; they feel dissatisfied, disillusioned,
and pose a potential threat to the forces of order (Bakunin, 47003[e], p. 2). This is the
case even if those soldiers who are kept in their ranks by an "iron discipline which
[deprives] them of any faculty of thought or any personal will" generally have no
"sense of fatherland nor of freedom." In such a case, they will have difficulty in
becoming agents of change (Bakunin, 49001[e], p. 2).

Finally, there is another group of agents that may be important to the Slavic revolution: "men of thought and good will," educated and from different social classes, including the dominant strata (bureaucracy, clergy, bourgeoisie, among others). Often, several of these men are young intellectuals from the nobility. They become revolutionaries to the extent that they adhere to popular demands, join the people, and contribute through their abilities and resources to the advent of the revolution. In this way they can understand "the instincts of the people" and carry, like the people, "the germ of the future in themselves" (Bakunin, 62002[e], p. 4).

Even if they originate from oppressive classes these people can, depending on the position they take in conflicts, become allies of the people. First, they must be in agreement with the "people's cause"; second, they must *approach the people and reconcile themselves with them*[6] (Bakunin, 62006[e], pp. 1, 28). It is not, therefore, about people who must use their knowledge and resources to provide the people with transformative capacity. More precisely, this means contributing to the strengthening of this people and their cause. When speaking of this relationship, in particular the role of the intellectualized youth—which can even be called "vanguard youth" (Bakunin, 62006[e], p. 23)—in their contact with the people, some considerations should be made.

> Without doubt, when we merge with the people, when we are accepted by the people, we can be very useful to them. Yes, we will bring to them the bitter experience of failed Western life that we know with it, the faculty of generalizing facts and determining them with precision, the clarity of conscience. By knowing history and being instructed by the experience of others, we can prevent them from being deceived and help them to express their will. That is all. We will bring to them aspects of life; they will give us life. Who will contribute the most? The people, of course, and not us.
>
> The question of our approximation to the people isuestiontion of life or death, not for the people, but for us, for all our activity. This proximity is necessary, but it is difficult, because it demands that we be totally reborn, not only externally but also internally. The Russian beard, the Russian costume, the rough hands, the coarse language do not yet make the Russian man. Our spirit must learn to know that of the people and our hearts must know how to beat in unison with their great heart, which is still obscure to us. We must not see them as a means but as an objective; we must not treat them as the raw material of the revolution, produced according to our ideas, as "flesh of liberation," but on the contrary we must consider ourselves, if they permit, servants of their cause. In short, we must love them more than ourselves, so that they may love us, that they may entrust us with their cause.
>
> To love passionately, to give oneself with all one's soul, to overcome difficulties and immense obstacles, to gain by the force of love and sacrifice the hardened heart of the people is the cause of youth. This is their mission! They must learn

from the people and not teach them. They must not elevate themselves, but elevate them [the people], and give themselves entirely to their cause. And then the people will recognize them. (Bakunin, 62006[e], pp. 30–31)

Therefore, even if strengthened by the presence of allies the revolution is popular, made by the people, without which there is no possibility of far-reaching changes.

Moving forward in relation to the way this revolution should be built, it should be noted that the main instrument of this movement is a "massive and courageous struggle" of the Slavic people and their allies (Bakunin, 49001[e], p. 2). First of all, the revolution is a mass revolution. But to strengthen it, secret political organizations can be beneficial or even necessary, which contribute to mobilization by exercising "influence over the people and the youth" (Bakunin, 62024[c], p. 3; cf., also: Bakunin, 62025[c], pp. 25–26). Just as those who are not part of the people by birth, but who ally themselves with them in the struggles, these organizations must contribute to becoming the "educated form of the popular conscience." By mobilizing the people, "above all the people of the countryside, the primary cause when it comes to Slavism", their members must do so not "as arrogant teachers, but as humble pupils"; the "right to guide the people" exists only when there is trust on their part. That is, these secret societies do not replace the people in the revolutionary process (Bakunin, 62025[c], pp. 5–6).

Although reforms, inside or outside Russia, could contribute to accelerating this revolutionary outcome, parliamentarianism was not an alternative; it was only a form of mediation and conciliation, harmful in those revolutionary times (Bakunin, 50001[e], pp. 14–15).

I have very little interest in parliamentary debates, and the era of parliamentary life, of constituent, national assemblies, etc. has passed, and anyone who [asks] the question honestly should admit that they have no more interest, or at least only a forced and chimerical interest in these outdated forms. I believe neither in constitutions nor in laws. Not even the best of constitutions could satisfy me. (Bakunin, 2010b, p. 52)

The most obvious case of a parliamentarianism that went against revolutionary practice was that of the Frankfurt Parliament. This initiative not only advanced in the field of reforms to the detriment of the revolution, but progressively distanced itself from the notion of the freedom of peoples. It demonstrated "German national selfishness" in that "the Germans wanted freedom for themselves and not for others." This parliament, "emerging from a revolt [...], began shortly afterwards to call the Italians and the Poles rebels and to consider them criminal adversaries who envied German greatness and omnipotence" (Bakunin, 1976b[e], p. 117). It was therefore essential to abandon expectations of parliamentarianism and invest definitively in a mass revolutionary movement.

To consolidate the great union of the Slavs, a collective basis for agreements is important, because "to have force against the common enemy, it is necessary to act together, and to act together, it is necessary to come to an agreement" (Bakunin, 62002[e], p. 14). This requires a determined investment in "the progress of popular consciousness" (Bakunin, 50001[e], p. 7). This common agreement aimed at awareness and action can only be implemented practically by means of a movement properly articulated and subjugated by values consistent with its ends: "Without discipline, without organization, without modesty in the face of the greatness of our goal, we will only amuse our enemies and will never achieve victory" (Bakunin, 62006[e], p. 32).

This basis of union of the Slavs, all of whom have been "victims of foreign oppression," imperialism, must support the gathering of people on the basis of "solidarity" around an anti-imperialist, national liberation struggle, which points to the "independence of all the peoples who make up the Slav race," and which can advance their claims. The goal of a future Slav federation, and even a European federation, capable of guaranteeing national liberation, peoples' self-determination, and popular emancipation, is also fundamental (Bakunin, 48004[e], pp. 1–2).

Finally, this revolutionary movement would need to find allies in other oppressed nation-races and among the European people. All oppressed peoples who could engage in this project should be supported. This was precisely the case for the Italians, who composed "this beautiful Italy corrupted by the subjection imposed by Austria." And also the "German people" —"not the despots of Germany" and their dominant sectors, of course—who demanded a "free German nation" and who were dispersed and oppressed, as were the Slavs. It was essential to direct Slavic hatred "towards the Germans" towards the imperialist German states and their upper classes—such hatred could not and should not be directed towards the German people, especially not towards their democratic sector. In the European revolution, the German struggle for democracy should be incorporated. Finally, even the Magyars, who in Hungary played an auxiliary role in Austrian oppression of the Slavs, should be sought in order to strengthen this "fraternal alliance" against the great agents of European despotism (Bakunin, 48020[e], pp. 9, 32–33; Bakunin, 1976b[e], pp. 139–40; Bakunin, 50001[e], p. 55; Berthier, 2010, vol. 2, pp. 46–47, 53, 83–84, 96).

9.3 CENTRALISM, DICTATORSHIP, ROLE OF THE TSAR AND THE BOURGEOISIE IN THE EMANCIPATION OF THE SLAVS, AND ANTI-GERMANISM

Finally, some aspects of Bakunin's revolutionary pan-Slavism that highlight certain divergences or nuances in relation to his project should be discussed in more depth. I will discuss his contention between 1844 and 1863 that freedom should be the path to freedom, and the need to build the autonomy of the Slavic people, and consider the extent to which his conception of revolutionary political organization and, above all, his defense of a temporary dictatorship in an eventual revolutionary government, are in agreement with such a project. In addition, I will discuss Bakunin's positions regarding the role that the tsar and the Russian bourgeoisie could play in this project, and finally, whether his positions towards the German cause and the Germans indicate anti-Germanism or Germanophobia on his part.

In these years, Bakunin states privately and publicly that freedom must be sought through freedom: "learning freedom," he writes, must be done through "freedom itself" (Bakunin, 50001[e], p. 65). He also points out that "for freedom to become for them [the people] a reality, they need *autonomy*"; only a people in conditions of self-determination is free. And autonomy and self-determination do not come "by the decree of a dictator, nor by the decision of a solemn parliament, which never fully expresses popular thought" (Bakunin, 62002[e], p. 5). They are conquered by means of popular revolution, and not even revolutionaries can deprive the people of this: "We are neither [...] sellers nor buyers of peoples, and we have neither the power nor the will to dispose of their destiny. We firmly and absolutely believe that this right belongs only to them." For us revolutionary pan-Slavists, "freedom with all its consequences is a supreme principle, outside of which we conceive nothing" (Bakunin, 62011[e], p. 10). That is, the principle of freedom guarantees that the revolutionaries who support it contribute to the autonomy and self-determination of peoples, and to attack it is to attack popular freedom.

However, two aspects seem to call into question such positions and deserve to be more thoroughly considered: first, the revolutionary model of political organization advocated by Bakunin; second, the post-revolutionary model of government prescribed by him. As Lehning explains (1974b, pp. 58–60), these aspects refer directly to Bakunin's concepts of revolutionary organization. His fundamental inspiration in this respect was the theoretical productions and practical experiences that had been conducted by Buonarroti, Babeuf, and the Conspiracy of the Equals during the French Revolution. Bakunin knew them through their own writings and works on the social history of France. He had contact with this tradition that was in force in the revolutionary movement of the nineteenth century and was inspired by it. His concept of revolutionary organization was influenced by this tradition, which was incorporated and, at the same time, modified in certain aspects.

With regard to the model of revolutionary political organization, a subject always dealt with in private documents, Bakunin maintains the need for a centralized, hierarchical, and disciplined secret society of cadres. It is a "secret society" articulated as a "revolutionary hierarchy," composed of other sub-societies "separated, independent and ignored by each other." Each of them "should be subject to a strict hierarchy and absolute discipline" and "should be limited to a small number of people" who should approximate a certain profile: "men of talent, of knowledge, of energy, of influence who, obeying the central direction, would in turn act on the masses, so to speak, in an invisible way." These sub-organizations "would be linked to each other by a central committee made up of three or, at most, five members [...] designated by election." This secret society would have to articulate a "joint conspiracy," a "common organization," "a centralized plan of action and direction" under the authority of a "central committee" (Bakunin, 1976b[e], pp. 142–43, 162, 164).

It can be noted that such a political organization is based on a model that has marked differences from the model of the future society conceived by Bakunin. Certainly there are some convergences: the function of the central committee (in the secret society) and that of the Council (in the Slav federation); the election of members of the central committee in the secret society and the more widespread elections in the Slav federation; the moderate centralism of the federal state and the strict centralism of the secret society. However, there are also differences. In these very cases, the elections are much less significant in the secret society than in the Slav federation, as is centralism. Moreover, it cannot be said that the revolutionary political organization is exactly a paradigm of equality and freedom. Such a society relies on the subordination of members and functional and decision-making power inequalities; therefore, it cannot be taken as a federation with internal democracy or self-government of the members and/or the sub-organizations that compose it.

Bakunin hoped to be one of the few members of the central committee of this revolutionary political organization. In the case of the Bohemian Uprising, he aspired to the role of "secret leader, without ostentatiously taking over at first in its central committee." If this insurrection were to come to pass, Bakunin says that "all the essential threads of the movement would be concentrated in my hands" (Bakunin, 1976b[e], p. 143). He was aware that this central committee could take the form of an "autocratic power," as in the case of the Warsaw Committee, but he accepted the fact, provided that it expressed the Slavs' "movement and national hopes" (Bakunin, 62011[e], p. 11).

As regards the post-revolutionary model of government, Bakunin even wrote that he "had no definite ideas." In the meantime, he outlined how he conceived a government after the revolution. First, he understood that the revolutionary political organization "should not disperse, but should strengthen itself, extend itself and gather living, really strong elements, and gradually embrace all Slavic lands." Such a society would have to make a decisive contribution by establishing a "dictatorship," a temporary "dictatorial power," which would be responsible for erecting the Slav federation and then the European federation (Bakunin, 1976b[e], pp. 110, 143). Bakunin arrived at and addressed this issue when he discussed the revolution in Russia and Prague. About the first case, he emphasized:

> I believe that in Russia, more than elsewhere, a *strong dictatorial power* will be necessary, a power which will be concerned exclusively with the *elevation and education of the masses*; a power free in its tendency and spirit, but *without parliamentary forms*; which prints books with free content, but *without freedom*

of the press; a power surrounded by partisans, enlightened by their advice, reinforced by their free collaboration; but *which is not limited by anything or anybody*. [...] The whole difference between this dictatorship [and monarchist power] consists only in the fact that the former, according to the spirit of its principles, *must tend to make its existence superfluous, since it would have no other end than the freedom, independence and progressive maturity of the people*, while monarchist power, on the contrary, by always striving to make its own existence indispensable, is thus obliged to keep its subjects in a permanent infantile state. (Bakunin, 1976b[e], p. 110, emphasis added)

About the second case, he explained:

In Prague, the seat of the revolutionary government endowed with *unlimited dictatorial powers* should be established. The nobility would be expelled, as would all the clerical opposition; the Austrian administration should be definitively abolished, officials dismissed, and only a few would be kept in Prague, among those most important and best informed, to give advice and, as it were, serve as a library for statistical data. All clubs, all periodicals, all manifestations of charlatan anarchy would equally be abolished. *Everything should be subject to a dictatorial power.* Youth and useful men, divided into categories according to their characteristics, their capacities and their personal tendencies, would be distributed throughout the country to ensure provisional, revolutionary and military organization. The masses would form two groups: some, somewhat armed, would remain in their homes to safeguard the new order of things, and would be employed, if necessary, in a *partisan* war. In return, all the young people, all the poor who could carry weapons, the industrial workers and craftsmen without work, as well as much of the educated bourgeois youth, would form an army, not *Freischar* [voluntary] but regular, formed with the help of retired former Polish officers, Austrian soldiers and non-commissioned officers, who would be elevated to different positions according to their ability and their zeal. The expenses would have been enormous, but I expected to cover them partly with the proceeds of what would be confiscated and the extraordinary taxes, but also with *assignats* similar to those of [Lajos] Kossuth.[7] (Bakunin, 1976b[e], pp. 135–36, emphasis added)

More than the revolutionary model of political organization, this post-revolutionary model of government is very different from the future society advocated by Bakunin. There is no prospect of freedom in it since it is a dictatorship without any limits. If one seeks equality imposed on the majority, it cannot be denied that there is a minority, the dictators, who have practically all access to power. It is an extremely centralized government, supported by a centralism that is much tougher than that of the secret society, because it does not tolerate elections and is not voluntary for the majority of the population.

There is therefore no prospect of autonomy, self-determination, or self-government; any construction of people's self-administration, of "self-government of the commune" or of a "liberated commune"—all this remains only as a future intention. On the basis of Bakunin's own argument in his anarchist period, it can be said that there is no prospect of a transition from this dictatorial government to the Slav federation. What is more, the way in which that government would be articulated would probably never allow for the development of a society of freedom, equality, and fraternity.[8]

Such ideas of defense of dictatorship were almost entirely developed in the "Confession" to Nicholas I of 1851. It could be questioned whether, for some particular reason or interest, Bakunin had lied to the tsar. This hypothesis seems mistaken, since, in some way, this defense of dictatorship appears at other times. In 1845, Bakunin (45002[c], p. 5), in a self-criticism to his brothers, came to say: "I have a great propensity for despotism." In 1860, in clearer evidence, Bakunin (60005[c], pp. 3, 22) defended Muraviev to Herzen, showing that he accepted the program of the former, of a "provisional iron dictatorship," which would aim at the "general interest" and "collective freedom." Finally, this position is expressed to a lesser extent when Bakunin questions, for some time, whether the tsar could play any positive role in the emancipation of the Slavs.[9]

Until 1850, Bakunin's criticism of Tsarism and Nicholas I remained the same, in accordance with the lines of criticism of despotism previously exposed. In 1849, Bakunin (49001[e], p. 2), in a public text, vehemently denies that "the emperor of Russia [...] is a Slav and a natural protector of the Slavs"; this is nothing more than "a lie, a lie, an abominable lie." This is because "Nicholas is not a Slav, but a German placed on the Russian throne, a German prince descended from the Holstein-Gottorp"—his allies are the other imperial rulers and any democratic people are his enemy.[10] To think that the tsar can save the Slavic people from "slavery" is "madness." In 1850, in his private letter to his lawyer, Bakunin (50001[e], p. 18), in a similar sense, states that "a single individual, however great, can establish a power of mechanical order, can subjugate peoples, but not create a free people. Freedom and life come only from the people."

In his "Confession" of 1851 Bakunin (1976b[e], p. 120) assumed that he was contemplating begging the tsar to help the "oppressed Slavs," welcoming them "under your powerful protection" and being "their savior and father." He thought that "after being proclaimed Tsar of all Slavs," Nicholas could "finally raise the Slav banner in Western Europe to the astonishment of the Germans and all the other oppressors and enemies of the Slav people." But one could doubtless question, like everything related to "Confession," whether Bakunin also writes this just to try to please the tsar. But, again, this hypothesis does not seem to be confirmed, if we look at Bakunin's subsequent conduct and his private and public texts between 1860 and 1863.

Obviously, there is an enormous rupture in Russia's history between 1855 and 1861, with the death of Nicholas I, the rise of Alexander II to the throne, Russia's defeat in the Crimean War, and the abolition of serfdom. With the substitution of the tsar and the war, "the inhumane creation of Peter the Great, Catherine II, Alexander I and Emperor Nicholas, that monstrous temple erected by despotism into slavery, the empire of Russia, was finally broken." Especially "after the Crimean catastrophe, everyone realized that the old system was dead and that a new one had to be erected." This was a "conviction so profound and general" that it even permeated "the highest spheres of the official world" and to everyone it seemed impossible to "revive the dead." "Public opinion [...] came to light" and began to speak openly "of the vices of military and civil administration" (Bakunin, 63003[e], p. 7).

The principles of Alexander II's government "were great. He decreed the freedom of the people, freedom and a new life after millennia of slavery"; it even seemed that he "wanted the Russia of the *zemstvo*." Moreover, in "February 1861, despite all the constraints, all the faults, all the monstrous contradictions and the no less monstrous narrowness of the decree of emancipation of the peasants, Alexander II was "considered by Russians "the greatest Tsar, the most beloved, the most powerful who had ever reigned in Russia" (Bakunin, 62006[e], p. 9).

In parallel with this moment of intense change, Bakunin was in exile in Siberia and, under the influence of Muraviev-Amurski, he recognized in a letter to Herzen in 1860 that if the Russian people lost their initiative—and this was what he thought was happening at that time, perhaps because of the isolation of the period of imprisonment and exile—it would be necessary to support changes from above. He saw in the figure and positions of Muraviev a possible way out of this dilemma (Bakunin, 60005[c], p. 16). Moreover, with the emancipation of the serfs the following year and the contact with Martyanov, Bakunin followed the general climate that was spreading in Russia and continued on this path of questioning some of his earlier certainties.

In 1862, he wrote publicly on the subject in "The People's Cause," assessing the possibilities for the tsar to unite with the people against the nobility and bureaucracy and to head the implementation of the necessary changes in Russia—thereby avoiding a violent and bloody revolution. However, Bakunin writes in the same breath that, even if it were possible, such an alliance would not happen. A more detailed analysis of this text reveals that it has at least three dimensions. In the first, more analytical dimension, Bakunin stresses that at least theoretically there would be a possibility of the tsar following this path, but that such a probability is practically non-existent. Even so, from the tone of the writing, there is at least a minimal expectation on Bakunin's part that this could happen. And precisely for this reason, there are the other two dimensions. Apparently, Bakunin dialogues with the revolutionaries, suggesting that if for some reason this happened, it should be positively received. He also apparently dialogues with the tsar himself, trying to convince him of this path and giving the broad outlines of what could be done (Bakunin, 62006[e]). In 1863, Bakunin returns to the subject in the writing "Letter Concerning Russia," already dealing with the subject in a more distant way, and only saying that this could have been a path adopted by the tsar following the liberation of the serfs (Bakunin, 63003[e]).

After the emancipation of the serfs, the Russian people seemed to wake up, announcing the conditions for a new revolution, which would bring the work begun by Alexander II to its ultimate consequences. The question, however, was what form this revolution would take: would it be a popular uprising along the lines of that of Pugachev, a *coup d'état* like that of Pestel's Decembrists, or a change from above, led by the tsar? The first two paths were necessarily violent; the third could be peaceful. It was therefore necessary to know: would this revolution "be peaceful or bloody?" For this, a fact of reality had to be taken into account: "the people are with the Tsar and against the nobility, against the officials, and against all who wear the German clothes," that is, the people see as their enemies all who are in "the official Russian camp, all except the Tsar. The majority of the people [...] have maintained their faith in the Tsar" (Bakunin, 62006[e], pp. 14, 16).

The awakening of the people, as well as their faith in the tsar—which, more than a simple belief in the emperor, showed a "*symbolic representation*" of a people who loved the "greatness and glories of the Russian land"—indicated the possibility of a transformative movement that could be carried out through an alliance between Alexander II and the Russian people. It was exactly the third path that could take place peacefully; the tsar "could bring about in Russia the immense and very beneficial revolution, *without shedding a drop of blood*. And he still can." On this "path, there is no danger, success is certain." This next revolution "will be peaceful and prosperous if the Tsar who takes the lead of the popular movement" takes the path of "radical transformation in Russia in the spirit of freedom and the *zemstvo*." He could put an end to internal oppression, to Russia's conquests, and contribute directly to the emancipation of other oppressed nations, including Poland, Ukraine, Belarus, and Finland. He could also found the great Slav federation and, even after that, remain a hereditary ruler. However, if Alexander II "retreats or stops at half-measures" the process will be horrible and "the revolution will take on the character of a ruthless carnage [...] as a consequence of the insurrection of the whole people" (Bakunin, 62006[e], pp. 7–8, 11–12, 14, 19, 34–35; Bakunin, 63003[e], pp. 8, 10).

In other words, "now Alexander Nikolaevitch has a terrible responsibility. He can still save Russia from definitive ruin, from blood. Will he do it? Does he want that?" In some way, is there "hope that this alliance [between Tsar and people] will be realized? *We say decidedly not*. Even if the people are undoubtedly devoted to the Tsar, the Tsar visibly fears them." And this fear stems from the fact that Alexander II does not love the Russian people, that he is unwilling to renounce his Germanic designs and his imperial pleasures, and also because he realizes that it is risky to play with the people. So, Alexander II does not appear to want "the freedom of the people," which "would be contrary to all his instincts." At that very decisive moment, in order to achieve the ends of the process he had begun, the tsar only thought of "strengthening, restoring and if possible extending the bisecular [two-century] cause of Russian immobility, the prison building of the State of Peter the Great, who hated the people." Finally, on the basis of this path, which would most probably be the one adopted, Alexander II "is ready to plunge Russia into a bloody revolution"—"he wants blood" (Bakunin, 62006[e], pp. 10, 15, 22–23, 39, emphasis added).

Thanks to the social formation of the countries where the Slavs were found, and also to recent events related to the June 1848 Revolution in Paris, Bakunin also wondered whether the bourgeoisie could play any positive role in the emancipation of the Slavs. For a brief moment (October and November 1848), in the unpublished drafts of the "Appeal to the Slavs" there was some doubt about this (Bakunin, 48019[e]). In the definitive writing that was published, the question ended up not being addressed (Bakunin, 48020[e]).

In these drafts, Bakunin presents two different analyses of the bourgeoisie (which is sometimes called the "middle class"), which do not have the same political-strategic implications. In the first, the bourgeoisie is considered a historical ally of the people in the fight against despotism. However, it seemed evident at the end of 1848 that there was a split between the two classes: such "division manifested itself above all in Paris in those fatal events of June." On that occasion, the bourgeoisie betrayed its historical allies and threw itself into the lap of reaction. Even so, Bakunin understood that this division, which was evident in the conduct during the conflicts, was to a large extent the result of the stimuli of the reaction, which aimed to weaken its enemies' bloc. This effort to "divide the classes," the bourgeoisie and the people, was a "fatal division," a way of "destroying the force of the revolutionary movement." It was "the division which the enemies of the movement sowed everywhere between the bourgeoisie and the people." Moreover, he thought that, even at the end of June 1848, it was still possible to distinguish two sectors in the bourgeoisie; the latter was "divided into two camps: the backward bourgeoisie and the revolutionary bourgeoisie," the latter "marching again with the people." The alliance between the revolutionary bourgeoisie and the people seemed fundamental to the defeat of despotism.

In the second analysis, the bourgeoisie is harshly criticized because of its restricted and exclusionary economic interests and its political indifference and insensitivity.

> Fortunately for us, with the exception of a few cities where the Germans
> managed to introduce elements alien to our Slavic customs, the bourgeoisie
> itself does not exist in our countries. Today it predominates in the West and
> that is where the misfortune and the curse of the time occurs. This class is the
> personification of narrowness, political indifference and selfishness; it imprints

upon all things a desolating character of pettiness and lies which is peculiar to it; it sterilizes everything and only lives by cover-ups and betrayals. It believes in nothing, sympathizes with nothing, is not touched by any suffering, by any misery, nor by any of the great questions involving the happiness and dignity of our species. It has no homeland, no political color, and can live equally in every country and under every regime, provided that it is allowed to enrich itself and enjoy its fortune in comfort. Make money! This is their goal and the only concern of their life. [...] The satisfaction of the bourgeoisie is always the opposite of the freedom of peoples; its interest is always diametrically opposed to the interest of the masses. (Bakunin, 48019[e])

This last judgment, that the bourgeoisie was a class opposed to the freedom of the masses, was maintained on the few occasions that the subject was taken up again later in that period. This was the case at the end of 1848, when Bakunin (48018[c], p. 1) clearly distinguished "bourgeois revolution" and "popular revolution" when discussing Germany, and also in 1862 when Bakunin (62008[e], p. 11) accused the bourgeoisie of being "the most conservative social class" and whose most characteristic trait would be "its philistine spirit." At that time, he argued, its members were already "bound by all that is the old traditional game"; notably on the occasions when they were able to make their interests prevail, they began to hate changes and to give preference to "sleepy calm and a disciplined order" provided, of course, that it guaranteed them "a well-filled pocket."

In sum, Bakunin addressed the question of the bourgeoisie only marginally in his work between 1844 and 1863. As far as the Slavic world was concerned, he understood that the bourgeoisie was not yet a relevant class; as far as Western Europe was concerned, the developments of the Peoples' Spring contributed to the formation of his critical position. Bakunin was hesitant in 1848—this is what the different positions of the drafts of the "Appeal to the Slavs" seem to indicate, apart from the fact that he did not deal with the subject in the definitive text. At the same time, however, it is possible to consider that the course of events, particularly in France, contributed to his having, after his imprisonment and exile, a vision more in tune with that of socialism (cf., also: Angaut, 2009, pp. 49–52).

Finally, some remarks can be made about Bakunin's views on the German question in general and the Germans in particular. Between 1844 and 1863, Bakunin (50001[e], pp. 44–47, 50–51, 55) understood that, in terms of strategic geopolitics, Germany was in a critical state. For, despite an enormous potential as a people, the Germans had not realized it, especially in political terms; the lack of unity left all their states subject to outside intervention. Unification was essential, not only for Germany to become a nation-race, but also to form a state capable of avoiding international pressure, including that exerted from Russia. And it was the German people who had to lead this unification.

A key player in this process, Prussia, with its outstanding military potential, would have to choose between alignment with Russia and Austria, sharing Germany with the latter, or the Prussianization of Germany and thus opposition to Russia and Austria. Both seemed to be feasible alternatives but would necessarily have problematic consequences. The solution to the German question was therefore to deal with the dilemmas of international relations involving Russia and Austria, and subsequently to resolve how their unification process would proceed.

As has been pointed out, in the period in question Bakunin expressed in most cases, especially by taking a public stand, support for the German people and democrats, seeking to channel Slavic hatred of the Germans towards German imperialism, Prussia, Austria, the rulers, and other upper Germanic classes. To achieve a European revolution, Bakunin (1976b[e], pp. 83–84, 139–140) recommends that the Slavs should ally themselves with the Germans by "fully and entirely recognizing the rights of the latter [Germans] to an independent existence and encouraging them to join the pan-European revolutionary cause."

But this issue did not receive homogeneous treatment throughout the period. Let us see, chronologically, how the arguments develop, highlighting the public or private character of the texts. In 1848, Bakunin (48020[e], p. 12) criticizes publicly the strategy of the despots who, in favour of their domination, "excite the Slavs against the Germans and the Germans against the Slavs." In 1850, Bakunin (50001[e], pp. 41, 44–45, 55) writes privately that "Germany is a magnificent country! [...] A people endowed with all that can constitute civilization, wealth, and progress, with a culture whose universality and depth are found nowhere else in the world!" Yet "Germany is not a nation, it is not [...] a true people." Because, as a nation-race at that time, it did not possess unity of conscience and politics, a feeling of its own strength, and was vulnerable to outside influences. "It is divided into more than 30 parts, which are governed by independent princes whose dynastic interests are diametrically opposed to the interests of Germany as a whole."

Germany, "in order to maintain its existence in the face of Russian pressure, needs unity," and it is not the governments or the upper classes who should lead this German unification but the people: "only the German people can create the organic unity of Germany" since "the German princes are at best capable of achieving a purely mechanical and yet very problematic union." German preservation is therefore necessary, since "the freedom and greatness of Germany are necessary conditions for the freedom of the whole of Europe, a necessary postulate for Russia to become free."

In this text of 1850, Bakunin (50001[e], pp. 71–73) acknowledged that "*hatred of the Germans, contempt for the Germans,* [...] are common to all Slavs." This hatred which "did not fall from heaven" but "was born of historical conditions" and which is "deeply rooted in history"—the Germanic oppression of the Slavs is the main aspect of this historical foundation. The fact that the Russian government employs several Germans in its bureaucracy, for example, contributes to "the persistence and reinforcement of this Germanophobia" among the Russians. However, Bakunin ponders anti-Germanism: "For my part, I completely condemn this antipathy when it concerns the entire German nation and not just the oppressive Germans." This "race hatred between Slavs and Germans would lead [...] to the most unfortunate consequences for the common cause of humanity and freedom."

Nevertheless, for him, "the Germans must agree: no matter how humane in their ideas, in all their culture, they have so far been extremely tyrannical in their foreign relations." Examples abound: "In Italy, against the Poles, against the other Slavs; everywhere they have been, they have taken slavery with them." The Germans "acted, it is true, only as instruments of their governments, but a Russian can also give the same excuse, for he too is an instrument of despotic power." So, Germany's necessary unity, greatness, and freedom cannot support Germanizing imperialism and the people must not be confused with their rulers or their state. Such objectives must be consolidated by "Germany remaining within its truly German limits and not beyond, and not indulging in that romantic extension sung in the patriotic hymn of the Teutonians."

In his "Confession" to Nicholas I of 1851, although it is not possible to know whether there was some exaggeration to please the tsar, Bakunin for the first time expounded an openly anti-Germanic position when relating the events of 1848:

> Before I left for Prague, the democrats in Breslávia had shown me great respect, but all my influence disappeared and was annihilated when I started defending the rights of Slavs in the democratic clubs. They all cried out against me and would not even let me finish; *it was my last attempt at eloquence in the Breslva club and in general in the clubs and public assemblies in Germany.* The Germans have since become so odious to me that I could not speak calmly to any of them; I could not hear their language, not even a German voice, and I remember when a German beggar asked me for alms once, and I had to restrain myself from hitting him. (Bakunin, 1976b[e], p. 118)

Still in this text, Bakunin (1976b[e], pp. 117, 139), though criticizing "German national egoism" —which, according to him, was based on the fact that "the Germans wanted freedom for themselves and not for others"—recounted all his efforts to lessen the fighting between Slavs and Germans in order to strengthen the possibilities of a revolution in Germany. He asked the Germans to change "their way of thinking about the Slavs" and at the same time to combat "the inveterate hatred of the Slavs against the Germans."

In 1862, Bakunin returned to the issue a few times. Remember that it was in that same year that he stated in a letter to his sister-in-law: "I preach systematically and by ardent conviction hatred of the Germans" (Bakunin, 62043[c], p. 3). In a less emphatic Germanophobic tone than that of the quotation from "Confession" and that letter, Bakunin (62025[c], 62006[e]) generalizes the German nation-race, treating the Germans almost in their entirety as dominators; he increasingly and indistinctively recognizes the majority of Germans as pan-Germanists and does not differentiate them from the state, the rulers, or the Germanic ruling classes. This is the case when Bakunin (62006[e], p. 37) publicly states that "going to war against the Germans is a good cause, and above all the necessary cause of the Slavs"; it would then be a "national war." War against which Germans and for what purposes? It happens similarly when Bakunin (62008[e], p. 7) writes, also publicly, that "the Germanic ferment certainly contributed to a rapid awakening of the two countries [Bohemia and Poland], but it also brought an enemy germ, to which both succumbed." What germ and what kind of submission?

In general, there are undoubtedly anti-Germanophobic as well as Germanophobic traits in these texts, although, depending on the private or public character, they are more or less emphasized.[11]

NOTES

1   I do not agree with Berthier (2010, vol. 2, pp. 3, 15, 168) when he defines pan-Slavism exclusively as "the doctrine that all Slavic peoples should be subject to the influence of Russia," and thus pan-Slavism would be only that "partisan to the submission of Slavic nations to the policy of the great Russian brother." Without doubt, this is *one possible* definition of pan-Slavism. Bakunin knew of the existence of this type of pan-Slavism—which he called "Petersburger pan-Slavism" and "Russian imperial pan-Slavism," and its defenders described by him as "centralizing pan-Slavists" (Bakunin, 63003[e], p. 2; Bakunin, 62025[c], p. 9; Bakunin, 62002[e], p. 11)—which he criticized harshly (Bakunin, 62008[e], p. 2; Bakunin, 62025[c], pp. 6–7, 9). Working with Berthier's narrow definition of pan-Slavism, it is certain that "Bakunin's writings leave no doubt that he is *not* a pan-Slavist." However, it must be pointed out that, at least since the Slavic Congress of 1848, there had been a dispute about the characteristics and the direction that pan-Slavism should take. Along with this concept of "Petersburger pan-Slavism," there were at least two others: one whose supporters wanted to transform the Austrian monarchy into a Slavic monarchy, later called *Austro-Slavism* (Berthier, 2010, vol. 2, pp. 68, 79); and that of the pan-Slavism advocated by Bakunin. Of these three currents, Bakunin considered the first two reactionary and the third, his own, revolutionary. It should also be noted that Bakunin was *fully aware of such a dispute*. In addition, as stated, between the end of the 1840s and the beginning of the 1860s, although Bakunin's political ideas as a whole were somewhat homogeneous, he referred to them as *pan-Slavism* only in 1862, the same year in which he asserted *Slavic socialism*. In 1862, Bakunin (62025[c], pp. 14, 16, 22) maintains that, in his view, "*pan-Slavism* is the conviction that the Slavic State, uniting 85 million individuals, will announce a civilization, a new and true living solution so that freedom may reign in the world." And he continues: "what I call *pan-Slavism* is the need for "all Slavism to unite and sublimate itself." Since "*anyone who is not like us, pan-Slavic, in this way that we understand, is not Slavic from the bottom of his heart*." Bakunin (62008[e], pp. 2, 9) also mentions, in a public text, the "formidable idea of *pan-Slavism*" and "our pan-Slavic program." Therefore—according to the history of Slavism and even Bakunin's understanding of this movement (Hepner, 1950)—Berthier's statement that Bakunin "is *not* a pan-Slavist" is incorrect. He is not pan-Slavist, only if pan-Slavism is understood as "Russian imperial pan-Slavism"; and pan-Slavism cannot be defined in this way, especially since this definition does not give an account of the historical phenomenon and differs from Bakunin's own reading. If pan-Slavism is defined as Bakunin did in 1862, Bakunin must be considered a pan-Slavist—it was precisely this definition that made him recognize himself as such that year. Such statements by Berthier (2010) are made in the volume covering the period 1848–61 of Bakunin's life and work (before he called himself a pan-Slavist); but in the volume covering the period 1861–68, nothing is mentioned about this concept of pan-Slavism and even Bakunin's claim to it. Berthier also considerably minimizes Bakunin's advocacy of dictatorship in "Confession" and in his interventions in favour of Muraviev-Amurski.

2   Cf. Herzen (2012, p. 35): "By Russian socialism, we mean the socialism that derives from the land and peasant way of life, from the effective distribution and existing distribution of the countryside, from communal tenure and communal government—and we advance with the workers' cooperatives towards that economic justice generally sought by socialism and affirmed by science."

3   In addition to the properly Slavic references (of Decembrists, Poles, and others), Bakunin is also influenced by Proudhon's federalism. In 1863, formalizing ideas previously held, Proudhon (2001, p. 90) will write: "FEDERATION, from the Latin *foedus, foederis* genitive, meaning pact, contract, treaty, convention, alliance, etc., is a convention by which one or more heads of families, one or more communes, one or more groups of communes or States, commit themselves mutually and equally to each other for one or more particular objects, the burden of which is especially and exclusively on the delegates of the federation."

4   Cf. Proudhon (1988, p. 244): "Individual *possession* is the condition of social life; five thousand years of property demonstrate: *property* is the suicide of society. Possession is within the law. Ownership is opposed to the law. I have suppressed property and I retain possession; and only with this change in principle will you change everything in the laws, the government, the economy, the institutions: you will expel evil from the land."

5   As Hepner (1950, pp. 264-265) points out, there is a parallel between the role which Bakunin attributes to the Slavs and those which, on the one hand, Marx attributes to the proletariat and that, on the other, Cieszkowski attributes to the Poles.

6   Since the 1840s, Bakunin has held to this idea, which will later have a great echo in Russia, that revolutionaries from the upper classes, especially the youth, should "go to the people." For example, in 1845, he recommends that these people must "be close to the people"; in 1848, he emphasizes that they must "merge with and lose themselves in the popular masses." In 1862, already as a character of some influence in Russian populism, Bakunin advised them to "merge with the people, to lose themselves in their ranks, to live and act with them" (Bakunin, 45001[e], p. 2; Bakunin, 48004[e], p. 2; Bakunin, 62002[e], p. 4).

7   It was these passages, which are included in this quotation and the previous one, which were the most used by Marxists who, immediately after the Russian Revolution of 1917, maintained that there were great similarities between what was advocated by Bakunin and the program of Lenin and the Bolsheviks.

8   This is a strategic contradiction which, sustained by an important part of historical Marxism, especially Marxism-Leninism, was proved during the revolutionary experiences of the twentieth century. In his anarchist years, Bakunin will argue that the notion of "dictatorship of the proletariat" should actually be understood as the dictatorship of a minority of bureaucrats over all workers. This dictatorship would be inadequate as a means of struggle to promote emancipation; it would tend to perpetuate itself and postpone indefinitely the abolition of social classes. However, between 1844 and 1863, Bakunin justified himself with an argument very similar to that of the Bolsheviks. The revolutionary dictatorship—which he approached critically from 1850 onwards, that which was protagonized by the Russian state inside and outside (Bakunin, 50001[e], p. 6)—differs from other dictatorships because it aims at freedom and intends to become increasingly superfluous, until it is no longer necessary.

9   For this discussion of dictatorship, cf., also: Angaut, 2009, pp. 41–43.

10 Also later, Bakunin (62008[e], p. 1) continues to maintain, according to Angaut (2005, p. 208), that "the Romanov dynasty is not a Russian dynasty, and that the Tsar is a Holstein-Gottorp." This is because, still according to Angaut, "Emperor Peter III—husband of the future Catherine II, who overthrew him after a year of reign—was, in 1762, in fact Duke of Holstein-Gottorp, a title he had inherited from his father Charles Frederico, Anne's husband, the eldest daughter of Peter the Great. This ruler, educated in Germany and completely foreign to Russia, distinguished himself effectively during his short reign by a clear pro-German orientation. It was from his marriage to Catherine that the future Tsar Paul I, father of Nicholas I and grandfather of Alexander II, was born."

11 There is an interesting note from Berthier (2010, vol. 2, pp. 97–98) in this regard, although it is not possible to identify whether it refers to Bakunin's pre-anarchist or anarchist period. In this note, he explains that Bakunin's criticisms of the Germans are for two main reasons: the historical oppression of the Slavs and the cult of authority, both of which were headed by the Germans. He also explains that

Bakunin usually distinguishes Prussia from Germany, and, as far as unification is concerned, prefers the Germanization of Prussia to the Prussification of Germany. Finally, Berthier emphasizes that when dealing with the Germans, Bakunin always does so by distinguishing the upper classes from the lower classes; his criticism is generally directed at the former. In any case, Berthier suppresses the most controversial passages in this respect, such as the aforementioned story of the beggar, which Bakunin notes in "Confession." On Bakunin's anti-Germanism between 1844 and 1863, cf., also: Angaut, 2005, pp. 225–27.

PART III

FROM SOCIALISM TO ANARCHISM (1864–76)

CHAPTER 10

"FREEDOM WITHOUT SOCIALISM IS PRIVILEGE, INJUSTICE; SOCIALISM WITHOUT FREEDOM IS SLAVERY AND BRUTALITY": FROM SOCIALISM TO ANARCHISM (1864–76)

This chapter describes Bakunin's political-intellectual trajectory in the period from 1864 to 1876, divided into two parts: 1) International Fraternity: Socialism, Federalism, and Anti-theologism in Italy (1864–67); 2) Anarchism, the Alliance, and International in Switzerland (1867–76). This second major part is broken down into six topics: Socialism, Federalism, and Anti-theologism: International League of Peace and Freedom in Switzerland; Public Alliance, Secret Alliance, and the International Workers' Association; Netchaiev, the Lyon Commune, and Paris Commune; The International: Sections, Representation, and General Council; Conflicts with Utin, Mazzini, Marx, and the General Council; Final Years. Finally, a third part provides important elements for the understanding of Bakunin's political theory in the period in question.

10.1 INTERNATIONAL FRATERNITY: SOCIALISM, FEDERALISM, AND ANTI-THEOLOGISM IN ITALY (1864–67)

Bakunin stayed in Italy for a little over three years, from the beginning of 1864 until September 1867, mainly in Florence and Naples. According to Lehning (1973, p. xv), arriving in that country, Bakunin and Antonia passed through Turin and went on to Genoa, where they were received by the first man of Garibaldi, who led them to the island of Caprera, where the hero of Italian liberation lived. The visit lasted a few days and enabled Bakunin to discuss with Garibaldi the Polish question and especially the situation in Italy. After all, he was a central character in recent Italian history.

Italy at that time was in the midst of the *Risorgimento*. The unfolding of the Peoples' Spring, with its national rather than social impacts in that country, resulted in an immense unification effort, marked by two wars of independence and the creation of the Kingdom of Italy in 1861. This effort ended in 1870 with the conquest of Rome. In this movement for Italian unification, Garibaldi had stood out since 1848, fighting against Austria for the liberation of Sicily and Naples. With his initiative he had obtained the support not only of Italian fighters and progressive sectors, but also of the dissatisfied masses, as in the case of the peasant uprising of 1860.

However, in the years immediately after the constitution of the Kingdom of Italy, the progressive liberating forces, of which Garibaldi and Mazzini were part—and which consisted of republicans, democrats, and Jacobins—lost ground to the constitutional monarchists and liberal conservatives, who then took the reins of building that new Italy. Under their influence, reinforced by the Italian ruling classes, the country was investing in the path of capitalist modernization, stimulating liberalism and, with it, industrialization. For, even with the pre-capitalist development that had taken place since the 1820s, especially in Piedmont and Sardinia, Italy remained almost completely agrarian. It overcame its feudal traits much less intensively than England and even France and Germany, and more than half of its population was illiterate (Hobsbawm, 2004a, pp. 71, 155, 243–69).

By early February 1864, Bakunin was already in Florence. There he worked especially with members of the Russian *intelligentsia*, who frequented his residence at weekly events, and tried to get volunteers to smuggle *Kolokol* into Russia. In the middle of that year his interest in Masonry was revived. Through Giuseppe Dolfi, a baker and Mazzinian leader, he joined the Florentine shop in order to take advantage of this network of relations for political purposes (Carr, 1961, p. 318). In an almost totally Catholic Italy, Freemasonry was at that time realizing a counterpoint to religious submission, actively promoting anti-clericalism and even atheism. In these almost two years of reestablishing links with Freemasonry, during which he reached grade 32,[1] Bakunin was deeply influenced by anti-theological ideas, rethinking definitively the relations between politics and religion (Leier, 2006, p. 171).

Although, as pointed out, his father was quite liberal with regard to traditions— at least at first—Bakunin was raised in the tradition of the Orthodox Church. Until the end of the 1830s, he understood himself to be a Christian and claimed to be a believer in God. In the first half of the 1840s, he related the idea of God to a God of freedom, of humanity. In the second half, he no longer considered himself a Christian and thought it necessary to seek God in man. During the 1850s, he said he was opposed to Christianity. From the 1840s until the beginning of the 1860s, there were references to God in his writings and letters, giving the impression that his belief was not very devout even though the very notion of God was resignified. With this re-entry into Freemasonry in 1864, anti-theological ideas and atheism were incorporated and, after 1866, became an essential part of his political-doctrinaire program. The mark of this passage was the "Fragments of Writings on Freemasonry" (or, simply, "Masonic Fragments") of 1865, the first philosophical writing in which the bases of what would be his scientific-naturalist materialism are delineated (Bakunin, 65001[e]).

As Nettlau (1964, pp. 44–45) points out, still during the Masonic period, in Florence, Bakunin began to formulate a set of ideas, through which he tried, unsuccessfully, to gain followers among the Masons. He then decided to continue developing such ideas in order to form a secret society—for him this was the most suitable form of organization for a revolutionary project at that time. Bakunin worked intensively on face-to-face and epistolary contacts to gain supporters. To this end he visited Stockholm in September and October 1864, where—in discussion with the chief editor of *Aftonbladet*, August Sohlman, a Scandinavian liberal and democrat professor and his main Swedish interlocutor (Mervaud, 1979)—he finished the writing of three texts that form the programmatic basis of the political organization founded that year, which Bakunin, in order to circumvent repression, referred to as "Adelaide," and which Nettlau proposed to call the International Fraternity.[2]

The three texts, produced in Stockholm between September and October 1864, which formalize the program of the Fraternity are: "Société Internationale Secrète de la Révolution: Programme Provisoirement Arrêté par les Frères Fondateurs" ["International Secret Society of the Revolution: Program Provisionally Drawn Up by the Founding Brothers], "Programme d'une Société Internationale Secrète de l'Émancipation de l'Humanité" ["Program of an International Secret Society for the Emancipation of Humanity"], "Projet d'Organisation de la Famille des Frères Scandinaves: Projet d'une Organisation Secrète Internationale" ["Project of an Organization of the Family of Scandinavian Brothers: Project of an International Secret Society"]. In them, a significant shift from previous writings can be seen.[3] While the national question remains one of the pillars, it is complemented equally with reflections on the social question.

Affirming the priority of facts over ideas, Bakunin interprets Europe in the key of *negative dialectics*, characterizing it by the *contradiction between oppression/reaction and freedom/revolution*. *Social classes* are more frequently used in the analysis of social relations, and underpin critiques of *national, religious, political-bureaucratic, and economic domination*. Religious critique has anti-theological foundations and, for the first time, elements with some deepening of *economic critique* appear in the discussion of private property and pre-capitalist and capitalist labour relations (exploitation). Bakunin continues to advocate freedom and peoples' self-determination, but also for the first time individual and collective *freedom* is intimately linked to notions of *economic equality and the ending of social classes*. Democratic communal *federalism* appears more clearly linked to *socialism*, which must be economically and politically organized from the bottom up (albeit guaranteed by a centralized revolutionary government). To achieve this, Bakunin sustains the need for a movement of peasants and proletarians led by upper-class revolutionaries committed to the cause of humanity. He advocates the ending of inheritance and armies, compulsory work for all, integral education, and the internationalization of the revolution. He dedicates himself with some depth, again for the first time, to subjects such as family, women, and children.

Public congresses are criticized and considered inadequate organizational forms/spaces for revolutionary articulation, especially for the ease of repression and lack of practical engagement by the majority of their participants. They serve, at most, for the selection of supporters for secret societies, which are, distinctly, organizational forms/spaces more conducive to such articulation—that is, the organizational path should not be public but secret. The revolutionary secret society must be based on internal unity and hierarchy and constitute itself internationally, being able, as far as possible, to become a public organization (Bakunin, 2014a[e], 2014b[e], 2014c[e]).

In October 1864, Bakunin left Stockholm and, on his return to Florence, spent a few weeks in London, Brussels, and Paris. In the English capital, he was with Herzen and met German tailor Frie'drich Lessner, a former member of the League of Communists. Through him, Marx was informed of Bakunin's presence in the city and proposed a meeting. They met in early November, breaking a 16-year hiatus. They talked about the defamations against Bakunin published in the *New Rhineland Gazette* and *Free Press*, about which Marx expressed dissatisfaction and disbelief. They discussed the Polish Uprising and more particularly the International, which had been founded two months prior and whose first documents Marx had just written (Carr, 1961, pp. 321–23). Informing Engels of the meeting immediately afterwards, Marx wrote: Bakunin "is one of the few people who, after 16 years, I believe to have moved forward and not backwards"; with the failure of the Polish Uprising, Bakunin said that he would, from then on, "get involved only with the socialist movement" (Marx and Engels, 2010c, p. 19).

Marx had been invited by English (mostly unionist) and French (mostly Proudhonian mutualist) workers, who had been working together since 1862, to join the discussions on the creation of an international workers' organization. At that time, the project was beginning to take shape, with the foundation—on 28 September, 1864, at Saint Martin's Hall in London— of the International Workers' Association (IWA or simply International). At the founding event, a committee was elected to articulate this new association, later called the General Council, and a subcommittee to draft an "Inaugural Manifesto" and the "Provisional Statutes"—both documents were eventually drafted by Marx in October (Guillaume, 2009b, pp. 43–44; Samis, 2015b, pp. 161–64). The manifesto gives an overview of the condition of workers in Europe, inviting them to unite in the struggle for their own emancipation. The statutes emphasize the role of the IWA as a means of communication and cooperation among workers and establish basic rules for the functioning of the organization (IWA, 1864a, 1864b).

In the meeting with Marx, Bakunin showed interest in the proposal of the International and agreed to contribute to its diffusion in Italian lands. After that, the relationship between them improved a lot, which can be noticed in the pleasant letters they exchanged for some time (cf., for example: Bakunin, 65004[c]). However, as much as Bakunin made some contributions to the IWA, as in the case of the copy of the "Inaugural Manifesto" that he sent to Garibaldi, his engagement was minimal. He remained non-believing in public organizations and preferred to continue secretly and intellectually articulating the revolutionary European intelligentsia in the Fraternity. This seems to have been his priority, both between October and November 1864 —when he passed through London, Brussels, Paris[4]—as well as between December 1864 and May 1865, the period in which he remained in Florence. At the same time, Herzen and Ogarev moved to Geneva, transferring *Kolokol*'s activities there. Bakunin spent the summer months of 1865 in Sorrento, Italy, where he was with his brother Pavel and his sister-in-law Natalia, and in October he went to Naples, where he stayed for almost two years.

As soon as he arrived in Naples in October 1865, Bakunin manifested himself a few times, polemically and anonymously—his texts were signed by "A Frenchman"—to the newspaper *Il Popolo d'Italia* [*The People of Italy*], of the Italian National Association. At that moment, the situation in Naples did not seem to offer great possibilities, as Bakunin (65017[c], p. 1) declared in a letter to Herzen and Ogarev: "the reaction does not grow daily, but hourly," and unless "something extraordinary, something unforeseen" happens in Europe, "the reaction will advance even faster." Despite this complicated scenario, the close relationship that was established with Princess Obolensky and the political circle that was forged around her brought certain perspectives.

Zoe S. Obolensky was a Russian aristocrat who had emigrated to Italy with her five children and a team of employees. Frankly progressive, she went to Europe with the aim of dissociating herself from her country and her husband's conservatism, gathering around herself and helping financially a group of revolutionaries of different nationalities whose trajectories were linked to the struggles of the late 1840s to the early 1860s. Besides Bakunin, this circle included the Polish Valerien K. Mroczkowski (the princess's lover) and Jean Zagorski, and the Italians Saverio Friscia (doctor), Carlo Gambuzzi (lawyer), and Giuseppe Fanelli (deputy). The members of this circle joined Bakunin's inner circle, continuing the experiment of the International Fraternity.

Contributing to the organization of the Fraternity, Bakunin wrote some documents in 1866. Some, less significant, briefly outline the organic elements of the Italian branch of the Fraternity (Bakunin 66001[e], 66004[e]). Two others, written in March, are much more important. Both are over a hundred pages long and are entitled "Principes et Organisation de la Société Internationale Révolutionnaire" ["Principles and Organization of the International Revolutionary Society"]; the first is known for its subtitle, "Catéchisme Révolutionnaire" ["Revolutionary Catechism"]; and the second has the subtitle of "Organisation."

"Revolutionary Catechism" states the objective and principles of the International Fraternity. According to Bakunin, the organization should promote world revolution and rebuild society on the foundations of freedom, equality, reason, justice, and work. He does this based on theoretical-philosophical assumptions that underpin the deepening of the concept of *anti-theologism* and the first more consistent formalization of the *concept of freedom*, from which equality is inseparable. The critique of the national question remains, but it gives way to the social question, which is increasingly becoming a priority. In the critique of national and social domination, the concepts of *social force*, *social classes*, and *class struggle* appear with importance, and the economy continues to receive attention, especially in reflections on *labour* and the *exploitation of labour*. The strategic paths for the revolution are not clearly exposed. What can be highlighted is that the focus is on the *political organization* that, investing in concomitantly secret and public activities, spreads its program and drives the revolution. In terms of future prospects, that democratic and socialist communal federalism remains, and the term "State" is still linked to the new political form of society (Bakunin, 2009c[e]).

"Organization" sets out the internal regulation of the Fraternity. For the first time, Bakunin formalizes in depth a notion of concentric circles, in which the organization is established in two distinct instances, the International Family and the National Families, the first of which has two levels of members, the Honorary Brothers and the Active Brothers. There is a distinction of rights and duties between the instances and, even within them, the members occupy hierarchically distinct positions. Even if there is an election for the positions, internally there is a chief-subordinate relationship (Bakunin, 66002[e]).[5]

In mid-1866, Obolensky moved with her children and employees to Casamicciola —on the island of Ischia, 50 kilometers west of Naples—where she rented an entire section of a hotel. It was there that she received, not infrequently for long days, friends and revolutionaries from her circle. Politics was constant in this routine, as was the enjoyment of boat trips and picnics. Bakunin, a frequent guest, participated and coordinated both activities. However, these pleasures in Ischia lasted less than a year— dissatisfied with his wife's political and amorous conduct, Obolensky's husband cut off the financial subsidies he provided to his wife, forcing her to curb expenses.

After May 1867—when Mroczkowski went on a political trip through Switzerland, France, and Belgium with a view to increasing the ranks of the Fraternity—the princess and her lover moved to Vevey, in Switzerland, where the cost of living was lower; they were followed by Bakunin and Gambuzzi.[6] Perhaps more than his companions' move weighed on Bakunin in his decision to leave Italy in August 1867: the increasingly moderate character of Garibaldi and Mazzini's Italian nationalism, as well as the threat of the Italian authorities, who spoke of deporting him for his revolutionary activities (Carr, 1961, pp. 329–36; Grawitz, 1990, pp. 274–83).

10.2 ANARCHISM, THE ALLIANCE, AND INTERNATIONAL IN SWITZERLAND (1867–76)

10.2.1 Socialism, Federalism, and Anti-theologism: International League of Peace and Freedom in Switzerland

Bakunin arrived in Switzerland between August and September 1867 and settled there until the end of his days. He lived in Vevey, then in Geneva, in Locarno, and finally in Lugano. He traveled practically all over Switzerland, concentrating his presence in Romanesque Switzerland (1867–70) and Italian Switzerland (1870–76). He left the country a few times, including in 1870 and 1874, when he participated in the insurrections in Lyon and Bologna, respectively.

The backdrop to Bakunin's trip to Switzerland was the change of companions, frustration with the direction of Italian nationalism, and threats of repression. But there was still another motivation. In June 1867, the democratic sectors of Europe were called to a congress that, in view of the growing conflict involving France and Prussia, intended to reflect on the paths to peace on the continent.

Since the 1850s, Europe had been marked by wars, in a process in which the high level of military conflicts accompanied the consolidation of national states and reconfigured the map of power in the region. Three of these wars stood out in the period: "France, Savoy, and the Italians against Austria (1858–59); Prussia and Austria against Denmark (1864); Prussia and Italy against Austria (1866)" (Hobsbawm, 2004a, p. 118). After this last conflict, international tensions grew even more, particularly between France and Germany. Under Napoleon III, France sought to strengthen itself through military interventions—in Syria (1860), China (1860), Indochina (1858–65), and Mexico (1861–67)—and annexations, as in the case of Nice and Saboia. At the same time, Germany, under William I and Otto von Bismarck, used its productive capacity to strengthen the army and invested, towards unification, in confederations, annexations, and conquests. By 1867, as Leier (2006, pp. 177–78) points out, "the balance of power in Europe was dangerously confused, and the leaders of France and Prussia [...] only saw opportunities in this imbalance." The basis for the Franco-Prussian War, which would break out in July 1870, was then being forged.

When Bakunin arrived in Switzerland, he had already decided with the members of the International Fraternity that they would participate in that Peace Congress. On the one hand, it was a good circumstance to gain adherents for the secret society, as stated above; on the other hand, the more democratic conditions in Switzerland offered possibilities for public intervention and activity of the Fraternity (Nettlau, 1964, p. 45).

According to Guillaume (2009a, pp. 115–34), the congress, organized by two Frenchmen, the pacifist Charles Lemonnier and the jurist Émile Acollas, was held in Geneva for four days in September 1867. It was attended by a massive 6,000 people, greatly encouraged by Garibaldi's presence—besides him, the congress received support from other political personalities such as John Stuart Mill, Victor Hugo, Blanc, and Herzen. During its four sessions, the public interventions revealed the contradictions among those present. What should have been, for many moderates, only an occasion for the approval of a motion against the war, turned into a stage of disputes involving various issues. There was no agreement on such perspectives to promote peace. Some defended bourgeois assumptions and pacifism, and others classist socialism and class struggle; some, reforms and conciliatory measures, and others revolution and social transformation; some, religion and theology, and others atheism or agnosticism. The positions in a certain sense were aligned, forming two great forces: one liberal, composed of Republicans and bourgeois Democrats, and the other socialist, composed mostly of delegates from the second congress of the International, which had just ended in Lausanne.

Bakunin was warmly received by the public. During the second session, he made a speech proclaiming himself Russian and socialist and aligned himself with the internationalists in this polarization. He spoke out against the great empires, including Russia, and the centralized states; he defended peoples' self-determination, socialism, and communal federalism as bases for international justice—this was, for him, the only way to peace and freedom, which was profoundly opposed to narrow nationalism and patriotism (Bakunin, 67007[e]). This intervention was in addition to his four previous public discourses, held in 1847–48 and 1863; it also definitively elevated him to the position of public figure and mass propagandist, which would be maintained in the following years thanks to his capacity for oratory and public persuasion.[7]

Among the positions exposed on the platform, it is worth highlighting that of the Belgian doctor and internationalist César de Paepe who—mediating between Proudhon and Marx and contributing directly to the improvement of Bakunin's ideas—emphasized that "political federalism supposes economic federalism" and that the latter "means: mutualism, reciprocity of services and products, suppression of all plundering of capital over labour, extinction of the bourgeoisie and the proletariat" (Guillaume, 2009a, p. 133). In addition, among the various internationalists present,[8] the Swiss Charles Perron (painter) and James Guillaume (professor), who spoke on behalf of Geneva workers and the IWA respectively, stand out. It was also during this congress that Bakunin received a copy of Marx's book *Capital: A Critique of Political Economy*, which had just been published, from the German internationalist Jean-Philippe Becker, founder of the International.

Even in the midst of the conflicts, the congress deliberated for the creation of the International League of Peace and Freedom, which was to organize annual congresses, as well as a permanent central committee, to which not only the moderates, but also Bakunin and other members of the Fraternity—Mroczkowski, Zagorski, Gambuzzi, and the Italian Alfredo Naquet—were elected. Finally, in spite of everything, the International Fraternity managed to have some impact on the deliberations, evident in the motion passed at the end of the meeting.

After the congress, Bakunin and Gambuzzi went to live around Vevey, close to Obolensky and Mroczkowski, who was now working as a photographer. They stayed there until mid-1868. Bakunin drew close to the revolutionaries who now frequented that circle of Vevey. Among them were: Jukovski, a journalist; his wealthy sister-in-law, Olga Levashov, who shared the group's ideas and to some extent guaranteed the financial support of its members; Nikolai Utin, a former member of Land and Freedom; Alexander Serno-Solovievich, brother of the martyr of Land and Freedom; Mikhail Elpidin, owner of a print shop in Geneva; Benoît Malon, a French internationalist worker, and his partner, André Léo (Léodile Bera), a novelist, socialist and women's rights activist (Guillaume, 1985, vol. I, pp. 45, 260; Carr, 1961, pp. 346–49).

From the 1860s to the 1870s, Switzerland was a country undergoing an accelerated process of population growth and industrialization, stimulated by the rapid changes brought about by the Swiss Peoples' Spring. Although the majority of the population was still living in the countryside, working in agriculture, cities grew rapidly and even though large industries were still in the minority—especially in the textile and, to some extent, chemical, pharmaceutical, agri-food and electrical engineering sectors—they expanded. At the same time, the cities had many artisan and qualified workers who, although still restricted to workshops (many of whom were family members), already lived with an established division of capitalist labour. Such was the case with the watch industry around the Neuchâtel mountains and the Saint-Imier Valley, regions where Bakunin was present.

Switzerland had low illiteracy rates and, compared with other countries, was a far more educated and learned country than the average. It was also affected by the liberalization of Protestantism. Politically, the new constitution of 1848 not only facilitated economic expansion—when it put an end to internal customs, created a single currency and instituted uniform labour rules—but also prepared a democratic institution strengthened by individual rights. It was a question of establishing a state that, if at that time was the object of a certain centralization, was also a multi-ethnic confederation in which the cantons had their own sovereignty guaranteed. In the late 1860s, proposals to increase popular participation in public administration were strengthened, particularly through referenda, and traditions concerning the reception of political exiles persisted. As a result, the presence of expatriate political agents, be they German, French, Italian, or other nationalities, was increasingly common (Hobsbawm, 2004a, 68–71, 395; Enckell, 1991, pp. 18–27).

Based in Vevey in late 1867, Bakunin visited Bern a few times for meetings of the International League of Peace and Freedom central committee. Since the first meeting in October, disputes between liberals and socialists had been harsh, often involving all excerpts from public documents and resolutions. To strengthen his proposal, Bakunin wrote a proposition, which was supported by his adherents and ended up constituting his first book: *Federalism, Socialism, and Anti-theologism*, which consolidates Bakunin's public return to philosophy and establishes a deepening of his ideas.[9] Picking up the philosophical elements of the "Masonic Fragments" of 1865 and of "Essenza della Religione" ["Essence of Religion"], published at the end of 1867 in the Neapolitan periodical *Libertà e Giustizia* [*Freedom and Justice*] (Bakunin, 2009a[e]), as well as the political elements of the 1864 and 1866 documents, Bakunin aims to provide the political-philosophical foundations for the transformation of the League—or at least part of it—into a materialist, socialist, federalist, and revolutionary political organization.

In this book, Bakunin realizes, through the critique of religion, the first formalization of the foundations of his *scientific-naturalist materialism*. Returning to Feuerbach and invoking Auguste Comte and Charles Darwin, always in a critical way, he affirms the need for a rupture with theology and the adoption of science as a paradigm of understanding reality. Society is considered part of nature, having to be understood through an approach that proceeds from facts to ideas; humanity is interpreted as the development of animality.

Rescuing *dialectics* theoretically, Bakunin postulates an approach to reality that takes as its basis the totality and its contradictions, in its dynamics of action and reaction, in which the individual is dependent on society. For the analysis of reality and political-doctrinaire lines, his great inspiration is Proudhon, but the recent influence of internationalists also plays a role, allowing for a radicalization of Proudhonism.[10] Bakunin considers *capitalism and the State* as *interdependent elements* and critiques labour exploitation and political domination. In this dynamic, he points out, social classes and class struggle play a preponderant role. He also analyzes the role that the *division between intellectual and manual labour* and education have in this capitalist-statist system, as well as the foundations for legitimizing this power. Liberalism in general, and Jean-Jacques Rousseau's theory in particular, are severely criticized. Taking up the notion of unity between theory and practice, Bakunin argues for the need for a political organization, not necessarily secret, endowed with unitary principles and programs, which focuses on society to advance certain objectives. More radicalized, he advocates, in this sense, *the abolition of private and state property*, as well as the *right of inheritance* and the *monopoly on education*. His *revolutionary socialism* is also based on democratic communal federalism and the freedom of peoples. And now, for the creation of a new morality, the need for the socialization of knowledge becomes more evident (Bakunin, 1988a[e]).

As Guillaume (2009a, pp. 165–66) demonstrates, Bakunin's work in the International League of Peace and Freedom bore fruit. At the committee meeting held in May–June 1868— at which it was decided that the next congress would take place in September in Bern—a declaration of principles was voted on, the most significant part of which reflects the positions of the members of the Fraternity. In a letter to Ogarev, Bakunin (68012[c], p. 7) commemorated this collective achievement.

At that moment, Bakunin was deeply and positively impacted by episdoes in the workers' movement. Two strikes in March 1868 with very different outcomes stand out in particular: a victory for the civil construction workers in Geneva, Switzerland,[11] and another defeated, of the miners of Charleroi, Belgium.[12] Both episodes are central to what Norte (1988, p. 78) characterized as "a process of radicalization" of the International, "which must be explained both by the escalation of social struggles and by the internal debates of the Association." Prominent moments of the "strikes in France, Switzerland, Belgium, which are growing from 1866 onwards," these two episodes also "end with massive adhesions to the International." These strikes, like others that followed them, considerably changed Bakunin's positions on the transformative capacity of workers and the centrality of their movements in general and the International in particular.

The International Workers' Association had held its first congress in Geneva in 1866[13] with a major discussion aimed at defining its statutes. In 1867, it held its second congress, in Lausanne,[14] discussing nine issues involving the international proletariat: the practical means to make the IWA a centre of action for the working class, credit and popular banks, the emancipation of the proletariat and its risks, labour versus capital, education and the women's question, and the State and political freedoms. Relevant in this congress were the affirmations of mutualism, federalism, the preaching of the ending of salaries, the recognition of the importance of education, the relationship between social emancipation and political emancipation, and the affirmation of capitalism as a class society divided into exploiters and exploited. With the aforementioned flux of radicalized social struggles, the International became an impressive political force in different countries (Samis, 2015b, pp. 164–72).

Recognizing the relevance of this process, Bakunin joined Elpidin in July 1868 in the Geneva section of the IWA; Perron joined shortly thereafter. In the August meeting of the League committee, he argued for and succeeded in getting the following excerpt included in the circular that would be sent to congress participants:

> To become an active and beneficial force, the *League* must become the pure *political expression* of the great *socio-economic interests and principles* that are now being so triumphantly developed and disseminated by the great *International Workers' Association* of Europe and America. (*Apud* Carr, 1961, p. 352, emphasis added)

In this quotation the foundations of the *organizational dualism* that would define Bakunin's political strategy in the next period are exposed for the first time. Differently from the interpretation offered by Carr (1961, p. 353) and other authors, this was not a doubling of organizations, but a very marked distinction between a political organization (comprising materialist, socialist, federalist, and revolutionary members) and an economic-social organization (involving workers of all kinds, regardless of their political or religious positions). Bakunin's intention seems clear: to shape this political organization to maximize the force of its principles, program, and strategy in the International.[15]

In order to get closer, the League committee sent a greeting to the IWA congress that would take place a few weeks later in Brussels. In the text, it invited the Internationalists to participate in its second congress, which would take place in Bern a few days after the International congress. In the first half of September 1868, the International held its third congress, which also accompanied the growth and radicalization of the workers' movement, in Brussels.[16] If since its inception the IWA had its main expression in mutualist federalism (or mutualism), this congress marked its transition to collectivist federalism (or collectivism), which would become hegemonic the following year. Among other decisions—concerning strikes and resistance societies, comprehensive education, reduced working hours, and other issues—the congress voted on the issue of property, positioning itself mainly from the perspective of collectivization: mines, quarries, railroads, arable land, canals, roads, communication lines, forests, tools, and machines should pass into the hands of workers. About the International League of Peace and Freedom, the Internationalists mostly understood that it had no *raison d'être* and recommended that the members of the League join the International (Samis, 2015b, pp. 172–77; Guillaume, 2009a, p. 157).

After a certain indisposition between Gustave Vogt, president of the League, and Bakunin (68019[c]) due to these developments, the second congress of the International League of Peace and Freedom was held—at the end of September 1868 in Bern. With much smaller participation, a little more than 100 delegates met and the polarization between liberals and socialists became more marked. Bakunin spoke at length five times. His speeches, more radicalized than the text of *Federalism, Socialism and Anti-theologism*—and whose foundations are found in the article "Наша Программа" ["Our Program"], published at the beginning of September in the first issue of the newspaper *Народное Дело/Narodnoe Delo* [*The People's Cause*][17]—advocate a socialism in which economic and social equality finds centrality, as well as the equalization/suppression of social classes. To this end, the workers are called upon to emancipate themselves. For the first time, Bakunin assumes himself to be a collectivist—a supporter of the socialization of property and the abolition of the State—opposing communism. At various times, he uses and defends Marxist ideas and even terminology (Bakunin, 68009[e], 68011[e]).

As Guillaume (2009a, pp. 172-173) relates, the second league congress ended, during its last session, in a split. The influence that Bakunin and his supporters achieved on the League committee did not extend to the congress as a whole, which for the most part remained faithful to democratic and bourgeois republicanism. The minority preferred to split rather than continue with the majority of delegates, who, as they pointed out, had spoken out "passionately and explicitly against the *economic and social equalization of classes and individuals.*" In this way, the majority broke, according to the minority's criticism, with the assumptions of revolutionary and democratic socialism, and even with those of peace and freedom. Among the 18 signatories of the document of the split are Bakunin, other members of the Fraternity—Mroczkowski, Zagorski, Jukovski, Friscia, and Fanelli; the French Reclus, Aristide Rey, Charles Keller, and the Italian Alberto Tucci—and the French Albert Richard, who would later become a member of the Alliance.[18]

10.2.2 Public Alliance, Secret Alliance, and the International Workers' Association

These militants—some of whom, like Bakunin, were already members of the International Workers' Association—ended up understanding that it was necessary to found a new political organization and did so immediately, naming it the

International Alliance of Socialist Democracy and pointing to the IWA as their favoured space for action.

> The International Workers' Association naturally presented itself as this better instrument. Bakunin became a member of the International in July of that year. He proposed to the socialist-revolutionary minority emanating from the League to enter the International en masse, while maintaining their intimate bond, that is, preserving their Alliance of socialist revolutionaries in the form of a secret society and expanding it. The proposal to join the International was unanimously adopted. However, as far as the Alliance was concerned, the French and the Italians wanted it to appear openly as a public organization under the name of the International Alliance of Socialist Democracy, while preserving its esoteric and intimate character as a secret society. They even wanted the Alliance to be organized completely independently of the International Association, content with its members being individual members of that Association. Bakunin opposed this because this new international organization would find itself in a rivalry with the workers' organization in no way desirable. These discussions resulted in the decision to found a public association under the name of the International Alliance of Socialist Democracy, and to declare it an integral part of the International, whose program was recognized as obligatory by every member of the Alliance. (Guillaume, 2009a, p. 178)

Although stimulating the redirection of the forces of the International Fraternity and its new associates to the IWA, Bakunin continued to defend organizational dualism, in which the public activity of the masses would be completed by the secret activity of cadres. However, his position was defeated by the French and Italians, and the militants ended up creating a public Alliance and a secret one, the trajectory of the former being a little more widespread and known than the latter, almost completely ignored.[19]

After the League of Peace and Freedom congress, Bakunin moved again. He left Vevey motivated by the rupture with Olga Levashov and arrived in Geneva in October 1868 with the expectation of being able to act in a place where the International was stronger—there he would stay for the next two years. Antonia and Zagorski accompanied him (Carr, 1961, pp. 360–61). It was probably in Geneva that Bakunin wrote the Alliance's documents during the autumn of 1868, describing the program and regulations of the public and secret organizations, and deepening his concept of organizational dualism.[20]

In programmatic terms, these documents formalize the elements of federalist and materialist socialism previously developed in *Federalism, Socialism and Antitheologism* but with the radicalism, stimulated by the historical context, which is found in "Our Program." There are two major differences from the previous texts. First, in terms of revolutionary transformation, the working masses are definitely pointed out as the subject of the process. For this reason, the Alliance is conceived not as a hierarchically superior political body but as a complementary organization that must stimulate workers in a strategic sense. Second, in terms of the perspective of future society, democratic communal federalism (more political, with a territorial focus) is replaced by democratic agricultural-industrial federalism (more economic, with a focus on the workplace). In organizational terms, the documents stipulate the criteria for the internal functioning of the public and secret organizations. They provide for an organization in which there is, among its members, political unity, expressed in a set of principles and programs, and individual-collective responsibility, between the militants and the organization. Based on the notion of concentric circles, they advocate different instances and levels of militancy, with corresponding rights and duties, without permanent hierarchies or privileges[21] (Bakunin, 68014[e], 68016[e], 2009d[e], 68022[e]).

With regard to the Alliance's dual objective, related to the level of masses and cadres, Bakunin pointed out:

> a.) It [the Alliance] will strive to propagate among the popular masses of all countries the true ideas about politics, about political economy and social economy and about all philosophical issues. It will actively advertise through newspapers, brochures and books, as well as through the founding of public associations. b.) It will seek to affiliate all intelligent, energetic, discreet and willing men sincerely devoted to our ideals—in order to form throughout Europe and in all possible localities, including America, an invisible network of revolutionaries devoted and empowered by this very alliance. (Bakunin, 68016[e])

Founded in Geneva, the public Alliance was formed between September and October 1868, incorporating members of the IWA, founding a central bureau, and sending a "Message to the Spanish Workers" trying to persuade them to contribute to the work of the International. It carried out a public activity at the end of October, aiming to broaden its membership and, at that time, reached 85 members. Besides Switzerland (Geneva), sections were established in other countries, under the leadership of some members: France (Lyon, with Richard; Marseille, with André Bastelica; Paris), Italy (Naples, with Gambuzzi) and Spain (Barcelona and Madrid, with Fanelli)[22] (Guillaume, 2009a, pp. 203–06, 227; Carr, 1961, p. 363).

According to Eckhardt (2016, pp. 2–4), at the end of November 1868, the Alliance submitted a request for admission to the General Council of the International through a confusing letter from Becker, in which, among other things, it affirmed the need for a vanguard for the workers' movement. Obviously, the letter aroused Marx's suspicion, who wrote to Engels on 15 December: "Mr. Bakunin, who is behind this, is condescending enough to want to place the workers' movement under Russian leadership" (Marx and Engels, 2010d, p. 190). Bakunin—motivated by a sounding from Marx to Alexander Serno-Solovievich, and possibly taking advantage of it to reinforce Becker's letter—wrote a friendly letter to Marx on 22 December, in which he recognizes his disciple and says to do at the moment what he had started more than 20 years ago (Bakunin, 68034[c]). However, that same day the General Council decided to refuse the request for admission, claiming that, as Bakunin had predicted, such an organization would contribute more to the disorganization than to the strengthening of the International (Marx and Engels, 2010a, pp. 34–36).

On the other hand, according to Bakunin's expectations, at that time the IWA was growing fast in Switzerland—Geneva was a centre of the movement and Bakunin was becoming increasingly popular among Internationalists. In that city, in the early days of 1869, 30 sections of French Switzerland met to found the Romanesque Federation, which would function as such until April 1870; the foundation was consolidating the preparations made since the previous October. Once founded, the federation decided on its statutes and the creation of a new newspaper, *L'Égalité* [*Equality*].

In this process, Bakunin and the Alliancists stood out: the statutes adopted were a simplified version of those proposed by Bakunin at the end of 1868 (Bakunin, 68018[e]); Brosset was elected president of the federal committee of the Romanesque Federation; Bakunin, Perron, and Becker took charge, along with seven other members, of the editorial board of *L'Égalité*. In addition, at this meeting Bakunin approached two Internationalists: Adhémar Schwitzguébel (recorder and delegate for Saint-Imier and Sonvillier) and Guillaume (professor, delegated by Locle and editor of *Le Progrès* [*Progress*]), to whom he spoke about the Alliance (Guillaume, 1985, vol. I, pp. 105–08).

Still in January 1869, the International Fraternity also held a congress in Geneva. Even if the only document that exists on this subject is a letter from Bakunin (69001[c]) to his supporters, it can be understood that: this organization existed until that time and had internal organization and discipline; it discussed issues related to the Alliance, including the composition of its board; Bakunin was possibly suppressed for his conduct, understood as authoritarian by the majority of the members, who decided to create another organization; Bakunin, deeply dissatisfied, withdrew from the process and said he did not know whether or not he would join the new initiative. Shortly afterwards, the Fraternity was declared dissolved.[23]

The document of dissolution of the Fraternity, written by Bakunin (Guillaume, 1985, vol. I, pp. 131–32) after the return of Fanelli from Spain, marked the differences with the Brothers Reclus, Malon, Mroczkowski, and Jukovski. As Nettlau (1977a, p. 21) explains, Fanelli had been sent to Spain at the end of 1868, together with Élie Reclus and Rey, to strengthen the Alliance's proposal in the region. This trip, although full of problems, produced very concrete direct and indirect results.

The nucleus and then the sections of the International were founded in: Madrid—the nucleus, which included the printer Anselmo Lorenzo and the engraver Tomás Gonzáles Morago, was constituted between November 1868 and January 1869; the Madrid section of the IWA was founded in December 1869; in Barcelona—the nucleus, which included the printer Rafael Farga-Pellicer, the doctor Gaspard Sentiñon, and the student José G. Viñas, was constituted between January and February 1869; the Barcelona section of the IWA was founded in May 1869; in Lisbon—in mid-1871. At that time, the Spanish International already had 40,000 members (Casas, 2006, pp. 44, 48; Nettlau, 1977a, pp. 57, 76–78). Concomitant to the constitution of the International, public and secret instances of the Alliance were created in Madrid, Barcelona, and Lisbon—of which Morago, Farga-Pellicer, Sentiñon, Viñas, and others, like Professor Charles Alerini, were part. Some of these, including Farga-Pellicer and Morago, joined the Geneva Alliance (Nettlau, 1977a, pp. 41–50, 60–61, 75).

According to Guillaume (1985, vol. I, pp. 140–41, 181), in the face of the General Council's refusal at the end of 1868 to admit the public Alliance, its members decided to declare the organization dissolved and transform its sections in Switzerland, Italy, France, and Spain into sections of the International. This position was communicated to the Council by Perron. Between March and July 1869, the issue between the Alliance and the Council was finally resolved, with the Section of the Alliance in Geneva, which had around 100 members, being admitted to the IWA.[24] At the same time, everything indicates that, despite this, the secret Alliance continued to exist.[25]

Despite negotiations with the General Council, the situation had not been resolved. Marx (2010d, pp. 332–33), dissatisfied, wrote to Engels on 27 July, 1869: "This Russian [Bakunin] obviously wishes to become the dictator of the European workers' movement. He should be careful, otherwise he will be officially excommunicated." Bakunin, unaware of this position, published during 1869 a series of ten articles in Guillaume's Le Progrès—a newspaper that until March belonged to the Locle workers' movement and after that became the journal of the Alliance Section—in which he exposed his ideas to the internationalists of the Locle and La Chaux-de-Fonds (Bakunin, 2009b[e]). He also published, in parallel, more than a dozen articles in L'Égalité, which were divided among various issues. Fully expounding his mature political theory, they go through different themes: criticism of the deviations from socialism; IWA, the workers' movement, strikes, resistance funds, and cooperation among workers; education and integral instruction; the European and Russian situation; persecutions and political trials.[26]

Also in 1869, still according to Guillaume (1985, vol. I, pp. 179–90, 195–213), Bakunin and the members of the Alliance intervened decisively in a conflict between two sectors, which occurred in the Geneva International: on one side "Construction" and on the other "Factory." The first, on the left and revolutionaries, were builders, carpenters, and workers, in most cases poorly educated immigrants (and therefore without citizenship or political rights) who came from France and Italy. The second, on the right and reformers, were watchmakers and jewelers, mostly trained Genevans (and therefore with citizenship and political rights). Bakunin made a decisive contribution to establishing the predominance of the revolutionary sector that, before his arrival, was subject to that of the reformists. This conflict provided the backdrop for the preparation of the IWA's Genevan sections for the fourth congress, which was to take place in 1869 in Basel. With regard to two important issues to be discussed at the congress, private property and the right of inheritance, the revolutionaries prevailed over the reformers, as well as in determining the number of delegates. In August 1869, Bakunin, president of the Alliance Section, warned that after the congress he would have to leave Geneva. He recommended the secretary Fritz Heng (recorder, from La Chaux-de-Fonds) to his post and Paul Robin (French professor, expelled from Belgium and newly settled in Geneva) to substitute him.

The Basel Congress took place in early September 1869,[27] consolidating the hegemony of collectivist federalism (collectivism), a camp to which Bakunin—a delegate of the silk textile workers of Lyon and the mechanics of Naples, representations obtained by Richard and Gambuzzi—and the Alliancists belonged. On the one hand, the collectivists voted similarly to the communists, supporters of Marx and with representation on the General Council, on some issues: both defeated the mutualists in the discussion on property, resumed from the previous congress, guaranteeing a position favourable to collectivization; both also contributed directly to the passing of two other resolutions: one, in favour of the need to strengthen the societies of resistance (unions), and the other, administrative, of increasing the power of the Council, whereby this body could approve and refuse memberships, suspend sections, and arbitrate conflicts. Bakunin believed that this measure would favour disputes with reformists, including those in Geneva.

On the other hand, collectivists and communists opposed each other in the discussion on the right of inheritance. On one pole, the commission in charge of the matter, in which Bakunin's position (69038[e]) prevailed; on the other, the General Council, whose position was that elaborated by Marx and defended by Johann Eccarius. The latter argued, through Eccarius, that since the question of collective property had been voted on and approved, there was no point in discussing the right of inheritance, a consequence of it. The former, through Bakunin's speeches (2016c[e]), contended that what was a consequence could, at a given moment, become a cause— it was, after all, a position similar to that which Bakunin held in relation to the State. Bakunin's proposal ended in victory and marked the first loss of the Council in the IWA's congressional bodies. Finally, the German Social Democrat Wilhelm Liebknecht, who had been close to Marx and the communists for years, had to apologize formally to Bakunin. The popular tribunal requested by the Russian at the congress ruled in his favour with regard to the accusations made by the German— one, old: Bakunin was an agent of the Russian government; another, new: Bakunin would have been interested in destroying the International. It was decided that the next congress of the International would take place the following year in Paris (see also: Samis, 2015b, pp. 177–83).

In summary, taking into account the deliberations and discussions of the congress, one can say that all the positions of the collectivists were victorious and that Bakunin rose to the position of one of their main leaders. In addition, the outcome of the controversy with Liebknecht strengthened his legitimacy and put his opponent and his circle in an embarrassing position.[28] In addition, the circumstance of the event provided conditions for Bakunin to deepen relations with other internationalists. Some of these belonged to the Alliance—like the tailor from Lyon, Louis Palix—and others would later belong to it—like the aforementioned Schwitzguébel, from Sonvillier, and the bookbinder from Paris, L. Eugène Varlin (Carr, 1961, p. 377; Guillaume, 1985, vol. I, p. 284).

10.2.3 Netchaiev, the Lyon Commune, and Paris Commune

At the end of October 1869, as planned, Bakunin left Geneva. He passed through Bern (where he saw the Vogts and the Reichels) and went to Lugano, but finally decided to settle in Locarno, where he stayed—albeit between seasons in Geneva, Milan, and Lyon—until mid-1874. Once settled, he dedicated himself to the translation into Russian of Marx's *Capital*, not without many difficulties.[29] During this period, even after Herzen's death in early 1870, Bakunin remained linked to Ogarev and drew close, in the first half of that year, to two young men: Emilio Bellerio, son of an Italian Republican refugee, and Mikhail P. Sajin, a Russian immigrant also known as Armand Ross, who would become a member of the secret Alliance (Guillaume, 1985, vol. I, pp. 282–83, vol. II, p. 61). In March 1870, Bakunin wrote "Наука и насущное революционное дело" ["Science and the Vital Question of the Revolution"] (Bakunin, 2009e[e]).

It was still early 1870 when he met the young Russian Serguei Netchaiev, who visited him in Locarno. According to Lehning (1977, pp. xiii–xvii), relations between the two had begun in March 1869 when they met in Geneva, and would continue until July 1870. It was certainly a brief period, but full of implications for Bakunin's political and personal life. Netchaiev came from a family of serfs and had been involved since 1868 with the revolutionary student movement that was growing in Saint Petersburg. With some of them, in early 1869 he had created a committee whose purpose was to prepare a revolution for February 1870. This initiative marked, to some extent, the political moment in Russia when populism was beginning to give way to nihilism. As Leier (2006, p. 203) explains, the fundamental feature of Russian nihilism was "the insistence that one should not believe in anything that cannot be shown to be true." It was therefore a movement that involved a "critical approach to practically everything" —politically, its growing contempt for the capacity of the masses brought them closer to Jacobinism.[30]

With the commencement of activities, the committee attracted the attention of repression and, in March 1869, two of its members ended up in prison. Immediately afterwards, Netchaiev left Russia for Switzerland, where he wanted to obtain training and propaganda material as well as financial resources. Before and during his trip, he invented and spread a story, without any support in reality, to Russians like Vera Zasulitch; he told them that he had been arrested and sent to the Peter and Paul Fortress, from which he managed to escape. Most probably, he sought with this story to build a martyr and hero image inside and outside his country (Barrué, 2015d, p. 270). When he arrived in Geneva, still in March 1869, Netchaiev sought out Bakunin. He presented himself as a delegate of the committee, told his story and shared his principles, showing enormous willingness and revolutionary spirit. He deeply impressed the old Russian, who wrote to Guillaume on 13 April: "I have here now one [...] of those young fanatics, who [...] have postulated as a principle [...] that they will not [rest] for a moment until the people lift themselves up. These young fanatics are admirable—fanatical godless believers and unsung heroes" (Bakunin, 69018[c], p. 2).

They united immediately. Bakunin issued a statement to Netchaiev stating that he was a fully empowered delegate of the Russian section of a non-existent General Revolutionary Alliance. The two then went on to work on producing written material and fundraising. Together with Ogarev, he wrote almost a dozen documents between April and July 1869. Among them are the controversial "Catechism of the Revolutionary" and "Принципов Революции" ["The Principles of the Revolution"], often attributed to Bakunin, but which, according to Leier's consistent argument (2006, pp. 208–10), were written by Netchaiev. Finally, in July, Bakunin obtained access to half the money from the Bakhmetiev fund—which in 1858 had been entrusted to Herzen and Ogarev by a landowner newly converted to communism in order to contribute to revolutionary propaganda in Russia—and handed it over to Netchaiev.

Between August and December 1869, Netchaiev remained in Russia, where he formed the People's Justice Society, a deeply hierarchical secret organization, of which he was part of the central committee. Under the amoral Jacobinism that guided his practices, he murdered, in November, a dissident of his group, Ivan Ivanov. Under suspicion, and with a police warrant of arrest, he fled to Switzerland, where he arrived in January 1870. When he visited Bakunin in Locarno, the Swiss authorities had already been called in, and Netchaiev was at risk of being deported for common crime. Both were worried about the precedent of a few months before, when the Swiss authorities, in cooperation with the Russian police, took Zoe Obolensky's children and sent them to his husband in Russia.[31]

Witnessing Bakunin's difficulty with the translation of *Capital*, Netchaiev convinced him to let him solve the matter with the editor, so that Bakunin could dedicate himself fully to revolutionary practice. In February, he wrote, without Bakunin's knowledge, a letter to Ljubavin, threatening him and saying that Bakunin would not finish the job and would not return the money advanced. With Bakunin's help, during the first months of 1870, Netchaiev met Natalie Herzen—the daughter of the late Alexandre, who had consideration among the revolutionaries and a large inheritance—whom he tried to exploit without greater success. Still, Bakunin's help and Natalie's influence were determinant for Netchaiev to inaugurate, in April 1869, the second season of *Kolokol*, publishing six weekly issues, and also for him to have access to the second half of the Bakhmetiev fund money.

However, the arrival of the Russian revolutionary German Lopatin in Geneva provided the opportunity for Bakunin to add to his perceptions the account of Netchaiev's true history in Russia. When questioned, Netchaiev continued to proceed in the same way and, after a fight with Bakunin, began to ignore him. The breakup, which in June 1870 seemed inevitable, came a few weeks later during Bakunin's visit to Geneva. Determined to flee, Netchaiev appropriated several of Bakunin's, Ogarev's, and Natalie Herzen's compromising documents and went to London. Concerned, Bakunin tried desperately to warn all his contacts and recognized, in a letter to Ogarev of 2 August, 1870: "We made a good fool of ourselves! [...] Herzen would laugh at us if he were here, and how right he would be! Well, there's nothing to do except swallow this bitter pill, which will make us more attentive from now on" (Bakunin, 70075[c], p. 1). For Bakunin, apparently it was the end of the Netchaiev case; but it would still have serious consequences. Netchaiev managed to escape from the police for some time and, arrested in mid-1872, was handed over to the Russian police and imprisoned in Peter and Paul Fortress, where he died ten years later (Avrich, 1987; Barrué, 2015d; Carr, 1961, pp. 396–409).

Immediately after the rupture with Netchaiev in mid-July 1870, the confrontation between Prussia and France, which had long been announcing itself, came to a head. It was the beginning of the Franco-Prussian War, which would last until the following year. Under the pretext of a dispute over the succession of Queen Elizabeth II of Spain, Napoleon III declared war on Prussia, imagining that this could increase support for him and his government from the French. On the other hand, Bismarck thought that this conflict would contribute to the unification of Germany, including the annexation of other territories. Even with the abstentions of Liebknecht and August Bebel, the German Reichstag supported the war. In almost a month and a half, the German military machine gained important positions in Metz and Sedan, France. Noting the incapacity of Napoleon III, the French masses overthrew their government at the beginning of September and thus ended the Second Empire and inaugurated a republican government of national defense. However, 15 days later, Paris was surrounded by the enemy. And even though the national government signed an armistice, the Parisian population decided to resist the German army and their own government (Leier, 2006, pp. 255–56).

Bakunin then began to write what would be called "Lettres à un Français" ["Letters to a Frenchman"] and "Lettres à un Français sur la Crise Actuelle" ["Letters to a Frenchman on the Current Crisis"].[32] These letters expose the application of

Bakunin's analytical frame of reference to the context of the Franco-Prussian War and the recommendation of a strategy that aims to *transform the war into a social revolution*—thereby reconciling the *national and social question*. For him, France could only be saved, and contribute to the salvation of other countries, through an insurrectionary movement of the people, who would have to confront the German troops and the French ruling classes concomitantly, through a popular army. This movement should be created by urban workers, should begin outside Paris (in cities like Lyon, Marseilles, and Rouen), should fight German soldiers from the rear, and should obligatorily involve peasants in the struggle, which are discussed in terms of their revolutionary limits and potential (Bakunin, 1977a[e]). Such arguments are also discussed, in this same context, in "La Situation Politique en France (Lettre a Palix)" ["The Political Situation in France (Letter to Palix)"] (Bakunin, 1977b[e]), which opens *The German-Knuto Empire and the Social Revolution.*

During the time of writing these letters, Bakunin corresponded with Richard from Lyon, France. At the beginning of September 1870, he decided to join him to try to intervene in the directions of the French mobilizations, arriving in Lyon on September 15. He had passed through Bern, Neuchâtel, and Geneva, where he met the veterans of the 1863 Polish Insurrection Vladimir Ozerov (Russian) and Walenty Lankiewicz (Polish), and went with them to France. With the fall of Napoleon III, a progressive movement in Lyon had formed a provisional government, settling in the Hôtel de Ville and proclaiming republic and municipal autonomy; it had also promoted municipal elections and tried to surrender itself to republican normality. But the Internationalists—who had been mobilizing intensely against the empire since March and who, despite being in the minority, composed and influenced the whole process—and other revolutionaries understood that it was necessary to take this struggle to its last consequences.

According to Guillaume (1985, vol. II, pp. 93–102), with the arrival of Bakunin, the revolutionaries gained force. Together with Alliancists Richard, Palix, and other Internationalists, he had decisive influence in shaping the new Committee for the Salvation of France, and in formulating its revolutionary strategy.[33] The Committee promoted the creation of similar bodies in other regions and recommended that, as federation of France's salvation, they promote a mass uprising which, from the interior, would travel to the capital to fight the siege of the Germans. On September 25, the central committee that headed this federation, of which Bakunin was a member, met and decided to invest in an insurrection that could advance its strategy and promote its program. Concrete measures of this program were formalized by Bakunin, approved by the central committee and, the next day, welcomed at a public meeting attended by a few thousand people. This program was then printed on red posters and fixed in various parts of the city.

This "red poster," as it became historically known, read as follows:

FRENCH REPUBLIC

REVOLUTIONARY FEDERATION OF COMMUNES

The disastrous situation in which the country finds itself; the impotence of official powers and the indifference of the privileged classes have brought the French Nation to the brink of the abyss.

If the people organized revolutionarily do not hurry to act, their future will be lost, the Revolution will be lost, everything will be lost. Inspired by the immensity of the danger, and considering that the desperate action of the People could not be delayed for a single moment, the delegates of the federal Committees of the Salvation of France, meeting in the Central Committee, propose to adopt immediately the following resolutions:

Article 1 - The administrative and governmental machinery of the State, having become impotent, is abolished.

The people of France enter into full self-possession.

Article 2 - All criminal and civil courts are suspended and replaced by the people's justice.

Article 3 - The payment of taxes and mortgages is suspended. Tax is replaced by the contributions of the federated communes, taken from the rich classes, in proportion to the needs of salvation of France.

Article 4 - The State, having been deposed, can no longer intervene in the payment of private debts.

Article 5 - All existing municipal organizations are dissolved and replaced in all federal communes by the Committees of the Salvation of France, which will exercise all powers under the immediate control of the People.

Article 6 - Each departmental administrative center committee will send two delegates to form the Revolutionary Convention of the Salvation of France.

Article 7 - This Convention will meet immediately at the Hôtel de Ville de Lyon, as this is the second city in France and the one that has the greatest conditions to vigorously ensure the country's defense.

This Convention, supported by all the People, will save France.

To arms!!! (Bakunin, 70026e)

Among the 26 signatories of this document were, besides Bakunin, the Alliancists and Internationalists Richard, Palix, Gaspard Blanc, and Bastelica (who had come from Marseille). However, the delay in the process, harshly criticized by Bakunin, allowed the enemy forces to organize themselves. On 28 September, a popular demonstration gathered in front of the Hôtel de Ville to protest the reduction in salaries, which had been determined by the new municipal government. Bakunin and the insurgents, among whom the worker Eugène Saignes, were among the demonstrators. Part of them occupied the hotel, and there was an immediate confrontation between the municipality and the national guard loyal to it, on the one hand, and the central committee and the insurgents, on the other. The latter demanded that the municipality adopt the demands (of the workers and the "red poster") or else renounce them.

During the conflict, aggravated by the presence of other members of the national guard from the bourgeois neighborhoods, the central committee installed itself in the hall of the municipality. But to Bakunin's despair, the committee—which, according to him, should act immediately to guarantee the continuity of the insurrectional experiment, among other measures, with the arrest of the enemy authorities—began to dedicate itself completely to issuing decrees. Gustave P. Cluseret, who had just been appointed general of the Lion's revolutionary army, began to mediate the conflict and, in a short time, encouraged the insurgents to leave the hotel. And, worse than that, Richard, his comrade, frightened by the situation, joined Cluseret, defending the departure of the demonstrators and the continuity of the session of the municipal government—he then "justified" himself by saying that he did not want to impose himself by violence... Bakunin, encouraging the resistance, was even arrested, but was released soon thereafter by a group of snipers. Finally, the National Guard managed to vacate the building, freeing it from the last resistance and guaranteeing the session of the municipality. The latter responded to the workers' demands, but not to the insurgents'. It was the end of that experience that became known as the Lyon Commune, a defeat that was harshly felt by the members of the International and the Lyon Alliance.

Two days later, Bakunin, who then attributed Lyon's defeat to Cluseret's betrayal and Richard's cowardice, was sent with other committee members to Marseilles to continue the revolutionary intent. There he stayed for two weeks, without, however, achieving greater results. In mid-October 1870, he had to leave France (for the last time) because of an arrest warrant issued against him by the local authorities. He thought about going back to Lyon or to Barcelona, but ended up fleeing through Italy, and—after passing through Genoa, Milan, Arona, and climbing Lake Major—at the end of the month, he was back in Locarno (cf., also: Angaut, 2010b; Moissonnier, 1972).

On Swiss soil, Bakunin continued the effort begun in September 1870 to formalize his reflections on the Franco-Prussian conflict. As on other occasions, the project grew considerably and became the book *The Knuto-Germanic Empire and the Social Revolution*, which was concluded in April 1871, amid the experience of the Paris Commune.[34] In this book, Bakunin dedicates himself, also through his framework of analytical reference, to a reflection on France and Germany at the same time historical, theoretical, and strategic. It takes up French history, focusing on the characteristics and movements of social classes in major episodes, including recent ones. It reclaims German history, with emphasis on the construction of its liberalism, its unification process, and its relations with Russia.

Starting from such reflections, Bakunin makes some predictions and theorizations. If on the one hand he considers France lost (in national and revolutionary terms)—and therefore does not foresee the outbreak of the Paris Commune—he correctly predicts the outcome of the war, with the victory of Prussia, and the position of the French ruling classes, who preferred submission to Prussia to a social revolution. He develops the concept of *imperialism*, taking as his basis the recent German paradigm. Still by means of his anti-theological critique, he continues the elaboration of a *theory of the State* which, enriched by a brief critique of capitalism based on Marx, contributes to reflections on the *interdependence between state and capitalism*. He enhances the concept of *social force*, based on the analysis of the forces at play in the war. According to him, the problem of the *domination of imperialism and statist-capitalism* only has a strategic possibility of being resolved in a *social revolution of workers and peasants*. In this discussion, besides taking up the problem of country-city relations and the peasantry in general, he finds a solution to the dilemma that involves the social question and national question, class struggle, and national liberation struggle.[35]

Bakunin criticizes not only monarchical and republican concepts, but also German communism which, as a political-doctrinaire paradigm, is insufficient for the battle it intends to wage. To the communists and other schools—non-socialist, reformist, and authoritarian—he counterposes the foundations of a *collectivist revolutionary socialism* that will later be called simply *anarchism*. Especially in the appendix "Philosophical Considerations about the Divine Ghost, the Real World and Man," he returns in a more systematic way to philosophy and, through theoretical-philosophical reflections, improves the contours of his analytical frame of reference. This framework is, by itself, called "scientific materialism" and later on will be discussed in depth and conceptualized as *scientific-naturalist materialism*. Based on Darwin, Comte, Feuerbach and, to some extent, Proudhon and Marx, this framework is a counterpoint to idealism and other forms of materialism—it acquires, in the aforementioned appendix, its most refined traits.[36]

In early 1871 Locarno, just before the conclusion of this book, Bakunin was deeply discouraged. This was due to the failure of Lyon and the Franco-Prussian War, which seemed to have put a hard end to local revolutionary possibilities. At the same time, this was also due to his enormous financial difficulties and the progressive deterioration of his health (Carr, 1961, pp. 425–26). However, he was deeply surprised when, in March, the Paris Commune burst forth in the French capital. According to Samis (2011, pp. 232–61), the Franco-Prussian War was continuing at that time, and the French, led by Louis A. Thiers's provisional government, were succumbing to the Germans, promoting an armistice. An independent movement of republican resistance to the Prussians had intensified since late February 1871 with the decisive participation of the National Guard, which remained armed and was composed mostly of workers from the poor districts of Paris. During early March, the Prussians occupied Paris and the seat of government was transferred to Versailles. In order to continue the French capitulation, Thiers tried to disarm the National Guard in an operation during the early hours of the morning. But to no avail, the attempt ended with the execution of two responsible generals and the expulsion of the Paris government's troops by the insurgents, who decreed the city's independence from Versailles.

It was 18 March, 1871 and the *communard* experience was beginning. The Central Committee of the National Guard, which was responsible for the government, hastened to promote elections for the Paris Commune. Despite its limits and defeat after 72 days, this experience brought the workers to the centre of a revolutionary political process in which many measures were taken on their own behalf.[37] Even with a more impressive numerical presence of Jacobins and Blanquists, the Commune ended up being decisively influenced by the Internationalists, who articulated themselves in the more than 30 sections of the IWA that existed then in the country. In line with the Internationalist positions and those of most French workers, this new communal power acquired markedly federalist traits. In addition to Varlin, the principal internationalist leader, and Lankiewicz—both of whom were murdered in the struggle—other militants from Bakunin's camp of relations—among them Rey, Malon, and the Reclus brothers—were part of this experience.

Even without having foreseen it, Bakunin endorsed the Paris Commune from the beginning. He wrote about it: "I am a supporter of the Paris Commune [...] above all because it was a bold, well-spoken negation of the State" (Bakunin, 2008e[e], p. 118). Still on 5 April, 1871, in a letter to Ogarev and Ozerov, he recognized that "all the merit of this revolution is precisely that it is a workers' revolution." Workers rose up in arms against the political and economic authorities, forming with the Commune an alternative to the State. For Bakunin, this was the formula of the *communard* experience that, to a great extent, materialized his expectations of social transformation. However, he predicted from that moment on, based on an analysis of the forces at play, that the defeat of the insurgents was imminent: "In all probability, the Parisians will succumb." But still, "they will not succumb in vain before they have accomplished their task, before they have raised the question" (Bakunin, 71003[c], p. 1). He argued that the impact and balance of this experience for European workers would be enormous and very positive—he recognized that, at that moment, "our task [...] is to do the preparatory work, to organize ourselves and understand ourselves in order to be ready when the devil awakens." And that, for this reason, "we should not sacrifice our scarce resources and our few men ahead of time" (Bakunin, 71004[c], p. 2).

And, indeed, a little more than a month after that, the Commune succumbed. At the end of April, Bakunin even went to the Jura to get closer to the border with France—he thought of joining the process, depending on how things went—but ended up returning to Locarno without having had any direct participation in the insurrection (Guillaume, 1907a, p. xlviii). In Sonvillier, he presented to the Swiss workers the "Three Conferences Made to the Workers of the Saint-Imier Valley" (Bakunin, 2008d[e]). As he had predicted, the French ruling classes preferred to submit to the Prussians rather than risk a social revolution. The repression of the *communards*—intensified during the so-called "Bloody Week" (21–28 May, 1871)—was enormous. It is estimated that the Paris Commune ended with more than 10,000 insurgents dead, more than 40,000 prisoners, and thousands of deportations to New Caledonia (Musto, 2014, p. 52). In June, the International expressed itself publicly through a Manifesto of the General Council.[38]

10.2.4 The International: Sections, Representation, and General Council

After the Basel Congress (September 1869), the International remained mobilized and on the rise, and the positions and conflicts enunciated on that occasion deepened. Between the end of 1869 and the middle of 1871, the IWA sections had different dynamics, depending on the country. In general, as Marcelo Musto (2014, pp. 43–44) puts it, "in 1869 the International obtained significant expansion throughout Europe." As in that congress, in most sections the concepts of collectivist federalism (collectivism) prevailed when compared to others (communists, social democrats, mutualists, etc.). At that time, there was already, as part of this collectivist current, a sector properly anarchist, whose members were Alliancists and whose most important leadership was Bakunin.

Among the countries that had played a considerable role in the IWA since its foundation—through its sections, trade unions, associations, and societies—are England, France, Germany, Switzerland, Belgium, Spain, and Italy.[39] According to the evaluations of Musto (2014, pp. 43–49), Berthier (2015c), and other authors, some notes can be made.

The English trade unions, protagonists in the early days of the IWA, had a significant number of members and, in the 1866 to 1869 congresses, had reduced representation.[40] As the years went by, they became less and less interested in the association, especially after the implementation of the electoral reform (Reform Act) of 1867. Since then, the engagement of British union leaders and rank-and-file members in the International declined progressively and, even when there were deliberations to strengthen this participation, they had often been disregarded. The moderate and pragmatic profile of unions and union leaders, who were almost exclusively interested in the immediate political and economic gains of workers, contributed to this (Musto, 2014, pp. 43–44; Berthier, 2015c, p. 10).

The French sections, also protagonists since the early years of the IWA, had a significant number of affiliates and, in the 1866 to 1869 congresses, had medium representation.[41] They came out of a crisis in 1868, due to imperial repression, to enter a phase of reconstruction in 1869. That was a moment of reconfiguration of the currents present in the association. On the one hand, the mutualists like Henri-Louis Tolain lost ground; on the other, the collectivists like Varlin, and especially the Blanquists, gained ground. As noted, the French Internationalists played an important role in the Lyon Commune in September 1870 and stood out in the Paris Commune between March and May 1871 when, even in the minority, they succeeded in influencing the course of events in a proportionally very significant way. But the brutal repression of the Commune, while in other countries it contributed to the growth of the IWA, complicated the activities of the Sections in France (Musto, 2014, pp. 44–45, 51–54).

The German sections never had substantial affiliations, but in spite of that, in the 1866 to 1869 congresses, they were well over-represented. Although there was significant work on the part of Becker in forming German militant sections both within and outside Germany, it is undeniable that as the workers' interest in social democracy initiatives grew, markedly after the founding of the Social Democratic Workers' Party (SDAP) in 1869, their willingness to cooperate with the International decreased. Unlike Musto (2014, p. 88), one should not include among affiliates to the International all the members of the SDAP. This is because, as Berthier (2015c, pp. 10, 85–90) demonstrates, based on correspondence from Engels, the SDAP's affiliation with the IWA was never more than a formality, without considerable involvement.[42] The Germans were increasingly interested in electoral disputes and gradually less in internationalism (Musto, 2014, pp. 47–48; Berthier, 2015c, pp. 77, 86–88).

The Swiss sections were very important in the history of the International. They were numerically significant, but did not have many affiliates, and at the 1866 to 1869 congresses they were also over-represented.[43] Concentrated in Geneva and the Jura region, these sections, after the foundation of the public Alliance, had the participation of Bakunin and were involved in a dispute over adopting the General Council line. In April 1870, at a congress of the Romanesque Federation, there was a split in which a federalist majority, which found in Guillaume its most impressive leadership, separated from a centralist minority under Utin's leadership. Strangely, in mediating the conflict, the Council granted the minority the name of the federation, forcing the majority to adopt a new name (Berthier, 2015c, pp. 68–71; Musto, 2014, p. 46). This was the motivation for Bakunin to write, in July 1871, "Protestation de L'Alliance" ["Protestation of the Alliance"] (Bakunin, 71011a[e], 71011b[e]), and for forming, in November of that year, the Jurassian Federation, later admitted to the International.

The Belgian sections were also very important in the history of the International, but only from 1868 onwards. They had a substantial number of affiliates and, in the congresses from 1866 to 1869, medium representation.[44] They grew from 1868, when, due to a great popular participation in strikes and victorious conflicts, they received massive affiliation. Their main figure César de Paepe, in addition to the impressive influence he had on Bakunin and on the IWA's own paths, was important until 1872 as mediator of the conflicts between centralists and federalists; after that, he aligned himself in a heterodox way with the latter (Musto, 2014, p. 45).

The Spanish sections had a significant number of affiliates—Berthier (2015c, p. 29) maintains that the Spanish Internationalists were by far the most numerous of the IWA—but at the same time, at the 1866 to 1869 congresses, they were the least represented.[45] As reported, the formation of the International in Spain is due to the work of the Alliance in general and Fanelli in particular. The Federación Regional Española (FRE), founded in mid-1870 and hegemonically collectivist under the influence of leaders such as Lorenzo and Farga-Pellicer, directly contributed to the Spanish IWA reaching its peak a few years later (Nettlau, 1977a, pp. 57–61; Musto, 2014, pp. 46–47).

The Italian sections, as well as the Belgian ones, formed late. They were the work of the Alliance in general, and of Gambuzzi and Friscia in particular. The sections began to grow more significantly in 1870, and reached their apex only a few years later, reaching a substantial number of affiliates. In the congresses from 1866 to 1869, taking into account their process, they had medium representation.[46] Also adhering to collectivist federalism in the majority, Errico Malatesta and Carlo Cafiero were two of their greatest leaders (Pernicone, 2009, pp. 31, 41, 44).

With regard to the aforementioned question of representation at the International's congresses from 1866 to 1869, it is possible to take into account the available statistics regarding the delegates present from each country and compare them, in relative terms, with the quantities of workers represented in each of these countries, even knowing the discrepancies between the latter figures (Musto, 2014, p. 86; Silva, 2017, p. 76). From this estimated comparison,[47] the following can be said: in terms of representation at the congresses, there are two over-represented countries (Germany and Switzerland), three intermediate countries (France, Belgium, and Italy), and two under-represented countries (England and Spain).

In view of the problem of the "platonic" relationship of German workers with the International, to use Engels' term, and considering that it was not right to include all SDAP members as IWA affiliates, Germany was certainly the country with the largest representation at the congresses. For various reasons, Switzerland was also over-represented—not only were three of the four congresses held in Switzerland, which made it easier to send delegations, but the bases of the sections were not as impressive in numerical terms. France had several delegates at all congresses. Belgium, later, had a much more active participation in the congress that was held in Brussels. Italy, even later, had few delegates to the congresses. In any case, all three countries were represented in relative terms. Among the underrepresented countries are England and Spain. The first had few delegates to the congresses and had bases that, although scarcely engaged with the IWA, were numerically significant. The second, completely underrepresented, had very few delegates to the congresses and had bases that, very engaged with the IWA, were numerically very impressive.

However, it was undoubtedly the members of the General Council—which, with an average of six delegates in each of these congresses and representing no section of workers—who, proportionally, had the most influence in the congresses of the International (Silva, 2017, pp. 109, 115, 129, 145). In fact, the question about the Council is a complex one, but at the same time indispensable for an adequate understanding of the trajectory of the International. Generally speaking, from the beginning there were different understandings about the role of this body in the IWA, and over the years as the association consolidated itself, a conflict, until then latent, became more and more evident and ended up being the great culprit of the "split" of 1872, which found its mark in The Hague Congress.

The body that would be called the General Council some time later was created in 1864, during the foundation of the International. In 1866, at the Geneva Congress, when the final statutes were voted on, the question of the Council was contemplated and, since that occasion, it was possible to perceive the different views of the subject. These differences expressed the positions of the two forces that were in dispute in the IWA until 1872. On the one hand, federalists; on the other, centralists. This is evident, for example, when one compares the original text of the statutes, in English (which expresses the centralist position of the General Council), with the translation made into French (which expresses the federalist position of the French sections). The very term "General Council," which would then be established as definitive, appears in the English document as "Central Council" and in the French translation as "General Council." Furthermore, in a passage that specifies the tasks of the Council, the English document speaks of coordination "under a common direction," while the French translation mentions "dans un même esprit" [in the same spirit] (Guillaume, 2009a, pp. 43, 62–73).[48] Thus, there are versions of the statutes that express the organizational concepts of each sector, and each one conceives this body and its functions distinctly. For the federalists, it was an executive body, with representation by the sections (Bakunin, 71023[e], p. 48); for the centralists, it was a governing body, with power over the sections.

Even though Marx (who had access to the French translations) and others perceived this question, they chose to keep the conflict latent. Regardless of this, as Guillaume (2009b) reports, until the Basel Congress in 1869, the General Council played a key role in the development of the IWA. It articulated sections from different countries, proposed relevant issues and debates, formalized section positions, and ensured unity around the principles validated at the Geneva Congress in 1866, especially on the occasion of disputes with sectors of dissenting positions. Recognizing this contribution and without much complaint, the sections approved, in 1867 and 1869, measures to expand the rights of the General Council: in 1867, it was given the power to incorporate new members; in 1869, it was given the temporary power to accept, refuse, and suspend sections, and also to arbitrate conflicts—temporary, since such measures should always be validated at the next congress of the association.

However, due to the complicated economic dynamics and the development of the International itself, the functions established in 1866 for the General Council were not fulfilled. For example, on that occasion it was approved that "each section is sovereign to appoint its correspondents in the Council" (Guillaume, 2009a, p. 73). But in practice, in general it was the Council members themselves who chose the correspondents, even against the position of the sections. Moreover, the fact that this body had always remained in London ended up almost exclusively favouring the participation of members who lived there. Sometimes supported by congressional decisions, and without support from others, the Council became increasingly influential in the routine of the sections. Now, when one observes the International's trajectory, it seems an unquestionable fact that, over the years, the General Council experienced a process of centralization and bureaucratization, accompanied by a growing detachment from the bases—a process that found in Marx and Engels its greatest architects.[49]

With the results of the Basel Congress of 1869—when the collectivists won the disputes with all the other forces, including, for the first time, the General Council itself (in the inheritance debate)—in addition to subsequent episodes, particularly related to conflicts in Switzerland, the Council took another direction. To this end, it took advantage of the increased power it had been granted in the congress, with the vote of the collectivists themselves, as well as a change in tactics, turning what was a latent conflict into an open conflict.

10.2.5 Conflicts with Utin, Mazzini, Marx, and the General Council

Beginning in 1870, Bakunin became involved in various conflicts in the IWA. He was a central figure in the plot that encompassed the Association's disputes in Switzerland and Italy, as well as that between the sections and the General Council.[50]

As Eckhardt (2016, pp. 35–36) explains, shortly after he moved from Geneva to Locarno in late October 1869, Robin, who had become the editor of *L'Égalité*, published some attacks on the General Council, with support from other Internationalists, between November and December, arguing among other things that it was not fulfilling its obligations. These attacks were related to the polarization that marked the IWA in Geneva at that time, which no longer included Bakunin. In January 1870, the opposing camp, closer to the General Council, was growing stronger. Utin took over *L'Égalité* and founded the first Russian section of the Association, promising to fight Bakunin's supposed tsarist pan-Slavism. Later that month, Marx sent a "Private Communication" on behalf of the General Council—having discussed the matter only in a subcommittee—to the federal councils of French Switzerland, in which he dedicated himself to answering the *L'Égalité* accusations brought by Robin.

Bakunin (71018[e]), who was no longer in Geneva, considered this attack by *L'Égalité* on the General Council "an unfair protest" and something "politically imprudent and absurd." But Marx held him responsible for the attacks, as can be seen in the letter he sent to Engels on 17 December, 1869, in which he states: "In this *L'Égalité* [...] you will see how brazen the *signõr* Bakunin is becoming." Fearful of Bakunin's influence in this and other newspapers linked to the International (not only in Switzerland, but also in Spain and Italy), Marx understands the attacks as "an open fight [Bakunin's] with us" and threatens, "he will be surprised" (Marx and Engels, 2010d, p. 404). Trying to bridge with De Paepe and articulating with Engels, Marx prepared a direct attack against Bakunin between the end of January and February. It would come in the form of a "Confidential Communication"—again on behalf of the General Council, and without having been discussed with its members (Eckhardt, 2016, pp. 41, 459)—sent at the end of March 1870 to the German Social Democrats.

In this communiqué Marx (2010a, pp. 112–124) maintains, amid a series of accusations, that the Russian sought "the transformation of the International into his personal instrument" and that if nothing was done, "the International would submit to Bakunin's dictatorship" (p. 115).[51] There is no way to discuss all the points of this document here, but it is possible to state without a doubt that most have no basis in reality. As far as Mehring (2014, p. 462)—a Marxist, Marx's principal biographer, and very unfriendly to the Russian—is concerned, he recognizes that, "Generally speaking, the more incriminating the accusations he makes of Bakunin, the less ground they have in reality"; in short, it is a document full of "errors in relation to Bakunin."[52]

The Swiss conflict culminated in the Congress of the Romanesque Federation in La Chaux-de-Fonds in April 1870. On that occasion, when Bakunin was not present, the Section of the Alliance had sent its delegates to the congress, waiting for a deliberation regarding its entry into the federation, which had been requested back in September 1869 and deliberately remained unanswered thanks to the conflict. And in congress, when the issue was finally voted on, 21 delegates (the majority) were in favour of the Alliance Section joining the federation and 18 (the minority) against. The majority was led by the Alliancists (Schwitzguébel, Guillaume, and others who belonged to other sections) and was mostly located in the Jura region. The minority was headed by Utin and was mostly located in Geneva. The minority did not accept defeat and preferred to split. Both the majority and the minority continued their congresses, concomitantly claiming to be the Romanesque Federation—a process that would still take a few months to resolve. As a result of the split in August 1870, Bakunin, Perron, Jukovski, and Henry Sutherland (son of Ogarev's second wife) were expelled from the Central Section of Geneva on the grounds that they were aligned with the opposition majority. Later that month, under Jukovski's leadership—and contrary to the positions of Bakunin, Guillaume, and other allies – the Alliance Section declared itself dissolved. Its members, together with ex-*communards*, founded the Section for Socialist Propaganda and Revolutionary Action in September (Guillaume, 1985, vol. I, pp. 217–18; vol. II, pp. 3–5, 75–76, 182–83).

The events of 1871, in particular the Paris Commune and its wide impact abroad, caused Bakunin to take part in another conflict, this time with Mazzini, to whom he had been relatively close years before. The Italian nationalist had published in his journal *La Roma del Popolo* [*The People's Rome*] between April and June of that year a series of articles attacking the *communard* experience. The heart of the criticism was that the communal autonomy proclaimed by the Paris Commune was a misunderstanding since it directly denied the very dear principle of national unity. His attacks in the Italian press continued, and in July he published in his journal a text proposing, with a harsh attack on the International, the holding of a workers' congress to establish a national pact. Mazzini denounced the Internationalists, responsible in a certain way for the course of the Commune in France, naming them as a threat to the workers, insofar as they denied God, the country/nation, and individual property (Lehning, 1973, pp. xxxvi–xxxviii).

Bakunin answered Mazzini immediately through an article, "Risposta d'un Internazionale a Mazzini"/"Réponse d'un International à Mazzini" ["Response from an International to Manzini"], published in August 1871 concomitantly in French (in *La Liberté*, Brussels) and Italian (in *Il Gazzettino Rosa*, Milan) (Bakunin, 1973a[e]). During the second half of 1871, amidst the conflict, Bakunin wrote a series of other articles that make up, together with the "Response," the book *Manzini's Political Theology and the International*, partially published at the end of 1871. In this book, Bakunin exposes and critically analyzes the foundations of Mazzinian doctrine, starting from its idealistic and religious bases and reaching its political consequences. He contrasts to this doctrine the philosophical, theoretical, historical, and strategic presuppositions that he developed previously when elaborating the foundations of his materialist and revolutionary socialism. He reaffirms and develops his *scientific-naturalist materialism* as an analytical frame of reference and counterpoint to Mazzini's idealism (theological, metaphysical/mystical, and political). He demonstrates, through his dialectic conception of reality, that in the contradiction between authority and freedom, the ideals of God and reaction are placed in opposition to the ideals of humanity and revolution. Therefore, he argues that Mazzini had to be considered as part of the reactionary camp. The IWA, as an expression of the mass strategy he advocated in his *anarchism*, would be exactly the humanitarian and revolutionary counterpoint to Mazzini's doctrine. Other themes received some attention: criticism of religious, political-economic, and national power; the relationship between religion and politics; the theoretical-philosophical and historical bases of human development from animality; the relationships between the inorganic world and the organic world and the particularities of social determinations; solidarity as an inseparable element of freedom and the basis of the moral conception of anarchism; the role of morality in social force; and the German-Slav question (Bakunin, 1973b[e]).[53]

From a workers' perspective, Europe was still complicated at the time. In 1870, due to the Franco-Prussian War, the International Congress scheduled for September in Paris did not take place. In 1871, after the Paris Commune and in a context of enormous repression, there was no possibility of holding a congress, be it in Paris or elsewhere. Therefore, at the end of July the General Council decided to replace the IWA congress with a conference. It would be held in September 1871 in London, allowing for the forwarding, even if temporarily, of relevant topics of the association.

As Leier (2006, pp. 262–64) argues, "there was no effort to represent the International in general" at the London Conference. This was because sections were arbitrarily excluded—as in the case of those that made up the majority of the Romanesque Federation, and which would then form the Jurassian Federation—and the immense majority of those present had no delegation from the sections to represent them—Engels, for example, answered for Italy, and the Italian sections, mostly collectivist federalists, had never granted him any mandate and did not even agree with his centralist conceptions.[54] According to Robin's impression—who, in exile in London, was part of the General Council—the London Conference, which he refers to as a "secret conference," was nothing more than an initiative by Marx to impose his program on the sections of the International through the General Council. When Robin realized what it was really about, he left the conference and went on to criticize it—he was then expelled from the council for this (Guillaume, 1985, vol. II, pp. 196–98).

This objective of Marx can be seen in the resolutions that were approved there. Among other things, the conference approved two measures that directly attacked the collectivists, the majority under Bakunin's strong influence. The first, with regard to the conflict in Switzerland, arbitrates in favour of the minority, granting it the name of the Romanesque Federation, and "decrees that the federation of the mountain sections [of the Jura] will be named: Jurassian Federation." The second, in a direct attack on the Socialist Propaganda and Revolutionary Action Section and the Alliance, resolves that "no longer shall any branch or society already admitted be allowed to continue to form a separatist group under the designation of 'Propaganda Section,' 'Alliance of Socialist Democracy' etc." However, the most important measure was found in resolution number nine. Taking up the documents of 1864 that had not been collectively endorsed at the following congresses, the conference passed, on the "political action by the working class" that "the proletariat cannot act as a class unless by constituting itself as a distinct political party" and that "its economic movement and its political action are inseparably united" (Guillaume, 1985, vol. II, pp. 212, 209, 203).

As Robin summarized clearly after the London Conference:

> I must remind you that there are two opinions in the International: some want workers to seek political power, inserting themselves, one by one, for want of something better, into the current parliamentary assemblies; others reject these means and desire the political organization of the proletariat *outside* the current State and against it. The former had the cunning to refer to their own position as "engaging in politics"; the others let them refer to theirs as "not engaging in politics." These vague expressions, used to represent clear ideas, served admirably for their inventors, Marx and co. They allowed them to put into the same bag the reactionary cooperators, later traitors, Tolain, Murat, Héligon, and the anarchist revolutionaries, whose ideas were well expressed by the former Alliance Section. (*Apud* Guillaume, 1985, vol. II, p. 204)

This conference in fact instituted, through a fictitious representation, the centralist thesis of the *Communist Manifesto*—constitution of the class in party and conquest of political power—as a principle of the association, which, since its foundation, had found a defense in a minority of the sections.[55] That is, it sought to resolve from the top down a dispute that had existed for years within the International, again in favour of a minority of the sections, whose positions were defended by the majority of the London delegates. Soon after the conference, at the end of 1871, Lafargue, Marx's son-in-law, was sent to Spain to obtain evidence against Bakunin for the General Council—there he would stay until mid-1872.

Right after the London Conference, the Jurassians, including Guillaume and Schwitzguébel, decided to convene a regional congress for November 1871 in Sonvillier. They intended to reorganize the federation and discuss what they understood to be the "dictatorial attitude of the General Council towards the sections." The various sections present at the Sonvillier Congress, claiming to be the legitimate Romanesque Federation, decided to dissolve it and found the majority federalist Jurassian Federation. The delegates voted on the new statutes, which advocated "autonomy of the sections," criticized the conference's maneuvers and demanded that an International Congress immediately be held. They sent a circular to the IWA sections denouncing the maneuvers of the General Council in London and instituted *La Révolution Sociale* [*The Social Revolution*] as the federation's journal (Guillaume, 1985, vol. II, pp. 226, 235–42).

The unfolding of events in the IWA can be understood even with the findings of a Marxist author:

> After the conference, Marx was convinced that the resolutions passed in London would receive the support of almost all the major federations and local sections. But soon after he had to reassess the situation. [...] Although the position of the Jura Federation was already predicted, Marx was probably surprised when, in 1872, signs of insurgency and rebellion in relation to his political line emerged from various quarters. In many countries, the decisions taken in London were received as a strong interference in local political autonomy and thus an unacceptable imposition. The Belgian Federation [...] began to take a rather critical stance on London. Then the Dutch also took a position of critical distancing. Even harsher were the reactions in southern Europe, where the opposition quickly gained remarkable consensus. The vast majority of Iberian Internationalists decisively turned against the General Council and welcomed Bakunin's ideas. [...] Also in Italy the results of the London Conference only generated negative reactions. (Musto, 2014, pp. 58–59)

The London maneuvers, if they aimed to align the sections under centralist principles, ended with a reverse effect: they stimulated a revolt of almost all the sections against the General Council. In May 1872, the General Council also tried to counteract them by issuing a long private circular to the sections entitled "Les Prétendues Scissions dans L'Internationale" ["The Fictitious Splits in the International"], written by Marx and Engels earlier that year. In it, the Council denied that the London Conference had split the International and tried, by means of administrative justifications, to show that things had occurred within the resolutions. For the most part, however, the circular directly and nominally attacked the Alliance and Bakunin. There he was accused, among other things, of defending pan-Slavism, of wanting to disorganize the IWA and replace the General Council with his personal dictatorship, of getting involved with Netchaiev, and of being linked to Richard and Blanc (Marx and Engels, 2010b, pp. 79–123, 664).[56]

At the end of 1871, as soon as he learned of the results of the London Conference, Bakunin sent several letters to his supporters and to the sections of the International with which he was close, especially in Switzerland, Italy, and Spain. This continued during 1872 and intensified after the spread of "Fictitious Splits." In these letters, he not only explains himself regarding the accusations and directly attacks Marx and the General Council, but also promotes his point of view both on the directions of International and his strategy of organizational dualism.[57]

In June 1872, Bakunin went to Zurich, accompanying Antonia and her two children, who would remain for a long stay in Russia. Antonia's brother had died in late 1871, and she was motivated to return, at least temporarily, to her native land. With the permission of the Russian government, which changed the position it had issued at the time of her departure, the trip was able to take place. After the family's departure, Bakunin stayed in Zurich for a few months during the second half of 1872; he joined a group of young Slavic people, with Russian and Serbian members, among whom was the Alliancist Ross. With them, he returned to the themes of the Slavic question and founded a secret group and a Slavic section of the International, which was linked to the Jurassian Federation.[58] Even without any contact with Netchaiev, Bakunin tried to intervene on his behalf during his arrest in Switzerland. He even publicly opposed his deportation to Russia, which ended up happening in October 1872.

In mid-1872, responding to pressure from the sections, the General Council decided to convene an IWA congress for September of that year in The Hague. The congress took place, even under the prior protest of the Swiss (Genevan and Jurassian), that the chosen location, being too far away, would make it very difficult or even prevent the delegations from participating. Bakunin himself was unable to attend, not only because of lack of money, but also because of the risk of arrest in France and Germany. As in London, the congress participants were far from representing the International. A majority of centralist "delegates" was forged—represented by the General Council, under the hegemony of Marx and Engels, reinforced by the Blanquists, and with only a few dissents—and a minority of federalist delegates—representing the immense majority of the sections and members of the International.

Even the Marxist Musto (2014, p. 62) recognizes that at The Hague Congress, the only one Marx attended personally, "the representivity of the delegates was absolutely biased. It did not mirror the true balance of forces within the organization."[59]

In this way, it was possible for the centralists to achieve their purposes. Two of them, quite evident since the 1871 conference: to approve positions about "political action by the working class" and definitively exclude the Alliancists, thus weakening federalist collectivism. In The Hague, it was adopted that "the working class cannot act as a class except by constituting itself into a political party" and that "the conquest of political power then became the great duty of the working class." It was also possible to expel Bakunin and Guillaume; Schwitzguébel and the Spanish Alliancists managed to save themselves. Not only did the accusations about the existence of the Alliance—considered a body hostile to the IWA, with a view to disorganizing it or dominating it, which was never proven—fall on Bakunin, but also on Netchaiev's actions, in particular the threat to the editor of *Capital*.[60] But a third, less obvious purpose was the approval of the transfer of the General Council to New York (IWA, 1872).

Differently from what has often been claimed in historiography, The Hague Congress did not mean the victory of the centralists or a personal conflict between Marx and Bakunin. Nor would it be appropriate to interpret it as a simple split between centralists and federalists. Berthier's thesis (2015c) that what really led to the conflict was the conduct of the General Council and the imposition of a political program on the International (the constitution of the class into a party and the quest for political power), provisionally realized in London and definitively in The Hague, and contrary to what was recommended by Bakunin (solidarity in the immediate economic struggle) seems correct. This was what motivated the general dissatisfaction and protest of the sections against the General Council.[61] With this body's subsequent determination that those who disagreed with resolutions would automatically be excluded, it ended up "excluding" from the IWA practically all of its sections and the immense majority of its members. The transfer of the General Council to New York provoked the withdrawal of even the Blanquists—who understood the measure as an organizational suicide— and anticipated, for 1872, the death certificate of the Centralist International, formalized four years later.

10.2.6 Final Years

In accordance with the proposal of the Italian Federation, after the Congress in The Hague in 1872, the federalists went to Switzerland to continue the work of the International. Bakunin was in Zurich discussing the secret Alliance with the Italian Internationalists Fanelli, Errico Malatesta, Vicenzo Pezza, and Ludovico Nabruzzi. They were joined by the Italian Cafiero, the Swiss Schwitzguébel, and the Spanish Morago, Farga-Pellicer, Alerini, and Nicolas Marselau (Nettlau, 1977a, p. 140). The organization consolidated and formalized its political principles and organizational foundations in a document written by Bakunin, "Programme de la Fraternité Internationale" ["Program of the International Fraternity"] (Bakunin, 72016[e]).

According to Guillaume (1985, vol. III, pp. 1–10), on 15 September, 1872, the Jurassian Federation met at a congress in Saint-Imier, Switzerland, to discuss the results of The Hague and prepare for the international congress proposed by the Italian Federation. On that occasion, the Jurassians formalized their non-recognition of the decisions of The Hague, which according to them had irreparably wounded the principle of autonomy of the internationalist sections, and reinforced their appreciation for Bakunin—who participated as delegate of the Sonvillier section— and Guillaume, who in their understanding had been unjustly expelled from the association. Finally, they delegated to Guillaume and Schwitzguébel the responsibility of representing them at the anti-authoritarian congress.

That same day, and extending until the following day, the International Anti-Authoritarian Congress also met in Saint-Imier, with four delegates from the Spanish Federation, six from the Italian Federation (Bakunin participated as one of the delegates), two from various French sections, one from two North American sections, and the two from the Jurassian Federation. It founded the Anti-Authoritarian International, which claimed to be the legitimate continuation of the IWA, and had four resolutions. All Hague decisions were rejected and the new General Council in New York was not recognized. A pact of friendship, solidarity, and mutual defense was established between the federations and sections present, seeking, under a federalist model of organization and without a general council, to continue the internationalist work. The organization of resistance on a large scale was encouraged so that the workers, immersed in class conflicts, could advance toward social revolution. The resolution on the "nature of the political action of the proletariat," countering the lines of London and The Hague, said the following:

1st. That the destruction of all political power is the first duty of the proletariat;
2nd. That every organization of a supposedly provisional and revolutionary political power to promote this destruction is nothing more than another lie, and something as dangerous to the proletariat as the governments existing today;
3rd. That, rejecting every compromise to accomplishing social revolution, the proletarians of every country must establish, outside all bourgeois politics, the solidarity of revolutionary action. (Guillaume, 1985, vol. III, p. 8)

The Anti-Authoritarian International thus adhered to the collectivist federalist positions promoted by the Alliancists and by Bakunin. The history of what remained of the Centralist International and the Anti-authoritarian International, from 1872, supports the interpretation that, as Berthier (2015c, p. 1) points out, "The Hague was the victory of the federalist current." Of course, this was not in formal terms, of the illegitimate delegates, but as a mark of the insurgence of the foundations of the association against its bureaucratic leaders. Practically all the sections with considerable bases joined the Anti-Authoritarian International, which held, in the following years, those that would be considered the sixth, seventh, and eighth congresses of the IWA, respectively in Geneva (1873), Brussels (1874), and Bern (1876). Its activities were carried out until 1877, when it also met its end. Curiously, among other factors, this end was again due to the imposition of a political program on the International—only this time the anarchists were responsible.

In October 1872, Bakunin returned to Locarno and produced two writings denouncing what had happened in the International.[62] At the beginning of 1873, he was feeling the health problems that affected him heavily, besides the usual absolute lack of resources. If his post-prison recovery seemed to have cured him completely, these problems were now aggravated by a rather unregulated life. Bakunin was obese and needed to eat, drink, and smoke less. But, contrary to medical recommendations, he could not escape the enormous amounts of food and the abundance of flour in his diet. Moreover, he smoked practically all day long, one cigarette after another.[63] He had asthma attacks, which made breathing difficult, and a problem in the prostate, which made him urinate permanently and which made it impossible for him to sleep, in addition to a heart problem (Leier, 2006, p. 290).

Even so, between January and August of 1873, he dedicated himself to writing what would be his last book: *Statism and Anarchy: The Struggle Between the Two Parties in the International Workers' Association*. Taking the conflicts in the IWA as a background, this book is dedicated at the same time to a harsh critique of statist socialism/communism and a more detailed exposition of anti-statist socialism (*anarchism*). Through his *scientific-naturalist materialism*, and the concept of *social force*, Bakunin takes up the history of the constitution of the modern State in Germany, Austria, and Russia, as well as historical elements of capitalism in general and German liberalism in particular. Uniting them to the dynamics of social classes in conflict, he points to a more robust elaboration of his *theory of the State*. Bakunin discusses the *theoretical frameworks for an understanding of social classes*, which are conceptualized in a multidimensional key, in which non-economic criteria are also relevant. He points to the bourgeoisification of a certain "labour aristocracy" and emphasizes the revolutionary potential not only of urban and rural workers, but also of peasants and the marginalized. He is concerned with the question of science and intellectuals, and warns of the risks of bureaucracy.

Reflecting on these aspects in a context of growing reaction in Europe—marked not only by the strengthening of *domination or statist-capitalist power*, but also by German *imperialism*, and by certain expectations in the face of representative democracy—Bakunin takes up the recent history of the International to show the inadequacy of the centralists' statism to transform this reality. He criticizes the positions of Marx, Lassalle, and the German workers. He argues that the seizure of the State, in a violent or peaceful way, would necessarily imply the constitution of a new social class, the bureaucracy, which, even on other bases, would continue the exploitation and domination of workers and prevent their emancipation. Moreover, he considers that the anti-capitalist and anti-statist struggle could not be dissociated from an anti-imperialist struggle, which would have to be carried out outside the nationalist, patriotic, and pan-Slavist frameworks. It was, therefore, a matter of reconciling the social question with the national question—in the latter sense, reflections on the German-Slav question are resumed. *The workers' and peasants' social revolution* remains a framework for transformation, and the fundamental strategy is still *organizational dualism* (IWA-Alliance). An appendix provides a critical discussion of cooperatives, and presents a revolutionary program for Russia (Bakunin, 2003a[e]).[64]

In the second half of 1873, Bakunin's trajectory was marked by two events. One, political, with the publication of the centralists' attacks and his departure from public political life. Another, personal, with the attempt to find a home in La Baronata. The main attack by the centralists was published in September: "The Alliance of Socialist Democracy and the International Workers' Association" by Lafargue, Engels, and Marx. As noted, these harsh personal attacks were considered false and unjust even by the Marxists themselves.[65] But, although recognizing that this was nothing more than the last gasp of that "International" that was perishing, Bakunin did not stop bothering. At the end of 1873, as a result of the developments of the competing Internationals, and taking into account his health and financial problems, aggravated by the unfair attacks he suffered, Bakunin decided to withdraw from public political life.

In October 1873, he wrote a letter to the Jurassian Federation, in which he acknowledged his affection for the Jurassians and the federalists' victory in the International:

> In spite of all the tricks of our common enemies and the infamous slanders they have cast against me, you have retained your esteem, your friendship and your trust in me. You were not intimidated by this name of "Bakuninians" that they threw in your faces. [...] Strongly assisted by your brothers from Italy, Spain, France, Belgium, the Netherlands, England, and America, you brought the great International Workers' Association back to the path from which Mr. Marx's dictatorial attempts failed to lead it. The two congresses just held in Geneva [the federalist and the centralist] were a triumphant, decisive demonstration of justice and, at the same time, of the strength of your cause. Your congress, that of freedom, brought together the delegates of the main European federations, except Germany. [...] The authoritarian or Marxist congress [was] composed solely of Germans and Swiss workers. [...] This congress was a funeral. (Bakunin, 2010h[c], pp. 157–58)

Also in this letter, he asked for his resignation from the Jurassian Federation and International:

> Yesterday [before the federalists' victory], [...] no one was allowed to abandon their lines. But today, when this victory became a fact, the freedom to act according to one's personal convenience has returned to each one. And I take this opportunity, dear comrades, to ask from you the kindness to accept my resignation as a member of the Jurassian Federation and a member of the International. I have many reasons to do so. [...] By my birth and by my personal position, [...] I would know nothing else but theoretical propaganda among you. [...] The time is no longer for ideas, but for facts and acts. What matters most today is the organization of the forces of the proletariat. But my age and my health do not allow me to do so. On the contrary, they ask me for solitude and rest. [...] I will be with you until death. (Bakunin, 2010h[c], pp. 158–60)

Shortly before that, in May 1873, Bakunin had gone to Bern to visit Adolf Vogt because of his health problems; Vogt had, with some frequency, been his doctor. Bakunin expressed to Vogt his concern about being deported to Russia, as happened with the sons of Obolensky and Netchaiev, and received the advice to try to obtain Swiss citizenship. One of the ways to do this was to acquire property in the country.

As Carr relates (1961, pp. 480–84), it was to this end, and in order to provide a dignified end to life for Bakunin and his family, that Cafiero, who had received a large inheritance at the time of his father's death, set out to acquire a property in the name of his Russian comrade. And so he did when he bought La Baronata in October 1873. The property, which had a house and a certain amount of land, was located in the canton of Ticino, a few kilometers from Locarno, still on the border with Italy. As agreed between Bakunin and Cafiero, La Baronata was to serve as both the Bakunin's home and a political space for Alliancists to pass through, take refuge or live in. In addition, the property was to be self-sustaining, and Cafiero invested in the planting of fruit trees and the purchase of some animals and equipment for work; the house also had to be renovated.

Away from Antonia since more than a year ago, Bakunin proposed that she come from Russia with her family to live in La Baronata. He did not mention the agreement with Cafiero, such that, for her, it seemed obvious that Bakunin's value corresponding to the family's inheritance had finally been sent by the brothers. With the agreement of Antonia—whose third son (Gambuzzi's) had been born shortly after his arrival in Russia—Bakunin sent remittances, also on loan from Cafiero, between the end of 1873 and the first months of 1874. So in May, Antonia left Russia for Switzerland accompanied by her three children, her parents, and her sister. After almost two years apart, the two finally met again.

But there was a huge setback in July 1874. At the beginning of that month, when Gambuzzi was accompanying Antonia and her family on their arrival, he commented with her on rumours that were circulating, noting that the purchase of La Baronata, attributed to Bakunin, had ruined Cafiero financially. Charged by his wife and deeply bothered, Bakunin went to Cafiero to ask that, with Ross, they deny the story. But she was greatly surprised when she learned, from Cafiero himself, that the rumours, in fact, were the harshest truth. The Italian had received a much smaller amount than expected, and would not be able to continue with the project of the property, which still required a lot of spending. This motivated a conflict and a temporary rupture on the part of Bakunin with Cafiero and Ross. So when Antonia and her family settled in La Baronata, the situation was already unsustainable.

However, after a few days, Bakunin left for Bologna. As Pernicone (2009, pp. 82–90) explains, since the second half of 1873, Italy had been immersed in a huge economic crisis and the population was agitated between strikes and protests. And the Italian disciples of Bakunin, aiming to take advantage of the moment to invest in practical propaganda of their ideas—and, at the same time, to distance themselves from the Mazzinians and Garibaldians—had been discussing for some time the possibility of leading an armed insurrection in the country, specifically in the region of Bologna. To this end, in December 1873, inspired by the Alliance, they founded the Comitato Italiano per la Rivoluzione Sociale (CIRS) [Italian Committee for the Social Revolution], whose most prominent leaders were Costa, Malatesta, and Cafiero. In February 1874, in Switzerland, Bakunin had met with Cafiero, Francesco Natta, and three ex-*communards*—Victor Cyrille, Louis Pindy, and Varry—and established the planning for what would be the Bologna Insurrection with them.

Costa and Malatesta coordinated the mobilizations—the first in central Italy and the second to the south in Mezzogiorno. Still in La Baronata, Bakunin hosted other meetings to discuss the insurrectional plans. Ross and Cafiero's wife bought and smuggled dynamite into Italy. Cafiero made a cash donation, with which weapons were acquired. But Bakunin only decided to leave for Bologna when Antonia and her family arrived in La Baronata. After a few days, the weather was terrible. Besides, Bakunin hadn't revealed that he had already removed his name from the property and transferred it to Cafiero. He then decided to leave for Italy, and did so telling his family that it was a routine trip to Zurich.

In fact, as he explained in a "Justification Memoir" sent to Bellerio to be forwarded to Cafiero, Bakunin went to Italy to die in the struggle for the revolution. Besides the health problems and political conflicts, this family crisis contributed a lot to everything. This memoir sought to clarify pending issues and provide the necessary guidelines for procedures after his death. Thus he said goodbye to his friends and to Antonia: "And now, my friends, I have nothing left but to die; goodbye. [...] Antonia, don't curse me; forgive me. I will die blessing you and our dear children" (Bakunin, 74001[e], p. 29; Guillaume, 1985, vol. III, p. 204).

Still according to Pernicone (2009, pp. 90–95), Bakunin arrived in Bologna in the last days of July 1874. There he stayed clandestinely for a week, planning more thoroughly how the uprising should be carried out with the insurgents. They hoped, on 7 August, 1874, to make a call to arms and, by example, bring the masses with them. They also counted on the arrival of thousands of revolutionaries from other regions, reinforcing the movement. But repression had been going on in Italy for some time, and even public activities were becoming more and more complicated. Fearing a revolutionary collaboration among the subversives, the authorities began to make preventive arrests in early August. They went after the Republicans and then the anarchists—Costa was arrested in Bologna on the 5th. Even seeing an imminent defeat due to repression, the insurgents decided to carry out what had been agreed. On the 7th, the third CIRS bulletin, written by Cafiero, called for workers, peasants, and soldiers to rebel against their masters. However, nothing went according to plan. The workers did not adhere to the call, and the thousands of revolutionaries who were supposed to support the uprising did not come either: on the night of 7 to 8 August, instead of the thousands expected, only 150 arrived, many of them unarmed. It was both a problem of repression and of the strategy adopted, which lacked roots among the masses. That same day, the police took the region and ensured the reestablishment of order—the revolutionaries were only left with dispersion. Bakunin remained in hiding and on 14 August fled in disguise by train. His attempt to die fighting, finally, was unsuccessful.

During the time Bakunin was in Bologna, Ross and Bellerio told the outcome of La Baronata to Antonia who, in three days, left the property with her family. They stayed in the Lake Maggiore region, first in Arona (Italy) and then in Lugano (Switzerland). Bakunin spent a few weeks in Sierre (Switzerland), reconciled with Ross and was invited by Antonia to join the family in Lugano; he arrived in early October 1874 after passing through Bern.

It was in Lugano that Bakunin spent the last period of his life. Initially in Antonia's house, with enormous financial difficulties, he tried to obtain the part of the family inheritance that belonged to him, together with the brothers in Premukhino. Hoping to receive it, he acquired a small property, Villa Bresso, where he moved in with his family in February 1875. There, he connected with a circle of local workers, received a visit from Malon and reconciled with Cafiero. He corresponded with Bellerio, the Vogts, the Reichels, and with Reclus. In light of his health problems, which were getting worse and demanded more and more care, not only family members and Gambuzzi were important, but also Alexandrina Bauler and two Italian workers: the shoemaker Andrea Santandrea and the refugee Filippo Mazzotti, who took care of him daily.

In a letter sent to Reclus on 15 February, 1875, Bakunin shows frustration with the advance of reaction in Europe and the lack of organization and the revolutionary passion of the masses:

Yes, you're right, the revolution at the moment has gone to bed, we have relapsed into the period of evolution, that is, into that of the underground, invisible and often even insensible revolutions. [...] I agree with you in saying that the hour of the revolution has passed, not because of the horrible disasters of which we were witnesses and the terrible defeats of which we were guilty, but because, to my great despair, I have noticed and see every day that revolutionary thought, hope and passion are absolutely not to be found in the masses, and when they are absent, there is no point in making useless efforts. [...] Poor humanity! It is clear that it can only come out of this quagmire through an immense social revolution. But how will this revolution come about? Never has Europe's international reaction been so formidably armed against every popular movement. It has made repression a new science that is systematically taught in military schools to lieutenants of all countries. And to attack this impregnable fortress, what do we have? The disorganized masses. But how can we organize them when they are not passionate enough for their own salvation, when they don't know what they should want and when they don't want the only thing that can save them?! (Bakunin, 2016b[c], pp. 541-43)

Noting the exacerbation of national conflicts, Bakunin speaks of the possibility of a "universal war. These immense military States must destroy and devour each other sooner or later. But what a prospect!" Moreover, he reflects on his own condition, saying he was "very old, very sick, very discouraged, and [...] very disillusioned" and that, in fact, he had definitely withdrawn from the struggle. "I will spend the rest of my days not in empty contemplation, quite the contrary, intellectually very active, and which, I hope, will not fail to produce something useful" (Bakunin, 2016b[c], pp. 542-43). At the end of his life, Bakunin expressed interest in recording his memoirs and writing a treatise on ethics, but neither project came to fruition.

The Premukhino inheritance arrived late and in small parcels. For this reason, the Bakunins, under threat of eviction, had to leave Villa Bresso in the middle of 1876. They planned to go to Naples, to live closer to Gambuzzi. While Antonia went to settle the matter of this move, Bakunin returned to Bern to meet and consult with Vogt. Arriving there on 14 June he had to be hospitalized due to serious health conditions. He spent the next few days in hospital talking with the Reichels and Vogts about politics, philosophy, and music. He would die due to bladder problem complications, on 1 July, 1876 (Carr, 1961, pp. 493-508).[66]

Bauler, Bakunin's last confidante and friend, informed the labour circle near him in Lugano:

When, from the threshold of the door, I pronounced these simple words "Michel and dead" [in Italian]—myself, terrified of what I had just said—the stupor was general. Bakunin's followers were not the only ones to fall into tears.

The Swiss workers, who had only heard about Bakunin from their fellow workers, also cried. Santandrea rolled on the ground, banged his feet like a child, and sobbed. (Lehning, 1999, p. 371)

Bakunin's death caused considerable commotion in revolutionary circles. His funeral took place on 3 July in Bern itself. Friends and workers' organizations expressed themselves in writing and in person. Among the Jurassians, Schwitzguébel read the farewell letters from friends and sections of the International, Guillaume recalled the calumnies against the deceased and his contributions to the cause of revolutionary socialism, and Reclus highlighted his personal and political qualities. Jukovski spoke for the Slavs, giving a short biography of Bakunin; Paul Brousse spoke for the French, Carlo Salvioni for the Italians, and Betsien for the Germans (Guillaume, 1985, vol. IV, pp. 36–37).

10.3 BAKUNINIAN POLITICAL THEORY BETWEEN 1864 AND 1876

I will now present some elements relevant to the understanding of Bakunin's political theory in the period in question. They introduce the theoretical discussion, which will be elaborated in more detail in the following chapters.

10.3.1 Revolutionary Socialist Period (1864–76)

This part deals with the years 1864 to 1876, when Bakunin proceeded from socialism to anarchism; this is his *revolutionary socialist period*, of which his *anarchist period* (1868–76) is the most relevant part. During those years Bakunin lived mainly in Italy and Switzerland, but also traveled to Belgium, France, England, and Sweden. He became involved in secret organizational initiatives such as the International Fraternity and the Alliance, the first of which occupied practically all his political efforts between 1864 and 1867, and from then on with public initiatives such as the League of Peace and Freedom and the International Workers' Association (IWA). He participated in two insurrectionary and revolutionary uprisings: the Lyon Commune in 1870 and the Bologna Insurrection in 1874.

In this period (1864–76), Bakunin wrote copiously—all his books and most of his articles and letters are from these years. His motivation for writing them was both the European context and the disputes with adversaries, especially in the context of the conflicts in the International. The conjunctural reconfigurations of those years, which involved the Franco-Prussian War and the conflicts that led to the Paris Commune; the unification of Germany, its growing international power and the reconfiguration of European geopolitics; the definitive passage of the bourgeoisie into the camp of reaction—as well as of the former progressives of the 1848 generation—assuming the position of a hegemonic social class; and the rise of workers' struggles, especially those linked to the International Workers' Association, were remarkable. The conflicts with Utin, Mazzini, Marx, and the bourgeois socialists and other mediators were also striking. The Bakuninian political theory of this period, which can be considered a *theory of revolution*, fits into this context and develops from these disputes.

The year 1864, which opens this period, was decisive. For Bakunin, it marked not only the resumption of an updated understanding of the European situation—since, between 1862–63, his reading basically reproduced the understanding of 1848–49, and reality had changed considerably—but it also defined the beginning of a new period, motivated by two events. First, Herzen's estrangement and the disillusionment with the Polish Insurrection of 1863, which motivated the passing of national and Slavic issues to a secondary level, with the social question and the emancipation of workers taking priority. Nevertheless, I do not agree with the position of authors like Nettlau (1964, pp. 41–43) who maintain that, in his pan-Slavic period, Bakunin experienced a "nationalist psychosis" from which he freed himself in 1864 in the direction of socialism. This is because the national question will continue to be asserted by Bakunin, but now as part of the social question. Second, Bakunin's return to Masonry, which supported a definitive break with religion. Through anti-theologism, incorporated into masonry and reinforced by the influence of Proudhon, and the study of other authors of the natural and social sciences in the following years, Bakunin definitively joined the camp of materialism.

There are, in these two aspects, central ruptures of a thematic and epistemological order that were further deepened in the following years, especially following Bakunin's entry into the IWA in 1868. For his political theory of the years 1864–76, both his practical experiences and Proudhon's work were fundamental, so that his anarchism can be considered as "Proudhon's anarchic system, which we have expanded, developed and released from all its metaphysical, idealistic, doctrinal clothing, and clearly accepting matter [nature] in science and social economy in history as the basis for all further developments" (Bakunin, 2014b[c], p. 93). Also important were the theoretical-philosophical contributions of Feuerbach, Comte, Darwin, Marx, and De Paepe.[67]

There is also a third aspect of rupture, concerning the question of the relationship between theory and practice, which had been present throughout Bakunin's life, but whose relative positions changed significantly. This revolutionary socialist period is characterized by a certain synthesis of the preceding periods. On the one hand, Bakunin returns to the theoretical-philosophical questions that had been practically abandoned since 1843; on the other, he gives continuity to concrete political practice, which characterized the priority of his life from that year on. In other words, the period 1864–76 is, to some extent, that of a conciliation between theory and practice. However, this conciliation is not made in the key of the "unity between theory and practice" of 1837–40 but in a materialistic key which, although theory is valued, continues to give greater importance to practice.

Bakunin's revolutionary socialism, like his anarchism, must be understood in its totality, which involves his philosophical and political-strategic positions. But one must not lose sight of the fact that the appropriation he makes of the different authors and the various practical experiences is done in a critical way and does not mean, therefore, unrestricted adhesion.

In philosophical terms, Bakunin operates within the framework of *scientific-naturalist materialism*,[68] establishing a definitive break with subjective and objective idealisms and with voluntarism. The definitive starting point of this rupture is the concept of anti-theologism, which, forged in religious criticism, allowed this critical reflection to extend to questions about nature and society.

According to McLaughlin, for Bakunin

Atheism or anti-theologism—the need to overcome the "divine ghost"— becomes a central component of his anarchist or anti-political program. It is in this sense that, as Lehning expresses it, "Bakunin's atheism [...] is linked to his political theory"; in fact, "anti-theologism [or] atheistic materialism [is] the cornerstone of Bakunin's philosophical conceptions." (McLaughlin, 2002, pp. 73–74)

With the theological principle being seen as the basis of authority, Bakunin (2014e[e], p. 258), like Proudhon, asserts the metaphor of Satan against God, "the eternal rebel, the first free thinker and emancipator of worlds," he who "shames man of his ignorance and beastly obedience," who "emancipates him and imprints upon his forehead the stamp of freedom and humanity, urging him to disobey and eat the fruit of science." As such, the religious criticism of those years is only the basis for a harsh criticism of idealism and a foundation for his materialism.

Bakunin's materialism is naturalistic since, for him, matter is synonymous with nature. Therefore, an important key to understand his texts from this period is to break with the nature-society duality, which is so incorporated in our midst and which will be the object of his criticism. When Bakunin states that something is natural, this does not necessarily mean that it is not social and vice-versa. Moreover, Bakunin's materialism is scientific because it relies on natural and social science to refute theology, even if it is opposed to the government of the intellectuals. It operates with the concepts of dialectics and history, among others, although it should not be considered a historical or dialectical materialism. His conception of dialectics maintains the foundations of the negative dialectics of previous periods, but now on a materialistic basis and, to a certain extent, modified by the influence of other authors, among them Proudhon. Even so, I consider as an exaggeration, without any historical proof, and with significant logical problems, the claim that Bakunin in his revolutionary socialist period would have adopted the Proudhonian serial dialectics.[69]

In political terms, Bakunin is a proponent of revolutionary socialism, collectivist socialism, or anarchism.[70] Starting from the concepts of history, society, social force, and social conflict, he elaborates a harsh critique of domination in all its forms and of the statist-capitalist system, the modern expression of this historical domination.

In this critique, the reflections of the previous period concerning Russia are deepened, and the economy becomes much more relevant in social dynamics. By exposing his concepts of social revolution, mass organization, and cadre organization—which are articulated in a *theory of organization*— Bakunin advances toward a transformational project of which a mass strategy is an essential part. His reflections on the International can be understood as the first more systematic elaboration of what would come to be called *revolutionary syndicalism* years later.[71]

10.3.2 Passage to Anarchism (1868)

When one intends to understand the precise moment of Bakunin's passage to anarchism, some considerations seem necessary. As pointed out, it is a gross methodological error to assume that everything Bakunin produced in his life should be considered anarchist. At the same time, it seems that taking the whole intellectual production from 1864 onwards as part of the same "anarchism" is also a mistaken procedure. Based on the analysis of Bakunin's life and work, and relating it to a strict definition of anarchism (cf., Corrêa, 2015), it should be considered that his conversion to anarchism occurred in 1868.

Discussing this conversion—and, consequently, the periodization of his work— Leier (2006, p. 172) and Angaut (2005, p. 10) point out that the year 1864 constitutes a first step, beginning with the foundation of the so-called International Fraternity and with the years that the Russian revolutionary remained in Italy. It was then that Bakunin developed an important part of the theoretical-philosophical tools that would be maintained and improved until the end of his life. For both (Leier, 2006, p. 190; Angaut, 2005, p. 20), this moment is characterized by Bakunin's reinsertion in the international political scene, after long years in prison, followed by the return to Europe and the defeat of the Polish Insurrection in 1863.

However, there are significant differences between his pre-anarchist period (1864–67) and his anarchist period (1868 onwards), which can be seen when, for example, three central writings from 1864 (Bakunin, 2014a[e], 2014b[e], 2014c[e]) are compared with his anarchist political thinking.

In 1864, the core of the two larger writings (Bakunin, 2014a[e] and 2014b[e]) is still to be found in national and political issues, as well as the federalism proposed as a model for the future society (Bakunin, 2014a[e], pp. 105–106). From 1868 onwards, the national and political question is approached as part of the social question and fits into a broader framework, with the economy and social classes assuming a decisive role and thus modifying the bases of federalism which, in a new society, forged from the IWA, has an economic foundation, although it may be articulated by territory.[72] In these writings, the main mechanism for achieving freedom and equality is still the abolition of the right of inheritance, with peaceful revolution being seen as a possibility and violent expropriation considered unnecessary (Bakunin, 2014a[e], pp. 100–101, 117). In the anarchist period, violent revolution and expropriation are generally seen as inevitable, and the right of inheritance, within a broader framework of the socialization of property (especially that of the peasants). In 1864, the popular masses were considered incapable of liberating themselves, and it was therefore necessary for minorities from the upper classes to organize themselves to act on the peasantry and especially the urban proletariat (Bakunin, 2014a[e], pp. 71–72, 114–16; Bakunin, 2014b[e], p. 133). From 1868 onwards, it is held that workers are able to emancipate themselves and that those with privileged origins, if they so desire, must take up the workers' cause and act together with peasants and proletarians in the struggle for emancipation.

In organizational terms, in these writings the favoured space is the secret society and therefore mass and public expressions are discarded, understanding that open congresses and even cooperatives have enormous limitations (Bakunin, 2014a[e], pp. 72–76, 115). In the anarchist period, Bakunin defends organizational dualism, reconciling secret and public, cadre and mass expressions. Finally, in 1864, the model of secret society proposed by Bakunin (2014b[e], pp. 133–35; 2014c[e], pp. 142–47) still has hierarchical and centralist features, which from 1868 onwards will be abandoned in favour of a federalist model of cadre organization.

Between 1864 and 1867, there are two important milestones in Bakunin's trajectory (theoretical and practical). First, in 1866, with "Principles and Organization of the International Revolutionary Society," of which "Revolutionary Catechism" is the best-known part. Second, in 1867–68, with *Federalism, Socialism and Anti-theologism* and the break with the League of Peace and Freedom. From then on, he will sustain political-strategic positions that will be maintained until the end of his life (Leier, 2006, pp. 172–91).

These changes are part of a larger transition, which also encompasses other positions. Bakunin's involvement in certain events—among them, his entry into the International and the founding of the Alliance—undoubtedly contributed to his passage to anarchism. In fact, such a transition formed part of a collective process that extended, in a relatively similar way, to a broader range of socialists and popular movements. Especially in Western Europe, but also in other localities, it was this process—which, in many cases, although not that of Bakunin, derived from a radicalization of Proudhonian mutualism—that laid the foundations for the emergence of the historical tradition of anarchism as a specific political doctrine. There are other details about how Bakunin relates to this process.

When in 1867 Bakunin sought the Peace and Freedom Congress, this initiative already marked an important step in his change of position. Certain elements of sufficiency and tutelage of the secret societies in relation to the working masses, present between 1864 and 1867, began to dissipate, culminating in his definitive entry into the IWA in 1868 (Berthier, 2011a, pp. 189–90).

Bakunin's departure from the League of Peace and Freedom also marks a rupture with a certain expectation, which still existed, of some productive dialogue with bourgeois democracy, hegemonic in that organization (Corrêa, 2014b). When, at the end of 1868, Bakunin wrote to Karl Marx "My homeland is now the International" (Leier, 2006, p. 231), he not only expounded on the change of priority of his political practice, but pointed out a fact that would directly influence his political positions.

Bakunin's participation in the International contributed immensely to the modification of his positions and to the solidification of his anarchist concepts. On the one hand, close contact with the workers' sections and the struggles of the Internationalists was decisive. He was unlikely not to suffer the effects of the whole wave of strikes that swept Europe[73] and, for Bakunin, the strikes in Belgium and above all in Switzerland in March 1868 had remarkable consequences (Guillaume, 2009a, pp. 147–49). On the other hand, the IWA provided the conditions for a relationship between Bakunin and many Internationalists, including Marx himself, but also others, such as the Belgian De Paepe, whose positions ended up contributing intensively to his development (Berthier, 2015, pp. 38, 51–52).

It was in this propitious environment that Bakunin developed and/or deepened a remarkable part of his anarchist concepts. Not only those that were mentioned— the relationship between politics and economics (the national question and economic federalism), notions of revolutionary subject (dispossessed classes as protagonists) and of revolutionary process (self-emancipation of workers, role of the abolition of inheritance), organizational conception (organizational dualism, federalism and complementarity of levels)—but also others: the International as a model of the future society, mass economic struggle as an inescapable step in the mobilization and stimulating the consciousness of the workers, mass organization as a practical school for revolution and socialism, organization of cadres as an auxiliary force, anti-imperialist struggle as part of the internationalist revolutionary program.

Besides this, even with all the historiographic difficulties, it is possible to affirm that the foundation of the Alliance, which took place in the same year of 1868, forges a camp around which to establish, in theory and practice, the political-doctrinaire skeleton that will shape anarchism in Western Europe (Corrêa, 2015, pp. 265–69). This influence of the IWA, which was present in Bakunin's trajectory, could not have left the Alliance itself intact. However much this organization presents some continuity with the so-called Fraternity of 1864, it breaks, especially because of this relationship with the IWA, with some authoritarian programmatic elements that are still in the programs of 1866 (Corrêa, 2014b). This change marks—again, from 1868 onwards— Bakunin's anarchist conception of the form and role of the cadre organization.

That is, even if we agree that the period from 1864 to 1867 represents a central development in Bakunin's trajectory towards anarchism, I consider, as Berthier (2008, p. 6), "Bakunin's properly anarchist period" to be from 1868 onwards.[74] Bakunin's positions produced in his texts of that year, from a logical perspective, seem to be in line with the anarchist ideas that will be developed in later years. Even in an analysis of Bakunin's historical trajectory, the milestone of 1868 and the continuity with the following years are evident (Leier, 2006, pp. 191–250).

Leaving Bakunin in the background and taking the historical formation of anarchism as a focus, the year 1868 is also a determining milestone. From the way the process of the emergence and diffusion of historical anarchism took place—I rely here on the "notions of totality and interdependence" between "anarchism, anarchists and social struggles" (Corrêa, 2015, p. 110)—this political-ideological tradition does not emerge and spreads through the thoughts of some great geniuses, but through the inseparable relationship between thinkers and popular movements, between anarchists and social struggles, in which both are influenced.

From this perspective, it seems incoherent to consider anarchism as a creation of Bakunin's mind or of any of the great libertarian classics, such as Proudhon. It is only possible to speak of *anarchism* when there is, historically, a group of people with relatively homogeneous thoughts and actions, people who relate to each other, who have common references and who participate in some way in the social struggles of their time. Until the present moment, it has not been possible for me to identify something of this kind before 1868.

The founding of the Alliance that year and the subsequent trajectory of its militants allow us to observe the existence of these aspects. In Western Europe, there are a number of revolutionary socialists, federalists, and collectivists who participate in the International— creating and strengthening its sections, influencing them, and being influenced by it—who communicate and meet frequently. Through travel, the sending of propaganda material and correspondence, they spread their positions on their continent and others. This constitutes, as I understand it, the first great international example of anarchism in full operation (Corrêa, 2015, pp. 265–69).

It seems reasonable, then, from a historical perspective, to locate the year 1868 as a milestone from which it is possible to situate both the emergence of anarchism and Bakunin's passage to anarchism.

NOTES

1   According to the Scottish Rite, degree 32 (Prince of the Royal Secret) is the second highest in the Masonic hierarchy, second only to degree 33 (Grand Inspector General).

2   The history of this organization, and of those that followed it, namely the Alliance, is far from adequately understood. On the one hand, this is because of the silence of its members during their lives and the lack of more in-depth records (letters, documents, etc.) about its course. On the other hand, it is because of the "official version" created later by the anarchists, who, trying to counter one of the reasons for Bakunin's expulsion from the International in 1872, stressed that there had never been a secret Alliance, which was only an invention of Marx (On the debate about the construction of this "official version", see Vuilleumier, 1964, 1979). However, there is diverse evidence of the existence of such organizations. In Bakunin's letters and writings it is abundant, as well as in the accounts and documents produced and/or leaked by his supporters, his opponents, and enemies, as in the aforementioned article by Lafargue, Engels, and Marx (1978). Even today it is not possible to know whether the organization Nettlau (1964) proposes to call the International Fraternity (founded in 1864) was a single society or whether there were multiple societies. Among the names of such an organization that appear in Bakunin's documents and accounts, we find: Fraternity, International Fraternity, International Secret Society of the Revolution, International Secret Society of the

Emancipation of Humanity, Family of the Scandinavian Brothers, International Revolutionary Society, Alliance of Social Democracy, Alliance of Socialist Revolutionaries, and Adelaide. In the case of some societies, there are also no explanations about the relationship between them (Bakunin, 64007[e], 2009c[e], 2014a[e], 2014b[e], 2014c[e]; Guillaume, 1985, vol. I, p. 77).

3   It is this change that substantiates, for some authors, the argument that Bakunin converted to anarchism in 1864. I disagree with this position for the simple reason that, as I have maintained (Corrêa, 2015, pp. 253–75), based on historical analysis, there was no anarchism or anarchists before 1868. Anarchism did not arise as a product of the thought of one or a few great theorists (whether Bakunin, Proudhon, or any other), but as a collective product of a popular movement which, in relation to some intellectuals, constituted itself concomitantly in action and thought, practice and theory; to this end, the historical context was decisive. Moreover, a comparison of Bakunin's writings with the anarchist historical tradition shows that the writings of the Russian revolutionary produced between 1864 and 1867 present certain elements which will be abandoned or modified from 1868 onwards, when they acquire, in political-ideological terms, much more similarity with the anarchist tradition. I agree with Berthier (2008, p. 6) that Bakunin became anarchist in 1868, and that *Federalism, Socialism, and Anti-theologism* (1867–68) is his writing of passage to anarchism. See Chapter 10.3.2.

4   During his stay in London, he associated himself with the Frenchman Alfred Talandier. During his time in Paris, he was associated with the internationalist brothers Élisée Reclus (geographer) and Élie Reclus (ethnographer), a bond that lasted until 1869. Talandier and the Reclus brothers were, as Guillaume (2009a, p. 175) points out, members of the Fraternity. It was during this same time in Paris that Bakunin met for the last time with Proudhon, who would die the following year (cf., also: Bakunin, 64037[c], p. 6; Nettlau, 1964, p. 44; Nettlau, 2008, pp. 149–50).

5   Just as the historical trajectory of the Fraternity is not known in greater detail, it is also not known to what extent this and other internal organizational regulations were put into practice.

6   Since Naples, Bakunin's marriage had been facing problems. It was not only the great difference of age with Antonia, but more importantly the incongruity of their interests. Bakunin was almost entirely dedicated to politics and Antonia preferred other pursuits. The attention she received from her husband was increasingly scarce, and as time passed she saw that situation with growing disapproval. The distance between the two became more pronounced, and Antonia ended up in love with Gambuzzi, a member of the International Fraternity who, still in Italy, became her lover with Bakunin's knowledge. Until the death of the Russian revolutionary the relationship remained like this: Bakunin was formally Antonia's husband and Gambuzzi her lover. All those who had a relationship with the couple knew about the situation. Even in Switzerland, the three lived under the same roof, with Gambuzzi and Antonia occupying the couple's room and Bakunin the living room. Antonia's three children that were born during Bakunin's life and received his last name—Carlo (Carluccio), Sofia (Zosia), and Maria (Maruschka) Bakunin—were in fact Gambuzzi's children. After Bakunin's death Gambuzzi formally united with Antonia, and had another daughter with her, Tania Gambuzzi (Lehning, 1999, pp. 282, 361, 366; Angaut, 2017).

7   The Russian positivist Grigori Vyrubov referred thus to Bakunin's speech that he witnessed in that congress: "I remember very well the extraordinary effect that his speech produced in the first session of the Congress. [...] Bakunin was not an orator; he was rather an excellent tribune, who could speak wonderfully well to the masses and, most notably, speak equally convincingly in several languages. His colossal stature [1.97m], his energetic gestures, his sincere and persuasive voice, his short, brilliant sentences, were all elements that made a great impression" (Lehning, 1999, p. 244; cf., also: Avrich, 1970, pp. 129–31).

8   Besides De Paepe, Perron, and Guillaume, a few dozen internationalists attended the congress, including the French Proudhonians Henri-Louis Tolain and Édouard Fribourg; the English members of the Reform League George Odger and William Cremer; the Germans Jean-Philippe Becker and Johann Eccarius, and the Swiss Pierre Coullery. As Guillaume (2009a, p. 117) stated: "This group, which had instinctively installed itself to the left, truly represented, during the duration of the Congress, the role of the *left* in a deliberative assembly".

9   For an excellent discussion of this return of Bakunin to philosophy, cf. Angaut, 2011.

10 It should be noted that Bakunin (2008e[e], p. 118) understands collectivism, in the midst of which anarchism arose, as "Proudhonism amply developed and taken to its ultimate consequences."

11   In March and April 1868, a strike of construction workers broke out in Geneva. The program, elaborated in January, demanded among other things a reduction in working hours, an increase in salaries, and wages per hour and not per day. In the face of the employers' refusal, the strike began at the end of March and emerged victorious at the beginning of April, with no further violent repercussions, with a retreat by the employers. This victory, in which the leadership of the construction worker François Brousset was decisive, weighed heavily on the solidarity that the Geneva workers received from their Swiss and French peers. In Geneva, the "Factory" workers—dedicated to the production of watches, jewelry, and music pieces; relatively well-educated and remunerated; Swiss citizens with political rights—showed solidarity with those in the construction industry—poorly educated and worse remunerated; mostly foreigners and without political rights—by setting up a strike fund to help the strikers. Despite the refusal of the British trade unions to contribute, the Paris-based IWA had a distinct position and contributed as much as they could, including financially (Guillaume, 2009a, pp. 147–49; Silva, 2017, p. 180; Becker, 1868). (As in this case, from here on the references to Silva, 2017 refer to the work of Selmo Silva.)

12   Still in March 1868, a strike by the miners of Charleroi did not have the same outcome. Harshly exploited in the coal mines, the Belgian workers had been facing reductions in wages since 1867 while the cost of living rose. When a new wage cut was announced at the end of March 1868, the workers went on a large and combative strike, marked by violence. Three thousand miners went to Épine, in Montigny-sur-Sambre, stopping work and breaking the office windows. Military troops were sent in, and under repression the workers reacted, throwing stones and threatening to destroy the ventilation system. The soldiers killed ten workers and left several others severely wounded. The repression marked the end of the strike and the defeat of the miners, who would still be prosecuted that year. Receiving solidarity from the International, the conflict, mediated by César de Paepe, finally guaranteed the acquittal of the accused. Following this, the IWA had massive subscriptions in Belgium (Defoort, 2004, pp. 131–34).

13   This congress was attended by 56 delegates representing 35 sections (Silva, 2017, p. 109).

14   This congress was attended by 72 delegates representing 57 sections (Silva, 2017, p. 115).

15   It is worth noting that, during all his time in the International, Bakunin (2001b[e], p. 27) believed that there was still a secret League of Communists or related organization, on the power of which Marx would rely in his work in the IWA. Bakunin (2014b[c], p. 90) writes in 1872 that the London Conference "sought to formulate this condemnation against us [the Alliance] in order to free the ground for its own conspiracy, the secret society which, under Marx's direction, has existed since 1848, founded by Marx, Engels, a late Wolff, and which is nothing more than the almost exclusively Germanic society of *authoritarian Communists.*" When Marx's correspondence became public, this view proved to be mistaken. Still, this does not mean that Marx was not part of an informal group, composed in general of members of the General Council and people from around him, with whom he discussed, articulated positions, and promoted a common line in the International.

16   This congress was attended by 100 delegates representing 129 sections (Silva, 2017, p. 129).

17   This newspaper, published in Russian in Geneva, was financed by Olga Levashov and existed between 1868 and 1870. Its first issue, 1 September, 1868, placed the entire edition under the responsibility of her brother-in-law, Jukovski, and Bakunin, who published the article "Наука и Народ" ["Science and the People"] (Bakunin, 2016a[e]). From the second issue on, Levashov passed control of the newspaper to Utin, generating bouts with the former editors and also between Bakunin and Utin (Carr, 1961, pp. 360–61).

18   Reclus was a member of the Fraternity (probably from 1864–65) until 1869. After that, he stayed away from Bakunin for a few years, returning in 1872, when he resumed his membership (probably in the Alliance) as an "independent brother" (Nettlau, 2008, pp. 149–50). Rey and Keller were already members of the Fraternity at that time (Guillaume, 1907a, p. xxxi) as was Tucci (Guillaume, 1985, vol. I, p. 120). Richard met Bakunin at the congress (Carr, 1961, p. 358). In addition to the members already mentioned, the Fraternity included Malon, Perron, A. Troussoff [Troussot?], V. Barténief, and his companion (Bakunin, 69001[c]; Guillaume, 1985, vol. I, p. 120).

19   The fact that Bakunin's position was defeated shows, as in other cases, the mistakenness of the argument that he would be the dictator of the Alliance, which was sustained, among others, by Lafargue, Engels and Marx (1978), and Carr (1961). As pointed out earlier in a note, for several reasons, the history of this organization, which Nettlau (1964) proposes to call the Alliance of Socialist

Democracy, is very little known. In its public expressions, it is a little more discussed. In its secret expressions, it is practically unknown; as far as the latter are concerned, it is not known exactly what its organizational status was and to what extent the statutes drafted by Bakunin were implemented. Nor is its relationship with the Fraternity, the Public Alliance, and the International known in detail. Among the names that appear in the historical documents drawn up by Bakunin and in other reports, we find: Alliance, Alliance of Socialist Democracy, International Alliance of Socialist Democracy, Section of the Alliance, Alliance of the International Brothers, Revolutionary Organization of the International Brothers, Society of the International Revolution, Secret and Universal Association of the International Brothers, Universal Alliance of Social Democracy, International Alliance of Social-Revolutionaries, and International Fraternity (Bakunin, 68014[e], 68016[e], 2009d[e], 68022[e], 69016[e], 70011[e], 71011a[e], 71018[e], 72016[e], 73002[e]).

20 These texts are the following. "Programme et Règlement de l'Alliance Internationale de la Démocratie Socialiste" ["Program and Rules of the International Alliance of Socialist Democracy"] (Bakunin, 68014[e]); a set of five "Statuts Secrets de l'Alliance" ["Secret Statutes of the Alliance"], whose subheadings are: "Organization of the Alliance of the International Brothers," "Secret Organization of the International Alliance of Socialist Democracy," "Program of the International Alliance of Socialist Democracy," "Program and Purpose of the Revolutionary Organization of the International Brothers," and one "Variant" (Bakunin, 68016[e]); "Program of the Society of the International Revolution" (Bakunin, 2009d[e]); "Fraternité Internationale: Programme et Objet" ["International Fraternity: Program and Purpose"] (Bakunin, 68022[e]). Another document, written the following year, is added: "Programme et Règlement de la Section de l'Alliance de la Démocratie Socialiste à Genève de l'A.I.T." ["Program and Rules of the Section of the Alliance for Socialist Democracy in Geneva of the IWA"], April 1869 (Bakunin, 69016[e]).

21 Despite certain variations it can be said, by way of example, that, in general, the public Alliance foresees three distinct instances: central bureau, national bureaus, and local groups (Bakunin, 68014[e]). And that the secret Alliance foresees three levels of militancy: international brothers, national brothers, and members of the public Alliance (Bakunin, 68016[e]).

22 The process of forming the public Alliance, which took place between September and October 1868, was the following: first, an initiating group was formed which elected a central bureau; then, organizational growth was sought with a public meeting. For the names of the initiating group, see Fribourg, 1871, p. 133 (or http://monde-nouveau.net/IMG/pdf/statuts_de_l_alliance.pdf). For the names of the central bureau, see Guillaume, 2009a, p. 173. For some names of the broader group which totaled 85 names, see Guillaume, 2009a, p. 206. Analyzing the three lists, two findings can be made. One, more obvious, is that the fact that Bakunin's name appears on all three lists highlights the relevance of his role in this organization. Another, less obvious, is the role that the members of the Fraternity had in the constitution of the Alliance. Crossing the names of the three lists with the known members of the Fraternity, we find the presence of Bakunin, Mroczkowski, Zagorski, Jukovski, and Perron, thus allowing us to affirm that the Fraternity also had a relevant role in the shaping of the public Alliance. Finally, it is worth mentioning, based on these three lists, some names of members who were part of the Alliance and have not yet been mentioned: Mikhail Elpidin, François Brosset (locksmith), Th. Duval (carpenter), L. Guétat (shoemaker), Jules Gay (journalist), Henry Perret (engraver), Victor Jaclard, Adolphe Catalan, and Marc Héridier.

23 According to the undated document in Guillaume (1985, vol. I, pp. 120, 131), the International Fraternity was declared dissolved shortly after the congress of January 1869. Guillaume states that after that the intimate relations with Mroczkowski, Obolensky, and Jukovski—who were then under Utin's influence—were broken off (Guillaume, 1985, vol. I, pp. 120, 131, 162). However, for lack of sources, it is not known whether another organization was created by the former members and, if so, whether or not Bakunin joined it. It is also not known whether or not former members of the Fraternity joined the secret Alliance. In any case, Bakunin's letter (69001[c]) is central to confirm Nettlau's thesis (1964, p. 45) that, at least until the beginning of 1869, besides the public Alliance, there was also another secret organization, possibly continuing the Fraternity. In this sense, he emphasizes: "But the bourgeois socialists [of the International League of Peace and Freedom] were insensitive to socialist ideas and, after that, Bakunin and some of his friends left the League, entered the [Geneva section of the] International and founded the Alliance of Socialist Democracy, within which, of course, the former secret group of the International Fraternity would continue to exist."

24   In this period, still according to Guillaume (1985, vol. I, pp. 140–41, 181, 218), the facts proceed as follows: In March, the General Council responded to Perron's letter by discussing the question of "the equalizing of classes" and demanding that it be replaced by "the abolition of classes"; the Alliance made the changes and adopted them at the end of April, when it became the Alliance of Socialist Democracy, a section of the International, or, as it will be known, Section of the Alliance, whose main member was Jukovski; in May, this section elects a committee (of which Bakunin is a member) and in June the former central bureau is also dissolved; finally, at the end of July the Council sends a letter admitting this section as part of the IWA. This link would be confirmed two months later, on the occasion of the fourth congress of the International, held in September 1869, when the delegation of the Section of the Alliance was recognized and authorized to participate in the deliberations.

25   James Guillaume and Constant Meuron (former revolutionary founder of the IWA section at Locle) were incorporated into Bakunin's "secret society" in February 1869. That same month, Malon, passing through Lyon, mentioned to Richard, of the Alliance, about the existence of the Fraternity, an act that was considered by Bakunin a betrayal (Guillaume, 1985, vol. I, pp. 130–31).

26   These are the articles, in chronological order and with the bibliographic reference (without Bakunin's name): "La Fraternité" ["The Fraternity"] (69001[e]), "Madame Leo et L'Égalité" ["Madame Leo and L'Égalité"] (69012[e]), "La Double Grève de Genève" ["The Double Strike of Geneva"] (2007d[e]), "En Russie" ["In Russia"] (69018[e]), "Le Mouvement International des Travailleurs" ["The International Workers' Movement"] (69020[e]), "L'Agitation du Parti de la Démocratie Socialiste en Autriche" ["The Agitation of the Party of Socialist Democracy in Austria"] (69025[e]), "Jugement Rendu en Faveur d'Albert Richard" ["Judgment in Favour of Albert Richard"] (69026[e]), "Les Endormeurs" ["The Misleaders/Sleepers"] (2008a[e]), "La Montagne" ["La Montagne"] (69033[e]), "L'Instruction Intégrale" ["Integral Instruction"] (2015[e]), "Le Jugement de M. Coullery" ["The Judgment of Mr. Coullery"] (69035[e]), "La Politique de l'Internationale" ["The Policy of the International"] (2008b[e]) and "De la Coopération" ["Of Cooperation"] (69039[e]). Between the end of June and the beginning of September 1869, Bakunin was the editorial director of L'Égalité as Perron, who held this position, was unavailable (Guillaume, 1985, vol. I, p. 180).

27   This congress was attended by 77 delegates representing 84 sections (Silva, 2017, p. 145).

28   Nevertheless, Moses Hess, a collaborator of Marx's at the congress, published an article titled "Les Collectivistes et les Communistes du Congrès de Basel" ["The Collectivists and the Communists of the Basel Congress"] in the newspaper Le Réveil in early October. It was yet another attack on Bakunin, accusing him of collaborating with reactionary pan-Slavism and damaging the International. Upon learning of the attack, Bakunin wrote a long response to the newspaper in which he challenged Hess's accusations and elaborated reflections on the Jews (Bakunin, 69043[e]). Liebknecht's accusations and Hess's article, both from 1869, further strengthened Bakunin's old suspicion that, because of his proximity, it was probably Marx who was behind the attacks. However, as he explained in a letter to Herzen on 26 October, 1869, Bakunin preferred not to attack him directly, and to focus his efforts on those around him who generally made public the positions Bakunin considered to be Marx's. This, Bakunin explained (69055[c], pp. 1, 4), was for reasons of justice and tactics. On the one hand, one had to recognize the "great services he [Marx] rendered to the socialist cause." On the other, it was necessary to act politically. For Bakunin, attacking the supporters and not Marx was to pursue three fronts: to set the communist adversaries against each other, that is, to "disunite" and "fractionize"; to avoid setting several internationalists who had regard for Marx against himself, for with "an open war against Marx himself, three-fourths of the members of the International would turn against me"; and to play with Marx's vanity, for he, "full of this malicious pleasure [. ...] he will be very happy to see his friends reprimanded."

29   Although Marx and Engels stated in the 1882 preface to the Russian edition of the Communist Manifesto that the first translation into Russian of that text was made by Bakunin in the 1860s, there is no evidence of this. This edition was printed at Kolokol's print shop and published—without indication of authors, translator, place, and date—in Geneva in 1869 (See Marx and Engels, 2003). While still in Geneva, Bakunin met a Russian named Ljubavin, who proposed for him to translate Capital. He agreed immediately. The proposal was in line with his project of working as a translator to solve his immense financial problems and, in addition, it provided conditions for the diffusion among the Russians of a work he admired very much. For example, in 1871 Bakunin (2007e[e], p. 17) wrote that, in this book, Marx presents "such a profound analysis, so enlightened, so scientific, so decisive" by "exposing the

formation of bourgeois capital and the systematic and cruel exploitation that capital continues to exert on the labor of the proletariat," even though it is "difficult to explain and almost inaccessible to most workers" for its relatively abstract style. In a letter to Ogarev dated 16 December, 1869, Bakunin (69064[c], p. 5), in Locarno, states that he had received one-third of the value of the work in advance and that "translation is terribly difficult," moving slowly at the rate of five pages a day (the edition that was with Bakunin had 784).

30 Many nihilists, like Netchaiev himself, knew Bakunin's history and writings and had a certain admiration for him. But although, with some difficulty, that "passion of destruction" of the Bakunin of 1842 could be approximated to nihilism, the positions of the anarchist Bakunin of 1869 did not find parallels with nihilism. Mainly because, from a political point of view, "nihilists did not have that [Bakunin's] belief in the masses," they did not believe in the revolutionary capacity of the masses; revolutionary nihilism had highly elitist traits. It often approached Jacobinism: "the logical politics for the nihilist was less anarchism than Jacobinism" (Leier, 2006, pp. 203–204).

31 Bakunin would denounce both situations in a March 1870 publication entitled "Les Ours de Berne et l'Ours de St-Pétersbourg" ["The Bern Bears and the Saint Petersburg Bear"] (Bakunin, 1998[e]).

32 "Letters to a Frenchman" were written between August and September 1870, but only an excerpt of them was immediately published (La Solidarité [Solidarity], August 1870). The six "Letters to a Frenchman on the Current Crisis" were written in the first half of September 1870 and published together in an anonymous brochure, edited by Guillaume that same month (Bakunin, 2000a; Nettlau, 1977b, pp. 17–18).

33 Musto (2014, p. 45) estimates that in Lyon, at that time, there were around 3,000 workers linked to the IWA.

34 The continuity between this book and the "Letters to a Frenchman on the Current Crisis" is evident in the first excerpt of this book, when Bakunin uses several excerpts from a long and important letter to Palix, dated 29 September, 1870. Later, this letter was elevated to the status of a text entitled "La Situation Politique en France" ["A Situação Política na França"] (Bakunin, 1977b[e]).

35 There is, on the part of different researchers, a minimization of the theme of national and anti-imperialist liberation in Bakunin's life and work from 1864 onwards. Perhaps this is explained—as in the case of the studies of anarchist historical experiences—by the fact that these researchers live, in most cases, in central countries of the North Atlantic axis. ·

36 The second part of The Knuto-Germanic Empire is entitled "Historical Sophisms of the German Communists' School of Doctrine" (Bakunin, 2014e[e]). In addition, there are some excerpts from this book that have been independently published and widely distributed: "The Paris Commune and the Concept of State" (Bakunin, 2008e[e]), "God and the State" (Bakunin, 2011a[e]), and "The Capitalist System" (Bakunin, 2007e[e]). Also in 1871, Bakunin formalized, in the independent article "The Principle of the State," some reflections on the nature of the State (Bakunin, 2008c[e]).

37 In 1871, the Paris Commune incorporated, as Samis argues (2011, pp. 260–61), a whole repertoire of the French working class, which was consolidated in the deliberations that opted for the abolition of the classic division between the three powers, the establishment of a type of federalist "popular power"—emanating from the working classes that were in the neighborhoods and articulated by a federal structure of revocable political delegations—and the organization of executive committees: War, Finance, General Security, Education, Subsistence, Justice, Labor and Exchange, Foreign Affairs, and Public Services. Among the many achievements of the Commune that benefited the working class, the following stand out: The replacement of the regular army by citizen militias, the separation between Church and State, the abolition of religious cults, measures related to work and housing (reductions in working hours, adjustments and salary equalization, end of fines, handover of abandoned workshops and buildings to workers), the granting of credit with reduced interest, the moratorium on debts, the return of items attached, free public schools, secular and polytechnic education, judicial reorganization, the confiscation of property from the ground up, and the role of women and artists.

38 The "Manifesto of the General Council of the International Workers' Association on the Civil War in France" was drafted by Marx between April and May 1871. His well-known book The Civil War in France was later composed of this manifesto and two other texts, produced in July and September 1870.

39 Especially from 1869 onwards, the following countries play a much less relevant role: United States, Netherlands, Denmark, Portugal, Ireland, and Austria-Hungary.

40 As Silva argues (2017, p. 76), there is no accuracy in the statistics on IWA affiliates and members. Even
    with this precaution, Musto (2014, p. 88) speaks of a peak in 1867 of 50,000 Internationalist members
    from England. Also, according to Silva (2017, pp. 109, 115, 129, 145), at the annual congresses from 1866
    to 1869 the English trade unions had, in terms of delegates and trade union associations represented,
    respectively, 1866: 1 delegate and 1 association; 1867: 5 delegates and 3 associations; 1868: 8 delegates
    and 7 associations; 1869: 3 delegates and 3 associations. The issue of representation in this and the other
    countries will be discussed in more detail below.

41 Musto (2014, p. 88) speaks of a peak in 1871 of over 30,000 Internationalist members in France.
    According to Silva (2017, pp. 109, 115, 129, 145), at the annual congresses from 1866 to 1869, the French
    sections had, in terms of delegates and sections represented, respectively, 1866: 14 delegates and 4
    sections; 1867: 19 delegates and 17 sections; 1868: 19 delegates and 22 sections; 1869: 25 delegates and 25
    sections.

42 Thus, Musto's statistics (2014, pp. 88, 47–48) are wrong, indicating a peak in 1870 of more than 10,000
    Internationalist members in Germany, i.e. virtually all SDAP affiliates. He himself signals this when he
    addresses the issue. According to Silva (2017, pp. 109, 115, 129, 145), at the annual congresses from 1866
    to 1869, the German sections had, in terms of delegates and sections represented, respectively, 1866: 3
    delegates and 4 sections; 1867: 6 delegates and 8 sections; 1868: 6 delegates and 6 sections; 1869: 12
    delegates and 13 sections. Berthier's argument is based on Engels himself who, in a letter to Cuno of 7–8
    May, 1872, stated: "In the meantime, the workers' movement in Germany was growing, freeing itself
    from the shackles of Lasalleanism [concerning Ferdinand Lassalle] and, under the leadership of Bebel
    and Liebknecht, joined the International *in principle*. [...] However, the relationship between the German
    workers' party and the International was never clear. This relationship remained purely platonic; there
    was no real affiliation of individuals (with a few exceptions), and sections were prohibited by law" (Marx
    and Engels, 2010e, p. 371). As Berthier (2015c, pp. 74, 88) points out, this argument of the laws and re-
    pression does not fully explain the Germans' lack of interest in the International. The French and Spanish
    experienced similar problems, in some cases much tougher, and did not stop mobilizing their sections.

43 Musto (2014, p. 88) speaks of a peak in 1870 of some 6,000 Internationalist members in Switzerland.
    According to Silva (2017, pp. 109, 115, 129, 145), at the annual congresses from 1866 to 1869, the Swiss
    sections had, in terms of delegates and sections represented, respectively, 1866: 20 delegates and 15
    sections, plus 13 delegates from Swiss labor societies representing 10 sections; 1867: 31 delegates and 22
    sections, plus 6 delegates from Lausanne labor societies representing 1 section; 1868: 8 delegates and 33
    sections; 1869: 24 delegates and 26 sections.

44 Musto (2014, p. 88) speaks of a peak in 1871 of over 30,000 Internationalist members in Belgium.
    According to Silva (2017, pp. 109, 115, 129, 145), at the annual congresses from 1866 to 1869, the Belgian
    sections had, in terms of delegates and sections represented, respectively, 1866: no representation; 1867:
    1 delegate and 1 section; 1868: 56 delegates and 57 sections; 1869: 5 delegates and 5 sections.

45 Musto (2014, p. 88) speaks of a peak in 1873 of 30,000 Internationalist members in Spain; Nettlau
    (1977a, p. 57) speaks of 40,000 workers represented at the Barcelona Congress in June 1870. According
    to Silva (2017, pp. 109, 115, 129, 145), at the annual congresses from 1866 to 1869, the Spanish sections
    had, in terms of delegates and sections represented, respectively, 1866: no representation; 1867: no
    representation; 1868: 1 delegate and 2 sections; 1869: 2 delegates and 3 sections. Berthier (2015c, pp. 11,
    66, 29) works with other numbers. He agrees with the 30,000 Spanish affiliates and speaks of the
    existence of 331 sections in 1873; he does not agree with the estimates of the other countries' sections,
    so he states that "around 1870, it [the Federación Regional Española (FRE)] had the same number of
    members as the rest of the IWA."

46 Musto (2014, p. 88) speaks of a peak in 1873 of some 25,000 Internationalist members in Italy.
    According to Silva (2017, pp. 109, 115, 129, 145), at the annual congresses from 1866 to 1869, the Italian
    sections had, in terms of delegates and sections represented, respectively, 1866: no representation; 1867:
    4 delegates and 4 sections; 1868: 1 delegate and 1 section; 1869: 3 delegates and 3 sections. Pernicone
    (2009, p. 44) states that in mid-1872 there were between 50 and 100 sections in Italy.

47 It is an estimated calculation and, to some extent, of little precision. However, it offers us important
    indications. For each country, I added up the number of delegates present at the congresses and
    divided it by the number of members estimated in the apex period; finally, I pondered the period of
    constitution of the sections.

48 For a more detailed discussion of the documents approved at the Geneva Congress of 1866, as well as
the problem of translations and disputes at that time, cf. Guillaume, 2009a, pp. 58–78. Marx certainly
knew about this problem because he had access to the French translations. But, possibly for tactical
reasons, he preferred not to intervene publicly on the topic.

49 The greatest evidence of this was the developments after the London Conference of 1871 and The
Hague Congress of 1872. After London, all the sections of the International with strong numbers
opposed the General Council. After The Hague, all these sections left the General Council and
founded a new International. The General Council, the "victor" in the votes at The Hague, ended in
isolation, without the backing of any expressive sections, giving a voluntary end to its organizational
project (Guillaume, 1985). But there is other evidence, such as a statement by John Hales, an English
member of the General Council, who, as General Secretary, could not even access the addresses of
correspondents in each country: "Those who did not know the former General Council closely have
no idea how the facts were distorted and how the information, which could have enlightened us, was
intercepted. There has never been a secret conspiracy whose action was more hidden than that of the
former General Council. So, for example, when I was the General Secretary of that council, I never
knew and never managed to get the addresses of the federations on the continent. Another example:
One day, the English federal council received an important letter from the Spanish federal council; but
whoever signed that letter, citizen Anselmo Lorenzo, forgot to put his address in the letter; the English
federal council then asked citizen Engels, who at that time was the Corresponding Secretary of the
General Council for Spain, to give him the address of the Spanish federal council; citizen Engels
formally refused. He then made the same refusal in relation to the Lisbon federal council" (apud.
Guillaume, 1985, vol. 3, p. 25; Berthier, 2015c, p. 29).

50 For a good theoretical approach to the conflict between Bakunin and Marx in the International, cf.
Angaut, 2007b.

51 Among the various accusations in the document, most of which are unfounded, is one relating to the
use of the Bakhmetiev fund. In this regard, Marx (2010a, p. 123) states that "Herzen, even if he was
personally rich, consented to the pseudo-socialist pan-Slavic party of Russia, with which he had good
relations, to pay him 25,000 francs annually for propaganda." Most likely based on Marx's version,
Borkheim wrote, in the pages of Der Volksstaat [The People's State] of April 30, 1870: "The rich Herzen
apparently received 25,000 francs a year from pan-Slavist committees in Russia and abroad for his
subversive activities in Europe. [...] With the death of Herzen, Bakunin wanted to appropriate this
salary of 25,000 francs a year for pan-Slavic subversion" (Eckhardt, 2016, pp. 44, 460–61). The Marxist
Mehring himself (2014, p. 462) considers this accusation absurd.

52 Eckhardt (2016, pp. 41–42) is even harsher than Mehring when commenting on the "Confidential
Communication." He emphasizes that "Marx conducted his campaign against Bakunin, surprisingly, in
a superficial and grossly unilateral manner." In this attack, as in others, Bakunin's positions "were
distorted while Marx's various presumptions and accusations were presented as facts." Moreover,
"apparently Marx was not taking the conflict seriously, and thus did not think it necessary to carry out
a more rigorous and substantial observation of Bakunin's ideas about federalist socialism." This attitude
will continue through the period of conflict between Bakunin and Marx, with the latter always refusing
to engage in a minimally serious debate with the former.

53 As part of this clash with Mazzini, Bakunin wrote his "Lettera Agli Amici d'Italia" ["Letter to (My)
Friends from Italy"] in October 1871 (Bakunin, 71022[e]). Despite Mazzini's criticism of the
communards and Internationalists, the IWA continued to grow significantly. With his death in March
1872, the Internationalists and Bakunin established their hegemony among the workers.

54 As Guillaume puts it (1985, vol. II, pp. 192–94), there were 23 participants in this conference: 13 of them
(more than half) had been appointed by the General Council itself, and they had no delegation from
the sections to represent them. Of the other 10, 6 represented Belgium (one of them was at the same
time a member of the General Council), 2 represented Switzerland (its minority sector, headed by
Utin, since the majority sector of the Jurassians was not invited), one represented Spain (the only one
that had an imperative mandate from the sections, certainly the most numerically representative at
that time) and one was unknown and without a mandate.

55 As I argued in a debate about Marx's political concepts (Corrêa, 2016b), I consider that there is no
evidence of a supposed "anti-statist Marx" after the Paris Commune. The positions taken by Marx in
1871 and 1872, as well as his subsequent relationships and alliances, highlight concepts similar to those

of the 1848 *Communist Manifesto*. The fundamental strategy, when it comes to the constitution of the class into party and the conquest of political power, is based, in most cases, on the dispute of elections and the conquest of the State. For a more in-depth elaboration of this thesis, cf. Corrêa, 2016a, Berthier, 2015c.

56   In 1872, Richard and Blanc abandoned internationalist collectivism and embraced Bonapartism. In "Fictitious Splits," Bakunin is accused for his link with both, and also with Bastelica, considered an accomplice of the other French. However, Bakunin's link with the three, which occurred between 1870 and 1871, was before Richard and Blanc's move to Bonapartism. As Guillaume (1985, vol. II, p. 23) states, "in 1870 and 1871 the three had the full confidence of the entire International; on 8 March, 1870, the General Council of London kept Albert Richard in his functions as correspondent secretary for Lyon, and in 1871, with Marx's full consent, Bastelica became a member of the General Council itself."

57   Among the documents produced on this occasion are the following, in chronological order and with the bibliographic reference (without Bakunin's name). At the end of 1871, "Letter to the Bologna Internationals" (2014g[e]), "Personal Relations with Marx" (2014h[e]), two letters to the editorial staff of "du *Gazzettino Rosa*" [the *Red Gazzette*] (71027[e], 72001[e]), "L'Italie et le Conseil Général de l'Association Internationale des Travailleurs" ["Italy and the General Council of the International Workers' Association"] (71028[e]). In early 1872, a long letter of 171 pages, "Aux Compagnons de la Fédération des Sections Internationales du Jura"] ["To the Companions of the Federation of International Sections of the Jura"] (72005[e]) and "Germany and State Communism" (2014j[e]). There are also two letters that have important contributions about the Bakuninian conception of anarchist cadre organization: "To Thomas Gonzales Morago" (2016a[c]), May 1872, and "To the Brothers of the Alliance in Spain" (2014b[c]).

58   On that occassion Bakunin wrote the program of this section: "Program of the Slavic Section of Zurich" (Bakunin, 2003b[e]).

59   The Italian sections—which were articulated in the Italian Federation, founded in August 1872, and had tens of thousands of members—were not represented in this congress. In its founding conference, this federation decided that it would not participate in the next congress as a form of protest for the maneuvers of the London Conference. Instead, it proposed that the anti-authoritarian (federalist) sections hold a separate congress in Switzerland, separating themselves from the centralists. Among others, the Internationalists, Celso Ceretti, and Andrea Costa maintained a close relationship with Bakunin. At The Hague Congress, which was held at a location chosen to make it difficult for federalist delegations (especially from Italy, Spain, and Switzerland) to attend, of the 65 "delegates" who were recognized as having participated (67 had presented themselves), 22 were from the General Council. Of these 65 "delegates," 40 were aligned with the centralists and 25 with the federalists. A more detailed analysis of the composition of the "delegations" of this congress reveals the bureaucratic maneuvering of the centralists. The centralist sections of the United States (of the Tenth Ward Hotel) sent two delegates; Sorge, one of them, received from these sections several blank mandates, handing them over to Marx, who remained with one and distributed others to his allies. The non-existent German sections (in Germany there were only a few individual affiliations) were "represented" by nine centralists. Moreover, even if they existed, these sections could not participate because they did not pay their dues. The French sections, clandestine because of the repression after the Paris Commune, could not confirm the delegates. Serralier, secretary of the General Council for France and a centralist, arrived at the congress with different mandates which, without any possibility of confirmation, were distributed to his supporters. The "Ferré Section", represented by the centralist Ranvier—which, according to him, had 3,000 members—actually had three members. The Spanish Federation, with tens of thousands of members and federalist, was represented, after overcoming the obstacles to its participation, by four delegates; Lafargue, the centralist "delegate," represented a Madrid "section" of nine members, and an alleged Lisbon "section." The Belgian sections, also with tens of thousands of members, sent seven delegates; the Dutch sections, much smaller but with some expression, were represented by four delegates; the Belgian and Dutch were federalists. The Swiss sections, also with some expression, were represented by three centralists and two federalists (Guillaume, 1985, vol. II, pp. 312, 321–33).

60   With the arrest of Netchaiev in October 1872, his story was widely exposed in the courts and by the press. Lafargue, Engels, and Marx (1978), taking advantage of this information, attributed everything that was done and produced by Netchaiev to Bakunin, as stated in the "conclusive" document on the matter, published in 1873.

61 Bakunin (71023[e], pp. 48–49) had already emphasized that "the unity, the strength, the life, the thought of the International are at the bottom, not the top; they are in the autonomous sections of all countries, freely federated from below and from the circumference to the center." And its existence "is only possible on condition that its General Council—as well as national, regional and local committees—does not exercise any power and does not constitute a government."

62 They are: "Lettre au Journal *La Liberté* de Bruxelles" ["Letter to the Journal *La Liberté* de Bruxelles"] (Bakunin, 2001b[e]), a letter that was never sent, and "Écrit Contre Marx" ["Written Against Marx"] (Bakunin, 2001a[e]), which is an excerpt that should complement *The Knuto-Germanic Empire*.

63 Bakunin's life was always marked by his enormous dimensions (tall and fat) and by the immense amount of food he ate at meals. In times of prison, for example, he even had to ask for permission to receive twice the ration of an ordinary inmate. He drank tea permanently and smoked around 60 cigarettes a day (Carr, 1961, pp. 215, 475; Lehning, 1999, p. 244).

64 `There is even a second appendix entitled "Программа славянской секции в Цюрихе" ["Zurich Slav Section Program"] of 1872 (Bakunin, 2003b[e]). In 1873 Bakunin also published, in Russian, "Куда идти и делать?" ["Where to Go and What to Do?"] (Bakunin, 2008f[e]).

65 Between late October and early November 1873, Engels also published an attack on Bakunin's Spanish disciples in *Der Volksstaat*. It is a collection of articles, which would soon be published as a booklet, *The Bakuninists in Action* (Engels, 1998).

66 Date of death according to the Gregorian calendar; according to the Julian calendar (in effect in Russia at that time), his date of death is 19 June.

67 Hegel's influence is rather residual, although it can sometimes be noticed.

68 On different occasions, Bakunin called his frame of reference or method *scientific materialism* (Bakunin, 68002[e], p. 1; Bakunin, 68009[e], p. 1; Bakunin, 1973b[e], p. 179; Bakunin, 2014[e], p. 256; Bakunin, 2014f[e], p. 403). In 1868, for example, he wrote: "I am happy to see the flag of *anti-theologism* bravely raised in France. A spirit wrapped in theological, metaphysical fictions, and bent before any authority, distinct from *rational and experimental science*, can only produce the political and social slavery of a nation. Regardless of what your official moral representatives and your spiritualist democrats say, *only scientific and humanitarian materialism is capable of founding freedom, justice, and therefore also morality*, in truly large and unbreakable branches" (Bakunin, 68002[e], p.1, emphasis added).

69 Despite the relevant contributions of Ferreira (2013, p. 4), Silva [Selmo] (2016, p. 84), and Brito (2014, p. 4) to Bakunin's studies, I disagree with them that in his anarchist period, the Russian revolutionary adopted Proudhon's serial dialectics. This is a hypothesis that I also considered plausible for some time—see my interview with Berthier (2014b, p. 9)—but by the end of this research, I consider it very likely that it will have to be discarded. Although the influence of the Frenchman has been decisive in many areas, this does not seem to be the case when it comes to dialectics. Bakunin's dialectics of this period is tributary, and to a certain extent continuous, to the negative dialectics that Bakunin himself elaborated in 1842, and which at maturity adjusted to his scientific-naturalist materialism. As for Proudhon, with the exception of the terminological adjustment of the terms in contradiction—when reaction-revolution/freedom are called authority-freedom (so that one can speak of a dialectic between authority and freedom for the two authors, even if they are different)—I do not believe there is any more evidence of this influence. And I say this based on two arguments, one of historical order and the other of logical order. Historically, I haven't found any evidence that Bakunin was interested in Proudhonian serial dialectics, both in Bakunin's work and in that of historians. On the contrary, different serious authors claim that Bakunin *is not* a tributary of Proudhonian serial dialectics: Berthier, 2014b, p. 9; McLaughlin, 2002, pp. 72–73, 102; Saltman, 1983, p. 22; Angaut, 2005, pp. 420–28. Logically, which is how the aforementioned authors proceed, in seeking similarities between Bakunin's and Proudhon's philosophical-political thinking, I also encountered two problems. The first, which explains why Bakunin refers to Proudhon as an idealist, is the fact that he relies on a split between nature and society, inappropriate in Bakunin's eyes. Second, when Proudhon states that "reconciliation is revolution" (Proudhon, 1969, p. 8) or when he proposes the "balance of authority by freedom and vice versa" (Proudhon, 2001, p. 47) it does not seem that they are holding the same positions. Bakunin, based on his negative dialectics, was completely opposed to any kind of reconciliation and proposed the destruction of authority for the construction of freedom.

70   When Bakunin refers to his doctrinal concept of this period, which encompasses both his
     philosophical and political-strategic concepts, he has a preference for the term *revolutionary socialism*,
     thus claiming to be *revolutionary socialist* (cf., for example: Bakunin, 2014d[e], pp. 169, 179, 265;
     Bakunin, 2003a[e], pp. 53, 218, 221). In some cases, Bakunin claims to be a *collectivist* or a *revolutionary
     collectivist*, giving to "collectivism" the meaning of opposition to communism, of asserting collective
     property and of adjective for socialism (as well as *materialism* and its synonyms and derivatives) (cf.,
     for example: Bakunin, 68011[e]; Bakunin, 2016c[e], p. 69; Bakunin, 2008e[e], p. 116). Finally, as
     Berthier (2014a) points out, the use of the term *anarchy* and its derivatives in these years is ambiguous;
     Bakunin permanently uses "anarchy" in the vulgar sense of chaos and disorder, but from 1870 onwards
     he also begins to confer on it the meaning of anti-statism. He claims to be *anarchist* a few times and
     the term *anarchism* appears only once in the whole work. However, for a discussion that extrapolates
     the terminological question and takes history as a basis for understanding Bakunin's passage to
     anarchism, see Chapter 10.3.2.

71   Leval (2007, p. 19) affirmed that "the true founder of revolutionary syndicalism was Bakunin."
     Although this position exaggerates the role of this "great man" and revolutionary syndicalism was a
     mass movement built by the very workers who were part of it, there is no doubt that Bakunin's
     discussion about the International contains, in political-strategic terms, much of what would be called
     revolutionary syndicalism years later. Bakunin's organizational theory allows for a proper
     understanding of the complex relationship between anarchism and revolutionary syndicalism, so
     poorly explained by other authors. As I have maintained, "like anarco-syndicalism, revolutionary
     syndicalism constitutes an anarchist strategy and cannot be, by means of a rigorous historical study,
     detached from anarchism" (Corrêa, 2015, p. 109). I think the key to understanding anarchism,
     particularly during the twentieth century, is to understand how and why anarchists, even though they
     had clear political positions that were markedly opposed to religion, proposed a model of mass
     organization, revolutionary syndicalism—in the midst of which, in the vast majority of cases, they
     were the hegemonic force—that was neither specifically anarchist nor anti-religious. The answer lies in
     the justifications presented by Bakunin.

72   Angaut (2005, pp. 463–66) considers that among the changes that mark Bakuninian thought in the
     period after 1864 is his conception of federalism. The political centrality of the first period would
     progressively give way to the centrality of the economy, and thus "economic federalism would be
     destined to supplant political federalism."

73   In an April 1869 article, reproduced in the works of Bakunin—although it is not known for certain
     whether the authorship was his or Charles Perron's, another Alliancist who had the same positions on
     strikes (cf. Bakunin, 1911[e], p. 48)—there is an excerpt that gives an idea of the relevance of the strikes
     in that context: "The news concerning the European workers' movement can be summed up in one
     word: strikes. In Belgium, strikes by printers in various cities, strikes by spinners in Ghent, strikes by
     carpenters in Bruges; in England, imminent strikes by manufacturing districts; in Prussia, strikes by
     zinc miners; in Paris, strikes by plasterers and painters; in Switzerland, strikes in Basel and Geneva"
     (Bakunin, 1911, p. 50). There is no doubt that they contributed directly to Bakunin's thought and action.

74   It should be taken into account that Bakunin's anarchist positions were established before he accepted
     and used the terms "anarchy" and its derivatives ("anarchism," "anarchist," etc.). Moreover, it should be
     noted that this is not about a complete and abrupt break in the passage from 1867 to 1868. This occurs
     gradually and differently, depending on the area of thought being analyzed. If in philosophical terms a
     coherence can be observed throughout the revolutionary socialist period (1864–76), in analytical and
     strategic terms things happen differently. There are some years of maturation and transition that
     analytically go from 1864–66 and strategically from 1864–67. Therefore, the coherence of this revolutionary
     socialist period varies: in philosophical terms, it goes from 1864–76; in analytical terms, from 1867–76;
     and in strategic terms, from 1868–76—this explains the periodization of chapters 11, 12, and 13.

CHAPTER 11

SCIENTIFIC-NATURALIST MATERIALISM, SCIENCE, AND FREEDOM (1864–76)

This chapter begins the exposition of Bakunin's political theory in his *revolutionary socialist period*, which runs from 1864 to 1876, and is divided into five parts: 1) Nature-matter and Science; 2) Animality and Humanity; 3) Genesis of Religion: Divine Authority and Human Authority; 4) Different Forms of Idealism; 5) Freedom, Society, and the Individual.[1]

11.1 NATURE-MATTER AND SCIENCE

Bakuninian scientific-naturalist materialism is a theoretical-philosophical frame of reference that, by bringing together philosophy, natural sciences, and social sciences,[2] proposes to provide an adequate understanding of reality. It has four foundations: the concept of nature-matter, the self-fulfilling theory of nature-matter, the concept of science, and the realistic method.

Roughly, nature-matter embraces the totality of reality and, therefore, breaks with the separation between nature-society, matter-spirit, and body-soul. According to the self-fulfilling theory of nature-matter, nature-matter in and of itself creates and recreates the universe and the worlds, in a dialectic movement that goes from the bottom up, from the simple to the complex. Humanity is conceived as part of nature-matter and, historically, as the development of animality, reason, and labour being the most important aspects of this passage—so that man possesses only quantitative differences in relation to non-human animals and other natural and material elements. Rational and positive science is an indispensable tool for understanding the general and particular laws of nature-matter. It must be carried out as a unity in diversity and through the realistic method, which proceeds analytically according to the development of life itself, going from the simple to the complex, from the bottom up, and having in conflicts and struggles its primary relationships. In short, it is an experimental, comprehensive, and critical method that aims to reconcile the particular and the general, history and theory.

* * *

In order to understand scientific-naturalist materialism in a deeper way, it is essential to define the concepts of matter, nature, science, and their implications.

At this point, the first two will be addressed, and it must be said that one and the other, *matter* and *nature*, have the same meaning and are equivalent to the broad definition of *reality*. "Matter is the same as nature (consequently, materialism and naturalism are synonyms)" (McLaughlin, 2002, p. 106). *Nature and matter are the totality of reality (effective reality or effectiveness, in Hegelian terms), the totality of the real world; they embrace not only the sum of all that really exists, but also its relations and transformations.* This "totality of the real world" that is, nature, is what we "abstractly call matter" (Bakunin, 2014e[e], pp. 286–87). In view of this conceptual equivalence, a hybrid concept will be used from now on for didactic purposes: *nature-matter*.[3]

The totality of nature-matter involves

> the whole scale of real beings, known and unknown, from the simplest organic bodies to the constitution and functioning of the brain of the greatest genius: the most beautiful feelings, the greatest thoughts, heroic deeds, acts of devotion, both duties and rights, both sacrifice and selfishness, everything, even transcendental and mystical aberrations [...] in the same way as the manifestations of organic life, properties and chemical actions, electricity, light, heat, the natural attraction of bodies, constitute to our eyes so many evolutions, no doubt different, but no less closely united, of that totality of real beings which we call matter [or nature].[4] (Bakunin, 1973a[e], p. 7)

That is, it encompasses

> everything that exists, the beings that constitute the indefinite whole of the universe, all things existing in the world, whatever their particular nature, both from the point of view of quality and quantity, the most different and the most similar, large or small, near or immensely distant, necessarily and unconsciously exerts, either through immediate and direct transmission, or through indirect transmission, a perpetual action and reaction; and all this infinite quantity of particular actions and reactions, when combined into a general and unique movement, produces and constitutes what we call *life, solidarity, and universal causality*, nature [or matter].[5] (Bakunin, 2014f[e], pp. 339–40)

Thus, nature-matter encompasses everything that exists in life, be it more or less complex, more or less known; the non-organic and organic world; everything that belongs to the mineral, vegetable, animal, human kingdom. It encompasses not only facts, but also ideas, not only objective elements, but also subjective—and, in addition, its transformations, its productions, and incessant reproductions.

This dynamic of action-reaction causes nature-matter to always develop into a "universal, natural, necessary and real combination," which is "in no way predetermined or preconceived, nor foreseen, *of this infinity of particular actions and reactions that all things actually in existence incessantly exert upon each other.*" It is a multicausal relationship between the parts and the whole that produces and reproduces the facts, processes, and procedures of life and the worlds: "each point acting on the whole (here is the universe produced), and the whole acting on each part (here is the universe producer or creator)." That is, it is nature-matter that *creates the worlds.*" The universe in general and our world in particular are a natural-material creation, which implied the foundation of a natural-material order. It was this movement "that determined the mechanical, physical, chemical, geological and geographical configuration of our Earth," a system of the world that *not only created and creates, but "continues to create, still, in the human world, society with all its past, present and future developments"* (Bakunin, 2014f[e], p. 340, emphasis added).[6]

Two aspects stand out here. First, that society is part of nature, and therefore there is no separation between nature-matter/society or between natural-material/human (Bakunin, 1973a[e], p. 9). Breaking with the anthropocentric philosophical traditions that support this separation, it is argued that "human society, considered in the full extent and breadth of its historical development, is [...] natural", so that human and social history is part of a broader natural-material development and subject to natural and socio-historical laws (Bakunin, 2014f[e], p. 346) Second, that nature-matter has created all that has existed, exists, and will support the creation of all that will exist. That is why, in broad terms, it must be understood as something that also involves the totality of potentialities, of what it can become. This is its sense of *universal causality*, and there is no chance, in view of this, of conceiving of any causality outside of nature. As such, nature-matter is the field of the possible, necessarily logical. To be natural-material consequently means to be logical, and that which is logical was, is being, or will be realized in nature-matter.

This opposition between the concrete and the possible supports a dialectical movement which, in Hegelian terms, can express itself as a contradiction between *Realität* (reality) and *Wirklichkeit* (effective reality or effectiveness). In the Bakuninian lexicon, it is explained as a contradiction between the *natural world* (existing reality, that which has been realized) and *nature* (logical totality, totality of possibilities, that which can also be realized). The relationship between the two poles of this contradiction (natural world and nature) is made by the *principle of immanent causality and matter.*

There is, therefore, a dialectic proper to nature-matter, which is permanently effective by itself, and not in function of something that is extrinsic, external. So that nature-matter must be considered as a living element and of its own dynamics, with inherent actions and movements, produced and executed by a set of properties and resulting from this contradiction between the natural world and nature (McLaughlin, 2002, pp. 106–107).

More or less regular natural-material facts and processes—that is, life itself—predate thought, human reason, and impose themselves on the human mind as a rational necessity. An important product of this development is science, which emerged at a certain moment in history and turned to nature itself, seeking to explain it rationally. This brings us to the third fundamental concept that has been mentioned, *science*.

In a rational and positive key,[7] *science "is nothing but the knowledge and understanding of the world by the human spirit," that is, it is the penetration of nature-matter by human knowledge, in order to reconstruct, through thought, the universe in its diversity.* Through it, truth is sought, in terms of the "just appreciation of things and facts, of their development or of the natural logic that manifests itself in them," of the "strictest possible conformity of the movement of thought with that of the real world." Thus science constitutes rational knowledge, based on natural and material evidence, whose object is the totality of known and unknown laws of nature-matter, and which intends to get as close as possible to the truth. It is only through science that such an understanding can be realized (Bakunin, 2014f[e], pp. 363, 396, emphasis added).

These natural and material laws are defined by the "constant reproduction *of the same facts by the same procedures*," that is, they are nothing more than "order in the infinite diversity of phenomena and facts." They are not laws inherent to nature-matter itself—for the latter, strictly speaking, has no laws—but which, elaborated by the human mind, try to reproduce in the most faithful way possible the aforementioned facts, processes, or procedures of nature-matter. Such laws are divided into two types: general and particular. General laws reflect facts and processes essential to all that is natural or material, for they are inherent in nature-matter— as in the case of the laws of physics and chemistry. The "particular laws [...] are proper only to certain particular orders of phenomena, facts and things, [... and] form among themselves systems or groups apart"—as in the case of the geological, physiological laws and the "social and ideal development of the most perfect animal on Earth, man" (Bakunin, 2014f[e], pp. 341–42; cf., also: McLaughlin, 2002, p. 109).

Now, even though natural laws are an object of immense diversity, our world is one; it is a *unitary world*. So too is human reason, independent of its countless historical representatives. It is a *unitary reason* because, regardless of conditions, human thought always develops according to certain natural and material laws. So this "immense diversity [...] constitutes the great unity of the human race." It is *unity in diversity*, which must be sought by science itself: "The great scientific unity is concrete: it is unity in infinite diversity" (Bakunin, 2014f[e], p. 396).

As can be seen, this concept of science differs from those that rely on the notion that only one or a few objects can or should be known, from those that understand science as something limited by historical or cultural factors, and also from those that conceive science as something individual. Rational and positive science aspires to universality, even if it is not fully effective. It is intended to be a *universal science*, and it is supposed to be a *trans-historical science*, without limitation of historical or cultural particularities (McLaughlin, 2002, p. 114). Finally, a *social-collective science* is proposed, since "the basis of science is the collective experience, not only of all contemporary men, but also of all past generations." For this reason, science can only improve itself adequately by accumulating what has been produced socially and collectively as a society (Bakunin, 2014f[e], p. 393).

The "scientific method" is the "*realistic method* par excellence", which breaks with religious and abstract presuppositions, and proceeds according to the logic of materialism-naturalism and the meaning of life itself: from the bottom up, from the simple to the complex, "from the details to the whole, and from the verification, from the study of facts, to their understanding, to ideas." It is then led, at least initially, by induction, from facts to ideas, from life to the understanding of life (Bakunin, 2014f[e], p. 392, emphasis added). This method has two procedures as a basis: *observation* and *understanding*. With the first, the scientist can find the reality of a phenomenon or a fact. With the second, he can discover and identify, in an empirical way, the properties, direct and indirect relationships between existing things. Thus, the scientist must distinguish, in these phenomena and facts, all that "which is accidental and variable, from that which is reproduced always and everywhere in an invariable manner." The law of a phenomenon or fact is exactly "the invariable procedure by which a natural phenomenon is constantly reproduced, whether externally or internally; the invariable succession of facts which constitute it." Although it is necessary to bear in mind that "this constancy and this repetition are not [...] absolute" (Bakunin, 2014f[e], p. 342).

The ideas resulting from these inductive procedures—that more generalized understanding of life, or what could be called a *theoretical "synthesis,"* which intends to explain reality rationally and more generally—should be only the "faithful exposition of the relations of coordination, succession and action or mutual causality that really exist between things and real phenomena." In other words, "its logic is not [and should not be] anything but the logic of things" (Bakunin, 2014f[e], p. 392, emphasis added). Moreover, this theoretical synthesis can never, as in the cases of theology and metaphysics, be "aristocratically" or "authoritatively" organized "from the top down, through [only] deduction and synthesis," ending up by "forcing nature to accept it." On the contrary, it must always be "the summary or general expression of a number of facts demonstrated by experience." At the same time, it must always be considered a hypothesis and can and should be, through deduction, tested and submitted to the reality of natural and material facts. This return movement, which goes from ideas to facts, must test ideas and submit them to facts. Not being "confirmed by the most severe experimental or critical analysis," the theoretical summaries should be updated, modified, or even discarded (Bakunin, 1988a[e], p. 44).

In contact with the studies produced by other researchers or thinkers, the realistic scientist has certain duties. First of all, they must take a *critical approach*, since science "admits no testimony uncritically." In the same way, they must: *know scientists and their methods*, prioritizing those of "realistic intelligence, developed and properly prepared by science," those who are serious, zealous and indeed concerned with the "reality of things"; *know the character and motivations of scientists*, making sure that they are (or were) honest men, "who hated lies, who sought the truth with good faith, with zeal"; *to always be open to criticism from others and to confirmation or refutation,* accepting that "nothing is as unfriendly to science as faith" and that "mutual criticism" must be permanent because it is the "severe and incorruptible guardian of the truth" (Bakunin, 2014f[e], pp. 393–95).

In this way, rational and positive science, through the realistic method, tries to contribute scientifically, so that the general and particular laws of nature-matter become known. This science, which is supposed to be both universal, trans-historical, and social-collective, relies on the "inductive method" and the "deductive method." It seeks, through observation, understanding and criticism, to base "its reasoning on experience" and to verify "incessantly its hypotheses through the most rigorous observation and analysis of facts" (Bakunin, 2016a[e], p. 92). Thanks to this, it differs from those irrational or abstract expressions of human thought, and also from that harder empiricism, seeking a science capable of reconciling the particular and the general, always prioritizing natural and material facts.

Now, even if one recognizes the enormous relevance of science, one cannot believe that it has any condition to replace life: "Science understands the thought of reality, not reality itself; the thought of life, not life." This is precisely its limit, which is "impassable [...] because it is based on the very nature of human thought, which is the only organ of science." However rigorous it may be, science will never be able to embrace the whole of life. It has a duty to approach this reality as closely as possible, but it will never be able to embrace it in its totality, much less replace this very totality of reality. For this reason, it must be stressed that "science is [and must be] the compass of life, but it is not life" (Bakunin, 2014e[e], p. 292). And, moreover, it cannot be believed that, because of its relevance, science (through scientists) should govern life—a subject that will be discussed below.

It is possible to talk about a *concept of nature-matter* and a *self-fulfilling theory of nature-matter* thanks to the contributions of the philosophy of science, the philosophy of history and science itself. This concept and this theory allow us to understand the development of nature-matter (of the universe, of the world) by means of an "interactive material causality, developing or emerging," that is, a dialectic causality that emerges from nature-matter itself and allows it to interact and develop (McLaughlin, 2002, p. 107). In short, nature-matter, which is at the same time the origin and object of humanity and of science, is produced and effective in a permanent manner, by a dynamic that is inherent to it. And since there is a creation and a natural-material order, the hypothesis of a personal creation, divine or human, should be discarded.

If, in the universe, order is natural and possible, it is only because this universe is not governed according to any system imagined beforehand and imposed by a supreme will. The theological hypothesis of a divine law leads to an evident absurdity and denial not only of every order, but of nature itself. Natural laws are only real because they are inherent in nature, that is, they are not fixed by any authority. These laws are simple manifestations, or else continuous modalities of the development of things and of the combinations of these very varied, passing, but real facts. The whole constitutes what we call "nature" [or matter]. Human intelligence and its science have observed these facts, have controlled them experimentally, then have gathered them into a system and called them laws. But nature itself knows absolutely no laws. It acts unconsciously, representing for itself the infinite variety of phenomena, appearing and repeating itself in a fatal manner. This is why, thanks to this inevitability of action, the universal order can and does exist. (Bakunin, 2008e[e], p. 132, emphasis added)

Thus natural and material creation and order exclude the possibility of any form of theologism: they deny the idea of God, theology, metaphysics, and even modern idealism, which start from the same point. In the light of the definitions and criteria of science and the realistic method, it is necessary to recognize that theologism, even if it intends to explain the world, does not do so in a satisfactory way.[8] It avoids experience, observation, understanding, criticism, and proceeds unilaterally, from top to bottom, from ideas to facts, producing only abstractions, without any support in the natural and material world. Natural laws, for example, have not been verified by it, but by human reason, by science, in a process of knowledge and explanation of reality much more rigorous than that.

And this was and is possible because the natural-material world can be known. For the subject is also part of this world and does not remain in relation to the object other than a quantitative difference, since humanity is part of nature. That is, the differences between the non-organic world and the organic world, between animality and humanity, between facts and ideas, are not qualitative but quantitative—all these are distinct elements of nature-matter (McLaughlin, 2002, p. 116).

Natural and material development is, in general, static or positive. However, it contains within itself the germ of change, which explains that from time to time there is an interruption of this development by transformations, negations. As part of nature-matter, the organic world proceeds similarly. Such is the logic of scientific-naturalist materialism, which rests on the notion that

the organic world is simply the direct development of the non-organic world, complemented by a new ingredient: organic matter. Organic matter is simply the product of new causal relationships operating at the level and under the conditions of non-organic matter. It is the denial and final determination of (mere) non-organic matter and produces everything that constitutes life, animal and others. The human—in all its forms (religious, political, economic, intellectual and moral)—is, in a similar way, the direct development of animality, complemented by a new and essential ingredient: reason. Reason is simply the product of new causal relationships operating at the level and under the conditions of organic matter, in particular the brain. Humanity is, therefore, the denial and final determination of the (mere) animal in man (*qua*, "spiritual" creature). (McLaughlin, 2002, p. 120)

This process is based on negation because "every development necessarily implies a negation, the negation of the base or the starting point." This is how the organic world develops, as negation of the non-organic world; animal and human life is the result of this negation. Consequently, "humanity is [...] essentially the rational and progressive negation of animality in men," a negation which is "as rational as it is natural, and which is only rational because it is natural, at the same time historical and logical, fatal, as are the developments and achievements of all the natural laws in the world" (Bakunin, 2014e[e], p. 257).

Therefore, men are nothing more than an evolution of non-human animals, which resulted from the negation of this pre-human condition. That is, "the whole history of man is nothing other than his progressive detachment from pure animality through the creation of its humanity" (Bakunin, 1988a[e], p. 55).[9]

11.2 ANIMALITY AND HUMANITY

According to Darwin's theory of evolution, the "new varieties and species" of "organic life" arise when alleged anomalies combine in different ways and fix themselves, establishing "new usual procedures, new ways of reproducing and being in nature." Thus, "after having started with a simple unorganized cell and having made it go through all the transformations of the plant organization, initially, and animal, it later became a man" (Bakunin, 1988a[e], pp. 59–60).

This is precisely what happened with human evolution. "Our first ancestors, our Adams and our Eves, were, if not gorillas, at least cousins very close to the gorilla, omnivorous, intelligent and ferocious animals." Such animals, in function of a natural evolutionary development, began at a certain moment to count on two faculties, that of thinking-speaking and that of revolting, which allowed them to become men. Through the "progressive action [of these faculties] in history" it was possible to form the "negative power in the positive development of human animality, and consequently everything that constitutes humanity in men was created" (Bakunin, 2014e[e], p. 257; Bakunin, 2014f[e], p. 351).

By developing their *reason* (their thinking, their faculty of abstraction, their capacity of speech) and revolting against their animal condition (negating it), the superior primates managed after a long effort to become men. A characteristic common to all men, *reason is what explains the passage from animality to humanity; it is what constitutes human nature itself.*[10] "As long as a man thinks [reason, has the capacity for abstraction], whatever his surroundings, his nature, his race, his social position and the degree of his intellectual and moral development, and even when he rambles or is unreasoning," his reason "always develops according to the same laws." And in this "is precisely what, in the immense diversity of ages, climates, races, nations, social positions and individual natures, constitutes the *great unity of the human race*" (Bakunin, 2014f[e], p. 396).

Reason can be defined as the human capacity to "combine the representations of both exterior and interior objects given to us by our senses" and to "form groups from them, then compare and combine these different groups again," going beyond the senses and arriving at rational human notions, "fixed by our memory" and transmitted from generation to generation. Through reason, men are able not only to understand the world—and therefore it is the foundation of science—but also to take advantage of certain objects and movements against others, following the social ideal that has been formed in them, and thus contribute to social change.

In this way, they extrapolate the instinctive and mechanical character of the animal will and, taking advantage of their intelligence, can "compare, criticize and order their own needs." Such are, precisely, the bases of the *rational will*, that tendency which every human being has to rationally seek to satisfy their needs, a will which can even be perfected by reason itself. However, this notion of will cannot be confused with that of free will if it is defined as "the spontaneous determination of man's individual will by itself, independent of any influence, both natural and social." In fact, free will, thus conceived, simply does not exist, for the independence of the human being, both in relation to nature-matter and in relation to society, is extremely limited.

That is, human will, even if rational, is always conditioned naturally and socially. "Every human individual" from the moment they are born "is entirely the product of historical development, that is, physiological and social." Throughout one's life, they— and, therefore, human action itself—will be determined by natural laws, by genetics, and by the social laws and structure of society (social structure) of which they are a part. Even so, there is no absolute determinism so that, even if conditioned and limited, human will and action have considerable transforming potential—it is they that allow man to arrive at revolt and the concrete denial of reality, the foundations of historical social change (Bakunin, 1988a[e], pp. 60–62, 68–69, 117; cf., also: Leval, 1976, pp. 24–40).

Thus, it is possible to affirm that "the principle of reason is concretely incorporated or realized in *science*," and that through science one can know the world. Added to will, reason is practically realized in the revolt for the transformation of the world: "The principle of revolt, the practical realization of reason, is concretely incorporated or realized in the (present) *freedom*." Reason is realized in labour, which is the basis of reason, will and revolt: "The principle of human animality, which is the fundamental principle that sustains all others (as naturalism demands), is [...] concretely incorporated or realized in the 'social and private economy'" (McLaughlin, 2002, p. 128).

But in order to understand these statements accurately, as well as the previous assertion—that reason is human nature—it is crucial to examine in greater detail the relationship between reason, on the one hand, and nature-matter, freedom, and labour, on the other.

First of all, it should be noted that reason (thought, the faculty of abstraction) is a material phenomenon.

> We call *material* all that which is, all that which is produced in the real world, both in man and outside him, and we employ the name *ideal* exclusively to the products of the cerebral action of man; but since our brain is an entirely material organization and, consequently, all its functioning is as material as the action of all the other things brought together, it follows that *what we call matter or the material world does not in any way exclude, but on the contrary, unfailingly embraces the ideal.* (Bakunin, 1973a[e], p. 7, emphasis added)

Such that the passage from animality to humanity is a natural and material development, since ideas, developed in relation to life, are nothing more than cerebral products.

Secondly, it is necessary to observe that, through reason, "man reaches the consciousness of his freedom in this natural environment of which he is the product." His freedom, distinct from what "Rousseau and his disciples" believed, is not found at the starting point, "at the beginning of history," but at the point of arrival, constituting the corollary or objective of human development. This means that such development is nothing more than a constant negation of slavery and affirmation of freedom.

In animality there was no freedom, only slavery—that pre-human man was completely subjugated to natural life as much as other animals. His situation was one of permanent suffering and threat: "hunger, privations of all kinds, pain, the influence of climates, seasons and, in general, the thousand conditions of animal life that keep human beings in almost absolute dependence on their surroundings." Moreover, there were "the permanent dangers" like that "perpetual fear which is the foundation of any animal existence and which dominates the natural and wild individual to the point that he finds nothing in himself that can resist and combat it." In the face of this, "none of the elements of the most absolute slavery are lacking [to this man]." So animality is absolute slavery, the complete lack of freedom. It was only when this man, slowly and "by the consecutive use of his reason" acquiring "awareness of himself" and of the "laws that govern the outside world," that he began to become aware of his freedom and to realize it.

Thirdly, it should be noted that if, through reason "man reaches the consciousness of his freedom," it is "only through labor that he realizes it." Such that, from reason, man proceeds to the consciousness of freedom and, through labour, he realizes freedom. Labour can be defined as *the very slow work of the transformation of the surface of our globe by the physical force of each living being, according to the needs of each one*, a work that is "more or less developed in all degrees of organic life." However, this activity only becomes *human labour* when the "application of man's muscular strength to the transformation of this world" is directed by man's reason, his knowledge of the outside world, and his rational will. Then, labour begins to serve the "satisfaction not only of the fixed and fatally circumscribed needs of the exclusively animal life, but also of those of the *thinking being, who achieves his humanity by affirming and realizing his freedom in the world*" (Bakunin, 1988a[e], pp. 67–68, 71–72; cf., also: Ferreira, 2013, p. 7).

As we can see, both the consciousness of freedom, which is achieved through reason, and the realization of freedom, which is achieved through labour, are natural and material processes. They are necessities inherent to being that force man to win his freedom. This is because freedom is a human faculty that, with time, tends to be realized, since "everything that lives [...], being carried away by a fatality that is inherent in it and manifests itself in every being as a set of faculties or properties, tends to be realized in the fullness of its being" (Bakunin, 2014f[e], pp. 373–74). Therefore, the transformation undertaken by man for his own satisfaction—which has taken place in the passage from animality to humanity, and which continues to take place—was a natural and material manifestation of freedom.

With this transformation, it would even be possible to say that man "dominated and overcame nature." But this statement may confuse rather than clarify. With it, one runs the risk of falling into the idealistic assumption that there would be a separation between humanity and nature. Let us remember that there is no spirit separate from matter, and it is therefore impossible for human beings to separate from nature. They are permanently subordinated to all those facts and processes which are understood as the general laws of nature, and many of those which are understood as his particular laws. Against this nature "there is no possible struggle." It would be more appropriate to say that, in this passage, man has dominated and overcome "*his exterior world*," that is, "the more or less restricted set of phenomena, things and beings that surround man." Against the exterior world, or against "this exterior nature, struggle is not only possible" but "fatally necessary, fatally imposed by universal nature to everything that lives, to everything that exists." In its development, humanity has progressively emancipated itself from complete subordination and absolute dependence on the outside world, succeeding in transforming them, through labour, with a view to better meet its needs (Bakunin, 2014f[e], pp. 376, 378–79).

Even so, this emancipation did not lead to man reaching full freedom. Far from it. In humanity, man's freedom is certainly greater than in animality, for there is no longer that complete slavery before the external world. But there is still an essential element in it, human slavery, which, thanks to the principle of solidarity, condemns all men to an enormous deprivation of freedom.

Human history has always been, as in every organic world, a history of struggle for life and therefore a history of conflict. It was characterized by a "fratricidal struggle" which, if it did not physically eliminate the opponents, ended with power, oppression, domination, "subjugation," and the "exploitation of some by others." Conflict and struggle are therefore the foundations of human history, and wars the characteristic marks of the beginning of that history and the expressions of such confrontations. Whether they are "race, nation, State wars" or even "class" wars, all "have never had any other objective than the domination, condition and guarantee necessary for enjoyment and possession." Through domination, some men began to "live and prosper at the expense of others" and this was done only through "plundering, the conquest of the riches of others and the subjugation of the labor of others."

Until the present, humanity has been marked by slavery or human domination, that is, by the *principle of authority*. Taken in a *broad* sense, this oppression of man by man has been expressed in history in different phases: "Men [...] began their history by anthropophagy," simply exterminating their enemies; after it, "slavery followed, after slavery serfdom, after serfdom wage labor"—all regimes of which exploitation was an essential feature (Bakunin, 2009b[e], pp. 53, 89).

At first, "men" (not yet human, but developed wild animals) were hunter-gatherers and lived, like other animals, having only their own body for hunting, fishing, obtaining fruits, and plants. And so they remained for centuries. The aforementioned passage from animality to humanity occurred, more precisely, when man began to produce tools.

> The first time he made use of the coarsest weapon, a simple staff or a stone, he made an act of reflection, and affirmed himself, no doubt without realizing it, as a thinking animal, as man; for the weapon, even the most primitive, must necessarily be adapted to the objective that man proposes to achieve, it supposes a certain calculation of the spirit, a calculation that essentially distinguishes man-animal from all other animals on earth. (Bakunin, 2009b[e], p. 91)

The original production of this weapon, this instrument of labour, was exactly what, through reason and labour, founded humanity, establishing its first degree of civilization. By using tools, men began to have more means of subsistence and, as a result, they multiplied with ease and in much greater quantity than before. In several cases, this process involved a sexual division of labour that, based on the absolute (non-relative) superiority of male physical strength, forged the power of men over women. It was in this way that "upon the woman [...] fell the heaviest and most degrading internal jobs." Those "unfortunate women, [...] natural slaves of the barbaric man" then began to succumb "under the burden of their daily labor" for the benefit of men.

It was only because, through thought and word, man was able to transmit knowledge from one generation to another that this human multiplication did not cease. This progressive reason was based "on the one hand, on tradition that preserves for the benefit of future generations the knowledge acquired by past generations, and, on the other hand" on its propagation, "thanks to this gift of the word that is inseparable from that of thought." With this, it supported the "unlimited capacity [of man] to invent new procedures to defend human existence against all the natural forces that are against it." Faced with the exhaustion of natural sources and the insufficiency of nature to feed everyone, man was able to produce other, artificial sources, extrapolating his previous limits.

Taking advantage of "their superiority of intelligence," instead of killing non-human animals to feed themselves, men began to domesticate them, making them serve their own purposes. "This is how, through the centuries, groups of hunters have become groups of shepherds," nomadic groups. In this second degree of civilization, the labour was not yet so heavy, and so there were practically no slaves, even though, very possibly, the subordination of women continued to exist in countless situations. In any case, with this new source of existence, man was able to multiply even more, and with this, the need to create new means of subsistence emerged once again.

With the exploitation of animals becoming insufficient, man began to exploit the land. "Nomadic peoples and shepherds" became, also in a journey that lasted for centuries, "cultivating peoples"—this was how agriculture emerged. It was in this third degree of civilization that mass slavery emerged, above all because "agriculture demands assiduous, daily and painful labor." Before, men had understood that there was an advantage in "making oneself be served by animals or exploiting them without killing them immediately" and soon understood the advantages that could be extracted from other living men, subordinate to them. "The defeated enemy was no longer devoured" but "became a slave, forced to do the labor necessary for the subsistence of his master." It's at that moment that "the slave assumes the role of the woman. An intelligent beast, forced to carry all the weight of corporal labor, the enslaved man creates the conditions for leisure and the intellectual and moral development of his master" (Bakunin, 2009b[e], pp. 92–95).

This massive oppression was gradually forming as a human fact, and little by little ideas were produced to legitimize it. This was the basis for the emergence of the first states, which, even without the intervention of legislators or divine prophets, aimed to guarantee the continuity of this power.

> The brutal fact of pillaging, conquest and enslavement, the material and real basis of all States past and present, always preceded the idealization of this fact by some religion and some legislation. First, the happy thief, the hero of history, founds the new State; then, often immediately after him, come the priests, prophets and legislators at the same time, who consecrate to the name of God and establish, as legal bases, the very consequences of this *fait accompli*. (Bakunin, 1973b[e], p. 56)

The State arises from the beginning as a result of oppression and exploitation among men, in order to perpetuate it. It was a fait accompli, which found in ideas—especially in religion—a very relevant legitimizing foundation, especially because of the moral that was established. However, in general terms, religion has not always had this role. When analyzed in the dialectics of history, it is necessary to note that it played a prominent—and, to some extent, liberating—role in the passage from animality to humanity.

11.3 GENESIS OF RELIGION: DIVINE AUTHORITY AND HUMAN AUTHORITY

Creation and the history of religion or the idea of God must be understood as part of the development of nature-matter in general and humanity in particular. What this means is that to study their trajectory is, to a great extent, to focus on human history, since both are human creations (Bakunin, 1988a[e], p. 39).[11]

It should be remembered that in man's immense struggle to overcome external nature and move on to humanity, reason and labour were central. At that moment, religion was fundamental to the progress of thought, of the faculty of abstraction of the human being, such that it must be seen as a particular form of development of reason: "We do not intend to deny the historical necessity of religion, nor to affirm that it has been an absolute evil in history." Even with all the problems it created—or those to which it actively contributed—religion was "the first awakening of human reason in the form of divine dementia," "the first twilight of human truth through the divine veil of lies," "the first manifestation of human morality, justice and law through the historical iniquities of divine grace," and, finally, "the learning of freedom under the humiliating and arduous yoke of divinity" (Bakunin, 1988a[e], pp. 85–86).

A genesis of religion shows that the first traces of consciousness arose in a context of fear in the face of a world that is indeed oppressive and full of threats. It was in trying to understand this world and himself that man, in all his doubts and uncertainties, ended up attributing everything that was unknown to him and gave him fear to an omnipotent superior entity. The idea of God, the basis of all religions, was thus born, helping that newly formed human being to remedy, in his own way, his own issues. So one can conclude that religion expresses man's absolute dependence in relation to nature, and that the basis of religious consciousness is the human consciousness of this dependence.

After creating the idea of God, humanity began to interpret it more and more as the source of life and as time went by subordinated themselves to that idea which, without knowing it, humanity itself had produced. Such was the case of fetishism, the first religion, which conceived nature-matter in an abstract way, fixing it and transmitting it through language. "Once the divinity was installed, it was naturally proclaimed the teacher, the source, the distributor of all things: the real world existed only through it, and man, after having created it without knowing it, knelt before it and declared himself its creature, its slave." The result of this movement was that "the more the sky became rich, the more humanity became miserable"; the more it was attributed to God, the less it was recognized by man (Bakunin, 1988a[e], p. 40).[12]

In this first religion, *fetishism*, "the natural, fetishized object, then becomes a supernatural object," and thus "reason, in the form of imaginary reflection or irrationality, creates religion in its purest and crudest form." Despite its simplicity, fetishism was very important, given the fact that it is the result of this first great step of humanity. It succeeded and in a certain sense coexisted with *witchcraft*, whose God exists only as an "all-powerful" essentially undetermined, totally without moral and intellectual content, and whose existence takes place through the mediation of the sorcerer, the "man-God" himself. However, with the development of thought, the "contradiction between the roles of the sorcerer as a limited man and the all-powerful God" becomes apparent. At a given moment, "neither the fetish (the God-thing) nor the sorcerer (the man-God)" became aware of embracing the divine, which was sought elsewhere. It was, for a time, found in the sun, in the moon, in the sky, beginning to embrace the universe.

This led to the emergence of the second religion, *polytheism*. Unlike fetishism, which conceived of "particular natural objects" as something living, supernatural and divine, polytheism perceived "natural objects as inert, but submitted to the will of the divine agents who govern objects of particular types." That is, while "fetishism divinizes the natural object, polytheism externalizes this divinity and, in fact, conceives of it as something separate from the natural object, related to it only to the extent that it governs it." When religion placed the divine outside the real, it placed the natural-material outside of itself, and inevitably began to negate it. It discarded the movement and energy of nature-matter and attributed "its manifestations and potentialities to the (necessarily unique) creator of all things, God, from whom all things *emanated*." The "transition from the materialistic polytheism of the pagans to the spiritual monotheism of Christians" was equally important.

As an interstice of this passage and culmination of polytheism, *pantheism* implied the beginning of the transcendence of the religious consciousness of its immediate nature. By conceiving of the complete identification between God and the universe as relational reality, this religious form allowed man to emerge as the first consciousness of the totality of real things in relation to each other, that is, of nature-matter. It allowed him to develop his reason and caused man, even in a very limited way and by a complete abstraction, to apprehend "the identity of the universe in its difference and the difference of the universe in its identity." This development of reason allowed man, made object of his own thought, to produce the abstract distinction between body and soul, attributing to the latter the government of the former— "transferring this abstract dualism to the natural world as a whole," man artificially divided nature into its parts, matter, and spirit.[13]

At the end of pantheism, the divine became a spiritual and extramundane God, universalized, it became the greatest and highest of all beings, forging the foundations of the third religion, *monotheism*. In this religion, this universal and spiritual God, a product of human creation because of his ignorance of nature-matter, became considered an objective and all-powerful being. All natural laws, all qualities of matter and man then came to be interpreted as divine creations, and God as the supreme being, creator and lord of all things and all people. The logical corollary of such a movement was that if the divine, God, was everything, the human, man, was nothing (McLaughlin, 2002, pp. 130–35).

> Thus reason, the essence of humanity with its means of "recognizing the truth," is transformed by religion into divine reason, a means of consecrating the absurd. Similarly, love, the basis of human solidarity, is transformed by religion into divine love and religious charity, historically the "poison of humanity." And justice, the basis of human equality, is transformed by religion into divine justice or, in theological terms, into divine grace, the basis of human conquest and privilege. [...] Yet it is only through religion that truth, equality, justice and freedom emerge in the first place—though submerged in falsehood, inequality, injustice and slavery. (McLaughlin, 2002, pp. 135–36)

Religion—necessary for the development of reason and, with it, for the very creation of humanity—is placed, from a certain point, as an obstacle to overcoming falsehood, inequality, injustice, and slavery. This can be observed very clearly in *Christianity*, which develops as part of monotheism and can be pointed out as absolute religion, the last religion, since it exposes very clearly the whole essence of religion. In theoretical terms, Christianity means the abdication of human reason, thus establishing itself as a form of theoretical or intellectual slavery. In practical terms, it expresses the denial of human freedom, thus constituting a form of real or practical slavery. Two aspects that in reality are one and the same thing.

> Christianity is precisely religion par excellence, because it exposes and manifests in its fullness the nature, the very essence of any religious system, which is *the impoverishment, subjection and annulment of humanity for the benefit of the divinity*. [...] Unable to find justice, truth and eternal life on his own, he [man] can only achieve this through a divine revelation. But who says revelation says revelators, messiahs, prophets, priests and lawmakers inspired by God himself; and these, once recognized as representatives of the divinity on earth, as holy educators of humanity, elected by God himself to direct it on the path of salvation, must necessarily exercise absolute power. All men owe them unlimited and passive obedience; for against divine Reason there is no human reason, and against the Justice of God there is no earthly justice that can stand. Slaves of God, men must also be slaves of the Church and the State,

insofar as the latter is consecrated by the Church. This is what, of all the religions that exist or have existed, Christianity has understood better than the others [because] it pretends to embrace all humanity. (Bakunin, 2014e[e], pp. 268–69)

It then becomes evident why there is a direct relationship between religion and politics. The divine authority, this God who takes everything from humanity, leaves man incapable of distinguishing between good and evil, and must have his morality imposed by God. And this is only done through self-defined divine lawmakers, so that divine authority comes to legitimize human authority and with it the power relations that are exercised in its name. Consequently, divine authority is inseparable from human authority, for God's power on earth is always exercised through men who claim to be his representatives. This is the principle that underlies not only the Church, but also the State (Bakunin, 65001[e]).

In short, humanity was forged in the midst of conflicts and struggles that resulted in domination and exploitation, in a political-economic submission, first of women, and then, with the emergence of agriculture, of women and men slaves. The first states were then founded, which were nothing more than instruments to guarantee this oppression. In an almost concomitant process, ideas were created to justify this fact, among which religion stood out. Developing from fetishism to polytheism, and from this to monotheism, religion attained its maturity in Christianity when the Catholic Church became the source of legitimacy of relations of class domination and exploitation throughout the Middle Ages.

Catholicism, starting from this abstraction that is the idea of God, was the religion that first recognized the "material relationship between power, wealth and spiritual faith, between political oppression, economic exploitation and spiritual propaganda." It was Catholicism which first admitted that "power generates wealth, and wealth produces power" and that, together, "power and wealth ([...] 'the two inseparable terms of the kingdom of divine ideality on earth,' that is, of divine authority in human form [...]) ensure the success of 'Christian propaganda.'" In this way, the Catholic Church formed a corporate structure which, in God's name, was able to make wealth flow from the base to the summit, and absolute authority impose itself from the top down (McLaughlin, 2002, pp. 143–44).

Later, Protestantism, in a similar way, leaned on this same relationship between power, wealth, and spiritual faith. But, averse to the centralized authority of Catholicism, it put it in check by putting an end to the struggle between Church and State that such authority implied: "The Reformation put an end to that struggle by proclaiming the independence of States." With this independence, "the right of the sovereign was recognized as coming immediately from God, without the intervention of the Pope or any other priest." And "thanks to this heavenly provenance, [the sovereign's] right was declared absolute. Thus on the ruins of the Church's despotism was erected the edifice of monarchic despotism." After a period in which the Church was the madam, "she became the servant of the State, an instrument of government in the hands of the monarch" (Bakunin, 2008d[e], pp. 60–61).

The Reformation meant the conquest of power by a distinct, non-clerical class, which instituted the modern State according to the same structure as the Church: a corporate structure that—no longer in the name of God, as the Catholic Church had done, but of the absolute right of the State—was also able to make wealth flow from the base to the summit and absolute authority impose itself from the top down (McLaughlin, 2002, pp. 144–45). For this reason, "the [modern] State ... is the younger brother of the Church" (Bakunin, 2009b[e], p. 58).

11.4 DIFFERENT FORMS OF IDEALISM

Idealism is the antithesis of materialism and, in its different forms, encompasses a wide range of theoretical and philosophical conceptions. Firstly, theology, metaphysics, and some forms of modern idealism in their most common forms will be critiqued: German idealism in general (Kant, Fichte, Schelling, Hegel), and Hegelianism in particular; liberal contractualism in general,[14] and Rousseau's theory in particular. Both in its religious and philosophical forms, idealism is based on the theological principle, more or less divinized. Whether starting with God, the absolute or abstract thought, these different forms of idealism have similar implications: they foster incorrect understandings of reality and always end with despotism.

Idealism not only separates matter and spirit, body and soul, but replaces or prioritizes the latter over the former. Reality is thus interpreted according to the abstraction of ideas—the divine, the spirit, thought, feeling, free will, etc.—which take the place of the concreteness of natural and material facts, in some of their forms, or precede them and are privileged in relation to them, in others. That is, in general, "the idealists maintain that ideas dominate and produce facts."

For them, matter is "the product of false abstraction," a being "inanimate, immobile, incapable of producing the slightest thing, a *caput mortuum*"—this "matter" of idealists is nothing more than a product of their imagination, of their abstraction. By unduly placing all the characteristics of matter outside nature, the idealists "removed from matter its intelligence, its life, all the determining qualities, the active relationships or forces, movement itself," and left to it "only the impenetrability and absolute immobility in space."

In the most evidently religious cases, the idealists "attributed all these forces, properties and natural manifestations to the imaginary being, created by their abstract fantasy; then, reversing the roles, they called this product of their imagination, this ghost, this God who is nothingness, 'the supreme being.'" And, finally, they "declared that the real being, the material, the world, was nothingness," beginning to think that "this material is incapable of producing something, not even of setting itself in motion" and that, consequently, it must have "been created by their God." And even in the most secular cases, the idealists proceeded in a similar way. They attributed to ideas, products of nature-matter, the role of a single source in the production of things and in the movement of the world, which, according to them, was the product of ideas. Both in the one case as in the other, this inversion caused the idealists to take the opposite path from the materialists: they did not recognize the self-creative capacity of nature-matter, and they conceived its movement only according to external influences.

Abstractly imagining a model of the world which, they thought, would start from the complex to the simple, from the top to the bottom, the idealists began to proceed in a similar way in their way of analyzing the world: "from the top to the bottom, from the complicated to the simple." They started from the "divine substance or idea," or else from pure ideas, in order to soon afterwards give "a terrible degradation from the sublime heights of the eternal ideal to the mud of the material world; from absolute perfection to absolute imperfection; from thought to being, or rather, from the supreme being in the midst of nothing." From complex ideas, theories, representations, they proceeded to simple facts, nature, matter (Bakunin, 2014e[e], pp. 256, 260–61).

Always showing itself to be far from rational and positive science and the realistic method, idealism, in its grossest forms, takes reality as the product of an idea, as in the case of creationism and blind faith. In its most refined forms, it considers life as the product of transcendent speculation or logical abstraction, as in the case of orthodox Hegelianism and liberal contractualist theories. Something that clearly exposes that "theoretical or divine idealism has as its essential condition the sacrifice of logic, of human reason, of the renunciation of science" (Bakunin, 2014e[e], p. 286). "This way of proceeding from idea to fact," of which "the idealists of all the Schools, theologians and metaphysicians have made eternal use," has already had its "final impotence [...] confirmed by history", because there is an "absolute impossibility" that "starting from the abstract idea" one can "arrive at the real and concrete fact" (Bakunin, 71011a[e], p. 53).

A certain logic can be identified in the different forms of idealism. As every development implies the negation of the starting point, those who begin, like idealists, with the abstraction of ideas, necessarily end up in the most degrading concreteness of facts: "idealism [...] serves, today, as a flag for material force, bloodthirsty and brutal, for shameless material exploitation." It "is part of divinity" or other ideals "to build slavery and condemn the masses to an endless animality." That is, "on whatever issue, you will find the idealists in flagrant crime of practical materialism and vile" (Bakunin, 2014e[e], pp. 286–87). When they reflect on life, "starting from the pure, absolute idea, and always repeating the ancient myth of original sin, which is only the symbolic expression of their melancholic destiny," the idealists "relapse eternally, both in theory and practice, into the material, from which they can never get free." And they fall into a material that is "brutal, ignoble, stupid, created by their own imagination, as an *alter ego* or as a reflection of their *ideal Self*" (Bakunin, 1973a[e], p. 7).

Such were, precisely, the cases of Catholic idealism, which resulted in the despotism of the Church, and Protestant idealism, which, after the French Revolution, resulted in the despotism of the bourgeoisie.[15] In various other historical circumstances, this logic remained the same, as in the case of Ancient Rome, which advocated the ideal status of the citizen and subjected him to the most brutal materialism of Caesarism, or even of modern Germany, which, the cradle of philosophical idealism, reached, with unification, the apex of Statist despotism (McLaughlin, 2002, pp. 143–44). It was also reproduced in the theoretical productions of liberal contractualists who like Rousseau set out from an abstractly free individual to arrive at the absolute domination of the State, the basis of the social contract and society (Bakunin, 1988a[e], pp. 89–90).

Idealism starts from abstract ideas—God, absolute, thought, feeling, free will, etc.—and, in order to develop, it negates its starting point, reaching concrete facts; starting from the superior, from the perfect, from freedom, reaching the inferior, the imperfect, the authority. With this, it animates humanity, reifies power and exploitation, founds the State and the Church—it is a movement of "continuous fall." It is no coincidence, that in political terms, idealists have always been linked to despotism, whether they were absolutist, constitutionalist, or liberal.

It is evident that this logic of idealism opposes the logic of materialism. According to what has been explained above, materialism, in a counterposed logic, starts from material facts and, in order to develop, negates its starting point, arriving at ideas; departs from animality arriving at humanity, departs from authority arriving at freedom. It is a movement of "progressive ascension" (Bakunin, 2014e[e], pp. 286–87).

> Whatever human question we want to consider, we always find this same essential contradiction between the two schools. Thus, as I have already observed, materialism departs from animality to constitute humanity; idealism departs from divinity to constitute slavery and condemn the masses to an endless animality. Materialism negates the principle of authority, because it rightly considers it to be the corollary of animality, and that, on the contrary, the triumph of humanity, which is for it the objective and the principal meaning of history, is only realizable through freedom. In a word, on any given question, you will find the idealists in flagrant crime of practical materialism; whereas, on the contrary, you will see the materialists pursue and realize the aspirations, the most vastly ideal thoughts. (Bakunin, 2014e[e], p. 287)

According to a materialistic understanding, humanity has developed with the negation of animality, affording a growth of freedom. But full freedom can only be achieved through a negation of humanity in general and the principle of authority or oppression of men by men in particular. The materialist must be able to scientifically and naturally analyze the present reality and, negating it, conceive the ideals that must guide the historical development of society.

The need for a social revolution and federalist socialism arises in this way. "Starting from the totality of the real world, or what we abstractly call matter," materialism "logically arrives at real idealization, that is, humanization, the full and complete emancipation of society." That is, "the flag of theoretical materialism, the red flag of economic equality and social justice, is raised by the practical idealism of the oppressed and hungry masses" in a revolutionary process "that tends to realize the greatest freedom and human right of each person in the fraternity of all men on earth" (Bakunin, 2014e[e], pp. 286–87).

In a second moment, this critique of idealism should also extend to other theoretical-philosophical conceptions which, more refined than those discussed— and, in some cases, even quite useful—continue to operate, to some extent, according to the logic of idealism. They are: positivism in general and Comte's disciples in particular, and revolutionary doctrinalism in general and German communism in particular. And, even if in much smaller proportions, anthropocentrism in general and the theories of Marx and Proudhon in particular.

Positivism, although it does not take the idea of God and the first cause as its starting point, does not reject them clearly. "The positivists have never directly denied the possibility of the existence of God" and, "always faithful to their system of reticence and equivocal statements, are content to say," as in the case of the idea of God, "that the first cause cannot be an object of science, because it is a hypothesis that science cannot verify." In this way they "open the door for theologians," leaving undue space for theologism. And this is done for political reasons, since, being "prudents and political conservatives," the positivists pretend, even without saying so, to be mediators between "scientific atheism" and their theological friends (Bakunin, 2014f[e], pp. 403, 411).

But there is still another aspect, common to the positivists of the Comte school and the German communist doctrinarians. Although, in both cases, the arguments are different, the result they arrive at is quite similar. They are based on an idealized notion of science and, by granting themselves the position of scientists, they despise the people and intend to govern them. This "government of science and of men of science, even if they call themselves positivists, disciples of Auguste Comte or even disciples of the doctrinal school of German communism, can only be impotent, ridiculous, inhumane, cruel, oppressive, exploitative, malefic" (Bakunin, 2014e[e], p. 292).

Positivism is "a sect, both political and priestly," which proposes to create "a new priesthood, not religious, this time, but scientific, called, according to it, to govern the world from then on." It starts from the principle that "the immense majority of men [...] are incapable of governing themselves" not because they are ignorant or because their daily reality has prevented them from "acquiring the habit of thinking, but because nature has created them that way." Thus the positivists maintain that these men are naturally less developed from the intellectual point of view, and therefore must be governed by the men of science, more educated than they (Bakunin, 2014f[e], pp. 400–401).

German communism, even if it claims to be materialistic, proceeds similarly. It forms a dogmatic system—of philosophical, theoretical, economic, and political foundations—which, even with many useful things, puts itself in the position of giving all the definitive answers for the understanding and government of the world. With this, "these doctrinarians instinctively aspire [...] to the domination of doctrine, of science over life; to the domination of a wise *intelligentsia* over society" (Bakunin, 2009e[e], p. 71). This is evidenced by the frequent use by Marxists and Lasallians of the terms "'scientific socialist', 'scientific socialism.'" The concepts that support this terminology, as well as the theories and practices of German communism, prove that the post-revolutionary state it advocates "will be nothing more than the despotic government of the proletarian masses by a new and very restricted aristocracy of true or purported scholars." In other words, "the people not having science, they will be completely freed from government concerns and fully integrated into the herd of the governed. Beautiful liberation" (Bakunin, 2003a[e], p. 213)!

As can be seen, in both cases a logic similar to that of religious idealism, theology, is evident. A product of human reason, science (or religion) is at a given moment idealized. It then dogmatically replaces natural and social life (or God is everything, life and men are nothing) and pretends to govern it (or the lack of human morality demands that God rules the world). The intellectuals, who hold scientific knowledge, are conferred representatives of science (or priests claim to be representatives of God) and therefore of the rulers of the people. Finally, they establish a government of the wise (or despotism of the Church), in which a minority oppresses the majority, understanding that it is legitimate to do so, in view of the popular inability to access scientific knowledge (or the word of God).

The common aspect to positivists and communists is that, through this procedure, they depart from an idealization (science is greater than life) and arrive at a cruel materialization (men must be governed by the wise). This is exactly why both defend the State, since in order to govern, it is necessary to have an instrument capable of guaranteeing the domination of a minority over the majority.

> Idealists of any nature, metaphysical, positivist, defenders of the primacy of science over life, doctrinal revolutionaries, all together, with the same ardor, although with different arguments, defend the notion of the State and of governmental authority, seeing it as the only completely logical means, according to them, of saving society. Completely logical, we can say, because, based on the deeply erroneous principle, according to our point of view, that the idea precedes life, the abstract theory of social activity, and that, in this way, sociology must be the starting point of revolutions and social transformations, they inevitably come to the conclusion that thought, theory, science, being, at least today, the appanage of a very small number of individuals, this small number is predestined to lead social life, as instigators, but also as drivers of all popular

movements, and that the day after the revolution a new social organization should be created, not by the free federation, from the bottom up, of associations, communes, cantons and regions, according to the needs and instincts of the people, but only by the dictatorial authority of this minority of men of science, who supposedly express the will of the people. (Bakunin, 2003a[e], pp. 168–69)

Finally, we must criticize another concept that, despite contributing to the understanding of reality, has its limits: anthropocentrism, represented by Marx's "economic metaphysics" (Bakunin, 70002[c], p. 2), more connected to the principle of authority, and Proudhon's "idealism" (Bakunin, 2003a[e], p. 175), more connected to the principle of freedom. In these two cases, what brings them closer to idealism is not the prioritizing of the spirit over matter or of the soul over the body, but the rupture between nature and society and the centrality that the latter receives to the detriment of the former. Both intend, to some extent, "to demonstrate the superiority of man-spirit over nature-matter" (Bakunin, 2014f[e], p. 376).[16]

Even with political limitations and risks, Marx's theory has ample relevance. Book I of *Capital*, his greatest theoretical contribution, is "an excessively important, erudite, profound work" (Bakunin, 71026[e], p. 17). This work is fundamental to understanding the process of economic development of capital and "the latter form of subjugation and exploitation which is called wage labor, or, the absolute rule of capital monopolized by the hands of a bourgeois oligarchy." In this and other works, Marx provided another essential contribution, confirming a profound and decisive truth that should guide the "study of the history of human civilization." It is the notion that "everywhere and always, religions, prejudices, ideas, customs, legal and political institutions, the social relations of individuals and peoples, war and peace, alliances and struggles," that is, everything that forms human history, the human world, "has never been anything other than a reflection, the equivalent expression of the different economic situations in which human society has successively found itself" (Bakunin, 71011b[e], pp. 3, 5).

However, there are some aspects of Marxist theory that, from the perspective of scientific-naturalist materialism, can be criticized. And, with this criticism, one can understand why Marx "could not, and will never, free himself from predominantly abstract and metaphysical thought" (Bakunin, 2003a[e], p. 163). First, because this is an anthropocentric theory, which rests on this division between the natural and the social. Marx conceives, almost theologically, the economy, a human creation, as the basis of matter, proceeding to a socialization of this matter that is inadequate—he exaggerates in the socio-historical aspect of nature. He still claims that man puts nature under his control, abstaining from the determination of its forces. As already argued, there is a continuity between nature and society, the second being part of the first. To be properly understood, matter must be naturalized, not socialized. After all, also as argued, although man can and must impose himself on external nature, he will never dominate or control nature, nor will he stop being subject to its laws (McLaughlin, 2002, pp. 168–69).

Second, even if, in society, we agree that the determination of the economy is "a profoundly true principle," it should thus be considered only "in its true aspect, that is, from a relative point of view." For "viewed and placed in an absolute way as the sole foundation and primary source of all other principles, as this school [of the German communists] does, it becomes completely false" (Bakunin, 2014e[e], p. 256). That is, economic determination must be seen as a true principle, not economic determinism, because in the study of nature and society one cannot want to universalize particularities.

To this preponderance of the economy must be added "the still evident reaction of political, legal and religious institutions to the economic situation." For even if we agree that "misery produces political slavery, the State," we must also take into account the fact that "political slavery, the State, in turn, reproduces and preserves misery" (Bakunin, 2001b[e], p. 39). Even agreeing that economics plays a huge role in defining class interests, we must also take into account that what keeps the "petty bourgeoisie" away from the "proletariat" is, in general, "prejudice."[17] And that what, not infrequently, throws peasants and workers into the lap of reaction is "their political, legal and [...] religious prejudices" (Bakunin, 71011[e], p. 8).

Therefore, as will be discussed below, it is not enough to socialize property, it is also necessary to abolish the State; social position does not automatically make a revolutionary subject, rational will being an essential element for this.

From another perspective, Proudhon, having "understood freedom much better than Marx," makes absolutely central contributions from the point of view of socialist theory. However, "despite all the efforts he made [...] to shake up the traditions of classical idealism, he did not cease to be an incorrigible, [...] and always metaphysical idealist, to the end of his fingertips." The main reason for this was also the rupture that operated between nature and society, but not only it. Proudhon's "great misfortune" was that he "never studied the natural sciences and did not appropriate their methods." In conceiving and theorizing society without relation to nature, he also bumped into the limits of the socialization of nature (Bakunin, 2014b[c], pp. 91–93).

Another reason for this was that, in taking the human world, Proudhon proceeded contradictorily in what concerns the relationship between facts and ideas, and between economy and other spheres of society. Sometimes he correctly maintained that "the ideal [...] is nothing more than a flower, whose material conditions of existence constitute the root," so that "the whole intellectual and moral, political and social history of humanity is a reflection of its economic history" (Bakunin, 2014e[e], p. 257; cf., also: Bakunin, 1988a[e], p. 26). However, he often took inspiration "from the Bible and Roman law," underestimating the role of economic relations and even facts in society (Bakunin, 2014b[c], p. 92). That is, he often conceived of a human nature that was psychologizing and, to a great extent, idealized (McLaughlin, 2002, p. 184).

11.5 FREEDOM, SOCIETY, AND THE INDIVIDUAL

Previously, the concept of freedom was utilized several times. It is now necessary to define it and explain it in its details.

At the outset, freedom can be defined from two perspectives, one positive and the other negative. *"From the positive point of view"*, freedom is *"the full development of all the [natural] faculties found in man"*; *"from the negative point of view"*, it is *"complete independence, not from natural and social laws, but from all laws imposed by other human wills, collective or isolated"* (Bakunin, 2015[e], pp. 279, 286, emphasis added; cf., also: Bakunin, 2008e[e], pp. 114–15; Bakunin, 2008d[e], pp. 73–74). Taking into account that every human being is endowed by nature with a set of natural faculties, freedom implies, on the one hand, the guarantee that all individuals will find conditions for the development of these faculties; on the other hand, it involves the guarantee that no individual or collective can impose their laws and wills on others. Obviously, it is a freedom that obeys natural-material and social determinations and therefore cannot be conceived, from any point of view, as a freedom capable of dispensing with nature-matter and society.

In general, authority is considered, dialectically, as the antithesis of freedom. But some notes must be made about this. Like freedom, authority can also be defined from two perspectives. One is *natural authority*, which "is imposed [on nature-matter itself and on all individuals] and determined by the pre-existing configuration of the natural world." Against this authority, there is no revolt or freedom possible, since this would be the very destruction of nature-matter and of society. So any freedom must respect that authority, which determines it and imposes insurmountable limits on it. The other is *artificial authority*, which is "intentionally and consciously imposed on men by the decision of certain individuals in human society" (Saltman, 1983, pp. 31–32). This authority is the antithesis of freedom and constitutes the foundation of all power, all domination, all oppression, all human exploitation, the former of which càn only take place to the detriment of the latter (Bakunin, 2014a[e], pp. 76–77; Bakunin, 65001[e]).

As argued, with the passage from animality to humanity, freedom has grown considerably. At the beginning of their history, prehuman men were completely subordinated to external nature, but from the development of their reason and through their labour, they gradually succeeded in subduing it, at least in what was possible. For "the first and last condition of this freedom are always, after all, the most absolute submission to the omnipotence of nature, our mother, and observation, the most rigorous application of its laws." It has also been seen that mankind has been characterized up to the present by the predominance of artificial authority, which, on different levels, has guaranteed the subordination of men to each other; and that, because of the solidarity existing among all men, this oppression of many for a few puts the freedom of the whole of society in check. In other words, even if, in relation to animality, humanity is characterized by a growth in freedom, its fullness is still very distant. In its fullness, human freedom means "independence from the despotic pretensions and acts of men," from the laws and artificial human wills that mark all fields of contemporary humanity. It means "science, labor, political revolt" and, "finally, the organization, rational and free at the same time, of the social environment, according to the natural laws that are inherent to every human society" (Bakunin, 2014f[e], p. 356).

This process makes explicit a *negative dialectic of history*: it is by negating the past (animality) that the present (humanity) has established itself; it is by negating the present (humanity) that the future (freedom) can constitute itself. Even between flows and refluxes, this human development has had as a basis the contradiction between authority and freedom, which continues to characterize the main conflict of humanity. Arriving at full freedom, therefore, demands that the conditions be created for it to emerge as a preponderant principle, in a reality in which artificial authority has been totally supplanted. And this is only done with the negation of artificial authority (still preponderant in contemporary humanity), which allows for forging affirmative ideals of a future society.

Artificial authority is based on the *principle of authority*, which can be defined as the "eminently theological, metaphysical, political idea that the masses, always incapable of governing themselves, should always suffer the benevolent yoke of a wisdom and a justice that, in one way or another, will be imposed upon them from above." Artificial authority is always produced by a minority of men who impose themselves on the majority. It can have different foundations—political, economic, religious, etc.—and implies the power of privileged minorities over the masses (Bakunin, 1988a[e], pp. 110–11).

> The materialistic, realistic and collectivist definition of freedom, totally opposed to that of idealists, is this: man only becomes man and only reaches the consciousness and realization of his humanity in society and only through the collective action of the whole society; he only emancipates himself from the yoke of external nature through collective or social labor, which is the only one capable of transforming the surface of the Earth into a place favorable to the developments of humanity; and without this material emancipation there can be no intellectual and moral emancipation for anyone. He can only emancipate himself from the yoke of his own nature, that is, he can only subordinate the instincts and movements of his own body towards his increasingly developed spirit through education and instruction; but both are eminently and exclusively social things; for outside of society man would have remained forever a wild animal or a saint, which means almost the same thing. Finally,

isolated man cannot be conscious of his freedom. To be free, for man, means to be recognized, considered and treated as such by another man, by all men around him. Freedom is not, therefore, a fact of isolation, but of mutual reflection, not of exclusion, but, on the contrary, of connection; the freedom of every individual is understood only as the reflection of his humanity or of his human right in the consciousness of all free men, his brothers and sisters, his equals. I can only consider myself and feel free in the presence and in relation to other men. (Bakunin, 71002[e])

A central aspect of the concept of freedom stands out here. Just as humanity has only surpassed animality collectively, freedom can only surpass humanity (and the artificial authority that cuts it from one side to the other) collectively. Alone, animal-man would have remained in animality, since reason and labour could only develop collectively; alone, human-man is condemned to perish in humanity, as a victim of artificial authority. For reason, science, labour, revolt, and the rational and free organization of a new world are only possible collectively and in society.

Society can be defined as *"the sum of all lives, all evolutions, all relationships, and all actions of the entirety of the individuals that compose it"* (Bakunin, 2016d[e], p. 149, emphasis added). It is therefore the totality of individuals, social relations, and human development that exists, connectedly, in a given community. It is part of nature and was produced by it, constituting the "last great manifestation or creation of nature on this Earth"—and, precisely for this reason, it is submitted to natural laws (Bakunin, 71002[e]). Society is "an ontological category" in that it "concerns the theory of being and subject," which was previously discussed (Ferreira, 2013, p. 7). In other words, it is a product predating the very formation of the individual-man—it was that which provided the conditions for the development of reason and labour, which, in turn, guided the passage from animality to humanity.

That which the "individualists of the school of Jean-Jacques Rousseau" and the "Proudhonian mutualists" advocate is a profound misconception. Both consider that "society is the result of a free contract of individuals who are absolutely independent of each other," and that the relationships and mutual dependence between them are nothing more than the fruit of voluntary agreement. However, society was formed by a natural and material necessity, which involved an involuntary and unconscious congregation: "individuals grouped together and associated not by their own will, not by common agreement, but independent of their conscience and will." These individuals "were not only grouped and associated, but engendered under the material, intellectual and moral aspect by the society of which they are the expression of material, intellectual and moral life." Therefore, the idea of free individuals, prior to society, establishing contracts and agreements, is profoundly false.

Individuals should be understood more properly as "agents, created and developed by society," as an inseparable part of it and inconceivable outside it.

Therefore, any revolt of the individual against society, any attempt by the individual to isolate himself is simply impossible. "The individual, his freedom and his intellect are the product of society, and not the product of individuals," such that the more the individual develops "the more he is the product of society, the more he has received from it and is indebted to it." But, in a way, society is also "in turn indebted to the individual" since its relations and actions also have, "albeit to a microscopic extent," an influence upon society itself (Bakunin, 2016d[e], pp. 149–50).

The natural and material basis of social relations between individuals is *mutual influence*; there is only life with relationship, with influence. This "*natural influence* that men exert upon one another" is none other than "the very basis, material, intellectual and moral, of human solidarity" (Bakunin, 2015[e], p. 280, emphasis added). Like natural authority, natural influence is always present in society, so that "the abolition of this mutual influence would, then, be death." When freedom in general or "freedom of the masses" in particular is asserted, it is not intended to "abolish absolutely any of the natural influences of any individual, of any group of individuals who exert their action over them [the masses]." Freedom is opposed to artificial authorities, as well as to artificial influences: "What we want is the abolition of artificial, privileged, legal, official influences" (Bakunin, 71011a[e], p. 72; cf., also: Saltman, 1983, pp. 36–37).

Every individual comes to the world in a society, in which he relates with others, influences them, and is influenced by them. As a result, they profoundly suffer the impacts of the "*social tradition*" that is in force in this society and is spread by "*education* [...] in the broadest sense." That is, the individual suffers an enormous influence from society, through a process that resembles what, during the twentieth century, will be called *socialization*.

This tradition and this education are responsible for transmitting to individuals, from the moment of birth until their death, what this society has accumulated. They "take the child from the first day of life that surrounds him, in every detail [...] of the social world in which he was born." "They penetrate in a thousand different ways into their consciousness, initially infantile, then adolescent and youthful, which is born, grows and is formed under their all-powerful influence." This *education in a broad sense*, which transmits the *social tradition* to the individuals, includes "not only instruction and moral lessons, but also and above all the examples that all the people around it give the child, the influence of everything it understands, of what it sees." It encompasses "not only the culture of its spirit, but also the development of its body through nutrition, hygiene, the exercise of its limbs and its physical strength." For this reason, "every child, every adult, every young person and finally every mature man is the pure product of the world that fed them and educated them in its bosom" (Bakunin, 1988a[e], p. 129).

In most cases, the individual will reproduce that which is in force in the society of which they are part. They may, of course, escape from some of their determinations, influencing, through their action, the social structure, since this determination is not absolute. But certainly, during their life, they will reproduce much more than they will modify that which is in force in society. "This power of society can be beneficial, just as it can be malefic." So this influence over the individual is not necessarily good or bad. It will be good in so far as it will strengthen "the development of science, of material prosperity, of freedom, of equality and of the fraternal solidarity of men"; it will be bad "when it has contrary tendencies" (Bakunin, 71002[e]). This reinforcement of science, material prosperity, freedom, equality, and solidarity is the foundation of what can be called "collectivist ethics," revolutionary socialist ethics, or anarchist ethics (Leval, 1976, pp. 88–94).

Just as nature-matter—which sets in solidarity the really existing things in accordance with the actions and perpetual reactions that they exert on each other—society also sets living individuals in solidarity, naturally and materially, thanks to their dependence, attachment, and influence on each other (Bakunin, 65001[e]). According to what has been pointed out, this was a decisive factor for humanity to survive. Individuals, with their very limited independence, submit themselves in society to the same natural laws and associate themselves for that which involves their humanity—they are in solidarity in their thinking, in their labour, and also in their freedom. "Finally, freedom is only just and complete in the entire solidarity of each one of us. There is no freedom in isolation; it is, by its nature, essentially mutual and social" (Bakunin, 2014a[e], p. 90).

Therefore, society is the basis of the individual's freedom, which cannot be conceived in an abstract or purely individual way. Freedom is not something external or previous to nature-matter or society—it is severely limited by nature-matter and by society itself, which is the condition for its realization. Thus individual freedom, as conceived by individualists and liberals, is impossible. Because of this solidarity, "man only realizes his individual freedom or his personality by completing himself with all the individuals around him, and only thanks to the labor and collective power of society"; that is, individual freedom is only realized in the collective freedom effective in society. "Society, far from diminishing and limiting, creates [...the conditions for] the freedom of human individuals. It is the root, the tree, and freedom is its fruit" (Bakunin, 71002[e]). Society, in this sense, does not contradict or place any restrictions on freedom—it is a premise for it.

I am truly free only when all human beings around me, men and women, are equally free. The freedom of the other, far from being a limit or the negation of my freedom, is, on the contrary, its necessary condition and its confirmation. Only the freedom of others makes me truly free, such that the more numerous the free men around me, and the more extensive and broader their freedom, the greater and more profound my freedom will become. On the contrary, it is the slavery of men that puts a barrier to my freedom, or, what is the same thing, it is their animality that is a negation of my humanity because, even once, I can only consider myself truly free when my freedom, or what means to say the same thing, when my dignity as a man, my human right, which consists in not obeying any other man and only determining my actions according to my own convictions, reflected by the equally free conscience of all, are confirmed to me by the approval of all. My personal freedom thus confirmed by the freedom of all extends to infinity. (Bakunin, 71002[e])

With this, two relatively common conceptions of freedom are discarded. In the first place, the perspective that an individual's freedom ends where that of the other begins is rejected. Individual freedoms are not competitors, but in solidarity. The freedom of the other is not an impediment to mine, but a condition for it. Therefore, the freer the others are, the freer am I; the less free the others are, the less free am I (cf., also: Bakunin, 2008c[e], p. 32).

In the second place, the perspective that freedom contradicts equality, or is established as its antithesis, is rejected. On the contrary, thus conceptualized, freedom demands and contains equality. Social and economic equality is indispensable for the full development of man's natural faculties, and for him not to be subject to the laws and wills of others. "Freedom, being the product and the highest expression of solidarity," "is only fully realizable in equality." "Political equality can only be based on economic and social equality. The realization of freedom through this equality— that is justice." Equality, it must be said, does not mean the end of diversity (Bakunin, 2009d[e], p. 78; cf., also: Bakunin, 2014a[e], pp. 90–91, 140).

Therefore, the full realization of freedom implies, on the one hand, the freedom of all, and, on the other, the effectuation of equality and the end of artificial authority in society. Freedom and equality are inseparable and together form the foundation of justice.

NOTES

1   The four books by Bakunin, as well as several relevant writings and letters, are from this period, which is discussed in this and the next chapters. When they were available, the Portuguese translations of this bibliography were almost always used as reference. In the case of "Letters to a Frenchman on the Current Crisis" I used the Spanish translation (Bakunin, 1977a). In other cases, I used the French material of the six volumes of the *Œuvres* (Stock, 1895-1913), the eight volumes of the *Œuvres Complètes* (Champ Libre, 1973–82), and the *CD-ROM Bakounine: Œuvres Completes* (IISH, 2000).

2   Cf. Feuerbach (1976, p. 25): "Philosophy must be united again with the natural sciences, and the natural sciences with philosophy. This union founded on a mutual need (*Bedürfnis*) on an internal need (*Notwendigkeit*) will be more lasting, more fortunate and fruitful than the marriage that has reigned until now between philosophy and theology."

3   In a frequent procedure, Bakunin makes use of "descriptive philosophical terms or categories in a more or less interchangeable (though not random) way, a habit of Feuerbach that he apparently adopted" (McLaughlin, 2002, p. 113). However, if on the one hand this avoids repetition, on the other it makes understanding difficult. In this case, the concepts of "nature" and "matter," which are already synonymous, are also referred to as "life," "universal causality," and "solidarity" (cf., for example: Bakunin, 2014f[e], pp. 339–40). I use here the concept of "nature-matter" because these are the terms most often used by Bakunin. They were thus ("nature-matter") exposed in Bakunin, 2014f[e], p. 376.

4   Such is Bakunin's definition of *matter*.

5   Such is Bakunin's definition of *nature*. Cf., also, references prior to 1864 and 1865: Bakunin, 2014a[e]; Bakunin, 65001[e].

6   Cf. Feuerbach (*apud* McLaughlin, 2002, p. 200): "What is nature? Feuerbach describes it, in effect, as the totality of causality, or as 'the sum of the [...] cosmic, mechanical, chemical, physical, psychological [and] organic causes' in interaction. Consequently, 'nature has no beginning or end. Everything in it is relative, everything is, at the same time, cause and effect, acting and reacting everywhere.'"

7   When referring to his concept of science, Bakunin refers to it in different ways: "rational science," "positive science," "universal science," "positive philosophy," and "rational philosophy" (cf., for example: Bakunin, 1988a[e], pp. 38, 43–45, 47; Bakunin, 2014e[e], p. 296; Bakunin, 2014f[e], pp. 392, 398, 400, 419).

8   Cf. Comte (1978b, p. 3), on the *law of the three states*: "In the theological state, the human spirit, essentially directing its investigations towards the intimate nature of beings, the first and final causes of all effects that touch it, in a word, towards absolute knowledge, presents the phenomena as produced by the direct and continuous action of more or less numerous supernatural agents, whose arbitrary intervention explains all the apparent anomalies of the universe. In the metaphysical state, which in the end is nothing more than a simple general modification of the former, the supernatural agents are replaced by abstract forces, true entities (personified abstractions) inherent in the various beings of the world, and conceived as capable of engendering by themselves all the phenomena observed, whose explanation then consists in determining for each a corresponding entity. Finally, in the positive state, the human spirit, recognizing the impossibility of obtaining absolute notions, renounces seeking the origin and destiny of the universe, knowing the intimate causes of the phenomena, in order to concern itself solely with discovering, thanks to the well combined use of reasoning and observation, its effective laws, namely, its invariable relations of succession and similitude. The explanation of the facts, then reduced to their real terms, is summed up from now on in the link established between the various particular phenomena and some general facts, the number of which the progress of science tends to diminish more and more."

9   Cf. Comte (*apud* McLaughlin, 2002, p. 208): "If we consider the course of human development from the highest scientific point of view, we will realize that it consists in revealing, more and more, the characteristic faculties of humanity, in comparison with those of animality; specifically those which man has in common with the whole organic kingdom. It is in this philosophical sense that the most eminent civilization must be considered as something that is in complete conformity with nature, since it is, in fact, only a more pronounced manifestation of the superior properties of our species."

10 Cf. Feuerbach (2007, pp. 63, 212): "This essence [of man] is nothing more than intelligence, reason or understanding"; in short, it is "reason or human nature."

11 Cf. Feuerbach (2007, pp. 22, 45–46, 164): "As a *specimen* of this philosophy which has as its principle the most positive real principle, i.e., the real entity or the realest possible, the true *ens realissimum*: man and not the substance of Spinoza, nor the *I* of Kant and Fichte, nor the absolute identity of Schelling, nor the absolute spirit of Hegel; in short, no abstract principle or only thought or imagined of this philosophy which produces thought by removing it from its opposite, from matter." In this philosophy, "the divine essence is nothing more than the human essence or rather, the essence of man abstracted from the limitations of the individual man, i.e., real, bodily, objectified, contemplated and worshiped as another essence of his own, different from his own—that is why all the qualities of the divine essence are qualities of the human essence." That is, "the concept of divinity coincides with the concept of humanity." Despite the proximity, it is important to point out that Bakunin denies Feuerbach's abstract and ahistorical conception of essence and human nature. He distinctly considers that both essence and human nature are natural and historical products (Bakunin, 2003a[e], p. 163; McLaughlin, 2002, p. 166).

12 From this idea derives the logical contradiction repeatedly pointed out by Bakunin: "God exists, therefore man is slave. Man is intelligent, just, free, therefore God does not exist" (Bakunin, 1988a[e], p. 41).

13 Cf. Comte (1978a, pp. 42–45), in his discussion about the theological state and its phases: fetishism, polytheism, and monotheism.

14 Bakunin's criticism also applies to Hobbes, especially because of the notions of the state of nature and the social contract that he sustains, which start from an abstract freedom that culminates in the despotism of the State. Even though he did not succeed in definitively breaking with idealism, Hobbes,

probably because of his reflections on sensations and the human mind, was considered by Bakunin (71004[e], p. 13) the "illustrious founder of English materialism."

15   Although, through the Reformation, Protestantism favoured the emergence of absolute monarchies, as the bourgeoisie began to rise, Protestant values served to legitimize its power project. When, after the French Revolution, the bourgeoisie established itself as the upper class, it greatly enjoyed Protestantism as a fundamental pillar in the consolidation of capitalism. "Imagine a society organized according to the pure principles of Protestantism. It would be a society of men full of contempt both for themselves and for others, and whose only serious concern in life would be the salvation of their own souls, each remaining isolated with God in his inner court, and only communicating with others to the extent that this was necessary for his own salvation. It is the religion of holy selfishness: 'Each one for himself and God for all'—a phrase dear to the bourgeoisie of all countries and which perhaps explains the kind of solidarity that has always existed between the bourgeoisie and Protestantism" (Bakunin, 2014a[e], pp. 80–81).

16   It is based on this position, and in agreement with McLaughlin (2002), that I consider it inappropriate to refer to Bakunin's "method," his frame of reference, in the terms of *historical materialism*—as Lehning (1970, p. 162), Guérin (1968, p. 31), Morris (1993, p. 78), and Monteiro (2013) do—or *sociological materialism*—as Ferreira (2013), Silva (2016), and Brito (2014) do. *History*, for Bakunin (2014e[e], p. 266), is "the revolutionary negation [...] of the past," the "progressive negation of man's first animality for the development of his humanity"; the rational progress of humanity towards freedom. Sociology for Bakunin (1988a[e], pp. 46–47) is the scientific field "which embraces the whole of human history as the development of the collective and individual human being in political, economic, social, religious, artistic and scientific life," that is, "the science of general laws which preside over all developments in human society." According to these definitions, both history and sociology refer to the human world. Moreover, Bakunin's concept of sociology (1988a[e], p. 52)—as "the science of the human world," as a science of the human sciences that should encompass "anthropology, psychology, logic, morality, social economy, politics, aesthetics, [...], theology and metaphysics, history"—goes back to the nineteenth century's Comtean pretensions, which proved to be unrealizable in the following century. So when one speaks of historical or sociological materialism, the impression is given, depending on the terms in question (I am not dealing here with content, but with form), that the naturalistic basis of Bakuninian materialism is left aside. That there is no continuity between nature, history, and society, and that the latter are not part of the former. Of course, this does not invalidate the contributions of these authors, nor does it mean that the naturalist aspects of Bakunin's work are not made explicit in his writings. As I have pointed out, this is just a terminological discussion of how best to refer to Bakunin's method or framework.

17   It is important to note that it is very common that, in his revolutionary socialist period, Bakunin often used the terms "worker," "proletarian," and "labourer" as well as their variants, as synonyms. As Cappelletti (1986, p. 353) points out, Bakunin, when referring to the terms "proletariat," "proletarians," etc., often "does not speak, like Marx, specifically and exclusively of the industrial proletariat, but of the working masses in general."

CHAPTER 12

HISTORY, SOCIAL FORCE, AND DOMINATION
(1867–76)

This chapter continues the exposition of Bakunin's political theory in his *revolutionary socialist period*—specifically based on the contributions from 1867 to 1876—and is divided into four parts: 1) History and Society; 2) Social Forces and Conflict; 3) Domination, Social Classes, and Class Struggle; 4) Statist-capitalist System: Domination at All Levels. In the second and fourth parts, there are three topics that briefly discuss episodes of European history: Forces at Play in the Franco-Prussian War; Historic Rise of the Modern State, Bureaucracy, Capitalism, and the Bourgeoisie; and Pan-Germanic Imperialism and the Slavs.

12.1 HISTORY AND SOCIETY
We have previously seen that society, in all its manifestations, is part of nature-matter, and consequently all that is social is both natural and material. And if "*man forms with all nature a single being and that he is nothing else but the material product of an indefinite number of exclusively material causes*," it can also be affirmed that human history is nothing else but a natural-material history and therefore a "necessary development" inasmuch as it is the "immediate continuation" of "organic and physical nature" (Bakunin, 1988a[e], pp. 50, 56).

History can be defined as a difficult process of "revolutionary negation of the past, sometimes slow, apathetic, asleep, sometimes passionate and powerful. It consists precisely in the progressive negation of man's first animality for the development of his humanity," as well as in the rational progress of humanity towards freedom (Bakunin, 2014e[e], p. 266, emphasis added). It is thus a dialectic movement of "man's intellectual and moral, political and social development," of society itself (Bakunin, 1988a[e], p. 53). It was also observed, in this sense, that the human past is animality (unconscious obedience to nature) and that it was by negating it that humanity was formed. Moreover, it was argued that the future of humanity lies in its own negation (because it is based on the *principle of authority*) for the constitution of full and self-conscious freedom (affirmation of the *principle of freedom*). The whole movement, the whole dynamism of history is explained by this negation (which can also be called the *principle of revolt*). It is this historical process of permanent negation that explains the development of society.

It is important to point out that this development is not necessarily progressive, evolutionary, teleological. In other words, "it cannot be said that in every epoch of history" development takes place in the same direction. Because it proceeds by ebbs and flows and, not infrequently, "by leaps." On certain occasions it "is very fast, very sensitive, very broad" and on "others it is slow or interrupted"; at "other times it even seems to go backwards completely" (Bakunin, 1977a[e], p. 160). Of course, no matter how much human beings tend to the realization of freedom, it will or will not be possible thanks to the confrontation of forces and subjects in conflict. In the constant contradiction between authority and freedom, reaction and revolution, the former often prevailed to the detriment of the latter, causing a regressive historical movement. In the case of the preponderance of the latter, humanity progresses in the direction of freedom (McLaughlin, 2002, p. 127).[1] After all, humanity has a "history without limits, without beginning and without end" (Bakunin, 1988a[e], p. 79).

The social world has been the object of scientific study in different fields: "anthropology, psychology, logic, morality, social economy, politics, aesthetics, [...] history" (Bakunin, 1988a[e], p. 52). And, even if these fields still have much to develop, it cannot be denied that they have advanced, and that they have contributed to a more adequate understanding of society and the individual. This is precisely the case with the "science of history," which "does not yet exist" as a fully consolidated field, since it has not yet been able to reproduce "a rational and reliable picture of the natural development of general conditions, both material and ideal, both economic as well as political and social, religious, philosophical, aesthetic and scientific, of societies that have had a history" (Bakunin, 2014e[e], pp. 296–97).

In the direction of a deepening of this knowledge of the human world, it seems that sociology—this "science that has just been born" and "that is still searching for its elements"— has many possibilities. It is defined as the scientific field "that embraces the whole of human history as the development of the collective and individual human being in political, economic, social, religious, artistic and scientific life," that is, "the science of general laws that preside over all developments in human society." It is thus a science of the human sciences, of the general laws of history, of society, which intends to encompass the knowledge produced by the aforementioned scientific fields, and even by others. For this reason, it is "the most difficult of all" sciences, and it must be admitted "that it will take centuries, at least a century, for it to be definitively constituted and become a serious science, somewhat sufficient and complete" (Bakunin, 1988a[e], pp. 46–47, 52).[2]

It was the sciences that focused on society in general and sociology in particular that identified certain aspects of their functioning, four of which have already been discussed and will now be summarized. The first, the very concept of society as the totality of individuals (inseparable and inconceivable outside of society), of social relations and human development that exists in an interconnected manner in a given community. The second, the existence of solidarity among all individuals in a given society, which is formed thanks to social relations, dependence, attachment, influence, perpetual actions, and reactions of some in relation to others. The third is the fact that the existing social tradition in a society, permanently spread by education in a broad sense, has a profound impact on its individuals—such that, in general, they tend more to reproduce such a tradition than to question and modify it.

The fourth is the relative economic determination of society. That is, on the one hand, it must be recognized that in the human or social world, "among all the facts, the economic and material facts, the facts par excellence, constitute the essential base, the main foundation, of which all the other intellectual and moral, political and social facts are nothing more than the necessary developments" (Bakunin, 2014e[e], pp. 256–57). It is fundamental to remember that this is a relative principle and that as an absolute principle it becomes false. On the other hand, because of the dynamics of action and reaction of nature-matter (and thus of society)—this universal causality according to which "all that exists is at the same time effect and cause"— there is not and neither can there be monocausal determinism (Bakunin, 2014f[e], p. 363). There is a relationship of interinfluence, sometimes a matter of interdependence between the economic and other elements.[3]

As pointed out, political, legal, and religious institutions can have, and indeed have had (historically speaking) influence over the economy; political oppression and the State can have, and indeed have had, influence over capitalist economic exploitation. What's more, even elements that could be narrowly called cultural have this characteristic. "The particular temperament and character of each race and people," which "are themselves naturally the products of a great number of ethnographic, climatological and economic causes, as well as historical," once given, "exert, even outside and independently of economic conditions [...] a considerable influence on their destinies, and even on the development of their economic forces" (Bakunin, 2001b[e], p. 40).

Thus, taking into account the continuity between nature and society, it can be argued that

> just as, in the world properly called material, inorganic matter (mechanical, physical, chemical) is the determining basis of organic matter (vegetable, animal, intelligent or cerebral), in the social world, which cannot be considered other than the last known level of the material world, the development of economic questions has always been, and continues to be, the determining basis of all religious, philosophical, political and social developments. (Bakunin, 1973a[e], p. 11)

In accordance with this definition of the most and least influential elements in the natural-material dynamics of action and reaction, we have that: in nature in general, inorganic matter is more influential (determinant) than organic matter; in society in particular, the economy is more influential (determinant) than political, cultural elements, etc.[4] But it is imperative to keep in mind that "in the history of human development, [...] it is the facts that precede ideas, which does not prevent the latter from later modifying and transforming the former in turn" (Bakunin, 2017f[e], p. 417).

Besides these aspects, the human sciences in general and sociology in particular have identified other traits of the functioning of society, which will now be discussed.

As with external nature—where, thanks to the struggle for life, "*the strong live and the weak succumb, and the former only live because others succumb*" (Bakunin, 2014f[e], p. 349) —society has as its essential characteristic struggles, contradictions, *conflicts* (Bakunin, 2009e[e], p. 34). "Every society is full of contradictions, and it is the theater of an endless struggle, scientific struggle, religious struggle, political struggle, economic struggle; struggle of the collectivity against the State; struggle of the parties and classes in the State; and, finally, struggle within the family." All these conflicts are motivated by the constant movement of formation and negation of order, which makes society something very different from a supposed heaven, where perfect harmony is in effect. "For happiness, for humanity, a perfectly harmonious social order does not exist and has never existed here down below" (Bakunin, 2016d[e], p. 151).

Even moments of a certain harmony, of a balance of forces, when a certain status quo is formed and maintained for some time, are nothing more than a temporary result of conflicts: "Harmony is established in it [the world] by struggle: by the triumph of some, by the defeat and death of others, by the suffering of all." It is clear that it is not only about suffering, but also about pleasure, which stimulates in the human being their "attachment to life." Now, in any case, "we must agree that nature is by no means the loving mother we speak of, and that in order to live, to keep themselves in her bosom, they [living beings] need a singular energy" (Bakunin, 2014f[e], p. 349).

It is conflicts that give movement to society and that make it develop. In the dialectics of history discussed before, this conflict movement is perceived: it was by negating the past (animality) that the present (humanity) established itself; it is by negating the present (humanity) that the future (freedom) can establish itself. Conflicts have marked and continue to mark this whole process. Since there is no humanity outside society, it can be affirmed that the present society constitutes an antagonism, a conflict between its past (animality) and its present (humanity)—whose fundamental trait is authority—and its future—whose essential characteristic is freedom.

In this way, present society—"the reality, that is, the political, civic and social order today and in all countries"—is nothing more than "the sum, or better, the result of struggle, conflicts, mutual annihilation, domination and, in general, of the conjunction and reciprocal action of the various forces that, inside and outside" act in or on it (Bakunin, 2009e[e], p. 34). The present reality of a society is therefore the result of confrontation between "many social forces" that relate to each other in a conflictive way. This result is always forged for a certain time—in view of the dynamism of the existing society due to its own conflicts—when certain forces prevail over others. When this happens, there is a temporary balance between the forces, a status quo is established in which the conflicts do not cease to exist, but at least become less apparent (Bakunin, 1973b[e], p. 59).

12.2 SOCIAL FORCES AND CONFLICT

A social force can be defined as the natural-material potential that individuals, groups, or social classes use in social conflicts to achieve certain objectives. It is a *real force*, resulting from the realization of a *potential force*, which previously existed as a latent possibility of becoming. Everything that belongs to the organic or inorganic world contributes to the formation of the surrounding environment. For this reason, "in society, the smallest human being represents a miniscule fraction of the *social force*." In social terms, it is possible to affirm that every individual, associated with others or not, contributes to the correlation of forces that forms a reality—the "balance between the forces that are manifested in a given society"— and therefore participates, voluntarily or involuntarily, in the production of its "social regimes." In other words, a social force can be an *individual force* or a *collective force* (Bakunin, 2009e[e], p. 34).

Individual force is part of the corporal power that an individual possesses, and can be increased in different ways (Bakunin, 2009c[e], pp. 51–52). Collective force starts with union, association, organization among different individuals, and, taking advantage of their individual strengths, can also be increased in different ways. However, just as society cannot be conceived as a simple grouping of individuals, a collective social force cannot be conceived as the simple sum of individual forces.

> The common effort of a few dozen individuals is much more effective than any individual effort, not only because the force of several units is always greater than that of a single one (in a society composed of millions of individuals, the sum of a few dozen small fractions compared to the immense sum of social forces is also almost equal to zero), but also because, when a dozen, or even more, individuals combine their efforts to achieve a common goal, a new force is constituted among them which goes far beyond the simple arithmetic sum of the individual efforts of each one. In political economics, this fact was first observed by Adam Smith and attributed to the natural action of the *division of labor*. Now, in the case I examined, it is not only the division of labor that acts, that is, engenders a new force, but also, and to an even greater extent, *union* and what necessarily completes it: the elaboration of a plan of action, then the best *possible allocation, and the systematic or reflected organization of sparse forces* in accordance with the established plan. (Bakunin, 2009e[e], pp. 35–36)

This fact, which was also verified and theorized by Proudhon,[5] shows, in the first place, that there is a substantial difference between collective force and individual force, in that the former cannot be considered the simple sum of the latter. It also shows that association is a determining tool for the increase of social force. It was only thanks to association that individuals were able to accumulate their reflections on understanding the world—and thus get to understand it more deeply—and establish lasting "productive forces" capable of ensuring their subsistence (Bakunin, 2009c[e], pp. 51–53; Bakunin, 2016a[e], p. 103).

It was only by means of union that certain individuals or groups were able to subjugate others, forging social orders that favoured them for long periods. However, it is not only organization that ensures the increase of social force. There are many other criteria—economic, political, legal, military, behavioral, moral, etc.—that contribute to this, and are essential for understanding the historical dynamics of a society. First of all, it should be noted that these criteria are related to the rooting and institutionalization of certain modes of systemic functioning (mode of production, power) and certain notions (ideas, habits, values, customs, etc.) in social structures and social tradition. This systemic functioning and these notions possess the force of reproduction, both by their own dynamics and by the broad education that spreads the social tradition (socialization). Therefore, a society always tends more to the maintenance of order than to change. Thus individuals, groups, or social classes that defend more structurally and institutionally rooted positions will always have greater ease in conflict than those who are acting in the direction of change (Bakunin, 2003a[e], p. 213; Bakunin, 2017d[e], p. 405; Bakunin, 1988a[e], p. 129).

In addition, criteria for increased social force include access to resources such as property, money—both often derived from inheritance and in some cases derived from the ownership of other people's own bodies—and natural resources. With ownership and the respective exploitation of labour, it is possible to multiply resources that, privately appropriated, become power. With money, it is possible to buy resources of all kinds, including influence in various sectors of society (Bakunin, 1973b[e], pp. 48–49, 60; Bakunin, 2003a[e], pp. 73, 108, 158). They also involve the occupation of hierarchical social positions, positions of command, the level of military organization, and access to arms. By occupying positions of power one is able to decide what concerns a broader range of people—to govern them—and, through military organization and weapons, to impose oneself on others, whether by the threat of or by the very use of violence (Bakunin, 2009d[e], p. 79; Bakunin, 1988a[e], pp. 105, 110; Bakunin, 1973b[e], pp. 60–62).

These criteria also include the ability of persuasion and the amount of popular support. When, through influence, people are able to directly or indirectly endorse a particular project, they can associate with it, providing the gain in force previously discussed or even contribute to the creation of favourable public opinion (Bakunin, 1988a[e], p. 25; Bakunin, 2003a[e], p. 101; Bakunin, 2014f[e], p. 442; Bakunin, 2016d[e], p. 148). Such capacity for influence is deeply related to knowledge, another criterion for increased force, which is acquired through education and instruction:

It is true, training is a force; and however deficient, superficial, deformed that of our upper classes may be, it is undeniable that, with other factors, it allows the privileged minority to retain power in their hands. [...] Knowledge is a strength; ignorance, the cause of social impotence. [...] Where has an uncultured spirit been seen, however powerful it may be by nature, superimposed on a confrontation with a collective intellectual force formed over centuries? This is why one often sees a man of the intelligent people capitulate before an imbecile who has received instruction. (Bakunin, 2009e[e], pp. 39, 43–44)

In a society that relies on the division between intellectual labour and manual labour it is much simpler for those who are educated to impose themselves on the uneducated (Bakunin, 2009c[e], p. 52). Finally, there are other criteria that, although pertaining to the broader field of ideas and subjectivities, deserve to be mentioned: morality, will, trust, discipline, and obedience. To believe deeply in an objective, to trust one's own proposal and strengths, to practice discipline (both self-discipline and imposed discipline) significantly increases the possibilities of victory in a conflict. In the same way, in a hierarchical organization or institution, the obedience of lower members to superiors does (Bakunin, 2014d[e], pp. 164, 166, 228; Bakunin, 1973b[e], pp. 62–63).

Based on these criteria, it is understood that in society a conflict can be more or less violent, and that social conflict does not necessarily mean violence. When a conflict is established, at least two social forces are formed and come into play, in confrontation. According to these criteria, each of the forces has, at first, a real and concrete power, which can be increased according to these very criteria, access to resources, and alliances with other forces. The confrontation may be of short or long duration, but it reaches a term when one force (or more) prevails over another (or others). An order or status is thus formed in which certain forces have prevailed over others.

However much this apparatus is used at other times to analyze the socio-political conjuncture, we will try now to explain how it can contribute to an understanding of the *longue durée* of history, with a more structural than conjunctural focus.[6] In this way, human history can be characterized as an arduous process of negation, on the part of the social forces supported on the principle of freedom, of those social forces supported on the principle of authority. In this way, society can be conceived dialectically as a permanent conflict between freedom and authority.[7] In this confrontation, the principle of authority has prevailed, more generally and from the earliest times of history, incarnated in minorities who impose themselves on majorities by means of domination.

When the beginning of humanity was discussed, it was pointed out that, in a first moment, men subordinated women, and in a second moment, men subordinated women and other men giving rise, with the appearance of agriculture, to mass slavery.

The struggles of men against women and of slaveholders against slaves are expressions of social conflict in those societies. Interpreting these events according to the concepts presented, we can say the following. Both the subordination of women and the enslavement of women and men were based on a confrontation between social forces. In both cases, the men who imposed themselves did so because they constituted a greater social force, probably through the use of criteria such as physical strength— and perhaps even others, which could include weapons, social position, knowledge. The oppressors then began to benefit from the oppression, taking advantage of the dominated, which revolved around labour and then spread to other fields. It was a movement of feedback, since domination is also a criterion for increasing social force, such that it allows the oppressor group to permanently increase its social force. The dynamism of those societies is explained by the negation that women and slaves realized of their own condition, on the one hand, and by the affirmation of that order on the part of the dominators on the other.

The logic of these events helps to understand the historical development of humanity. Thanks to their greater social force, certain groups impose themselves on others, creating plunder, conquest, and enslavement, and then seeking in social rules and beliefs the legitimacy for this fact. In turn, these instruments of legitimization contribute to guarantee the continuity of domination. While the preponderance of a certain force lasts, there is a social order, a status quo, within which more or less open social conflicts arise, which are forged by the rejection of this circumstance by oppressed groups. At a certain moment, when this conflict emerges openly, and to the extent that the oppressed groups manage to accumulate greater social force than the dominators—managing to supplant their movements of reaction and conservation of order— changes occur, revolutions take place.

12.2.1 Forces at Play in the Franco-Prussian War

The concepts presented above contribute to a reading of relations between France and Prussia in the context of the Franco-Prussian War, between 1870 and 1871.

The context in question has already been mentioned. France, under Napoleon III, and Prussia, under William I and Bismarck, had been increasing their state forces and the conquests of other territories was fundamental to this: it both explained this increase in might and indicated new possibilities in this regard. Both states were at the heart of an international dispute for the hegemony of Europe, such that the conflict between France and Prussia existed even before the Franco-Prussian War. The beginning of the war changed the terms of the conflict, which began to be expressed by open armed violence. That is, the war reconfigured a previous conflict, opening the possibilities for a change in the balance of European forces and putting two state social forces into open confrontation: France and Prussia, which from July 1870 began to mobilize their forces in the war.

The August battles already made it clear how the forces would be put into play in the war and which state had the greatest social force and therefore the greatest chances for victory:

> It is evident today [25 August, 1870] that the last battle of 18 August in Gravelotte was, for the French, a disaster. Beaten, discouraged, slaughtered, badly organized, badly administered and badly led [...], starting already to suffer from hunger [...], the 100,000 men of Bazaine find themselves in the presence of 250,000 Germans, all replenished by the looting of Alsace and Lorraine and by the immense supplies of all sorts that were snatched from the three bodies of Frossard, Du Failly and Mac-Mahon. [...] The Germans, on the contrary, are in an excellent disposition. They are commanded by good officers, wise, conscientious, intelligent, fierce, and in whom science and military intelligence are joined by abnegation and the discipline of slaves in front of their crowned chief. [...] They are commanded by equally intelligent generals. [...] They follow a plan that has long been thought out, agreed upon, and that has not needed to be modified until now, while the French army, having initially conducted itself without a plan, without an idea, reduced to the extreme, has yet to create one, inspired by despair. The Prussians [...] have the intelligent study, preparation and execution of an established plan which they follow systematically, uniting great audacity with great prudence. [...] It is clear that, from the point of view of strategy and tactics, in a word, of the military position, all the advantages are on the side of the Prussians, all the probabilities are theirs. (Bakunin, 1977a[e], pp. 72–74)

In military terms, the war demonstrated Prussian superiority at the time, mainly because it succeeded in mobilizing greater force by the following criteria: number of soldiers, quantity of provisions, level of organization and strategy, knowledge, and discipline. Prussia's position in the war is also explained by the advantages it had in economic and political terms, and the mood of its population and its combatants. "The economic position of Germany *at the moment* is a thousand times better than that of France" for "the simple reason that the war is being waged not in Germany but in France." "Germany is administered a hundred times better than France, looted at this moment by the Germans and the imperial administration." Moreover, while on the Prussian side there is "Germanic exaltation" and enormous motivation and willingness for war, on the French side there is only "abatement, discouragement, complete prostration" (Bakunin, 1977a[e], pp. 74–76).

It was because of the greater mobilization of social force in the conflict that Prussia began to convert what was initially a "war of self-defense" into a "war of conquest," into a "war of German despotism against the freedom of France" (Bakunin, 2014d[e], p. 220). It was not, however, a popular war, based on the natural forces of the German people, but an "aristocratic, monarchical and military invasion" headed by the ruling classes of Prussia against all the classes of France even if, obviously, the oppressed classes suffered the greatest consequences (Bakunin, 1977a[e], p. 143).

In September 1870, following the Battle of Sedan, Napoleon III was overthrown and a republican government of national defense was established in France; refusing a peace agreement, Bismarck initiated the siege of Paris. The armed confrontations continued and Prussia prevailed for the reasons listed above. In addition, the siege was decisive for another criterion of strength: supplies became increasingly scarce for the French, so that, as we know, at one point the bourgeoisie began to feed on the zoo animals and the poor on rats.

Finally, Paris capitulated at the end of January 1871 when Thiers achieved an armistice with Bismarck. In analyzing the reasons for the Prussian victory, some notes can be made. First, that there was the contribution of the countless betrayals of the French ruling classes (Bonapartists and Republicans) who from the beginning abandoned the salvation of France.

> In every city in France, the proletariat demanded arms and general recruitment against the Germans, and it would undoubtedly have accomplished this purpose had it not been paralyzed, on the one hand, by the ignominious fear and widespread betrayal of the majority of the bourgeois class, who preferred to submit a thousand times to the Prussians instead of entrusting weapons to the proletariat, and, on the other hand, by the reactionary countermeasures taken systematically by the "government of National Defense," in Paris and in the interior, as well as by the no less anti-popular opposition of the dictator, the patriot Gambetta. (Bakunin, 2003a[e], pp. 41–42)

Second, that "France did not succumb [just] because its armies were destroyed"; to this was added the fact that "the French nation itself was in a state of disorganization and demoralization that made it absolutely incapable of spontaneously mounting a serious national defense." In other words, in addition to greater military, economic, and political capacity, there was an important moral force that impacted on the conflict (Bakunin, 1973b[e], pp. 61–62, 67).

However, this imposition of force by Prussia was not immediately consolidated, thanks to the eruption of the Paris Commune in March 1871. With it, new forces came into play in this conflict, which would only be resolved in May, when the allied forces of the upper French and Prussian classes bloodily imposed themselves on the social force of the *communards*.

12.3 DOMINATION, SOCIAL CLASSES, AND CLASS STRUGGLE

Since its inception, humanity has had in social conflict the reason for its development and, although oppressive groups and superior social classes have changed, the principle of authority has always prevailed. For this reason, it is possible to argue that the common trait of humanity is power, oppression, exploitation—or, in synthesis, domination.

Domination is a social relationship that results from the confrontation between social forces, in which some (in general a minority with greater social force) impose themselves on others (in general a majority with less social force) and take advantage of this imposition to become artificial authorities and obtain economic and non-economic privileges. It is, therefore, a relationship between a privileged minority and an underprivileged majority for the benefit of the former and to the detriment of the latter (Bakunin, 2014d[e], p. 181; Bakunin, 2008e[e], p. 125; Bakunin, 2009e[e], p. 39; Bakunin, 2017f[e], p. 428). "Domination is only real when everything that hinders it is subjugated to it. One force only supports another when it is forced to, that is, when it feels powerless to destroy or overthrow it" (Bakunin, 2008c[e], p. 28).

This relationship of imposition is at the same time a relationship of power which, to endure in time and space, demands the permanent oppression of those who have been subordinated in order that they may continue to produce the privileges of the dominators. As can be seen, *domination, power, and oppression function as synonyms, and are directly opposed to emancipation.* "He who says power [...], says domination" and "where there is domination, there must necessarily be men, a more or less large part of the society that is dominated," and those "who dominate must necessarily repress, and consequently oppress those who are submitted to their domination" (Bakunin, 1998[e], pp. 30–31).

Domination is found in the different fields of society. In the economic field it is expressed as "*economic domination*," whose most common form is "*exploitation of labor*" (Bakunin, 2014d[e], pp. 172, 174; Bakunin, 2003a[e], p. 35).[8] In the political field it is expressed in the relationship between states and nation-races as *national domination* and/or *imperialism*, and in the relationship between rulers and ruled, where violence is a determining aspect, such as "*political domination*" or state (Bakunin, 2014e[e], pp. 255, 265, 274, 333). In the field of "intellectual and moral culture" it expresses itself as *intellectual and moral domination*, with inequality of knowledge (education, instruction) and the "domination of the Church" being its main forms (Bakunin, 2014a[e], 77, 85; Bakunin, 71010[e], 38). However, these forms of domination should only be separated analytically, since in history, they have generally been associated with each other, reinforced by the dynamics of action and reaction.

In historical terms domination expressed itself in various ways. One can mention, for example, the case of the national domination of Slavic peoples by Russia, Prussia, Austria, and the Ottoman Empire. As part of this relationship many Slavs have been submitted to the harshest German yoke and a growing process of (Pan-)Germanization (Bakunin, 2003a[e], pp. 57–62). It is also possible to cite the case of the racial domination of blacks by whites: "Our century [...] had the distinguished honor of emancipating Blacks" from slavery which, in the United States, persisted until the 1860s.

Finally, one can mention the case—very significant for its antiquity—of male domination, of the oppression of women by men. Even though she was "endowed with the same capacities as the man," the woman was subjugated because he was "naturally stronger" in absolute terms, and was able to impose himself physically. This fact of "the real subordination of women in the natural organization of families and society" was then legitimized by a range of ideas, which includes "religious, mystical and juridical theory" and also "the metaphysics of their [women's] bodily, but above all intellectual and moral inferiority." Ideas that, incorporated into the consciousness of society, later became effective causes of the fact "of an increasingly real inferiority" of women (Bakunin, 2017f[e], pp. 417–19).

However, the most common historical expression of domination has been class domination: "until now history has known no other civilization than class civilization" (Bakunin, 2009e[e], p. 45). Until the present, society has been completely traversed by a schism between social classes, putting the oppressed on one side and oppressors on the other:

> For as long as there has been a history, the human world has been partitioned into two classes: the immense majority, chained to more or less mechanical, brutal and forced labor; the millions of workers, eternally exploited, spending their sad lives in misery close to hunger, ignorance and slavery, and condemned, therefore, to eternal obedience. Then, on the other hand, the more or less happy, educated, refined, exploitative, dominant, ruling minority, consuming the best part of the collective labor of the popular masses and representing the whole civilization. (Bakunin, 2017a[e], pp. 453–54)

Class domination also results from confrontation between social forces. In general terms, the contradiction between *dispossessed (or dominated, oppressed, inferior, exploited) classes and superior (or dominant, oppressive, privileged, exploitative) classes* can be interpreted as a historical conflict between "two great" antagonistic "categories" of social forces. The imposition of the latter (minority) over the former (majority) is based on a range of criteria, among which are: access to wealth, power, and knowledge, and also the level of organization.

Practically without access to these resources and lacking organization, the oppressed classes—which comprise "the millions and millions of individuals who constitute the mass of the people," that is, this "sum of unconscious, instinctive, traditional, as it were, spontaneous and poorly organized forces, even though full of life"—have been subordinated. Those who have always imposed themselves on them are the dominant classes—who have rich and powerful people who have access to these resources and are more organized, that is, this "incomparably smaller sum of conscious forces, conjugated, deliberately associated, acting according to a given plan, and systematically organized according to that plan." This is what explains why "society is divided into a minority composed of exploiters and a more or less consciously exploited immense mass" (Bakunin, 2009e[e], p. 36).

In statist and capitalist modern society social classes are also essential aspects, and are constituted from the production and reproduction of social relations:

> In human society [...] the difference between classes is, however, very marked, and the whole world will know how to distinguish the noble aristocracy from the financial aristocracy, the upper bourgeoisie from the petty bourgeoisie, and the latter from the proletarians of factories and cities; thus also, the great landowner, the tenant farmer and the peasant landowner who cultivates his land; the farmer, from the simple proletarian of the countryside. (Bakunin, 1988a[e], pp. 15–16)

In this passage, some concrete social classes (which have historically existed) are distinguished more or less clearly: nobility, landowners, bourgeoisie, proletariat (of the city and the countryside), and peasantry. It is also possible to point out the existence of other concrete social classes: "priestly class," "bureaucratic class," and "ragged proletariat." Thus, in addition to the classes listed above, there are at least three others: clergy, bureaucracy, and the marginalized in general or "lumpen proletariat" in Marxist terminology (Bakunin, 2009b[e], p. 60; Bakunin, 2003a[e], pp. 30, 79).

For the definition of social classes, the binomial domination-privilege is the main foundation. Owing to the relevance of the economic field in society, economic domination and privileges are crucial criteria in this conceptualization: "exclusive ownership of land" (the privilege of nobility in the second half of the nineteenth century) and "the monopoly of capital and both industrial and commercial enterprises" (the privilege of the bourgeoisie of that same period) constitute the bases of economic domination, both of the owners of the means of production and distribution in relation to the wage-earning workers of the city and the countryside, as well as of the landowners in relation to the tenant farmers or even small landowners. The difference between rich and poor, based on ownership of capital, also implies another important economic privilege, and contributes to class domination. Ownership of the means of production—including land—distribution, and capital implies "the exploitation of the subjected labor, or forced by hunger, of the popular masses" and thus increases social inequality, making the rich richer and the poor poorer (Bakunin, 68006[e], pp. 2–4).

But, avoiding economic determinism, these should not be considered the only criteria to define social classes. The control of administration and all that this implies (wars, decisions, laws, justice, defense, coercion), non-economic privilege, is in the hands of a "privileged [...] class of men," the bureaucracy, which has "solidarity with the interests of the State" and for this very reason is devoted "body and soul to its prosperity and existence." The ability to massively promote a certain understanding of the world—a non-economic privilege also of the clergy and other wise men in the second half of the nineteenth century—comes from the "difference in education and instruction." Through it, one can guarantee "the artificial and forced development of the stupidity of peoples" and with this contribute to "a mass of slaves" being subjugated by "a small number of dominators" (Bakunin, 68006[e], pp. 1–2; Bakunin, 2015[e], p. 267). Thus, besides the economic criteria, there are others, fundamental to defining social classes: ownership of the means of administration, control, and coercion (political criteria), as well as ownership of the means of knowledge in society (cultural criteria).

In short, social classes are defined on the basis of the concept of domination and are formed in a relationship of multicausal determination between economic, political, and cultural (intellectual-moral) phenomena. They express a social stratification that evidences the different privileges in a society: in the economic field, ownership of the means of production, including land, distribution, and capital; in the political field, ownership of the means of administration, control, and coercion; in the cultural field (intellectual-moral), ownership of the means of knowledge. In general terms, economic privileges imply economic domination (exploitation of labour), political privileges imply national domination (imperialism) and political domination (government), and cultural privileges imply knowledge inequality and religious submission.

During the nineteenth century, the dominant classes included: the nobility/latifundium (landowners), the bourgeoisie (owner of the means of production and capital), the bureaucracy (owner of the means of administration, coercion and control), and the clergy and the intellectuals (owners of the means of knowledge). The oppressed classes included: the proletariat of the city and the countryside (wage-earning workers), peasantry (tenants or small landowners), and the marginalized (unemployed, beggars, miserable, illiterate, thieves, etc.).

Obviously, there were class fractions and "gray areas" among these large categories. However, in theoretical terms, the finding of the existence of those points that are not exactly black or white[9]—which exist to the extent that it is "impossible to establish a demarcation line between the possessing and dispossessed classes" and since, in these zones, they are confused "by a quantity of intermediate and imperceptible nuances"—cannot in any way support the argument of the non-existence of social classes. As in everything in nature, it is impossible to know rigorously and exactly where the "demarcation lines" that, for example, separate animality from humanity or day from night, pass. But it is not because it is not known precisely at what historical moment animals became men, or at what instant day becomes night, that animality, humanity, day, and night do not exist. Such that "despite the intermediate positions that form an insensitive transition from one political and social existence to another, the difference between classes is nevertheless very marked" (Bakunin, 1988a[e], pp. 15–16).

Class struggle (or class war) is exactly the expression of the conflict between social classes that puts oppressive and oppressed, which have unequal access to economic, political, and cultural privileges, on opposing sides (Bakunin, 2001a[e], 68). It emerges above all because of the social position that individuals and groups occupy in society, which is the basis of their class interests, but it is enhanced by the consciousness and actions of these subjects (Bakunin, 2009e[e], pp. 59–60; Bakunin, 2014d[e], p. 209). On the one hand, class struggle manifests itself in particular social relations: workers and bosses, peasants and landowners, etc. On the other hand, its broader manifestation involves general social relations, formed by two broad groups of dominators and dominated, which also go beyond structural determinations and involve class interests and the class position assumed in the conflict. This is the basis of class conflicts, in which social classes have sought to mobilize social force to impose themselves.

To verify this second (larger) manifestation theoretically requires working, in more abstract terms, a reduction of the forces at play—in this case, of the concrete and historical classes in struggle at that time:

> All these different political and social existences [concrete and historical social classes] today allow themselves to be reduced to two main categories, diametrically opposed to each other, and natural enemies of each other: the *political classes* [or dominant, oppressive, superior, privileged classes], composed of all the privileged, both of the land and of capital, or even only of bourgeois education, and the *working classes* [or dominated, oppressed, inferior, dispossessed classes], disinherited from both capital and the land, and deprived of any education and any instruction. (Bakunin, 1988a[e], p. 16)

Although this quotation does not include all the criteria that are used in the definition of social classes, it shows how this reduction can operate theoretically. The social conflicts that emerge in a society due to the existence of economic, political, and cultural privileges, and confrontations in different fields, are reduced to two large groups. One, superior, with members who accumulate wealth, power, and knowledge, and the other, inferior, deprived of all this. As will be seen below, these privileges relate to and reinforce each other. It should be noted that the basis of this reduction is not the centrality of these groups at a given historical moment, nor their perspective of future evolution, but class interests and the role played by these classes in the more general process of class struggle.

Contemporary society is first and foremost—like previous societies—the result of the confrontation between social forces of class and a real depiction of the imposition of superior classes on the dispossessed. However, it differs from previous societies in that it relies on modern forms of domination.

12.4 THE STATIST-CAPITALIST SYSTEM: DOMINATION AT ALL LEVELS

. In the contemporary world, domination is expressed as a *statist-capitalist system.*[10] A historical social structure composed of different related parts and that articulates forms of domination at all levels for the benefit of certain social classes. With the rise of the bourgeoisie and capitalism, this systemic domination has been characterized by an articulation between the governments of the modern State and its bureaucracies on the one hand and capitalist economic exploitation on the other. In some cases this articulation resulted in imperialism and, in all of them, it was legitimized by education and the religions in force.

12.4.1 The Modern State: Imperialism, Physical Coercion, Bureaucratic Domination

The modern State, in all its government forms or regimes, is *a political instrument of class domination that has a dominating nature, class character, and function of guaranteeing class domination.* Under the threat of being conquered or failing to maintain order, the State needs to permanently seek to increase its social force and does so by reconciling its imperialist and enslaving vocations. In the first case, conquering or trying not to be conquered; in the second, seeking the maintenance of the status quo. It does this through various mechanisms that involve, in some cases, national domination (imperialism) and, in all cases, political domination (government, or physical coercion and bureaucratic domination), in addition to other forms of domination.

The function of the State to guarantee class domination implies different forms of domination, which makes the State and domination permanently and inseparably related: "Whoever says State, necessarily says domination [...], that is why we are enemies of the State" (Bakunin, 2003a[e], p. 212).[11] Understanding how and why this relationship occurs, however, requires a more detailed explanation. To fulfill its function, the State needs to *permanently increase its force*, above all for two reasons: to not be conquered or dominated by other states and to be able to establish the internal maintenance of order.

The political power of the State tends to concentrate itself and seek hegemony through the constitution of empires. There is, thus, a similarity between the dynamics of the State and that of capital: "The same competition that, on the economic level, crushes and devours small and even medium-sized capital, industrial establishments, land properties and commercial houses, crushes and devours small and medium-sized states for the benefit of empires." If, on the economic plane, big capital defeats small capital in the process of competition, tending to be concentrated, in politics, "every State that is not content to exist on paper and by the grace of its neighbors, for as long as they want to tolerate it, but wishes to be a real, sovereign, independent State, must necessarily be a conquering State." In the international dispute between national states it is necessary, for the maintenance of sovereignty, that the State conquers or at least that it is not conquered, because if this occurs it will remain subjugated or even disappear (Bakunin, 2003a[e], p. 66).

In order to participate adequately in this dynamic, states must strengthen themselves militarily, especially through standing armies: "The modern State, by its essence and by the objectives it sets itself, is by force a military State," which must necessarily "become a conquering State; if it does not launch itself into conquest, it will be conquered, for the simple reason that wherever force exists, it must show itself or act." The modern State needs to be large and strong to safeguard and impose itself in international relations. Just as capitalist initiatives tend toward monopoly, "the modern State, military by necessity, carries within itself the irresistible aspiration to become a universal State"—that is, it tends toward generalized hegemony (Bakunin, 2003a[e], p. 36).

However, it is clear that not all states have this vocation for conquest or even have the ability to carry it out. If, on the one hand, the big and powerful states tend to conquer the smaller ones, the latter are left to increase their defense forces in an attempt to avoid being conquered (Bakunin, 2008c[e], p. 27).

The consequence of this process is the exacerbation of conflicts: "among all the States that exist, one next to the other, war is permanent and peace only a truce" (Bakunin, 2008c[e], p. 28). The tendency to concentrate political power and this "imperialist vocation" (Cappelletti, 1986, p. 222) of the modern State therefore implies constant confrontations between states, often leading to armed conflict, in this struggle for domination and its confrontation with national resistance. As in any relationship of domination, moments of peace do not mean that power has ceased to exist.

Moreover, for the modern State, it is essential to guarantee the maintenance of order in its own territories: "To maintain internal order, to preserve its unity imposed under duress," the modern State needs not only "a great army" but also "a police force, a gigantic bureaucracy" (Bakunin, 2003a[e], p. 87). In normal circumstances, order is preserved by mechanisms of legitimization produced and reinforced, among other agents, by the State itself. When this is not enough, the threat of violence or violence itself unleashed by the State in the form of repression surfaces and guarantees the preservation of the status quo. These police-military and bureaucratic arms of the State act by more or less violent means, depending on the circumstance, and their agents— police, military, rulers, judges—embody this task, controlling entire populations and ensuring that the essential aspects of the social structure are not undermined.

The preservation of the status quo implies the continuity of the privileges of the dominant classes.[12] The State not only guarantees, but itself creates the conditions for the monopoly of political power by the bureaucracy, which enjoys the privilege of making decisions concerning the rules of society, the solution of conflicts, the execution of deliberations, coercion, and punishment. A privilege that, at the same time, relates to the economic benefits that the bureaucracy also enjoys, and in accordance with which it often acts. The effect of the State is "to directly and unfailingly consolidate the political and economic privileges of the ruling minority and the economic and political slavery of the popular masses" (Bakunin, 2003a[e], p. 169). It is also the State that guarantees the exploitation of labour, through the submission of the masses, inasmuch as the State aims at "organizing, on the widest scale, the exploitation of labor, for the benefit of capital concentrated in very few hands." Because this capital constitutes "the soul of every political State," above all because it finances it, the latter guarantees the former "the unlimited right to exploit the labor of the people" (Bakunin, 2003a[e], pp. 35, 228). Landowners and capitalist industries are thus guaranteed their privileges in the appropriation of part of the product of labour by peasants, industrial and other workers. This is what characterizes the "enslaving vocation" of the modern State (Cappelletti, 1986, p. 223).

The greatest threat to the maintenance of order is social revolution, since it implies not only the "abolition of all exploitation and of all political or legal, governmental or administrative oppression, that is, the abolition of all classes through the economic leveling of all goods" but also, and indispensably, the "destruction of their last bastion, the State." In this way it puts "the State on one side, the social revolution on the other," characterizing a clear contradiction between the oppressed in their search for an end to domination and class privileges and the political instrument that guarantees them (Bakunin, 2003a[e], pp. 73, 44).

Therefore, in order not to be conquered or dominated by other states and to maintain internal order, the modern State must permanently increase its force. In this process, it starts conflicts with other states and with its own people:

> All States [...] are condemned to a perpetual struggle: struggle against their own populations, oppressed and ruined, struggle against all foreign States, of which each is powerful only on condition that the other is weak; and since they can only preserve themselves in this struggle by increasing their force each day, both internally, against their own citizens, and externally, against the neighboring powers—it follows that the supreme law of the State is to increase its force to the detriment of interior freedom and exterior justice. (Bakunin, 1998[e], p. 41)

Reinforcing the argument of the constant need for increased force, and concerning the dynamics between the conflicting social forces of society, it is in the nature of these forces that the larger ones impose themselves on the smaller ones. Even one of the latter "cannot endure any other, neither superior nor equal" and only submits itself "when it is forced to, that is, when it feels powerless to destroy or overthrow it" (Bakunin, 2008c[e], p. 28). In the dynamics of the State, this means that if one is not increasing its force, others may be, including proletarians, peasants, and the marginalized. In this way, there is a risk in relation to its power. If the State wants to ensure it, externally and internally, and thus fulfill its function, it must ensure constant strengthening, its greatest guarantee that it will not be threatened by external or internal factors.

The most appropriate way for the State to increase its force is through the conciliation of its imperialist and enslaving vocations to transform outer and inner domination into social force—such dominations constitute its most relevant sources of force. There are at least eight mechanisms that allow a state to obtain force and to increase it: extension and type of territory, presence in "free territories"; financial, organizational, and military resources; extension, support, and limit of political participation of the population.

Some remarks can be made about these mechanisms. The larger the territory of a state, the greater its force, because of the space and resources it can benefit from, which include possibilities of the exploitation of mines and other natural resources, space for industries, agriculture, livestock, housing, etc. Conquests are important tools for the annexation of new territories and, in case they occur in developed regions, there may still be other resources to be exploited. Depending on the type of territory one has or conquers, there are greater or lesser possibilities of increasing force, especially due to its dimensions and the resources that exist in it. There are great advantages in territories that have port regions and thus access to the oceans, since navigation and maritime commerce provide distinct benefits. A presence in free territories such as seas and air space is also significant.

The financial resources of the State can be obtained through external domination (wars, colonialism, imperialism), internal domination (taxes, direct exploitation), and even through borrowing and pure and simple theft—in order to obtain money, the State supports the owners, the bankers, and the large merchants. The State can leverage its own organizational resources, in particular through centralization and rational administration with a view to efficiency. In military terms, the following are important: the number of personnel, the quantity and level of equipment, the degree of discipline and organization, the quality of the commanders, and the level of commitment to the State.

The larger the population of a state, the more that population supports the State and the more the State can keep its management in the hands of a minority, giving the impression that it represents the majority, the greater its force. Above all, more people means greater financial resources and possibilities for the army to grow with people who, at least in theory, are more faithful to the State than mercenaries. The support of this population is central, and therefore patriotism and submission of the bodies and minds of the governed become fundamental. Guaranteeing control of the State by a minority that appears to defend general interests, if it does not increase, at least maintains the force of the State and makes it more legitimate, and therein lies the value of representative democracy (Bakunin, 2003a[e], pp. 32, 117–18, 127, 133–34, 228).

Although, as explained, social force is not summed up as brute force, physical coercion and militarism, these aspects cannot be downplayed. "The State is precisely synonymous with coercion, domination by force, camouflaged, if possible, and, if necessary, brutal and naked." In other words, the monopoly of violence is a determining aspect in maintaining the status quo, even if it takes place in a disguised manner: "the State, whatever it may be, even assuming the most liberal and democratic forms, is necessarily founded on supremacy, domination, violence, that is, despotism, camouflaged if it is preferred, but in this case even more dangerous" (Bakunin, 2003a[e], pp. 47; 58–59). This physical coercion—whether in fact carried out, with the use of violence, or potentially used in the form of a threat—is certainly one of the most important means of state action. As noted, beyond this force *stricto sensu*, the State invests in means involving diplomacy and most importantly in mechanisms of self-legitimization.

> The State is force, and has, above all, the right of force, the triumphant argument of the rifle. But man is so singularly made that this argument, however eloquent it may seem, is no longer sufficient with the passing of time. To impose respect on him, some moral sanction is absolutely necessary. Moreover, this sanction must be both so simple and so evident that it can convince the masses that, after having been reduced by the force of the State, they must be led to the moral recognition of its right. (Bakunin, 2011b[e], p. 124)

Such sanction, which has in education and in religions privileged sources, can also be reinforced by the State itself, by forming a particular morality: "Everything that serves it is good, everything that is contrary to its interests is declared criminal, such is the morality of the State" —such is the reason for the State (Bakunin, 2008c[e], p. 28). The State plays a decisive role in the production and reproduction of discursive propositions that have moral effects and that avoid the permanent use of violence and thus the wearing down of the State itself. Violence is ineffective if it is constantly used. That is why it is necessary to convince the masses that the situation of domination experienced by them is normal, just, correct—and every mechanism of legitimization, including those produced by the State itself, goes in this direction. With the progressive rationalization of society, the State has developed other mechanisms of legitimization, among which are representative democracy and modern forms of law (Berthier, 2011f, pp. 69–73). Even so, as will be discussed below, this legitimization is supported by processes that go beyond politics in the strict sense.

Another central aspect of the State is that, in this permanent search for increasing force—which, as stated, is required so that it is not conquered or dominated by other states and so that it can guarantee the internal maintenance of order—it produces different forms of domination.

When they seek to expand their territory and resources, some states promote conquest, which "is not only the origin, but also the supreme goal of all States, large or small, powerful or weak, despotic or liberal, monarchic or aristocratic, democratic and even socialist" (Bakunin, 2008b[e], p. 27). This imperialist vocation of the modern State—which is always effective when the conditions are right—is not only behind many wars, but also national domination or imperialism, carried out by a restricted number of states to the detriment of others, involving privileges and submission of economic, political, and cultural order.

For the practice of government and the realization of its enslaving vocation, the modern State produces two other forms of domination: physical coercion and bureaucratic domination. It has been seen that the State is based on supremacy and on the domination of violence, which is mobilized through threat or de facto use— and these are the foundations of physical coercion. But there is another aspect: the State also seeks to guarantee that its management remains concentrated in a minority, since "the government of the immense majority of the popular masses is done by a privileged minority" (Bakunin, 2003a[e], pp. 213). This split in society between a governing minority and a governed majority implies a contradiction between the restricted group of people who manage the State and make the political decisions (the bureaucracy, the rulers) and a broad range of people who are distant from these decisions—and who obey the decisions made by others, despite the fact that these decisions concern them. This has one consequence: "the more the yoke that is kept on them [the popular masses] is overwhelming, the more the people are left with the impossibility of exercising control over themselves, the more the administration of the country moves away from management by the people themselves" (Bakunin, 2003a[e], p. 79). The more the State strengthens and monopolizes decision-making, the more the governed weaken, given the impossibility of their self-government over themselves. This split between a governing minority and a governed majority characterizes bureaucratic domination.

12.4.2 Capitalism: Exploitation of Labour

Capitalism, taken in its economic dimensions, is a *regime based on private property that has its core in the exploitation (a form of economic domination) of the wage-earning working class*, although it coexists with previous forms of exploitation and often integrates with them. Capitalist labour relations put workers—who are forced to the market by hunger, with greater risk and, once employed, collectively produce value through their labour—and capitalists, who go to the market seeking profit (with less risk) and who individually take advantage of this value to increase their own wealth. In structural terms, capitalist competition favours monopoly, promotes poverty, social inequality, and broad proletarianization.

"Neither property nor capital produce anything if they are not fertilized by labor" in such a way that, in a society, value is always produced by labour, this application of human force in the transformation of the world (Bakunin, 2007e[e], p. 4). Without labour, both property and capital are incapable of creating value. On the one hand, "the land and the factory do not produce by themselves." Even in the case of land, which has a "natural productive force," if it is "left without cultivation, it [becomes] incapable of producing social values, incapable of providing wealth or even enough food for a somewhat civilized man." On the other hand, "capital [...], as monetary value represented by the sums of gold, platinum, silver, copper or banking papers [...], produces nothing by itself." Abandoned, such capital also does not reproduce and is incapable of creating value (Bakunin, 71023[e], pp. 6–7).[13]

As the workers are the ones who perform the labour, the labour relationship based on property and capital means that those who produce value and wealth collectively are deprived of it, since part of the product of their labour is unduly appropriated by those who own the means of production and capital. Since "labor isolated from individuals would barely be able to feed and clothe a small people of savages," every society that produces considerable wealth does so through "collective labor, organized in solidarity." Therefore, "it would seem logical that the enjoyment of these riches should also" be collective. However, what has been seen for a long time is the "isolated, private enjoyment" of the owners, which is done to the detriment of the dispossessed masses (Bakunin, 2008d[e], p. 97). It is precisely this relationship— between landlords and the dispossessed, in which the former take over part of the labour of the latter—that characterizes the exploitation of labour, an economic form of domination that, even though it is anterior, continues to be in force in capitalism.[14]

The peculiarity of capitalism—"the great financial, commercial and industrial exploitation, the great international spoliation; a few thousand men internationally in solidarity with each other and, through the power of their capital, dominating the whole world" (Bakunin, 69020[e], p. 1)—is that, even living with pre-capitalist forms of exploitation, human labour is transformed into a commodity and the labour relation starts to occur through wage (or salaried) labour. Thus, the worker (proletarian in the restricted sense) offers "his own labor as [...] a commodity to be exchanged for the salary offered by the capitalist" (bourgeois) and, in doing so, by selling "his labor, his particular labors, the productive forces of his body, mind and soul, which are in him and inseparable from his person," he ends up selling himself (Bakunin, 2007e[e], pp. 13, 15). In short, everything becomes a "vile commodity" (Bakunin, 71023[e], p. 28).

Since "only labor produces new wealth, it is therefore labor, that is, the workers who pay the capitalist's expenses and earnings" (Bakunin, 71023[e], p. 9). By saying that labour is only performed by workers, it is understood that what the capitalist considers his own labour is nothing more than "administration and exploitation," an unproductive labour for which he is "remunerated with a value far greater than that of the workers." It is in this sense that it must be understood that capitalists enrich themselves "without having to labor" (Bakunin, 2007e[e], p. 9).

As can be observed, the greatest economic problem of capitalism is the exploitation of workers, which is made effective with wage labour. When a capitalist hires a worker, he demands of him a job that produces value and wealth, and remunerates him with a salary that guarantees only his reproduction and that of his family. The rest (which also includes the fruits obtained thanks to the collective association of workers) is appropriated and, after deducting the costs, forms the basis of the capitalist's profits, which allow him to have comfort, wealth, and even increase his capital. This capitalist has two mechanisms for increasing his profits. Making "the workers [have] to labor more," which makes "*the existence of each worker more painful*" and with less "*free time*" (Bakunin, 2017f[e], p. 427). Or "reducing the cost of production," which can be done in "different ways: by using new methods, new machines, searching for raw materials that cost less, by a new and more productive division of labor, by introducing a cheaper and simpler administration" (Bakunin, 71023[e], pp. 33–34).[15]

Contrary to liberal rhetoric—which functions as a mechanism of legitimization—under capitalism there is no free labour and not even free competition. Because, first of all, what drives capitalists and workers to the market are very different motives and, when they meet, both have relationships without any equity.

Do both [capitalists and workers] not find themselves in the market as two equal merchants [...]? Of course, none of this is true. What attracts the capitalist to the market? It is the will to enrich, to increase his capital, to satisfy his social ambitions and vanities, to be able to indulge in every conceivable pleasure. And what brings the worker to the market? Hunger, the need to eat today and tomorrow. So while the capitalist and the worker are the same from the legal point of view, they are anything but the same from the point of view of the economic situation, which is the real situation. [...] What happens in the market is the meeting between one initiative for profit and another for hunger, between you and your slave. Legally they are both equal; but economically the worker is a servant of the capitalist, even before the business by which the worker sells his person and his freedom for a while is concluded. The worker is in the position of a servant because this terrible threat of hunger, which daily hangs over him and his family, will force him to accept any conditions imposed by the profitable calculations of the capitalist, the industrialist, the employer. (Bakunin, 2007e[e], pp. 13–15)

That is, while capitalists search the market with the intention of profit, workers do so for the fear of hunger.[16] And legal equality means nothing when, in a labour relationship, two economic agents are so disparate in terms of social force (for which the capitalist's possibility of waiting and the worker's urgency to get out of unemployment also count)—surely the capitalist will impose himself in this relationship.

"But the capitalist, the owner of the business, runs risks, they say, while the worker does not run any risks." It is necessary to say that "this is not true." Because in the market, the risks of the capitalist are much lower than those of the workers. There is no doubt that "the owner can conduct his business in an unfortunate way, he can be left with nothing in a bad negotiation, or be the victim of a commercial crisis, or of an unforeseen catastrophe; in a word, he can ruin himself." But no matter what happens, he won't face the risk of hunger, nor will he live like an ordinary worker— "it happens so rarely, that we could very well say 'never.'"

Two reasons explain why this is so: because of their "family and social relationships" and their "knowledge." Even a ruined capitalist may resort to his relatives and friends, as well as to the education and formal or informal instruction he obtained, so as to be able to be employed in "the highest positions of work, in administration," or else "to be a State employee, to be an executive in a commercial or industrial business." Even if he ends up more "dependent," he will undoubtedly have "a higher income than those he [...] paid to his former workers." On the contrary, when the risks of the workers are analyzed, the scenario is quite different. Deprived not only of property and capital, but also of family and social relations and knowledge, if "the establishment in which he is employed goes bankrupt, he will remain for several days and sometimes for several weeks without work. And this, for him, is more than ruin, it is death; because, every day, he eats what he earns" (Bakunin, 2007e[e], pp. 10–11).

Capitalism is not, therefore, a regime of freedom, but of "true slavery"— "voluntary from the legal point of view, but compulsory by economic logic (Bakunin, 2007e[e], p. 16). And "this so-called free contract" advocated by the liberals should be more properly called "the pact of hunger, the slavery of hunger for the masses and the exploitation of hunger by minorities who devour and oppress us" (Bakunin, 2008d[e], p. 75).

When analyzing competition, it cannot be said either that capitalism promotes freedom—not even among capitalists themselves, much less when workers are taken into account. First of all, because there is a tendency toward monopoly that, in competition, causes big capital to impose itself on small and medium-sized companies:

> In this competition, in this fight for the lowest price, the big capitals must
> necessarily crush the small capitals, the big bourgeoisies must ruin the small
> bourgeoisies. A huge factory can naturally make its products and sell them
> cheaper than a small or medium size factory. [...] Producing proportionally
> much more, it can obviously sell its products at a much lower price than the
> small or medium manufacturers; but by selling them cheaper, it equally forces
> the small or medium manufacturers to lower their price, without which their
> products would not be bought. But as the production of these products costs
> them much more than the big producer, by selling them at the price of the big

producer they ruin themselves. This is how big capital kills small capital, and if the big encounter bigger ones than themselves, they are, in turn, crushed. (Bakunin, 2008d[e], pp. 99–100)

That is, even for capitalists, the market does not imply free competition; by the logic of social forces applied to the economic field, the conditions of the large imposed on the small are immensely greater than the opposite. Let us remember that this dynamic of capitalism is similar to that of the State: competition tends to do away with the small in favour of the big, and capital tends to become universal, to become a "capitalist monopoly." With this, "a growing number of small or medium sized capitalists, speculators, merchants or industrialists" are being forced to occupy lower social positions and even reach the condition of wage earners—a movement of proletarianization that even extends to the peasantry (Bakunin, 2007e[e], p. 6; cf., also: Saltman, 1983, p. 83).[17]

However, capitalist competition is even more harmful to workers. Forced to sell "the products of the workers they exploit [...] at the lowest possible price," the capitalists have to pay the workers "the lowest possible wages" and as a result, they seek "the labor that is sold, which is forced to be sold, at the lowest value" (Bakunin, 2008d[e], pp. 101–102). This value is that "*strictly necessary* for the daily maintenance of their families" (Bakunin, 71023[e], p. 35).[18] And, since the workers "have no other means of existence besides their own manual labor, they are driven, for fear of being replaced by others, to sell it for the lowest price." This need imposed on workers adds to the tendency of capitalists to buy labour for the lowest price and "constantly reproduces and consolidates the poverty of the proletariat." This is the logic that keeps the worker in poverty: "since he is in a state of poverty, the worker is forced to sell his labor for almost nothing, and since he sells this product for almost nothing, he sinks into increasingly greater misery" (Bakunin, 2007e[e], pp. 6–7).

It should also be observed that this competitive dynamic of capitalism is structural and therefore is not "determined by the will of the capitalist, but by the competition" between capital and labour, by what is called "*supply* and *demand*" (Bakunin, 71023[e], p. 28). Thus, the greater or lesser exploitation of labour does not result from the goodness or badness of the capitalist, but from this dynamic of capitalism itself.

Therefore, "the economic organization of today's society" can be characterized, on the one hand, by the fact that "the capital or raw materials and labor instruments necessary for production [remain] monopolized in the hands of this bourgeois oligarchy" and, on the other, by the fact that the "proletariat" is forced "into fatal competition to escape hunger" and has to "continue to sell its labor—the one, the only producer—as a commodity, at the lowest price, always more or less determined by the price of what is absolutely necessary so that its productive force does not die of starvation." The necessary consequence of this is "*the increase of the misery and suffering of the proletariat,"* which is *"always the direct reason for the growth of wealth or what is called the development of material interests and economic prosperity"* of the bourgeoisie. Moreover, "the more wealth or capital is monopolized by an ever-smaller number of bourgeois oligarchs, the more the necessary consequence will be the middle bourgeoisie being pushed to the small, and the small bourgeoisie to the proletariat" (Bakunin, 71011b[e], pp. 5–6).

The fallacy of bourgeois discourse, which insists that in capitalism it is possible to prosper thanks to one's own willpower and free enterprise, is then clearly seen:

> Bourgeois society says to all these individuals: fight, fight for the prize, the well-being, wealth, political power. The winners will be happy. Is there at least equality in this fratricidal struggle? No, not at all. Some, in small numbers, are armed from head to toe, strong because of their education and their inherited wealth, and the millions of men of the people present themselves in the arena almost naked, with their ignorance and their equally inherited misery. What is the necessary result of this supposedly free competition? The people succumb, the bourgeoisie triumph, and the chained proletarian is forced to labor as a force for its eternal victor, the bourgeois. (Bakunin, 2008d[e], p. 98)

This discourse has no relation with reality—it is, as mentioned, only a mechanism of legitimization of capitalism. Because, in this regime, when one analyzes the trajectory of capitalists, it is evident that the immense majority of them did not reach their position through their own efforts alone. In general, they come from rich, powerful, educated, well-connected families, and all this is transmitted to them by a formal and informal inheritance, which allows them to access the market accompanied by all the advantages. In this competition, the privileged is the "eternal winner" and not infrequently the exceptions to this rule are used to show that it is possible for the dispossessed to win and be happy.[19]

12.4.3 The Statist-capitalist System and Other Mechanisms of Legitimation

However, although the State and capitalism can be separated analytically, their concrete, historical functioning does not manifest this division. Thanks to the dynamics of action and reaction that exist in society, even if the economic aspects of capitalism have a certain preponderance over the political aspects of the State, and therefore political power is always greatly influenced by economic power, the State is indispensable to the functioning of capitalism. For this reason, the State and capitalism must be considered interdependent elements which, in permanent relation, reinforce each other, forming a statist-capitalist system, at the same time political and economic (Saltman, 1983, pp. 80–81).

In fact, this interdependence is the modern expression of an ancient relationship between power and wealth, which have always been together for mutual benefit.

"Political power and wealth are inseparable." On the one hand, "he who is powerful possesses all the means to acquire wealth and must acquire it, for without it he would not keep power for long." On the other hand, "he who is rich must necessarily be powerful, for if force is not on his side, he who has it will dispossess it." This relationship explains, for example, both the emergence and maintenance of private property. In this way, the world of workers—those who have always been deprived of wealth and power, "at all times and in all countries"—was always "impotent because it was in misery, and remained miserable because it had no organized force" (Bakunin, 2009e[e], p. 49; cf., also: Bakunin, 71023[e], p. 18).

In the statist-capitalist system, it is inevitable, owing to the relative determination of the economy, that the State expresses the interests of the economically dominant classes in its government (laws, decisions, power of arms), as well as in the solution of legal conflicts (Bakunin, 71023[e], pp. 27–28). But it happens that, owing to the influence that politics can exert on the economy, it is the State that makes viable and guarantees the economic exploitation of capitalism. After all, to exploit, capitalists must have the power and right to exploit, and for this the State is indispensable (Bakunin, 2007e[e], p. 4).

> Modern capitalist industry and banking speculation need, in order to develop to the full extent desired, these large State centralizations, which alone are capable of subjecting to their exploitation the millions and millions of proletarians of the popular mass. [...] The capitalist industry and banking speculation accommodate themselves very well with so-called representative democracy, for this modern State structure, founded on the pseudo-sovereignty of the pseudo-will of the people, supposedly expressed by false representatives of the people in pseudo-popular assemblies, meets the two preconditions necessary to achieve its ends, that is, State centralization and the effective subjection of the sovereign people to the intellectual minority that governs them, that is, that represents them and exploits them in an inevitable manner. (Bakunin, 2003a[e], pp. 35–36)

Capitalism cannot develop without the State, and in the modern world bourgeois representative democracy functions very well as a legitimizing mechanism, in that it brings the State closer to its population and contributes to the discourse of political participation.

In addition, there is a legal element that is essential in maintaining social inequality: the "right of inheritance," this "faculty for the children of the rich to be born in wealth, and for the children of the poor to be born in misery" (Bakunin, 2008a[e], p. 26). Inheritance explains, at least in part, that aforementioned inequality of birth, which allows some to access the market in conditions far superior to others, the immense majority. For inheritance is a guarantee that property, passed on from one generation to another, will remain in the hands of the same families and continue to perpetuate the existence of social classes and privileges (Bakunin, 69038[e]).

Finally, capitalist expansion can only be understood as a phenomenon that occurs together with the expansion of the modern State. The "capitalist system of monopolies [...], everywhere and always, accompanies the progress and expansion of statist centralization." And the result of this double development is "privileged capital concentrated in very few hands," which has become "the soul of every political State." Financed by capital, it "assures it, in return, the unlimited right to exploit the labor of the people" (Bakunin, 2003a[e], p. 228).

But that's not all. As in all previous modes of power, a cultural, intellectual, and moral legitimizing framework always emerges from the political-economic relationship of domination. It has been seen that, in the statist-capitalist system, some of these mechanisms are produced by the State and by capitalism; but two more should be mentioned: religion and education.

In the case of religion, as previously stated, the appeal to the theological implies the abandonment of reason and concern for human relations. And as the respect and adoration of the divine increases, so does the contempt for the earth—directly or indirectly, cruelty among men is sustained. It should also be pointed out that "all past and present religions, without in any way excluding Christianity, were the religion of the strongest." For this reason, they have played an important role in legitimizing the dominant interests, not only by stimulating submission, silencing the "inclination to injustice" and development "contrary to all inequality and all privilege," but also by directly contributing to "excluding the majority in favor of the oppressive, powerful and divinely privileged minority." "Such is the secular work of religion," which continues to be carried out in the modern world, especially by Protestantism and Catholicism, but not only them (Bakunin, 2009a[e], p. 20).

In the case of education, or even science and technology in general, it is also possible to make some notes. First, in statist and capitalist society, education—this form of "brain capital," mental or intellectual (Bakunin, 2009a[e], p. 44)—is a class education. With it, the directions and purposes of teaching, scientific, and technological development are made with the aim of promoting and guaranteeing the domination of the privileged classes (Bakunin, 2015[e], p. 268). With it, the rich are educated and the poor are forcibly condemned to ignorance:

> As long as the people labor not for themselves but to enrich the owners of property and capital, the instruction they can give their children will always be infinitely inferior to that of the children of the bourgeois class. [...] The child endowed with the greatest faculties, but born into a poor family, into a family of workers, living the daily life of their crude daily labor, is condemned to ignorance, which, instead of developing it, kills all its natural faculties: it will be the worker, the worker, the one forced to support and feed the bourgeois who,

naturally, are much more stupid than him. The son of the bourgeois, on the other hand, the son of the rich, however foolish he may be, will naturally receive the education and instruction necessary to develop, as far as possible, his poor faculties: he will be an exploiter of labor, the boss, the legislator, the governor – a lord. However foolish he may be, he will make laws for the people, against the people, and he will govern the popular masses. (Bakunin, 2008d[e], pp. 81–82)

It is, as we can see, an education that is, at the same time, the effect and cause of class society, and that knowledge is decisive in the division that exists between intellectual and manual labour. Thus, as stated, the monopoly of knowledge contributes, along with other privileges, to the maintenance of the dominant classes' class position (Bakunin, 2015[e], p. 269).

Consequently, access to the mass production of knowledge, be it religious or scientific, allows the diffusion of ideas that are fundamental to legitimizing the statist-capitalist system; spreading submission, subservience, functional value to that system or even depriving workers of an integral education collaborates with the creation of a mentality consistent with statism and capitalism.

Finally, there is an understanding of the whole statist-capitalist system and the forms of domination present at all levels. In the economy, there is the exploitation of wage labour, which coexists with previous forms of exploitation, especially those linked to land ownership. In politics, there is national imperialist domination and political domination, both of which are led by the modern State. In culture, there is intellectual and moral domination, a remarkable factor of legitimization based on religion and education.

This systemic functioning can be playfully illustrated through the imaginary utterance of a capitalist to a worker. He would say:

You see, my children, I have a little capital, which by itself can produce nothing, because something dead can produce nothing. I have nothing productive without the labor. So I can't profit by consuming it unproductively, since, consuming it, I would have nothing else. But thanks to the social and political institutions that govern us and that are all in my favor, in today's economy my capital must also be a producer: it brings me profit. From whom this profit must be taken—and it must be from someone, since, in reality, it produces absolutely nothing by itself—doesn't matter to you. It's enough, for you, to know that it generates profit. Alone, this profit is not enough to cover my expenses. I'm not a simple man like you. I can't be, nor do I want to be, happy with little. I want to live, to live in a beautiful house, to eat and drink well, to ride a carriage, to look good, in short, to have all the good things in life. I also want to give my children a good education, make them gentlemen, and send them away to study, and in the end, having received much more education than you, may they someday dominate you, just as I dominate you today. And since education alone is not enough, I want to leave them a great inheritance, so that by dividing it among them, they will remain almost as rich as I am. Consequently, besides all the good things in life that I want for myself, I still want to increase my capital. How will I reach my goal? Armed with this capital, I propose to exploit it, and I propose that you allow me to exploit it. You will labor and I will collect, appropriate and sell, to my own benefit, the product of your labor, passing on to you nothing but a part, which is absolutely necessary so that you don't die of hunger today and, at the end of tomorrow, still labor for me under the same conditions; and, when you are exhausted, I will throw you away and replace you with others. Know this, I will pay you such a small salary, and I will impose on you such a long working day, under such severe, despotic, as cruel working conditions as possible; it's not for evil—it's not for feeling hatred for you, nor for wanting to do you any harm— but for the love of well-being and quick enrichment; because the less I pay you and the more you labor, the more I will earn. (Bakunin, 2007e[e], pp. 11–13)

In this section it is possible to observe a relevant part of the functioning of modern class struggle. However, it is also necessary to point out that this contradiction between bourgeoisie and proletariat, as fundamental as it is—and in fact it is, because it expresses the economic relationship typical of capitalism—is not the only one and cannot even be understood as the primary one, for two reasons. Because the contradiction between the former landowners and the peasants is still significant, especially in its quantitative expression. And because class struggle is not expressed only in the economic field. So, with the bourgeoisie, old and new landowners, the State bureaucracy, the clergy and the intellectuals must be included among the upper classes. And with the proletariat, the peasants, the rural proletariat, and all the poor and marginalized must be included among the dispossessed classes.

12.4.4 Historic Rise of the Modern State, Bureaucracy, Capitalism, and the Bourgeoisie

This understanding of the statist-capitalist system can be complemented with a historical reflection, which allows us to understand more precisely how the modern State and capitalism, the modern bureaucracy, and the bourgeoisie ascend.

In the first place, this requires evaluating the social forces at play at that moment of statist and capitalist ascension, especially class forces. Second, to start from two historical events central to this process: the Reform and the French Revolution. For it was these "two historical events," these "two memorable revolutions" that instituted "what we call the modern world, the world of bourgeois civilization": "the religious revolution of the 16th century, known as the

Reformation, and the great political revolution of the last century [18th]," the French Revolution (Bakunin, 2008d[e], pp. 59, 71).

Remember that until the first half of the Middle Ages, the clergy were the dominant class—they selected their members from among all the other classes and owned the land.[20] At that time the power and rights of kings and emperors had to be recognized and consecrated by the Church. The period extending from the twelfth to the fifteenth century is characterized by ever more acute conflicts between sovereigns and the Pope—between political power and clerical power—especially from the fourteenth century, when the bourgeoisie was beginning to rise thanks to communal freedoms and commercial and industrial development.

With the sixteenth-century Reform, there was the separation—and with it the minimization of conflicts—between political and clerical power; the independence of states was proclaimed. Thus, the modern State emerged.

> From this revolution [the Reform] came a new power, not yet that of the bourgeoisie, but that of the [modern] State, monarchic, constitutional and aristocratic in England, monarchic, absolute, nobiliocratic, military and bureaucratic throughout the continent of Europe, with the exception of two small republics, Switzerland and the Netherlands. (Bakunin, 2008d[e], p. 60)

The Reform was responsible for a marked change of position concerning the perception of the source of power and political rights. If before it was considered that the power and rights of sovereigns originated in the Church, after the Reformation it was believed that they emanated directly from God—and, in this way, sovereigns became absolute.

With this, power relations are changed and, upon the ancient domination of the Church, statist, monarchic domination is established. Before that, the Church submitted itself to the State, becoming an instrument of government in the hands of sovereigns. This movement occurred "not only in Protestant countries, where, without excluding England, especially by the Anglican Church, the monarch was declared head of the Church, but also in all Catholic countries, without even excluding Spain" (Bakunin, 2008d[e], p. 61). That is, with the Reformation, "the crowned sovereigns of Europe have usurped the power of the Church, creating a secular authority based on the notion of divine right—hence, the birth of the modern State" (Newman, 2012, p. 11).

In this way the Church lost power and relied more and more only on itself. But to guarantee its continuity and even some influence, even if subordinate, it was necessary for it to win the support of the sovereigns. And this would only be possible if it was able to contribute to their financial and political interests, and to prove itself worthy of that support. Breaking with the position it took at various times prior to the Reformation, when it confronted the rulers, the Church found its opportunities in all countries, including Switzerland, allying itself with the State against the bourgeoisie and the people (proletariat and peasants).

This was possible because the Church proved to be a substantial institution for legitimizing this new form of domination that had emerged with the Reformation. It gave itself "as a mission to preach to the popular masses resignation, patience, obedience and, consequently, the renunciation of the goods and fruitions of this land, which the people, it said, must abandon to the happy and powerful of the land in order to secure for themselves the heavenly treasures" (Bakunin, 2008d[e], pp. 61–62). In this way, the Church converted its ability to influence the masses and legitimize the status quo into a social force so as to find in the relationship of privileged submission to sovereigns a less costly way out of the unfolding of the Reformation. These were the foundations for building a new state morality that was also an important mechanism for legitimizing this new state power.

A concrete relationship between social forces that results in this power has, as a consequence, the formulation of ideas to legitimize it and, from them, a legal framework is built to guarantee its conformity with the laws. It proceeds therefore from the facts of domination to ideas, and from ideas to law (Leval, 1976, p. 199). The universality and absolutism attributed to states then place them in a growing conflict with each other, and wars of conquest are increasingly frequent. This legitimizing content—intellectual, moral, and legal—becomes the justification for countless crimes against humanity, committed thanks to statist interests.

The nobility (especially the feudal lords) faced a similar process, becoming, after the Reform, a "privileged servant" of the State, of the sovereign (Bakunin, 2008d[e], p. 62). Before that, the nobles had, like the Church but in different circumstances, stood against them—even forming a rival or enemy social force. However, with the Reformation, the correlation of forces changed and—above all because it filled almost all the military and civil functions of the State and occupied a significant part of the courts—the nobility also ended up in a position of privileged submission to the sovereigns.

No matter how much they remained more or less exclusive owners of the land, the feudal (noble) lords lost their political independence. And even though they were submissive to the sovereigns, they continued to exploit the bourgeoisie and the people, no longer in their own name and under the support of divine right, but in the name of the sovereign and under the justification of state interest. "This character and this particular situation of the nobility have been preserved almost entirely, even in our days, in Germany." And "proof of this is the ignoble, atrocious barbarities" of the Franco-Prussian War, "the very recent formation of this terrible Germanic empire, which is undeniably a threat to the freedom of all the countries of Europe," and which is based on "the brutal despotism of an emperor-police officer and soldier at the same time, and on the stupid insolence of his villainous scoundrel" (Bakunin, 2008d[e], p. 63).

Through the Reform, the bourgeoisie found itself completely free from tyranny and plunder by the feudal lords, as independent and private bandits or thieves; but it found itself handed over to a new tyranny and plunder now regularized under the name of ordinary and extraordinary State taxes, by those same lords made servants, that is to say, bandits and legitimate thieves, of the State. [...] Reform, by the way, has made the [bourgeois] middle class lose in freedom perhaps twice as much as it safely gave them. Before the Reformation, it had generally been the ally and indispensable support of kings in their struggle against the Church and feudal lords, and had skillfully taken advantage of it to gain a certain degree of independence and freedom. But from the moment the Church and the feudal lords subjugated themselves to the State, the kings, no longer needing the services of the middle class, gradually deprived it of all the freedoms they had once granted it. (Bakunin, 2008d[e], pp. 63–64)

By providing the conditions for the rupture of the power of the Church, the cornerstone of the power of the feudal lords (nobility), the Reformation ended up favouring the bourgeoisie, which had been strengthening itself for two centuries, although this also brought it certain problems. Communal freedoms and commercial and industrial developments gave force to the bourgeoisie, while reinforcing them—it was the emergence of the capitalist economy. The bourgeoisie ended up surrendering to the new despotism of the State, now regularized, which began to affect it, especially through taxes, which were constantly increasing in view of different causes.

The increase in state spending was directly reflected in taxes. Among the factors that contributed to this increase were: "the ceaseless wars [...] that these States, made absolute, have waged among themselves"; "the growing luxury of sovereign courts"; "the need to maintain great permanent armies," and "to feed this privileged crowd that filled the highest functions in the army, the bureaucracy and the police" (Bakunin, 2008d[e], p. 64). However harshly the taxes affected the people, they did not alleviate the bourgeoisie much less in the period between the Reformation and the French Revolution. Unlike the Church and the nobility, the bourgeoisie before the Reformation had, on several occasions, been allied with the sovereigns in the struggle against the clerical and feudal forces. For this reason, it had a certain level of independence. However, with the Reformation—and the described process of privileged subordination of the Church and the nobility—the sovereigns no longer needed the bourgeoisie, which ended up losing much of its independence.

The situation of the people, the peasantry and the proletariat, in that context has also changed. It should be emphasized that the people were responsible for paying the majority of taxes. At the beginning of the Reform, the peasants of central Europe, Germany, Holland, and in part, Switzerland, became involved in an emancipatory movement that ended up being betrayed by the bourgeoisie, cursed by bourgeois Protestantism and suffocated in blood. This situation eventually bound the peasants to the land—becoming "serfs by right, de facto slaves" —until 1789–93 in France, 1807 in Prussia, and 1848 in almost the rest of Germany (Bakunin, 2008d[e], p. 65). The proletariat of the cities was also in a situation analogous to that of the peasants, falling into two categories: those organized in corporations and those not organized. The former were immobilized and oppressed by their bosses (heads of corporations); the latter were deprived of all rights and were exploited by all.

In Europe, the intermediate period between the Reform and the French Revolution was characterized by the consolidation of the Old Regime (absolutism and mercantilism), the expansion of Western civilization—including colonization initiatives—and the continued rise of the bourgeoisie, for which mercantile strengthening was determinant, even if servitude was still a condition of most peasants. The power of the State was thus progressively strengthened.

Together with the Industrial Revolution, the French Revolution collaborated in a decisive way to the development of modern society, even if, since the seventeenth century in England, the bourgeoisie had established itself hegemonically. With the crisis of the Old Regime, this era of revolutions had as its fundamental mark the more widespread establishment of bourgeois domination and the formation of capitalism. It should be remembered that history has always been the history of class struggle, permanently crossed by divisions between ruling minorities and governed majorities, in a process in which "the minority plays the role of a hammer and the majority represents the anvil" (Bakunin, 2008d[e], p. 69).

But with the French Revolution, the condition of the bourgeoisie changed dramatically:

Until the great Revolution, the bourgeois class, although to a lesser degree than the popular masses, had been part of the anvil. And that is why it was revolutionary. [...] The bourgeoisie, represented, in this struggle against the Church and the State, by its noblest spirits and by its greatest qualities, believed in good faith that it worked equally for the emancipation of all. The two centuries that separate the struggles of the religious Reformation from those of the great Revolution were the heroic period of the bourgeois class. A powerful journey for wealth and intelligence, it audaciously attacked all the respected institutions of the Church and the State. It undermined everything, initially by literature and philosophical criticism; later it overthrew everything by open revolt. It was the one that made the revolutions of 1789 and 1793. No doubt it could only make use of popular force; but it was it that organized this force and directed it against the Church, against royalty and against nobility. It was it that thought and that took the initiative of all the movements that the people executed. The bourgeoisie had faith in itself, it felt powerful because it knew that behind it, with it, there was the people. (Bakunin, 2008d[e], pp. 69–70)

Thus, the French Revolution was an important milestone for the establishment of bourgeois and capitalist domination, even though its hegemony was not fully, immediately, and concomitantly consolidated in all European countries. However, it should be noted that, in spite of benefitting from the popular forces, this political revolution, even though it exchanged hands of political power and favoured the establishment of the hegemony of the bourgeoisie, maintained the structures of domination, including the State, but above all class society and thus the exploitation and oppression of workers in general.

In Europe, the domination of bourgeois interests and politics—"bourgeois domination" and capitalism (Bakunin, 2014e[e], p. 312)—ended in 1830, "mainly in France, England, Belgium, the Netherlands and Switzerland." In other countries, such as "Germany, Denmark, Sweden, Italy, Spain and Portugal," even though "bourgeois interests" had "overwhelmed all others," "the political government of the bourgeois" had not yet been established (Bakunin, 2008d[e], p. 93).

With the conflicts of 1848, the bourgeoisie placed itself definitively in the camp of reaction. The revolution "unmasked and demonstrated the impotence and harmfulness of the bourgeoisie. During the days of June, the bourgeois class openly renounced the religion of its parents," the one that took "freedom, equality and fraternity as principles and bases. As soon as the people took equality and freedom seriously, the bourgeoisie, which exists only through exploitation, that is, through economic inequality and social slavery of the people, relaunched into reaction" (Bakunin, 2008d[e], pp. 104–105).

It was the crowning achievement of the statist-capitalist system—of "capital domination" associated with the modern State (Bakunin, 2003a[e], p. 240)—which was formed and operated in Europe for the benefit of the bourgeoisie, the bureaucracy, and other upper classes, and to the detriment of workers, peasants, and other dispossessed classes.

12.4.5 Pan-Germanic Imperialism and the Slavs

Finally, we must make brief comments about a relevant phenomenon in the statist-capitalist system of the 1870s: Pan-Germanic imperialism, which grew and became responsible for different national oppressions, among which that of the Slavic peoples. As previously argued, "Germany has a long history of conquests and attempts to Germanize other States and nation-races," and this case of the Slavic nation-race is a striking example. Although "in all its international relations, Germany" has always been "invading, conquering," its recent unification process has greatly increased its social force and with it, its capacity for conquest. For this reason, "since it became a unitary power, [it] has become a threat, a danger to the freedom of the whole of Europe" (Bakunin, 2014e[e], p. 284).

From an emancipatory perspective, one can assure that, considering all possible scenarios, this process ended up being accomplished in the worst possible way. It was a "half forced and half voluntary unification of all the States of Germany under the royal scepter of Prussia," eminent representative of German imperialism. This provided the conditions for "the constitution of the most powerful empire in the heart of Europe" both in military and geopolitical terms (Bakunin, 2014d[e], p. 214).

This "Knuto-Germanic empire" is the largest imperialist state in Europe. Under the responsibility of that "official, bureaucratic, military, nobiliocratic, bourgeois Germany"—that is, of the German ruling classes—it has imposed itself in the region, headed different national dominations, and through them promoted an "execrable pan-Germanism," that is, Germanization. As a "conquering State" it is now "forced to keep subjugated by violence many millions of individuals of a foreign nation" (Bakunin, 2014d[e], pp. 161, 221; Bakunin, 2003a[e], pp. 61, 66–67).

In terms of historical formation, five main causes can be identified for Germany's rise to this position as an imperialist state. The first, "the feudal nobility whose spirit, far from having been defeated as in France, was incorporated into Germany's current constitution"; the second, "the absolutism of the sovereign sanctioned by Protestantism and transformed by it into an object of worship"; the third, "the persevering and chronic servility of the bourgeoisie of Germany"; the fourth, "the invincible patience of its people"; and the fifth, "very close, indeed, to the first four, is the birth and rapid formation of the totally mechanical and totally anti-national power of the State of Prussia" (Bakunin, 2014d[e], p. 227).

With regard to the events of the 1870s, the German state succeeded in substantially increasing its social force, not only with unification, but through seven other criteria:

> Because it achieved brilliant victories over Denmark, Austria and France; for having seized all of the latter's weaponry and all of its military stocks; for having forced it to pay five billion; for having occupied, against it, by annexing Alsace and Lorraine, both in a defensive and offensive aspect, a military position of first order; not only because the German army, by its personnel, its weaponry, its discipline, its organization, by the spirit of obedience and the military science of its officers, but also of its petty officers and soldiers, not to mention the undeniable superiority of its staff, today supplants all the armies existing in Europe; not only because the masses of the German population are made up of citizens who can read and write, who are industrious, who produce, who are relatively educated, not to say cultured, and, moreover, docile, respectful of authorities and laws, and that the administration as much as the German bureaucracy has achieved, so to speak, the ideal to which the bureaucracy and administration of all the other States aspire in vain. (Bakunin, 2003a[e], p. 133)

The organization, resources, and military victories, as well as the money, the new territories, the national traits of the German population, and their positions were therefore determinant for this empire to be constituted.

Among the nation-races that have been suffering the effects of German imperialism are the Slavs (Cipko, 1990, p. 10). It has been seen that there has been a historic effort on the part of the Germans to "conquer Slavic lands, exterminate, pacify and civilize, that is, to Germanize the Slavs" and that in the face of national resistance—whose foundation is the "indestructible idea and the hope that the Slavs will one day free themselves"—a national conflict of considerable proportions has been established.

With the formation of the German empire and owing to the increase in its social force— the largest of all the European states—the oppression of the Slavs increased. All Slavs who are under threat or under Germanic yoke will continue to suffer and suffer even more, both from "Austria" as well as from "Lithuania," [from] Poland, [from] Little-Russia, and" even "Great Russia." For the historical artificial Germanization of the Slavic peoples will be further deepened, contributing directly to putting an end to their way of living, acting, and thinking; and to putting an end to their territories and their national identity (languages, conditions, feelings, etc.) (Bakunin, 2003a[e], pp. 60–61).

And, as if German imperialism were not enough, Austrian and Russian Slavs have claimed forms of pan-Slavism which, completely mistaken, will end up making Slavic national liberation from pan-German imperialism impossible.

NOTES

1 In general, Bakunin uses the term "progress" in two senses: of historical development; of progress towards freedom. Cf., for example: Bakunin, 2008f[e], pp. 85, 90; Bakunin, 2009e[e], pp. 25, 45, 50, 70.

2 Cf. Comte (1978a, p. 89): "We have thus gradually discovered the invariable hierarchy, at once historical and dogmatic, equally scientific and logical, of the six fundamental sciences, mathematics, astronomy, physics, chemistry, biology and sociology. The first necessarily constitutes the exclusive starting point, and the last the only essential goal of every positive philosophy, considered from now on as forming, by its nature, a truly indivisible system, in which every decomposition is radically artificial, without being in any way arbitrary, since everything finally refers to Humanity, the only fully universal conception."

3 If the exposition of Bakuninian materialism in this book intends to counteract authors who, like Carr (1961, p. 451), claim that Bakunin, even in later life, was an idealist, it also intends to contest authors who, like Ferreira (2014, pp. 50–51), although correctly recognizing Bakunin's rejection of economic determinism, deny the predominant role of the economy in society (relative economic determination). On numerous occasions, Bakunin, in his anarchist period, emphasized this preponderance. "At the basis of all historical, national, religious and political problems, there has always been, for the world of labor, as well as for all classes and even for the State and the Church, the economic problem, the most important, the most vital of all" (Bakunin, 2009e[e], p. 49). "While the idealists maintain that ideas dominate and produce facts, communists, agreeing here with scientific materialism [that is, with *Bakuninian materialism*], say, on the contrary, that ideas are born of facts, and that these are never anything but the ideal expression of faits accomplis; and that, among all facts, economic and material facts, facts par excellence, constitute the essential basis, the main foundation, of which all other

intellectual and moral, political and social facts are nothing more than the necessary developments. [...] Yes, the whole intellectual and moral, political and social history of humanity is a reflection of its economic history" (Bakunin, 2014e[e], pp. 256–57). "This law is particular in the sense, as I said, that it does not apply to the things of the inorganic world, but is general and fundamental to all living beings. It is the question of food, the great question of the social economy, which constitutes the real basis of all subsequent developments in humanity" (Bakunin, 2014f[e], pp. 365–66). "In the social world [...], the development of economic issues has always been, and continues to be, the determining basis of all religious, philosophical, political and social developments" (Bakunin, 1973a[e], p. 11). "Mr. Marx, contrary to him, enunciated and demonstrated the undeniable truth, confirmed by all ancient and modern history of human society, nations and States, that the economic fact preceded and continues to precede political and legal law. One of Mr. Marx's main scientific merits is to have enunciated and demonstrated this truth" (Bakunin, 2003a[e], p. 175).

4   Bakunin still seems to hierarchize politics, especially the State, in relation to other non-economic and more abstract human factors. Thus, if economics is more influential than politics, it would seem to be more decisive than religion, philosophy, and other elements of society more tied to the field of thought.

5   Cf. Proudhon (1988, p. 103, emphasis added): "The capitalist, it is said, paid the workers' *daily rates*; to be exact, it must be said that the capitalist paid a daily rate as many times as the workers he employed per day, which is not the same thing. For *the immense force that results from the harmony and union of the workers, from the convergence and simultaneity of their efforts, he did not pay. Two hundred granadiers raised the obelisk of Luxor on the base in a few hours; could one man, in two hundred days, do the same?* However, in the capitalist's account, the sum of the wages was identical."

6   I understand that, with such reflections, Bakunin continues his *method of political analysis*, described in Chapter 5—although the idealistic traits of that period have been replaced here by the foundations of scientific-naturalist materialism. Taking this into account, the questions that guided the elaboration of this analytical tool, and which were explained in a note in the aforementioned chapter, are still valid here ("What are the forces at play?" etc.) Furthermore, with his reflections from later life, Bakunin seems to broaden the scope of his tool, so as to support not only conjunctural but also structural analyses of society.

7   In 1864, Bakunin (2014a[e], pp. 76–77) characterizes this dialectic thus: "The world is more than ever divided between two eternally opposed systems: the theological principle and the humanitarian principle, that of authority, and that of freedom. The old system starts from this fundamental idea that humanity is bad for itself, and that to recognize the truth it needs divine revelation, to recognize justice, divine laws, and, to observe them, divine authorities and institutions [illegible], both religious and political, of the *Church* and the *State*. The theological principle, in its two different, parallel but invincibly linked accomplishments, the Church and the State, is essentially based on contempt for humanity, of which it highly proclaims incompetence, inferiority, unworthiness, in short, nullity, not only before God, but also before all missionaries and privileged representatives of justice, or rather, of divine grace, before all established authorities: priests, princes, nobility, doctors of science, aristocrats of capital, armed forces, police, magistrates, bureaucrats, spies, jailers and executioners."

8   Bakunin does not work with the relatively common distinction between exploitation (economic) and domination or oppression (political and/or social). Although, for him, exploitation is an economic category, it is at the same time a form of domination, of oppression. Thus, exploitation and domination/oppression are not parallel or competing concepts; the former is included in the latter. This position is reinforced when one understands the relationship between economics and politics (capitalism and the State), which will be discussed below.

9   As, for example, in the case of Russia in the 1870s, where in addition to those who are exclusively exploiters and exploited, there is an intermediate sector, with members who are both exploiters and exploited. "Let us now look at the quantitative relationship of these three social categories. Of the 70 million inhabitants of the Empire, the part of the lower category composed solely of exploited is at least 67 or 68 million. That of the consummate and conscious exploiters, that is, the most malevolent, does not exceed three, four thousand, say ten thousand. Two or three million remain for the intermediate category composed of individuals who are at the same time, although to different degrees, exploiters and exploited. This category can be divided into two branches: on the one hand, the immense majority of those who are more exploited than exploiters, on the other, the minority of those who are little exploited and more or less consciously exploiters; if we add this last branch to the

category of the finest and most conscientious exploiters, we find that out of 70 million inhabitants, there are a maximum of 200,000 authentic and ferocious exploiters, such that for each exploiter there are approximately 350 exploited" (Bakunin, 2009e[e], pp. 38–39).

10   Bakunin (2003a[e], pp. 168, 228) speaks of a "statist system" and "capitalist system." Thanks to his concept of interdependence between politics and economics, the State and capitalism, I use, for didactic purposes, the concept of the *statist-capitalist system*.

11   Cf. Proudhon (1988, p. 69; 1969, p. 108): "our civil State [...], a State that was initially despotic, then a monarchy, then an aristocracy, today a democracy, and a tyranny always." "Experience shows, in fact, that everywhere and always the government, however popular it may have been in its origins, has aligned itself with the most enlightened and richest class against the poorest and most numerous; that, after having shown itself to be liberal for a while, little by little it has become exceptional, exclusive; that, finally, instead of upholding freedom and equality among all, it has worked obstinately to destroy them, by virtue of its natural inclination to privilege. [...] The history of governments is the martyrology of the proletariat."

12   Cf. Proudhon (1969, pp. 242–43): "What is the purpose of this body [the governmental system]? To maintain *order* in society, consecrating and sanctifying the obedience of the citizen to the State, the subordination of the poor to the rich, of the villager to the noble, of the worker to the parasite, of the layman to the priest, of the civilian to the soldier."

13   Cf. Marx (1985, p. 47): "Therefore, a value of use or good has value only because abstract human labor is objectified or materialized in it. How then to measure the greatness of its value? By means of the quantum contained in it of the 'substance constituting the value', the labor. The amount of work itself is measured by its duration, and the time worked has, in turn, its unit of measurement in certain fractions of time, such as time, day, etc."

14   Cf. Proudhon (1988, pp. 16, 18): "Property is theft! [...] Yes, everyone believes and repeats that equality of conditions is the same as equality of rights; that *property and theft* are synonymous terms; that all social preeminence, granted, or rather usurped under the pretext of superiority of talent and service, is iniquity and rapine: everyone, I say, attests to these truths in the depths of their soul; it is only a matter of making them perceive them."

15   Cf. Marx (1985, vol. I, p. 251): "The added value produced by the extension of the working day is called absolute added value; the added value that, on the contrary, results from the reduction in working time and the corresponding change in the proportion between the two components of the working day is called relative added value."

16   Cf. Marx (1985, vol. I, p. 145): "The old possessor of money marches on as a capitalist, followed by the possessor of labor power as his worker; one, full of importance, smiling satisfied and eager for business; the other, timid, cringing, like someone who has taken his own skin to the market and now has nothing left to expect, except the tanning."

17   Cf. Marx and Engels (2007, p. 47): "The lower layers of the middle class of old, the small industrialists, small shopkeepers, those who lived by peasants' and artisans' rents [*rentiers*], fall into the ranks of the proletariat; some because their small capital does not permit them to employ the processes of big industry and they succumb in competition with the big capitalists; others because their professional skills are depreciated by the new methods of production. Thus, the proletariat is recruited from all classes of the population."

18   Cf. Proudhon (*apud* Bakunin, 2007e[e], p. 8) "Price, compared to value (in the real social economy) is something essentially mobile, therefore, essentially variable, and that, in its variations, is no more regulated than by cooperation, cooperation which, let us not forget, as Turgot and Say agree, causes the necessary effect of not adding to the workers' wages beyond what is strictly necessary to prevent deaths by hunger, and to maintain the class in the necessary number."

19   For a good discussion of Bakunin's critique of capitalism, cf. Saltman, 1983, pp. 80-95.

20   According to Berthier (2011e, p. 117), Bakunin's theoretical reflections on the bureaucracy that aspires to power—which was deepened in his critique of state communism—are based on the priestly domination of that period: "his [Bakunin's] theory of the priestly class of the Middle Ages" identifies "a dominant class without individual titles of ownership," which possesses "in an oligarchical way the means of production" and which governs "by a centralized apparatus whose structure is strictly hierarchical and which is reproduced by absorption of the elites of society."

CHAPTER 13

SOCIAL REVOLUTION, MASS ORGANIZATION, AND CADRE ORGANIZATION (1868-76)

This chapter concludes the exposition of Bakunin's political theory in his *revolutionary socialist period*, but it does so specifically from the contributions of his anarchist period, which lasted from 1868 to 1876 and is divided into five parts: 1) Destruction-construction Dialectics: Collectivist-federalist Socialism and Social Revolution; 2) Social Force, Organization, and Federalism; 3) Mass Organization: The International; 4) Cadre Organization: The Alliance; 5) Dictatorship of Allies and Anti-Semitism.

13.1 DESTRUCTION-CONSTRUCTION DIALECTICS: COLLECTIVIST-FEDERALIST SOCIALISM AND SOCIAL REVOLUTION

According to the logic of materialism and the materialistic, naturalistic, and scientific analysis of reality, the ideals for social transformation towards freedom can be conceived through negation. This means, dialectically, to achieve affirmation through negation, to achieve construction through destruction: through negation-destruction of the present society the affirmation-construction of the future society is made. "These two sides of the same question, one negative and the other positive, are inseparable" for "no one can want to destroy without having at least a distant imagination [...] of the order of things that should [...] succeed that which exists in the present." Such a positive imagination is done by the negation of that which one wants to destroy such that "destructive action is always determined [...] by the positive [and constructive] ideal which constitutes its first inspiration, its soul" (Bakunin, 71011a[e], p. 51).

It should be remembered that this movement (negation-affirmation, destruction-construction) is motivated, on the one hand, by the germ of change that exists in society: the contradiction between the concrete (or "natural world," that is, the existing reality, in which domination-authority is a fundamental trait) and the possible (which is contained in nature as the perspective of the realization of freedom). On the other hand, it is driven by the negation of subjects who concretize their rational will through action, towards revolt and respecting the limits imposed by nature-matter and by natural and socio-historical laws.

In general terms, through the negation of domination, authority, and statism-capitalism one arrives at the affirmation of emancipation, freedom, and *collectivist-federalist socialism* as a perspective for the future. This emancipated society is free, egalitarian, and does not rely on any form of domination, privilege, and artificial authority. It is a classless society, whose crucial mark is widespread socialization—not only economic, but also political and cultural. It is therefore a socialism with freedom spread throughout all social camps, legitimized by means of a new ethics.

More specifically, through the denial of economic domination and the exploitation of labour, the need to destroy private property, inheritance, social inequalities, and the construction of collective property for workers, compulsory collective labour that upholds rights,[1] and social equality that respects diversity— precisely that which conforms to the economic foundations of *collectivism*—is affirmed.

Thanks to the decisive role of the economy, a free society demands the "*definitive and complete* economic emancipation of the workers"—the realization of the "principle of *economic equality*, which is to say": "*the complete return of capital to labor*," "*social liquidation*," and the implementation "of collective labor and property" (Bakunin, 2008b[e], pp. 61–62; Bakunin, 2008e[e], p. 116). To this end, the "taking over (of possession) by autonomous collectivities, workers' associations, agricultural or industrial, and communes"— that is, the expropriation by workers and their organizations—"of all social capital, all ownership of land, mines, dwellings, religious and public buildings, instruments of labor, raw materials, precious metals, precious jewels and stones, and manufactured products" (Bakunin, 72016[e], pp. 3–4).[2]

Through the negation of national domination (imperialism) and political domination (government) one arrives at the affirmation of the need to destroy the State and to build workers' own decision-making bodies, such as agricultural and industrial associations. This is because "the State, however popular its forms, will always be an institution of domination and exploitation." Ultimately, "there is no other way to emancipate the peoples economically and politically, to give them well-being and freedom, but through the abolition of the State, of all States" (Bakunin, 71011a[e], p. 24).

With the ending of the State, there is no longer a political body with an enslaving and imperialist vocation, with power merging into society and no longer existing as something apart and above it: "In this system, there is no longer any power properly speaking. *Power merges into collectivity*, and becomes the sincere expression of each one's freedom, the faithful and sincere realization of everyone's will" (Bakunin, 2014d[e], p. 166, emphasis added). State and power are therefore replaced by the aforementioned workers' organizations (Bakunin, 71011a[e], p. 24). This establishes *federalism*, which articulates economic and political institutions by workplace and/or region, from local to regional, from regional to national, and from national to international levels (Bakunin, 1998[e], p. 31; Bakunin, 2008e[e], p. 116).

Through the negation of intellectual and moral domination, the inequality of knowledge, and religious domination one arrives at the affirmation of the need to end the division between manual and intellectual labour, that integral education be guaranteed to all from their first years. Since reconciling manual and intellectual labour is "the only way to elevate and humanize manual labor" and thus to guarantee "real equality among men."

Everyone in society must be able to develop intellectually and to this end must have free time, leisure—of which manual workers are deprived (Bakunin, 2008a[e], p. 31). Moreover, "all children of both sexes, from birth to adulthood" must have "equal means of development, that is, livelihood, education and instruction at all levels of science, industry and the arts," and knowledge "must truly become the property of everyone" (Bakunin, 68014[e]; Bakunin, 2014e[e], p. 298). However much religious freedom must be guaranteed—as must all individual liberties[3]—institutionalized religions, especially those with governmental pretensions, must be abolished.

Through the negation of the domination of women and children within marriage and the family, the affirmation of gender equality and the end of "patriarchal right" is achieved. That is, "the equalization of the rights of women with those of men" and the abolition of the "despotism of husband and father" over women and children (Bakunin, 2009d[e], p. 82).[4]

In short, from the negation of present society, a socialist, collectivist, and federalist program emerges that can guide the construction of the future society, which will feature

> the ending of deprivation, of misery, and the full and complete satisfaction of all their material needs through collective labor, obligatory and equal for all; then, with the ending of patronage, of all domination, and the free organization of their social life, according to their aspirations, not from top to bottom, as in the State, but from bottom to top, by the people themselves, outside governments and parliaments of any kind; as the alliance of agricultural and industrial workers' associations, of communes, regions and nations; and finally, in the more distant future, as the universal brotherhood whose triumph will assert itself upon the rubble of all the States. (Bakunin, 2003a[e], p. 57)

In this society, all forms of domination no longer exist: exploitation of labour, imperialism, government of a majority by a minority, inequality of knowledge, religious submission, and patriarchal law. It is, as can be seen, a society without classes, whose structure has been completely transformed and socialized. Taking into account the decisive role of the economy in society, to ensure the end of social classes is to socialize the means of production, distribution, and capital. But owing to the interdependence between politics and economics and the reactions that politics and culture can have on the economy, ensuring the ending of social classes also means socializing the means of administration, control, and coercion and the means of knowledge. For the State and the inequality of knowledge will not automatically disappear with the end of property, and if they are maintained, they will preserve or recreate class society—which may be different, but certainly no less oppressive.[5]

Because this society is constituted "from the bottom up," "from the circumference to the center," it reproduces the movement of nature-matter itself and becomes an environment conducive to the development of man's natural faculties, to the realization of freedom, equality, justice (Bakunin, 68016[e]). On the one hand, it provides the conditions for the economic, political, and cultural self-organization of workers in the cities and countryside, in their own social bodies, with decisions being taken by the grassroots. On the other hand, it guarantees the chances for the articulation of these industrial and agricultural bodies, by region or place of work, conciliating city and countryside and relying on shared decisions and delegations controlled by the base, revocable and for a determined time.

In accordance with the conception of history discussed earlier, this socialism— the result of a historical social change—cannot be conceived as a necessary and obligatory development nor as an involuntary product of a crisis of statism-capitalism, or even of misery and social inequality. "General, public and private bankruptcy" is a "condition of social revolution" but it is not enough to unleash it, and "misery, even united with despair" is also "not enough to trigger social revolution." The structural, conjunctural, and historical aspects of society make transformation possible or impede it, favour it more or less, and place themselves as a condition and premise to it—but they are not sufficient elements.

Collectivist-federalist socialism is the result of a revolutionary process that, if it takes advantage of these conditions of statist-capitalist society, also demands the rational will of workers—"a general idea of their rights and a deep, ardent, one might even say, religious faith in those rights"—committed to building a social force capable of supplanting the force of the dominant classes. "When this idea and this faith are united in the people," together with the structural, conjunctural, and historical conditions, "the social revolution is near" (Bakunin, 2003a[e], pp. 53, 56).

The workers' and peasants' social revolution is the moment of transition from the statist-capitalist system to collectivist-federalist socialism. More precisely, it is a moment of broad, profound, and violent[6] transformation, in which oppressed classes, the "people of the countryside and of the cities" (Bakunin, 71022[e], p. 71)—having accumulated greater social force and applied to the social conflict—overwhelm the upper classes and their movements of the conservation of order. It is the interstice between humanity and freedom.

"The triumph of social revolution" means that "the working [and peasant] masses will definitively destroy the detested secular yoke, completely destroy bourgeois exploitation and the civilization built upon it," promoting "the abolition of all that is called the State." As can be seen, this revolution, which transforms all aspects of the statist-capitalist system, is distinct from political revolution, which modifies only some of these aspects and preserves the principle of authority and domination—as in the case of the countless revolutions that have replaced rulers and/or regimes but preserved the State. Unlike political revolution, the social revolution is "the path of real emancipation and the most complete, accessible to all," that is, it is "the path of anarchist social revolution hatching by itself in the people, destroying everything that opposes the impetuous flow of people's lives, so that from the depths of their being, the new forms of a free community are then created" (Bakunin, 2003a[e], pp. 44, 165).

However, promoting a social revolution requires not only the right conditions and the will of the workers, but also "preparatory organization," without which "the most powerful elements are impotent and null" (Bakunin, 71022[e], p. 71).

> We want, both from the point of view of the creation of the new economic and social order and from that of the formation of the revolutionary potential and the inevitable struggle of the insurgent masses against reaction, *the spontaneous organization of insurgent groups* of all the rebellious countries, under the same principle of popular demands, in provisional communes, without any consideration for the territorial divisions and current borders of the States; the immediate sending of delegates from all the communes, with imperative mandates, to the revolutionary spaces; urgent federation of both communes and these spaces, permanence of the barricades and revolutionary uprising aiming at the common defense of all points of the insurgent countries, federation of the popular forces which are organizing themselves spontaneously for the struggle; division of all delegates into committees perfectly distinct and independent from each other, but which must understand each other, complement each other and support each other whenever necessary. (Bakunin, 72016[e], pp. 4–5)

Only with adequate organization is it possible to achieve the social force necessary to make a change of these proportions and to ensure that it is maintained. For this, the "*local and federal committees* [...] *of revolutionary defense*" and of bodies responsible for the transition are fundamental. In the defense of the revolution, an "effective alliance or even the fraternal fusion of socialist revolutionaries of all countries against all reactions and all sorts of reactionaries" is necessary, but not only that. Above all, one must be concerned with "those who, under the mask of the revolution, will promote authority, seek, serve or advocate dictatorship." Revolutionaries must fight both this open reaction and this disguised reaction, which do not let themselves be forms of "counter-revolution." It is also important to be concerned with the transition between the old and the new world. As much as this in no way means the maintenance of the State, it is necessary to invest in the creation of "*local and federal committees* [...] *of provisional detention of capital, temporary handing over of capital and labor instruments to agricultural and industrial associations*" that will mediate the revolutionary situation and general socialization (Bakunin, 72016[e], pp. 5–6).

13.2 SOCIAL FORCE, ORGANIZATION, AND FEDERALISM

Discussing organization of the revolution requires a return to previous reflections on the concept of social force. It has been seen that a reality results from the confrontation between social forces, some of which impose themselves on others. In the case of the statist-capitalist system, it expresses the preponderance of the social force of the privileged classes (owners of the means of production, distribution, capital; of the means of administration, control, and coercion; of the means of knowledge)—a tiny minority—over the dispossessed (proletariat, peasants, and marginalized)—the vast majority.

Transforming these relations so as to advance a revolutionary process toward collectivist-federalist socialism requires therefore that the oppressed classes (the workers in general) conceive and implement means for the increase of their class social force. For this "transformation [...] is never accomplished except by a profound change in the balance of forces," and the conversion of the potential (spontaneous, natural) force of the workers into a real force is necessary (Bakunin, 2009e[e], p. 34).

> It is true, there is a lot of spontaneous [potential] force in the people; this is incomparably greater than the force of government, including that of the [dominant] classes; however, for lack of organization, spontaneous [potential] force is not a real force. It is not in a position to sustain a long struggle against much weaker but well-organized forces. On this undeniable superiority of organized force over the elementary force of the people rests all the power of the State.
>
> This is why the first condition for the victory of the people is *the union* or *the organization of popular forces*. (Bakunin, 2009e[e], p. 67)

That is, the organization of the oppressed classes will provide the conditions for the formation of this real social force which, besides being a collective force, will enjoy the determinant benefits of association in order to potentiate itself. It will ensure the possibilities for the association of workers, for "the elaboration of a plan of action, then the best possible distribution and the systematic or reflected organization [of] forces [...] in accordance with the established plan." In this way, the oppressed classes will be able to intervene much more effectively in the social conflict.

Therefore, "the question is not whether the people are capable of rising," whether they have the potential to do so, because history has numerous cases of workers' mobilizations both in the countryside, like the uprising of Pugachev, and in the city, like the Paris Commune. The real question is whether the people "are capable of forming an organization that can ensure the victory of the uprising, a victory that is not ephemeral but lasting and definitive" (Bakunin, 2009e[e], pp. 35–36, 87). This is even more challenging when one considers that the ruling classes are also organized and, because they have been in power for a long time, have the institutional structure and values of society playing to their advantage.

But it is not enough to advocate for organization. It is indispensable to define it, stipulating with some precision what it is and what it is intended to negate and affirm with it. In discussing the organization of future society, the negation of the statist-capitalist system led to collectivist-federalist socialism. Since the organizations of the privileged classes, which have been imposing their social force, are based on dominant and bureaucratic organizational conceptions (which enjoy the exploitation of labour, the monopoly of decisions, and the subservience of members), it is necessary to negate such conceptions to arrive at a new one. Moreover, to "organize a force, [...] it is necessary to establish its purpose, since the very nature of its purpose essentially depends on the mode and nature of its organization" (Bakunin, 72005[e], p. 145). This means that the form of an organization must be determined by the ends it intends to achieve. This strategic coherence advocates that adequate means are needed to achieve certain ends, and that therefore, depending on these ends, some organizational conceptions are more appropriate than others. That is, "the organization, being linked to a particular objective, cannot contradict this objective; it must contain the objective, it must be of the same nature as it" (Berthier, 2015c, p. 31).

Negating dominating and bureaucratic organizational conceptions, and taking into account that the purpose of this organization must be collectivist-federalist socialism, one arrives at federalism—previously used to explain the organization of future society from below and from the circumference to the centre, and reproducing the movement of nature-matter— which also supports this "how" of the organizational conception of the workers' struggle. In this sense, *federalism*, practiced by both the International and the Alliance, can be defined as an *organizational conception based on the principle of freedom, which allows the means of struggle to be coherently related to the ends of collectivist-federalist socialism, to counter bureaucracy and bureaucratization, and to carry out delegation with control from the grassroots.* Federalism *guarantees the strategic coherence of the revolutionary project, thanks to the promotion of federalist means and the protagonism of the workers in their organizations and struggles.*

Unlike authoritarian organizations, which use domination to increase their social force, federalism rejects privileges and permanent hierarchies, and proposes voluntary and emancipatory means for the necessary gain of social force as well as for the solution of differences of perspectives and conflicts among its members. Thus, for the increase of its social force, a federalist organization does not take advantage of the exploitation of labour, the monopoly of decisions, the coercion of weapons, and subservience, both among its own members and between its members (and its own organization) and others. It benefits, in addition to organization, from the natural influence to win popular support and engagement, from workers' own knowledge and education, from self-discipline, self-confidence, and the rational will of its members (Saltman, 1983, pp. 36–37).

In this way, workers' organizations have to be founded on federalism, thus forging the foundations of a new world. Thus organized, they "still carry the living germs of the *new social order* that must replace the bourgeois world. They create not only the ideas, but the very facts of the future" (Bakunin, 71011b[e], p. 17). In this way, federalism allows the building of a new society within the old, prefiguring the future in the present. "The central idea [...] is that the organization of workers, in its form, should not be built on the model of the organizations of bourgeois society"; the organization of the oppressed "should be founded on the basis of the internal needs of the workers' [and peasants'] struggle and, as such, constitutes a *prefiguration of the socialist society.*" Consequently, the federalist organization of workers is characterized by coherence with its objective, contributes to its approximation and does so by anticipating the future in the present (Berthier, 2011b, p. 56, emphasis added; cf., also: Berthier, 2015c, pp. 51–52).

However, this does not mean creating a perfect world on the fringes of society, isolated and incapable of influencing its course.[7] It is a matter, distinctly, of building a powerful organizational tool, strategically coherent and capable of contributing to the revolutionary transformation of society. Such an instrument cannot be in contradiction with the new order it intends to create: "freedom can only be created by freedom"—one does not reach socialism, a classless society, by means that reinforce domination. With federalism as its base, this tool allows "revolutionary organization from the bottom up and from the circumference to the center," which is totally in line with the "principle of freedom" and clearly distinguishes itself from the authoritarian model, which advocates organization "from the top down," "from the center to the circumference." The logic that "to free the popular masses, one should begin by subduing them" seems inconceivable. That is, even if domination provides greater social force, it contradicts emancipatory ends, and is therefore the very guarantee that they will not be attained (Bakunin, 2003a[e], p. 214; Bakunin, 68016[e]).

The most common example in this sense is the use of the State as a means of revolutionary transformation, as the communists call for. This institution has remained, throughout its history, an instrument of class domination, of division between a governing-exploiting minority and a governed-exploited majority, of hierarchy and subservience of some classes to the advantage of others. Such that, as a means of submitting the masses, it cannot contribute to an emancipatory end. The consequences of the seizure of the State by socialist workers would be disastrous to any emancipatory pretension: "as soon as [these workers] become rulers or representatives of the people, they will cease to be workers" and will begin "to observe the proletarian world from the State above." With this, "they will no longer represent the people, but themselves and their pretensions to govern them." Even if, with this, the old dominant classes find their end, these former workers—who will have become bureaucrats—will themselves form a new privileged class, which will govern a society that will continue to be characterized by the principle of authority and domination (Bakunin, 2003a[e], p. 213).

According to what the International recommends, "the emancipation of labor must be the work of the workers themselves" and the realization of this emancipation must be "necessarily *subordinated to their theoretical and practical participation* [concours]". (Bakunin, 71011a[e], pp. 75–76). Consequently, workers must "take into their own hands the direction of their own affairs [affaires]" and participate widely and actively, through their thinking and action, in that organization which will emancipate them. Because this exercise is an indispensable element to advance toward an emancipated society (Bakunin, 1973b[e], p. 32).

Fundamental to this is the elimination of bureaucracy and the bureaucratization of workers' organizations, to which federalism also contributes. An organization "can only become a tool of emancipation for humanity when it has first emancipated itself." This implies that such an organization is not "divided into two groups: most of the blind instruments and most of the wise machinists" (Bakunin, 71011a[e], p. 79). Observing certain deviations of the International one can understand "perfectly how this separation between the base and the leaders causes a growing indifference, engenders a lack of initiative and, finally, tends to reduce the association to its committees, thus emptying it of its substance" (Vuilleumier, 1979, p. 124). When crystallized, this split between leaders and led, between those who obey and those who make decisions, operates with the monopoly of decision-making by a restricted privileged group, the *bureaucracy*. The creation and maintenance of this separation is what is called the *bureaucratization of workers' organizations*.

In workers' organizations, bureaucratization not only reproduces the mechanisms of the State, but also makes them "the worst of all States," since their despotism "carefully conceals itself under an apparent obsequious (courteous or servile) respect for the will and resolutions of the sovereign people." This bureaucratization is "a detestable and inevitable consequence of authoritarianism once introduced into the organization," which ends up being very "favorable to the development of all kinds of intrigues, vanities, ambitions and personal interests" that are "fatal to the proletariat." It should also be noted that, in accordance with the materialistic dynamic between social position and will (structure and action), the positions occupied by bureaucrats will be more determinant in what they do than their eventual goodwill.

The ending of the permanent separation between leaders and led, as well as the elimination of bureaucratic domination, indispensably implies that all workers have the autonomy to deal with their concerns in their own organizations. Broad participation prevents ignorance and indifference on the part of the workers, and thus makes generalized empowerment possible. The full involvement of the masses in the processes of struggle is central to their knowledge and awareness: "the ignorant and indifferent masses are only capable of creating a *fictitious power*, not a *genuine one*," ending up not properly potentializing their social force for an emancipative project.

It should be pointed out, however, that bureaucratization is not only fortified by the position and the will of the bureaucracy. The absence of workers' participation also contributes to this process. The more they show "indifference to general issues," the more they pass on "all decisions to their committees," and the more they cultivate a "habit of automatic subordination," the more they become "unthinking instruments of the thought and will" of a restricted set of members. Thus, the greater the involvement of workers in the daily life of the organization, the more they participate in relevant decisions and refuse subordination, the more they avoid bureaucratization.

Now, advocating an end to bureaucracy and bureaucratization does not mean promoting assemblyism, in which everyone always participates in everything and the division of tasks and functions is prohibited—that would not be desirable either. Federalism provides for delegation, a means by which one or more people are invested with responsibility for carrying out certain tasks/functions, or for taking decisions in certain circumstances, often being substituted by rotation. Depending on the circumstances, it can take two forms: delegation with prior deliberation at the grassroots on function or task, or delegation without prior deliberation and with rotation. In both the first and second cases there is grassroots control, since "the best men are easily corruptible, especially when [... there is] a lack of serious control and permanent opposition" (Bakunin, 71011a[e], pp. 1, 6–7, 79).

In the first case, "to constitute a federation" it is necessary to have "delegates" who are "invested with mandatory, responsible and revocable mandates." This *imperative* federalist mandate allows the delegate to uphold positions previously discussed and deliberated on by the base of the organization. Grassroots control is exercised both before the delegation itself, when it makes the decisions to be represented by the delegate (*a priori* control), and after the delegation, evaluating the delegate in question immediately after they have played their role (*a posteriori* control) (Bakunin, 68016[e]).

In the second case, delegation is different:
At the moment of the action, in the middle of the struggle, the roles are mutually divided, according to each one's aptitudes, appreciated and judged by the whole collectivity: some direct and command and others execute the commands. But no function is petrified, fixed and irrevocably linked to any person. Order and hierarchical progression do not exist, so that the commander of yesterday can become a server today. No one rises above the others, and if he rises, it is only to fall again after an instant, like the waves of the sea, returning to the healthy level of equality. (Bakunin, 2014d[e], p. 166)

Here the delegation of the organization's decisions is foreseen, or even the distribution of functions and tasks based on the personal competences of the members. Even if there are officers and directors, such positions are not permanent or crystallized. Both grassroots control (*a posteriori*) and the rotation of militants in decision-making bodies ensure that the organization does not become bureaucratic.

There is yet another notion that complements federalism and that could be called *concentric circles*. It is not an organizing principle, but a tool that can contribute to the gaining of social force and the practical application of federalism. Concentric circles are the different levels or ambits that exist in an organization, be it mass, cadre, or hybrid. Their logic provides conditions for the participation of various types of members, reconciles the different levels of participation with federalism and guarantees the complementarity of the levels and the correspondence between rights and duties among the members of the organization (Bakunin, 71011a[e]; Bakunin, 68016[e]; Bakunin, 72016[e]).

In terms of a *theory of organization* one can say that the federalist organization of workers has two levels: a mass movement, the International, which is complemented by a party of cadres (anarchist political organization), the Alliance.

> The Alliance is the necessary complement to the International...—But the International and the Alliance, tending towards the same ultimate objective, pursue different objectives at the same time. One has the mission of gathering the working masses, the millions of workers, with their differences of professions and countries, across the borders of all States, into one immense and compact body; the other, the Alliance, has the mission of giving the masses a truly revolutionary direction. The programs of one and the other, without being in any way opposites, are different by the very degree of their respective development. That of the International, if taken seriously, contains in germ, but only in germ, the whole program of the Alliance. The program of the Alliance is the ultimate explanation of the [program] of the International. (Bakunin, 72015[c], p. 8)

Based on the notion of concentric circles, both the International and the Alliance can be properly organized to, in a complementary relationship, mobilize the social force necessary for workers to promote a revolution that leads to socialism. This organizational dualism supported in concentric circles can be explained as follows. In the case of the International, there is a dual structure, based on three criteria that define it: type of organization (grouping the masses by professions and minorities by region), function of organization (economic and economic/political/cultural), and profile of militants (more and less prepared) (Bakunin, 71011a[e]). In the case of the Alliance, there is a three-part structure based on three criteria that define it: locality (international, national, local/regional), character of the instances (public and secret), and profile of the militants (less and more prepared, with this distinction accompanying the difference in power of decision-making) (Bakunin, 68016[e]; Bakunin, 72016[e]).

As will be discussed below, it is the social force of the mass organization that must be able to supplant the statist and capitalist forces, but the organization of cadres makes this possible.

13.3 MASS ORGANIZATION: THE INTERNATIONAL

Through an analytical and prescriptive reflection on the International Workers' Association (IWA or "mass organization"), theoretical-strategic reflections on the mass *revolutionary syndicalist* organization, involving its objectives, character, functions, and structure, can be elaborated.[8]

13.3.1 Constitutive Aspects, Emancipatory Objectives, Internationalist and Mass Character

As its name reveals, the International is an international mass organization founded from the experience (actions, thoughts, struggles, and lessons learned) of the dispossessed classes, in a context of the development and internationalization of the statist-capitalist system (Bakunin, 71011a[e], p. 47). By bringing together members for the immediate economic struggle, it proceeds to a practical education for the class struggle, which increasingly promotes the radicalization of its members and the gaining of social force, in order to advance it towards social revolution and collectivist-federalist socialism—towards the complete emancipation of the workers, of which this organization is the greatest protagonist.

Differentiating itself from the typical form of organization of the bourgeoisie—which "groups citizens on the basis of a constituency," "corresponds to the capitalist system," and possesses its "real power" emanating "from the control of the means of production"—the mass organization "does not group citizens, but producers," workers and the poor in general, in its own organic structures, such as "union, workers' council, factory committee," and is based in federalism (Berthier, 2011b, p. 67).

Since the IWA adopts federalism as an organizational concept—articulating from the bottom up, from the circumference to the centre, and thus arriving at a form appropriate to the ends it aims to achieve—it is a "natural organization of the masses" capable of offering an essential counterpoint to authority, "artificial and violent, strange and hostile to the natural developments of popular interests and instincts"—which is why it is a spontaneous organization (Bakunin, 71011a[e], p. 68; Berthier, 2011b, p. 67).[9] In this way, it prefigures the future in the present and "constitutes a new world, the world of solidarity of the proletariat of all countries," the germ of an emancipated society (Bakunin, 2001a[e], pp. 76-77; cf., also: Morris, 1993, p. 140).

The goals of the mass organization are "the definitive and complete emancipation of the workers." That is, the elimination of "the yoke of all the exploiters of this [popular] labor" and the "complete liquidation of the present political, religious, juridical and social world" as well as the building of "a new economic, philosophical and social world." The International is the organization that must lead the social revolution and provide the basis for the construction of collectivist-federalist socialism (Bakunin, 71011a[e], p. 63). This means—in order to avoid the mishaps of bourgeois political revolutions and parliamentarianism—an emphatic search for the *"complete economic emancipation of the worker"* (Bakunin, 2008b[e], p. 67). But, at the same time, the politics of "total abolition of the State"[10] and the formation of a "new social philosophy" capable of intellectually and morally supporting the entire camp of the oppressed (Bakunin, 71011a[e], pp. 24, 77).

The increasing internationalization of the statist-capitalist system and the solidarity between the oppressing classes of different countries[11] demands that the IWA has an *internationalist character* and embraces workers from all over the world. For "to guarantee itself against the exploitative and ever-increasing oppression of the bosses, it is not enough to organize local solidarity." It is essential to unite workers "not only from the same region or country, but from all countries," conceiving of an "organization that is not only local or even national, but truly *international*" (Bakunin, 71011a[e], p. 43). And such internationalism is central not only to the immediate confrontation of the upper classes, but also because revolution and socialism are inconceivable if restricted to one locality, one region, or even one country.

Moreover, the social force of the class enemies demands that the IWA has a *mass character* articulating all "the people, the mass of workers: these hundreds of millions of unknown proletarians," that is, the "eternally sacrificed human beings who, since history has existed, serve as pedestals to all the civilizations of the world, and who have always been the victims of history" (Bakunin, 71011b[e], p. 25). During the process of struggles and confrontations, all members of the oppressed classes are able to become *revolutionary subjects*: not only the urban-industrial proletariat, but also the rural proletariat, the peasants and the marginalized. In fact, considering the context of Western and Eastern Europe of the 1860s and 1870s, the realization of a social revolution obligatorily depends on the involvement of the peasantry (Bakunin, 71022[e], pp. 71–72).

Now, although it is a revolutionary and socialist organization, the International has less radicalized entry criteria. It allows the participation of all the workers who have understood the class struggle, taken sides with the workers, and who have the will to promote the struggle against the bosses for immediate improvements, accepting the need for an organization to do so (Bakunin, 2008b[e], pp. 39–42, 48–49, 56). Beyond social position and the condition of exploitation, its unifying foundation involves a certain level of class consciousness and an agreement for the immediate economic struggle for improvements, and should be sought "in the aspirations of the proletariat of all countries for material or economic emancipation." After all, what mobilizes workers is much more the concreteness of facts than the pure abstraction of ideas (Bakunin, 72015[c], pp. 11–12).

Besides that, this mass character demands an adaptation of organizational criteria to the concrete reality of the workers. Especially when they are not organized, the majority of these workers are religious, depoliticized, and not interested in theoretical or philosophical issues. And even when these workers, organized or not, have political-doctrinaire and theoretical-philosophical positions, they differ a lot from each other.

> We believe that the founders of the International Association acted with great wisdom in initially eliminating all political and religious issues from the Association's program. Without a doubt, they were not lacking in political opinions or well-defined anti-religious opinions; but they abstained from expressing them in this program, because their main objective was to unite above all the working masses of the civilized world in common action. They necessarily had to seek a common basis, a series of simple principles on which all workers, whatever their political and religious aberrations, inasmuch they may be serious workers, that is, harshly exploited and suffering men, do and must agree. (Bakunin, 2008a[e], pp. 42–43)

That is, the International should not demand that its members take positions that separate them from each other. It should not prevent workers from entering and participating because of their political or religious positions or lack thereof. Nor can it establish official and binding political and religious positions for all its members, because in the process of class struggle, they separate more than they unite the workers. Which does not mean that the different political, apolitical, religious, and non-religious conceptions cannot or should not be the subject of debate among the workers of the mass organization (Bakunin, 2001a[e], p. 75; Berthier, 2015c, pp. 20–21).

"For the International to be and remain a power, it must be able to attract, embrace, and organize the immense majority of the proletariat of all countries," and this can only be accomplished with "an excessively general, that is, undetermined and vague program" (Bakunin, 2001a[e], p. 59). It is thus understandable that the indoctrination of mass organizations, in the sense of imposing a political-doctrinaire program—even if it is anarchist—is incongruent with its character and ends (Bakunin, 72015[c], p. 10).[12]

13.3.2 Economic Struggle and Practical Education of the Class Struggle

Another relevant criterion for the mobilization of workers is that it cannot be achieved only through advertising and education in a restricted sense. Without a doubt, these means are beautiful and have a certain importance, but alone—because they operate more in the field of ideas than of facts—are insufficient for a more meaningful engagement. Because of the way the world works and the concrete condition of the workers, this mobilization should be done, as a matter of priority, through practice, with engagement in concrete struggles for immediate conquests, and around simple, everyday problems.

Few are engaged by a noble ideal, but many mobilize for the resolution of a concrete problem. For this reason, the IWA must give "to the workers' agitation in all countries an *essentially economic* character, setting as its objective the reduction of the working day and the increase of wages; as a means, *the association of the working masses*, syndicalism, the formation of the *resistance funds*" (Bakunin, 2008b[e], pp. 52, 68; Bakunin, 71011a[e], p. 55; Bakunin, 69041[e]).

> To interest and draw the whole proletariat into the work of the International, it was necessary, and still is, to approach it not with general and abstract ideas, but with a concrete and living understanding of its real woes. [...] To touch the heart and win the trust, approval, adherence and participation of the uneducated proletariat—and the immense majority of the proletariat, unfortunately, is still in that state—one must begin by speaking to it, not of the general woes of the entire international proletariat, nor of the general causes that provoke them, but of their particular, daily and private woes. He must be told about his own profession and the conditions of his work, precisely on the local level, the weight and the excessive duration of his daily labor, the insufficiency of his salary, the evil of his boss, the high cost of food and the impossibility for him to adequately feed and support his family. [...] He must first be offered such means that his natural good sense and daily experience cannot ignore their usefulness nor repel them. (Bakunin, 71011a[e], pp. 55–57)

This economic character of the struggle makes it possible to guarantee the unity of the workers as a class and a concrete approach to organization and class struggle. Through this involvement with the demands and daily issues, the workers enter a pedagogical experience, guaranteed by a practical education that will contribute in a decisive way to their political training. This *revolutionary and socialist education through the class struggle* promotes a better understanding by the workers of the world around them, of social relations, their situation, their interests, and their class project. It also contributes to the radicalization of workers in a revolutionary and socialist direction.

There are certain precautions to ensure that this education is carried out properly. Since the workers have engaged in mass organization for the immediate economic struggle, they should not be preached to about the maximum program at the beginning, as this would probably drive them away. Patience is essential so that the "collective experience" of their struggles can be constituted and assimilated. This process is gradual and does not result from radicalized discourses or decontextualized actions, but from this experience that demands time, maturation, and planning (Bakunin, 2008b[e], pp. 46–47, 53). With time, workers, living elements of this praxis, educate and instruct each other in a movement that progresses as the struggles develop; that produces and enjoys a tool of practical knowledge that goes far beyond what is transmitted at school or in theoretical, philosophical, or even political proselytizing.

This practical education begins with the economic struggle and, little by little, addresses other issues that go beyond the economy and are indispensable in the formation of the revolutionary subject:

> If the *aspiration to well-being and more freedom* [...] is just in itself, something more than the elementary class struggle and the systematic, methodical organization, however perfect, of the proletariat at the level of the economy, is necessary to realize it. [...] One cannot remain on the sidelines of the complex facts that often determine social events; ignore the political and psychological factors that intervene in human relations and the evolution of societies; ignore the techniques of science; despise the culture that develops intelligence and allows one to embrace the vast activities and the whole of social life whose organization requires, in order to be properly coordinated, and at least to the extent that this depends on the welfare and activity of the workers, a little more than the initial instruction. (Leval, 2007, p. 70)

In other words, this emphasis on the economic struggle should not be confused with a defense of economic determinism. This "exclusive concern with only economic interests would be, for the proletariat, death." Because, if taken as an end in itself, this struggle is incapable of emancipating the workers. So asserting it means considering it as a starting point which, expanded by the educational process in question, becomes a social, political, philosophical project. "If the political and philosophical issues had not been introduced into the IWA, the proletariat would unfailingly introduce them." For it is inevitable that, by participating in social conflicts, workers will become interested in these issues. And even though they should not become official and mandatory in mass organization, they have to be discussed and deepened whenever possible (Bakunin, 2001a[e], pp. 74–75).

Revolutionary and socialist education through class struggle also contributes in a decisive way to the growth of class solidarity—a feeling of affinity and identification among workers, motivated by a similarity of social position—and of class consciousness, which gradually emerges in this process, and is defined by the workers' understanding of their situation, of their class interests, and project (Bakunin, 71011a[e], pp. 41, 45–46; Berthier, 2012, p. 2). In the International, the creation and strengthening of solidarity and class consciousness among workers must be permanently encouraged. And this must also be done in conformity with naturalism: from the concrete to the abstract, from the simple to the complex, from the particular to the general.

In more didactic terms, it would be possible to speak of four steps that—although they often manifest in a not-so-linear way—help to understand how to stimulate solidarity and class consciousness. First, it is necessary to encourage experiences of confrontation in the workplace and reinforce a particular class struggle against the immediate and direct oppressors (bosses and middlemen). Second, it is fundamental to encourage "the extension of this solidarity to all workers against all the bosses of the same profession, in the same locality." With this, the scope of the struggle is broadened and the exclusivity of the workplace is extrapolated; it encompasses the totality of those who do the same kind of work in the same region, who begin to understand themselves as allies in a broader struggle against the employers of that sector. This is the moment when workers must actively participate in a section of the trade, the grassroots and most elementary instance of mass organization.

Third, "once he has entered the section, the neophyte worker learns many things." At first, "it is explained to him that the same solidarity that exists among all the members of the same section is equally established among all the different sections or among all the bodies of office in the same locality." And also "that the organization of this wider solidarity [...] has become necessary because the bosses of all trades have agreed among themselves to reduce all [workers] to ever more miserable conditions." In this way, solidarity and class consciousness expand: they pass from those that involve workers of their own trade to the group of workers of a locality who have different occupations. Fourth, and finally, it is made clear to the worker "that this double solidarity of workers of the same craft, at first, and then among the workers of all trades or of all the bodies of the craft organized in different sections" should not be confined locally. It must go beyond "all frontiers, embracing the whole world of workers, the proletariat of all countries strongly organized for defense, for resistance, for war against bourgeois exploitation." With the expansion of these feelings, knowledge, and projects, the workers will be able to intervene more effectively in the international class struggle (Bakunin, 71011a[e], pp. 57–58).

But practical education is not limited to contributing to this expansion of solidarity and class consciousness—it is also capable of leading workers to adopt a revolutionary and socialist perspective. First of all, it must be taken into account that the convincing and conversion of workers to revolutionary and socialist positions is greatly facilitated by their social position, according to which corresponding instincts emerge. To make workers consciously adhere to a revolutionary and socialist position is therefore something that implies making manifest, real, and effective, that which exists in them as a latent potential.

> This solidarity [of the masses in the economic struggle] has so far shown immense results. First, it deepens a chasm between the bourgeoisie and the proletariat, and at the same time pushes the proletariat to revolution. Secondly, it gives the proletariat, through the practice of action and collective struggle, feeling, thought and force, a *socialist education and instruction*, not poured on it in small doses and from above, but developing spontaneously and widely, in

FREEDOM OR DEATH

the very bosom of the masses, enlightened by collective passion and thought...
It develops through a daily practice, the thought of justice, equality, and the
great popular freedom, incompatible with the authority of some tutors and
doctors of whatever nature. This is what our great Association does—it *prepares
the ground for the international and social revolution.* (Bakunin, 72015[c], p. 14)

Once a member of the IWA and inserted into this process, the worker will abandon
his religious beliefs and improve his political positions: "engaged in the struggle, he
will inevitably end up understanding the irreconcilable antagonism that exists
between these supporters of the reaction and his most dear human interests"; he "will
not fail to *recognize himself and clearly position himself as a revolutionary socialist*"
(Bakunin, 2008b[e], p. 54, emphasis added).

Determining factors in this collective pedagogical experience are strikes, this
"beginning of the social war of the proletariat against the bourgeoisie, still within the
limits of legality." But they acquire enormous importance, since, on the one hand,
they "electrify the masses, strengthen their mental energy, and awaken in them the
feeling of deep antagonism that exists between their interests and those of the
bourgeoisie." On the other hand, they "contribute immensely to provoking and
constituting among the workers of all trades, all localities and all countries, the
consciousness and the very fact of solidarity" (Bakunin, 2001a[e], p. 78). "Strikes are
necessary" and without them "it would be impossible to launch the masses into the
social struggle and organize them." This is because "the strike is war" and "the popular
masses do not organize themselves except in war and for war." This war is class war,
class struggle, the confrontation between dominant and oppressed classes (Bakunin,
70011[e], p. 37).

In addition, the power of strikes increases even more when, united to each other,
they can constitute a *general strike*:

When strikes spread from one point to another, it means that they are very
close to becoming a general strike; and a general strike, with the ideas of
liberation that prevail in the proletariat today, could only lead to a great
cataclysm, which would give society a new face. No doubt we're not at that
point yet, but everything is leading us to it. However, it is necessary that the
people be ready, that they don't let themselves be deceived by the talkers and
dreamers as in 48, and, therefore, they must be strongly and seriously
organized. (Bakunin, 1911[e], p. 51)[13]

Strikes create the conditions for the necessary mediation between the immediate
economic struggle and greater social transformation, between reforms and revolution.
"While waiting, an indispensable prelude to the general strike, partial strikes
constituted training in the practice of workers' solidarity and organization, and

provoked the formation of the necessary unanimity of spirit" (Leval, 2007, p. 58).

Once participating in the mass organization, in the struggles and strikes that it has led, the workers—with the results of class struggle education, which imply a leap in solidarity and class consciousness as well as considerable radicalization toward the revolutionary and socialist perspective—will find themselves in a position to overcome economic determinism, as well as corporatism (the exclusive defense of the interests of one category at the expense of others) and reformism (which sees reform as an end in itself, abandoning a revolutionary project) that often accompany immediate economic struggles.

> Bakunin understood very well the purpose of the IWA: to unite all the workers determined to resist the employers and, through the practice of real solidarity among them, through the struggles for demands and through the strikes, to lead them to a clearer awareness of their social position and to make them glimpse the path of their complete emancipation. It is, therefore, through practice, through the collective experience of struggle, that the International would enable workers to develop the germs of socialist thought that they possessed within themselves and to become aware of what they instinctively wanted but had not been able to formulate. Therefore, the primordial importance of this mass organization. (Vuilleumier, 1979, p. 124)

However, the organizational *how* of the IWA is not yet completely exposed. Since class struggle education does not occur mechanically, in each and every case, it must be stimulated and strengthened. And this is done in two ways: with a certain structuring of the mass organization, which will now be discussed, and with the complement of a cadre organization, to be addressed later on.

13.3.3 Professional Sections and Central Sections

In a given location, the IWA must have as its main organizational structure the *sections*, groupings of workers. There are two types of sections: the professional sections and the central sections. The former act in a vertical logic, of mainly economic base, grouping workers by profession in professional unions. The second act in a horizontal logic, of economic, political, and cultural base, aggregating militants of different professions, in interprofessional structures. In each location there are several trades sections and a central section, aggregating the most advanced workers of various professions. This structure intends to facilitate and contribute to the totality of the mass organization, from the captivation of militants to the achievement of their emancipatory objectives.[14]

Thus, "the International consisted of two federated structures: a 'vertical' structure, formed by 'professional sections' (equivalent to trade unions), and a geographical or interprofessional structure, formed by the 'central sections' (equivalent to *bourses du travail* or local unions)." There is a complementarity between "these two processes, between these two organizational instances," with the result of this relationship "establishing class organization with the forms that will allow it to constitute itself as a substitute for statist organization" (Berthier, 2014c, pp. 95–96).

A trade section is equivalent to one trade union per profession and constitutes the most basic instance of the mass organization in a given locality. There, the IWA has several professional sections, thus forming a grouping of unions, each of which unites workers by profession. These sections articulate workers "from the bottom up [...], taking as their starting point the social existence of the masses, their real aspirations, and provoking them, helping them to group themselves, harmonize and balance themselves in accordance with this natural diversity of occupations and situations." In a federalist organization, the professional sections, grassroots groupings, are essential, since they constitute the body of the organization, where the foundations of its social force are found and its daily praxis is developed.

It is only the professional sections that give the International a mass character, since each one of them is also a grouping of the masses, obviously smaller and more restricted than the IWA as a whole. *It is they, and only they, that allow the potential force of workers to be transformed into a real force* because without these sections there is no mass organization, no real social force, and no revolutionary possibility. And it is only in their bosom that the experience that provides the conditions for practical education and, therefore, for the radicalization of workers towards an emancipatory project takes place (Bakunin, 71011a[e], pp. 60, 73–74).

A central section is an interprofessional structure that brings together the most advanced workers from various professions in a given location. It is an organization of minorities, not masses, since these workers usually exist only in limited numbers. "The central sections do not represent any particular industry, since the most advanced workers from all possible industries are gathered in them." In these sections, one does not enter "as a special worker of this or that trade, with a view to the particular organization of that trade"—since this happens in the professional sections—but as a worker "in general, with a view to the emancipation and general organization of labor and the new social world founded on labor, in all countries."

The members of the central sections are also workers, but of a different kind; "workers of the idea, of the propaganda and of the organization of both the economic and militant potential of the International Workers' Association: workers of the social revolution." Workers who have understood the aims of the organization, the "ideal of the International,"[15] and who are dedicated to promoting, through their daily practice, the creation, growth, strengthening and radicalization of the professional sections, taking as a basis this objective, this ideal (Bakunin, 71011a[e], pp. 50–53).

It can be seen that the central sections have a completely different and even diametrically opposed character to that of the craft sections. While the latter, following the path of natural development, begin with the fact to arrive at the idea, the central sections, on the contrary, following the path of ideal or abstract development, begin with the idea to arrive at the fact. It is evident that, in opposition to the so completely realistic or positive method of the professional sections, the method of the central sections presents itself as artificial and abstract. (Bakunin, 71011a[e], p. 53)

This distinction explains why the professional sections are able to bring together the masses of workers (majority) and the central sections, the more advanced workers (minority). The former are based on a method that goes from facts to ideas, from concrete to abstract, and therefore can attract the millions of workers, even if less prepared. The latter are based on an inverse method, going from ideas to facts, from the abstract to the concrete and consequently a reduced potential for attraction, although from more prepared militants.

In a mass organization, both types of section are important—they are complementary and interdependent. Each has an indispensable role in the organizational functioning of the International and does not function alone, but only in conjunction. The professional sections, if taken in isolation, although they bring together the masses essential to the revolution, involve considerable organizational risks, particularly those related to economic determinism, corporatism, and reformism. Easily, the unions can take the economic struggle as the sole basis of their praxis, defend each one's own interests, dedicate themselves exclusively to the immediate struggles, and surrender the revolutionary perspective.

The central sections minimize these risks. Its members, advanced workers aware of the organization's final objective, carry out a type of militancy that goes beyond the economic field, stimulating the relationship and solidarity between the professional sections and the necessary advance of the immediate banners to the revolutionary and socialist perspective. However, the central sections, if taken in isolation—in spite of bringing together the most advanced workers—are powerless, since they fail to embrace the masses of workers and, for lack of social force, do not concretize an emancipatory program in practice. "If there had only been central sections of the International Workers' Association, there is no doubt that it would not have attained even the one hundredth part of the power so serious of which it now glorifies itself." These sections "could never drag and take in but a very small number of workers." Even if they were "the most intelligent, the most energetic, the most convinced and the most dedicated," "the immense majority, the millions of proletarians, would be left out" (Bakunin, 71011a[e], pp. 53–55).

Finally, the trade and central sections are the two concentric circles of mass organization. There are three criteria that define these levels in the International: 1) *Type of organization.* The professional sections are groupings of the masses by professions, and the central section is a grouping of minorities by region; 2) *Function of the organization.* The professional sections are functional to economic struggles, and the central section is functional to economic, political, and cultural struggles; 3) *Profile of the militants.* The professional sections have the least prepared members, whose focus is mainly on immediate economic struggles, and the central section has the most prepared, whose focus is both on contributing to these struggles and their radicalization, and on promoting the "ideal of the International," its emancipatory ends. Both circles guarantee the correspondence between members' rights and duties.

13.3.4 National Liberation Struggles and Anti-imperialism

There is one last aspect related to the Bakuninian mass strategy, but not necessarily linked to the IWA project: that of national liberation struggles or anti-imperialism.[16] In fact, Bakunin takes up a series of ideas from the previous period (1844–63) and, making some adaptation to the changes in his political theory, argues the need for participation in these struggles and a position that is frankly opposed to nationalism.

In the same way as conflicts linked to the social question, struggles related to the national question can also advance towards a social revolution, depending on how they are pursued. But, just as in the case of the IWA the struggle must be properly organized for this to be possible. To this end, it is essential to "reject the confusion [conflation] of anti-imperialism [...] and national liberation with the specific ideology of nationalism," since both positions differ greatly in terms of composition and class perspective, in relations with members of other nationalities and mobilized subjects, and in the character of the confrontation (Van der Walt, 2014, p. 12).

Let us remember that national domination or imperialism is defined by the imposition of social force of the dominant classes of one state on the entire population of another state or of a nation-race (people or homeland) for the benefit of those who impose themselves and to the detriment of those who are subjected (Bakunin, 2003a[e], pp. 66–67). And that this form of domination derives from the conquest and/or influence—that is, from the imperialist vocation—of states and can be observed when a people, because of its nationality-race, is the victim of persecution, discrimination, imprisonment, murder; when it experiences the subordination of its culture, its religion, its institutions; when it is the victim of economic dependence and/or exploitation.

"Both in international relations as well as in relations between classes" one must "always be on the side of those who others want to civilize" (Bakunin, 1977a[e], p. 131). That is, just as in the case of class domination it is necessary to be on the side of the workers, in the case of imperialism it is fundamental to ally oneself with oppressed nations and peoples. The defense of internationalism and anti-imperialism in no way means abandoning national liberation struggles and anti-imperialism. After all, engagement in these causes does not inevitably imply support for the State since it is not synonymous with nation, race, or homeland:

The State is not the homeland [the nation, the race, or the people in the national sense], but the abstraction, the metaphysical, mystical, political, legal fiction of the homeland. The popular masses of all countries deeply love their homeland; yet this is a natural, real love. The patriotism of the people is not an idea, but a fact. Political patriotism, love for the State, is not the just expression of this fact, but a denatured expression of a deceptive abstraction that always benefits some exploitative minority. Homeland, nationality, like individuality, is a fact both natural and social, psychological and historical; it is not a principle. Only that which is universal, common to all men, can be called a human principle; yet nationality separates them: it is not, therefore, a principle. What is a principle, however, is the respect that each one must have for natural, real or social facts. Nationality, like individuality, is one of these facts, and therefore we must respect it. Violating it is an evil and, using Mazzini's terms, it becomes a sacred principle every time it is threatened and violated. And that is why I feel, frankly and always, *the patriot of all the oppressed homelands*. (Bakunin, 71022[e], p. 55, emphasis added)

Thus, while the State is an artificial political instrument of class domination, the homeland is a natural fact: it "represents the undeniable and sacred right of every man or group of men—of all associations, communes, regions and nationsto live, feel, think, want and act in their own way", something that "is always the undeniable result of a long historical development" (Bakunin, 71022[e], p. 55). So state patriotism—this love for the State, *nationalism*—is also artificial and must therefore be fought. Nationalism here has to be understood as what, between 1844 and 1863, was called national exclusivism, narrow nationalism, patriotic exclusivism, and narrow patriotism. On the other hand, the patriotism of nationality, of nation, being natural, must be defended, especially in cases of national domination or imperialism.

This is because an emancipatory project cannot disregard the issue of peoples' self-determination: this notion that "every people, weak or strong, every nation, large or small, every province, every commune has the absolute right to be free, autonomous, to live and govern themselves according to their particular interests and needs" (Bakunin, 2015a[c], p. 110). When, because of national domination or imperialism, this self-determination is being undermined, it is the duty of every revolutionary socialist to adopt this *patriotism of oppressed homelands*—that is, an *anti-imperialist perspective*.

But when talking about supporting national liberation struggles from an anti-imperialist perspective, certain precautions are indispensable. It is "important to be cautious about the methods to be used in this struggle if one wants to avoid replacing imperialist domination with a national form of exploitation and despotism" (Lehning, 2017, p. 4). What, then, would this method, this form of organization be?

FREEDOM OR DEATH

First of all, it is necessary to know that "any movement for national liberation [must] be directed towards social objectives, to prevent it from [becoming] a bourgeois revolution" (Cipko, 1990, p. 11). That is, the ends of the anti-imperialist struggle cannot be restricted only to national liberation, but to social revolution and collectivist-federalist socialism. And just as one must reject reformism and political revolutions, it is crucial to reject nationalism with exclusively political ends. It is also crucial to participate in such struggles and movements "to push them as far as possible in the direction of a classist, anti-statist and internationalist social revolution." And, although "some cooperation with the nationalists" is necessary, it needs to be based on a "critical commitment" (Van der Walt, 2014, p. 12).

Such are the foundations of anarchist anti-imperialism: it is classist, anti-statist, internationalist, and aims at a new completely emancipated society. Moreover, like any revolutionary and socialist movement, it must be a mass movement.

These foundations can be better understood through a counterpoint—the negation of nationalism. In terms of class composition, while nationalism is intended to be a multi-classist movement, with the presence of all social classes of the oppressed nationality, anarchist anti-imperialism supports the need for a movement concentrated on the dispossessed classes. As far as the future perspective is concerned, if nationalism does not intend to do away with classes and the State in the nation struggling for liberation, anarchist anti-imperialism claims the concomitant end of both national domination and class and state domination in the struggling nation for liberation.

Within the oppressed nation, while nationalism *a priori* has no enemies—except those who may be considered agents of the dominant state—and assumes its entire population as potential allies, anarchist anti-imperialism judges the privileged classes, eventual agents of the dominant state, as enemies, and sees the dominated classes as its potential allies. In the dominant state, if nationalism views its entire population as enemies, without potential allies, anarchist anti-imperialism judges only the oppressive classes of that state as enemies. This is because, as mentioned, imperialism is characterized as the domination of the upper classes of one state over the entire population of another state or nation. Hence the dispossessed classes of this oppressive state are considered potential allies (Bakunin, 70016[e], p. 2).

In the case of the bourgeoisie, for example, its patriotism is not a natural patriotism, but a state patriotism. The "nationalism defended by the bourgeoisie" is "essentially economic" and subordinated to its class interests. Such that "a national revolution led by this stratum would have terrible consequences for the masses" (Cipko, 1990, p. 11).

The bourgeoisie [...] loves the homeland, and only because the homeland, represented by the State and completely absorbed by the State, guarantees it its political, economic and social privileges. A homeland that stopped doing so would no longer be a homeland for it. Therefore, for the bourgeoisie, the homeland is the State. A patriot of the State, it becomes an angry enemy of the popular masses whenever, tired of serving as a chair for the government and a passive pedestal and always sacrificed to the State, they rebel against the State. (Bakunin, 1977a[e], p. 80, translation adjusted based on the original)

Bourgeois nationalism and that of any ruling class is state nationalism and the anti-imperialism of the workers must be that of the nation, of the people—a classist and anti-statist national liberation movement. The patriotism of the dominant classes is sustained until such time as their privileges are challenged—when, then, they will be willing to submit willingly to any other state, provided that they have preserved their privileges.

In the case of the national liberation of the Slavs,[17] for example, it is necessary to fight its enemies (the Germanic privileged classes) and seek in all countries allies in the oppressed classes. The Slavic peoples "must and can [...] free themselves from foreign domination, above all from Germanic domination, which for them is the most hateful." But this liberation needs to be achieved with the Slavs "rising up in solidarity *with all the European proletariat through the social revolution*" (Bakunin, 2003a[e], p. 65, emphasis added).

The Slavs will be able to free themselves; they will be able to destroy the German State they abhor, not by vain efforts to subjugate the Germans to their domination and turn them into slaves of their Slavic State, but only by calling them to freedom and universal fraternity on the ruins of all the present States. But States do not collapse on their own; only social revolution, embracing all peoples, all races, in every country of the world, is able to destroy them.

To organize the popular forces to carry out this revolution—this is the task, the only task, of men sincerely eager to free the Slavic people from the secular yoke. (Bakunin, 2003a[e], p. 70)

Finally, as far as the perspectives of national relations are concerned, in case the struggle for national liberation is victorious, while nationalism sees no problem in eventually establishing itself as a new imperialist or subimperialist agent—for the sake of truth, such is the utopia of many nationalists—anarchist anti-imperialism intends to build the self-determination of peoples and federalism on an international level, without oppressive and oppressed nations (Bakunin, 70016[e], p. 1; Bakunin, 2003a[e], pp. 67, 70). And, finally, while nationalism commands a movement for national reforms or a revolutionary movement (which generally proceeds from the top down), anarchist anti-imperialism intends to build a revolutionary movement that proceeds in accordance with federalism, from the bottom up, from the circumference to the centre.

13.4 CADRE ORGANIZATION: THE ALLIANCE
Through a reflection on the Alliance (or "cadre organization/party"), theoretical-strategic reflections can be elaborated about the *anarchist* cadre organization, involving its objectives, its character, its functions, and its structure.[18]

13.4.1 The Need for a Complementary Organizational Level
When dealing with the organization of workers in general, the IWA was discussed in more detail and it was pointed out that, even with the central sections, this association needs a complementary organizational level to achieve its emancipatory objective: an organization of cadre, the Alliance.

> To those who ask us what good the existence of the Alliance is for, when there is the International, we will answer: the International, it is true, is a magnificent institution, it is undoubtedly the most beautiful, the most useful, the most benevolent creation of the present century. It has created the basis for the solidarity of workers throughout the world. It has given them a start in organizing across the borders of all States and outside the world of exploiters and the privileged. It has done more; it already contains today the first germs of the organization of future unity, and at the same time it has given the proletariat of the whole world the feeling of its own force. It is true, this is the immense service it has rendered to the great cause of universal and social revolution. But *it is not an absolutely sufficient institution to organize and direct this revolution.* (Bakunin, 2014b[c], p. 82, emphasis added)

The mass organization is able to associate the workers concerned on the basis of immediate economic struggle and to proceed to the practical education of the class struggle, which collaborates with the development of the workers' solidarity and class consciousness, and even to bring them closer to more frankly revolutionary and socialist positions—elements undoubtedly indispensable for a social revolution. However, the IWA lacks organizational and leadership components of the revolutionary process: "the International [...] is an immense favorable and necessary means for this [revolutionary organization of the masses], but it is not yet this organization"—to this end, the Alliance is indispensable (Bakunin, 2014b[c], p. 83).

It is not, as must already have been evident, a matter of considering that workers in their class organizations are incapable of thinking and acting beyond their short-term interests. It has been seen that the emancipation of workers must be done by the workers themselves, and that it is therefore the masses and their organizations that must lead the revolutionary transformation. The workers have the capacity for both the economic struggle and the political and cultural struggle, both for the struggle for reform and the revolutionary struggle. It has also been observed that class consciousness and transformative capacity do not come from outside, nor should they be formulated and divulged to the workers by a nucleus outside them. The revolutionary subject constitutes itself in the class struggle, and the mass organization and its praxis are irreplaceable in this sense.

In such a way that *organizing and directing the revolution* does not imply an entity foreign to the workers that uses them, in a hierarchical relationship of domination, as an auxiliary force for a revolutionary process, in which the cadre organization is the leader and whose immediate end is the taking of the State—such are the bases of Blanquism, quite distinct from anarchist socialism.[19] On the one hand, the Alliance must strengthen the functions of the central sections in the International and assume them in case they do not exist. On the other hand, it must provide a solution to the problem of the organizational nature of the IWA and ensure the preponderance of anarchist positions in the internal disputes of this association, especially those of a strategic and tactical order. Organizing and directing the revolution is therefore to stimulate and guarantee the empowerment and radicalization of the masses, ensuring the programmatic line previously exposed and, through it, the process of change that will lead to freedom and equality.

In its mass work, the cadre organization aims to "exert a more effective and powerful influence on the spontaneous movement of the popular masses" and to prevent its organizations from "degenerating" or turning into "government or [...] official dictatorship." But for this to happen, its members must discard the means of domination and relate in an anti-authoritarian way with the workers, relying on natural influence and enjoying this two-way relationship. Alliancists "always have much more to learn from the people than to give them"; they must work to be only "more or less qualified midwives of the revolution" and never its "creators and [principal] actors" (Bakunin, 72016[e], pp. 6–7, 16–17).

At first, the cadre organization can contribute to the above-mentioned process of practical education in the IWA, helping to combat economic determinism, corporativism, and reformism; where there are central sections, they should be reinforced in this task. However, thanks to historical contingencies, such sections may not exist or function as desired, and in such cases the Alliance must assume their functions. It also has to account for the problems surrounding the syndical nature of the International in general and the sections of office in particular. When it comes to the latter, the International articulates "the public and legal struggle of workers in solidarity from all countries against the exploiters of labor, capitalists, owners and entrepreneurs of industry, but never goes beyond that." Even if in these instances it is possible to carry out "the theoretical propaganda of socialist ideas among the working masses"—which, like the immediate economic struggle, is very useful and necessary "in preparation for the revolution of the masses"—this "is far from the revolutionary organization of the masses" (Bakunin, 2014b[c], p. 83).

But the justification for the cadre organization goes beyond that. It relates to the "public and legal struggle" and the limits of the mass organization because, even assuming the existence of the central sections, the International continues to be a public association that acts within the law, at least in countries that allow initiatives of this kind.[20] A dilemma arises here. It is only the masses that are able to accumulate the necessary force, and it is they who must lead the emancipation of the workers; and an association that gathers and mobilizes the masses can only be a public organization, because the clandestine articulation of these enormous contingents is unviable.

When reflecting on the ends of the IWA, it becomes clear that they require articulations and actions that cannot be done in public, at the risk of compromising the entire organization and its members, and that such ends go beyond the legal limits of any statist and capitalist society. A work that has "a practical, revolutionary objective, mutual understanding, which is its necessary condition, cannot be done publicly." A considerable part of this effort, if carried out in public, "would draw against the initiators the persecutions of the whole official and unofficial world, and they would find themselves crushed before they could have done the slightest thing." In view of the repression of the State and the upper classes—a concrete threat of any revolutionary initiative—an organization that can act secretly, fulfilling indispensable functions, becomes indispensable (Bakunin, 2014b[c], p. 89).

Organizational dualism intends to solve this dilemma since it advocates, on one hand, a public and mass International and, on the other, an Alliance of cadres that acts secretly and also publicly. The social force of the masses is thus reconciled with the demands for clandestinity of revolutionary and socialist praxis.

> In any case, one can never lose sight of the limits of a cadre organization: Revolutions [...] cannot be carried out by individuals or secret societies. They derive from circumstances, from the inevitable course of events, and can only succeed if they have the support of the masses. There are moments in history when revolutions are impossible and others when they are inevitable. [...] But propaganda and action can prepare the revolution. All that a well-organized secret society can do is, first, to contribute to the outbreak of the revolution by spreading ideas that correspond to the instincts of the masses, and then to organize, not the army of the revolution—the army must always be the people—but a kind of military staff composed of sincere, hard-working, devoted friends of the people, "without ambition or vanity" and "capable of acting as intermediaries between the revolutionary idea and the popular instinct." (Lehning, 1974b, p. 65)

In other words, the Alliance is concomitantly indispensable and quite limited. It has an important role in the relationship with the International, but it is not able and cannot carry out the social revolution itself. It is, therefore, the dual organization of workers—mass organization and cadre organization—that has adequate responses to the dilemma posed.

In addition, there is another justification for the existence of a cadre organization that works in the IWA: the various internal disputes, especially those of a strategic and tactical nature. Based on the concept of social force, it is known that any space that aggregates people around a purpose involves disputes between its members, which, at the limit, define their character, function, trajectory, etc. If this is a fact for society as a whole, it is also a fact for any organization—it seems evident that, in the case of the mass organization, this is no different.

The IWA, in all that pertains to it, is nothing more than the result of confrontations between all the social forces mobilized by its members, groups, sectors, sections, and also between the association itself and the forces outside it. Its objectives, its strategic-tactical line and its structure are the product of these confrontations, in which its militancy and its groupings (formal and informal), the structural factors of society and the action of other collectivities (dominant classes, repression, etc.) interact. For this reason, anarchists need to have an organizational structure that provides them with the conditions to adequately and effectively intervene in this dispute with other more or less articulated divergent forces.

> To act in the midst of the working class, it is necessary to recognize a struggle of tendencies, and that not all paths lead to Rome. This is what Bakunin did in the First International. The Russian revolutionary understood that there were two ways of conceiving the International, that its horizon was represented by two different "parties." The full title of his 1873 work is quite clear in this respect: *Statism and Anarchy: the struggle between the two parties in the International Workers' Association.* [...] The central point of Bakunin's idea is to *realistically assume the diversity of tendencies within a mass organization. Diversity that necessarily leads to ideological struggle.* In this sense, personalities like Engels and Utin can be thought of, without major problems, as part of a more or less organizational line, of a tendency; they are partisans of *a determined vision of how to build socialism.* Although Bakunin exaggerates the real situation of the "Marxist party", I believe that his analysis refers to a more fundamental issue: *the inherent recognition of the ideological struggle within labor organizations.* (Rivas, 2014, pp. 50, 54, emphasis added)

A mass organization that does not function under the limits of a political-ideological line that is obligatory and homogeneous for all its members—that is, the IWA, according to the programmatic lines explained above—has a diversity of tendencies, of social forces that represent different political conceptions and, for this very reason, includes political-doctrinarian struggles among supporters of the different positions.

This, as in society itself, is natural and healthy. The existence of these tendencies is explained by the fact that, even if the emancipation of workers is advocated through revolution and socialism, there are disparate conceptions about what precisely these objectives are, and how they should be pursued. Such responses are not obvious and, in a way, explain the diverse tendencies of a mass organization such as the International.

The Alliance is the organization that promotes—in an articulated manner, and taking advantage of the benefits of the collective social force—the aforementioned IWA program. This mass line requires an organization that constantly stimulates it, ensuring that it can prevail in the dispute with other tendencies. The central sections, though very significant, are insufficient, since they do not realize the fact that these very ends are in constant dispute, as well as the ways to reach these ends, that is, the strategy and tactics that must be adopted by the mass organization.

13.4.2 Constitutive Aspects, General and Specific Objectives, Internationalist and Cadre Character

The Alliance is *an internationalist organization* thanks to the way it conceives the revolutionary process and the character of the mass organization, both of which are international and internationalist at the same time. It is *a political organization of a partisan type*, since it gathers its members according to well-defined political-doctrinaire principles, an explicit and in-depth program, and common positions in the different camps. It is a *secret organization* that can, depending on the circumstances, at once make itself *secret and public*. It is *a minority organization, a party of cadres*, because it gathers a restricted number of members, based on qualitative criteria, among which are: capacity of influence, polyfunctionality, and certain personal characteristics. Finally, the Alliance is a

> secret organization formed within the International itself, to provide the latter with a revolutionary organization, to transform it, and all the popular masses outside it, into a force sufficiently organized to annihilate the political-clerical-bourgeois reaction, to destroy all the economic, juridical, religious and political institutions of the States. (Bakunin, 2014b[c], p. 89)

And, also, to forge the foundations of an emancipated society, of collectivist-federalist socialism. It was argued previously that "the International and the Alliance, tending towards the same ultimate objective, pursue different objectives at the same time." Both the organizational levels, of masses and cadres, have the same finalist objective, but at the same time each of these levels has specific objectives. In broad terms, the IWA "has the mission of bringing together the working masses, the millions of workers [...] in one immense and compact body" and the Alliance "has the mission of giving the masses a truly revolutionary direction" (Bakunin, 72015[c], p. 8).

The objectives of the cadre organization should thus be understood: first, a final objective, which is similar to that proposed for the mass organization; second, some specific objectives, which define the specific purpose of the Alliance in the relationship with the International and workers in general.

> To form all these revolutionary organizations, indispensable for the triumph of the popular cause, to impel and stimulate them, to, on the one hand, direct them and, on the other, prevent them from degenerating or becoming governments, even if only provisionally, the need for a force, for an invisible collective organization is evident that, obeying a frank and completely revolutionary program and taking it to its ultimate consequences, itself abstains from any manifestation, from any governmental or official interference, and can thus by itself exert an even more effective and powerful influence on the spontaneous movement of the popular masses, as well as on the action and all the revolutionary measures of its delegates and its committees. This is the sole object of the Y. [Alliance]. (Bakunin, 72016[e], pp. 6–7, emphasis added)

This means that, if on the one hand the mass organization needs to build a social force capable of supplanting the statist and capitalist forces of the dominant classes, on the other hand the cadre organization has to form a social force with the capacity to impose itself on others, in the inner disputes of the dispossessed classes themselves, guaranteeing a strategic course for the IWA.

In sum, the Alliance has one final objective and three specific objectives. Its final objective is: *to destroy the statist-capitalist system, social classes, and domination in general; to build collectivist-federalist socialism from the associations of workers and peasants, guaranteeing their full freedom and equality.* Its specific objectives are: *1) To build a revolutionary cadre organization based on principles, program, and strategic and tactical lines; 2) To seek the growth of social force and influence of this organization among the workers and the implementation of its program; 3) To ensure that the cadre organization does not become a new organ of domination and subjugation of the masses, but rather stimulates and enhances their leading role.*

The cadre organization has, like the mass organization, an internationalist character, but is distinguished from it owing to its (political) character of cadres. While the former is a political, secret or secret and public cadre (minority) organization, the latter is a social-popular, mass (majority), and public organization. These characteristics have direct implications on the way the Alliance organizes itself and on the profile of the members it assembles.

The Alliance is a *political organization* both because of its objectives and functions and because of its cadre nature. It does not intend to dispute or conquer the State by means of elections, reforms, or revolution; it is distinctly a "party that refuses to participate in elections, that refuses even to take political power, because it is an instrument of return to domination and therefore is not intended for any institutional existence" (Angaut, 2005, p. 553). Its action is political in that it stimulates and influences a revolutionary workers' movement that has, among its objectives, the abolition of the State. "We do not form a theoretical or exclusively economic institution. The Alliance is neither an academy nor a workshop; it is an essentially militant association." It is a party organization that gathers members with homogeneity in the field of thought and action around anarchist political-doctrinaire positions, and expresses them through principles, programs, and strategic and tactical lines, which intend to support an effective intervention both in the correlation of forces of the International and of workers and society itself. Therefore, in comparison with the mass organization, the program of the cadre organization is "more explicit and more determined on the aspect of political [anarchism], religious [atheism] and social [lines and objectives] questions" (Bakunin, 2014b[c], pp. 82–83).[21]

Since the Alliance is characterized as a party, it must also be said that, in view of the already classic distinction, it is a party of cadres and not masses. "The number of these individuals [members of the Alliance] must not, therefore, be immense." For each European country, "a hundred strong and seriously allied revolutionaries are enough" and for "the organization of the largest country," "two, three hundred revolutionaries will suffice" (Bakunin, 68016[e]). The Alliance is distinguished both from the International, a majority organization— and for this it has more flexible entry criteria and more limited principles and program—and from the mass parties, whose conditions of entry and participation are modest. It is a minority organization, which has tougher requirements in terms of membership, participation, and conduct of its members, and which has well-defined political and other principles and an explicit and in-depth program, which are mandatory for all members.[22]

In addition, the cadre organization is primarily secret—it needs to be able to constitute itself in this way to accomplish all that cannot be done publicly—which also reinforces the fact that the Alliance has to be a minority organization. But it does not have to be completely secret; it can rely on the necessary flexibility to adapt to the context and, if necessary, to take advantage of public instances and activities, depending on the possibilities and circumstantial necessities. In other words, the Alliance can become a secret and public organization at the same time.

The Alliance's cadre character is reinforced by the profile of its members, with the entry and participation criteria prioritizing quality rather than quantity. These cadre[23] are above-average militants, who have political-doctrinaire and programmatic agreement with each other and who stand out for their natural influence among workers, their multi-functionality and their personal characteristics.

The cadre organization must

ensure the participation of all popular leaders. I call popular leaders individuals most of the time emanated from the people, living their lives with them, and who, thanks to their intellectual and moral superiority, exert a great influence on them. There are many among them who abuse this influence and use it for their personal interests. They are very dangerous men, and it is necessary to avoid them like the plague, to fight and annihilate when possible. You must seek the good leaders, those who don't seek their own interest but everyone's interest. (Bakunin, 2014b[c], p. 88)

In terms of class origin, the Alliancists cadre is a worker, but they do not necessarily have to be one; they can also be a member emanating from the dominant classes who has taken the side of the oppressed in the class struggle. This cadre needs to be able to *influence* the workers, to be a leader among them and, thus, to succeed, through their natural influence, to persuade them, to convince them of their positions, to engage them in their political project. However, this needs to be done by means that lead to the desired ends and that obey certain ethical assumptions. Authoritarian criteria for increasing social force must be discarded, among which are domination of the masses and the substitution of a collective project of transformation by individual or group mobility.

Moreover, the Alliance's cadre is multi-functional, that is, they perform various functions, external and internal to the organization, which do not obey the hierarchical division between intellectual and manual labour—a separation of the organization into a leadership that decides and a base that executes. And since this cadre is first and foremost the link between the Alliance and the working masses, the means by which a determined mass line is promoted, their most important function is "propaganda and organizational work."

In relation to propaganda, it is a matter of producing and disseminating, by the most diverse means, the political-doctrinaire line of the cadre organization, as well as those positions that strengthen it among the public: programmatic-strategic positions, structural and conjunctural analyses and readings, etc., so that it promotes the organization's points of view among the workers. And this "propaganda" has to be done "not only through words, but through facts." That is, it does not involve only discursive forms, but is based above all on practices that can be multiplied by the force of example. In relation to the organizational work, it is a matter of carrying out what come to be called *grassroots work* during the twentieth century, stimulating the creation, growth, and radicalization of the professional sections and the whole of the International, seeking to implement the Alliance's program and fulfilling certain organizational criteria (Bakunin, 72016[e], p. 11).

But there are still other functions to be performed by the cadres: the definition and guarantee of organizational functioning, in what concerns the different levels of the organization, its deliberative and executive instances, its organizational processes and the functions of its members; the discussion, definition, and improvement of structural and conjunctural analyses, of the political-doctrinaire, programmatic, strategic, and tactical positions of the organization; the elaboration and promotion of a permanent politics of recruiting, capacitating, and training of militants; the establishment and management of a finance policy and a common fund; the preparation, archiving, and distribution of the organization's documents; the ensuring of relations among militants and the solution of conflicts between them according to organizational rules; the establishment of relations with other organizations and people (Bakunin, 68016[e], 72016[e]).

Regarding the characteristics of a cadre of the Alliance:

> The qualities required of all international brothers [full cadres of the Alliance] —except those that constitute a good and devoted revolutionary conspirator, such as true revolutionary passion, firmness, constancy, discretion, prudence, energy of character, intelligence, courage—are: the ability to rise naturally and spontaneously above all the narrow inspirations of personal ambition and vanity, of family and patriotism, and this other quality, even rarer among men of energy and intelligence, the ability to submerge one's own personal initiative in collective action.
>
> For each international brother, our program, as well as our politics and revolutionary tactics, must be more than the result of a vain philosophical abstraction, more than the expression of uncertain and vague aspirations. It is necessary that they become your life, your dominant passion, your conscience and your everyday instinct, at the same time reflected and ardent. Externally, in the coldest possible way; internally, so ardently that no exterior seduction can ever prevail over them, and that no sophistry, theoretical or practical, can divert them from their path. (Bakunin, 72016[e], pp. 13–14)

It is understood here that the member of the cadre organization must *have, or seek to have over time*, a set of qualities that need to be incorporated into their daily lives and that can be divided into two parts: one, common to all good and devoted conspirators, and the other, particular to the Alliancists, because of the ends they propose to achieve and the means they consider valid for this purpose.

In the first case, the Alliancists must be: passionate about the revolution, firm, constant, discreet, prudent, energetic, intelligent, and courageous. In the second, they must be "sincerely devoted to our [the Alliance's] ideas," "capable of serving as intermediaries between the revolutionary idea and the popular instincts," and therefore act as midwives of the revolution. This revolutionary passion, which can be referred to as "having the devil in the body," requires "the greatest sacrifices to be imposed." The Alliancist cadre therefore has a high level of dedication: "every brother [militant] is on a permanent mission." This is because "every day, from morning till night, his thought and his dominant passion, his supreme duty, must be the propaganda of the principles of the Alliance, its development and the increase of its potency" (Bakunin, 68016[e]; Bakunin, 72016[e], p. 22).

These militants must not only have good will and honesty, but discard (personal, family, and patriotic) ambition and vanity, and fuse their individual work into a collective revolutionary project. They must also exercise criticism and self-criticism, and respect the ethical foundations that regulate all relations of the Alliance's cadres among themselves and with the workers. Among other things, these foundations advocate that, as far as "domination" and "exploitation [...] of the masses" are concerned, the Alliancists must have "renounced exercising them, in whatever form"; for those who do, will be "mercilessly excluded" (Bakunin, 68016[e]; Bakunin, 72016[e], pp. 15–16).

13.4.3 Principles, Program, and Conduct Criteria

The cadre organization has a set of principles, program, and conduct criteria that will now be discussed. It should be remembered that "science understands the thought of reality, not reality itself" (Bakunin, 2014e[e], p. 292). Therefore, conjunctural and structural analyses of reality must be more flexible, adapting to a more precise understanding of the world, in the same way as concrete plans of action, which are adapted to the analyses aimed at promoting the strategic program.

Distinctly, the maximum program, but above all the organizational principles, the political-doctrinaire principles and the ethical foundations (including the conduct criteria of the members) are less flexible and therefore modify less in temporal and spatial terms. The frameworks of the Alliance must be "inflexible in all that concerns our principle, our supreme law, our morality, transparency and mutual solidarity in all undertakings and actions," that is, they must be "inflexible in all that concerns the common interest of the Alliance" (Bakunin, 72015[c], p. 6).

The organizational principles of the Alliance are: 1) Common thought (principles, theory, analysis of reality, program, plan of action); 2) Common action (practice, implementation of the program and plan of action); 3) Commitment among members (fraternal self-control of members and mutual responsibility between each member and the Alliance as a whole).

Members are required to "think and act only in common" (Bakunin, 72015[c], p. 6). And that "in both the big and the small things that have any relation to common work, we must from now on strive to think, want and act in common." It is also prescribed that, in the organization of cadres, "there can be no different parties," that everyone must have "absolutely the same program, the same politics and the same revolutionary tactics, and also the same method of recruitment," and that "all its members" must act "according to a collectively established plan of action" (Bakunin, 72016[e], pp. 13, 19, 22, 25).

This unit is achieved through a federalist decision-making process, in which the members participate through the appropriate instances; they can perform the organizational functions, elect and be elected in case of delegation. They are primarily responsible for implementing the deliberations in the daily life of the organization and ensuring that they are executed. In the decision-making process, it is up to each one to contribute "to the organization all that is best in thinking, in such a way that a thought, once emitted by the individual and accepted by the collectivity, becomes, therefore, a thought not of him but collective" (Bakunin, 72015[c], p. 6).

This collective process of natural discussion and influence—in which all members, on the same basis, exchange information, points of view, perspectives, influence and are influenced, persuade and are persuaded—intends to arrive at a common denominator, if possible through unanimity (consensus), but not necessarily. The Alliancists "consult each other, reaching, as far as possible, unanimous resolutions" (Bakunin, 72016[e], p. 22). Seeking unanimity "as far as possible" means that the cadre organization prioritizes consensus among members in its decisions, but that it accepts, in many cases, majority (simple, 2/3, etc.) voting, depending on the case (Bakunin, 68016[e]).

Providing the conditions for broad discussions among members and for all their individual positions to be presented and debated, once deliberated, the questions and positions taken become binding on all, at least until different decisions are taken. In the case of the highest instance of the cadre organization, it

> will discuss and determine the Alliance's general plan of revolutionary action, a plan which, once established, can only be revoked by it; and until it has been revoked by it, it will be *absolutely* obligatory for all national Councils, which must, at all costs, have it carried out in their respective countries, under the constant vigilance of the Central Bureau, which will have not only the right but the duty to remind them, whenever necessary, of the strict and active observance of this plan. (Bakunin, 72016[e], pp. 26–27)

Besides the deliberative instances that serve for decision making and rely on the self-discipline of the members for execution, there are control bodies (such as the bureau) that guarantee the fulfillment of what has been decided. The "fraternal control of all over each and each one over all" is encouraged (Bakunin, 72016[e], p. 18). Unlike the International, which has the autonomy of the sections, the members of the Alliance "cannot take any action regarding propaganda and revolutionary organization without the consent of the neighboring brothers" and, more specifically, "no brother will accept public functions without the consent of the neighboring brothers" (Bakunin, 68016[e]). And only those who agree with the historically accumulated positions become members.

The political and doctrinal principles of the Alliance are: 1) Negation of the theological understandings of the world, including liberals and individualists, and the adoption of a materialistic, naturalistic, and scientific framework of analysis of reality; 2) Understanding the individual as a product of society and labour as the only producer of value and the foundation of society, which implies that man can only emancipate himself in the midst of society and through labour; 3) Understanding society as a terrain of relations of domination at all levels (which includes exploitation), especially between classes—in which case a privileged minority dominates a majority of workers and supports the existence of a class struggle; 4) Rejection of domination at all levels, especially those of a class-based nature, but not only them; 5) Affirmation that freedom, the product of historical development, must guide all human relations, be collectively and individually sought, together with economic and social equality— this must constitute the ethical foundation of society; 6) Conviction that the possibility of an emancipated future resides only in the workers, in the dispossessed classes, who, by freeing themselves, will free all humanity (Bakunin, 2009d[e], pp. 69–81).

The strategic program (maximum program) of the Alliance is: 1) Extinction of established religions and authoritarian theological influence on life; 2) Ending of social classes, exploitation of labour and domination in general, including those related to women; 3) Socialization of property (distribution according to the labour done), ending of the right of inheritance (having in mind the possible maintenance of small peasant properties that do not benefit from exploitation), and democratization of knowledge (integral education for everyone under society's responsibility); 4) Abolition of states and their replacement by agricultural and industrial associations of workers; 5) Freedom and equality at all levels, with preservation of diversity; 6) Promotion of a revolutionary, classist, and internationalist politics—and therefore contrary to nationalism—that strengthens the workers in their class struggle and prevents them from any conciliation or alliance with their enemies; 7) Guarantee of a libertarian and egalitarian socialist society based on workers' associations, organizing and articulating itself through federalism (Bakunin, 68014[e]; see also: Angaut, 2005, p. 554). This program guides the more restricted strategies and tactics of the Alliance, and thus the "general plan of revolutionary action of the Alliance" and the "revolutionary tactics of Y. [Alliance]" (Bakunin, 72016[e], pp. 9, 27).

In terms of the criteria for the conduct of the members of the cadre organization we have the following. First, the need for agreement with the principles and the program. Secondly, certain rules of behaviour and relationship among members, from which values are derived that should be cultivated and promoted, configuring a type of internal ethics. "Each international brother will be for all the others more a brother than a natural brother" (Bakunin, 68014[e]). And he must cultivate and practice, with each other, affection, respect, sincerity, trust, solidarity, dedication, faithfulness, and generosity (Bakunin, 72016[e], p. 19).

They commit themselves to abandoning manipulation and lying to each other: "Jesuitical systems of manipulation and lying" need to be totally excluded, since they involve "harmful, dissolving and degrading means and principles" (Bakunin, 2017a[c], p. 135). Alliances must be sincere with each other and exercise "transparency without reserve for everything that relates to their own lives, both public and private." But for the sake of security, no one should know more than necessary: "indiscretion and meaningless curiosity are completely anti-revolutionary defects" (Bakunin, 72016[e], pp. 20, 32).

"Everyone dedicates themselves to each one and each one to everyone. Each brother is saved and must sacrifice himself for all the others to the limits of what is possible" (Bakunin, 68014[e]). Furthermore, the members cultivate a critical spirit, but one which is at the same time constructive, and which values this organizational strengthening (Bakunin, 72015[c], p. 6). Individual limits and problems exist and will always exist, but they must be overcome, or at least minimized and corrected, by the collective qualities of the organization. These strengthen each member of the organization: "each one of us feels the need to complete, correct and fortify ourselves by the intelligence, morals and energy of our entire collectivity, and the force, virtue and spirit of all must become that of each one of us" (Bakunin, 72016[e], p. 20).

In this way, responsibility is cultivated between one and all, individual and collective, which is exercised with the "open fraternal control of everyone by everyone," which allows avoiding, identifying, and treating the most varied problems. However, such control can never be "annoying, mean and, above all, malevolent"; it must replace "Jesuitical control" and exclude "bad mistrust, perfidious control, espionage, and reciprocal delusions." It must be done through "moral education, with the pillar of force of each member, on the basis of mutual fraternal trust, on which all the inner and therefore outer force of the association will be founded" (Bakunin, 2017a[c], pp. 131, 136). If problems are identified, the solution must be sought not only through the aforementioned preferences for (re-)education in relation to punishment and generosity, but through consideration of the effort and fidelity of the members involved: "we must act frankly and promptly, never behind the one who is being accused, but directly, either addressing him alone or making the necessary observations to him in the presence of all the other brothers" (Bakunin, 72016[e], p. 21). Political and personal differences between members can never be brought into the public arena, much less in the courts of the State: the Alliancists "never attack each other or expose their quarrels in public or in the courts" (Bakunin, 68014[e]).

This process of dealing with problems, misunderstandings, and conflicts is based on the expectation that all members of the organization need to cultivate a constructive spirit of criticism and self-criticism—they must know how to speak and listen, persuade and be persuaded, educate and be educated by this collective process.

Finally, the cadre organization also operates according to the logic of concentric circles. The Alliance is divided into three geographic levels—International, National, and Regional/Local—and operates with two levels of members: International Brothers and National Brothers. It relates these levels in a federalist way and proposes to guarantee the organizational effectiveness and the correspondence between the rights and duties of the members (Bakunin, 68014[e]; Bakunin, 72016[e]; Bakunin, 72015[c]).

13.5 DICTATORSHIP OF ALLIES AND ANTI-SEMITISM
Finally, we must discuss two aspects of this Bakuninian anarchism that show divergences in relation to his project presented. It should be remembered that between 1868 and 1876, Bakunin, supported by scientific-naturalist materialism, harshly criticized both domination in general, national domination, and imperialism in particular, and narrow nationalism and patriotism. In contrast, he defends popular emancipation, national liberation, anti-imperialism, internationalism, classism, and the self-determination of peoples. From such bases, both the call for a collective dictatorship of the allies and the demonstration of frankly anti-Semitic positions seem incongruous with his political theory.

As far as the issue of dictatorship is concerned, from a general perspective of Bakunin's work, in the vast majority of cases he uses the term "dictatorship" as a synonym for domination and power, that is, authoritarian imposition of a minority on a majority for the benefit of the former and to the detriment of the latter. This is exactly why it relates, in all these cases, to the political issue in general and to the State in particular.

> Between revolutionary dictatorship and statist centralization, all the difference lies in appearances. Basically, both are just one and the same form of government of the majority by the minority, in the name of the supposed stupidity of the former and the supposed intelligence of the latter. That is why both are, to the same degree, reactionary, both having the effect of consolidating, directly and unfailingly, the political and economic privileges of the ruling minority and the economic and political slavery of the popular masses. (Bakunin, 2003a[e], p. 169)

This is also the meaning used in the criticism of authoritarian socialists, who sustained the need for a transitional dictatorship between the society of exploitation and the classless society:

> According to them, this statist yoke, this dictatorship is a necessary transition phase to arrive at the total emancipation of the people: anarchy or freedom being the objective, and the State or dictatorship, the means. Therefore, in order to liberate the popular masses, one should begin by subjugating them. [...] No dictatorship can have any other goal than that of lasting as long as

possible and that it is capable only of engendering slavery in the people who suffer it and educating the latter in this slavery; freedom can only be created by freedom, that is, by the insurrection of the whole people and by the free organization of the working masses from below. (Bakunin, 2003a[e], p. 214)

These two examples summarize well the concept of dictatorship that is criticized by Bakunin in almost the whole of his revolutionary socialist period. He uses this term to critically qualify historical regimes—"military dictatorship" being the most frequent case (cf., for example: Bakunin, 2014d[e], pp. 181, 183, 230)—but also to criticize statist socialists and to refer to the conflict in the International—the period from 1870 to 1872, for example, is qualified as "dictatorship of the General Council" (Bakunin, 2001a[e] p. 58). Even when he referred to the Alliance and wrote its programs, he stated that "there could be no question of dictatorship among us, that our law was collective action" (Bakunin, 71018[e]) and that, in its action, the Alliance had to renounce "all pretension of official leadership of the people and, consequently, all that is called provisional dictatorship or provisional government" (Bakunin, 72016[e], pp. 1–2).

However, in private correspondence in the first half of 1870 with two interlocutors, Richard and Netchaiev—both of whom had authoritarian conceptions and whom Bakunin mistakenly thought were being convinced by his proposals—he seems to contradict his positions (Bakunin, 2017a[c], 2017b[c], 2017c[c]).

To the first he wrote: "we must foster, awaken, unleash all passions—we must produce anarchy—and, invisible pilots in the midst of the popular storm, we must steer it, not by any ostentatious power whatsoever, but by the *collective dictatorship of all Allies*." And further: "There is only one power, one dictatorship whose organization is healthy and possible: it is this *collective and invisible dictatorship of the allies*" (Bakunin, 2017c[c], pp. 114–15, emphasis added). To the second he wrote: "With what authority, with what force will we administer the popular revolution? [...] Through the *collective dictatorship of our organization*," that is, "the *collective dictatorship* of the secret organization" (Bakunin, 2017a[c], pp. 124–25). It is clear that Bakunin is calling here for the "collective dictatorship" of the Alliance.

Even so, it is important to understand what Bakunin understands by this dictatorship in these letters. In explaining it to his two interlocutors, he emphasizes that such a dictatorship can be characterized as "revolutionary anarchy, directed upon all points by a collective and invisible force," that it will not be public, and "will not be vested with any official power, nor of any ostensible character" (Bakunin, 2017c[c], pp. 112, 115). Furthermore, it will be based on natural influence and will not involve the privilege of the dictators. It is thus a dictatorship based on "the natural action of all socialist revolutionaries" (Bakunin, 2017b[c], p. 107), which are articulated in groups that "seek nothing for themselves, neither profit nor honor nor authority." Such groups exercise their dictatorship to the extent that a broader collective of people is "naturally subject to their influence" (Bakunin, 2017a[c], p. 125). In short,

Such a dictatorship is not absolutely contrary to the free development and self-determination of the people, nor to their [bottom-up] organization according to their [habits] and instincts, since [it acts on them] exclusively through the natural and personal influence of its members, who are deprived of all power and [disseminated] through its invisible network, in all regions, districts and [communes]. They strive, by common accord and each in their town, to [steer] the spontaneous revolutionary movement of the people according to a prior and well-defined [common established] plan. (Bakunin, 2017a[c], p. 126, translation adjusted based on the original)

In an analysis of this question, one can conclude that, in fact, there is a contradiction in the use of the term dictatorship, because, in these months only (March to June 1870), it is positively asserted. However, I do not believe there is a significant contradiction in content, since, as explained, the dictatorship of the allies is nothing more than the preponderance of the social force of the Alliance in the revolutionary movement, which is materialized through the natural influence of the Alliancists. In any case, since this happened only these times and with two interlocutors whom Bakunin knew had recently become authoritarian (and who would soon show that they had not abandoned him), my hypothesis is that by using this term, probably asserted by both, Bakunin sought to give this form the content of his own program. I consider, independently of this, that there is a risk in this tactic, that what it posed was misunderstood, both by his interlocutors as well as later (which, in this case, actually occurred).[24]

As far as the problem of anti-Semitism is concerned, this is a trait of Bakunin's work that appears since the 1840s. At that time, Bakunin criticized the Jewish people—who he understood as a nation-race, and not just as a group of religious adepts—and often equated them with the Germans, especially for the historical role attributed to both in the Germanization of the Slavs (Berthier, 2010, vol. 2, p. 138). Since then, Bakunin made certain generalizations both of Jews and Germans, affirming characteristics of these peoples that admit few exceptions. Such generalizations will be found in writings and letters until the end of his life.

In 1869, Bakunin (69043[e], pp. 3–4, 10) wrote a long letter to the editors of *Le Réveil* [*The Awakening*] to respond to Hess' slanderous attacks. Although he claims not to be "in any way an enemy or detractor of the Jews," he attacks his opponent harshly, and does so not by criticizing him for being a slanderer, or even a centralist, but, to a great extent, for being Jewish. He tries to justify himself, recognizing that there were and are great representatives of the Jewish people, including Jesus, St. Paul, Spinoza, Marx, and Lassalle—but points out that Hess, distinctly, belongs to the group of "Pygmy Jews."

These positions culminate in a document from early 1872 entitled "To the Comrades of the Federation of the International Sections of the Jura." In this text,

Bakunin (72005[e], pp. 1, 9, 89) states that there is a "conspiracy of German and Russian Jews against [him]," and that he is being slandered by "Jews and Germans" thanks to his condition as "Russian and Slavic." Proceeding with some more of the aforementioned generalizations, he argues, already in very anti-Semitic tones, that "the Jew is [...] authoritarian by position, by tradition and by nature," which seems to him to be "a general law that admits few exceptions." And more:

> I said that the Jews of Eastern Europe are sworn enemies of every truly popular revolution, and I think that, without any injustice and with very few exceptions, the same can be said of the Jews of Western Europe. *The Jew is bourgeois, that is, exploiter par excellence.* (Bakunin, 72005[e], p. 7, emphasis added)

In other words, the Jewish, in their national condition as Jewish, would almost entirely be an authoritarian and exploitative people. In the first place, because of their historical formation as a people, they would have become "representatives and pioneers of German civilization, order, discipline and the German State." Secondly— and despite the great Jewish who "honor their race"—because the majority of these people are "filthy little Jews": "bankers, usurers, industrialists, merchants, [...] and speculators" who, even if individually powerless as a "legion" are powerful and threatening. For this reason, the parallel can be made between the Jews and the German bourgeoisie, since both, by their condition, "pay homage to all the established powers in the country where they live" (Bakunin, 72005[e], pp. 6, 9–12).

This "Jewish exploitation [that] exercises its most ruthless and excessive depredations" on society explains why, "in all these countries, the people hate the Jews." This feeling is manifested when, in "every popular revolution," the people carry out "a massacre of Jews." And even this does not take the Jewish away from this position and drive them to revolution. For, in fact, the condition of Jew prevails over all others: "basically, the Jews of each country are only friends of the Jews of all countries, regardless of all the differences that may exist between their social positions, their levels of education, their political opinions and their religious cults" (Bakunin, 72005[e], pp. 5–8).

Bakunin's more clearly anti-Semitic positions have their Slavic opposition to German national oppression as their basis and become more evident as conflicts with centralists in general and Marx in particular escalate. It should be remembered that, in 1869, Marx was placed among the Jewish greats by tactical decision—Bakunin, at that time, attacked Marx's allies and preserved him. But some time later, especially when the conflict with him became public, Bakunin attacked him countless times, as he had done with Hess, not only because of his political ideas and practices, but because of his Jewish heritage—and he did the same with Utin, Liebknecht, and others. It is strange, to say the least, that Engels, who was deeply active among the centralists, as well as Lafargue and others, was not taken as an obvious example that his argument of the concerted attack by German Jews was unfounded.

Even if Bakunin had never advocated any kind of violence or relationship of domination towards Jews, it must be emphasized that his anti-Semitism is indefensible and contradicts his positions of the revolutionary socialist period, above all by substituting the classist analysis and position with the national posture, and by showing traces of that narrow nationalism or patriotism, which he himself so harshly criticized. Possibly, such conceptions are explained (but not justified) by his Slavism of the previous period, of which some traces remained until the end of his life.[25]

NOTES

1   When Bakunin advocates compulsory work for all and as the basis of rights, he considers that children, the elderly, and the disabled should be spared this obligation and supported by the community. As he said, in an emancipated society: "No one can exploit the labor of others anymore. Everyone must work to live. Everyone will be free to die of hunger for not working, unless he finds an association or a commune that consents to feed him out of pity. But then, it will probably be fair not to recognize any political right while he, being able to work, prefers the shame of living off the work of others; all political and social rights should only be based on one's work" (Bakunin, 2009d[e], p. 85).

2   Cf. De Paepe (*apud* Guillaume, 2009a, p. 133): "We too are republicans and federalists; but we do not want a nominal republic and an illusory federation. We want the republic in the facts, and above all in the economic facts, which prevail among all the others in our time: not only do we not want a hereditary monarch who calls himself emperor or king, or a temporary monarch who calls himself president, but we also want to suppress the monarch called capitalist, or the oligarchy called national banks, financial companies, etc., which despotically govern the circulation of values and whose civil registry is called interest or dividends; but we want to suppress the monarch who is called owner, who reigns as absolute lord over the soil and whose civil registry is called rent or lease. Federalism, we want it not only in politics, but in social economy; we want not only to decentralize power, but also to decentralize capital; as we want each citizen to be his own sovereign, we want each producer to be his own capitalist, that is, capital and labor to be brought together on the same head; as we want the law to be nothing but a contract between citizens, that is, an exchange of services, we want production, trade, credit, consumption to be nothing but an exchange of services. So what would be the point of decentralizing the nations, the provinces, the communes, if in each of these groups the capital remained centralized in the hands of a few? In republics as well as in monarchies, does not capital rule, and does not misery cause servitude? Political federalism supposes economic federalism, without which it is only a decoy; and economic federalism means: mutualism, reciprocity of services and products, suppression of all the plundering of capital over labor, extinction of the bourgeoisie and the proletariat."

3   In 1866, Bakunin (2009c[e], p. 24) recommended: "The freedom of every adult individual—man and woman— must be absolute and complete; freedom to come and go, to profess openly all possible opinions, to be lazy or active, immoral or moral, to dispose, in short, of his own person and his good and his goodwill, without giving an account of it to anyone, freedom to live, either honestly by one's own labour or by exploiting [living at the expense] shamefully charity or private trust, provided that this charity and trust are voluntary and are provided only by adult individuals."

4   In 1864 Bakunin (2014a[e], pp. 92–94, 117) called for "the emancipation of women" and "freedom in marriage and the family." He maintained: "Woman, different from man, but not inferior to him, will be recognized as equal. She will enjoy the same political and social rights, with no other limits than those imposed naturally, but not legislatively, by her sex. Just as for man, labor, this unique foundation of freedom, will be for her a duty—and the only means of her individual sustenance and emancipation." For this to be possible and fair, "children of both sexes, until they reach the age of adult, will find themselves under a double tutelage: the natural tutelage of parents and the superior tutelage of a committee for education and instruction." Furthermore, "marriage will be free," it will have as its origin "a free agreement between two individuals of different sexes" and "it will not need a priest's sanction." It "being for which "sufficient the will of one of the spouses for the marriage to be broken off." Such emancipation "will deal a mortal blow, the last blow to the patriarchal, theological and sacred family,"

which is based on "the terrible authority of the father, the spouse, the elder brother, and in general the brothers over the sisters." With this, the family will not—and must not—cease to exist, but will reject in its bosom any manifestation of domination.

5   Bakunin (2003a[e], p. 213) stated: "Thus, from whatever angle one is placed to consider this question, one arrives at the same execrable result: the government of the immense majority of the popular masses by a privileged minority. This minority, however, say the Marxists, will consist of workers. Yes, of course, former workers, but as soon as they become rulers or representatives of the people, they will cease to be workers and will place themselves to observe the proletarian world from the State above, they will no longer represent the people, but themselves and their pretensions to govern it."

6   Bakunin always stresses that the revolution must confront social positions much more than people. So it is not enough to replace those who occupy the structures of domination and class in society without putting this structure in check (Bakunin, 2008a[e], pp. 12–13). However, he does not see any concrete possibilities that a social revolution, thanks to the magnitude of the changes it implies, can be carried out without violence: "Revolutions are not children's games, nor academic debates, where only vanities enter into play, nor literary disputes, where only ink is spilled. Revolution is war, and those who say war say destruction of men and things. It is undoubtedly unpleasant for humanity that it has not yet invented a more peaceful means of progress, but up to the present moment every new step in history has only really been taken after it has received the baptism of blood" (Bakunin, 1998[e], p. 22).

7   In the case of cooperatives, for example, Bakunin (2003a[e], pp. 240–41) considers that, even though they constitute "an equitable and rational form of the future system of production," in order for them to contribute to the "emancipation of the laborious masses," "land and capital [...] must be converted into collective property. Until this is done, cooperation will, in most cases, be crushed by competition." He also points out that "under the present conditions of the social economy, cooperation cannot provide emancipation for the laboring masses." Even so, it offers at least one advantage: "to get workers used to coming together, organizing themselves, and conducting their own interests" (cf., also: Bakunin, 71023[e]).

8   These reflections by Bakunin were part of the program promoted in the International by federalist-collectivists in general and by Allancists in particular. Since 1868, this program guided most of the organization's deliberations. These deliberations were also based on concrete examples from French Switzerland: the Romanesque Federation, especially between 1869 and 1870, and the Jurassian Federation from 1871. So here both Bakunin's reflections on what the Swiss sections of the IWA were and how they functioned are combined with those on how the IWA should be and function. Berthier (2011b, pp. 62, 72) points out in this direction that "Bakunin observes the sections of the International in Switzerland [...] and is content to describe how they functioned, but will from then on develop a true theory of organization."

9   In Bakunin, the concept of spontaneity should not be confused with antithesis of organization. For him, spontaneity refers to something that is natural, that is self-effective in itself and is built dialectically from the bottom up, from the simple to the complex. Or, according to Berthier (2015c, p. 24), "a phenomenon is 'spontaneous' if it develops through its own internal dynamics, without external intervention."

10 When, reflecting on his strategy of masses and cadres, Bakunin sometimes equates politics with power and the State and therefore rejects politics. A common view among federalist internationalists: "From the very beginning, the dominant idea [in the IWA] was the repudiation of all legal and parliamentary politics; the political question was placed solely on the revolutionary terrain [...]. This mode of action was characterized by an unfortunate and inexact term borrowed from Proudhon, that of political abstention" (Malon, 2014, p. 53). On this, Bakunin (71011a[e], p. 24) is clear: "It is not true that we make abstraction from politics. [...] Our politics, the only one we admit, is the total abolition of the State and of politics, which is its necessary manifestation." It was, in fact, the rejection of using the State, by revolutionary or parliamentary means, to promote socialism. The politics advocated by Bakunin was a "*revolutionary politics*" (72016[e], p. 9) aimed at the realization of anarchist principles, that is, "the true politics of the workers" (2008b[e], p. 45).

11 Bakunin (71011a[e], pp. 43–44) notes that, during the nineteenth century, it was possible to notice an internationalization of capitalism, in which competition was present in favour of bosses and to the detriment of workers. Not infrequently, in situations of crisis and strike, "the workers of the same craft,

of any place, join forces, demand from their bosses an increase in salary or a decrease in working hours" and the employers, in response, bring workers "from other localities or regions of the same country or even from abroad." At the same time, in order to increase profits and flee workers' mobilizations, and thus be able to maintain lower wages and longer working hours, "the capitalists transport[ed] their capital and the employers their credit and their exploitative activity" to businesses and locations that provide them with more advantageous conditions.

12   Discussing the case concretely and justifying the risks of giving the International the program of the Alliance, Bakunin (72015[c], p. 10) writes that to impose "the program of the Alliance on the International" would mean that "the International will not have more than 2 or 3 thousand members in the whole of Europe." Such members would undoubtedly be "precious men, the most developed, the most energetic and sincere socialist revolutionaries in Europe" but who, in the face of "the coalition power of the rich classes and the State," would conform to nothing more than "absolute impotence." It is known, from Nettlau, (1977, pp. 30–31) that Bakunin rebuked G. Fanelli—the member of the Alliance who was instrumental in the creation of the Spanish International—for having made a mistake in proposing and having the program of the Alliance approved among the militants who initiated the International in Spain. In doing so, Fanelli, even though he did not know it, contributed to the creation of what could be called today the first expression of anarcho-syndicalism in the world.

13   In the note presenting this text, which became known as "Organisation et Grève Générale" [Organization and General Strike], Guillaume explains its origin: The text consists of two small anonymous writings, which were originally published "in the issue of L'Égalité which contains the article 'The Double Strike of Geneva.'" Guillaume explains that both writings "seem to have been written more by Perron [Charles Perron, an Alliancist] than by Bakunin. However, he justifies: "We reproduce them here [in Bakunin's works] because the thoughts they express fit well with the kind of ideas that underpinned the propaganda made by Bakunin in the International" (Bakunin, 1911[e], p. 48).

14   In this case, "vertical" and "horizontal" do not refer to hierarchical and/or federalist organization. In Bakunin's conception, the mass organization, in all its structure, is federalist. Based on Berthier (2014c), the terms refer only to professional and interprofessional, economic and economic-political-cultural structures. It should also be noted that when the term "union" and its variants are used, it is intended to facilitate understanding of the discussion, since these terms were not widely used at the time. At that time, it was more common to refer to unions as "resistance societies" (Guillaume, 1985, vol. I, pp. 204–206), although Bakunin preferred other terms, such as "professional sections" (71011a[e], p. 53), "trade-unions" (2008b[e], p. 52; 69039[e], p. 3), "associations for collective resistance" (71023[e], p. 15), and "corporate societies" (69041[e], p. 1), among others. As Vuilleumier points out (1979, p. 124), the "professional sections constitute the first embryos of the present unions."

15   Bakunin (71011a[e], pp. 50–51) defined this "International ideal" thus: "It is the emancipation not only of the workers of one industry or one country, but of all possible industries and countries of the world. It is the general emancipation of all those who, in the world, painfully earn their miserable daily existence through some productive labor, who are economically exploited and politically oppressed by capital, or rather, by the privileged owners and intermediaries of capital. Such is the negative, bellicose or revolutionary force of the ideal. And the positive force? It is the foundation of a new social world, established solely on emancipated labor, creating itself on the ruins of the old world, through the organization and free federation of workers' associations liberated from the economic and political yoke of the privileged classes."

16   This theme—which, as I stated, has been downplayed in Bakunin's life and work—is discussed by him throughout his revolutionary socialist period and even in writings that address the International. However, it is likely that due to the strategic directions being taken by the IWA (with its almost exclusive focus on the social question), as well as the profile, nationality of its members, and the struggles that were taking place, Bakunin did not want to link his ideas about national liberation and anti-imperialist struggles to the project of the International.

17   It is true, as Barrué (2015c, pp. 261, 265) points out, that "after 1863, the liberation of the Slavic peoples will move to the second level of Bakunin's concerns." However, I do not agree with him that "it was already time, in 1863, for Bakunin's concerns for the International Workers' [Association] to supplant the Federation of Slav peoples," nor with Nettlau (1964, p. 43) when he said that "in the autumn of 1863, he [Bakunin] withdrew entirely from the Slavic national movements, and it is likely that he

reconsidered the situation completely." This is because his project of national liberation of the Slav peoples was not *supplanted* or *completely reconsidered*, but incorporated into his revolutionary socialism—the national question continues to receive attention, but becomes linked and subordinated to the social question.

18   These reflections by Bakunin were made in the writings and letters that discuss the Alliance. As the history of this organization is almost unknown, it is not possible to know exactly to what extent what is advocated here found practical support or not.

19   For a discussion on the difference between the Bakuninian and Leninist organizational models, cf. Berthier, 2012.

20   Historically, the International was banned in different countries and had to deal with the dilemma of insisting on a public organization and facing repression or becoming clandestine.

21   Historically, this set of principles and program of the Alliance must be considered anarchist, and therefore the organization of Bakuninian cadres is an *anarchist political organization*, an anarchist party. However, when it is said that Bakunin advocates the party as an organizational form, it is fundamental to point out that this term is used by him in two distinct ways. First, in the sense used since the 1840s, in which party, in its broad sense, is understood as part, camp, tendency. This is what is expressed, for example, by the subtitle of *Statism and Anarchy: the struggle between the two parties in the International Workers' Association* (Bakunin, 2003a[e]). It is therefore a dispute between two camps, two tendencies: federalist and centralist. Second, in the specific meaning of an organizational form that differs from others (movement, pressure group, etc.), for being concretely articulated around common principles and program. It is in this sense that statements like those of Angaut (2005, p. 554) that "Bakunin conceives the Alliance as a party" should be understood. This is confirmed by Bakunin himself (2003a[e], p. 221, emphasis added), when, as he returns to the history of the founding of the Alliance in 1868, he mentions the "split, which occurred for the first time in this Congress [of the League of Peace and Freedom], between the bourgeois socialists and democrats and the *revolutionary socialists* who were supporters of the *party called the Alliance* or who entered it *a posteriori*." Moreover, even if he does not necessarily refer to the Alliance, Bakunin (1977a, p. 121, emphasis added), in the context of the Franco-Prussian War, outlines his concept of a party, claiming to be a member of one. "It was absolutely necessary to keep the banner of *theoretical principles* high, to clearly expose these principles in all their *purity*, in order to form a *party, however small it may be*, but *composed only of men who were sincere, full and passionately attached to these principles*, so that *each one*, in time of crisis, could count *on all the others*. Now it is no longer a question of recruiting..We have managed to form, well or badly, a *small party*—small in relation to the *number of men* who join it with *knowledge of the cause*, immense if one takes into account its *instinctive adherents*, the *popular masses* of whom it *represents the needs* better than any other party."

22   Bakunin (1988[e], pp. 4–5) was aware of this correlation between the depth of an organization's principles and program and its number of members. The greater the demands in this regard, the smaller the number of members and vice versa. "There is no doubt that if we avoid determining our real character, the number of our members may become very large. [...] But, says the proverb, whoever embraces too much scarcely embraces. [...] It is evident, on the other hand, that if we proclaim our principles openly, the number of our adherents will be more restricted; but at least they will be serious adherents on whom we can count."

23   Usually called "brothers" or "allies" by Bakunin (cf., for example: Bakunin, 68016[e], 72016[e]).

24   For a good discussion of the dictatorship of the allies, cf. Angaut, 2005, pp. 553–64.

25   For a good discussion of the anti-Semitism question, cf. Angaut, 2005, pp. 571–77.

"IN POLITICS THERE IS NO POSSIBILITY OF HONEST AND USEFUL PRACTICE WITHOUT A THEORY":

AN ASSESSMENT OF BAKUNIN'S POLITICAL THEORY AND TRAJECTORY

After all that has been discussed, a brief assessment of Bakunin's political theory and political-intellectual trajectory can be made, indicating this book's principal contributions. More generally, its greatest contribution is to provide the reader, as set out in the Introduction, with "a good starting point for understanding Bakunin's work and life," which had not existed until then—at least in the form presented here. I reiterate that this was done by seeking seriousness and honesty, and taking as a basis all the writings of the Russian revolutionary, his main letters, as well as his most important commentators and historians.

More specifically, its first contribution is to prove that Bakunin has significant contributions to the field of political theory. That is, to show that he was not only a man of action—as no doubt attests his trajectory exposed in Chapters 7 and 10 (and, to a lesser extent, in Chapter 2), but also *a theorist of substance and breadth*. Both the title of the thesis that gave rise to this book and these final considerations refer to this argument, possibly the most important of all research: Bakunin's life can be characterized as a "real unity of thought and action" (Bakunin, 2014g[e], p. 139) and, if *"in politics there is no honest and useful practice without a theory"* (Bakunin, 1988[e], p. 2, emphasis added), one must consider that Bakunin's political practice was, throughout his life, supported by a theory, which can be reconstructed based on his work, produced between 1836 and 1876.

The second contribution of this book is, through this reconstitution, to expound what these contributions by Bakunin were, in fact, and, before them, to face the argument about their incoherence, supported by several studies. In this respect, there are two more conclusive points.

1) That Bakunin's theoretical production is relevant to the field of political theory, especially for contributing, in dialogue with great classics of philosophical and political thought (Fichte, Hegel, Feuerbach, Herzen, Comte, Proudhon, Marx) to the critical understanding and judgment of reality and to the general lines of social change capable of providing solutions, or at least mitigating, the greatest problems of modernity. This can be seen when one analyzes the concepts that, in each period, title the theoretical chapters and are discussed in them: In the Fichtean period (1836–37), love-liberty, and emancipation; in the first Hegelian period (1837–40), alienation, reconciliation with reality, and theory-practice unity; in the second Hegelian period

(1841–42), theory of revolution and negative dialectics; at the moment of departure from philosophy (1843), primacy of practice and self-government of the people; in the pan-Slavist revolutionary period (1844–63), state, nation-race, imperialism, national liberation, and self-determination of the people; in the socialist revolutionary and anarchist period (1864–76), scientific-naturalist materialism, science, freedom, history, social force, domination, social revolution, mass organization, and cadre organization.[1]

2) That both Bakunin's theoretical contributions and the relationship between them and his political practice are quite coherent, as long as they are analyzed in an adequate periodization of his life and work. There is no doubt that Bakunin's political-philosophical thinking underwent impressive changes, and even ruptures, during the 40 years that it was produced (1836–76). Therefore, it is obvious that, without the mentioned periodization, this coherence does not exist—as in the immense majority, if not in the totality, of authors intellectually active for a similar time. The periodization of Bakunin's life and work is also a relevant contribution of this book, as it establishes the temporal parameters for its analysis and allows us to locate in a precise way the greatest changes and ruptures in the author's political-intellectual trajectory.

I maintain that there were two major ruptures in Bakunin's political-philosophical thought, both in epistemological and thematic terms, which also relate to his trajectory. One, in 1843–44, when the period of more exclusively philosophical interest and theoretical reflections about the world and man came to an end, and a new period of rupture with philosophy opened up, in which the national (Russian-Polish and then Slavic) question replaced the previous theme and supported a concrete political practice. Another, in 1863–64, when the period of rupture with philosophy (and theory in general) and of priority focus on the national question comes to an end, a new period of materialistic conciliation between theory and practice is opened in which the national question will be inserted within a broader framework, with the social question and the emancipation of workers then being given priority. It is on the basis of these ruptures that one can speak of the three great periods of Bakunin: that in which he proceeds from philosophy to praxis (1836–43), that in which he sustains revolutionary pan-Slavism (1844–63), and that in which he proceeds from socialism to anarchism (1864–76).

Within these periods, this book also allows one to identify the less drastic changes in Bakunin's philosophical-political thinking. In philosophical terms, his change from subjective idealism to objective idealism in 1837; from this to voluntarist realism in 1841; and from this to scientific-naturalist materialism in 1864. In political terms, his change from progressive romantic idealism to French republican radicalism in 1841; the complementing of this with revolutionary pan-Slavism, in 1844; and the change from this to revolutionary socialism in 1864 and finally to anarchism in 1868.

Considering all these aspects, it is possible to make some more conclusive remarks about the internal coherence of Bakunin's political theory, as well as the coherence between this theory and the author's political practice.

In the first period (1836–43), I consider that there is coherence both in the primarily philosophical interests and in the reflections that take as their theme the human interpretation of reality, the problems of man and the modern world, and the paths to change. At the same time, this is a period of Bakunin's rapid and constant evolution and, in my opinion, this is what explains the changes in his philosophical (in 1837 and 1841) and political (in 1841) references—changes that seem to demonstrate this progress of the revolutionary rather than his incoherence.

In the second period (1844–63), I maintain that there is coherence in the priority that practice acquires over theory (and philosophy), in the philosophical referential that supports the analysis of reality (voluntarist realism) and in the thematic centrality of the national question. Both the passage from the Russian-Polish cause to the Slavic cause and the modification of the political referential—which complements French Republican radicalism with Slavism resulting in revolutionary pan-Slavism—also seem to me to respond more to Bakunin's development than to his contradictions. Such contradictions are more identified, albeit as a very minority part of his thinking and action, in three moments: in the defense of a Jacobin model of political organization (in 1851 and 1862) and of the dictatorship as a model of post-revolutionary government (in 1851 and 1860); in the flirtation with the tsar and with exclusivist and narrow nationalism in 1851 and 1860–62; in the anti-Germanic and even Germanophobic aspects of 1850–51 and 1862.

In the third period (1864–76), I consider that there is coherence in the philosophical defense of scientific-naturalist materialism, in the materialist conciliation between theory and practice, in the treatment of the national question as part of the social question, and in the thematic focus on the emancipation of workers. As far as the passage from socialism to anarchism is concerned, it also seems to me more like Bakunin's progress than a contradiction. That is why I see the years of this passage (1864–67)—in analytical and strategic terms, and in the relationship between labour and life—as part of a transition that undoubtedly highlights certain inconsistencies. In any case, even with the periodization of the three chapters that deal with this period, there are contradictions in two moments—although, again, they constitute a very minority part of Bakunin's thought and action. These contradictions appear both in the positive assertion of the term "dictatorship" in 1870 and in the anti-Semitic and, in some cases, anti-Germanic positions, which were exacerbated from 1869 onwards.[2]

Finally, this book also serves to counter a number of arguments that have been and are being sustained in studies of Bakunin. With it, it is possible to understand how Bakunin developed his revolutionary conceptions and, therefore, discard the hypotheses of the Oedipus complex and sexual impotence.[3] It is also possible to assure that, based on his work and life from 1836 to 1876, Bakunin was not a conservative, reactionary, precursor of fascism, apostle of destruction and chaos, individualist, and disciple of Stirner or Rousseau. And that in his anarchist period, he was not idealistic, opposed to organization, or a pan-Slavist (in the sense of defending a Slavism under the hegemony of the tsar), and neither can his ideas and actions be considered petty bourgeois.

Moreover, it allows us to establish what Bakunin's due responsibility in the Netchaiev case was and that the former cannot be held responsible for everything that the latter wrote and did.[4] And it also makes it possible to sustain that: Bakunin and the Alliance never intended to disorganize or destroy the International. It is certain that the secret Alliance existed—something which, if it in no way legitimizes the deliberations of the London Conference of 1871 and The Hague Congress of 1872, at least challenges the official account of the anarchists who have vehemently denied such an existence ever since. Bakunin was not the dictator of the Alliance and that it was not a Jacobin organization nor (anachronistically speaking) a precursor to Bolshevism, but a federalist cadre organization compatible with the organizational model of the International.[5]

NOTES

1   One can mention in detail, as an example, an aspect of Bakuninian political theory that shows his relevance and predictive capacity. When—in the discussion with socialists about how to promote the emancipation of workers—Bakunin maintains the need to abolish the State while still in a revolutionary context, it is because he considered that, if this were not done, the revolution would not lead to socialism and would not emancipate workers. It would create a new class regime, in which the bureaucracy would continue to dominate and exploit the workers. Such a reflection foresaw, in general terms, the fate of *all* the revolutionary processes headed by the communists and experiences with "real socialism" in the twentieth century.

2   Finally, it is possible to question the extent to which two other questions highlight differences or even contradictions between Bakunin's thought and action: the relationship with Netchaiev (with the relativization of certain ethical assumptions, in the name of a supposed revolutionary impetus of the young Russian); and the participation in the Lyon and Bologna uprisings (with a notable detachment of the workers' bases which undoubtedly puts Bakunin's mass strategy in check).

3   Just out of curiosity, for what I could verify during this research, the Oedipus complex never existed and the sexual impotence cannot be proved by lack of evidence. And, even if there were proof, they certainly would not explain Bakunin's revolutionary positions.

4   It should be noted that this case allows us to draw an important lesson: that in an emancipatory project, besides the revolutionary impetus of the members, there are ethical and moral criteria that are indispensable and, therefore, cannot be dismissed.

5   To state that Bakunin was a precursor of Bolshevism would require a more detailed study of the revolutionary's historical influence in Russia and the extent to which his ideas had an impact on people and movements that somehow contributed to the construction of Bolshevism. Something that has not existed to date, at least that I know of. By proceeding with the pure comparison of ideas, one can identify similarities and countless and irreconcilable ruptures.

FROM ANARCHISM:
BAKUNIN FOR THE TWENTY-FIRST CENTURY

by Rocio Soledad Lescano

This work by Felipe Corrêa is without a doubt a significant contribution to both political theory and the history of political thought. After reading the book, what prevails is the sense of complexity inherent in Bakunin's thought. We are far from being able to affirm that this important figure was univocal in his affirmations, or that he always maintained a straight line in his reflections. It also forces us to definitively abandon a reading that sees his work as an always coherent set of static ideologies.

In this sense, this important work contributes a new dimension to the theoretical elaboration of this progenitor of anarchism, to understand his work in his context of production and debate. Corrêa also humanizes this figure who was above all a militant, who far from remaining on the platform of intellectual debate, constantly sought to put his analyses and proposals into practice, in a back and forth that enriches each of his elaborations. The disorder of his papers, the fragmentary nature of his work, the complexity of the reconstruction of his archive, give us a clue to this profile. So does the value of his words for his contemporaries and later generations. Undoubtedly, beyond his advanced analyses, he managed to synthesize and systematize key tools and elements for those who want to change society from an anarchist perspective.

Now, if Bakunin in his complexity, in his political and theoretical thought was following the path that Corrêa reconstructed in his work, it remains for the anarchists of the present to think about why he continues to be one of the most important figures of our movement today. The simplicity with which other ideologies would respond to similar questions (if there were interest in formulating them) cannot exhaust the concerns within anarchism. Leaders, the idealization of people, bosses, are alien to our ideology, and not only that, but we fight them tooth and nail every time they slip into our interpretations.

Recognizing people from the past and the present who, because of their worth, their commitment, solidarity, and humanity, are worthy of being remembered, is a necessary operation for those who inscribe themselves within a political-ideological current, but the nature of the operation can have varying degrees of depth depending on the objective sought. It also has the potential to be an identity trait, a marker of what is inside and what is outside, especially when we speak of something like anarchism, which has been and is prone to refer to a multitude of meanings and ascriptions within its broad mantle.

We could suggest that the validity of Bakunin's thought does not reside only in its historical importance, but today finds its explanation in its intrinsic value, in its contribution to social struggles, and in the methodological clues it leaves for those of us who try to change the world from a perspective of socialism and freedom. He was a theorist of mixed papers, of publication in newspapers, of fragments and letters, of much imprisonment and cinematic escapes, and with little arrival in the academic debate. A militant who knew how to insert himself, among other things, within the debates of socialism itself and to give shape to a series of ideas and political proposals that have made a great contribution to social struggles and to worldwide militancy. It is also in this unsystematic way that his purely theoretical contribution had been collected, analyzed, and disseminated.

In this sense, as Corrêa also states, the systematization and accessibility of his work is in itself a key component of its possibilities of use and its impact within different "worlds." Thus, the gravitation of Bakuninian thought in the academic field escapes the concerns of this brief epilogue, but its contribution to a project of social transformation linked to anarchism is central.

A quick tour through the history of anarchism, from its emergence in the last third of the nineteenth century,[1] framed in European debates and struggles, to its present day throughout the planet proves difficult to synthesize. It is more than a century of organizational initiatives, of revolutionary attempts, of pre-figurative practices, and of great objectives of social transformation for the children of the people. In this framework Bakunin's thought was always recovered, reread, republished, rethought, and updated, with all the limitations and possibilities to which the author has already referred. And from anarchism, as has been said, we can affirm that dogma or the profile of the enlightened intellectual is alien to this operation. What prevails here is the continuity of a large part of the problems to which this militant dedicated reflection and advanced a reading, where his production gives an answer to a series of questions that we continue to ask ourselves.

Thinking about the contemporary context, it is worth starting from what has already been pointed out: since the 1980s the ideological field of anarchism has experienced a worldwide resurgence. This is easily verified in Latin America, where in countries such as Argentina or Brazil anarchism is once again present in different spaces of social struggle after decades of absence. For this, the contribution of the Uruguayan Anarchist Federation (FAU) was undoubtedly key, which, with more than sixty years of existence, became a pole from which Latin American anarchism promoted further organization. *Especifismo*, as a Latin American variant of organized anarchism and platformism, takes up the main lines of Bakunin's thought, among other militants. And it is in this framework where theory also becomes relevant for the movement and the rereading of Bakunin's thought contributes to anarchists and their political projects.

We will now point out some of what we believe to be the most important contributions proposed by Bakunin that are still valid today and are being put into practice by a portion of contemporary anarchism. It is not the objective of these remarks to develop Bakunin's postulates, but to rescue his theoretical contributions that are applicable to current militancy, such as organizational dualism, revolutionary strategy, anti-statism, and the notion of freedom, among others.

In the first instance, the need arises to distinguish mass organization, or social organization, from anarchist organization. In the case of Bakunin, as has already been exposed throughout the course of the text, this distinction is based on the experience of the Alliance and the IWA. And it is in this framework that Bakunin constructs a proposal of what will be organizational dualism, or this double affiliation of the anarchist militants.

In this proposal, on the one hand, there are the mass organizations, whose objective is to bring together the oppressed for the immediate struggle, to win demands and progressively gain experience in the class struggle and thus strengthen the consciousness of their own forces and advance towards a revolutionary transformation. Today we are talking about social organizations where those who share a class condition converge. Anarchist militants thus contribute to the formation and development of organizations in union, student, neighbourhood, and peasant sectors, among others. The purpose of this organization, as has been said, is the progressive conquest of demands, from the most immediate to the most systemic. The revolutionary subject is built in the framework of the class struggle and the organization of the masses and their actions are indispensable for this. Anarchists participate in it as just one more of its members, but seeking to influence and share theoretical and methodological tools.

However, the proposal put forward by Bakunin also includes the formation of a specifically political organization, which brings together anarchists, organizes the efforts of militants, and gives guidelines for militancy in these sectors. This organization is far from being an authority that imposes its proposals on the mass organization or a vanguard that takes advantage of the social organization for its own ends outside the agenda thereof. The anarchist organization seeks to guarantee the performance of anarchist militancy in social spaces, contributing to organizing and influencing the revolutionary course and the radicalization of the social struggle, ensuring the revolutionary project, and contributing to social transformation. It is conceived as a small, dynamizing engine, which does not impose but promotes, drives, and offers tools to the mass organization.

Moreover, the changes in the contexts and the different conjunctures have demonstrated that this organization is the one that can keep functioning, even in moments of persecution and clandestinity, enabling the modification of tactics and strategy as the context requires.

Likewise, these organizations should also contribute to the construction of the revolution, understood as the culmination of an organizational process where the mass or social organizations take the lead. The task of anarchist organizations is in this respect to contribute to this process, to the participation and growth of influence within the framework of popular struggle and organization. This path proposes what would be the self-emancipation of the oppressed, where social organizations are the principal agents.

On the other hand, in a twenty-first century where the brutality of the system of capitalist domination continues more than ever, but the hopes of transformation often find a channel within the institutions and the very structure of the state apparatus, the anti-statism promoted by Bakunin also becomes relevant to be recovered. In this sense, from the perspective of the Russian thinker, the need for the abolition of the State is given even in the revolutionary context, understanding that it is the only guarantee for the revolution to lead to socialism and the emancipation of the oppressed. The survival of the State from this point of view would bring nothing more than the prolongation of the class regime and the perpetuation of domination over the workers and other oppressed classes.

In this sense, this affirmation of an anarchist identity, which remains more valid than ever, allows us to escape interpretations, which today also survive where forces of the statist left appeal to the use of the same tools of the system in the hope of contributing to the transformation of reality. If today there is a proliferation of discourses that appeal to the "citizens," and why not the "voters," from anarchism the ideological certainty, but theoretically grounded by thinkers like Bakunin, that the same tools of domination will not bring any fundamental transformation poses a possible alternative path.

Another of the fundamental axes of Bakunin's thought during his revolutionary socialist period that we can find in the anarchist organizations of the present is the importance given to freedom. But the notion of freedom differs profoundly from the prevailing notion at this stage of the system of neoliberal capitalist domination. For Bakunin freedom is understood as purely social. As has been pointed out throughout Chapter 11, the realization of freedom implies the freedom of all as well as the effective guarantee of equality and the end of the State and all artificial authority within society.

Freedom and equality are thus inseparable from and form the very foundation of justice. There is a frequent quotation of Bakunin in this respect, accurate words that for that reason have been published and republished an infinity of times. He tells us that "I am truly free only when all human beings around me, men and women, are equally free. The freedom of the other, far from being a limit or the negation of my freedom, is, on the contrary, its necessary condition and its confirmation."[2]

Rocio Soledad Lescano is an Argentinian historian and professor at the National University of Rosário; and an anarchist and syndicalist militant (Anarchist Federation of Rosario, FAR).

NOTES

1   As Corrêa points out in this book, from a historical perspective the year 1868 can be put as the date of the emergence of anarchism (p. 302).

2   Cited p. 341.

BIBLIOGRAPHIC REFERENCES[1]

BAKUNIN'S COMPLETE WORKS
BAKUNIN, Mikhail. *CD-ROM Bakounine: Œuvres Complètes* (BOC). Amsterdam: IIHS, 2000a.

BAKUNIN'S WRITINGS
BAKUNIN, Mikhail. *Œuvres*. 6 vols. (ed. Max Nettlau and James Guillaume). Paris: Stock, 1895–1913.

____. [1869] "Organisation et Grève Générale." In *Œuvres*. Tome V. Paris: Stock, 1911.

____. [1871] "Réponse d'un International à Mazzini." In *Œuvres Complètes*, vol. I: Michel Bakounine et L'Italie 1871–1872, première partie. Paris: Champ Libre, 1973a.

____. [1871] *La Théologie Politique de Mazzini et l'Internationale*. In *Œuvres Complètes*, vol. I: Michel Bakounine et L'Italie 1871–1872, première partie. Paris: Champ Libre, 1973b.

____. [1842] "A Reação na Alemanha." In BARRUÉ, Jean; BAKUNIN, Mikhail; NETCHAIEV, Serguei. *O Anarquismo Hoje / A Reacção na Alemanha / O Catecismo Revolucionário*. Lisbon: Assírio & Alvim, 1976a.

____. [1851] *Confesión al Zar Nicolas I*. Barcelona: Labor, 1976b.

____. [1870] "Cartas a un Francés sobre la Crisis Actual." In: *Obras Completas*. Tomo I. Madrid: La Piqueta, 1977a.

____. [1870] "Carta [A Palix]. La Situación Política de Francia." In: *Obras Completas*. Tomo I. Madrid: La Piqueta, 1977b.

____. [1838] "Hegel's *Gymnasium Lectures.*" In DEL GIUDICE, Martine. *The Young Bakunin and Left Hegelianism: Origins of Russian Radicalism and Theory of Praxis (1814–1842)*. Montreal: McGill University (PhD dissertation), 1981a.

____. [1839] "From Philosophy, part I." In: DEL GIUDICE, Martine. *The Young Bakunin and Left Hegelianism: Origins of Russian Radicalism and Theory of Praxis (1814–1842)*. Montreal: McGill University (PhD dissertation), 1981b.

____. [1839–1840] "From Philosophy, part II." In: DEL GIUDICE, Martine. *The Young Bakunin and Left Hegelianism: origins of Russian radicalism and theory of praxis (1814–1842)*. Montreal: McGill University (PhD dissertation), 1981c.

____. [1837] "My Notes." In: DEL GIUDICE, Martine. *The Young Bakunin and Left Hegelianism: origins of Russian radicalism and theory of praxis (1814-1842)*. Montreal: McGill University (PhD dissertation), 1981d.

____. [1867–1868] *Federalismo, Socialismo e Antiteologismo*. São Paulo: Cortez, 1988a.

____. [1870] "Os Ursos de Berna e o Urso de São Petersburgo." In: *Novos Tempos*, num. 2. São Paulo: Imaginário, 1998.

* * *

Writings from the CD-ROM Bakounine: Œuvres Complètes
BAKUNIN, Mikhail. [1837] "Article sur *Hamlet* de Shakespeare." In *BOC*. Amsterdam: IIHS, 37003.

____. [1845] "Lettre a *La Réforme*." In *BOC*. Amsterdam: IIHS, 45001.

____. [1846] "Lettre au *Constitutionnel*." In *BOC*. Amsterdam: IIHS, 46001.

____. [1847] "Discours 17e Anniversaire de la Révolution Polonaise." In *BOC*. Amsterdam: IIHS, 47003.

____. [1848] "Lettre a *La Réforme*." In *BOC*. Amsterdam: IIHS, 48002.

____. [1848] "Principes Fondamentaux de la Nouvelle Politique Slave." In *BOC*. Amsterdam: IIHS, 48004.

____. [1848] "Projet de Lettre à *Die Reform*." In *BOC*. Amsterdam: IIHS, 48014.

____. [1848] "Appel aux Slaves par un Patriote Russe" (draft). In *BOC*. Amsterdam: IIHS, 48019.

____. [1848] "Appel aux Slaves par un Patriote Russe" (published). In *BOC*. Amsterdam: IIHS, 48020.

____. [1849] "Appel aux Tchèques." In *BOC*. Amsterdam: IIHS, 49001.

____. [1849] "La Démocratie Tchèque." In *BOC*. Amsterdam: IIHS, 49003.

____. [1849] "La Situation en Russie." In *BOC*. Amsterdam: IIHS, 49005, 49006, 49007, 49008, 49009, 49010.

____. [1850] "Ma Défense." In *BOC*. Amsterdam: IIHS, 50001.

____. [1861] "*Amur*, Quelques Mots sur la Vie Sociale d'Irkutsk." In *BOC*. Amsterdam: IIHS, 61001.

____. [1861] "Article Dans *Amur*, Journal de la Sibérie Orientale." In *BOC*. Amsterdam: IIHS, 61002.

____. [1862] "Aux Russes, Polonais, et Tous les Amis Slaves." In *BOC*. Amsterdam: IIHS, 62002.

____. [1862] "La Cause du Peuple. Romanov, Pugatchev ou Pestel?" In *BOC*. Amsterdam: IIHS, 62006.

____. [1862] "Bakunin sur les Slaves." In *BOC*. Amsterdam: IIHS, 62008.

____. [1862] "Le Comité Central de Varsovie et le Comité Militaire Russe: Réponse au Général Mieroslawski." In *BOC*. Amsterdam: IIHS, 62011.

____. [1863] "Discours de Malmö." In *BOC*. Amsterdam: IIHS, 63002.

____. [1863] "Lettre sur la Russie." In *BOC*. Amsterdam: IIHS, 63003.

____. [1863] "Discours Prononcé au Banquet à Stockholm." In *BOC*. Amsterdam: IIHS, 63006.

____. [1863] "La Russie Officielle et le Peuple Russe." In *BOC*. Amsterdam: IIHS, 63008.

____. [1864] "Région Scandinave: Adélaïde." In *BOC*. Amsterdam: IIHS, 64007.

____. [1865] "Fragments d'Écrits sur la Franc-Maçonnerie" (7 documents). In *BOC*. Amsterdam: IIHS, 65001.

____. [1866] "Branche Italienne." In *BOC*. Amsterdam: IIHS, 66001.

____. [1866] "Principes et Organisation de la Société Internationale Révolutionnaire" (includes "Revolutionary Catechism" and "Organization"). In *BOC*. Amsterdam: IIHS, 66002.

____. [1866] "Programme de la Révolution Démocratique-Sociale Italienne." In *BOC*. Amsterdam: IIHS, 66004.

____. [1867] "Discours Prononcé au Congrès de la Paix et de la Liberté, Deuxième Séance." In *BOC*. Amsterdam: IIHS, 67007.

____. [1868] "Lettre à *La Démocratie*." In *BOC*. Amsterdam: IIHS, 68002.

____. [1868] "La Russie: La Question Révolutionnaire dans les Pays Russes et en Pologne." In *BOC*. Amsterdam: IIHS, 68006.

____. [1868] "Notre Programme." In *BOC*. Amsterdam: IIHS, 68009.

____. [1868] "Discours au Deuxième Congrès de la Paix et de la Liberté" (5 documents). In *BOC*. Amsterdam: IIHS, 68011.

____. [1868] "Programme et Règlement de l'Alliance Internationale de la Démocratie Socialiste" (3 documents). In *BOC*. Amsterdam: IIHS, 68014.

____. [1868] "Statuts Secrets de l'Alliance" (5 documents). In *BOC*. Amsterdam: IIHS, 68016.

____. [1868] "Projet de Statuts pour la Fédération des Sections Romandes de Suisse Proposé par les Sections Genevoises." In *BOC*. Amsterdam: IIHS, 68018.

____. [1868] "Fraternité Internationale: Programme et Objet." In *BOC*. Amsterdam: IIHS, 68022.

____. [1869] "La Fraternité." In *BOC*. Amsterdam: IIHS, 69001.

____. [1869] "Madame Léo et *L'Égalité*." In *BOC*. Amsterdam: IIHS, 69012.

____. [1869] "Programme et Règlement de la Section de l'Alliance de la Démocratie Socialiste à Genève de l'A.I.T." In *BOC*. Amsterdam: IIHS, 69016.

____. [1869] "En Russie." In *BOC*. Amsterdam: IIHS, 69018.

____. [1869] "Le Mouvement International des Travailleurs." In *BOC*. Amsterdam: IIHS, 69020.

____. [1869] "L'Agitation du Parti de la Démocratie Socialiste en Autriche." In *BOC*. Amsterdam: IIHS, 69025.

____. [1869] "Jugement Rendu en Faveur d'Albert Richard." In *BOC*. Amsterdam: IIHS, 69026.

____. [1869] "*La Montagne*." In *BOC*. Amsterdam: IIHS, 69033.

___. [1869] "Le Jugement de M. Coullery." In *BOC*. Amsterdam: IIHS, 69035.

___. [1869] "Rapport de la Commission sur la Question de l'Héritage." In *BOC*. Amsterdam: IIHS, 69038.

___. [1869] "De la Coopération." In *BOC*. Amsterdam: IIHS, 69039.

___. [1869] "Contre-Rapport sur les Caisses de Résistance." In *BOC*. Amsterdam: IIHS, 69041.

___. [1869] "Aux Citoyens Rédacteurs du *Réveil*. Étude sur les Juifs Allemands." In *BOC*. Amsterdam: IIHS, 69043.

___. [1870] "L'Alliance Universelle de la Démocratie Sociale: Section Russe. À la Jeunesse Russe." In *BOC*. Amsterdam: IIHS, 70011.

___. [1871] "L'Empire Knouto-Germanique et la Révolution Sociale: Suite (Dieu et l'État 4)." In *BOC*. Amsterdam: IIHS, 71002.[2]

___. [1871] "L'Empire Knouto-Germanique et la Révolution Sociale: Fragments et Variantes (Fragment C)." In *BOC*. Amsterdam: IIHS, 71004.[3]

___. [1871] "L'Empire Knouto-Germanique et la Révolution Sociale: Avertissement." In *BOC*. Amsterdam: IIHS, 71010.[4]

___. [1871] "Protestation de l'Alliance." In *BOC*. Amsterdam: IIHS, 71011a.[5]

___. [1871] "Protestation de l'Alliance: Suite." In *BOC*. Amsterdam: IIHS, 71011b.

___. [1871] "Rapport sur l'Alliance" (3 documents). In *BOC*. Amsterdam: IIHS, 71018.

___. [1871] "Lettre à Mes Amis d'Italie." In *BOC*. Amsterdam: IIHS, 71022.

___. [1871] "Lettre aux Rédacteurs du *Proletario Italiano*." In *BOC*. Amsterdam: IIHS, 71023.

___. [1871] "Lettre à la Rédaction du *Gazzettino Rosa*." In *BOC*. Amsterdam: IIHS, 71027.

___. [1871] "L'Italie et le Conseil Général de l'Association Internationale des Travailleurs." In *BOC*. Amsterdam: IIHS, 71028.

___. [1872] "Lettre au Rédacteur du *Gazzettino Rosa*." In *BOC*. Amsterdam: IIHS, 72001.

___. [1872] "Aux Compagnons de la Fédération des Sections Internationales du Jura." In *BOC*. Amsterdam: IIHS, 72005.

___. [1872] "Programme de la Fraternité Internationale." In *BOC*. Amsterdam: IIHS, 72016.

___. [1873] "L'Alliance Internationale des Sociaux-Révolutionnaires." In *BOC*. Amsterdam: IIHS, 73002.

___. [1874] "Mémoire Justificatif." In *BOC*. Amsterdam: IIHS, 74001.

* * *

___. [1872] "Escrito Contra Marx." In *Escritos Contra Marx*. São Paulo: Imaginário, 2001a.

___. [1872] "Carta ao Jornal *La Liberté* de Bruxelas." In *Escritos Contra Marx*. São Paulo: Imaginário, 2001b.

___. [1873] *Estatismo e Anarquia*. São Paulo: Imaginário, 2003a.

___. [1872] "Programa da Seção Eslava de Zurique." In *Estatismo e Anarquia*. São Paulo: Imaginário, 2003b.

___. [1842] "La Réaction en Allemagne." In ANGAUT, Jean-Christophe. *Bakounine Jeune Hégélien: La Philosophie et Son Dehors*. Lyon: ENS, 2007a.

___. [1843] "Le Communisme." In ANGAUT, Jean-Christophe. *Bakounine Jeune Hégélien: la philosophie et son dehors*. Lyon: ENS, 2007b.

___. [1843] "Carta a Arnold Ruge de maio de 1843." In ANGAUT, Jean-Christophe. *Bakounine Jeune Hégélien: la philosophie et son dehors*. Lyon: ENS, 2007c.

___. [1869] "A Dupla Greve de Genebra." In LEVAL, Gaston. *Bakunin, Fundador do Sindicalismo Revolucionário*. São Paulo: Imaginário/Faísca, 2007d.

___. [1871] *O Sistema Capitalista*. São Paulo: Faísca, 2007e.

___. [1869] "Os Enganadores" ["Os Adormecedores"]. In *Os Enganadores / A Política da Internacional / Aonde Ir e o Que Fazer?* São Paulo: Imaginário/Faísca, 2008a.

___. [1869] "A Política da Internacional." In *Os Enganadores / A Política da Internacional / Aonde Ir e o Que Fazer?* São Paulo: Imaginário/Faísca, 2008b.

___. [1871] "O Princípio do Estado." In *O Princípio do Estado e Outros Ensaios*. São Paulo: Hedra, 2008c.

___. [1871] "Três Conferências Feitas aos Operários do Vale de Saint-Imier." In *O Princípio do Estado e Outros Ensaios*. São Paulo: Hedra, 2008d.

___. [1871] "A Comuna de Paris e a Noção de Estado." In: *O Princípio do Estado e Outros Ensaios*. São Paulo: Hedra, 2008e.

___. [1873] "Aonde Ir e o Que Fazer." In *Os Enganadores / A Política da Internacional / Aonde Ir e o Que Fazer?* São Paulo: Imaginário/Faísca, 2008f.

___. [1867] "Essência da Religião." In *Essência da Religião / O Patriotismo*. São Paulo: Imaginário, 2009a.

___. [1869] "O Patriotismo: Aos companheiros da Associação Internacional dos Trabalhadores no Locle e em La Chaux-de-Fonds." In *Essência da Religião / O Patriotismo*. São Paulo: Imaginário, 2009b.

___. [1866] "Princípios e Organização da Sociedade Internacional Revolucionária. Catecismo Revolucionário." In *Catecismo Revolucionário / Programa da Sociedade da Revolução Internacional*. São Paulo: Imaginário/Faísca, 2009c.

___. [1868] "Programa da Sociedade da Revolução Internacional." In *Catecismo Revolucionário / Programa da Sociedade da Revolução Internacional*. São Paulo: Imaginário/Faísca, 2009d.

___. [1870] *A Ciência e a Questão Vital da Revolução*. São Paulo: Imaginário/Faísca, 2009e.

_____. [1871] *Deus e o Estado*. São Paulo: Hedra, 2011a.

_____. [1864] "Programa de uma Sociedade Internacional Secreta da Emancipação da Humanidade." In FERREIRA, Andrey C.; TONIATTI, Tadeu. *De Baixo para Cima e da Periferia para o Centro: textos políticos, filosóficos e de teoria sociológica de Mikhail Bakunin*. Niterói: Alternativa, 2014a.

_____. [1864] "Projeto de Organização da Família dos Irmãos Escandinavos: projeto de uma organização secreta internacional." In FERREIRA, Andrey C.; TONIATTI, Tadeu. *De Baixo para Cima e da Periferia para o Centro: textos políticos, filosóficos e de teoria sociológica de Mikhail Bakunin*. Niterói: Alternativa, 2014b.

_____. [1864] "Sociedade Internacional Secreta da Revolução: programa provisório convencionado pelos irmãos fundadores." In FERREIRA, Andrey C.; TONIATTI, Tadeu. *De Baixo para Cima e da Periferia para o Centro: textos políticos, filosóficos e de teoria sociológica de Mikhail Bakunin*. Niterói: Alternativa, 2014c.

_____. [1870–1871] "O Império Knuto-Germânico e a Revolução Social." In FERREIRA, Andrey C.; TONIATTI, Tadeu. *De Baixo para Cima e da Periferia para o Centro: textos políticos, filosóficos e de teoria sociológica de Mikhail Bakunin*. Niterói: Alternativa, 2014d.

_____. [1871] "Sofismas Históricos da Escola Doutrinária dos Comunistas Alemães." In FERREIRA, Andrey C.; TONIATTI, Tadeu. *De Baixo para Cima e da Periferia para o Centro: textos políticos, filosóficos e de teoria sociológica de Mikhail Bakunin*. Niterói: Alternativa, 2014e.

_____. [1871] "Considerações Filosóficas sobre o Fantasma Divino, o Mundo Real e o Homem." In FERREIRA, Andrey C.; TONIATTI, Tadeu. *De Baixo para Cima e da Periferia para o Centro: textos políticos, filosóficos e de teoria sociológica de Mikhail Bakunin*. Niterói: Alternativa, 2014f.

_____. [1871] "Carta aos Internacionais de Bolonha." In *Escritos Contra Marx*. São Paulo: Imaginário, 2014g.

_____. [1871] "Relações Pessoais com Marx." In *Escritos Contra Marx*. São Paulo: Imaginário, 2014h.

_____. [1872] "Aos Redatores do Boletim da Federação do Jura." In *Escritos Contra Marx*. São Paulo: Imaginário, 2014i.

_____. [1872] "A Alemanha e o Comunismo de Estado." In *Escritos Contra Marx*. São Paulo: Imaginário, 2014j.

_____. [1873] "Ao *Journal de Genéve*." In *Escritos Contra Marx*. São Paulo: Imaginário, 2014k.

_____. [1869] "Instrução Integral." In *Obras Escolhidas*. São Paulo: Hedra, 2015.

_____. [1868] "A Ciência e o Povo." In *Educação, Ciência e Revolução*. São Paulo: Intermezzo, 2016a.

____. [1868] "Discurso do Cidadão Bakunin a uma Assembleia Pública de Socialistas Estrangeiros." In *Obras Seletas 1*. São Paulo: Intermezzo, 2016b.

____. [1869] "Dois Discursos no Congresso da A.I.T. em Basileia." In *Obras Seletas 1*. São Paulo: Intermezzo, 2016c.

____. [1870] "As Intrigas do Sr. Utin." In *Educação, Ciência e Revolução*. São Paulo: Intermezzo, 2016d.

____. [1873] "Carta aos Companheiros da Federação Jurassiana." In *Obras Seletas 1*. São Paulo: Intermezzo, 2016f.

____. [1868] "Primeiro Discurso no Segundo Congresso da Paz e da Liberdade." In *Obras Seletas 2*. São Paulo: Intermezzo, 2017a.

____. [1868] "Quinto Discurso no Segundo Congresso da Paz e da Liberdade." In *Obras Seletas 2*. São Paulo: Intermezzo, 2017b.

____. [1868] "Fraternidade Internacional: programa e objeto." In *Obras Seletas 2*. São Paulo: Intermezzo, 2017c.

____. [1869] "Como se Apresenta a Questão Revolucionária." In *Obras Seletas 2*. São Paulo: Intermezzo, 2017d.

____. [1869] "O Movimento Internacional dos Trabalhadores." In *Obras Seletas 2*. São Paulo: Intermezzo, 2017e.

____. [1870–1871?] "História do Socialismo." In *Obras Seletas 2*. São Paulo: Intermezzo, 2017f.

____. [1871] "A Oligarquia Burguesa." In *Obras Seletas 2*. São Paulo: Intermezzo, 2017x.

CUTLER, Robert (ed.). *The Basic Bakunin: Writings 1869–1871*. New York: Prometheus, 1992.

DOLGOFF, Sam (ed.). *Bakunin on Anarchy: Selected Works of the Activist-Founder of World Anarchism*. New York: Vintage Books, 1972.

LUTA LIBERTÁRIA (ed.). *Bakunin: Socialismo e Liberdade*. São Paulo: Luta Libertária, 2002.

MAXIMOFF, G. P. (ed.). *The Political Philosophy of Bakunin: Scientific Anarchism*. New York and London: Free Press, 1964.

MINTZ, Frank (ed.). *Bakunin. Crítica y Acción*. Buenos Aires: Anarres, 2006.

PAUVERT, Jean-Jacques (ed.). *Conceito de Liberdade*. Porto: RÈS, 1975.

BAKUNIN'S LETTERS[6]

BAKUNIN, Mikhail. "Aos Pais (20 de setembro de 1831)." In *BOC*. Amsterdam: IIHS, 31005.

____. "Às Irmãs (28 de março de 1833)." In *BOC*. Amsterdam: IIHS, 33016.

____. "Às Irmãs (26 de janeiro de 1834)." In *BOC*. Amsterdam: IIHS, 34002.

____. "Aos Pais (19 de dezembro de 1834)." In *BOC*. Amsterdam: IIHS, 34012.

____. "A Sergei Muraviev (fim de janeiro de 1835)." In *BOC*. Amsterdam: IIHS, 35001.

____. "À Tatiana Bakunin (17 de fevereiro de 1836)." In *BOC*. Amsterdam: IIHS, 36014.

____. "À Tatiana e Varvara Bakunin (28–29 de fevereiro de 1836)." In *BOC*. Amsterdam: IIHS, 36017.

____. "À Nathalie Beer (fevereiro/março de 1836)." In *BOC*. Amsterdam: IIHS, 36019.

____. "À Varvara Bakunin (9 de março de 1836)." In *BOC*. Amsterdam: IIHS, 36029.

____. "À Varvara Bakunin (11 de março de 1836)." In *BOC*. Amsterdam: IIHS, 36030.

____. "À Tatiana Bakunin (17 de março de 1836)." In *BOC*. Amsterdam: IIHS, 36033.

____. "À Alexandra e Nathalie Beer (primavera de 1836)." In *BOC*. Amsterdam: IIHS, 36034.

____. "À Alexandra Beer (4 de abril de 1836)." In *BOC*. Amsterdam: IIHS, 36043.

____. "À Tatiana Bakunin (20 de abril de 1836)." In *BOC*. Amsterdam: IIHS, 36049.

____. "À Tatiana e Varvara Bakunin (23 de abril de 1836)." In *BOC*. Amsterdam: IIHS, 36052.

____. "À Tatiana e Varvara Bakunin (10 de agosto de 1836)." In *BOC*. Amsterdam: IIHS, 36074.

____. "Aos Irmãos (11 de setembro de 1836)." In *BOC*. Amsterdam: IIHS, 36088.

____. "À Varvara Bakunin (10 de janeiro de 1837)." In *BOC*. Amsterdam: IIHS, 37007.

____. "À Alexandra, Nathalie e Konstantin Beer (22 de julho de 1837)." In *BOC*. Amsterdam: IIHS, 37038.

____. "À Alexandra e Nathalie Beer (27 de julho de 1837)." In *BOC*. Amsterdam: IIHS, 37039.

____. "A Alexandre Bakunin (15 de dezembro de 1837)." In *BOC*. Amsterdam: IIHS, 37055.

____. "Às Irmãs (começo de março de 1838)." In *BOC*. Amsterdam: IIHS, 38014.

____. "À Varvara Bakunin (fim de março de 1839)." In *BOC*. Amsterdam: IIHS, 39008.

____. "À Alexandra e Tatiana Bakunin (13–14 de março de 1840)." In *BOC*. Amsterdam: IIHS, 40024.

____. "À Alexandra e Nathalie Beer (9 de setembro de 1840)." In *BOC*. Amsterdam: IIHS, 40057.

____. "A Alexandre Herzen (23 de outubro de 1840)." In *BOC*. Amsterdam: IIHS, 40061.

____. "A Tatiana Bakunin (13 de fevereiro de 1841)." In *BOC*. Amsterdam: IIHS, 41002.

____. "A Pavel e Varvara Bakunin (27 de outubro de 1841)." In *BOC*. Amsterdam: IIHS, 41009.

____. "A Família (3 de novembro de 1841)." In *BOC*. Amsterdam: IIHS, 41010.

____. "A Pavel e Varvara Bakunin (dezembro de 1841)." In *BOC*. Amsterdam: IIHS, 41016.

____. "A Alexandra e Tatiana Bakunin (fim de dezembro de 1841–3 de janeiro de 1842)." In *BOC*. Amsterdam: IIHS, 42001.

___. "A Alexandra Beer (janeiro de 1842)." In *BOC*. Amsterdam: IIHS, 42002.

___. "A Nikolai Bakunin (10 de fevereiro de 1842)." In *BOC*. Amsterdam: IIHS, 42005.

___. "À Varvara Bakunin (2ª quinzena de junho de 1842)." In *BOC*. Amsterdam: IIHS, 42010.

___. "À Tatiana Bakunin (verão de 1842)." In *BOC*. Amsterdam: IIHS, 42014.

___. "À Família (9 de outubro de 1842)." In *BOC*. Amsterdam: IIHS, 42016.

___. "A Pavel Bakunin (6 de novembro de 1842)." In *BOC*. Amsterdam: IIHS, 42019.

___. "A Pavel Bakunin e Ivan Turgueniev (20 de novembro de 1842)." In *BOC*. Amsterdam: IIHS, 42026.

___. "A Arnold Ruge (11 de março de 1843)." In *BOC*. Amsterdam: IIHS, 43010.

___. "A Pavel e Nikolai Bakunin e às Irmãs (abril de 1843)." In *BOC*. Amsterdam: IIHS, 43012.

___. "A Família (meio de maio de 1843)." In *BOC*. Amsterdam: IIHS, 43015.

___. "A Louise Vogt (9 de fevereiro de 1844)." In *BOC*. Amsterdam: IIHS, 44002.

___. "A Reinhold Solger (14 de outubro de 1844)." In *BOC*. Amsterdam: IIHS, 44004.

___. "A Pavel Bakunin (29 de março de 1845)." In *BOC*. Amsterdam: IIHS, 45001.

___. "As Irmãs e aos Irmãos (1 de maio de 1845)." In *BOC*. Amsterdam: IIHS, 45002.

___. "A Louise Vogt (5 de agosto de 1847)." In *BOC*. Amsterdam: IIHS, 47001.

___. "A Karl A. V. von Ense (12 de outubro de 1847)." In *BOC*. Amsterdam: IIHS, 47003.

___. "A Georg Herwegh (fim de dezembro de 1847)." In *BOC*. Amsterdam: IIHS, 47011.

___. "A Walery Wieloglowski (31 de dezembro de 1847)." In *BOC*. Amsterdam: IIHS, 47012.

___. "A George Sand (9 de julho de 1848)." In *BOC*. Amsterdam: IIHS, 48007.

___. "A Georg Herwegh (1ª quinzena de agosto de 1848)." In *BOC*. Amsterdam: IIHS, 48009.

___. "A Pierre-Joseph Proudhon (12 de dezembro de 1848)." In *BOC*. Amsterdam: IIHS, 48018.

___. "A Alexandre Herzen e Nikolai Ogarev (verão de 1858)." In *BOC*. Amsterdam: IIHS, 58004.

___. "A Alexandre Herzen (7–15 de novembro de 1860)." In *BOC*. Amsterdam: IIHS, 60005.

___. "A Alexandre Herzen (8 de dezembro de 1860)." In *BOC*. Amsterdam: IIHS, 60006.

___. "A Mikhail S. Korsakov (10 de setembro de 1861)." In *BOC*. Amsterdam: IIHS, 61006.

___. "A Anton Joann Frič (12 de maio de 1862)." In *BOC*. Amsterdam: IIHS, 62024.

___. "A Josef Václav Frič (12 de maio de 1862)." In *BOC*. Amsterdam: IIHS, 62025.

___. "A Natalia Semenovna Bakunina-Korsakova (16 de junho de 1862)." In *BOC*. Amsterdam: IIHS, 62043.

____. "A Alexandre Herzen (24 de março de 1863)." In *BOC*. Amsterdam: IIHS, 63025.

____. "A Alexandre Herzen e Nikolai Ogarev" (1 de agosto de 1863)." In *BOC*. Amsterdam: IIHS, 63037.

____. "A Pierre-Joseph Proudhon (11 de novembro de 1864)." In *BOC*. Amsterdam: IIHS, 64037.

____. "A Karl Marx (7 de fevereiro de 1865)." In *BOC*. Amsterdam: IIHS, 65004.

____. "A Alexandre Herzen e Nikolai Ogarev" (8 de outubro de 1865)." In *BOC*. Amsterdam: IIHS, 65017.

____. "A Nikolai Ogarev" (14 de junho de 1868)." In *BOC*. Amsterdam: IIHS, 68012.

____. "A Gustav Vogt" (31 de agosto de 1868)." In *BOC*. Amsterdam: IIHS, 68019.

____. "A Karl Marx" (22 de dezembro de 1868)." In *BOC*. Amsterdam: IIHS, 68034.

____. "Aos Membros da Fraternidade Internacional" (26 de janeiro de 1869)." In *BOC*. Amsterdam: IIHS, 69001.

____. "A James Guillaume" (13 de abril de 1869)." In *BOC*. Amsterdam: IIHS, 69018.

____. "A Alexandre Herzen" (26 de outubro de 1869)." In *BOC*. Amsterdam: IIHS, 69055.

____. "A Nikolai Ogarev" (16 de dezembro de 1869)." In *BOC*. Amsterdam: IIHS, 69064.

____. "A Nikolai Ogarev" (2 de agosto de 1870)." In *BOC*. Amsterdam: IIHS, 70075.

____. "A Nikolai Ogarev e Vladimir Ozerov" (5 de abril de 1871)." In *BOC*. Amsterdam: IIHS, 71003.

____. "A Nikolai Ogarev" (9 de abril de 1871)." In *BOC*. Amsterdam: IIHS, 71004.

____. "A Anselmo Lorenzo (7 de maio de 1872)." In *BOC*. Amsterdam: IIHS, 72013.

____. "A Tomás Gonzáles Morago (21 de maio de 1872)." In *BOC*. Amsterdam: IIHS, 72015.

____. "A Arnold Ruge (19 de janeiro de 1843)." In ANGAUT, Jean-Christophe. *Bakounine Jeune Hégélien: La Philosophie et Son Dehors*. Lyon: ENS, 2007.

____. *Revolução e Liberdade: Cartas de 1845 a 1875*. São Paulo: Hedra, 2010a.

____. "A Georg Herwegh (primeira quinzena de agosto de 1848)." In *Revolução e Liberdade: Cartas de 1845 a 1875*. São Paulo: Hedra, 2010b.

____. "A Franz Otto (2 de novembro de 1849)." In *Revolução e Liberdade: Cartas de 1845 a 1875*. São Paulo: Hedra, 2010c.

____. "A Mathilde Reichel (16 de janeiro de 1850)." In *Revolução e Liberdade: Cartas de 1845 a 1875*. São Paulo: Hedra, 2010d.

____. "A Mathilde Reichel (16 de fevereiro de 1850)." In *Revolução e Liberdade: Cartas de 1845 a 1875*. São Paulo: Hedra, 2010e.

____. "Aos Irmãos e Irmãs (fevereiro de 1854)." In *Revolução e Liberdade: Cartas de 1845 a 1875*. São Paulo: Hedra, 2010f.

____. "A Alexandre Herzen (15 de outubro de 1861)." In *Revolução e Liberdade: Cartas de 1845 a 1875*. São Paulo: Hedra, 2010g.

___. "Aos Redatores do Boletim da Federação do Jura" (12 de outubro de 1873)." In *Revolução e Liberdade: Cartas de 1845 a 1875*. São Paulo: Hedra, 2010h.

___. "A Anselmo Lorenzo (10 de maio de 1872)." In *Escritos Contra Marx*. São Paulo: Imaginário, 2014a.

___. "Aos Irmãos da Aliança na Espanha (12–13 de junho de 1872)." In *Escritos Contra Marx*. São Paulo: Imaginário, 2014b.

___. "A Jules Barni (3 de janeiro de 1868)." In *Obras Escolhidas*. São Paulo: Hedra, 2015a.

___. "A Alexandre II (14 de fevereiro de 1857)." In BRUPBACHER, Fritz. *Bakunin, o Satã da Revolta*. São Paulo: Intermezzo/Imaginário, 2015b.

___. "A Tomás Gonzáles Morago (21 de maio de 1872)." In *Obras Seletas 1*. São Paulo: Intermezzo, 2016a.

___. "A Élisée Reclus (15 de fevereiro de 1875)." In *Obras Seletas 1*. São Paulo: Intermezzo, 2016b.

___. "A Serguei Netchaiev (2 de junho de 1870)." In AVRICH, Paul. *Bakunin & Netchaiev*. Aparecida de Goiânia: Escultura, 2017a.

___. "A Albert Richard (12 de março de 1870)." In *Obras Seletas 2*. São Paulo: Intermezzo, 2017b.

___. "A Albert Richard (1 de abril de 1870)." In *Obras Seletas 2*. São Paulo: Intermezzo, 2017c.

BAKUNIN'S OTHER WORK
BAKUNIN, Mikhail. [1837] "Resumo da *Enzyclopädie der philosophischen Wissenschaften im Grundrisse* de Hegel." In *BOC*. Amsterdam: IIHS, 37001.

___. [1871] "Histoire de Ma Vie: Première Partie – 1815–1840." In *BOC*. Amsterdam: IIHS, 71030.

STUDIES ON BAKUNIN
ABRUNHOSA, Rafael. *Fundamentos Político-Pedagógicos a Partir do Pensamento de Mikhail Bakunin*. Fortaleza: Universidade Federal do Ceará (Master's thesis), 2015.

ANGAUT, Jean-Christophe. *Liberté et Histoire chez Michel Bakounine*. 2 vols. Nancy: Université Nancy 2 (PhD dissertation), 2005.

___. *Bakounine Jeune Hégélien: La Philosophie et son Dehors*. Lyon: ENS, 2007a.

___. "The Marx-Bakunin Conflict at the International: A Clash of Political Practices." In *Actuel Marx*, 41. Paris: PUF, 2007b.

___. *La Liberté des Peuples: Bakounine et les Révolutions de 1848*. Lyon: Atelier de Création Libertaire, 2009.

___. "Bakounine et le Cercle de Stankevitch." In Atelier de Création Libertaire, 2010a.

___. "Bakounine à Lyon: chronologie des événements." In Atelier de Création Libertaire, 2010b.

___. "Le Statut de la Philosophie chez le Dernier Bakounine." In Atelier de Création Libertaire, 2011.

___. "Amour et Mariage chez Bakounine." In Atelier de Création Libertaire, 2017.

ARVON, Henri. *Bakunine: ou a vida contra a ciência*. Lisboa: Estúdios Cor, 1971.

___. *Bakounine: Absolu et Révolution*. Paris: Cerf, 1972.

___. "Bakounine et la Gauche Hegelienne." In CATTEAU, Jacques (ed.). *Bakounine: Combats & Debats*. Paris: Institut d'Estudes Slaves, 1979.

AUGUSTO, Acácio. "Revolta e Antipolítica em Bakunin." In *Verve*, num. 26, 2014.

AVRICH, Paul. "The Legacy of Bakunin." In *The Russian Review*, vol. 29, num. 2, 1970.

___. *Bakunin & Nechaev*. London: Freedom Press, 1974. Revised in 1987.

BARRUÉ, Jean. "Introdução." In BARRUÉ, Jean; BAKUNIN, Mikhail; NETCHAIEV, Serguei. *O Anarquismo Hoje / A Reacção na Alemanha / O Catecismo Revolucionário*. Lisboa: Assírio & Alvim, 1976.

___. "Bakunin e a Educação." In BAKUNIN, Mikhail. *Instrução Integral*. São Paulo: Imaginário, 2003.

___. "Caderno de Notas." In BRUPBACHER, Fritz. *Bakunin, o satã da revolta*. São Paulo: Intermezzo/Imaginário, 2015a.

___. "Bakunin e os 'Anais Franco-Alemães' (1843)." In BRUPBACHER, Fritz. *Bakunin, o satã da revolta*. São Paulo: Intermezzo/Imaginário, 2015b.

___. "Bakunin Pan-Eslavista?" In BRUPBACHER, Fritz. *Bakunin, o satã da revolta*. São Paulo: Intermezzo/Imaginário, 2015c.

___. "Bakunin e Netchaiev." In BRUPBACHER, Fritz. *Bakunin, o satã da revolta*. São Paulo: Intermezzo/Imaginário, 2015d.

BEKKEN, Jon. "Bakunin and the Historians." In *Libertarian Labor Review*, num. 13, 1992.

___. "Bakunin and the Historians Revisited." In *Anarcho-Syndicalist Review*, num. 63, 2015.

BERLIN, Isaiah. "Herzen and Bakunin on Individual Liberty." In *Russian Thinkers*. London: Penguin, 1978.

BERTHIER, René. *Bakounine Politique: Révolution et Contre Révolution en Europe Centrale*. Paris: Éditions du Monde Libertaire, 1991.

___. "Bakounine, L'État et l'Église." In *Réfractions*, num. 7, 2001.

___. *L'Autre Bakounine*. 3 vols. Monde Nouveau, 2010.

___. "Bakounine et les 'Sociétés Secrètes.'" Monde Nouveau, 2011a.

___. *Do Federalismo*. São Paulo: Imaginário, 2011b.

___. "Action et Organisation." Monde Nouveau, 2011c.

____. "Elementos de uma Análise Bakuniniana da Burocracia." In: BERTHIER, René; VILAIN; Éric. *Marxismo e Anarquismo*. São Paulo: Imaginário, 2011d.

____. (signed as Éric Vilain) "Bakunin Fazia Política?" In: BERTHIER, René; VILAIN; Éric. *Marxismo e Anarquismo*. São Paulo: Imaginário, 2011e.

____. "Bakounine: Une Théorie de l'Organisation." *Monde Nouveau*, 2012.

____. "O Emprego do Termo 'Anarquia' em Bakunin." In: *Revista da Biblioteca Terra Livre*, year I, num. 1, 2014a.

____. "Teoria Política e Método de Análise no Pensamento de Bakunin: entrevista a Felipe Corrêa." Instituto de Teoria e História Anarquista, 2014b.

____. "Postface." In ANTONIOLI, Maurizio. *Bakounine: Entre Syndicalisme Révolutionnaire et Anarchisme*. Paris: Noir et Rouge, 2014c.

____. "Atualidade de Bakunin." In BAKUNIN, Mikhail. *Obras Escolhidas*. São Paulo: Hedra, 2015a.

BONOMO, Alex B. "Introdução." In: BAKUNIN, Mikhail. *Deus e o Estado*. São Paulo: Hedra, 2011.

____. *Introdução ao Pensamento Político de Bakunin*. São Paulo: Ascaso, 2017.

BRITO, Luciana. "Da Reconciliação com a Realidade à Instrução Integral: contribuições filosóficas de Mikhail Bakunin às questões educacionais." In *Filogênese*, vol. 7, num. 1, 2014.

____. "Uma Polêmica com Silvio Gallo a Respeito de 'A Instrução Integral' de Mikhail Bakunin." In *Posição*, year I, vol. 1, num. 2, 2014.

BRUPBACHER, Fritz. *Marx y Bakunin: Uma contribuición a la historia de la Asociación Internacional de los Trabajadores*. Toulouse: Cenit, 1955.

____. *Bakunin, o satã da revolta* (with comments from Jean Barrué). São Paulo: Intermezzo/Imaginário, 2015.

CAFIERO, Carlo; RECLUS, Elisée. "Apresentação." In BAKUNIN, Mikhail. *Deus e o Estado*. São Paulo: Imaginário, 2000.

CAPPELLETTI, Angel. *Bakunin y el Socialismo Libertario*. Madri: Leega/Minerva, 1986.

____. *A Evolução do Pensamento Filosófico e Político de Bakunin*. GEAPI, 2014.

CARR, E. H. *Michael Bakunin*. New York: Vintage Russian Library, 1961.

CATTEAU, Jacques (ed.). *Bakounine: Combats & Débats*. Paris: Institut d'Estudes Slaves, 1979.

CIPKO, Serge. "Mikhail Bakunin and the National Question." In: *The Raven: Anarchist Quarterly*, vol. 3, num. 1, 1990.

CODELLO, Francesco. "Mikhail Bakunin: a educação como paixão e revolta." In: *"A Boa Educação": experiências libertárias e teorias anarquistas na Europa, de Godwin a Neill*. São Paulo: Imaginário, 2007.

COÊLHO, Plínio A. (ed.). *Bakunin*. São Paulo: Imaginário, 1994.

COLOMBO, Eduardo. "Introdução." In BAKUNIN, Mikhail. *O Princípio do Estado e Outros Ensaios*. São Paulo: Hedra, 2008.

CONFINO, Michael. *Violence dans la Violence: Le Débat Bakounine-Necaev*. Paris: Découverte, 1973.

COPOAG (Coletivo Pró-Organização Anarquista em Goiás). *Anarquismo Coletivista: o bakuninismo. Elementos de um Programa Anarquista*. Originally published in 2005, revised in São Paulo: Biblioteca Virtual Faísca, 2013.

CORRÊA, Felipe. "Introdução" / "Cronologia." In BAKUNIN, Mikhail. *Revolução e Liberdade: cartas de 1845 a 1875*. São Paulo: Hedra, 2010a.

___. "A Bibliografia de Mikhail Bakunin." In Anarkismo.net, 2010b.

___. "Bakunin Ontem e Hoje: entrevista à editora Hedra." Hedra, 2010c.

___. "Mikhail Bakunin e o Anarquismo." In CABRAL, Alexandre et al (eds.). *Filosofia: um panorama histórico-temático*. Rio de Janeiro, Mauad X, 2013.

___. "Federalismo, Socialismo e Antiteologismo de Bakunin." In Instituto de Teoria e História Anarquista, 2014b.

___. *Teoria Bakuniniana do Estado*. São Paulo: Intermezzo/Imaginário, 2014c.

___. "A Lógica do Estado em Bakunin." In MATEUS, João G.; ATAÍDES, Marcos (eds.). *A Destruição do Leviatã: críticas anarquistas ao Estado*. São Paulo: Faísca, 2014e.

___. "Social Classes and Bureaucracy in Bakunin." In Instituto de Teoria e História Anarquista, 2016b.

___. "Contexto e Implicações da Relação Bakunin-Netchaiev." In AVRICH, Paul. *Bakunin & Netchaiev*. Aparecida de Goiânia: Escultura, 2017.

CORNÉLIUS, Gabriel. *O Bakuninismo: um estudo sobre o coletivismo*. Goiânia: UFG (monograph in History), 2008.

CRIADO, Demétrio. *Ética y Poder Político em Mijail Bakunin*. Bilbao: Universidad de Deusto, 1993.

CUTLER, Robert. "Bakunin and the Psychobiographers: The Anarchist as Mythical and Historical Object." Article based on a presentation held at IVth World Congress for Soviet and East European Studies, Harrogate, UK, 21–26 July, 1990.

___. "Introduction." In *The Basic Bakunin: Writings 1869–1871*. New York: Prometheus, 1992.

___. "Bakunin's Anti-Jacobinism: 'Secret Societies' for Self-emancipating Collectivist Social Revolution." In *Anarchist Studies*, vol. 22, num. 2, 2014.

DEL GIUDICE, Martine. *The Young Bakunin and Left Hegelianism: Origins of Russian Radicalism and Theory of Praxis (1814–1842)*. Montreal: McGill University (PhD dissertation), 1981.

___. "Bakunin's 'Preface to Hegel's *Gymnasium Lectures*': The Problem of Alienation and the Reconciliation with Reality." In *Canadian-American Slavic Studies*, vol. 16, num. 2, 1982.

DOLGOFF, Sam. "Palabras Previas." In: BAKUNIN, Mikhail. *Obras Completas. Tomo 1*. Madrid: La Piqueta, 1977a.

___. "Prefacio." In BAKUNIN, Mikhail. *Obras Completas. Tomo 2*. Madrid: La Piqueta, 1977b.

___. "Prefacio." In BAKUNIN, Mikhail. *Obras Completas. Tomo 3*. Madrid: La Piqueta, 1979a.

___. "Prefacio." In BAKUNIN, Mikhail. *Obras Completas. Tomo 4*. Madrid: La Piqueta, 1979b.

___. "Prefacio." In BAKUNIN, Mikhail. *Obras Completas. Tomo 5*. Madrid: La Piqueta, 1986.

DRAGOMANOV Mikhail (ed.). *Michail Bakunins sozial-politischer Briefwechsel mit Alexander Iw. Herzen und Ogariow*. Stuttgart: Cotta, 1895.

___. "Preface." In BAKUNIN, Mikhail. *Correspondance de Michel Bakounine: Lettres à A. Herzen et à A. Ogareff*. Paris: Librairie Académique Didier, 1896.

DUNOIS, Amédée. "Mikhail Bakunin." In BAKUNIN, Mikhail. *Obras Seletas*, vol. 1. São Paulo: Intermezzo, 2016.

ECKHARDT, Wolfgang. "Rezension. Madeleine Grawitz: Bakunin." In *Internationale wissenschaftliche Korrespondenz zur Geschichte der deutschen Arbeiterbewegung (IWK)*, Notebook 1. Berlin, 2000.

___. *The First Socialist Schism: Bakunin vs. Marx in the International Working Men's Association*. Oakland: PM Press, 2016.

FERREIRA, Andrey C. "Trabalho e Ação: o debate entre Bakunin e Marx e sua contribuição para uma sociologia crítica contemporânea." In *Em Debate*, num. 4, 2010.

___. "Materialismo, Anarquismo e Revolução Social: o bakuninismo como filosofia e política do movimento operário e socialista." In XXVII Simpósio Nacional de História (ANPUH), Natal, 2013.

___. "Anarquismo, pensamento e práticas insurgentes: fenômeno da 'Primeira Internacional'?" In FERREIRA, Andrey C.; TONIATTI, Tadeu (eds.). *De Baixo para Cima e da Periferia para o Centro: textos políticos, filosóficos e de teoria sociológica de Mikhail Bakunin*. Niterói: Alternativa, 2014.

FERREIRA, Andrey C.; TONIATTI, Tadeu. *De Baixo para Cima e da Periferia para o Centro: textos políticos, filosóficos e de teoria sociológica de Mikhail Bakunin*. Niterói: Alternativa, 2014.

GORELIK, Anatol. "Bakunin e a Ditadura do Proletariado." In BAKUNIN, Mikhail. *Obras Escolhidas*. São Paulo: Hedra, 2015.

GRAWITZ, Madeleine. *Michel Bakounine*. Paris: Plon, 1990.

GUILLAUME, James. "Notice Biographique." In BAKUNIN, Mikhail. Œuvres. Tome II. Paris: Stock, 1907a.

____. "Avant-propos: L'Empire Knouto-Germanique et la Révolution sociale." In BAKUNIN, Mikhail. Œuvres. Tome II. Paris: Stock, 1907b.

____. "Avant-propos: Articles pour le journal L'Égalité." In BAKUNIN, Mikhail. Œuvres. Tome V. Paris: Stock, 1911.

____. "Avant-propos: Protestation de Alliance." In BAKUNIN, Mikhail. Œuvres. Tome VI. Paris: Stock, 1913.

____. "Mikhail Bakunin." In BAKUNIN, Mikhail. Táticas Revolucionárias. Teresina/Parnaíba: GEAPI, 2015.

____. "Introdução de 'Os Ursos de Berna e o Urso de São Petersburgo.'" In Obras Seletas 2. São Paulo: Intermezzo, 2017.

HEPNER, Benoît-P. Bakounine et le Panslavisme Révolutionnaire. Paris: Rivière, 1950.

ISWOLSKY, Hélène. La Vie de Bakounine. Paris: Gallimard, 1930.

JOYEUX, Maurice. "Bakunin na França." In BAKUNIN, Mikhail. Obras Escolhidas. São Paulo: Hedra, 2015.

KAMINSKI, Hanns-Erich. Michel Bakounine: La Vie d'un Révolutionnaire. Paris: Montaigne, 1938.

KELLY, Aileen. Mikhail Bakunin: A Study in the Psychology and Politics of Utopianism. New York: Oxford University Press, 1982.

KLOOSTERMAN, Jaap. "Les Papiers de Michel Bakounine à Amsterdam." IIHS, 1985/2004.

LEHNING, Arthur. From Buonarroti to Bakunin: Studies in International Socialism. Leiden: Brill, 1970.

____. "Introduction." In BAKUNIN, Mikhail. Œuvres Complètes, vol. I: Michel Bakounine et L'Italie 1871–1872, première partie. Paris: Champ Libre, 1973.

____. "Introduction." In: BAKUNIN, Mikhail. Œuvres Complètes, vol. II: Michel Bakounine et L'Italie 1871–1872, deuxième partie. Paris: Champ Libre, 1974a.

____. "Bakunin's Conceptions of Revolutionary Organizations and Their Role: A Study of His 'Secret Societies.'" In ABRAMSKY, Chimen (ed.). Essays in Honour of E. H. Carr. London: Macmillan, 1974b.

____. "Introduction." In BAKUNIN, Mikhail. Œuvres Complètes, vol. III: Michel Bakounine et les Conflits dans L'Internationale 1872. Paris: Champ Libre, 1975.

____. "Introduction." In BAKUNIN, Mikhail. Œuvres Complètes, vol. IV: Étatisme et Anarchie 1873. Paris: Champ Libre, 1976.

____. "Introduction." In BAKUNIN, Mikhail. Œuvres Complètes, vol. V: Michel Bakounine et Ses Relations avec Sergej Necaev 1870–1872. Paris: Champ Libre, 1977.

___. "Introduction." In BAKUNIN, Mikhail. *Œuvres Complètes*, vol. VI: Michel Bakounine et Ses Relations Slaves 1870–1875. Paris: Champ Libre, 1978.

___. "Michel Bakounine et les Historiens: Un Aperçu Historiographique." In CATTEAU, Jacques (ed.). *Bakounine: Combats & Débats*. Paris: Institut d'Estudes Slaves, 1979a.

___. "Introduction." In BAKUNIN, Mikhail. *Œuvres Complètes*, vol. VII: Michel Bakounine sur la Guerre Franco-Allemande et la Révolution Sociale en France 1870–1871. Paris: Champ Libre, 1979b.

___. "Introduction." In: BAKUNIN, Mikhail. *Œuvres Complètes*, vol. VIII: Michel Bakounine, L'Empire Knouto-Germanique et la Révolution Sociale 1870–1871. Paris: Champ Libre, 1982.

___. *Bakounine et les Autres*. Paris: UGE, 1976. Reissued as *Conversaciones con Bakunin*. Barcelona: Anagrama, 1999.

___. *Bakunin for Anti-Imperialists*. [Originally *Spheres of Influence in the Age of Imperialism*, 1972]. Fordsburg, South Africa: Zabalaza Books, 2017.

LEIER, Mark. *Bakunin: The Creative Passion*. New York: St. Martin's Press, 2006.

LEVAL, Gaston. *La Pensée Constructive de Bakounine*. Paris: Spartacus, 1976.

___. "Bakunin e o Estado Marxista." In *Os Anarquistas Julgam Marx*. São Paulo: Imaginário, 2001.

___. *Bakunin, Fundador do Sindicalismo Revolucionário*. São Paulo: Imaginário/Faísca, 2007.

___. *A Pedagogia de Bakunin*. GEAPI, 2014.

LIARTE, Ramón. *Bakunin: la emancipación del pueblo*. Barcelona: Salud, 1995.

LUTA LIBERTÁRIA. "Biografia: Quem foi Bakunin" and "Discussão: Bakunin, seu tempo e suas ideias." In BAKUNIN, Mikhail. *Socialismo e Liberdade*. São Paulo: Luta Libertária, 2002.

MARQUES-ALVARES, Carlos. "Bakunin in Spain: The Alliance and the Ideological Diffusion That Wasn't." In *Anarcho-Syndicalist Review*, num. 63, 2015.

MARTINS, Angela. "A Pedagogia Libertária e a Educação Integral." Presented at VIII Seminário Nacional de Estudos e Pesquisas: História, Sociedade e Educação no Brasil. Campinas, UNICAMP, 2009.

MATEUS, João G. "O Conceito de 'Liberdade' em Mikhail Bakunin." In: *Espaço Livre*, vol. 6, num. 11, 2011.

MATEUS, João G.; SOUSA, Wanderson; SADDI, Rafael. "Educação Libertária: Instrução Integral em Mikhail Bakunin." In *Revista Enfrentamento*, year IV, num. 7, 2009.

MCLAUGHLIN, Paul. *Mikhail Bakunin: The Philosophical Basis of His Anarchism*. New York: Algora, 2002.

MENDEL, Arthur P. *Michael Bakunin: Roots of Apocalypse*. New York: Praeger, 1981.

MERVAUD, Michel. "La 'Societé Internationale Secrète de l'Émancipation de l'Humanité' (Bakunin et Sohlman)." In CATTEAU, Jacques (ed.). *Bakounine: Combats & Débats*. Paris: Institut d'Études Slaves, 1979.

MONTEIRO, Fabrício. "A Construção da 'Teoria' Social como Construção de Relações Sociais: o materialismo histórico de Mikhail Bakunin." In *História e Perspectivas*, num. 48, 2013.

MORAES, José D. "Mikhail Bakunin e a Educação na AIT: notas sobre a instrução integral." In Academia.edu, no date.

MORRIS, Brian. *Bakunin: The Philosophy of Freedom*. Montreal: Black Rose Books, 1993.

NASCIMENTO, Fabiana. *Bakunin e a Educação*. Belo Horizonte: PUC Minas (monograph in Philosophy), 2005.

NASCIMENTO, Jonathan. *Bakunin e a Gênese Histórica da Ideia de Divindade na Consciência dos Homens*. São Paulo: Universidade São Judas (monograph in Philosophy), 2014.

NETTLAU, Max. "Introduction." In BAKUNIN, Mikhail. *Œuvres. Tome I*. Paris: Stock, 1895.

___. *Michael Bakunin, eine Biographie*. London, 1896–1900.

___. "Michael Bakunin: A Biographical Sketch." In MAXIMOFF, G. P. *The Political Philosophy of Bakunin: Scientific Anarchism*. New York and London: Free Press, 1964.

___. "Notas a la *Confesión al Zar Nicolas I*." Barcelona: Labor, 1976.

___. *Miguel Bakunin, la Internacional y la Alianza en España (1868–1873)*. Madrid: La Piqueta, 1977a.

___. "Prólogo." In BAKUNIN, Mikhail. *Obras Completas. Tomo 1*. Madrid: La Piqueta, 1977b.

___. "Prólogo." In BAKUNIN, Mikhail. *Obras Completas. Tomo 2*. Madrid: La Piqueta, 1977c.

___. "Prólogo." In BAKUNIN, Mikhail. *Obras Completas. Tomo 3*. Madrid: La Piqueta, 1979a.

___. "Prólogo." In BAKUNIN, Mikhail. *Obras Completas. Tomo 4*. Madrid: La Piqueta, 1979b.

___. "Prólogo." In BAKUNIN, Mikhail. *Obras Completas. Tomo 5*. Madrid: La Piqueta, 1986.

NOMAD, Max. *Apostles of Revolution*. New York: Collier, 1933.

NORTE, Sérgio. *Bakunin: sangue, suor e barricadas*. Campinas: Papirus, 1988.

___. "Bakunin versus Marx: conflito de titãs na Associação Internacional dos Trabalhadores (AIT)." In BAKUNIN, Mikhail. *Escritos Contra Marx*. São Paulo: Imaginário, 2001.

OLIVEIRA, Ivan. "A Filosofia Política de Bakunin e a Pedagogia Libertária: reflexões acerca da educação integral e da Escola Moderna de Barcelona." In: *Filogênese*, vol. 7, num. 2, 2014.

PÉCHOUX, Pierre. "Écrits et Correspondence de Bakounine: Bilan des Publications." In CATTEAU, Jacques (ed.). *Bakounine: Combats & Débats.* Paris: Institut d'Études Slaves, 1979.

PELLETIER, Philippe (ed.) *Actualité de Bakounine, 1814–2014.* Paris: Monde Libertaire, 2014.

PINO, Ramon. "Mikhail Alexandrovitch Bakunin." In *Libertários 1.* São Paulo: Imaginário, 2002.

PIRUMOVA, Natalia. *Бакунин* [Bakunin]. Moscou: Molodaja Gvardija, 1970.

___. *Социальная доктрина М. А. Бакунина* [The Social Doctrine of M. A. Bakunin]. Moscow: Nauka, 1990.

POMPER, Philip. "Bakunin, Nechaev and the 'Catechism of a Revolutionary': The Case for Joint Authorship." In *Canadian-American Slavic Studies*, vol. 10, num. 4, 1976.

PYZIUR, Eugene. *The Doctrine of Anarchism of Michael A. Bakunin.* Chicago: Gateway, 1968.

RAVINDRANATHAN, T. R. *Bakunin and the Italians.* Montreal and Kingston: McGill-Queen's University Press, 1988.

RAYNAUD, Jean-Marc. "Mikhail Bakunin e a Educação Libertária." In BAKUNIN, Mikhail. *Instrução Integral.* São Paulo: Imaginário, 2003.

RESENDE, Paulo-Edgar. "Apresentação: A Luta entre as Duas Tendências na Associação Internacional dos Trabalhadores." In BAKUNIN, Mikhail. *Estatismo e Anarquia.* São Paulo: Imaginário, 2003.

RIBEIL, Georges (ed.) *Marx / Bakunin: socialismo autoritario, socialismo libertario.* Barcelona: Madrágora, 1978.

RIVAS, Gabriel. "Introducción: La Organización Política en el Pensamiento Bakuniniano – presentación a la Carta a Netchayev, 2 de junio de 1870." In BAKUNIN, Mikhail. *Carta a Nechayev.* Santiago: Pensamiento y Batalla, 2014.

SALTMAN, Richard B. *The Social and Political Thought of Michael Bakunin.* Westport/London: Greenwood, 1983.

SAMIS, Alexandre. "Bakunin, Ciência e Revolução." In BAKUNIN, Mikhail. *Obras Escolhidas.* São Paulo: Hedra, 2015a.

SHATZ, Marshall. "Mikhail Bakunin and His Biographers: The Question of Bakunin's Sexual Impotence." In MENDELSOHN, Ezra; SHATZ, Marshall. *Imperial Russia (1700–1917).* DeKalb: Northern Illinois University Press, 1988.

___. "Bakunin, Turgenev and Rudin." In OFFORD, Derek (ed.) *The Golden Age of Russian Literature and Thought.* New York: St. Martin's Press, 1992.

___. "Mikhail Bakunin and the Priamukhino Circle: Love and Liberation in the Russian Intelligentsia of the 1830s." In *Canadian-American Slavic Studies*, num. 33, 1999.

SILVA, Pablo Abufom. *Reconciliación y Revolución: la juventud hegeliana de Mijaíl Bakunin*. Santiago: Universidad ARCIS, 2010.

SILVA, Selmo N. "A Anarquia Social: resistência, insurgência e revolução social na teoria de Bakunin." In *Em Debate*, num. 11, 2014.

___. "O Bakuninismo: ideologia, teoria, estratégia e programa revolucionário anarquista." In MORAES, Wallace; JOURDAN, Camilla (eds.). *Teoria Política Anarquista e Libertária*. São Paulo: Via Verita, 2016.

STEKLOV, Yuri. Михаил Александрович Бакунин. Его жизнь и деятельность [*Mikhail Aleksandrovitch Bakunin: His Life and His Work*]. 4 vols. Moscow and Leningrad: Gosizdat, 1926–1927.

TRAGTENBERG, Maurício. "Introdução." In BAKUNIN, Mikhail. *Federalismo, Socialismo e Antiteologismo*. São Paulo: Cortez, 1988a.

___. "Introdução." In BAKUNIN, Mikhail. *Deus e o Estado*. São Paulo: Cortez, 1988b.

UNIPA (União Popular Anarquista). "A Alma e o Corpo: o bakuninismo e a organização anarquista," 2003. In *Série Documentos, Política e Teoria*, vol. 1.

___. *Revista Via Combativa*, num. 1. *O bakuninismo e a teoria da revolução social*, 2009.

VENCIA, Alexis. "Bakunin e a Ação Revolucionária na Rússia." In BAKUNIN, Mikhail. *Obras Seletas*, vol. 1. São Paulo: Intermezzo, 2016.

VUILLEUMIER, Marc. "Bakounine et le Mouvement Ouvrier de Son Temps." In CATTEAU, Jacques (ed.). *Bakounine: Combats & Débats*. Paris: Institut d'Études Slaves, 1979.

COMPLEMENTARY BIBLIOGRAPHY

AIT [Associação Internacional dos Trabalhadores]. "Inaugural Address" (written by Karl Marx). In Marxist Internet Archive, 1864a.

___. "Provisional / General Rules" (written by Karl Marx). In Marxist Internet Archive, 1864b.

___. "The Hague Congress: Resolutions." In Marxist Internet Archive, 1872.

ANDERSON, Benedict. *Comunidades Imaginadas*. São Paulo: Companhia das Letras, 2013.

___. *Sob Três Bandeiras: anarquismo e imaginação anticolonial*. Campinas and Fortaleza: UNICAMP and UECE, 2014.

ARANTES, Paulo E. "Hegel: Vida e Obra." In: G. W. F. HEGEL, *Os Pensadores*. São Paulo: Nova Cultural, 1999.

BALL, Terence. "Aonde Vai a Teoria Política?" In *Revista de Sociologia e Política*, num. 23, 2004.

BECKER, Jean-Philippe. *L'Association Internationale des Travailleurs et la Grève Genevoise en Mars-Avril 1868*. Geneva: J.-C. Ducommun and G. Oettinger, 1868.

BEER, Max. *História do Socialismo e das Lutas Sociais*. São Paulo: Expressão Popular, 2006.

BERLIN, Isaiah. *Russian Thinkers*. London: Penguin, 1978.

BERTHIER, René. *Essai sur les Foundements Théoriques de l'Anarchisme*. Monde Nouveau, 2008.

___. "Estado, Direito e Legitimidade." In KROPOTKIN, Piotr et al. *Justiça e Direito: uma abordagem libertária*. São Paulo: Imaginário, 2011f.

___. "Introdução a *Escrito Contra Marx*." In BAKUNIN, Mikhail. *Obras Escolhidas*. São Paulo: Hedra, 2015b.

___. *Social-Democracy & Anarchism in the International Workers' Association (1864–1877)*. London: Anarres, 2015c.

BERTHIER, René; VILAIN; Éric. *Marxismo e Anarquismo*. São Paulo: Imaginário, 2011.

BEVINGTON, Douglas; DIXON, Chris. "Movement-Relevant Theory: Rethinking Social Movement Scholarship and Activism." In *Social Movements Studies*, vol. 4, num. 3, 2005.

BRANDÃO, Gildo. "A Teoria Política é Possível." In *Revista Brasileira de Ciências Sociais*, vol. 13, num. 36, 1998.

BURKE, Peter. *História e Teoria Social*. São Paulo: UNESP, 2011.

CASAS, Juan Gómez. *Historia del Anarcosindicalismo Español*. Madrid: La Malatesta, 2006.

COLE, G.D.H. *Historia del Pensamiento Socialista*, vol. II (Marxismo y Anarquismo 18501890). Mexico City: Fondo de Cultura Económica, 1975.

COMTE, Auguste. "Discurso sobre o Espírito Positivo." In *Comte: os pensadores*. São Paulo: Abril Cultural, 1978a.

___. "Curso de Filosofia Positiva." In *Comte: os pensadores*. São Paulo: Abril Cultural, 1978b.

CORRÊA, Felipe. *Rediscutindo o Anarquismo: uma abordagem teórica*. São Paulo: Universidade de São Paulo (Master's thesis), 2012.

___. "Entrevista com o professor e militante anarquista Felipe Corrêa. Entrevistadora: Eloísa B. de Andrade." In *Kínesis*, vol. VI, num. 12, 2014a.

___. *Bandeira Negra: rediscutindo o anarquismo*. Curitiba: Prismas, 2015.

___. "Debate: Marx Antiestatista?" In Instituto de Teoria e História Anarquista, 2016a.

CORRÊA, Felipe; SILVA, Rafael V. "Anarquismo, Teoria e História." In CORRÊA, Felipe; SILVA, Rafael V.; SILVA, Alessandro S. da (eds.). *Teoria e História do Anarquismo*. Curitiba: Prismas, 2014.

DAHRENDORF, Ralf. "Ciência Social e Juízos de Valor." In *Sociedade e Liberdade*. Brasília: UNB, 1981.

DEFOORT, Hendrik. "Charleroi Confrontation Between Miners and the Military." In SCHLAGER, Neil (ed.). *St. James Encyclopedia of Labor History Worldwide*. 2 vols. Farmington Hills: The Gale Group, 2004.

DEMO, Pedro. *Metodologia Científica em Ciências Sociais*. São Paulo: Atlas, 2011.

DOLLEANS, Edouard. *História del Movimiento Obrero*. 3 vols. Madrid: Zero, 1969.

DRAPER, Hal. *Karl Marx's Theory of Revolution*, vol. 3: The Dictatorship of the Proletariat. London: Macmillan, 1978.

___. *Karl Marx's Theory of Revolution*, vol. 4: Critique of Other Socialisms. New York: Monthly Review, 1990.

DROZ, Jacques. *História Geral do Socialismo*. 9 vols. Lisboa: Horizonte, 1976.

DRYZEK, John; HONIG, Bonnie; PHILLIPS, Anne. "Introduction." In *The Oxford Handbook of Political Theory*. Oxford University Press, 2006.

DUCLOS, Jacques. *La Première Internationale*. Paris: Éditions Sociales, 1964.

ENCKELL, Marianne. *La Fédération Jurassienne: les origines de l'anarchisme en Suisse*. Saint-Imier: Canevas, 1991.

ENGELS, Friedrich. *Los Bakuninistas en Acción*. Barcelona: Debarris, 1998.

___. "Democratic Pan-Slavism." In *Marx & Engels. Collected Works*, vol. 8: Marx & Engels, 1848–1849. London: Lawrence & Wishart, 2010.

FERREIRA, Andrey C. "Luta de Classes e Insurgências no Brasil: o mito da classe média, a aristocracia operária e o proletariado marginal no capitalismo flexível." In *Pensamento e Práticas Insurgentes: anarquismo e autonomias nos levantes e resistências do capitalismo no século XXI*. Niterói: Alternativa, 2016.

FEUERBACH, Ludwig. *Tesis Provisionales para la Reforma de la Filosofía*. Barcelona: Labor, 1976.

___. *A Essência do Cristianismo*. Petrópolis: Vozes, 2007.

___. "Necessidade de uma Reforma da Filosofia." In Lusosofia Press, 2008.

FICHTE, Johann G. "Conferências sobre a Vocação do Sábio." In Lusosofia Press, no date.

FRAZER, Michael. "Three Methods of Political Theory: Historicism, Ahistoricism and Transhistoricism." Annual meeting. Ottawa: Canadian Political Science Association, 2010.

FREYMOND, Jacques. "Étude sur la formation de la Première Internationale." In *Revue d'Histoire Suisse*, vol. 30, 1950.

FRIBOURG, Ernest E. *L'Association Internationale des Travailleurs*. Paris: A. le Chevalier, 1871.

GARCIA, Victor. *La Internacional Obrera.* Barcelona: Jucar, 1978.

GRAHAM, Robert. *We Do Not Fear Anarchy, We Invoke It: The First International and the Origins of the Anarchist Movement.* Oakland: AK Press, 2015.

GUÉRIN, Daniel. *O Anarquismo: da doutrina à ação.* Rio de Janeiro: Germinal, 1968.

GUILLAUME, James. *L'Internationale: Documents et Souvenirs.* 4 vols. Paris: Gérard Lebovici, 1985.

____. *A Internacional: documentos e recordações,* vol. I. São Paulo: Imaginário/Faísca, 2009a.

____. "A Internacional dos Trabalhadores: de sua fundação até o Congresso da Basiléia." In Anarkismo.net, 2009b.

HEGEL, G.W.F. *Escritos Pedagógicos.* Librodot, no date.

____. "Lectures on the History of Philosophy." In Marxist Internet Archive, 1805/1806.

____. *Ciencia de la Lógica.* Buenos Aires: Solar, 1982.

____. *Fenomenologia do Espírito.* Parte I. Petrópolis: Vozes, 1992.

____. *A Razão na História: uma introdução geral à filosofia da história.* São Paulo: Centauro, 2001.

HERZEN, Alexander. *My Past and Thoughts.* Los Angeles: University of California Press, 1982.

____. "St. George's Day!" In PARTHÉ, Kathleen (ed.). *A Herzen Reader.* Evanston: Northwestern University Press, 2012.

HOBSBAWM, Eric. *Revolucionários: ensaios contemporâneos.* São Paulo: Paz e Terra, 2003.

____. *A Era do Capital (1848-1875).* São Paulo: Paz e Terra, 2004a.

____. *A Era das Revoluções (1789-1848).* São Paulo: Paz e Terra, 2004b.

INWOOD, Michael. *Dicionário Hegel.* Rio de Janeiro: Zahar, 1992.

KOLPINSKY, N. Y. "Epílogo." In MARX, Karl; ENGELS, Friedrich; LENIN, Vladimir. *Acerca del Anarquismo y el Anarcosindicalismo.* Moscow: Progresso, 1976.

LAFARGUE Paul; ENGELS, Friedrich; MARX, Karl. "La Alianza de la Democracia Socialista y la Asociación Internacional de Trabajadores: informes y documientos publicados por orden del Congreso Internacional de La Haya." In RIBEILL, Georges (ed.). *Marx/Bakunin: socialismo autoritário, socialismo libertario.* Barcelona: Madrágora, 1978.

LIST, Christian; VALENTINI, Laura. "The Metodology of Political Theory." In *The Oxford Handbook of Philosophical Methodology.* Oxford University Press, 2016.

MALON, Benoit. *A Internacional: sua história e seus princípios.* São Paulo: Imaginário, 2014.

MARCUSE, Herbert. *Razão e Revolução: Hegel e o advento da teoria social*. Rio de Janeiro: Saga, 1969.

MARX, Karl. "Teses sobre Feuerbach." In Marxist Internet Archive, 1845.

____. *O Capital: crítica da economia política*. São Paulo: Nova Cultural, 1985.

____. *Crítica da Filosofia do Direito de Hegel*. São Paulo: Boitempo, 2010.

____. "Resumo Crítico de *Estatismo e Anarquia*, de Mikhail Bakunin (1874)." In *Crítica do Programa de Gotha*. São Paulo: Boitempo, 2012.

MARX, Karl; ENGELS, Friedrich. "Prefácio à edição russa de 1882." In *Manifesto Comunista*. São Paulo: Instituto José Luis e Rosa Sundermann, 2003.

____. *Manifesto Comunista*. São Paulo: Boitempo, 2007.

____. *Marx & Engels. Collected Works*, vol. 21: Marx & Engels, 1867–70. London: Lawrence & Wishart, 2010a.

____. *Marx & Engels. Collected Works*, vol. 23: Marx & Engels, 1871–74. London: Lawrence & Wishart, 2010b.

____. *Marx & Engels. Collected Works*, vol. 42: letters 1864–68. London: Lawrence & Wishart, 2010c.

____. *Marx & Engels. Collected Works*, vol. 43: letters 1868–70. London: Lawrence & Wishart, 2010d.

____. *Marx & Engels. Collected Works*, vol. 44: letters 1870–73. London: Lawrence & Wishart, 2010e.

MARX, Karl; ENGELS, Friedrich; LENIN, Vladimir. *Acerca del Anarquismo y el Anarcosindicalismo*. Moscow: Progresso, 1976.

MAZZONI, Marcelo de M. *Como Surgiu o Anarquismo? A Associação Internacional dos Trabalhadores e sua expressão na Suíça* (monografia de conclusão de curso em Ciências Sociais), UNESP, 2015.

MEHRING, Franz. *Karl Marx: a história de sua vida*. São Paulo: Sundermann, 2014.

MÉSZÁROS, István. *Para Além do Capital: rumo a uma teoria da transição*. São Paulo: Boitempo, 2006.

MIZRAJI, Pablo (ed.). *Dossiê 100 Anos da Revolução Russa: anarquismo, revoluções russa e ucraniana*. In Instituto de Teoria e História Anarquista, 2017.

MOISSONNIER, Maurice. *La Première Internationale et la Commune à Lyon (1865–1871): spontanéisme, complots et "luttes réelles."* Paris: Éditions Sociales, 1972.

MORAES, Wallace dos S. "A Revolta dos Governados do Inverno-Primavera de 2013 no Brasil e Suas Interpretações." In FERREIRA, Andrey C. *Pensamento e Práticas Insurgentes: anarquismo e autonomias nos levantes e resistências do capitalismo no século XXI*. Niterói: Alternativa, 2016.

MUSTO, Marcelo. "Introdução." In *Trabalhadores, Uni-vos!: Antologia política da I Internacional*. São Paulo: Boitempo, 2014.

NETCHAIEV, Serguei. "O Catecismo Revolucionário." In BARRUÉ, Jean; BAKUNIN, Mikhail; NETCHAIEV, Serguei. *O Anarquismo Hoje / A Reacção na Alemanha / O Catecismo Revolucionário*. Lisboa: Assírio & Alvim, 1976.

NETTLAU, Max. *História da Anarquia*. 2 vols. São Paulo: Hedra, 2008.

NEWMAN, Saul. "Anarchism, Marxism and the Bonapartist State." In The Anarchist Library, 2012.

ORTELLADO, Pablo; JUDENSNAIDER, Elena; LIMA, Luciana; POMAR, Marcelo. *20 Centavos: a luta contra o aumento*. São Paulo: Veneta, 2013.

PERNICONE, Nunzio. *Italian Anarchism, 1864–1892*. Oakland: AK Press, 2009.

POCOCK, John G. A. "Theory in History: Problems of Context and Narrative." In *The Oxford Handbook of Political Theory*. Oxford University Press, 2006.

____. "Quentin Skinner: a história da política e a política da história." In *Topoi*, vol. 13, num. 25, 2012.

PORTAL, Roger. *Os Eslavos: povos e nações*. Lisboa and Rio de Janeiro: Cosmos, 1968.

PROUDHON, Pierre-Joseph. *General Idea of the Revolution in the 19th century*. New York: Haskell House, 1969.

____. *O que é a Propriedade*. São Paulo: Martins Fontes, 1988.

____. *Do Princípio Federativo*. São Paulo: Imaginário, 2001.

RANDOLPH, John. *The House in the Garden: The Bakunin Family and the Romance of Russian Idealism*. Ithaca and London: Cornell University Press, 2007.

ROCHA, Bruno L. et al. "'Ou se vota com os de cima ou se luta com os de baixo': presença e a (re)organização do anarquismo em tempos neoliberais no Brasil (1980–2013)." In SANTOS, Kauan W. SILVA, Rafael V. (eds.). *História do Anarquismo e do Sindicalismo de Intenção Revolucionária no Brasil*. Curitiba: Prismas, 2018.

ROSSELL, Thyde. "A Internacional na Itália." In BAKUNIN, Mikhail. *Obras Escolhidas*. São Paulo: Hedra, 2015.

SAFATLE, Vladimir. "Dialética Hegeliana, Dialética Marxista, Dialética Adorniana" (Postgraduate course). São Paulo: Departamento de Filosofia da Universidade de São Paulo, 2015.

SAMIS, Alexandre. "Pavilhão Negro sobre Pátria Oliva." In COLOMBO, Eduardo (ed.). *História do Movimento Operário Revolucionário*. São Paulo: Imaginário, 2004.

____. *Negras Tormentas: o federalismo e o internacionalismo na Comuna de Paris*. São Paulo: Hedra, 2011.

____. "A Associação Internacional dos Trabalhadores e a Conformação da Tradição Libertária." In CORRÊA, Felipe; SILVA, Rafael V.; SILVA, Alessandro S. da (eds.). *Teoria e História do Anarquismo*. Curitiba: Prismas, 2015b.

SANTOS, Kauan W. SILVA, Rafael V. (eds.). *História do Anarquismo e do Sindicalismo de Intenção Revolucionária no Brasil*. Curitiba: Prismas, 2018.

SEWELL JR., William. *Logics of History: Social Theory and Social Transformation*. Chicago and London: University of Chicago Press, 2005.

SILVA, Rafael V. *Elementos Inflamáveis: organizações e militância anarquista no Rio de Janeiro e em São Paulo, 1945-1964*. Curitiba: Prismas, 2017.

SILVA, Ricardo. "O Contextualismo Linguístico na História do Pensamento Político: Quentin Skinner e o Debate Metodológico Contemporâneo." In *Dados*, vol. 53, num. 2, 2010.

SILVA, Selmo N. *Greves e Lutas Insurgentes: a história da AIT e as origens do sindicalismo revolucionário*. Rio de Janeiro: UFF (PhD dissertation), 2017.

SOLANO, Esther; MANSO, Bruno P.; NOVAES, Willian. *Mascarados: a verdadeira história dos adeptos da tática Black Bloc*. São Paulo: Geração, 2014.

THOMPSON, E. P. "La Lógica de la Historia" (Source: *Miséria da Teoria*). In THOMPSON, Dorothy. *Edward Palmer Thompson*. Barcelona, Crítica, 2002a.

___. "Agenda para una Historia Radical" (Source: "Agenda for Radical History"). In THOMPSON, Dorothy. *Edward Palmer Thompson*. Barcelona, Crítica, 2002b.

___. "La Historia desde Abajo" (Source: *The Times Literary Supplement*). In THOMPSON, Dorothy. *Edward Palmer Thompson*. Barcelona, Crítica, 2002d.

TOZO, Lucas. "A Ideia de Método na Teoria Política Normativa." In *Teoria & Pesquisa*, vol. 25, num. 3, 2016.

TRAGTENBERG, Maurício. *A Revolução Russa*. São Paulo: Faísca, 2007.

VAN DER WALT, Lucièn. "Anarchism, Syndicalism and Violent Anti-imperialism in the Colonial and Post-colonial World (1870-1940)." Article for Politics seminar, Rhodes University, 22 August, 2014.

___. "Revolução Mundial: para um balanço dos impactos, da organização popular, das lutas e da teoria anarquista e sindicalista em todo o mundo." In FERREIRA, Andrey C. *Pensamento e Práticas Insurgentes: anarquismo e autonomias nos levantes e resistências do capitalismo no século XXI*. Niterói: Alternativa, 2016a.

___. "Fora das Sombras: a base de massas, a composição de classe e a influência popular do anarquismo e do sindicalismo." In FERREIRA, Andrey C. *Pensamento e Práticas Insurgentes: anarquismo e autonomias nos levantes e resistências do capitalismo no século XXI*. Niterói: Alternativa, 2016b.

VAN DER WALT, Lucien; HIRSCH, Steven. "Rethinking Anarchism and Syndicalism: The Colonial and Postcolonial Experience, 1870-1940." In *Anarchism and Syndicalism in the Colonial and Postcolonial World, 1870-1940*. Leiden: Koninklijke NV, 2010a.

___. "Final Reflections: The Vicissitudes of Anarchist and Syndicalist Trajectories, 1940 to the present." In *Anarchism and Syndicalism in the Colonial and Postcolonial World, 1870-1940*. Leiden: Koninklijke NV, 2010b.

VEGA, Rafael S. "Entre el Contextualismo de Skinner y los 'Perennial Problems': una propuesta para interpretar a los clássicos." In *Praxis Filosófica*, num. 43, 2016.

VIANA, Nildo. "A Comuna de Paris Segundo Marx e Bakunin." In *Letra Livre*, num. 41, 2004.

___. "Gênese e Significado da Religião Segundo Bakunin." In *Espaço Acadêmico*, num. 172, 2015.

VUILLEUMIER, Marc. "Les Archives de James Guillaume." In *Le Mouvement Social*, num. 48. Paris: Les Éditions Ouvrières, 1964.

NOTES

1 For the distinction between "Bakunin's Writings," "Bakunin's Letters," and "Bakunin's Other Productions," I follow the IISH approach on the CD-ROM *Bakounine: Œuvres Complètes* (Bakunin, 2000a); in it, some important letters have been "hiked" to the position of writers.

2 Excerpt from *The Knuto-Germanic Empire and the Social Revolution* published by Nettlau in 1895, with the title "God and the State." It is a different text from the "God and the State" (excerpt from "Historical Sophisms of the Doctrinal School of the German Communists") that is known worldwide. Not included in Ferreira and Toniatti (2014).

3 Excerpt from *The Knuto-Germanic Empire and the Social Revolution* corresponding to pages 95 to 140 of the original manuscript. Not included in Ferreira and Toniatti (2014). To locate this fragment in the *Complete Works*, access: Écrits -> Numbering: 71004CEF.

4 "Advisement" to the second part of *The Knuto-Germanic Empire and the Social Revolution*. Not included in Ferreira and Toniatti (2014).

5 "Protestation of the Alliance" has two parts. This one (71011a) is the one that was translated into Portuguese (in *Obras Seletas 1*. São Paulo: Intermezzo, 2016). The other (71011b) is only in the original French.

6 Only those cited in the book.

BAKUNIN'S WRITINGS (1837–76)

As previously mentioned, this appendix presents a list of all Bakunin's writings. With this, I intend to contribute to further research and to the selection of writings that will be published and translated in the future. This list is based on the texts that, in the complete works organized and published by the IISH—*Bakounine: Œuvres Complètes* (Bakunin, 2000a)—were classified as *writings*, distinguishing themselves from letters and other productions.

This is a review/update of that inventory I made in "A Bibliografia de Bakunin" ["Bakunin's Bibliography"] (Correa, 2010b). Not included in this list, as well as in that one, are very excerpts and small fragments; differently to that one, not included in this list are the writings of which Bakunin's authorship is uncertain, as well as those that had only minor adjustments or revisions on his part.

I also took the opportunity, after this study, of making a change in the indication of Bakunin's most important writings. In "Bakunin's Bibliography," I had only highlighted which ones seemed to me the most important at the time; here, I redid and deepened this classification, differentiating, in order of importance: books, most important (primary) articles, secondary, and tertiary articles.

Such a classification was made on the basis of the relevance that such writings have in Bakunin's trajectory and political theory. To understand it, the following legend should be followed: the books are in bold and specified; the most important (primary) articles are highlighted with an asterisk; the secondary articles with two asterisks and the tertiary (less important) articles with three asterisks.

1837
*   Article about Shakespeare's *Hamlet*

1838
**   Hegel's *Gymnasialreden*. Foreword by the translator.

1839
**   From Philosophy.

1842	
*	The Reaction in Germany

1843	
***	Letter to Arnold Ruge
**	Communism

1845	
***	Letter to *La Réforme*

1846	
***	Letter to *Constitutionnel*

1847	
**	Speech: 17th Anniversary of the Polish Revolution

1848	
***	Letter to Count Duchâtel, Minister of the Interior
***	Letter to *La Réforme*
**	Fundamental Principles of the New Slavic Politics
***	Letter to *Die Allgemeine Oder-Zeitung*
***	The Wallachian Uprising and Russian Intervention
***	Draft letter to *Die Reform*
***	Draft letter to *Die Neue Rheinische Zeitung*
***	Draft letter to *Die Reform*
***	Draft letter to the editor of *Die Reform*
***	Objection Addressed to the Prussian National Assembly
***	Objection Addressed to the Second Chamber of Saxony
*	Appeal to Slavic Peoples by a Russian Patriot

1849	
**	Appeal to the Czechs
*	The Situation in Russia. The Army.
*	The Situation in Russia. The People.
*	The Situation in Russia. The Nobility.
*	The Situation in Russia. The Church and Priests, Officials and Finances

1850

**	My Defense

1851

*	Confession

1860

***	Letter to the editor of *Kolokol* concerning the duel between Beklemitchev and Nekljudov
***	Reply to *Kolokol*

1861

***	*Amur*: a few words on Irkutsk's social life
***	Article in *Amur*, East Siberian newspaper

1862

*	To the Russians, the Poles and All My Slavic Friends
***	Letter to *Working Man*
***	A few words to the Southern Slavs
*	The People's Cause: Romanov, Pugatchev or Pestel?
**	Bakunin on the Slavs
***	Preface to a brochure on Poland
***	The Warsaw Central Committee and the Russian Military Committee. Reply to General Mieroslawski
***	Article for *Przeglad Rzeczy Polskich*

1863

***	Draft Proclamation to the Poles
***	Speech from Malmö
**	Letter on Russia
***	Speech given at the banquet in Stockholm
***	Official Russia and the Russian people

1864

***	International Secret Society of the Revolution. Program Provisionally drawn up by the Founding Brothers

*   Program of an International Secret Society for the Emancipation
          of Mankind
***   Letter from a Democrat I
**   Project for the Organization of the Family of the Scandinavian Brothers.
          Project of an International Secret Society
***   Scandinavian Region: Adelaide
***   Letter from London
***   Letter from a Democrat II

1865

**   7 Fragments of writings on Freemasonry
***   5 Articles for *Il Popolo d'Italia*

1866

***   Italian Branch
*   Principles and Organization of the Revolutionary International Society.
          Revolutionary Catechism
**   Principles and Organization of the Revolutionary International Society.
          Organization
***   Program of the Italian Social-Democratic Revolution

1867

**   The Essence of Religion
***   Letter to *Kolokol*
***   Excerpt from a letter to *Kolokol*
**   The Slav Question
***   Speech given at the Congress of Peace and Freedom, second session

1867-1868

BOOK   Federalism, Socialism and Anti-theologism

1868

***   Letter to *La Démocratie*
***   A Final Word to Senhor Mieroslawski
***   Russia: the revolutionary question in Russian countries and Poland. Preface
**   Russia: the revolutionary question in Russian countries and Poland.
          Fragment
***   A Necessary Explanation
***   Our Program

**	Science and the People
***	Confidential Letter
**	5 Speeches at the Second Congress of Peace and Freedom
**	Program and Regulations of the International Alliance for Socialist Democracy. Program and Regulation
***	The Situation
**	Secret Statutes of the Alliance: Organization of the International Alliance of Brothers
**	Secret Statutes of the Alliance: Secret Organization of the International Alliance for Socialist Democracy
**	Secret Statutes of the Alliance: Program of the International Alliance for Socialist Democracy
**	Secret Statutes of the Alliance: Program and Object of the Revolutionary Organization of International Brothers
***	Speech at a Public Assembly of Foreign Socialists
**	Draft Statutes for the Federation of Romanesque Sections in Switzerland Proposed by the Geneva Sections
***	Letter to the commission of the newspaper *L'Egalité* in Geneva
***	From the Geneva International Workers' Association to Spanish Workers'
**	Program of the Society of International Revolution
***	International Fraternity. Program and Object

1869

***	The Fraternity
**	9 Letters on Patriotism. To the Fellows of the International Workers' Association at Locle and La Chaux-de-Fonds
***	Ms. Léo and *L'Égalité*
***	How the Revolutionary Question is presented
***	A Few Words to the Young Brothers in Russia
**	Program and Regulations of the Section of the Alliance for Socialist Democracy in Geneva of the IWA
**	The Geneva Double Strike
***	In Russia
***	The International Workers' Movement
***	The Agitation of the Party of Socialist Democracy in Austria
***	Judgment in Favor of Albert Richard
***	Letter to Ludwig Bulewski
**	The Deceivers/Sleepers [*Endormeurs*]

***   *La Montagne*
**   Integral Instruction
***   The Judgement of M. Coullery
*   The Politics of the International
***   Committee report on the issue of inheritance
***   Cooperation
***   Counter-report on Resistance Funds [*Caisses de Résistance*]
**   2 Speeches at the IWA Congress in Basel
***   To the Citizens Editors of *Réveil*. Study on German Jews

---

1870

**   To Russian Army Officers
***   Alexandre Herzen's necrology
***   The Death Penalty in Russia
***   Letter from Netchaiev and Bakunin to *Progrès*
***   The Swiss Police
**   Science and the Vital Question of the Revolution
***   The Universal Alliance of Social Democracy. Russian Section.
        To Russian Youth
**   The Bears of Bern and the Bear of Saint Petersburg
***   Letters on the revolutionary movement in Russia, addressed to citizen
        Liebknecht, editor-in-chief of the *Volksstaat*
***   Letter to the editors of *Kolokol*
***   Pan-Slavism
***   Letter from Sergei Netchaiev and Mikhail Bakunin to the editor
        of the *Volksstaat*
**   The Intrigues of Lord Utin
*   Letters to a Frenchman on the Current Crisis (includes Letters
        to a Frenchman)
***   Revolutionary Federation of Communes
***   The Awakening of Peoples
**   The Political Situation in France. Letter to Palix

1870–71	
BOOK	The Knuto-German Empire and the Social Revolution. Social Revolution or Military Dictatorship
	Excerpts from this book
	Philosophical Considerations on the Divine Ghost, on the Real World and on Man
	Historical Sophisms of the Doctrinal School of the German Communists
	The Paris Commune and the Notion of State
	God and the State
	The Capitalist System
	4 Fragments of Writings, 1870–71

1871	
**	The Principle of State
**	Three Conferences Made to the Workers of the Valley of Saint-Imier
*	Protestation of the Alliance
*	An International's Response to Mazzini
BOOK	Mazzini's Political Theology and the International
***	The Bourgeois Oligarchy
***	Report on the Alliance
***	Reply to *Unità Italiana*
***	Letter to My Friends in Italy
***	To the Delegate Workers at the Congress of Rome
**	Letter to the editors of *Proletario Italiano*
***	Article against Mazzini
**	Letter to Bologna Internationals
***	Personal Relations with Marx
***	Letter to the editorial staff of *Gazzettino Rosa*
***	Italy and the General Council of the International Workers' Association

1872	
***	Letter to the editor of *Gazzettino Rosa*
***	French article
***	Letter to the editorial staff of *Die Tagwacht*
***	To the comrades of the Federation of the International Sections of the Jura
**	Germany and State Communism
***	To the Russian Revolutionaries
***	Article for Polish magazine *Gmina*

***   Program of the Polish Social-Revolutionary Society of Zürich
**   To the Comrade Editors of the Bulletin of the Jurassian Federation
***   Program of the Zürich Slav Section
***   Call of Russian Emigrants to Swiss Authorities
***   Netchaiev: Political Criminal Or Not?
***   Program of the Serbian Socialist Party
*   Program of the International Fraternity
**   Letter to the *La Liberté* Journal of Brussels
**   Writing Against Marx

1873
***   The International Alliance of Social Revolutionaries
***   Socialism in Belgium
BOOK   **Statism and Anarchy**
***   Letter to the *Journal de Genève*
**   Letter to the Comrades of the Jurassian Federation
**   Where to go and what to do?

1874
***   Justification Memoir

1875
***   Revolutionary Socialism in Russia

1876
**   On Europe
***   On Democracy in France

No date
***   Project of an international and revolutionary society
***   Fragment on the Fraternity
***   Revolutionary association project
***   Note on Poland
**   History of Socialism

BAKUNIN'S PERIODIZATION, THEORETICAL AND POLITICAL POSITIONS (1836–76)

	Period	Sub-period	Main residence	Theoretical Philosophical position	Political-strategic position	Key concepts
1836-1837	Philosophical period	Fichtean period	Russia	Subjective idealism	Progressive romantic idealism	Love-freedom, emancipation
1837-1840	Philosophical period	First Hegelian period	Russia	Objective idealism	Progressive romantic idealism	Alienation, reconciliation with reality, unity of theory and practice
1841-1842	Philosophical period	Second Hegelian period	Germany	Voluntarist realism	French Republican Radicalism	Revolution, negative dialectics
1843	-	Moment of departure from philosophy	Switzerland	Voluntarist realism	French Republican Radicalism	Primacy of practice, self-government of the people
1844-1863	Revolutionary Pan-Slavic period	-	Switzerland, Belgium, France, Austria, Poland, Prussia, Prisons (Germany, Austria, Russia + escape), England	Voluntarist realism	French Republican Radicalism/ Revolutionary Pan-Slavism	State, nation-race, imperialism, national liberation, self-determination of peoples
1864-1876	Revolutionary socialist period	-	Italy (until 1867)	Scientific-naturalist materialism	Revolutionary socialism	Scientific-naturalist materialism science freedom, history, social force, domination, social revolution
1868-1876	Revolutionary socialist period	Anarchist period	Switzerland (from 1867 onwards)	Scientific-naturalist materialism	Revolutionary socialism (anarchism)	Ditto + mass organization and cadre organization (organizational dualism)

Ask your local independent bookstore
for these titles or visit blackrosebooks.com